RAF Little Rissington

The 'Waterfront' at RAF Little Rissington circa 1962, shortly after the new control tower and visitors' pan were opened. (*John Severne*)

RAF Little Rissington

THE CENTRAL FLYING SCHOOL YEARS 1946 - 1976

Roy Bagshaw
Ray Deacon
Alan Pollock
Malcolm Thomas

Pen & Sword
AVIATION

First published in Great Britain in 2006 by
Pen & Sword Aviation
An imprint of
Pen & Sword Books Ltd
47 Church Street
Barnsley
South Yorkshire
S70 2AS

Design and layout by David Hemingway

ISBN 1 84415 381 9
ISBN 978 1 84415 381 7

A CIP catalogue record for this book is available from the British Library

Printed and bound in Singapore
By Kyodo Printing Co. (Singapore) Pte Ltd

Pen & Sword Books Ltd incorporates the Imprints of Pen & Sword Aviation, Pen & Sword Maritime, Pen & Sword Military, Wharncliffe Local History, Pen & Sword Select, Pen & Sword Military Classics and Leo Cooper.

For a complete list of Pen & Sword titles please contact
PEN & SWORD BOOKS LIMITED
47 Church Street, Barnsley, South Yorkshire, S70 2AS, England
E-mail: enquiries@pen-and-sword.co.uk
Website: www.pen-and-sword.co.uk

Front cover: With Flt Lt I.K. 'Snowy' Mckee in the lead Jet Provost, the CFS Red Pelicans aerobatic team perform a loop over the Cotswold countryside in 1962. (*CFS Archive*)

Back cover: top; The CFS Historic Training Flight Vampire and Meteor display team ahead of a Meteor F.8 and Battle Of Britain Flight Lancaster during the 1971 ROC Day. (*Adrian Balch*)

Back cover: bottom; Most of the types then operating with Training Command are represented in this flypast over Little Rissington on 11 October, 1974, performed by Examining Wing staff. Flt Lt Dennis Barber was captain of the Varsity but knew little about leading large formations, so Wg Cdr Alex Wickham was in the other seat providing the expertise. The Jetstream was flown by Sqn Ldr R.C. (Mac) McKinlay with Flt Lt Tony Oldfield. Piloting the Dominie was Sqn Ldr Ken Pollard with the Commandant, Air Cdre John Severne, in the co-pilot's seat. Pilots for the Hunter and Gnat were Flt Lts Alastair Holyoake and Ross Payne respectively. Sqn Ldr Bruce McDonald (Meteor) and Flt Lt Pete Bouch (Vampire) were the Vintage Pair pilots. (*Alex Wickham/Dennis Barber*)

Contents

Forewords

Air Vice-Marshal Sir John Severne KCVO OBE AFC DL

1948	CFS student
1950-53	CFS Staff Instructor
1974-76	CFS Commandant

Royal Air Force Little Rissington has a very special place in the hearts of all those fortunate enough to have served, in whatever capacity, at that splendid station on the top of a Cotswold hill. The station was held in high esteem by the local community and their continued support sustained a close and happy relationship throughout four decades. All this is reflected in the pages of this book where many individuals have told their own stories of life at 'Rissy'.

Most aviation publications tend to concentrate on aircraft or their pilots but this one is significantly different in that it also gives considerable weight to the thoughts of those on the ground. Thus it is a well balanced story of all that happened there.

Whilst the content is about RAF Little Rissington from its beginnings just before the War, the concentration is on the Central Flying School because CFS was the dominant unit from the time of its arrival just after the War to 1976 when the station closed.

Reading the book has brought back many happy memories to be shared with those of the thousands of servicemen and women, civilians, families and visitors who made 'Rissy' such a unique place in our affections. The authors are to be congratulated on their painstaking research and for their tireless efforts in contacting the many people who have contributed to this fascinating and detailed record.

AV-M Sir John Severne on the flight deck of a Nimrod at RAF St Mawgan, when Commander Southern Maritime Air Region at Plymouth, 1978-80. His flying suit still bears the distinctive pelican badge of the Central Flying School. (*Sir John Severne*)

Air Chief Marshal Sir Patrick Hine GCB GBE ADC FRAeS

1954-55	CFS student with No 165 Course
1956-57	CFS staff instructor

As Patron of the Central Flying School (CFS), it gives me real pleasure to provide a foreword to this well-researched book which, with its many personal accounts and anecdotes, should be of particular interest to all those who served at RAF Little Rissington during the 30 years that CFS resided there. 'Rissy' (or 'Hell-on-the Hill' as some irreverently called it) was a very active and happy station with a tangible esprit de corps, which was immediately felt by those posted to this relatively small airfield perched on top of a 730 ft hill. I spent my final bachelor days there being very well looked after in that beautiful 1920s style Officers' Mess before getting married in late 1956 and moving down to Bourton-on-the-Water.

ACM Sir Patrick Hine, then Joint Commander British Forces, is pictured here during the 'Desert Storm' conflict with Iraq in 1991. (*Sir Patrick Hine*)

CFS, as Little Rissington's 'heartbeat', was the RAF's custodian of pure flying and instructional flying standards that were (still are) second to none and very highly regarded by air forces around the world. Literally thousands of QFI trainees passed through this lovely station, some like myself to return 'home' later to serve on the staff or with the Examining Wing (the so-called 'Trappers'). I for one wore the CFS Red Pelican flying badge with elitist but justifiable pride, and the flying experience and expertise gained then stood me in very good stead for the rest of my flying life.

Everyone will have his or her fond memories of their time at Little Rissington, of the beautiful surrounding Cotswold villages, and of the lively social life both on the station and in the local taverns and community. This book will not only refresh those memories but enable its readers to share the recollections of many others who were fortunate enough to serve at 'Rissy' in whatever capacity during what was a golden era for CFS, the RAF and indeed for military aviation in general. All this comes through vividly in the following pages, as does the 'Rissy' team spirit, and I commend the authors for their dedication, editorial skill and attention to detail in producing such an interesting and readable record. RAF Little Rissington made a major contribution to the RAF's history and this book describes it well.

Introduction

The Royal Air Force and the airfields from which it has operated has provided a rich vein of material for those interested in aviation. Over the years many books have been written embracing countless aspects of the service, its aircraft and operations with a large proportion concentrating on the more eye-catching, high profile units of Fighter and Bomber Commands. Little attention has been given to units operating in the more supportive but vital roles. Within these pages, the authors have sought to redress this imbalance somewhat by concentrating on the sizeable indirect contribution to RAF history and British air power of a lesser known Flying Training Command airfield and station, Little Rissington. In the three decades between 1946 and 1976, the Central Flying School, which was based there, produced over 6,000 fledgling Qualified Flying Instructors and continually endeavoured to monitor and improve the wider Royal Air Force's standards of flying, based on sound, proven instructional methods and a wealth of tradition extending back to Upavon in 1912.

In the mid-1930s, with the possibility of a war against Germany looming, the government of the day decided to implement an unprecedented programme of airfield construction. One of these airfields was located on a Cotswold ridge some 730 ft above sea level, close to the village of Little Rissington. Building work commenced in 1936 and the station was opened in August 1938. Operating as a grass airfield initially, concrete runways were laid during the war years. Right from the outset RAF Little Rissington performed a dual role, with flying training operations from the northern side and aircraft maintenance and storage on its southern flank.

Despite occasional attention from the Luftwaffe, wartime hostilities caused few problems for the flying training programme, although disruption from severe winters and difficult weather conditions was a common occurrence. The Maintenance Unit was kept busy receiving aircraft from manufacturers and issuing them to front line squadrons. At times several hundred aircraft would pass through each month and many were parked on hard standings in fields beyond the airfield's southern perimeter. With the cessation of hostilities in 1945, the station's role took on a new dimension with the arrival of the Central Flying School (CFS) from RAF Upavon in the following year. The main function of CFS was to fulfil RAF requirements and assist some Commonwealth air force requirements for flying instructors. RAF Little Rissington became CFS's important focal base for the next thirty years.

During that time, CFS expanded so that a number of 'permanent' detachments were made by the fixed-wing squadrons to other nearby RAF stations. A CFS helicopter squadron, formed at South Cerney in the mid-1950s, moved to RAF Tern Hill in 1961. Government cutbacks in the defence budgets following the 1973 oil crisis saw a spate of RAF station closures. Little Rissington succumbed in 1976 when CFS was split into separate units and relocated to three separate airfields. The station, handed over to the Army for a few years, was later utilised as an emergency hospital facility by the American forces for a further decade, before being sold off for use by commercial enterprises.

Each year since 1998 a public Air Day is held at the former RAF base at Kemble with many former CFS personnel meeting there for a reunion. From these gatherings and conversations it became apparent that many felt their time at Little Rissington was the best of their service careers, despite more interesting and exciting tours elsewhere. This was sufficient to convince the authors that something had to be done to record more fully the story of this much loved station and they set about the task of collating material.

Selecting a basic structure and deciding which material to include and what to leave out were difficult choices. Both the amount and complexity of officially recorded information on RAF Little Rissington are substantial, allowing only a small fraction to be included in a single volume.

A representative cross-section of factual information from 1946 to 1976, extracted from records at the National Archives at Kew, the RAF Museum at Hendon and the Central Flying School at Cranwell, linked with other published material, form the skeleton of this compressed history. Anecdotes and recollections from service and civilian personnel based at Little Rissington help to bring these unfolding years to life.

Extracts have been chosen for their general interest and portrayal of flying training and station activities during different eras. With many excellent photographs to choose from, our main criteria for selection were to focus on those which best depicted general life on the station or enhanced the flavour of any particular story or period. Descriptive analysis and factual snapshots are introduced where available to avoid monotonous repetition.

Sadly, because of limited space we had to exclude coverage of the Maintenance Units and the Helicopter Squadron over at South Cerney, although mention of important milestones are made in the appropriate sections.

The challenge of compiling this short history of a once proud flying training base has given the authors a great deal of pleasurable interest over several years. The task has enabled their meeting, speaking and corresponding with many former colleagues, acquaintances and Little Rissington personalities. We hope you reap a similar enjoyment from reading this tribute to an unusual but surprisingly busy Royal Air Force station.

Roy Bagshaw, Ray Deacon, Alan Pollock
and Malcolm Thomas

Acknowledgements

Even collectively it is impossible to thank adequately all those whose generous co-operation has made this book possible. In sending our appreciation and gratitude to everyone who submitted photographs, anecdotes and stories for our project, we recognise that this book would have been far less comprehensive without your enthusiastic support. Initially the authors tried to include most contributions but it soon became apparent that strict selection would necessitate anything not related directly to CFS activities or Little Rissington airfield having to be omitted. We pass on our apologies for any disappointment this action may cause but many of these are expected to be garnered by five QFIs in two later books with provisional working titles "Flying and Training" and "Flying and Fighting" during the Cold War era.

Throughout nearly four years we have had the pro-active support and encouragement from the CFSA Patron, many members of the Central Flying School Association and in particular Sir John Severne, who offered continuing advice and encouragement: he facilitated access to the important memoir family papers of Air Cdre Christopher Paul, who died a few weeks before we were to visit him. We send sincere thanks to Mrs Sharon Keable and for the help received from Central Flying School staff between 2003 and 2005 at RAF Cranwell and the access given to the School's archives and records. We wish to register the guidance received from the National Archive staff in Kew through the maze of documentation, followed by the ready involvement of Ray Flack and Bill Kelley, respective long suffering editors of the Aircrew Association's 'Intercom' and 'The Haltonian', which gave swift access to earlier post-war CFS technical and flying generations. Similarly we record the value of Colin Cummings's superb set of publications, which allowed us to extract the extensive list of accidents sustained by CFS aircraft and recognise Ashley Bailey's generosity in allowing us to extract information from the Little Rissington website.

While every endeavour was made by the authors to acknowledge the photographers who took the photographs in this book, we offer sincere apologies for any mistaken accreditations that may appear. The authors and publishers would welcome any information in this regard.

Special mention should also be made of David Watkins, who unstintingly supplied a large number of photographs and substantial supplementary information from his comprehensive files on aircraft issued to CFS. We acknowledge the painstaking proof reading and valuable comments of Alan East, with further assistance from Alasdair Liddle, in scrutinising the final draft and highlighting various errors. Thanks also to Michael Blundell whose help in researching documents at the National Archives significantly reduced the workload of the authors. Without the enthusiastic support and the co-operation of Pen & Sword Books this work would certainly have been a much slimmer volume.

Finally but by no means least a special thank you to our wives Hilary, Rose, Patricia and Teresa for their support, encouragement and understanding.

RAF Little Rissington: Its Origins

Heritage

Little Rissington is situated on the edge of the Midlands of England, on a limestone ridge 730 feet above sea level, open to all the winds that blow. This ridge of limestone, which runs from Bath in the South through Gloucestershire and Oxfordshire to Lincolnshire, then north of the Humber through the East Riding of Yorkshire and out to the sea at Scarborough and Whitby, is known by various names. Between Bath and Banbury it is known as the 'Cotswolds', with a steep edge to the north-west and a gentle, undulating slope to the south-east down to the Thames Valley at Cricklade, Abingdon and Oxford.

Centuries ago Man built his houses and made his pathways on high ground above the forest line, away from the haunts of wolves and other wild animals. Long before the Romans came to Britain the area was inhabited and there are many of these Neolithic remains visible as 'Tumuli' even today. Under the Romans this was a wealthy area and Cirencester, founded in 60 AD, soon became the second largest town in England. It was an area rich in agriculture and was well-liked by Roman settlers. At Chedworth, between Rissington and Cheltenham, can be seen the remains of a prosperous Roman's home.

In later centuries the district grew rich on the wool trade and the magnificent churches at Chipping Campden, Kingham, Cirencester, Northleach and Burford are evidence of the prosperity and the piety of the merchants of the fourteenth and fifteenth centuries. They spent their fortunes in the area where they made them and left a wonderful heritage of churches, manor houses and well-planned small towns.

The prosperity of later centuries, based on coal, iron and steam power, left this part of England unmarked and the Cotswolds remained an agricultural area, well known for its bracing uplands and its sheltered valleys. The only industry, which has maintained its place, is the blanket industry of Witney. In our own time new industries have appeared at Cheltenham and Witney, for example, but the area retains its agricultural importance, its large open fields and still quiet villages, its windswept uplands and sheltered valleys with their lazy winding streams.

Although Little Rissington at first sight appears to be isolated and 'in the middle of nowhere', it is in fact in the middle of one of the most interesting and beautiful regions of England. All around are villages with inns and churches of great architectural interest. Cheltenham, 20 miles to the west is the nearest shopping centre, while Oxford 25 miles to the east is also within easy reach. Although at times the winter weather is bleak and one would wish to be almost anywhere else, the long warm days of summer are compensation.

In this area Romans built, Britons worshipped, Normans conquered and many a grim battle was fought out. It is fitting that this spot should have been chosen on which to establish a school to train modern warriors.

The Expansion Period

During the mid 1930s it became clear to those in government that the situation within Germany could easily threaten United Kingdom and her allies. Therefore during this period steps were taken to strengthen Britain's Armed Forces. This era became known as 'The Expansion Period' with the construction of a large number of airfields across the country and Little Rissington was one of these airfields.

Construction begins

Situated some 730 ft above sea level on a Cotswold plateau, Little Rissington was the highest mainland RAF airfield. The station was built by the War Office's contractors following consultation with the Council for the Protection of Rural England (CPRE). This body ensured that the station's buildings were in keeping with the local surroundings, with such attractive villages as Bourton-on-the-Water, Little Rissington and Great Rissington. Hence the station benefited from dry-stone walling and many buildings were constructed from Cotswold Stone.

The airfield was designed for use as both a Flying Training School and as a Maintenance Unit for the storage of aircraft, the majority of buildings, including instructional facilities, workshops, main stores, and four C-type hangars being built on the northern side of the airfield site. An impressive Officers' Mess was constructed on the northern edge of the camp with single rooms for 108 officers. The Sergeants' Mess could accommodate 65 SNCOs and Barrack blocks were of three types: Type P (for 52 airmen and three NCOs), Type Q (for 64 airmen and three NCOs) and Type R (for 84 airmen and three NCOs). The two Type R blocks were located outside the main camp on the west side of the Great Rissington road and comprised mainly single rooms. To the north of the parade ground were a

NAAFI and Airmen's Mess which could seat 450 personnel at one sitting.

A number of maintenance and Lamella storage hangars, which were to be in much demand as the war progressed, were dispersed to the south and east of the airfield. As with most airfields constructed during this period, the 'landing area' consisted of marked out runways on a grass field. It was felt that grass runways were acceptable for the lightweight aircraft of the late thirties.

CO appointed

Little Rissington's first RAF Commanding Officer was Gp Capt A. ap Ellis CBE. He was a popular man locally, as he took a keen interest in the Station during the latter stages of its construction and was able to have a few extras installed, including an attractive Cotswold wall along the roadway beside the Sergeants' Mess and the Married Quarters. He also ensured as many trees as possible were retained in the domestic and technical areas and was even successful in getting a gardener established by ensuring that the area which had been staked out for a garden by the AMWD mysteriously became enlarged one dark night to just over an acre – the minimum size required to qualify for a gardener. And so it remained until the Station closed.

First unit moves in

An advanced party of No. 6 Flying Training School arrived at Little Rissington on 11 August 1938, shortly after the completion of the Station, and a fortnight later all personnel and equipment were installed. Aircraft on the inventory at that time included Audaxes, Furies, Harts and twin-engined Ansons. It was June 1939 before more 'modern' machines arrived, in the shape of Harvard trainers.

On 11 October 1938, No. 8 Maintenance Unit (MU) formed at the station and was declared operational on 7 November under Sqn Ldr D.W. Dean. Originally intended for the storage of motor vehicles, in March 1939, Maintenance Command decided that the MU should become responsible for the preparation and storage of aircraft. As a result the MT vehicles were transferred to another MU and the first aircraft, Blenheims, Spitfires and Wellingtons, were received by 8 MU on the 27th of the month.

World War 2

In common with other Units of the Royal Air Force, Little Rissington began to prepare for war in August of 1939. On the 23rd, the day the Auxiliary Air Force and part of the Reserve were called out, No. 41 Group ordered No. 8 MU to make every effort to prepare Immediate and Ready Issue aircraft. Key personnel of both the MU and FTS were recalled from leave the following day and orders were received to put war-time markings on aircraft, adopt the blackout system and observe security on Wireless Transmission. General security on the Station was tightened up in the following days, wardens were armed and emergency passes issued.

On the day war was declared 268 aircraft were in storage with 8 MU. The FTS was renamed No. 6 Service Flying Training School and 215 Squadron moved in with its Wellingtons for a brief period from RAF Bassingbourn as it was feared that the eastern airfields would be subject to immediate air assaults by the Luftwaffe. Many other East Anglia based squadrons were similarly dispersed during this period, but 215 Squadron was not destined to stay in the Cotswolds for very long. Two days after the beginning of hostilities it was decided that all training aircraft should have their undersides painted yellow.

During the first winter of the war the weather played havoc with the airfield. Heavy snows formed deep drifts and a sea of mud following the thaw, and several patches of the field were unusable for many weeks. During January part of the SFTS moved to Kidlington and for the first two months of 1940 flying at Little Rissington was

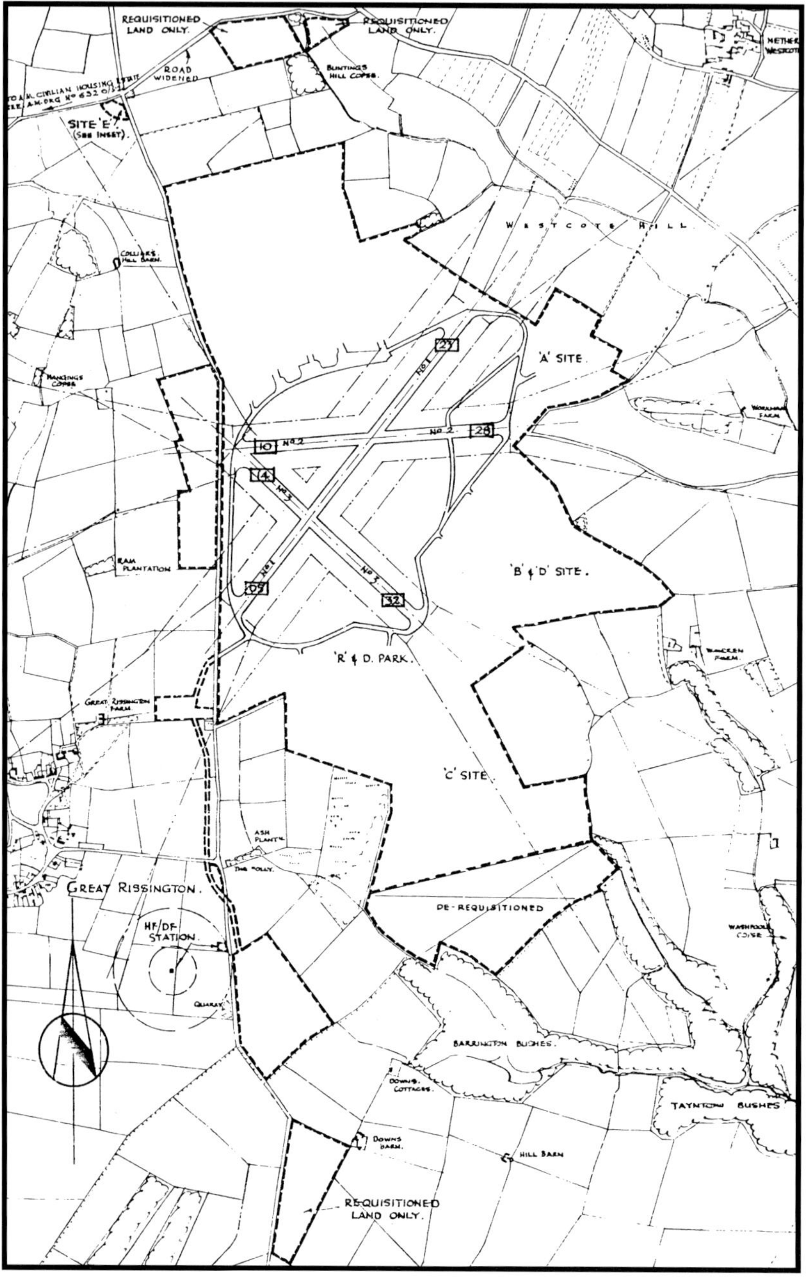

Map showing the outer boundaries of the land requisitioned by the Air Ministry for the construction of an airfield at Little Rissington. (*RAF Museum, Hendon*)

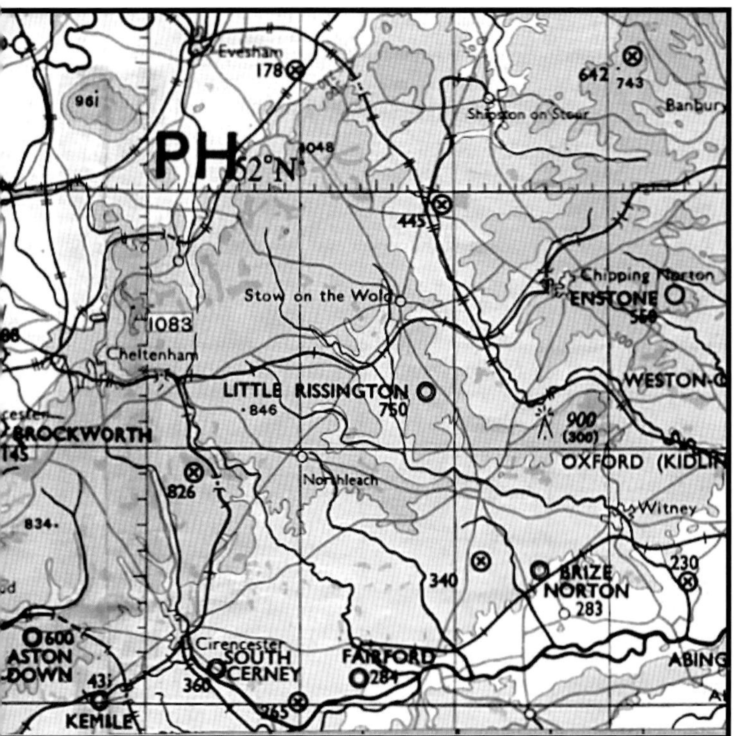

This 1960 map shows the location and proximity of Little Rissington in relation to other RAF airfields in the Cotswolds area.
(HMSO via Alan Pollock)

reduced to a minimum. In March a Type 4 Meteorology Station was opened, obtaining weather reports and forecasts from Abingdon and passing back the weather at Rissington.

The enemy closes in

It was not until after some months of 'phoney' war that the enemy began paying attention to the area near Rissington. Alerts had started by June, 1940 and on the night 25/26th of that month a few bombs fell nearby but the Station suffered neither casualties nor damage. Until mid-1942 the airfield A.A. defences were manned by Army detachments. Air Force personnel were trained to use lighter weapons of various sorts. Included among the aircraft held by 8 MU at this time were 58 Battles, 39 Hampdens, 21 Magisters, 30 Spitfires and 21 Tiger Moths. Close on 100 Blenheims delivered during the following month caused some concern as to their security.

In July, 1940, 6 SFTS became a Group 2 unit, training pupils on Oxfords. At that time the course was of fourteen weeks duration with a planned intake of forty pupils every 3 weeks. Pupils completed the intermediate and advanced stages of their training at 6 SFTS. Wings were awarded on completion of the intermediate stage and pupils went forward to Operational Training Units (OTUs) after the advanced stage. By late summer the course length was reduced to 12 weeks and the pupil strength raised to 160 in order to increase the flow to the OTUs.

By now there were some 400 aircraft in the care of 8 MU, although some of these were stored at Little Rissington's satellite airfields - Kidlington in Oxfordshire and Windrush, a few miles to the south of Rissy. No. 6 SFTS also made use of Windrush airfield during this period for flying training.

'A lighter shade of Pale Blue'

AC2 Reg O'Neil was posted to Little Rissington on completion of his basic training and wrote about his wartime experiences on camp in a book called 'A lighter shade of Pale Blue', extracts from which provide a flavour of life on the base during those dark days.

> *"The main task for the airfield and its supporting personnel,"* writes Reg, *"was to train pilots to fly twin engined aircraft, Avro Ansons, later to be joined by Airspeed Oxfords. There were one or two North American Harvards, which were single-engined and would awake the whole camp every morning at about 06:00 when the night watch would run and warm up the engines. The Harvard must have been one of the noisiest aircraft; it was so loud that it even drowned out the sound of the few 'Rolls Razor' owners as they prepared for the daily shave! The main activities were centred around the flying school and of course, most airmen would be found in the areas of the hangars, 'Flights' as they were known. Life was easier going as compared with the training centres we had left after completing square-bashing. Airmen were seldom marched to their duties, with the exception of the student pilots, who were subjected to the rigorous discipline as part of their training. The everyday 'working' airmen (permanent staff) enjoyed a less demanding life in that respect. Apart from the occasional 'fatigues' it was pretty much a normal working day for most.*
>
> *As the winter of 1940/41 turned to spring, the CO, a Group Captain who it was said would not have WAAF on his station, was posted out. A much younger Group Captain was to take his place and it was understood that he would welcome a contingent of the WAAF to join us. This was indeed a morale booster and it was noticeable how much smarter the ranks began to look. All airmen billeted in what originally were 'Married Quarters', were to move out and occupy a couple of marquees that were hastily erected between barrack blocks. Then came the official announcement that a group of WAAF would shortly join us and that everyone should do all they could to receive them and make them feel at home. A welcome party was arranged, tables and chairs were to be taken out from the NAAFI and placed on the square, this Holy of Holies! No one dared put a foot on it whilst the ensign was flying at the masthead, unless one was on parade. The punishment for taking a quick cut across the square was seven days' 'jankers'."*

The Luftwaffe drops by

The Luftwaffe made its first visit to the area on 29 July 1940, when a stick of 17 bombs dropped harmlessly in fields nearby. This attempted raid prompted the issue of a Spitfire to the staff pilots of 6 SFTS as it was envisaged that a single Spitfire might have some deterrent effect on the enemy.

During the night of 18/19 August, an Anson from Little Rissington

Airmen awaiting the arrival of the first WAAF contingent on the parade ground. Note the extensive use of camouflage and saplings by Station HQ. *(Reg O'Neil)*

recorded the station's first kill, a Heinkel 111, in bizarre circumstances. In reporting the incident, the 'Times' newspaper stated that

> *"The third (German bomber) was destroyed by the sergeant pilot of an unarmed Anson aircraft of Training Command. Whether he intentionally rammed the raider will never be known. The two aircraft collided and fell to the ground interlocked."*

Sgt. B. Hancock of No. 21 Course was the pilot and Flying Training Command endeavoured to find out if he had in fact rammed the Heinkel but, as both he and the enemy crew were killed, no ruling could be made.

Reg O'Neil witnessed many of the events that occurred during this tense period.

> *"Although Little Rissington was a flying training school, we were not exempt from the attentions of the Luftwaffe and during the Battle of Britain the enemy were to be heard passing over quite frequently. One bright sunny afternoon the air raid warning was sounded, but nothing seemed to happen in our air space. However the neighbouring airfield at Brize Norton was heavily attacked creating much damage. The smoke from the attack could be seen quite clearly over the Cotswolds. From the air this airfield looked much the same as ours as it was built at the same time in 1936 to a similar design. The following day at almost the same time, the warnings were sounded again and it was thought by everyone that this would be our turn. Fortunately, it appeared that the enemy mistook Brize Norton for our airfield and in consequence, they received another hammering. Again the smoke could clearly be seen from where we were.*
>
> *Shortly after these attacks, the Germans switched to the night bombing of cities and we seemed to be on the path of the bombers attacking the industrial Midlands. We could hear them drone overhead throughout the night. Very strict blackout regulations were observed on the camp. A few miles away in the wilds of the hills a decoy flare path would be lit to distract the enemy aircraft, this was kept a secret known only to the airmen who serviced the site. On mentioning this to a local farmer during a recent visit to the area, he took me to an underground bunker that once housed the generator for the flarepath. It was located at Goms Hole, near Clapton-on-the-Hill.*
>
> *A few miles to the south of Rissy, at Windrush, a satellite airstrip was installed for night flying training as it was considered too risky to fly from the main airfield during air raids. One night, 'Jerry' was passing overhead and several of us were standing at the door of the billet watching for evidence that London was being bombed, as we could usually see a glow in the sky from that direction when a raid was in progress. On this particular night we were startled to hear the sound of machine guns to the south, followed by a bright burst in the sky accompanied by the sound of an explosion. It was, as we discovered later, a Heinkel III, that on seeing one of our training aircraft coming in to land at Windrush had made an attack with machine guns. The flying instructor, Sgt Plt Hancock was hit in the stomach. Being an unarmed training aircraft, Sgt Hancock decided to pull back on the stick and ram the Heinkel, which he did as we saw for ourselves. Both aircraft became locked together and crashed in flames on the runway. There were no survivors. In September 1990, a plaque commemorating this gallant airman was installed in the wall of the churchyard in the village of Windrush."*

As activity by German raiders continued to intensify, 8 MU increased the numbers of aircraft it turned out each week. In a three week period during September 1940, when the Battle of Britain was at its height, the MU issued 142 aircraft of various types, among them much needed Spitfires.

By now it was evident that the Germans were planning an invasion of Britain. The defence of the local area was increased in August by the formation of a Home Guard unit recruited from 60 volunteers among the civilian staff of the SFTS and the MU. Training was organised by the Squadron Leader Admin. Some fourteen block houses and twelve pillboxes round the airfield perimeter were manned by the Station Defence Force, and at the end of the month twelve Home Office shelters became usable — a big improvement on the trenches which till then had been used as shelters.

During the 'Battle of Britain' summer of 1940 No. 6 SFTS was selected to train pilots on twin-engined aircraft, which led to the Harvards being replaced by more than 150 Airspeed Oxfords, supported by a few Ansons which were to soldier on for some months.

With so much activity at Little Rissington, the Relief Landing Ground (RLG) at Windrush was used for most night time training. A second RLG was allocated during November 1940 and, on the 16th, No. 6 SFTS commenced circuit training at RAF Chipping Norton.

In addition to Little Rissington's training duties, No. 8 MU was also very busy, with a wide variety of aircraft arriving for storage and refurbishment. Only more fragile aircraft were now being stored in hangars, with the more hardy airframes dispersed around the large airfield site. Storage problems eased a little when Satellite Landing Grounds (SLGs) at Barton Abbey, Middle Farm, Great Shefford, Stoke Orchard, Watchfield and Worcester became available during late 1940 and early 1941. Despite the use of SLGs, records show 120 Oxfords, 27 Hampdens, 10 Curtiss Mohawks, 39 Proctors and 37 Spitfires amongst the mixed bag of aircraft still stored by No. 8 MU at Little Rissington.

Three distinguished visitors paid calls on the Station during 1941: Marshal of the RAF Sir Edward Ellington in March, Sir Archibald Sinclair, Secretary of State for Air, on 13 September and Air Vice-Marshal HRH The Duke of Kent on 1 November.

In October 1941 No. 23 Blind Approach Training (BAT) Flight formed, with eight Oxford Mark IIs. The BAT units were conceived to train pilots in the use of 'blind flying aids', the forerunner of today's Instrument Landing Systems. No. 23 BAT Flight was renumbered as No. 1523 BAT Flight early in 1942 and the unit remained at Little Rissington until November 1945.

Change of role

With the Battle of Britain over, the air war against Germany had commenced in earnest in 1941. The major role of the Station changed on 22 April 1942 when No. 6 SFTS became No. 6 (Pilots) Advanced Flying Unit (PAFU). The mission of the renamed unit was to run short courses to familiarise pilots returning from training in Canada, USA and South Africa with European weather conditions, a culture shock after training in the sunshine. Special attention was paid to navigation, with night flying and beam approach training included in the syllabus. No. 1523 BAT Flight carried out part of the beam approach training commitment.

A local civilian named Jim, seen here, worked as barman in the Sergeants' Mess, for the full duration of the war. (*Reg O'Neil*)

The 115 Oxford and Anson aircraft with the unit provided the final training to pilots, sharpening their skills before they were posted to Bomber Command, most probably through an OTU. Despite the large number of aircraft assigned, the need for pilots was so great that an additional 34 Oxfords were assigned to No. 6 PAFU in July 1942. Due to the intense training activity, Little Rissington gained another Relief Landing Ground, at RAF Akerman Street, Oxfordshire, to the South East.

Tarmac runways

Up until now, Little Rissington had used grass runways, which could become extremely boggy during inclement weather, and severely curtail flying operations. During 1942, by making greater use of the three RLGs, it was possible to construct three concrete runways which enabled greater utilisation of the airfield during most weathers. The runways were laid out in the standard "A" pattern associated with many of the bomber stations and helped to secure continued operations at Little Rissington after the war.

A notable event in the Station's history was the arrival in July 1942 of the RAF Regiment. The Army gunners that had manned the Anti-Aircraft(AA) defences of the Station for 2¾ years, were stood down after June and No. 4174 AA Flight of the RAF Regiment was stationed at Little Rissington until 18 May 1943. During the Army's last month on the Station the WAAF celebrated its third birthday with a birthday cake, a ceremonial church parade and a free cinema show and dance. At the time there were 315 airwomen on the strength of the Station.

To keep the personnel of 8 MU occupied while runway construction progressed, Horsa and Hotspur gliders were assembled from kits in preparation for the invasion of France. By coincidence, No. 8 MU had been heavily involved in the servicing of Audax, Hart, Hector and Hind glider tugs from Glider Training Schools, so in July, it was decided that the Heavy Glider Conversion Unit should form at Little Rissington. The Unit's stay however, was short lived as the AOC-in-C Flying Training Command, Air Marshal Sir William Welsh, decided it should be based at RAF Brize Norton. Once the runways had been completed, the gliders were towed-off by Whitley bombers.

Records show that during May 1943 there were 350 pilots under training with No. 6 PAFU. To cater for this number of students, the unit had an establishment of 163 Oxford Mark I and II aircraft, 4 Ansons and a single Tiger Moth. Three RLGs continued to be used for flying training, in addition to Little Rissington itself.

By increasing specialisation 8 MU made steady improvement throughout 1944 in the numbers of aircraft prepared until by the end of the year it was consistently exceeding its target figure.

The PAFU was not lacking in technical achievement either. In September of that year work began fitting a Rissington version of a modification to the Oxfords which prevented the inadvertent retraction of undercarriages on the ground, a fairly common mishap. During the same month one of the Unit's Oxfords broke up in mid-air, the first time that this had been known to happen on this type. It was believed that the aircraft had been overstressed during recovery from unusual positions.

The year 1944 saw a change of emphasis for No. 8 MU, as the unit was tasked with the dispersed storage of over 700 Wellington aircraft of different marks. One year later, 1,388 aircraft were being stored by this unit. The same year also saw two new units at Little Rissington, when Nos. 1516 and 1517 BAT Flights were transferred from Pershore and Chipping Warden respectively.

The last year of the war saw some slackening of the pace. No. 8 MU began to accept aircraft for storage and there were a number of pilots at the PAFU who had completed their courses but who had not been posted out. Some anxiety was felt about the Oxfords which had done yeoman service but whose age had caused deterioration in their performance when on one engine. Many aircrew were uncertain about their futures as the war in Europe drew to a close and contraction became inevitable.

The end of the war brought redundancies among pilots on the unit as the requirement for aircrew decreased. In October six instructors went to Upavon for Harvard conversion courses and on the 23rd of the month orders were received that No. 6 PAFU was to cease all training with effect from 26 November 1945.

No. 6 PAFU was in existence for three years and seven months. It was based at Little Rissington the entire time and acclimatised 5,541 pupils in all, among them members of most of the Allied and Dominion Air Forces. Ex-pupils gained 705 awards for gallantry, including four Victoria Crosses and various Allied awards.

On 17 December 1945, No. 6 SFTS reformed at Little Rissington equipped with Harvards. Owing to the lack of aircraft publications and tools it was necessary, to begin with, to send aircraft to Upavon for Minor Inspections. Coupled with this was the problem of fluctuating manpower due to releases from the Service which caused minor hold-ups. In spite of such difficulties training recommenced at Little Rissington. Four months later the SFTS moved to RAF Ternhill.

Where it all began! Instructors and students of No. 1 Course, the first ever run by the Central Flying School, pose for an official photograph at Upavon in 1912 with; *back row (l to r)*; Lt R.B. Martyn, 2nd Lt R. Abercrombie, Lt P.A. Shepherd, 2nd Lt D. Young, Lt F.F. Waldron, Lt G. Wildman-Lushington, Lt I.T. Courtney, Lt D. Allen, Lt J.W. Pepper, Capt C.E. Risk: *centre row (l to r)*, Lt E.V. Anderson, Maj J.F.A. Higgins, Lt R. Cholmondeley, 2nd Lt R. Smith-Barry, Capt J.H. Becke, Lt G.B. Stopford, Lt K.P. Atkinson, Lt S. Winfield-Smith, 2nd Lt T.O.B. Hubbard, Maj H.M. Trenchard: *front row (l to r)*, Capt R.H. Cordner, Maj E.R. Gerrard, Lt A.M. Longmore, Lt Col H.R. Cooke, Capt G.M. Paine, Capt J.D.B. Fulton, Eng Lt G.R.J. Randall, Asst Pay J.H. Lidderdale, Lt Q.M.F. Kirby. (*CFS Archive*)

Central Flying School Foundations

The Central Flying School is the longest serving flying school in the world, a record of which this country is understandably proud. The concept of a British military air force was born in 1911 when Herbert Asquith, the then Prime Minister, instructed the Committee of Imperial Defence to examine the questions of naval and military aviation and suggest measures to create an efficient air force. The Committee recommended the formation of a Royal Flying Corps comprising a military wing, a naval wing, a reserve, the Royal Aircraft Factory at Farnborough and a flying training school which subsequently became the Central Flying School (CFS).

Although the cost of CFS was to be borne equally by the Army and the Navy, its administration was the responsibility of the War Office. In compensation, a naval officer, Captain Godfrey Paine RN was chosen to be the first Commandant. He was informed by the First Lord of the Admiralty, Winston Churchill, that he must learn to fly within two weeks if he was to take up the appointment. He successfully completed his somewhat rushed conversion at Eastchurch under the eye of Lieutenant Arthur Longmore RN.

The CFS was formed at Upavon in Wiltshire on 12 May 1912. The primary aim was not to produce aviators as such, but professional war pilots. This was to be achieved by accepting for advanced training only men who already held a Royal Aero Club Certificate, although they were offered a refund of part of their expenses incurred in private tuition. Having obtained their Pilot Certificates in order to qualify for the course, the students were taught to fly all types of aircraft available at the school. The inventory then consisted of Maurice Farmans, Henri Farmans, Shorts, Avros and Bristol Bi-

planes. The first ever course was completed on 5 December 1912 and graduates could carry out short cross-country flights and local flights of 20 to 30 minutes duration, at heights around 1500 ft. The ground training syllabus included theory of flight, map reading, strength of materials, military and naval aviation history, hints on flying and practical work on Gnome and Renault engines and aircraft repair. The standard for a pass was 50% in each subject and 60% overall.

One of the successful students on this first course was Major Hugh Trenchard who was later to become Lord Trenchard and first Marshal of the Royal Air Force. One of his fellow students became, in later years, Marshal of the Royal Air Force Sir John Salmond, the succeeding Chief of the Air Staff. After his course Trenchard was appointed Senior Staff Officer at Upavon, although he had not then qualified for his military brevet. However, one of his duties was to set the examination papers, arrange and invigilate the examinations, correct the papers and assess the results. So he regularised the situation by setting himself a flying and ground examination, correcting his own paper and awarding himself his 'wings'.

Very soon aircraft began to take on a more military form and CFS quickly became one of the main centres for experimental and research flying. Bomb dropping experiments began, and in July 1914, a fourteen-inch torpedo was launched from a Short seaplane. One of the first tasks was to gain the confidence of commanders in the field by showing that the Royal Flying Corps was not just a fine weather Service, and it was with pride that the Secretary of State for War told the House of Commons in 1913, that CFS carried out experiments in flying in strong winds. What had been achieved was an aircraft with a maximum speed of 57 mph taking 16 minutes to cover 400 yards into the teeth of a gale. This was quite an advance, since only a year before it had been considered dangerous to fly in winds of 15 mph.

By the outbreak of war in August 1914 the CFS had contributed 93 pilots to the Royal Flying Corps. A rapid expansion took place and by the end of 1915 the basic training policy was for all pupils to do their ab-initio flying at one of the Reserve Squadrons, and then pass on to CFS or to a service squadron for advanced training.

A major fault of the Royal Flying Corps at this time was its lack of standardisation. One of the main critics in the field was Major Smith-Barry and in 1916 he put his thoughts on paper. He wanted a School for Instructors in flying where all instructors would have their flying brought up to a high standard necessary to enable them to teach with confidence and ease, and where they would be given definite lines upon which to instruct. He also recommended the introduction of dual controls so that pupils could learn to fly to the limits of their aircraft.

Smith-Barry was brought home from France and given command of a squadron at Gosport where he could put his ideas into practice. He soon had his school operating on dual controlled Avro 504Js, Blériots and Bristol Scouts. The standard of flying improved still more after the introduction of the Gosport tube which enabled the instructor to converse easily and comfortably with his pupil; a capability which had previously been restricted to the few moments of quiet before and during a stall. Pilot training became both quicker and more efficient and the system was adopted throughout the training school. In September 1917 the first syllabus for Instructor Training Courses was produced – probably the first ever evolved in the history of flying – written by Major Parker of the School of Special Flying at Gosport:

Lesson I

Demonstrate use of controls and their effect on the machine
Straight flying, level and climbing
Turns (with engine on)
Use and effect of controls in turning
Getting into the turn and keeping the machine turning
Getting out of a turn
Difference in right and left turns
Misuse of controls and detection of faults
Turns (with engine off)
Difference in effect of controls on the machine
Faults in turning
Glide

Lesson II

Taking off into wind
Repeat lesson landings into wind
Normal and short circuit landings

Lesson III

Brief repetition of Lessons I and II
Steeper turns, with and without engine
Taking off in a cross wind, and climbing turns
Landing cross wind
Side-slipping, various degrees and uses of
The approach for landing on fixed mark
Flatter glide

Lesson IV

Lesson III repeated, but not that part taught in Lessons I and II
Forced Landings: Practice in choosing right field
Detection of wind
Approach

Lesson V

General repetition of advanced training
Harder Manoeuvering
Looping
Rolling
Spinning
Stalling turns
Manoeuvering against another machine

The Instructor should, when possible, remain in the air half-an-hour with a pupil and the lessons have been set out to occupy about that time.

Various aircraft types then operated by CFS are visible in this historic view taken outside the unit's hangars at Upavon in 1913. (*CFS Archive*)

In 1918 the Royal Flying Corps and the Royal Naval Air Service were amalgamated to form the Royal Air Force and, as part of the reorganisation, CFS became the Flying Instructors School tasked to carry on the work started at Gosport.

Between the Wars

As a result of a further reorganisation in 1926, CFS moved from RAF Upavon to RAF Wittering. The Air Ministry decided that in between the courses the staff should visit flying training schools to check whether the system and standard of instruction was being maintained. This was the emergence of the Examining Wing. In 1927, a Refresher Flight was formed and pilots from all over the world were being trained in some form of flying at CFS.

It was at about this time that the idea of a formation aerobatics team emerged and a five-man team led by Flt Lt D'Arcy Greig began displaying in de Havilland Genet Moths. Their repertoire was quite extensive and would do the Service justice at Farnborough even today. Formation aerobatic displays by CFS instructors became a traditional item at the Hendon Air Displays in the early thirties and the team of five red and white striped Tutors led by Flt Lt, later Air Chief Marshal Sir Hugh Constantine, made a great impression in 1933 with its inverted formation flying.

The idea of an annual get-together of past and present members of the staff was born in 1930 and the first dinner was held at RAF Wittering. Among the 40 to 50 who attended were Air Vice-Marshal Sir Godfrey Paine, Marshal of the Royal Air Force Lord Trenchard, the then Air Marshal Sir John Salmond, who followed Lord Trenchard as Chief of Air Staff, and Air Vice-Marshal Longmore. The Central Flying School Association developed in 1951 from this beginning and now has a membership of over 700. The colours of the Central Flying School Association were chosen with the multi-service genesis in mind, green to represent land and the Army, purple to represent the Engineering Branch of the Navy, from which most of the original engineering staff had been drawn,

Upavon again a decade later and Gp Capt Vesey-Holt inspects a line of Avro 504ks and CFS personnel. (*CFS Archive*)

silver for the River Avon and black for the unknown future. Less respectful persons have preferred to believe that black stands for the old tarred huts at Upavon, purple for the first Commandant's language and green for the innocence of his Chief Staff Officer.

The following year CFS became one of the first Royal Air Force units to receive its own armorial bearings. Briefly, the Arms symbolise the origin and work of the CFS. The Pelican represents a seat of learning; the Crown and Tower the School's naval and military genesis; the pilot's brevet, the anchor and sabre the 3 Services. The White and Blue wavy lines serve as a reminder of the original site of the CFS that was close to the banks of the River Avon. The motto can be interpreted to mean "Our Teaching is Everlasting". However, the school has been running refresher courses for some years now. The Pelican is a strong aviator, despite its shape and there is no truth in the rumour, freely spread about the CFS students, that it was chosen because of the size of its mouth and its poor flying performance.

By 1930 interest was being shown in 'pilotage without exterior visibility'. Flt Lt W.E.P. Johnson was sent on a course at the Farman Factory near Paris and on his return he pioneered the teaching of instrument flying in the Royal Air Force. By 1934 the international situation had deteriorated to such an extent that Mr Baldwin, the Prime Minister, announced a new expansion programme for the Services.

CFS was again enlarged and became a unit within Flying Training Command and moved back to RAF Upavon. The expansion continued but the Air Council realised that, if war came, all the training stations in the United Kingdom would not be able to meet the aircrew requirements and the Commandant, Group Captain James Robb, was sent across the Atlantic to pave the way for training facilities in Canada.

With powerful and modern aircraft coming into service and squadrons re-equipping rapidly, a new role for CFS began to develop. Careful conversion training was necessary during the transition from comparatively slow biplanes to the new generation of Hurricanes and Spitfires and standard publications explaining the handling characteristics of the new machines required. Thus 'Pilot's Notes' were evolved. It was decreed that one machine of each new type would in

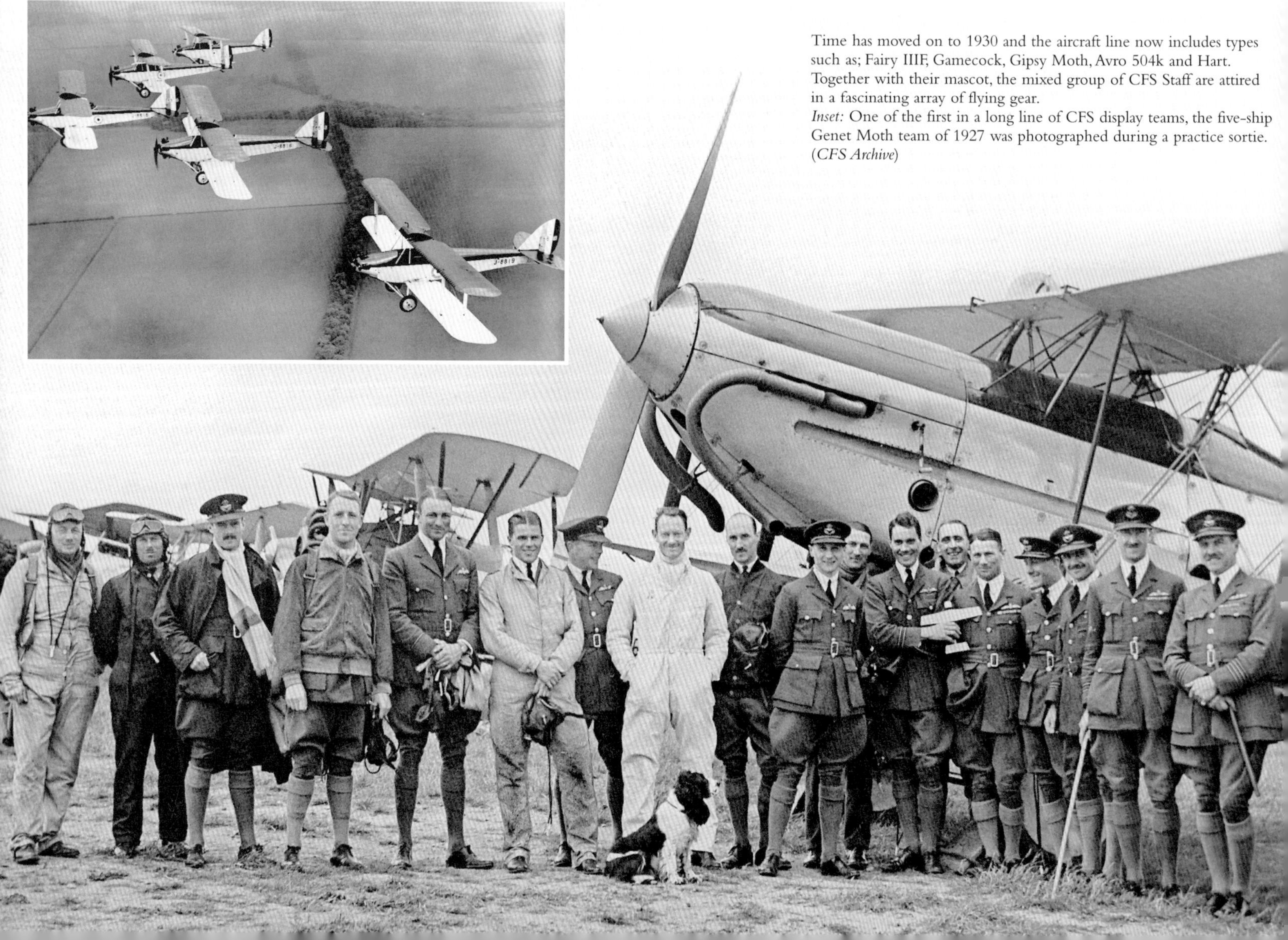

Time has moved on to 1930 and the aircraft line now includes types such as; Fairy IIIF, Gamecock, Gipsy Moth, Avro 504k and Hart. Together with their mascot, the mixed group of CFS Staff are attired in a fascinating array of flying gear.
Inset: One of the first in a long line of CFS display teams, the five-ship Genet Moth team of 1927 was photographed during a practice sortie. (*CFS Archive*)

future be sent to RAF Upavon to enable its characteristics to be assessed and written up in the form of Pilots Notes for squadron use.

The War Years

It was in this form, carrying on the high rate of production of Qualified Flying Instructors (QFIs) and testing new aircraft, that CFS entered the War. The first wartime QFI course, which began on 18 September 1939, was reduced from 9 weeks to 4 weeks and RAFVR uniforms began to appear as full mobilisation took place. The Refresher Squadron began to receive an assortment of pilots from all backgrounds who had volunteered for the newly formed Air Transport Auxiliary (ATA), which was to relieve the pilot shortage by ferrying aircraft from the factory to the squadron. The ATA became locally construed as 'Ancient and Tattered Airmen' when elderly and bald pilots, young pilots and not particularly fit pilots, some with only one eye or arm, arrived. But by no means all the ATA pilots were of these categories. Early in 1940 there arrived at CFS some young ladies who were far from ancient and tattered. Some were old hands like Amy Johnson and Winifred Crossley, who had given aerobatic displays with Alan Cobham's Circus, but at least one, Joan Hughes, was only 17 years old and almost certainly the youngest pilot ever to pass through CFS.

In the 12 months before September 1939 the fighter defences of Britain had improved from a force of about 600 aircraft of which all but about 90 were obsolescent biplanes, to one of 35 squadrons of which 22 were equipped with the Hurricane and Spitfire; these were to increase to 38 within another 6 months.

CFS played its part in this expansion by writing Pilot's Notes for the new types but it became obvious that the efforts were on too small a scale. There was a lack of uniformity in handling techniques and furthermore, the new aircraft were not giving the increased fighting power and efficiency that had been hoped for, because they were not being flown to best advantage. To overcome this the Air Ministry introduced the 'Examining Officers Scheme' that established a flight of 8 experienced officers to maintain liaison between CFS and the operational squadrons and to instruct the latter in up-to-the-minute techniques.

Twice in 1940 the intake of pupils was increased and by the end of the year 90 pupils were accepted in each 5 week period. The examining officers had by now been absorbed into the Refresher Squadron and continued their duties world-wide. Some of today's familiar procedures can be traced back to this period. It came to their notice that while a party of Army officers was being flown from Iraq to Palestine in a Bombay transport one of them became badly airsick and made for the toilet at the end of the cabin. Three of his friends followed to help him and shifted the C of G so much as to make the aircraft uncontrollable. This incident began the now familiar procedure of load sheet compilation and Centre of Gravity calculation.

Another procedure introduced during this period followed from the introduction of the newer more complex aircraft. Many of the early accidents happened because pilots forgot some operation that had not been necessary in earlier types and therefore the now universal mnemonics for the take-off and landing checks were introduced. Those who have flown the Chipmunk will remember "My Friend Fred Has Hairy B★★★s" as the downwind checks! The Examining Officers Scheme contributed much to the efficiency and safety of the RAF but it became impractical to deprive the operational squadrons of so many experienced officers in wartime and they were dispersed to command squadrons and to the operational training units.

RAF Upavon was home to the Central Flying School for many years and several aircraft types operated by the unit can be seen in this 1938 view. (*CFS Archive*)

CFS had become much like any of the other flying instructor schools and the Air Ministry felt the need for a 'training conference in permanent session'. Thus, in 1942 a new unit was formed, the Empire Central Flying School (ECFS), at RAF Hullavington in

Wiltshire under the command of Group Captain Down. ECFS took many of the staff from RAF Upavon but left behind sufficient to form the nucleus of No. 7 Flying Instructors' School (FIS). The ECFS was intended to draw the wide experience of the course members into a common pool for the benefit of all the training schools. Handling Squadron was responsible for preparing Pilot's Notes for all new types of aircraft coming into Service and for advice on aircraft handling. Examining Flight was given the job of inspecting the Flying Instructors' School in the United Kingdom and re-categorising instructors. A Research Flight was formed to investigate the practical and psychological problems of flying instruction. Eventually the Day/Night Development Unit was added to advance the all-weather flying aspects. The school was responsible for co-ordinating and revising untidy theories concerned with the art of flying and from its AP1732, the modern instructor's 'Bible', the AP3225 Instructors Handbook, was evolved. It had been intended to retain ECFS after the war as a permanent centre of flying training research but in 1946 the Central Flying School was revived and moved to RAF Little Rissington.

ECFS was renamed the Empire Flying School and continued in existence for a few years before being disbanded. The nucleus of the staff was transferred to RAF Manby in Lincolnshire to open the Flying College. Manby later became the home of the College of Air Warfare, part of which was the School of Refresher Flying.

Central Flying School Commandants at Little Rissington

Gp Capt E.A.C. Britton DFC 1946
Gp Capt W.M.L. MacDonald CB CBE DFC 1946-48
Gp Capt G.D. Stephenson CBE ADC 1948-50
Gp Capt G.T. Jarman DSO DFC 1950-51
Air Cdre A.D. Selway CB DFC 1951-53
Air Cdre G.J.C. Paul CB DFC 1954-56
Air Cdre N.C. Hyde CBE 1956-58
Air Cdre J.N.H. Whitworth CB DSO DFC 1958-61
Air Cdre H.P. Connolly CB DFC AFC AFM 1961-63
Air Cdre H.A.C. Bird-Wilson CBE DSO DFC AFC 1963-65
Air Cdre F.L. Dodd CBE DSO DFC AFC 1965-68
Air Cdre I.G. Broom CBE DSO DFC AFC 1968-70
Air Cdre F.S. Hazlewood CB CBE AFC 1970-72
Air Cdre R.H. Crompton OBE BA 1972-74
Air Cdre J. de M. Severne MVO OBE AFC MBIM 1974-76
Air Cdre J.M.D. Sutton 1976-77

RAF Little Rissington Station Commanders

Gp Capt A. ap Ellis CBE 1938-40
Gp Capt C.E. Barraclough 1940-43
Gp Capt M.H. Kelly OBE 1943-45
Gp Capt E.P. McKay 1945-46
Gp Capt E.A.C. Britton DFC 1946
Gp Capt W.L.M. MacDonald CB CBE DFC 1946-48
Gp Capt G.D.S. Stephenson 1948-50
Gp Capt G.T. Jarman DSO DFC 1950-51
Wg Cdr A.J. Trumble OBE 1951-53
Gp Capt P.W.D. Heal AFC 1953-54
Wg Cdr D.D. Rogers CBE 1954-55
Gp Capt C. Scragg CBE AFC 1955
Gp Capt R.K. Cassels DFC AFC 1955-56
Wg Cdr R.O. Buskell DFC 1956-57
Wg Cdr J.B.A. Fleming OBE 1957-60
Wg Cdr C.K. Gray DFC 1960-62
Gp Capt R.U.P de Burgh OBE 1962
Gp Capt H.M. Chinnery MVO AFC 1963-64
Gp Capt J.F.J. Dewhurst OBE DFC AFC 1964-67
Gp Capt D.A. Trotman AFC 1967
Gp Capt B.P. Mugford 1967-70
Gp Capt M. Adams OBE AFC 1970-72
Gp Capt R.J. Barnden 1972-73
Gp Capt M.R. Williams MA 1973-76
Wg Cdr M.C.D. Felton 1976

Central Flying School Armorial Bearings

Granted in 1931, the arms symbolise the origin and the work of the Central Flying School. The School's motto, 'Imprimis Praecepta' is best translated, 'Our Teaching is Everlasting'.

To all and singular to whom these presents shall come Sir Gerald Woods Wollaston, Knight, Member of the Royal Victoria Order, Garter principal King of Arms, Arthur William Steuart Cochrane, Esquire, Commander of the Royal Victorian Order, Clarenceux King of Arms and Algar Henry Stafford Howard, Esquire, upon whom has been conferred the Decoration of the Military Cross, Norroy King of Arms, send greeting, Whereas John Eustace Arthur Baldwin Esquire is Companion of the Distinguished Service Order, Officer of the Most Excellent Order of the British Empire, Aide-de-Camp to his Majesty the King, Group Captain the Royal Air Force and Commandant of the Central Flying School, represented unto the most Noble Bernard Marmaduke Duke of Norfolk, Earl Marshal and Hereditary Marshal of England, that on the Thirteenth day of May One thousand nine hundred and twelve the Central Flying School situate at Upavon in the County of Wiltshire was created for the purpose of training Officers for the Royal Flying Corps and that the said School was subsequently transferred to and is now situate at Wittering in the County of Northampton under the control and authority of the Royal Air Force, That the Commandant and Staff of the said school being desirous of having fit and proper Armorial Bearings assigned to be borne and used for the said School he therefore as Commandant requested the favour of His Grace's Warrant for our granting and assigning such armorial Ensigns as might be proper to be borne and used for the said Central Flying School on Seals, Shields, Banners or otherwise according to the laws of Arms and Forasmuch as the said Earl Marshal did by Warrant under his hand and seal bearing date the Twenty-fifth day of August last authorize and direct us to grant and assign such Armorial Ensigns accordingly, know ye therefore that we the said Garter Clarenceux and Norroy, in pursuance of His Grace's Warrant and by virtue of the Letters Patent of Our several Officers to each of Us respectively granted do by these Presents grant and assign the Arms following for the Central Flying School that so to say: Sable on a Fesse wavy Argent between in Chief two Wings conjoined and inverted or and in base an Anchor of the third and a sword proper Pommel and Hilt Gold in saltire two Bars wavy Azure And For the Crest On a Wreath of the Colours Upon the Battlements of a Tower proper a Pelican Gules rising from her Nest and gorged with a Naval Crown Or as the same are in the margin hereof more plainly depicted to be borne and used for ever hereafter for the Central Flying School on Seals, Shields, Banners or otherwise according to the Laws of Arms in witness whereof we the said Garter, Clarenceux and Norroy King of Arms have to these presents subscribed Our names and affixed the Seals of Our Several Offices this Ninth day of December in the Twenty second year of the Reign of Our Sovereign Lord George the Fifth by the Grace of God of Great Britain Ireland and the British Dominions beyond the Seas King, Defender of the faith and in the year of Our Lord One thousand nine hundred and thirty-one.

Central Flying School Charter

The CFS Charter, the Original of which was signed by Sir Ralph Cochrane in 1950, reads:

1. The tradition of organized flying instruction, which was born at Gosport in the days of the first world war, has grown with the passage of time and is now a major factor influencing RAF efficiency in peace and war. The Central Flying School is the guardian of that tradition, and is responsible for the technique of flying instruction, in particular for ensuring that it does not lag behind the developments in operational flying.
2. Its chief task is to train flying instructors who, by their skill, knowledge and enthusiasm, will raise the flying efficiency of the Royal Air Force. The syllabus is to be designed to teach students:
   - a. to master the art of instructing, both in the air and on the ground;
   - b. (i) to fly single-engined training aircraft accurately, and to their limit, under all weather conditions by day and by night;
     - (ii) to fly representative service-type aircraft;
     - (iii) to be able to teach on those service-type aircraft which they are qualified to fly;
   - c. to understand the problems and the practical methods to be followed in training cadets to be officers; and
   - d. to organise flying instruction so as to obtain the best results from the resources of instructors, technical personnel, and aircraft, available in a training unit.
3. The Examining Wing. The Examining Wing at the Central Flying School is:
   - a. to provide an inspectorate of flying training for all commands in the United Kingdom, and for the Rhodesian Air Training Group;
   - b. to undertake the examination and recategorisation of flying instructors of category B and above;
   - c. to appoint examiners under the RAF instrument rating scheme;
   - d. to ensure that the latest instructional technique is being used by qualified flying instructors;
   - e. to provide liaison between units employing qualified flying instructors, and the Central Flying School;
   - f. to feed back to the Central Flying School information on the latest ideas on operational flying which may affect instructional technique; and
   - g. to provide examiners, when necessary, to accompany composite teams of examiners in the operational roles, on their visits to commands abroad.

(Originally signed by Air Chief Marshal Sir Ralph A. Cochrane GBE KCB AFC then AOC-in-C Flying Training Command.)

12 January 1950

CHAPTER 1

Little Rissington Welcomes CFS

1946

Wg Cdr Ron A.E. Allen was trained to fly in the USA in 1942 after his UK training was curtailed into a mere grading course of about 12 hours on Magisters at Kingstown, 3 miles north of Carlisle, when no further ab initio flying training courses in Britain were permitted to begin after 1 June 1942.

"This was largely to assist with sheer airspace management and facilitate that massive expansion in the number of active airfields to allow the Anglo-American build up for the Allied strategic bomber offensive and support of air operations up to and beyond the invasion of Normandy," Ron explains. *"By 1945 and the war's end there would be a grand total of 687 active airfields, a total confirmed by my carefully counting them off a Met Office 1945 airfield chart, corroborated by the total of 586 or so airfields historically hosting front line RAF squadrons. For the last three years of WW2 ab initio flying training was provided abroad by the Commonwealth Air Training mainly in Canada, South Africa and Rhodesia and the two Arnold Schemes of training in USA, firstly the 50:50 Anglo-American scheme and secondly the 100% British Flying Training Schools in Texas. By early 1946 therefore in UK there was now an urgent requirement to drive towards re-building the status and output of CFS in both quality and quantity. Already the Empire tag on the ECFS was beginning to seem dated with its earlier mixture of Australian, New Zealand, South African, Rhodesian, Canadian and even American links and to re-designate this as the Commonwealth CFS also made less sense. In 1949 the Examining Wing came under CFS and for only a few months they were housed across at RAF Brize Norton before co-locating with their parent unit at Little Rissington."*

New beginning

Following the cessation of hostilities in Europe and the rapid introduction of jet powered aircraft in the RAF, staff at 7 FIS soon realised that the unit would have to find a location offering tarmac runways and supporting facilities: the abundance of redundant airfields provided the ideal opportunity to relocate. Legend had it that the reason for siting CFS *on top of a mountain* at RAF Upavon was to symbolise the highest honour a pilot could attain, a posting to the staff of CFS. When the School was re-formed at RAF Little Rissington, *on top of Everest* may have seemed more apposite as, at 730 ft. above sea level, Little Rissington was the highest operational RAF airfield in the U.K.

On 22 January 1946, RAF Ramsbury became a satellite of Upavon and plans were made to move 7 FIS there. However, flying ceased on 15 April and two days later packing started for the move to Little Rissington, the Ramsbury plans having been dropped. While preparations continued it was decided to split the move between Little Rissington and RAF South Cerney. An advance party left for Little Rissington on 24 April followed a week later by the main party. The last aircraft to depart were half-a-dozen Oxfords. Aircraft colour schemes were changed to overall yellow then silver with yellow bands and new black code letters began to appear, e.g. Oxford T.1, HM696 FDL-F and Harvard T.2b, FX199 FDM-P. During May, 7 FIS became the nucleus of a reformed Central Flying School. The rear party arrived at Little Rissington and South Cerney on 7 May.

The 7 FIS Commanding Officer, Gp Capt E.A.C. Britton, was appointed CO Little Rissington and on 2 May transferred from Upavon with his staff to form a nucleus of CFS staff. In place of the small, uneven grass field to which they had been accustomed, they found a fine, large aerodrome with proper paved runways, all the hangar accommodation they could wish for and a spacious mess. The CFS was officially re-formed there on 7 May with four squadrons: No. 1 Squadron (Lancaster, Vampire, Spitfire, Auster and Harvard), 2 Squadron (Harvard, also Prentice from July 1947), 3 Squadron (Harvard and Tiger Moth) and 4 Squadron (Mosquito).

Flying commenced on the 6th of the month and the unit name reverted to Central Flying School on the following day. By the end of the month, unit strength had risen to 1,038 personnel and the School achieved a remarkable 1,240 flying hours with 85% serviceability of aircraft.

Early memories

W O Gill Davies served 38 years in the RAF and spent two tours at Little Rissington. The first began in 1945 as WO in charge of the Aircraft Servicing section and he remembers some of the station and social activities of the early post-war era.

"Each morning a flying instructor would be detailed to carry out a weather test in a Harvard or Oxford and on his return would file his findings with the OC Flying and Met Officer. In addition, it was the

Line-up of ECFS aircraft at RAF Hullavington, home to Examining Wing and a wide range of types, many of which were transferred to Little Rissington when the unit joined CFS. (*CFS Archive*)

duty of the Air Traffic Control Officer to carry out a safety inspection of the airfield and taxiways and to ensure that the emergency services, equipment and personnel were in place.

The SWO at the time was WO Watt who had boxed for the RAF and was known as 'Boxer Watt'. Discipline was high in his agenda and it was most unwise to upset him – sitting in his chair in the Sgts' Mess being the biggest of sins. He and the PTI formed a boxing club which was a great success with the young airmen.

Having received permission to fish the local landowners' lakes for no charge, a fishing club was also formed and many happy hours were spent by all ranks on the banks of the Windrush and the Thames at Lechlade.

Relations between service personnel and the local communities were excellent during the early post-war period. As television was not widely available the CO gave permission for civilians to use the Station Cinema. The local bus company, Pulhams of Bourton, provided regular daily services to remote villages and schools, as they do to this day. The health and well-being of base personnel was taken care of by the base's Sick Quarters which maintained close links with local medical practices. Although a small chapel was provided in the ground training block, many personnel attended the churches and chapels in Bourton, Stow and Little Rissington village. A number of civilian police provided support for the service police manning the guardroom.

The Sergeants' Mess provided a good all round social life for mess members and their guests. Summer balls were held and one had to attire oneself accordingly in full evening dress. Many WOs and SNCOs had seen operational service during the war and one of their more common expressions was 'I was upside down in the cloud and nothing on the clock'.

One of the duties of the Orderly Officer was to accompany the Orderly Sergeant on an inspection of the Airmen's Mess and asking for complaints concerning the food. These rarely came to anything as the OO had the last word."

Sorry Sir, you just missed them!

Gp Capt Tony Talbot-Williams remembers his early days as a Flight Lieutenant at CFS.

"As a specialist in pilot navigation – rather more important in the days of limited radio aids, and when it was considered a failure to call for a QDM – I was posted from instructing with 20 FTS at RAF Church Lawford to CFS at RAF Upavon on 7 May 1946. As was the fashion in those days, I merely bundled all my kit and my bicycle into an Anson and flew down. On landing at Upavon I was informed by the one man in the control tower that CFS had left for Little Rissington the previous week. The personnel staff had not caught up with this surprising event as CFS had been at Upavon since the beginning of the First World War

when Major Trenchard was the CO. So I took off again and arrived at Little Rissington, unloaded my gear and sent the Anson back to Church Lawford. This extra short flying leg had entailed doing those 120 turns of the manual undercart handle twice instead of once.

My other memories were of the living conditions in that large type 'A' Officers' Mess. It was less than 12 months since the end of the war and, with the huge numbers still serving, we accepted that it was necessary for three Flight Lieutenants to have to share a bedroom, and the rest of the mess was equally crowded. Food rationing and petrol rationing had been part of life for years but that did not stop Flt Lt Dickie Stoop driving fast to and fro across the front of the mess and doing 180° power turns at either end of the straight in his Fraser Nash BMW special, the engine of which he had somehow got from Germany. Dickie was the son of one of England's greatest rugby players of the pre first war era and later he frequently drove in the Le Mans race. The station commander, a little man called Gp Capt E.A.C. Britton DFC, added tone to the mess car park with his superb vintage Rolls-Royce tourer. For most of us, doing up pre-war cars – there were no new ones – was an essential Flying Wing pastime.

There were masses of 'civilians' still serving. A prep school headmaster, Sqn Ldr Langhorne, was the CGI and he later returned from being a wartime pilot to schoolmastering. I remember lecturing on Navigation and Met, as well as conducting the morning met briefing using the question and answer technique, which at least kept the 'hung over' students awake. Harvards were the chief training vehicle but my logbook records driving Oxfords and Ansons on what appear to have been quite a few 'jollies' to visit old friends elsewhere."

That the other ranks approved of their new station was enforced by the visit of AV-M F.F. Inglis, AOC No. 23 Group, on 3 July to present a trophy for the best WAAF quarters.

Gp Capt W.M.L. MacDonald CBE DFC took over command of the Station on 7 September, just in time to host the Battle of Britain open day which was held on the 14th. Low cloud restricted the flying display and was probably the reason for an attendance of only 300 members of the public.

Unexpected guests

Bad weather often caused the cessation of flying at Little Rissington, so the unscheduled arrival of an Irish Airways Dakota carrying four crew and 21 passengers on a flight from Dublin to Croydon on 1 October was cause for some excitement, all 25 being held to await the arrival of customs and civil police. In a similar incident not requiring the services of the civil authorities, Marshal of the RAF Sir Sholto Douglas, shortly to be Lord Douglas of Kirtleside GCB MC DFC RAF, initiated a precautionary landing on 29 December during bad weather.

CFS staff portray the dress code for the immediate post-war period, the most notable item of which is the forage cap. (*From l to r*), Flt Lt Reeve, Sqn Ldr Morgan, Wg Cdr Boult, Gp Capt MacDonald (OC), Sqn Ldr Granby, Sqn Ldr Tew, Sqn Ldr Webber. (*CFS Archive*)

1947

The big freeze

Heavy snow fell throughout much of Britain during the early part of 1947 and it was particularly bad at Little Rissington during February. With flying curtailed for most of the month, members of No. 98 Course, which got underway on 1 January, were sent home on indefinite leave. Twelve days later they were recalled, as there seemed a good chance of being able to get back into the air but no sooner had they returned to Rissington than the snow returned with a vengeance. The station was snowed in and cut off completely from the outside world.

W O Vic Deboni was a student on 97 Course at the time and remembers how bad it became:

"1946/7 was one of the worst winters in Britain. Never mind clearing the runways to fly, it took us all our time to dig through to Bourton-on-the-Water. As I remember it, the road lay between two steep banks topped by hedges and heaving the white stuff up there was good exercise. The road was the only means of supplying the station. In fact we were sent home several times when the station virtually closed down. Much of my gratuity vanished in a most enjoyable way!"

Every able-bodied male was issued with a shovel and a start was made on digging a path to Stow-on-the-Wold. When an officer at the front discovered that the metallic object he had struck was the top of a 'Halt at Major Road Ahead' sign, the decision was taken to dig through Sandy Lane to Bourton-on-the-Water instead. Spurred on by the thought of a pint at the Old New Inn, the breakthrough came after two days allowing the first supply truck to pass down the lane, its top just visible above the snow. As most service personnel were stuck on camp, food and fuel shortages became a major concern. A supply drop by transport aircraft replenished some food stocks but restrictions on heating remained in force throughout the freeze. A thaw began during the last week of March enabling No. 98 Course to recommence flying but it had to be extended by 14 weeks.

Students from Course No. 97 take time off to relax. (*back row, l to r*) Flt Lt Butterworth, Fg Off 'Paddy' Kinnin, W O Baker, Flt Lt Harper. (*front row, l to r*) Flt Sgt Whincup, W O Eccles, Flt Sgt Cooper, Flt Sgt Morgan, Flt Sgt Kefford, Flt Lt Ernett. (*Vic Deboni*)

Vic continues:

"Scattered in the fields surrounding the airfield were hundreds of Wellingtons parked nose-to-tail with their wings removed.

The CFS staff were marvellous. Sqn Ldr Langhorne, who was the CGI, showed us how a lecture on the dreariest subject could, with preparation, a good delivery and a bit of humour, hold everyone's attention. Our Flying Instructors Flt Lt 'Chunky' Ormrod (mine) and Fg Off Paddy Kinnin, were outstanding, both professionally and personally.

Although not an official entity, the Little Rissington Camera Club was popular while I was based there and a lot of 97 Course members developed an interest in photography at about the same time. One of the Course Officers whose identity I no longer recall offered to run a photography course. Many of us were enthusiastic and he obtained use of the Station Dark Room and equipment for the odd evening. Starting without any knowledge at all, we learned how to handle, develop and fix the film, the importance of solution temperatures; how to make contact prints and how to produce enlargements. My own camera was a Kodak 127 VPK (Vest Pocket Kodak 7). Film was not readily available – wartime shortages in Britain continued for many more years – but when you did find some film it was a nameless brand prepared from surplus RAF stocks. Thick and stiff to handle when processing, it was orthochromatic – not sensitive to red, unlike panchromatic. For me it was the beginning of what became almost an obsession."

A little humour goes a long way

Vic also remembers an amusing incident that happened during a lecture.

"Course 97 was typical of any group of males of differing and unknown personalities. One particular member possessed to the nth degree a quality that enabled him to charm … let us say, the birds off a tree – where the opposite sex was concerned. It was no secret that he used that quality to the utmost. Let's just call him 'X'.

Sqn Ldr Langhorne, Chief Ground Instructor at the time, had lectured us on various subjects and, on this day, was dealing with the drives to which individuals are subject, keeping in mind the importance of the instructor supporting the drive which urges the student pilot to achieve success in his flying career. Probably oversimplifying on Freud, he drew a diagram like a horizontal strip of ribbon with a dividing line midway to the width and running along the length. The upper portion was labelled 'Power Impulse' and the lower one 'Sex Impulse'. The total width he labelled 100% and he pointed out that any increase in one part resulted in an equivalent decrease on the other. As an example he mentioned the typical elderly spinster, who had never had any interest in sex but strived to dominate everything and everyone within reach, typical of a person whose power impulse is close to 100%.

He continued: 'On the other hand, we all know the sort of person who has no interest in power or dominance, but is eternally searching for some hole into which he can insert himself.........'.

He got no further. As one – every single head in the classroom turned

RAF Little Rissington airfield North side (*previous page*), depicting the accommodation, administration and hangars allocated to CFS, circa 1947. South side (*above*) with the MU hangars to the right and the peri-track link criss-crossing the Great Rissington/Barringtons road, leading to the aircraft storage pans and hangars in fields further south, circa 1947. (*RAF Museum*)

to look at 'X'. Like a glass being filled with red wine, so his face reddened from the neck upwards until it glowed like a beacon. The class collapsed in hysterics. I doubt that any of those present will have forgotten the occasion. A bit of humour in the classroom goes a long way."

CFS trophies returned

Instruction was received in March that all CFS trophies were to be returned to CFS at Little Rissington from the Empire Flying School at RAF Hullavington where they had been on loan for several years. The trophies concerned are believed to have been the CFS Trophy and the Clarkson Trophy as these were once again awarded from course No. 100. Flt Lt Gibbons was the first recipient of the Clarkson Trophy when he flew in the 'Aerobatic and Forced Landing' competition, the name by which it was then known. Over the ensuing years several new competitions and trophies were instituted and details can be found in the Appendices.

Courses increase in number and length

When it was realised that the allotted Course duration was too short, irrespective of weather conditions, it was extended from 12 to 18 weeks, with new intakes of 45 students arriving every 10 weeks. Increasing tensions due to the 'Cold War' saw a rapid increase in the number of students and course frequency. As one course progressed from elementary flying on Tiger Moths to advanced flying on Harvards, another was ready to take its place.

Course 100

Having returned from a tour in the Far East in the winter of 1946/47, Flt Lt John Gibbons arrived at Little Rissington as a student on No. 100 Course.

"This was the first full post war Instructors course. Because of the bad weather it was delayed until April. In January we dug our way out down the little lane one day and the next night it filled up to the hedgerows and we had to dig it out again. Then we were cut off completely and eventually relied on an air drop of food from a Dakota."

Instrument Rating Scheme

In 1947 an important development took place, which rapidly improved the overall standards of RAF flying. This Instrument Rating Scheme spread throughout the service to become so accepted and useful that its benefits were rapidly and universally taken for granted from that time forward. Although he was not yet at CFS, this major innovation affecting every RAF Command can best be covered through the recollections of Flying Officer Ron Allen, who would transfer to Little Rissington a few months later as one of the four IREs (Instrument Rating Examiners) at CFS.

"On 8 October 1947, while still at RAF Church Lawford, I had become the seventh instructor to be selected and tested on the ground and in the air to be awarded the new Green Instrument Rating Card just being introduced into RAF usage. As one of the first two 'IRE' Harvard examiners at Church Lawford, I had to return and help bring in this then brand new Instrument Rating Scheme (IRS) at my unit. The Air Ministry's aim was to create a truly modern 'all weather Air Force' by improving the overall flying capability of all its pilots. There would be regular instrument flying training conducted by a system of categorised examiners training and testing all pilots annually to much more rigorous standards. Earlier I had carried out the short specialist Standard Beam Approach (SBA) course at Watchfield near Swindon. We were able to train and operate down to 100 ft cloud bases and less than 150 yds in visibility because of the beam's accuracy and the inner marker's note allowing one to fly the aircraft in for landing at a set, safe and dwindling

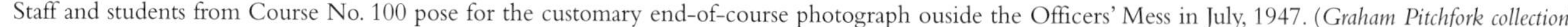
Staff and students from Course No. 100 pose for the customary end-of-course photograph ouside the Officers' Mess in July, 1947. (*Graham Pitchfork collection*)

Mosquito T.3, HJ978, undergoing attention outside No. 1 Hangar. (*Les Lane*)

rate of descent, if correctly positioned. By the mid 1950s technical developments internationally in avionics, dramatically illustrated by a few early excellent US base GCA controlled talkdown facilities in Britain, would tend increasingly towards the ILS and radar approach systems, which first complemented and then replaced SBA. Reverting to SBA training sorties in 1948, the honeypot airfield in UK to go to and practise SBA approaches and to land off the beam was RAF Honiley (south west of Coventry), also developing radar and talkdown GCA procedures. Instructional aircrew at CFS and elsewhere were universally agreed that the prettiest WAAF in the service at that time was working up in Honiley's air traffic control!

The IRS, which initially only consisted of Unrated, White and Green Card ratings, was largely the brainchild of Wg Cdr Shelfoon at ECFS RAF Hullavington, who subsequently ended up as DT(F) Director of Flying Training. At CFS I well remember the discussions of whether recovery, inevitably on limited panel (see note below), from a fully developed spin should be a separate element in its own right for the annual Instrument Rating Test (IRT) beyond the 'Recovery from unusual positions' exercise. Certainly in the Harvard, you had to bring the nose right up a long way and fly the aircraft determinedly to enter any spin. Many will have carried out a full spin on limited panel but CFS policy evolved and prevailed that this full spin recovery on limited panel should not be made a mandatory part of the formal IRT exercise. The correctness of this policy had been reinforced by the death of a fellow CFS instructor who had flown off to RAF White Waltham. He had been practising such manoeuvres in marginal weather and had crashed straight in and there had been a few other similar fatalities. One could argue over the value of this directive but this decision does seem correct with hindsight. A flexible variety of 'unusual positions' could be set by either safety pilots or examiners to suit UK's frequently prevailing cloudy weather flying conditions at medium altitudes. Instrument flying sorties or I/F segments of mixed sorties could thus maximise training value without unnecessarily increasing flight safety hazards."

Limited panel was instrument flying without using the prime instrument – the Artificial Horizon. In those days the Artificial Horizon would topple if you went inverted and would take a little time to reset. It was therefore important to be able to fly on the remaining instruments, the Airspeed Indicator, Altimeter, Turn and Slip Indicator, Vertical Speed Indicator and Compass. By cross-referring to all these you could work out which way was up!

"Flying instructors would agree how fundamentally useful the IRS proved to be in improving operating flying standards across the whole of the Royal Air Force – there were also other additional indirect but real benefits in completely different aspects of applied and operational flying. With the later introduction of the Master Green card category this did allow experienced pilots even more independence and flexibility. Rated pilots, flying into and out of other airfields and those of different Groups or Commands, could fly off in and down to their rating minima. At or away from one's home base, diverting or visiting aircrew, as much as the supervisory commanders on host stations and diversionary airfields, would find the Unrated, White, Green and Master Green cards scheme invaluable in changing or marginal weather conditions. Coupled to the use in Fighter Command of Master and Diversion Airfield status operational and present weather 'states' of Black, Red, Amber 3, 2 and 1 then Green, the IRS dramatically assisted more aircraft operational re-deployments, in turn enhancing force capabilities. This 'Green' airfield weather state in this instance means open and excellent weather, good visibility and a high cloudbase, suited for Unrated and White card less experienced pilots, so should not be here confused with those IRT Green and Master Green cards awarded to more experienced leaders and pilots, flying down to those much worse 'Amber 3' and 'Red' weather margins. The logging each month of every pilot's 'simulated' (training with a safety pilot or instructor) and 'actual' (within cloud) I/F within his overall flying also recorded the increasing experience necessary for Green and Master Green rating cards.

Personally I found the blue goggles in the Harvard were better with a ventilator fitted to avoid their misting up. Before this blue goggles and amber screen system for simulation of cloud flying and the later helmet visors, there had already been a two stage amber system. The Link trainers, which virtually all flying stations had but which had no natural feel, were only used at CFS for a couple of hours a month. These were gradually phased out at the same time as the departure of SBAs and the advanced piston trainer aircraft in the middle and second half of the 1950s. Simultaneously the declining day to day importance of signals squares and certain other procedures were accelerated by the ever increasing reliability of radios and the introduction of supporting radar and navigational aids."

1948

New magazine

In March 1948, the Central Flying School's first magazine was produced. Priced at one shilling and edited by the education officer, Flt Lt K.S. Tayler, the Foreword was written by the Commandant, Gp Capt W.L.M. MacDonald, who said that he was sure the magazine would be a great asset to CFS in building up team spirit and keeping in touch with CFS aims and events.

A lady at the wheel

Betty Smith holds the distinction of being the first civilian lady motor transport driver at Little Rissington, having joined No. 8 MU as early as 1941.

"During my time as a driver" says Betty, *"I drove many different vehicles including Hillman, Bedford and Chevrolet trucks, and BSA motor cycles. I was often nominated to pick up VIPs arriving at the camp, one of the most famous being Amy Johnson and her husband Jim Mollison when they flew Spitfires into Rissington for armament furnishing by 8 MU.*

The airmen assigned to the MU could not go off camp very often due to the lack of transport. On one occasion I almost got caught smuggling a number of airmen out for a day in Broadway in the back of a Hillman during a routine trip to Honeybourne. On the return journey I picked them up before heading off back towards the camp, when disaster struck on Stow Hill; the front wheel suffered a puncture. With no tools or spare wheel, I had to contact the camp for assistance to be sent to fix the wheel. Meanwhile, the airmen, not wanting to drop me in the cart, hid behind a high stone wall until the wheel was fixed. The airmen treated me like an angel.

During the war years the YMCA in Bourton was a regular haunt for airmen based at Rissington, where tea and beans on toast became their special treat. At my suggestion, attempts were made to hold a dance there for the airmen. Sgt Chapel, who played in the station band, said they could supply the musicians if the Station Adjutant granted permission. My brother, who ran the local butcher's shop, went in his butcher's van up to the camp to see the Adjutant, Sqn Ldr Cording, who agreed it was OK by him. He required the CO's permission who was then in the Officers' Mess. So he and the Adjutant went off to the Mess in the butcher's van, which had the slogan 'We supply the Best Sausages' painted along the sides. The sight of the Adjutant in this most unusual mode of transport drew sniggers from officers and airmen encountered en-route. However, the CO agreed to my request and the Station band played at many YMCA dances over the following years."

Cartoon depicting Betty's predicament (*Betty Smith*).

Course Curriculum

By the spring of 1948 the CFS was charged with training 240 instructors a year on 4 courses, each comprising 24 weeks. The unit was now reorganised with three Wings; Training, Technical and Administrative. Four Squadrons, with two Flights in each, operated under Training Wing. The establishment of each Flight was a Flight Commander, five instructors and 15 students, and an additional instructor was assigned to each Squadron to cover for leave or sickness.

The course curriculum required each student to fly a total of 110 hours, broken down into 62 dual and 48 'mutual', where two students fly together, each taking it in turn to act as instructor. To say that the Rissy circuit was busy would be a gross understatement, a total of around 13,200 hours being flown per annum.

Before students were selected for CFS courses, they were required to have a minimum of 500 hours in their log-books, and their suitability was judged on their arrival at Little Rissington, the Commandant having the final word. Students from the Dominions' Air Forces and Royal Navy were accepted without an interview. Air Observation Post courses were run for Army pilots as requirements demanded.

Instructor Categorisation

At the end of their courses students were given a rating category which was dependent upon their capabilities and until 1947, three main categories were used, A, B, or C. In May 1947, Vic Deboni received a C rating which, he understood,

"meant that it was a probationary category which could not be held indefinitely. A test had to be taken with an A category instructor to be recategorised to B. This occurred in the following August after I had been instructing at RAF Tern Hill and had my recat test with the Sqn Ldr OC Flying. Recategorised to B, this entitled me to an assessment of Average as Pilot, Average as Instructor – as long as I remained on Harvards. I could not authorise a first solo or test a C. I could remain a B forever and many did. In March 1948 I flew to ECFS at RAF Hullavington and after testing in the air and on the ground was

recategorised to A2. 'A' categories were published in AMOs. I was now entitled to an Above Average Assessment as Pilot and as Instructor as long as I continued instructing on Harvards. The really ambitious who rose to A1 category (and which was expected of anyone instructing at CFS) would then be entitled to an assessment of Exceptional."

Sometime during 1948 the ratings were reclassified as follows: Category 'B.1' (a capable instructor) or 'B.2' (an instructor on probation who had been taught the elements of flying instruction, who had the makings of a good instructor, but who required guidance in his work). The latter could be re-categorised to 'B.1' standard by his Chief Instructor after a period of three months instructing experience. 'B' graded instructors could be re-categorised to 'A.2' (a very capable and skilful instructor with considerable experience) or 'A.1' (an instructor of exceptional ability, skill and experience) by the Examining Squadron of the ECFS only.

CFS and Type Flying: a most attractive course for pilots

"My Central Flying School tour at Rissington in 1948 was most rewarding in several ways", says Ron Allen, *"since this also enabled me to qualify, mostly as QFI, on eleven new aircraft types. CFS in early 1948 was already much prized as a highly attractive course, more so than at any other time. The enthusiasm of pilots was so high, largely because of the additional experience of the type flying on Lancaster B.Mk.7, Mosquito T.Mk.3, Spitfire F.Mk.16 and Vampire F.Mk.3. To understand one must put these four 'type experience' aircraft in the context of that time, not only for the variety of these aircraft but that all were still up to date or operational front line aircraft types. Word spread rapidly and many aircrew wanted to come to CFS in those days. One of my own proudest achievements was to be able to take all four of my student instructors right through their complete course on Harvards and then supervise myself, all four individually, on each of their four type check outs and type training. We had a strict limit of only six hours of dual instructional flying allowed to send our under training instructors off solo on the Mosquito. At times some students only achieved this with quite a struggle, since this early post-war era was still a settling down period with a great mix of backgrounds of those arriving at CFS. This might have been one element in some of those accidents, which occurred at this time; in aircraft terms these losses were partly ameliorated by the fair number of Mosquito aircraft still being available. Remember too that the Mosquito T.3 had no war bomb load and was thus the most light and potent Mosquito to fly with its higher power to weight ratios. No. 8 MU at Rissington was always short of pilots, which provided even more available flying for the 'waterfront' QFIs, if they wished.*

On arrival at CFS in the spring of 1948, I had more than 2,000 hours with my instructional experience split roughly down the middle between Oxfords and the Harvard. There were about 10 to 12 QFIs who also came to Little Rissington from Lulsgate. Initially I had been invited down by CFS Chief Instructor, Wg Cdr Ben Boult, for a five man board interview. The CI's deputy as Chief Flying Instructor was Sqn Ldr Alf Knowles, who earlier had been an engineer before his pilot training. At that time I was still a Flying Officer until promotion a few months after my arrival. Anxious to go off to an operational squadron, I was not at all enthusiastic of yet a third tour, now to instruct new instructors. Bombarded with a mixture of seniority, charm and persuasiveness, I succumbed to their blandishments as they spoke of CFS's expanding commitments, which underpinned their dire need of my two tour instructional experience, my 1,100 hours on Oxford twins and 900 hours on Harvard.

Digressing on to the Harvard itself, what a magnificent trainer this aircraft really was – in my five and a half years I can only remember one return to dispersal with a magneto drop on that excellent Junior Wasp engine and virtually no emergency or problems in the air – she was what any trainer should be, robust and reliable as well as pleasant to fly and instruct on. The Percival Prentices, seen far more over at Cerney's Basic Training Squadron, climbed all too slowly and very much in a nose down attitude. They were 'modern' in the sense of having an enclosed cockpit, brakes, flaps, radio, a variable pitch propeller and full tailwheel, compared to the Tiger Moths they replaced. Apart from primitive biplane nostalgia, I found the Tiger less comfortable by far. Being tall, my head was stuck out too far into the airstream in any weather and often in too low temperatures for my liking. Comparatively the Harvard was a purpose-built trainer from its inception unlike the Gnat, which was really a modified lightweight fighter concept altered to the market opportunity of a trainer. Many of the Gnat's emergency systems were meant just for occasional emergencies and not designed for such frequently repeated practice in the air of these quite complicated systems. The Gnat, although lively and much loved, demanded regular extra coverage of its idiosyncratic flying control characteristics and standby emergency procedures. Greatly underestimated were the cost and time in servicing and spares support to allow this, plus some of those inherent design deficiencies such as Dzus panels just beyond and above air intakes to the sheer tyre wear inevitable from the geometry of the outwardly splayed main undercarriage wheels. By comparison the Harvard's own emergency systems were so straightforward. The virtually foolproof undercarriage operation system of the Harvard must have been one of the best ever designed to prevent the dangers of untimely u/c selections by u/t pilots.

In those now distant days, particularly at CFS, type checkouts were more a question of an individual's own experience being trusted along with using those invaluable drills and succinct texts of the 1940's and 1950's Pilot's Notes, which seemed thereafter to double or more in size with each decade which followed.

The CFS course was three months to become an instructor and then a further three months to cover further consolidation and a variety of type flying, all of which were advanced and operational or nearly so at that time, such as the Lancaster, Mosquito, Spitfire, Vampire and later on the Meteor T.Mk.7. During this time there would be four differently phased 60 strong courses going through with 320 officers in the Mess – this number of well over 300 officers on the station at this time, I can verify because there had been a financial scandal just before my arrival. Because of this I was volunteered to become a most diligent and careful 'Wines Member for the Mess', heavily involved with the large number of social occasions required."

Bottle of wine, Sir!

An unusual incident that occurred during the Dining In night for No. 104 course on 4 May, involved Indian Air Force officer, Fg Off Jafar Zaheer. Earlier in the day he had been suspended from the course and, shortly after the toast 'The King', he poured a bottle of white wine over the Chief Instructor.

More students

The increasing need for instructors brought about the further reorganisation and expansion of CFS in August 1948 enabling the number of students under training to rise to some 360 per year. Each course became twenty-seven weeks in duration with sixty students entering at nine-week intervals. Two courses were conducted at Rissington the remainder at RAF South Cerney. Having a grass surface that could not be used by the larger aircraft, students reported to South Cerney (later Brize Norton) for the first two months of their Course, before moving on to Little Rissington for more advanced training. To accommodate this expansion the number of squadrons was increased from four to six. Numbers 1, 2, 3 and 4 Squadrons were based at Little Rissington with numbers 6 and 7 Squadrons operating out of South Cerney; there was no number 5 Squadron.

The aircraft inventory during this period comprised 34 Harvards, 17 Tiger Moths, 10 Mosquitos, 7 Lancasters, 4 Spitfires, 3 Vampires and a number of Prentices.

Early course experiences

As a young Flying Officer, John Severne had enjoyed his flying training towards the end of the war so much (Tiger Moths and Harvards), and also his first tour on a Mosquito Night Fighter Squadron just after the war ended, that he decided he wanted to put something back into flying. Thinking this could best be done by becoming a test pilot or by instructing, he soon realised he did not have the academic skills to be a test pilot and so opted for the CFS course.

Recalling that early period in his RAF career, John continues;

"There was little chance in those days (1948) of being stuck for ever as a QFI and I was prepared to take the risk. I admit that there was a certain attraction in going to CFS at that time because the course included the type flying. All CFS students in those days had to fly solo, not just on the types on which they were going to instruct, but also on the Lancaster, Mosquito, Vampire and Spitfire. Obviously it was not cost effective and I believe the scheme only lasted for about four courses before the Treasury put an end to it and the number of types was reduced.

I have particularly happy memories when I was selected to do the course at Little Rissington to learn how to become a flying instructor and have always felt that the type flying on that course did my flying far more good than hundreds of hours on a single type. I also came to realise that the best way to learn about flying was to try to teach it to someone else.

I well remember my first solo on the Lancaster. After 2.5 hours dual, my instructor, Flt Lt Graham Hulse who was subsequently killed in Korea, wanted to send me solo. The problem was that the flight engineer had been flying all morning and needed a spot of lunch and no other flight engineer was available. Graham, wanting to keep the aircraft flying, said: 'I will be your flight engineer, and so that I can have no possible influence on your flying I will lie down in the back so that I can watch the engine gauges!'

Looking back, one of the great joys of flying during my Tiger Moth training was that you had your head in the fresh air, there was no Air Traffic Control, no radio, no proper blind flying instruments and no navigation aids other than a wobbly magnetic compass and a map. It was great!"

A formation of Tiger Moths, with N9369 leading DE255, flies sedately over the Cotswold countryside during the summer of 1948. (*Christopher Blount, via John Severne*)

Admiral Sir Raymond Lygo KCB RN

Onetime Commanding Officer of HMS Ark Royal, later Chief of Naval Staff, then Chief Executive and Chairman of British Aerospace, and since 1996 President of FAA Officers Association, Sir Raymond Lygo reminisces on the arrival at Little Rissington of the 22-year old Lt R. Lygo RN in 1946.

"Rissington was perhaps one of the happier periods of my life and I remember the place with great affection. I first arrived on the second post-war instructors' course, which must have been some time in 1946. At that time there was a shortage of practically everything and for quite a bit of the time we had to go haymaking with the German prisoners of war! I well remember my first instrument flight with my instructor. As we walked back from the aeroplane, I apologised to him for the very rough performance I had just given. His answer rather stopped me in my tracks, when he said 'Well no, that's perfectly normal for an RN student'. At this time I quickly realised how lucky I had been to survive the war, flying in all kinds of instrument conditions and not really being on top of it – this was before the widespread introduction of the Instrument Rating and annual Card renewal system, which was a decided step forward in our RAF and RN weather flying capabilities.

After a year of instructing at RNAS Lee on Solent, I was asked to go back on the CFS staff, which I was delighted to do. Gp Capt Stephenson was then the CO and Commandant, later sadly killed on a flying exchange with the US Air Force. In those happy days we were allowed to fly and instruct on the types with which our students were going to be faced on their first instructor's assignment. This meant Mosquito, Tiger Moth, Harvard and Lancaster aircraft, so my claim from this policy was to be the only A1 instructor in the Navy qualified on a four-engined bomber!

At that time I had a dog called 'Buck', a bull terrier, who became quite enthusiastic about flying after I mistakenly took him up with me in a Mosquito and put him on the back shelf. After that, whenever he saw me in anything approaching flying uniform, he proceeded to go mad, wanting to come airborne with me. In those days, with the swirling propellers, there was always a danger that the dog would get off the lead and rush towards me and get chewed up on the way.

One minor episode might be amusing. One day when I was acting Flight Commander, I was asked to deal with a rather slack airman who had been late on parade. As he was wheeled in front of me and I was about to harangue him, my bull terrier, which was asleep in the corner, suddenly woke up. 'Buck' saw me facing this man, leapt out and attacked him. The Flight Sergeant said to me afterwards 'I don't think he'll come in front of you again, Sir!'

Among my 'secondary duties' in RAF parlance, I managed to run the station amateur dramatic section. Firstly I produced 'Dangerous Corner' and later both produced and appeared in 'Rookery Nook'. I then left CFS to go down to EFS to do the conversion course on to Meteors. At its end I was asked to go back to the RAF at the College of Knowledge, about to be opened at Manby. At the same time I was given the option of going on an exchange tour to the United States Navy and, for better or worse, I decided to do that.

As a result of this detachment to the RAF, I was able to avoid the Royal Navy at a particularly bad and dangerous time, when the accident rate was really rather alarming. Mind you, it wasn't particularly good at CFS because we were still in the midst of limit flying – I remember we spent more time on our Mosquito flying single-engined than we did twin-engined.

In summary there were only happy memories of Central Flying School. Your readers may be interested to know that I am still flying, as I have my own Cessna 421. How long this will go on for, I'm not quite sure."

A busy and happy station

Posted to No. 3 Squadron and a friendly welcome, Ron Allen ended up enjoying his CFS tour immensely.

"My first squadron commander was Sqn Ldr Roy Edge and I joined the staff formally after flying one brief introductory trip with him. After only twenty minutes he was kind enough to say: 'Well you certainly can make this bird sing – just take me back now for a flapless landing and that will be fine'. Roy was succeeded six to eight months later by Sqn Ldr Frank Dodd, another great character and successful Mosquito and Beaufighter pilot who would return to Little Rissington as Chief Instructor and later still, Commandant.

We flew once together and again he kindly said: 'You obviously have plenty of experience so I will have to listen to what you say on the Harvard, as I was mainly a Mosquito man'. Wg Cdr Ben Boult, our Chief Instructor, was from the pre-war 'old school' days, a precise officer but thoroughly insistent that our clear aim was to maintain and exceed pre-war flying standards. Subsequently Ben handed over to Tom Keen, who in turn himself handed over to Wg Cdr C.D. Tomalin, both again fine and well suited CIs. CFS was a happy station and Frank Dodd, a sterling individual among other fine officers and NCOs, also was determined to create a CFS renowned for its flying excellence. He helped set a well balanced mix of professional flying and high morale to achieve CFS's major task of turning out plenty of and ever better instructors. With few exceptions I do believe that the Central Flying School's role throughout the Royal Air Force was a significant and important factor in the improvement of flying standards and the steady reduction in flying accidents by the early 1960s, without any excessive reduction of that vital operational press on spirit in the air needed in a fighting air service.

New Commandant

Remembering little of my few months' overlap with Gp Capt W.M.L. McDonald, I saw more of his replacement, Gp Capt Geoffrey D. Stephenson, a pre-war Cranwellian. Having been captured as a POW early on in the war he had in fact a relatively few number of flying hours. This was something not that unusual among a range of officers in those early post-war years of re-alignment back into a peacetime RAF. After the drastic post-war contractions, officers came from a wide variety of previous jobs and backgrounds, which meant that there were several squadron leaders on the courses with only 300 or so flying hours and one

Wg Cdr with just over 400. The Commandant coped well with the demands of his extremely active responsibilities and would later become Commandant at the Central Fighter Establishment before being killed in a F-100 accident on an extended visit to the USA in November 1954.

Known as 'GD', I once had to fly him to RAF Hendon in a Prentice, a fast and easy way of getting to Air Ministry meetings via tube train up to central London. United States Army Air Corps Dakotas then also used Hendon for similar London visits. Here I witnessed a bizarre sight, having taxied in and parked fairly close to one such Dakota, which had a dozen or so rather untidy GIs lounging around aimlessly on the grass eating apples. In their full view 'GD' had quickly shed his flying suit and withdrawn from the back seat of the Prentice in his pinstripe city suit jacket, his rolled umbrella and bowler hat. Thus instantly kitted out, this City Gent apparition strode purposefully off from the antique looking Prentice, both so strange to the American airmen. The sight became just too much for their jokey mood and soon not just ribald comments overtook GD but several apple cores. Just beyond range and with a remarkable degree of both savoir faire and sang froid, the Commandant turned in their direction took off his bowler, bowed graciously and shouted out: 'Good day gentlemen, each and every one of you missed!'

A distant but distinct recollection was of an Indian officer at a Dining Out night being so upset at his final assessment given of his flying ability that he had upended the remnants of his wine bottle over the Chief Instructor's head to express his displeasure, not too long before he was quickly escorted away back to his room! From this train of thought I come to the definite historical watershed of the other big differences and special arrangements, which had to be made immediately after the British withdrawal and Partition in India, after all had been smooth before. All the Indians had to be grouped together and moved into rooms at one end of the Mess and all the Pakistanis to the other. At the same time all had to be segregated and placed on entirely separated squadrons, including only Indians or Pakistanis. Likewise from then on no Pakistani student could ever be sent off for mutual flying with an Indian.

Also on the courses were Egyptians, Belgians and I recall a Thai, whose name was Funyankanteratna, such a mouthful that he was universally known, wherever he went and to his own great delight, as 'Smithy'! Standards of achievement of some overseas students could inevitably not be kept as high as CFS might have wished for but their governments with or without assistance were paying for these courses. Internal mechanisms were in place to provide additional supervisory safeguards where necessary. However it was not always and only overseas students who led to those 'little local difficulties' on the ground or in the air for our instructors on the waterfront – I can remember a furious confrontation with a 44-year old, later Air Cdre in my Lancaster, after he had only had an accelerated part Harvard course after Defence College to help increase his experience before going to his staff job. Over this sort of incident one needed and virtually invariably received the unqualified support of one's CI and superiors - Tom Keen was great in backing up his instructors in this important respect of loyalty downwards.

Courses were just as lively in those earlier days at Rissington or even more so! One Dining in Night, where one of the courses had a Red Indian style pow-wow, complete with fire, in the entrance hall, their members ended up with a share of more than £800 being divided out across their mess bills, a most costly business in those days, with money worth about 18 times more in parity terms to now. There was an absolute maximum bar bill charge limit in those days set at £15."

This 1949 view of a Tiger Moth T.2 portrays the early post-war, four-letter style of coding used on CFS aircraft. T6274's career at Little Rissington was short-lived, lasting a mere two months. (*Dave Watkins*)

Battle of Britain

Battle of Britain day was held on the 18 September and was open to the general public from 13:45 to 18:00 hours. In the workshops and hangars displays of the various types of flying and ground support equipment were laid-out and demonstrations of some of the activities needed to maintain the base's flying commitments. On show in the static park were examples of each type of aircraft operated by the CFS, and a Spitfire and a pair of Tiger Moths participated in the flying display.

Boxing team shines

On the sporting front, the boxing team, AC Deed, Cpl Parking, AC Dunford, AC Way, LAC Sullivan and LAC Beard, performed brilliantly and brought the 'Lord Wakefield' senior trophy back to the station.

By contrast, the solitary Auster AOP.5, TW440, to operate with CFS, remained at Little Rissington from 1948 until 1951. Retaining its camouflage livery it carries the unit code FDMZ. (*Ray Sturtivant*)

1949

When Gp Capt G.D. Stephenson took over as Commandant in May 1949, the Berlin blockade had just been lifted but, with the number of trouble spots around the globe on the increase, the never-ending requirement for additional pilots placed increased demands upon CFS and operations at Little Rissington. This caused a big upheaval within the organisation, No. 2 Squadron being detached to RAF Brize Norton between September 1949 and March 1950 and the formation of a Type Flight (Meteor, Prentice, Tiger Moth, Auster and Anson) to replace 4 Squadron by September 1949. When the Empire Flying School at RAF Hullavington was absorbed into the RAF Air University at RAF Manby, the Examining Wing returned to CFS, its home unit before the war on 22 April 1949. On 30 June 1949, the Wing relocated to Brize Norton only to return to Little Rissington in May 1950.

Falling standards

Flt Lt Caryl Gordon, a close friend of John Severne, began his association with CFS and Little Rissington on Course No. 97 and on completion, was posted to 2 FTS at RAF Church Lawford as a Harvard instructor.

"I was also appointed PA to the AOC No. 23 Group, Air Marshal Ledger, when he carried out a repeat inspection of Little Rissington which had failed the previous one. When the WAAFs were marching smartly past, the 'undercarriage' of one young lady fell down – she was forced to a stop and had to be removed by ambulance. The AOC's face was a picture."

Rissy's uniquely sloping runway

On the Rissington runway topic, Ron Allen wishes to remind readers,

"of the inbuilt 6½° 'wing down to port' slope across the threshold of Runway 23, which may or may not have had some bearing on the Meteor incident described in the next paragraph. With Rissington's hump-backed, 1,600 yd length uphill and downhill, main runway slopes, one remembered also the airfield's other idiosyncrasies, with its 1,200 and 1,100 yd subsidiary runway lengths, those unusually gapped approach lights at night or in bad visibility, and its record airfield height. The Harvard's tailwheel lock had a 13° traverse limit either side of centreline, which meant one could spring it free and unlocked beyond 13½°, if one hit and jerked it. Because one always landed with that inbuilt corrective, transverse gradient component, it was necessary to land without too much drift in crosswinds. Care with torque and weathercocking considerations were needed to avoid the danger of ground looping.

Gloster test pilot Sqn Ldr W.A. Bill 'Split' Waterton's actual arrival at Rissy on 30 April to deliver the first Meteor T.Mk.7 trainer, VW437, after a few preliminary aerobatic manoeuvres over the airfield, ended by having a starboard undercarriage mishap on touchdown, with the wing tip then digging in and a departure off the runway."

Increasing workload

Having regained much of its pre-war reputation overseas, the number of students from foreign air forces undergoing CFS courses had begun to increase by October 1949 as can be gauged from the figures:

1 Squadron, Course No. 112
RAF (Officers) 26, RAF (Other Ranks) 16, RAAF 3, RIAF 3, RPAF 6, AOP 2.

2 Squadron, Course No. 111
RAF (Officers) 38, RAF (Other Ranks) 6, RIAF 3, RPAF 6, AOP 2, Egypt 2.

3 Squadron, Course No. 113
RAF (Officers) 43, RAF (Other Ranks) 8, Royal Navy 8, RIAF 1, Egypt 2, Iraq 2 and USAF 1.

Operation 'Bulldog' took place in October with the CFS playing a major role. Twenty-four Harvards and their crews were involved in the exercise their objective being to fly reconnaissance sorties over

Off-site trips were a rare occurrence, but in 1949 a group from Technical Wing participated in a visit to the Bristol Aerospace Company, the highlight of which was a tour round the Brabazon airliner then under construction. (*Les Lane*)

RAF Middle Wallop to assess the fighter strength of the base.

Trainer evaluation

In order to appraise the suitability of new aircraft in the flying training role, CFS carried out a familiarisation and evaluation trial of the Boulton Paul Balliol T.Mk.2 and Avro Athena T.Mk.2 piston-engined trainers. Two examples of the Balliol, VR593 and VR594, and a pair of Athenas, VR566 and VR567, arrived at Little Rissington in late October 1949 for the trial which lasted until July the following year. Neither aircraft saw further service with CFS.

Meteor makes public debut

The following extract is from the Gloucestershire Echo:

"The CFS had received its first Meteor T.7s some three months ago and was anxious to show them to the public at the Battle of Britain day, 17 September 1949. The team was initially led by Sqn Ldr Stimpson, who had the 'brilliant' idea of tying the aircraft together for the display; the other members were not too keen on this and the idea was subsequently dropped! The team first flew together on 1 September and had a further eight rehearsals before Stimpson left and was replaced by Tony Brown. They appeared at four displays on the 17th; twice at Little Rissington and once each at South Cerney and Hullavington, and at RNAS Yeovilton on 24 September. Their final display was at the School of Land and Air Warfare at RAF Netheravon on 5 October. The team comprised Flt Lt A.G. 'Tony' Brown, Flt Lt G. 'Graham' Hulse, and Lt (A) A.R. 'Ray' Rawbone, RN.

The BoB Day, which appears to have been quite an event according to the newspaper, included a mass flypast of 31 Harvards, a formation of USAF Superfortresses, and a handicap air race. 10,000 people turned up to watch the event."

(*Inset*), Avro Athena T.2s, VR566 and VR567, flying in formation while on loan to CFS at Little Rissington. The pilot presses the start button and the Rolls Royce Merlin on Boulton Paul Balliol T.2, VR594 (*Below*), roars into life at the start of another evaluation flight. (*MAP*)

From USA and Mossies to Rissy

Fg Off M.F.H. Dobson went to the USA for his Wings course, at Ponca City, Oklahoma. On completion he returned to the UK and went on to fly Mosquitos with 98 Squadron (2 TAF) and 109 Squadron at Coningsby. On 19 September 1949, Fg Off Dobson joined No. 113 Course with an initial phase at RAF Brize Norton.

"When transferring to Rissington on 21 November, Flt Lt Netherwood was my main instructor and Sqn Ldr Frank Dodd was then OC No. 3 Squadron. Wg Cdr Tomalin was OC Flying and Wg Cdr Bunce Chief Instructor. Living down in Bourton in that particularly bad winter of 1949, at times because of its icebound hill, any journey into Rissy was completely impossible. Unusually 113, maybe as an experiment, had eight Royal Navy aviators, unusually high by future numbers – perhaps this near self-sufficient group did rather keep to themselves without integrating so well like the more normal later two or three. Coping with language and patter was not that easy, coupled to the flying workload for some of the four pilots we had from Egypt and Iraq, plus one from India. Our one USAF fellow student was a very capable ex-wartime medium bomber pilot."

Harvard tragedy in bad weather

Flt Lt W.M. 'Paddy' O'Kane was a most popular and competent Pilot Navigation Instructor (PNI) with whom Ron Allen played soccer for Little Rissington at wing half.

"Unfortunately on 6 December 1949, after abandoning a Navex in Harvard FT331, his aircraft struck rising ground in cloud south of the airfield, perhaps without the regional pressure setting on his altimeter being correctly set – Paddy was killed but fortunately his Iraqi student survived the crash. In this type of situation with poor visibility and low cloudbase conditions, the rear seat vision was not of the best in the Harvard, one element often neglected in the side by side versus tandem cockpit layout trainer bar debates. In contrast other types of lateral vision required, as for joining up in formation flying echelons etc, could be much safer with the tandem layout, without any 'blind' side restricted by the other pilot's bulk."

1950

Following Government calls for economies, the Commandant instituted yet another reorganisation. The services of the satellite station at South Cerney were dispensed with and the duration of the courses was reduced from twenty-seven to twenty-four weeks at the beginning of 1950. The number of students on each course was reduced to forty and a new intake occurred every six weeks. This saved money without seriously affecting the quality or volume of the instructor training programme. The course content was revised and consisted of the following elements; six weeks at RAF Brize Norton for officer training and an introduction to the CFS syllabus. Two weeks leave was then followed by sixteen weeks flying and ground instruction at Little Rissington. Twelve weeks instruction to Air Publication 1732 standard preceded a final four weeks flying the various aircraft types on CFS strength; 7.5 hours on the Harvard, 9 hours on Tiger Moth and Chipmunk, 2 hours on Valetta and 8 hours on the Meteor.

Type flying was limited to the new Meteor T.Mk.7 jet trainers as these aircraft could not only cover most aspects of the training syllabus that were beyond the capabilities of the Harvards, but also provided students with an exciting finale to their Course.

Sporting hero

Rissy again found another sporting hero among its numbers when eighteen year old AC Tony Porter won the RAF Senior Sculls championship at the RAF Regatta which was held at Reading on 29 April 1950. After rowing some thirty miles during his cup-winning weekend, Porter's only comment was, *"I simply don't like short distance rowing"*.

Effects felt of Korean war

The convenience of having all Squadrons of the CFS at Little Rissington was short-lived as Britain found itself involved in another conflict, the Korean War which started on 25 June 1950. Concerned that it might develop into something more serious, the RAF began a drive for expansion, and preparations were put in hand to increase the number of training schools. With an increased obligation to turn out 750 students a year from the CFS, Gp Capt Stephenson had no choice but to reopen the South Cerney operation and reduce the Course duration to 16 weeks.

Some relief was provided by Volunteer Reservists many of whom had considerable experience as instructors. They were brought up-to-date on the latest techniques and passed out as 're-treads' after only a short six-weeks course at Cerney on Prentice basic training aircraft.

After two years instructing at RAF Cranwell on the Prentice and Harvard, Flt Lt John Severne was posted to the staff at CFS in 1950 where he says,

"I had three very happy years. Initially I was teaching qualified pilots how to instruct on the Harvard, but I was then fortunate enough to join the Meteor Flight where each student was sent solo on the Meteor. For most of them it was their first experience of the joys of jet flying. During this time I used to display the Meteor and I was also PA to the Commandant, Air Cdre 'Mark' Selway.

In those days there were no g limits laid down in pilot's notes and we knew little about metal fatigue. Furthermore there were no accelerometers fitted on the instrument panel. I was interested to find out when I blacked out so I made myself a simple accelerometer with a bolt on the end of a spring; I calibrated it by adding additional bolts to represent 2g, 3g etc. I got it up to about 7g before blacking out although things had got a bit fuzzy! (there were no g suits at that time). It was no wonder that several Meteors broke up in the air in those days because we were obviously overstressing the aircraft. There were no height limits laid down for display flying for CFS staff pilots at that time. What fun! Perhaps it is not surprising that some of us killed ourselves.

It was around this period that Jan Zurakowski, the Gloster test pilot, did his famous cartwheel at the SBAC Show at Farnborough. He was flying a prototype ground attack Meteor fitted with tip tanks. He would pull up to the vertical as if to do a stall turn, but instead of rotating through 180 degrees to face vertically downwards, he did 1.5 complete turns before descending - very impressive! For the next few weeks there were Meteor pilots throughout the RAF trying to complete this dramatic manoeuvre, but all we could do was one complete turn. We were thus facing vertically upwards and going backwards downhill! This didn't do the aircraft much good and rivets were popping all over the place! Within days we were forbidden to attempt the Zurakowski Cartwheel. The reason he was so successful was that he had fuel in the tip tanks and the momentum kept him going for that extra half turn!"

'Fine body of men!'

Having returned to Little Rissington to take up his post as Flight Commander in 1950, Flt Lt Peter Gilpin was appointed as Officer in charge of the Guard of Honour.

"The Commandant was Gp Capt G.T. Jarman DSO DFC, who later achieved unfortunate notoriety in the newspapers by being called on to resign his commission because he had used airmen and RAF materials in service time to assist in the building of a boat – at this stage he was stationed somewhere up in NE England.

The 1950 AOC's Inspection misfired on a number of aspects, culminating in the formal inspection of the Officers' Mess. The AOC opened an airing cupboard door to find a workman taking a snooze in the warmth. The Inspection terminated instantly and the AOC did not stay for lunch. The Inspection was to be repeated at a later date. I am pleased to say that the Guard of Honour was about the only thing that had really gone well. Readers can imagine that life was hell on the station for those next two months.

When Her Majesty was Queen Elizabeth, she paid her first visit to Cheltenham on 16 March 1953, and I had the honour of having my CFS Guard of Honour lined up on the town's boundary to greet her arrival. She stepped down out of her car and inspected the chaps, who all were splendid. The Guard of Honour was restricted to 50 men but I always had more trained up to cater for leave, sickness and other eventualities. That day the hardest decision was to weed out a number to reduce the total to 50. I had told them all earlier that I would have to do this but it would be no reflection on them, as they really were superb. All were taken on the day so that they would be able to see HRH."

One overstressed Meteor and lucky escape

"The Meteor breaking up phenomenon seemed normally to be associated with high speed, often with the port u/c D-door panel first opening slightly, with or without 'g', and then this high speed airflow rushing inside and entirely destabilising the wing structure into disintegration," explains Ron Allen who goes on to tell of one such incident involving Flt Lt Graham Hulse. *"Graham was the man who did much to demonstrate the Meteor T.Mk.7 at CFS with flair early on, often inverted and well up to and beyond its limiting speeds of 490 kts or 590 mph, often to push up before pulling back through on to the runway centreline. However, it didn't always go to plan! On 29 June 1950, and watched with some awe, Graham pulled up in T.7, WA668, and was passing through 500 ft or so and at about a 40° climb angle, when he initially lost both sides of his tailplane and continued another 1,000 ft or so before gradually shedding the rest of the airframe as wings and fuselage broke up, leaving him flying in some sort of fashion more or less upwards, still strapped in his seat. Releasing his harness and pulling his ripcord he was fortunate to land in a rather dishevelled state beyond the north side of the airfield in a field. Gathering in his parachute and shroudlines, he noticed a car slowly coming down the nearby road. He rushed to the road to flag down an elderly lady driver so as to get a lift back to Little Rissington. As the lady pulled to a halt, she wound down the window and asked him: 'Were you the pilot of that aircraft I just saw breaking up, young man?'. 'Yes, ma'am, that was me' was all he could think of in reply to her beady gaze. 'Well then, young man', she said with deliberation, 'I really do think you should be much more careful'. She wound up the window with a sanctimonious air and drove sedately off, leaving Graham stranded and completely speechless.*

Graham married a wealthy and attractive lady, who presented him with an Armstrong Siddeley for a wedding gift. Not before long he managed to do a complete 360° roll in this remarkable gift and at a speed reputedly at over 70 mph – he and his new wife, with no safety straps at all, were lucky to survive with barely a bruise and little damage to the car's expensive bodywork!

Another incident involving Graham was when he was airborne in a Lancaster when, shortly after take off in the climb out, the whole instrument panel fell out forward and down on to him without any instruments then being visible. For well over an hour he circled to burn off fuel above cloud before getting a random sight of the Gloucester road and somehow managing to fly back down again and land safely, without any shepherd aircraft despite his instrument-less predicament – this said something for what could be done by a CFS pilot in good flying practice. Both the Lincoln and Lancaster had an element of natural feel through their flying controls and there were adequate warning buffet signals at lower airspeeds approaching the stall but still this was a good practical example literally of an experienced CFS pilot having to fly completely 'by the seat of his pants'! Sadly in the Korean war, Graham Hulse would be one of those killed on active service there when flying an F-86 Sabre."

Another person to witness Graham's Meteor breakup was Flt Lt Ian Roxburgh, writing in *People, Planes & Providence*:

"In 1946 I was offered a permanent commission, which under pressure from my brand new wife and my parents, I turned down. It did not take me long to find out that I was not well suited to civilian life. When the Berlin blockade arose, with the possibility of further hostilities, I decided I had better take up the offer of a permanent commission, which fortunately still stood.

So after a gap of three years I was back in the RAF. On rejoining I was sent to a flying school to be 'refreshed' and then posted to CFS, the very font of flying, as a flying instructor. One of its many traditions is to provide air displays. Flt Lt Graham Hulse had a close call when rehearsing for a display in a Meteor jet. Round about the same time 'Birdie' Wilson, a later Commandant, had a similar experience in a Meteor.

Graham Hulse was a delightful chap and a brilliant pilot. Soon after this incident he was sent out to the USA for three months to demonstrate the Balliol Trainer. He became so popular in the US that a request was made for him to join the USAF on an exchange posting and thus he joined a Sabre fighter squadron in Korea, where he was shot down. A helicopter almost managed to rescue him but was unable to do so because of the arrival of enemy troops. Graham was captured and never heard of again."

The sound of Merlins droning over Rissy was a common sound at the turn of the fifties, most notably from the half-dozen Lancasters operated by CFS. The Mark B.7, NX737, depicted here carries the unit code FDIB and a yellow training band round the rear fuselage. (*Ray Sturtivant*)

Hobson's choice!

Air Cdre John F. Langer CBE AFC has clear memories about his decision to become an instructor.

"After $2^{1}/_{2}$ exciting and happy years as a Flight Commander on No. 33(F) Squadron, flying Tempest IIs in Germany, Singapore, Malaya and Hong Kong, I returned to the UK expecting a flying job within Fighter Command. To my horror I was posted to RAF Little Rissington in October 1950 to attend No. 123 CFS Course. When I objected strongly, I was told that the alternative would be a ground job at RAF College Cranwell – so my becoming an instructor was Hobson's choice. Fifty of us reported for the course, 47 completed it successfully – more by luck than good judgment. I came fourth in the order of merit thereby, unwittingly, making a return to the CFS staff a distinct probability – perish the thought!

The course was unremarkable but was livened up by the Chief Flying Instructor, Wg Cdr Tomalin, an Olympic high diver, who revelled in showing off his aerobatic skills during progress checks. I thoroughly enjoyed my flight with him, being accustomed to high 'g' loads and inverted flying but many of the students with Bomber, Coastal or Transport backgrounds came down to earth very much the worse for wear."

Balliol T.Mk.1

Three months after the conclusion of the Balliol T.2 trials at CFS the prototype Mark 1, VL892, arrived at Little Rissington on 25 October 1950, presumably for evaluation as the Mark 2 had already entered service. The Mark 1 differed in that it had a Mamba turbo-prop engine, but delays in the development programme saw the Merlin-powered Mark 2 ready for service first. Although VL892 was the world's first turbo prop, single-engined aircraft, it never went into production.

Flt Lt Severne undertook nine flights in the aircraft while it was with CFS and recaptures his experience of flying a turbo-prop for the first time.

"I don't honestly know why we had this aircraft. VL892, was certainly at CFS from 25 October 1950, when I first flew it, to 9 January 1951, when I force landed it at RAF Strubby!

VL892 was a fascinating aircraft to fly. Turbo-props have a high idling speed and a narrow range of operating RPM, so an efficient variable pitch prop with a rapid pitch change is the order of the day. I seem to remember this one changed pitch at a rate of 60 degrees per second. As the throttle is opened the fuel is injected, but the rapid pitch change keeps the RPM the same – just the thrust changes very quickly. This meant that the sudden increase in power could be quite dramatic. I remember trundling along to let a Harvard formate on me and I thought I would show him what this remarkable aircraft could do. I slammed the throttle open (literally) and the Balliol shot forward in a way that even I as its pilot was surprised!

It had one disconcerting quality in that if it detected an engine failure the propeller automatically feathered. On my last flight I was delivering VL892 to Strubby and as there was no-one in the circuit I arrived at high speed at about 1,000 ft and did a very tight turn over the top of the airfield when the engine decided to fail. A second or two later I saw a stationary propeller in front of me accompanied by a deafening silence! I was ideally placed for a forced landing and chose a runway which was not the runway in use. As I came to a halt on the runway the Wing Commander Flying drove up in his car, not looking particularly pleased, and said: 'do you usually land those things like that?' What I had not appreciated was that I had forgotten to turn off the fuel cock (I suppose I was too intent on landing safely) and consequently unburnt avtur was pouring into a hot jet pipe creating a dramatic smoke trail. What with that and landing a single-engined aircraft with a feathered prop on the wrong runway, I suppose anyone would have been a bit surprised!"

Prototype Balliol T.1, VL892, seen on a flight test some time before its short sojourn at Little Rissington. (*MAP*)

CHAPTER 2

Into the Jet Age

1951

The aircraft inventory at the beginning of the year included the following aircraft types:

Meteor T.7, Prentice T.1, Chipmunk T.10, Harvard T.2b, Lincoln B.1, Valetta T.3, Firefly, Spitfire and Wellington.

Unit strength comprised:

Staff	156
Airmen	764
WRAF	52
Airmen/Aircrew	10
Total	982

A flight commander's tale

Flt Lt John Gibbons returned to Rissy on a staff posting in January 1950.

"Together with a friend of mine, I participated in the 1950 Farnborough air show performing synchronised aeros in two Chipmunks. The highlight of our display was to approach head on and do a flick roll as we passed each other.

In January 1951 I was made flight commander of the Meteor Flight. Our main task was to give students air experience in jet aircraft as the final part of their CFS course. These comprised 30-minute trips to 35,000 ft, talking all the time in an unpressurised cockpit four to five times a day. It was very hard work. At that time the Service was experiencing unexplained accidents with Meteor 7s. We discovered that many occurred during simulated single engine approaches where the QFI had left the air brakes out. This disturbed the air flow around the aircraft causing it to spin out of control and dive into the ground. Very nasty! I received my AFC for that discovery.

Another incident that comes to mind was when a Flight Sergeant in my flight suddenly found his ailerons jammed. He managed to maintain control using the rudder and returned to a safe landing at Rissy. It was subsequently discovered that a spanner had been left in the works and we

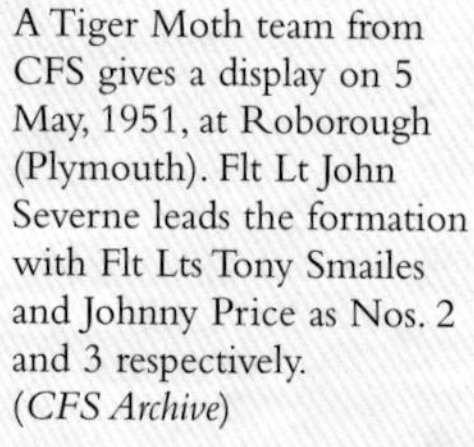

A Tiger Moth team from CFS gives a display on 5 May, 1951, at Roborough (Plymouth). Flt Lt John Severne leads the formation with Flt Lts Tony Smailes and Johnny Price as Nos. 2 and 3 respectively. (*CFS Archive*)

traced it back to the factory at Gloucester where the aircraft was built. I even managed to trace the tool to one particular floor in the factory during a personal visit but the Unions closed ranks and I was unable to find the person responsible."

From Whitleys to Harvards

As a Flight Sergeant Pilot, Peter Crouch undertook his first CFS course in 1951.

"My aviation life had been pretty mundane, Whitleys, Halifaxes, Hastings, Ansons but the first two had a glider attached to them now and then, and there was nothing mundane about that – it was quite frightening at times! The last two years, beginning January 1949, had seen me flying the Anson Mark 21 out of Hullavington with navigators under training and CFS 'Trappers' paid us periodic visits during which I had to demonstrate my flying ability. Late in 1950 one of them said: 'You seem to have been here some time, where are you going to be posted to?' I had to confess that I didn't know what openings there were for a Flt Sgt Pilot with just under two thousand hours. 'The Central Flying School, Flight Sergeant, that is where you should go. Become a flying instructor.' he said, 'And I will fix it.' I said a very doubtful 'Thank you, Sir', wondering what I had let myself in for and would I not have been better to go as a Link Trainer Instructor or Target Towing!

Things moved pretty fast – before I knew it I was at RAF Little Rissington for an interview, which I presume I passed because I was off to RAF Oakington for a single engine refresher course on Harvards. I remember my first slow roll, I lost 5,000 ft but I did get better by the end of the course. Having been refreshed and given one landing from the back seat (which nearly caused me to go AWOL), I went back to Little Rissington to join Course No. 123, which started on 1 January 1951.

Mary and I lived in a caravan and I was lucky enough to get a parking site behind the local pub, where they sold an intoxicating brew called Yankee Bitter. It was a gill of Best Bitter and a gill of rough cider. The course lasted six months: to begin with I could manage a half, maybe even a pint of this potent brew, but by the end of the course I could drink two pints before anaesthesia took over. I graduated as a below average instructor but my ability on the dartboard was rated as above average and occasionally exceptional, depending on how much I drank.

As students we were lectured, taught what to say and how to say it, and then we got airborne in the Harvard and practised teaching each other to fly. They gave me a ride in a Prentice and to this day I am not sure if it really was meant to fly or just someone's idea of a joke. Then one morning in April I was told to report to Type Flight to fly the Meteor.

I am basically a 'heavy' pilot and have an inbuilt mistrust of 'Fighter types'. My Granny once told me never to let my sister marry a fighter pilot and NEVER buy a second hand car from one. So it was with some misgivings that I trotted down to Type Flight. My instructor was Flt Sgt (later Master Pilot) Vic Brown and, on 25 April 1951, I was kitted up, taken around the aircraft for an exacting pre-flight inspection looking for loose rivets and skin ripples, before being introduced to the front seat of the Meteor T.7. Not a lot of room, I thought to myself, and indeed it was a close but comfortable fit. I followed Vic's comments around the pre-flight checks and under his control I started the engines. No noisy bangs with big things rotating, just a gentle hum and a slight vibration ... very nice I thought. As we taxied out I was impressed with the positive control of the nose wheel and the wonderful visibility forward. What a difference from the Harvard!

Percival Prentice T.1, VR267-FDIO, in standard livery and CFS codes of the era in which Flt Sgt Peter Crouch would have undergone his QFI training. (*MAP*)

The take off was a revelation, there was the positive push from the back of the seat, as we surged forward and, as our speed increased, so did the wind noise and the slap, slap, slap of the wheels as we crossed the runway expansion joints. Then the nose came up and the slap, slap, slap stopped and I was told to retract the wheels. There was a quick thump, thump, thump, as I moved the lever up, and the wheels were all tucked up and the undercarriage warning lights were out. The airspeed indicator was winding itself up and Gloucestershire was falling behind and below very rapidly. I could now feel a part of this wonderful bird that was opening new horizons for me.

I see from my log book that the exercise was aerobatics and circuits and landings. I remember we climbed to about 25,000 ft and I had reached there, higher and faster than ever before. We did a couple of clearing turns and went into the aerobatic exercise. I was very impressed by the ease with which it was possible to loop, roll and stall turn and I began to experience a little of what Plt Off Magee wrote so poetically about in 'High Flight'. We dived back towards Little Rissington when at about 4,000 ft the whole cockpit canopy misted over. I was definitely unhappy. I like to be able to look around but fortunately the front heated window was still clear but it was not very big! The voice from the back seat told me that we had to fly around at about three hundred knots to warm the canopy up and clear the mist; we did this and things returned to normal but I was not impressed and knocked off some 'brownie points' for this somewhat dangerous exercise. Landings were easy compared with tail draggers. Again I experienced the power of the jet and the exhilaration of the acceleration, as we flew a rapid couple of circuits and landings before we had to call it a day because our fuel state was getting low.

I was completely hooked. I did another flight with Vic Brown a week later when we investigated the asymmetric qualities of the aircraft – I realised that I needed a strong leg at times to keep control. I went back to flying the Prentice at 70 knots for a week before I was called back to Type Flight for another ride, this time with Flt Lt Devillez. We climbed to 35,000 ft for an introduction to compressibility at high Mach number then a let down back to Little Rissington for a couple of circuits and landings before the fuel state made us taxi in!"

Harvard tragedy

The year 1951 got off to a bad start when two Staff instructors from No. 2 Squadron, Flt. Lts. R.B. Jackson DFC and L.A. Green DFC were killed when their Harvard, FX307, crashed near Pebworth, Warwickshire on 24 January.

Fifty-three students on the first day of No. 124 Course assembled at Little Rissington on 20 February for administration prior to moving to the CFS detachment at RAF Moreton-in-Marsh. No. 121 course, which had just completed, moved back in the other direction. The number of hours flown during February by the Flying Wing amounted to 3,365 while the Examining Wing achieved 290.

Leadership Squadron

On 2 March, the Instructors Leadership Squadron moved to RAF South Cerney, where it became an integral part of CFS. All students undertook a three-week course with the Squadron before commencing the flying stage of instructor training. The task of the Squadron was to refresh students in the basic elements of leadership, and to instruct them in the art of teaching officer cadets to be leaders and officers of the standard required by the RAF. Particular attention was paid to fostering independence of mind, initiative and physical fitness. The prime importance of personal smartness, self discipline and an adventurous spirit were emphasised. Included in the wide variety of activities were lectures on leadership, morale, management and discipline, each followed by discussion. There was also instruction on law and basic administration. On the practical side, the training included drill, PT, organised games and a small escape exercise. The course was concluded with a five-day camp under canvas in South Wales.

Entertainment

Geographically, Little Rissington was not the best of RAF stations for local entertainment but it did boast an 'Astra' Cinema, which showed films on every day but Friday. The following films were advertised as some of the forthcoming attractions in the CFS magazine.

22 March, for one day only

Gregory Peck and Millard Mitchell in 'The Gunfighter'. *This is a film to please all Western fans, plenty of all that's good in a super cowboy drama.*

27 March, for two days

Orson Welles and Nancy Guild in 'Black Magic'. *A story set in medieval Europe, full of dark mysterious deeds, with Orson Welles at his horrifying best.*

3 April, for two days

Van Johnson and George Murphy in 'Battleground'. *A thrilling and authentic story of a GI unit in the bitter fighting after D-Day.*

17 April, for two days

Richard Widmark and Linda Darnell in 'No Way Out'. *A gripping drama that no Widmark fan will want to miss.*

22 April, for two days

'They Were Not Divided'. *A film for every man and woman who served.*

24 April, for two days

'On the Town'. *An all star cast including Gene Kelly, Vera Ellen, Frank Sinatra and Betty Garrett, make this one of the best musicals of the year.*

CFS Repertory Company

In addition to the Cinema showing films Little Rissington had its own CFS Repertory Company which made use of the Cinema on a Friday. Forthcoming plays included Ivor Novello's 'Full House', 'Arsenic and Old Lace' and 'Castles in the Air', by Alan Melville, plus two other undecided productions.

The Bourton Vale Players was a local repertory company whose productions were enjoyed by personnel from the station for many years. It began life in 1941 as "The Forty-One Club" and was founded by Ernie Joy, a civilian radio engineer who worked for the MU on the other side of the airfield. Although it became a village society after the MU was closed, several RAF folk became members over the years. Three productions were usually presented upstairs in the Village Hall over a winter season, each usually running for three nights. In the early nineteen seventies, the group's production of 'The Heiress' won the Rosebowl for the best amateur full-length play in Gloucestershire.

Reluctant instructor!

Having been 'invited' to attend an interview at Little Rissington on 31 January 1951, Sgt Maurice Biggs flew over from Germany in a Vampire Mk.5 of 16 Squadron.

"My tactics at CFS were to try and convince the Board that I really needed more experience before becoming an instructor and also, since my twin girls were just over a month old, we were not yet ready to travel as a family. This was a ploy on my part to stay for a second tour in Germany, as at that time I considered being an instructor the worst flying job there was. In my innocence I thought I had convinced them but was told that the decision was not theirs and I should put a letter in requesting a delay through my CO when back on the Squadron. In any case, they went on to say that it would only be for one tour and then I could return to the Squadron – nowadays such a statement would be categorised as being 'economical with the truth'. It was Saturday morning before I arrived back at Wunstorf. On the Monday at the Squadron, ready to submit my letter straightaway, I was greeted with the news that my posting to the CFS course had already arrived. The RAF could always be relied upon to give one the bad news quickly.

Arriving at South Cerney for No. 125 Course, the first part was on the Prentice, known to us as the 'mechanical mouse'. An interesting time! Memories include the whole Course standing on tables in best uniform

to be inspected by OC Instructor Leadership Squadron. We also spent a few days at a training camp at a grass airfield, believed to be Southrop, slightly north of Lechlade. The various activities, largely forgotten now, included erecting all the tents plus the construction of a tripod to lift a 50-gallon drum of bleach. The Squadron CO, invited to stand underneath to prove our confidence and his faith in our structure, politely declined. Our flying on the Prentice was along the unchanging CFS lines of dual trips then two students flying together on 'mutual', trying out the appropriate 'patter' for the various flying exercises. This was sometimes at the expense of the flying and often caused unplanned variations not part of the idealised spiel. One of my fellow students was Fg Off Finnimore, who ended up years later on Examining Wing. Once during our course, flying was transferred to Blakehill Farm, a de-commissioned airfield, perhaps because our grass airfield was so wet and exceedingly muddy. The wheel spats were removed from the Prentices for these few days. Another test of our initiative was the midday meal, which had to be prepared by students. There was not a lot of briefing before our flying and absolutely none one day when, in extremely poor weather, my fellow student and I were told to go off to do an hour's flying on Standard Beam Approach procedures. Neither of us had used this system since our flying training school and had not been that proficient then. It was a good job that the same thick cloud prevented our progress through the air being seen by anyone below!

On completion of our Prentice flying, we arrived at Little Rissington on 28 May 1951 to start on Harvards. Several memories of the second half of our course do spring to mind. Accommodation for the NCOs was in a new accommodation block on the other side of the road just outside the Guard Room. The trees were all in full bloom, a sight never to be forgotten. Our flying instruction now moved up a gear on this Harvard Advanced stage. The Harvard was not such a shock for me as we had had one in Germany for instrument flying and as a general transport hack, later replaced by a Meteor T.7. By this time as Harvard students we were used to the usual instructional patter techniques. One aspect of flying which does stand out in my memory was the 'negative R/T' technique used in the circuit. Different types of aircraft flew circuits at different heights, with some landing on the grass on either side of the runway, leaving the high performance machines to use the hard tarmac bit. This was all good fun but, when leading a formation landing, you certainly needed to keep your eyes well peeled. One great and useful 'perk' in those days was the possibility of using an aircraft at weekends. This was ideal for me as my family were now living in the middle of Norfolk – only a modest contribution to the coffee fund was the usual fee for my having an aircraft for the return flight.

Part way through training, our Directing Staff gained the impression that some students were not serious enough about their future as instructors, though it was neither my attitude nor that of the majority. To concentrate people's minds on the course, we were told that anyone failing would certainly not get a good posting afterwards. Within a couple of weeks one pilot was removed from the course for some unknown failing but was then quickly posted to a Photo Recce Squadron. This annoyed me considerably as this was the one flying posting I wanted and for the rest of my service career I never did manage to get into that PR role. Just over three months after starting, I completed the course, not exactly covered in glory but surviving to become a practising B.2 flying instructor. Fortunately, my initial posting to an Oxford Training School in Northern Ireland was changed to 102 AFS at North Luffenham. There I instructed on Vampires and a Meteor 7. This I enjoyed, since I seemed to be the only QFI flying the Meteor. Thus was my future career set firm and ever more deeply in the instructional role, an outcome not to change for many a long year."

No. 128 COURSE – By a Member

An extract from a 1951 copy of the CFS magazine. " 'A likely bunch of thugs' – salutary comment from the immaculate Squadron Leader gave some clue to the trend of forthcoming events, and the nondescript collection of types, poised at uneasy 'Attention', prepared themselves for the worst. Their deepest forebodings were masterpieces of understatement. By the time the steadily increasing toll of haircuts, new hats and red-cotton stitched gloves had been levied, their ignorance underlined by ineffectual attempts at quiz-papers, their obvious inadequacies at drill routine brought to light, the new entrants of CFS had resigned themselves to their fate.

Survivors of the initial spate of admin. lectures and parade technique, were permitted to scramble madly over the Welsh mountains in the middle of the night, clinging grimly to their health, strength and corned beef; their joyous greeting of the dawn strangling in their throats as they realised they were enveloped in eight-eighths cloud. One unit of embryo leaders squatted negligently on the edge of a yawning precipice calculating their slim chances of survival whilst another unit, with bags of 'Actual' time, casually scaled the wrong range of mountains.

A tented camp and accompanying exercises provided unlimited scope for development of leadership, and being lowered sixty feet by highly amused fellow-students obviously imbues some quality in the unfortunate bod strapped to the stretcher. Home cooking, benevolent weather and battling on the beaches gave the Course a veneer of vital self-sufficiency as they crisply performed the final ILS ceremonial parade and marched into the next phase of their training.

Alas! the veneer couldn't take it .... The all-up weight of the literature issued for student study was sufficient to unbalance an unemployed Samson, and the list of 'things to do' before the mighty Prentice could thunder into the air, provided enough straw to sort out a complete herd of camels. Lectures and flying, flying and lectures, pre-flight briefings, post-flight briefing – 'Do a roll,' 'I have control,' ' Speak up,' 'Don't shout,' 'Pretend I'm your pupil,' 'Don't be sarcastic.' The increasing tempo of the malevolent machinations soon undermined the façade of self-sufficiency, and, as the fleeting days passed, the bewildered students wallowed deeper in the morass of knowledge and instruction. SCIENCE proved they applied peculiar forces all over the place, 'MET' proved that it does rain, and PRINCIPLES OF FLIGHT proved that they *could* fly even if their flying instructors considered the possibility unlikely. The days were full, and the nights were also a trifle crowded, with aerofoils, aerobatics and tendencies to blow bits of paper off the tip of the nose. Mid-term examinations were coupled rather neatly with night-flying, and this somnambulistic set-up undoubtedly accounted for the results.

The inspired heroes had barely time to convince their sceptical families of the rigours of their existence when their leave period ended and they started the final stage of their instruction.

Suppressing the slight anoxia resulting from their new and elevated Station, the Course applied themselves to bigger and better checks, before, in, and after flight, meanwhile bracing themselves to withstand a fresh onslaught by dynamic instructors. They backed a little at precession of gyros, recoiled even more at trigonometry or a Warm Front and dissolved completely when the Angle of Attack didn't alter when the Flaps went down. The 'champagne' effect of whistling to 35,000 ft in a Meteor raised their flagging morale and piston-engined aircraft were mentally discarded as sissy stuff. This, despite a recognised ineptitude at back-seat landings in the humble Harvard and other trivialities that kept their flying instructors slightly hoarse, and prematurely aged. The maelstrom of information battered them into the Final Exams. and the catalytic night-flying produced the same unbelievable results as before. They were QFI's.

As the highly polished Course disintegrated, the glittering fragments were scattered far and wide to spread the gospel of CFS. Disciples with heads slightly bowed with the weight of knowledge, shoulders slightly bowed with the weight of their responsibilities, but sporting a very nice line in red-cotton stitched gloves."

Flt Lt McConville

128 COURSE – By an Instructor

"The course transferred from South Cerney to Little Rissington immediately before the August Grant, and, though already worn out by leave, accepted some more time off with good grace. It is not, therefore, surprising that the advanced stage became, as it were, the retarded stage. Flt Lt Nicholson summed things up neatly by saying 'Ils ont eu leurs frites.'

Certain course members fancied their chances as aircraft designers, and set about altering the effective dihedral angle of Harvard mainplanes by the usual unusual method. Obviously they had made a careful study of the Prentice. Another pair made a landing in a Meteor, which resulted in a near overrun, so near that they had to get out and walk. The *force* was OK, but the *time* element wasn't!

Finlayson's Academy has been a hive of industry, and more tea cups have been washed up per student sleeping hour than at any period in the past 'n' courses. Naturally there have been attempts to get lectures going, but invariably these have been halted by Flt Lt 'Mac' Noon who incisively gets words in edgeways – thereby making a kind of verbal sandwich of truth, half truth and untruth. This is always a source of delight to Group 2, and makes the NAAFI tea taste much sweeter.

Fg Off Gaywood recently developed a new art – that of thinking. He managed to do this with his eyes at 170° to the horizontal, flashing steady whites at the lecturer. The new technique gained several supporters towards the end of the course, but the CGI is not prepared to state that the final average mark will be influenced for the better by these deep thinkers.

The Senior Service is represented on the course by Lt Hook – known inevitably as 'The Captain'. He can always be relied upon to come out of his shell when the conversation becomes in any way fishy or will not hold water. In class the Captain sits next to 'Sweeney' Todd, who, we are glad to relate, has not yet started making pies – Flt Lt Brown is fairly plump and should watch out. Talking of the Senior Service reminds one of Flt Lt Senior, who is noted for the fact that he doesn't take notes – presumably he has not time.

Off duty is off duty – and here sport comes into its own. Wet elbows may be seen dripping their way to bed each evening, their owners having once more tested the relative merits of Black and Tan, and Pernod. Darts are always popular, and though 'Mr' Mercer hasn't a clue on the stability of these projectiles he can throw a nifty one. Further, in company with 'Lars' Nielsen and 'Old' Moores, he makes one realise where the poker comes in poker dice.

At the moment of writing the course is approaching its close, and examinations loom on the horizon. Despite examinations and night flying, however, the tempo is increasing and is expected to work up to a peak by the end of August. This should effectively reduce everyone to the same level of incoherence and may result in the quietest Dining-In Night for some time BUT I DOUBT IT.

Flt Lt J.R. Goodman

New appointments

Since the move to Little Rissington in 1946, an officer of Group Captain rank was appointed as both Station Commander and Commandant of the CFS, but this policy changed on 8 May 1951 when Air Cdre A.D. Selway DFC, took over the role of Commandant from Gp Capt G.T. Jarman DSO DFC. On 3 August Gp Capt L.H. Anderson arrived to take up his appointment as the new Station Commander. The Commandant's responsibilities lay with the Flying Training of QFIs whilst the Station Commander's prime task was to provide the facilities to enable the CFS to operate.

Also joining the ranks of the CFS Staff was Flt Lt Caryl Gordon.

"In June 1951 several of us moved to the Meteor Flight and I was paired up with Flt Lt David Dick to convert. After twelve flights taking it in turn to be pupil and instructor, I was let loose for an average of five or six sorties daily converting others. Exceptions to this routine were rare and formation aerobatics was one of them."

Personalities in the CFS magazine

LACW May Matthews first joined the WAAF in 1941 as a Balloon Operator; she can always tell of the incident when "One got away." She was demobbed in 1946 and worked for some time in a Plastics Factory. Missing the company of the Service, however, she rejoined in 1947 and spent three years in the Gymnasium at Tern Hill as the local "Muscle Girl" before moving to Rissy. She is particularly well known as the Gestetner operator and as an Usherette in the Station Cinema. Her chief ambition for the future is to emigrate to Canada and, although she professes no marital ambition, rumour has it that she has been seen occasionally in the company of men.

Flt Sgt Brown joined the Service in 1937 as an armourer. On the outbreak of war he went to France with the BEF moving to the Middle East in June 1940. From there he went to Rhodesia, where he was awarded his wings in September 1943. He remained there as an instructor until 1945. He came to CFS in 1948 and was awarded the AFM in 1949 for his instructional work. He has completed a total of almost 4,500 flying hours. Flt Sgt Brown, who is married with one daughter, has not only represented the Station at soccer, badminton and cricket, but in soccer has been goalkeeper for three Commands in which he has served, including Flying Training Command.

Mr Frederick Jeffries has been on the Station as assistant barrack warden for the last five years. This has made him almost too well known to the married families for his help in supplying coal and furniture. During the war he served in Burma, South Africa and India as a Royal Artillery Sergeant Major, and is now a member of the Territorials at Moreton. He has lived at Lower Slaughter for a long time and helped to build RAF Little Rissington in 1937. His main interests apart from his family are 12-bore shooting and helping to train Bourton Rovers Football Club.

LAC Hobbis or "Lofty" as he is known to his friends is an Engine Mechanic on the "Snag Gang" of the CFS detachment, RAF Moreton-in-Marsh. Before he joined the Service he was apprenticed as a Maintenance Engineer to a bullion firm where he handled gold bars worth thousands of pounds. He is interested in motor cycling but as a National Serviceman cannot afford his own machine. He plays cricket for a local team and has also 'boxed' his way to the Quarter finals of the Wakefield Cup. Once he was fined 10/- for the gentlemanly action of seeing someone else's lady friend home on his cycle cross-bar.

Grunters

An article written by Flt Lt Greenhow in the June 1951 edition of the CFS magazine.

"The object of the Station pig farm is not to bring home the bacon to the starving troops of Central Flying School, but to replenish the ever-hungry coffers of the PSI. Consider for one moment where the money comes from which enables you to blast away at the skeet range. Who pays for the football and cricket gear and what provides the money for the transport which takes you to Cheltenham to immerse yourself in the healing waters of the bathing pool. The simple answer is–them there pigs–there's gold in them there sties.

The gold which flows into the PSI fund has a strange history. It starts in humble mood, squeaking its way round a colossal mammy in a nice warm sty and watched over by the farm staff. The gold grows into a rather dainty little animal full of skittish pranks and joyful squeaking noises, and poised like a ballerina on its claw feet. At this stage the young gold has no interest in the 'luverly grub' which flows in a rich cascade down a chute into the trough–after all, what is a big fat mammy for? After a few weeks, however, Goldie delicately nibbles at the crust you left over from breakfast and follows up rapidly with a bit of queer stuff you could not eat; then Goldie eats all that's put before him. Now he has a lovely life; he is wakened in the morning by the staff who tidies up after him. He eats, drinks and is merry from dewy morning to shadowed eve; he lazes in the sun and has a good-natured grunt for all comers. Who, I ask, would not be a pig.

Goldie is now high, wide and handsome, but evildoers have been at work plotting his downfall. Fate, very much in the shape of the sword of Damocles, intervenes and Goldie, the loved, cherished child of Destiny is whisked away to the happy hunting grounds.

This does not complete the strange eventful story. His body is consumed to the accompaniment of appreciative noises rather like those, which Goldie himself made at feeding times, but his soul hovers with those of his forbears among the rafters in the barn where he was born."

A touch of Kew!

"The Central Flying School gives Little Rissington what has been rather aptly called 'a rarefied atmosphere of its own.' It is evident immediately you enter the main gate. There are acres of neatly trimmed lawns, beds ablaze with flowers that would do credit to Kew Gardens, imposing mellow-brick buildings that suggest that there is a big country estate rather than an RAF Station, and, in summer, colourful sunshades arranged outside the Sergeants' Mess." Thus read this extract from the August edition of the 'RAF Review' which records the first impression of an unbiased observer visiting Little Rissington in June 1951.

New aircraft for the inventory

To augment continuation training for Examining Wing instructors, a Chipmunk was collected from RAF White Waltham and a Vampire fighter from RAF North Luffenham on 2 July for the CFS fleet. To these were added a Firefly on the 3rd, an Oxford on the 7th, a Buckmaster on the 19th and a Spitfire on 25th.

Throughout the month, several Examiners were flown to RAF Kinloss to convert onto the Shackleton MR.Mk.1, which was just entering RAF service.

In 1951, Flt Lt Roy Clee was a student on No. 129 course.

"At the time, there was pressure to produce more pilots for the expanding Service, due to the Korean war. As a result, when there was no need for refuelling of our long serving Harvards, we used to change over details without stopping the engine. So out the door went the pre-flight check. Tut, tut, not good procedure but we had to take appropriate steps in our pursuit of the holy grail of monthly target hours. I remember that on Harvards at Ris, with the flight offices being attached to the hangars, the taxiway between them and the control tower was used for changing crews. The Harvards taxied in two parallel rows. The nearest row stopped engines to refuel and change crew. The others kept their engines running, having sufficient fuel for a further sortie, and changed crew on the run, so to speak. Positions reversed for the next sortie. I never saw that procedure used anywhere else.

One incident I remember related to the mutual flights we did with fellow students, practising both the patter, and the attempt at accurate flying to go with it. Two students on my 129 course, had taken off to do just that, and had inadvertently selected transmit, instead of intercom. This of course meant that all their commentaries were being heard by both the tower and whoever was airborne at the time. As an example, pattering a slow roll, might be interrupted by a violent curse, as the exercise went wrong. It was so entertaining, that people were rushing to get on the radio to hear it all. And believe it or not, as the language got more blue, members of the WRAF on duty in the tower, were ushered out of earshot, to spare blushes. It's true! Fortunately as I recall, there were no criticisms of the staff, although I do know a case at another station, in similar circumstances, where whilst still taxiing, the Wing Co Flying was being slated and who also happened to be on the ground and on air. Unable to contact the culprits, he was standing up on his seat waving his fist at those who he thought were guilty. And he was right, as the guilty parties saw him, they were heard to comment, 'There's the silly bugger now. What's he doing, he must have gone mad'.

And that dreadful Percival Prentice! It was designed with extra seats, so that an instructor could take both of his students flying together, the one in the back being able to observe the performance of his fellow student, perhaps from the inside of a sick bag. I can't imagine what the already abysmal performance of the aircraft was, with a passenger. It took ten minutes of hard climbing to achieve a minimum altitude for spinning. And that was on a good day!!!

Incidentally, at that time, there was no Meteor course for jet instructors, only a handful on the air experience flight to give us a taste of what the new world was like. I was lucky to have one trip but, in the main, I think it was purely a vehicle kept for the benefit of the staff, who could then show off to us poor down trodden students. One particular instructor was a John Severne who used to indulge in outside loops, well the bottom half going up, which was hardly an approved manoeuvre at the time. My own version of jet CFS was carried out by the very experienced senior instructors on 205 AFS at RAF Middleton St George.

My memory of our dining out night was that the Station Commander referred to us as 229 course and the teaching of Socrates. To which the Chief Instructor, a Gp Capt Cole, commented somewhat cuttingly, that he hoped he was as far removed from 229 course, as Socrates was from flying."

From carriers to Hell on the Hill

Fg Off M.A. Vickers began his flying career during WW2 with the Fleet Air Arm flying Avengers from Manston, Thorney Island and HMS Formidable. He arrived at Little Rissington in July 1951 to begin his QFI training on No. 130 Course and would return for two further tours with CFS on Examining Wing, firstly in March 1954 for two years and then in 1968 as a Sqn Ldr until November 1970 and, with other visits witnessed CFS history over three decades.

"In 1946 I left the Fleet Air Arm and went to college before deciding to join the Education Branch of the RAF in 1949. This soon palled, so having requested a return to flying I found myself at CFS for assessment as to my suitability to become a flying instructor. Although I do not remember a great deal about the course I do recall a three-week leadership course at Pembrey immediately beforehand. We clambered around the Black Mountains, swung ourselves over static water tanks and were informed by the boss that the art of leadership had four stages, analysis, organising, deputising and then supervising! Eventually I fell out at the far end of the course, categorised as a B2 (below average) QFI. This, I thought to be in need of some improvement.

My first posting was to No. 6 FTS at RAF Tern Hill, where they too had recently been on the receiving end of an Examining Wing visit and, likewise, had been assessed as 'below average'! I was quickly pitched into instructing on the venerable old Harvard T.2b and found that I actually enjoyed the experience. My first brush with CFS occurred in February 1952, when volunteers had been requested from No. 6 FTS for QFIs to become Instrument Rating Examiners (IREs). I was specially selected for the honour from a field of one – me. So I drove a Harvard down to Ris and managed to fool them into approving me for the job. A short time before this I had passed the B1 (average) test with the CI. My second brush with the trappers was in October that same year when I passed the A2 (above average) test. In the meantime the School had been completely re-vamped – new CO, new CI, new OC Standards and new CGI, so the trappers found the School's performance to be satisfactory on their next visit, by which time I was now a member of Standards Flight. The next trappers' visit was in May 1953, when I took and passed the A1 (exceptional) test – so below average to exceptional in 18 months – I had redeemed my poor start and was asked to join Examining Wing."

Sad story of "The Inflated Bootlace"

The end of course report reproduced here was first published in the CFS magazine:

'130 Course knocks CFS average for six'

Number 130 course has just passed out which is just as well because the Instructional Staff nearly passed out with it.

Despite the recent 'At Home' and an evasion exercise, the course managed to 'keep on the line' at flights. This pleased OC No. 4 Squadron because at this time the hours available always seem to be less than the hours required. This is disconcerting, as Arthur Sharples will agree.

The Major was not so pleased with occurrences involving runway centres of gravity in Harvards. One young man was heard to remark after one of these fabulous efforts *"Who the heck put wing-tips on Harvards anyway?"*

Finlayson's College was hard pressed. So many dome-headed gentlemen attended the course that the erstwhile sublime became ridiculous and the CFS average was knocked for six. Flt Lt McNeile better known as the 'Inflated Bootlace,' rose to the dizzy heights in Principles of Flight but fell down in the final exam, gaining 297 out of a possible 300 marks.

Mac and his sidekick, Flt Lt Pembridge (joint CFS Trophy winners), were highly mathematical. It is said they persuaded Fg Off Bennett that all couples had their moments. This was a triumph, for Ben who had begun the final stage under the impression that 'cos theta' was a special kind of lettuce.

'Basildon' Bond had difficulty in completing the course owing to pressing duties as a French interpreter. His logic won all the hearts while his knowledge of degrees of bank and yaw required to achieve equilibrium on asymmetric power won him a posting to Shawbury – on Ansons. When is a master green?

Mess life was enlivened when Flt Lt Hayter-Preston. 'HP' held his fellow sufferers spell-bound by declaiming ersatz modern poetry in the bar; it was possible to recognize bits of the CFS syllabus here and there. Rumour says that 'Hateful' fooled a local longhaired gent and the latter is now on the warpath with a hatchet.

The majority of the course has gone to jet units to do some 'Barrier Bashing' and doubtless Mighty Joe Young will soon be tearing through the wall, enclosed in his own Mach Cone.

Fg Off Shorter however, off to pound the circuit on cloth bombers, will soon have a fine pair of bowed legs as may be found on any Wimpey unit.

The course has now dispersed and we wish them all 'Happy Landings-Right Way Up'.

Flt Lt Hayter-Preston's letter to CFS

The course at CFS is a major historical event in a pilot's life and like all history is best regarded in retrospect. The odd thing about the Central Flying School is that no one seems to be particularly happy when he finishes the course. With examinations over, with final handling tests passed, students who previously moaned of the pressure of work became moody, feeling and looking like potential suicides.

This is partly due to normal post-course anti-climax. But the realisation that now you are leaving your friends is a sad business. You get to know people pretty well when you have been frightening the life out of each other in the air, or dangling on the end of a rope while undergoing the Dyer treatment at ILS. It is morally right, however that having had the course, one should pass the required knowledge on to others, that the boot should be on the other foot for a change.

It is only when a man starts to lecture that he realises what an incredibly disheartening job it can be. We must now express our admiration at the incredible way in which a science instructor can remain cheerful, faced with moronic students refusing to be scientifically indoctrinated. No student likes filling the role of a human sponge; absorbing knowledge, or trying to, every day for three months. But at least he can play the part sitting down.

Every course has students who fall to sleep during lectures. Some snore. All miss parts of lectures. Many are woken up. Few avoid black looks. 130 Course had its sleepers. One in particular was a genius at the art of academic dozing. His technique not only defied detection but also earned him the reputation of being the most attentive student. It was really easy, when his brain shut up, his eyes stayed open. They looked a little glassy, but now on another course and with a little more practice should add the finishing touches to a truly remarkable attainment.

It speaks highly of CFS reputation that its products are regarded as walking Encyclopaedia Aeronautica. Such was my own experience. On reporting to my unit as a newly qualified flying instructor all was confusion. Examining wing was about to descend, 'Just the man, just down from CFS, got all the gen,' there was an endless stream of questions. I must confess that I was unable to answer all of them, but my notes could. Now I have an empty loose-leaf file and the job of trying to recover the contents. Worse still I cannot officially admit I need the notes. My principles of flight instructor at South Cerney is now my adjutant.

It is a human failing that we look upon our own as the best. 130 Course was probably just another load of trouble. To us it was the hardest working, hardest suffering and friendliest course ever. Possibly the staff remembers us with horror. But undoubtedly members are still preening themselves with the thought of the Chief Instructor's modified tirade on the last night. No greater praise than that.

Formal appreciations invariably sound stilted but nonetheless sincere. Members of 130 Course would like to thank Air Cdre Selway, his staff and all his instructors for our training.

A very special Spitfire

Air Chief Marshal Sir James Robb GCB KBE DSO DFC AFC had a long association with CFS going back to his first solo flight from Upavon in 1916. He twice served on the staff of the School, first as chief instructor and then as Commandant in the difficult years before the war. On his last day in the Royal Air Force, 21 September 1951, he flew his personal Spitfire LF.Mk.XVIe, SL721, into Little Rissington and handed it to the Commandant, Air Cdre Selway, as a gift to CFS.

On 26 September, the CFS detachment at RAF Moreton-in-Marsh was disbanded and reformed at RAF South Cerney as 2 FTS.

Air Cdre Selway greets ACM Sir James Robb on his arrival in SL721 at Little Rissington. Note his initials on the aircraft's fuselage. (*CFS Archive*)

134 course and night patter to a Texan

"The 35 members of No. 134 Flying Instructors Course, assembled at Little Rissington in September 1951, were mostly pilots with active RAF service during WW2", recalls Flt Lt Alan Robertson MBE. *"There were eight NCOs and twenty-seven officers, of whom two were Royal Thai Air Force, one Israeli Air Force and a Fleet Air Arm*

Commissioned Pilot. Most officers held flight lieutenant rank, though there were a couple of squadron leaders and a rather flashy wing commander, sporting a red-lined, RAFVR-style tunic and an impressive 'Flying Officer Kite' moustache. We suspected we had been chosen for flying instructor training because of our accumulated flying experience and being too long in the tooth for operational flying in Korea. We were all eagerly looking forward to flying the Meteor, even though we were only destined to fly Harvards and Percival Prentices, chief trainer workhorses in 1951. The powers-that-be dictated that all QFIs should have some jet experience, since most students would be going on to jet aircraft after their training. Apart from the exacting flying programme, a challenging ground school component ran in parallel for the three months of air training. All instructors had to be proficient in navigation, airmanship and theory of flight. The emphasis was on precision, in the air and on the ground. Our two Thai officers had the extra task of learning flying sequences in English and lecture in their second language. We all marvelled at their ability to think and cover such difficult topics as 'The aerodynamic forces in play when changing the pitch of an airscrew.' Our Wingco colleague gained little comfort from ground school lectures, tending to dismiss the whole exercise as one of futility. Over a beer in the bar he could be heard proclaiming the gospel of flying by the seat of one's pants: 'No time for all that nonsense, old boy, when we were flying the Spit - too busy to think about lift, drag or those flying limitations in Pilot's Notes. Had to win the bloody war!'

Major Cole, our USAF exchange officer, administered my final handling test, consisting of my giving him the full pre-flight briefing normal for any student, followed by demonstrating a particular flying exercise, in our case night circuits and landings. Each exercise had its own unique 'patter', which described exactly what the instructor was doing. The student would hear, something like this: 'Having completed our final checks for take-off, we are parked at forty-five degrees to the active runway, as we await permission to line up and hold for take-off. We now have a green from the control tower – I'm releasing the brakes to apply sufficient power to turn on to the runway, after checking the approach – lining up with the runway lights, I set the gyro to three-six-zero, standard practice for our bad weather circuits – we have another green, so I'm applying full take-off power with enough touch of rudder to prevent the aircraft swinging, as the tail comes up and we reach flying speed. With a gentle backward stick movement, we're airborne and onto our six master instruments to ensure a safe, positive rate of climb, scanning airspeed, altimeter, artificial horizon, climb rate and gyro compass. Wheels coming up, trim forward slightly, as we prepare to raise the flaps.' After a couple of demonstration circuits, the 'instructor' handed over control to the 'student' and lightly 'followed through' on the controls. A difficulty facing the Harvard instructor was the poor vision ahead from the rear seat, particularly in the final stages of landing. On this particular December night the weather, always significant at Britain's highest operational airfield, was forecast as 1,000ft cloud base, 3 miles visibility with occasional light rain showers. As our flight progressed, the cloud base dropped to five hundred feet and we were flying through wet snow, making the eternally emphasised 'circuit Lookout' trickier for us both. At our crew room de-briefing, Major Cole complimented me on adapting the running commentary to the weather conditions but added a wry comment in his lazy Texan drawl. 'Y'all did good on the flight and I'm goin' to give you a pass but, when you're talkin' the student in for a landin', try to keep your voice in a lower pitch. Sounded to me as if you had a rattler in your shorts, when you flared out a tad high. You need to give the student the confidence you don't really have yourself."

Yes it did; ah, no it didn't!

If asked the question was the Brigand operated by CFS the factual answer is yes as Brigand B.1, RH759 was delivered to Little Rissington on 9 October 1951. Three days later the aircraft swung on take-off and crashed into a number of parked trucks. The badly damaged airframe was transported to 19 MU and CFS had no further association with the type.

Korean War dragnet for 300 ex-QFIs

Fg Off Bill Higgens, who had finished his flying training in early 1942, returned to UK and was posted to a Flying Instruction School (FIS) against his will, where he flew Oxfords at RAF Church Lawford before moving on to Tiger Moths at Cambridge.

"Demobbed in 1946, I finished my teacher training before re-joining the VR in mid-1949. In October 1951, 300 ex-QFIs were called up for 18 months instructional duties. We were given a refresher course, probably the normal course, of 45 hrs on the Prentice at South Cerney followed by 52 hrs on the Harvard at Little Rissy. I did not exactly get off to a good start with my instructor, one Fg Off Sharples, who wondered how I had ever achieved my wings, let alone QFI status. I admit I found the Harvard strange at first, never having flown a single-engined or any service aircraft at all for nearly 6 years. In the end it took me 4½ hrs to solo on the Harvard against less than 2 hrs on the Meteor. For me the Meteor flying was the highlight of the course with not enough of it. I soon began to enjoy the Harvard, especially when another pupil introduced me to the thrill of night aerobatics.

The main difference to war-time instructing seemed to be the dropping of the 'patter' learnt by heart to ensure standardisation, whereas we could now describe a manoeuvre in our own terms. I remember little of social life at Rissy, if any. One of our group had a small car, out of the boot of which a seat emerged for two people to sit but fully exposed to every vagary of winter weather. However we had some good trips around the countryside, mainly exploring the various hostelries.

Posted from CFS, I was sent to help open up a Service Training School at RAF Wellesbourne Mountford, a delightful spot east of Stratford – best of all I was now flying Oxfords."

Instructors for the new RAF

This extract from the Birmingham Post of November 1951, identifies one of the major problems facing a rejuvenated post-war Air Force and the important part CFS plays in its resolution that year.

"One of the most reassuring aspects of the expansion of the RAF has been the appearance of three new aircraft – two four-engined jet bombers and one all-weather fighter – in the past six months. Such progress by British aircraft designers and constructors is essential to bring the RAF back to a modern operational standard comparable with that held by it at the end of the war.

Orders for one of the bombers, the Vickers Valiant, were placed while the plans were still on the drawing board, and the aircraft industry is now slowly and reluctantly cutting production of airliners and civilian light planes and re-tooling for the Valiant and other new designs. But new machines bring fresh problems. Anxious though it is to have the jets, the RAF has not the necessary young (and the emphasis is on their youth) pilots, navigators and bombardiers. In June the then Secretary for Air, Mr. Arthur Henderson., said there was "*some anger*", that the supply of trained aircrews is falling behind the supply of the advanced jet aircraft which were to be delivered.

Part of the answer to the problem is being provided at the highest aerodrome in Britain, RAF Little Rissington, which is reputed, too, to have the coldest weather of any aerodrome in England, high up in the Gloucestershire Cotswolds. There, at the Central Flying School, experienced pilots, who will later teach young aircrews to fly these new machines and others which, it can safely be assumed, will appear in the next year or two, are learning the art of instruction.

Hand-picked pilots from many units in the RAF are sent to the school as fast as they can be dealt with. In four months they take a course, which took six months during the war. Afterwards their teaching careers begin, flying day after day with young pupils fresh from civilian life or lecturing on the principles of flight or intricacies of piston and jet engines. Others go on for further training at advanced flying schools, where they learn all that is at present known, and perhaps cover a bit more, about teaching men to handle the latest aircraft, which are in cases capable of flying 'through the sonic barrier' – in plain English, faster than the speed of sound. Little Rissington is typical of many Training Command stations – tidy, expansive and at the same time businesslike. The work has increased so much because of the expansion that the main aerodrome has two satellites, at South Cerney and Moreton-in-Marsh.

Flying goes on 24 hours a day, and even cloud down to 150 ft and stretching up solidly to 30,000 ft is not enough to ground Harvards and two-seater Meteors. In such conditions, of course, the number of aircraft flying into and leaving the airfield is restricted, because they have to be 'talked down' and are unable to make visual approaches.

Dual-control machines are not used only to carry an instructor and the pupil instructor. Often, two pupils fly together, one acting as instructor and practising his teaching knowledge upon the other. All of them are experienced pilots and their ranks may be anything from Sergeant to Wing Commander. A few Naval pilots and fliers from Western European and Commonwealth countries are among them, for although the expansion of the RAF is the main purpose of the Central Flying School, the importance of standardisation of methods with the Navy and Allied nations is not forgotten.

Not every candidate sent to the station is chosen for the course. Flying ability and experience are only two of the qualifications needed by an instructor, and many are sent back to their units as unsuitable. Although excellent pilots these often can not fly well and instruct clearly at the same time."

"Just the chap we want here"

Wg Cdr Maurice 'Mo' M. Foster recounts how in 1951, as Plt Off M.M. Foster, he was not the only one to have heard, on his first encounter with CFS and its Chief Instructor, similar welcoming words.

"On 22 November 1951, towards the end of my Meteor Wings course and about to become a reluctant 'creamy', I was sent in our station Oxford from No. 203 AFS at RAF Driffield to Rissy with Mike Hughes. We were interviewed individually by Bill Coles, then both Assistant Commandant and Chief Instructor. He asked each of us if we wanted to become QFIs to which we both replied that 'I would much rather go off to a fighter squadron'. Bill responded, 'Just the chap we want here'. There then followed interviews with the Commandant, Air Cdre Selway.

During my first instructional tour after CFS I had to send one of my own students off to Rissy for interview, but before he departed I briefed him on my experience, saying it was up to him if he wanted to try the trick of being an enthusiastic volunteer, so as to try to get rejected. He tried using this ploy and received exactly the same response from Bill: 'Just the chap we want here'!

Some years later, while refresher flying on the Jet Provost at Rissy, and late for lunch, I was sitting alone in the dining room away from the Station Commander's party. Bob Barnden, the Station Commander, happened to be top tabling Bill Coles (by then AM Sir William Coles KBE CB DSO DFC AFC and Controller of the RAF Benevolent Fund). From where I sat, I could easily overhear him repeat exactly the same story to his guests, presumably from his own identical experience.

Two memories stick in my mind from my time on course in 1951/2. Wg Cdr J.D.W. Willis, our 'press on' CI, was on a morning weather check in a Meteor Mark 7 when he managed to blow out both engines just above some very low cloud. He received the standard ATC response to his Mayday call, 'What is your fuel state?' Rather irrelevant in his predicament but he did manage a wry smile and to relight both engines before landing safely back at Ris.

The second incident concerned my first CFS Meteor ride with Mick Swiney, when an undercarriage red warning light refused to go green on our return to the airfield. We carried out the usual fly-by of the tower for their inspection, while yawing the aircraft to check the main leg. Suddenly the yaw became excessive and, as the nose dipped, I found myself looking through the windscreen at a startled ATC observer standing on the tower balcony. We managed to recover OK but our pelican feathers were somewhat ruffled. This was not caused by the phantom dive problem, with airbrakes out with sequencing undercarriage drag differentials, as we discovered on landing that a quantity of fuel remained in one drop tank and as this slopped around it tended to lever our Meatbox round its own axis. A particularly memorable moment!"

Early 'Creamy' experience

Flt Lt Brian Ashley recalls his being an early Pilot Officer 'creamy' with Plt Off Bob Barnden, at a time when the RAF needed to quickly expand its pilot strength to respond to the Korean War and the deteriorating international situation.

"I arrived at RAF Little Rissington in late 1951 as a member of No. 136 Course. Already having survived the Basic half of the course flying Prentices at RAF South Cerney, we were now ready to tackle the second part on the Harvard. I was one of the newly introduced 'Creamed-Off' QFIs, who had been taken straight out of training as ab initio instructors in the hope of alleviating a shortage of potential QFIs caused by the sudden expansion necessary in the service at that time. My co-student, who had been with me at No. 4 FTS Heany in Southern Rhodesia, at No. 2 FTS for a Rhodesian Refresher Course and at South Cerney for CFS 'A', was Plt Off Bob Barnden. Bob and I shared Plt Off Alfie Camp as our CFS instructor.

On 22 January 1952, I was detailed to fly a solo exercise, while Alfie and Bob went off with Bob in the front seat and Alfie in the back to give Bob a low flying training sequence. As part of my flight I needed to make a practice forced landing and was setting myself up and looking for a suitable field in the Chedworth area, south west of Rissington for my practice approach, when my attention was attracted by the flash of rather bleak sunshine on an aircraft low flying across my intended forced landing area. It was flying very low and entering a left turn. As I watched, its left wing tip touched the ground. This upset the balance of those forces on an aircraft, about which we had been taught in Ground School – the next few seconds were quite spectacular. The engine hit the ground and the aircraft cart-wheeled. The starboard wing separated from the fuselage closely followed by the port wing. The tail section broke off just aft of the cockpit. The engine broke away and continued bounding along, leaving a very sorry looking cockpit section lying on its side.

Abandoning any idea of my practice forced landing, I called Little Rissington to describe what I had seen. The scene below looked like a scrap merchant's yard and I could not imagine there would be any survivors. Going down low to make a better assessment, I soon saw the identification letters FT424 on the fuselage side, which told me that it was Bob and Alfie's aircraft. I was passing this devastating information to Rissington when I noticed movement in the front cockpit. Very slowly Bob was dragging himself out of what was left of the aircraft. He took a few wobbly steps to orientate himself before setting about the task of rescuing Alfie. In a few minutes Bob had Alfie out of the cockpit and I was happy to tell Rissington that they were both on their feet again.

Later, back at the base, I was discussing this with a bruised but otherwise intact Bob. He told me that Alfie had given him the copybook low flying exercise before he said, 'That's for the students. Now I'll show you the real thing.' The CFS course was always full of interest!

While on No. 136 Course, Little Rissington qualified for the final of the RAF Station Rugby Championship and the needle match was to be played at RAF Halton. Our Station Commander, Gp Capt Bill Coles, decided we would show support for our team by his leading a mass formation of Harvards to Halton. As many Harvards and pilots as possible were mustered for the occasion and I felt lucky to be given an aircraft with a fellow student, Flt Lt Ron Bradley, in the back seat.

By hook or by crook we all got airborne to set course for the sleepy Chilterns in a formation of about 30 Harvards, the sound of which is guaranteed to put paid to any such somnolence. Our arrival at RAF Halton called for some clever juggling but we all finished up approaching down the hillside and side by side into the grass airfield. This was quite a sight to behold. Due to the superb piloting skills of CFS pilots, we all arrived intact and the rugby match began.

Since I had had my moment of glory, Ron Bradley was delegated as pilot for the return journey. Formation flying was over for the day so we set course independently for our return to Rissington. I settled down in the back seat with my rudder pedals pushed fully forwards to enjoy my return to base and savour the view of the English countryside. Our arrival in the circuit at Rissington was right out of the manual, with the approach as steady as a rock. The three-point landing was right on the runway markers and all was well with the world, until the nose of the aircraft began to swing left. The swing continued and, at 90 degrees to the runway, the starboard wing tip hit the runway. The rate of turn was reduced but we still finished slowly rolling backwards along the runway. It was a beautiful evening for one's first and last ground loop. I never managed to make a ground loop during my FTS course but the training at CFS was very thorough: this manoeuvre completed my education!

The period of our course ran over the fairly hard 1951/2 winter, particularly at our high airfield elevation, but we kept near to schedule by flying in marginal weather conditions. For my co-student, Bob Barnden, and me, this was our first UK winter flying. As creamed off QFIs we did not have a lot of hours in our logbooks and far less time in bad weather, so we found this aspect quite a challenge.

The course began to be delayed in January and February 1952, with the main obstacle being night flying. At first we encountered the usual night-time fog but then it snowed. The temperature stayed below freezing level and the snow became compacted. Since the end of the course was approaching, the decision was made to fly from the hard snow. To complicate the issue further a fresh wind now settled in from the north,

Backbone of the CFS syllabus, the Harvard T.2b exemplified here by a very smart FX301-FDNQ. (*MAP*)

so we had no option but to fly from the short runway 14,800 to 900 yards long but with no runway lighting. All RAF airfields had a ready supply of kerosene-fuelled gooseneck flares, so what was the problem? There were no approach lights and the approach and undershoot areas were just solid blackness.

A pilot in the front seat of a Harvard could not see a lot at night because of the broad engine cowling but from the back seat all that could be seen was the back of the head of the lucky lad in the front seat. Before take off the most important check was to ensure that the aircraft was accurately lined up on the centre line of the runway. A little help from the front seat was always welcome. On what was virtually an instrument take off, it was essential to curb the ever present tendency to swing to the left and then check both sides of the cockpit to ensure that the flares were passing by evenly at the same distance. With any luck the aircraft became airborne before it ran off the runway.

The trickiest problem was getting the beast back on the ground again. On our first night flying session Alfie Camp, our instructor, gave both Bob and me the night flying sequence from the back seat. Then we climbed in again, this time with Bob in the back seat to give the exercise to me. In the next 40 minutes we discovered a lot about landing a Harvard at night but fortunately the wind was not straight down the runway, allowing our drift angle to provide glimpses of the runway to be seen down the side of the nose. The next night it was my turn in the back seat to give the sequence to Bob. To make life more exciting, the wind was absolutely straight down the runway. The most essential requirement was to fly the downwind leg and base leg as accurately as possible to ensure that the straight in final approach was commenced from the correct place. From then onwards everything ahead was black. If a runway light was seen you were not lined up and a correction was urgently needed. The use of the correct throttle setting ensured that the aircraft usually reached the runway and not the undershoot area but it was a great relief to see the flare path appear with lights on both sides of the aircraft. The short length of the runway did not allow us the luxury of landing well down the runway and one was often grateful for the odd suggestion from the front seat that perhaps a little more power might prove appropriate.

The easy solution to landing from the back seat on snow at night would be to make a 'main wheels only' landing with the tail still off the ground but this was blasphemy at CFS. Here we were required always to make three point landings. Any lack of concentration after the landing would invite a ground loop before an embarrassing interview with the Squadron Commander. Thankfully we completed all our night flying on the short snow-packed runway without incident.

Bob and I both passed out as B1 QFIs. After our excellent training on the Prentice and Harvard, Bob went to No. 208 AFS RAF Merryfield to instruct on Vampires, while I went to No. 207 AFS RAF Full Sutton to instruct on Meteors. Landing a Meteor 7 from the back seat at night was another trick but one I found easy in comparison to the Harvard on that short Rissy runway without lights. QFIs are very adaptable. I returned to Rissington in 1965 on Examining Wing and Gp Capt Bob Barnden returned a little later as the Station Commander."

1952

Clouded Call Sign

On 2 January 1952, Flt Lt Alan Robertson was detailed for initial dual and solo Meteor flights from Rissington's satellite airfield at Kemble with Flt Lt Caryl Gordon,

> *"who was then something of a celebrity as HRH Prince Philip's instructor"*, writes Alan. *"After twenty-five minutes' dual and a couple of circuits, Gordon sent me off solo with the admonition 'Look out for the weather!'. My Meteor at that time was the only aircraft in the circuit. As I turned on to the downwind leg, the tower radioed the following message to me: 'This is Sun-Up. We are now Subside'. Concentrating hard on completing my downwind checks, maintaining my heading, speeds and height, I interpreted this gobbledygook as an immediate recall for all aircraft. As I turned onto the base leg I called: 'This is Oboe Uncle turning final, three greens.'*
>
> *After taxiing round to the tower and reporting to the Duty Air Traffic Controller, I asked him for the meaning of his cryptic message. 'Oh, sorry about that, old chap', came the reply, 'we were just changing callsigns – absolutely nothing to do with the weather!' I never will forget my truncated first solo sortie in a Meteor."*

From dark blue to light blue

Former wartime Fleet Air Arm (1943-1946) pilot Sub Lt (A) James Primrose, RNVR, who at the age of 20 was mentioned in dispatches flying Seafires from HMS Implacable against Japan, took up a career in teaching Physical Education until invited to re-join when the Korean War started.

> *"The Royal Navy interviewing officer in London said I could join within three weeks, there would be three weeks of refresher flying and three weeks later I would be aboard a carrier in Korean waters. I could not see my wife being permitted to share my cabin in an aircraft carrier, so I trotted along The Strand to where a building displaying a huge sign saying 'THERE IS A PLACE IN THE ROYAL AIR FORCE FOR YOU!' Once within, a young Flight Lieutenant enquired about my Naval service before asking me if I would like to join the RAF as a flying instructor. So I signed on.*
>
> *In January 1952, I arrived at RAF South Cerney for a month's enjoyable refresher flying on Harvards. Thence to Rissy where this light blue 'rookie' Flying Officer found himself on a No. 143 Course which comprised twelve Squadron Leaders, a score of long in the tooth Flight Lieutenants and sundry others, plus one Naval Commissioned Pilot, Lt(A) Tony Read. Our course would last four months and Tony and I became good friends, with myself being the most junior guy on the course by far. On 1 April 1952, the twelve Flight Lieutenants were promoted to Squadron Leader, the start of four promotion lists a year instead of the usual two. With 24 Squadron Leaders now on my course, I had to salute and 'Sir' them all.*
>
> *Tony and I revised our work in the evenings and for two or three hours, if the mood took us, at the weekends. Neither of us had a car and*

everyone else did or so it seemed. My family came down from Stirling to Cheltenham for three weeks in a hotel and I visited my wife and son twice in the week by bus. One night I walked from Cheltenham to Bourton-on-the-Water where an RAF mail van gave me a lift up the hill to Rissy in time for breakfast, but no sleep. I could not tell Kath how short the money was but CFS was a fantastic course and I loved every minute of it. Tony knew how important this was for his career, while I just did my best. At a ground school roll call one day an instructor calling my name said, 'Henceforth you will be known as TULIP'. After a bit of leg pulling for a few days, the name didn't stick.

No seating plan was displayed before our Graduation Dinner and no Order of Course Results. Only upon entering the dining room was the seating plan displayed. Surprised to find myself seated next to the Commandant, I was the only student on the top table, with Tony Read at the head of the right side table. I had won the CFS Trophy and Tony Read was a close runner up, almost a Fleet Air Arm coup. When the Commandant stood up to speak, he asked for my indulgence for a few minutes, placing a hand momentarily on my shoulder. He then addressed his remarks to the 24 Squadron Leaders on the course and berated them for failing to perform to the same standards achieved by Tony and myself. After dinner one of them came up to me and said, 'Thank .. You .. Very .. Much … And Congratulations!' Four of us had competed for the Clarkson aerobatic prize and the winner was a delightful, small Polish pilot, Flt Lt K.I. Dolicher, more usually known by the nickname 'Dolly'. Pretty well every student on the course got his chosen posting except for me. I wanted the Flying School at Bulawayo in Rhodesia, but was told that my posting was automatic and non negotiable. My first flying instruction tour would begin at the RAF College, Cranwell on Chipmunks and that was that. At tourex, I was initially posted to the CFS Basic staff at Cerney, but this rapidly changed into an extended tour with the Examining Wing at Rissy, where I gained my A1 category and my first Queen's Commendation".

Flying Wing reorganisation

At the turn of the year, plans were put in place for a complete reorganisation of CFS to incorporate a certain number of qualified jet instructors from the normal intake and to provide a jet aircraft conversion course for experienced QFIs.

The new structure came into being on 1 May 1952 with the creation of CFS (Basic) and CFS (Advanced). CFS (Basic) was formed at RAF South Cerney, by redesignating No. 2 Flying Training School and comprised 1 Squadron (Prentice, Auster and later, Provost) and 2 Squadron (Harvard and later, Provost). CFS (Advanced) formed at Little Rissington and consisted of 1 Squadron (which included a Communications Flight with Anson, Valetta and later, Provost), 2 Squadron, 3 Squadron (Meteor and Vampire), 4 Squadron (Vampire) and a Type Flight.

The course duration was increased from twelve to sixteen weeks and the Instructor Leadership Training phase, which until then had been held at the beginning of each course, was absorbed into the Basic stage of the new curriculum. Thereafter, courses commenced every four weeks with 64 students per course. Allowing for four wastages (failures) in the Basic stage, 46 students progressed onto the Harvard and fourteen onto the Meteor. Six QFIs joined each course at the beginning of the Meteor stage for conversion to the jet trainer.

The first half of the flying course was carried out at South Cerney, 22 miles from Rissington on Prentice basic trainers, before students progressed on to either Harvard or Meteor advanced trainers, with Harvard instructors also carrying out a few hours of Meteor and Vampire flying for jet experience before completing their courses.

At this particular time the RAF's required expansion of the course's output, which had doubled over the past two years, was assisted by the re-introduction of the wartime policy of 'creaming off' some above average pupils from the advanced stage of their flying training straight into instructor training.

As it continued to expand, CFS had absorbed the entire station at South Cerney by the spring of 1952. Until this time it had been occupied on a shared basis with No. 2 FTS. The two Basic Squadrons based there were responsible for the whole of Basic stage training on Prentice T.1 aircraft.

Meteor 3-ship special

On 29 March, New Zealander Sqn Ldr George Brabyn led a formation of three Meteor T.7s on a photographic sortie during which air-to-air photographs were taken of him flying his Meteor inverted with the other two aircraft in close formation and the right way up on either side, by Air Ministry photographer Mike Chase. In itself nothing special you might think, but considering that the Meteor was limited to 15 seconds of inverted flying before the engines flamed out, it was quite an achievement. Flt Lts D.D. James and J.D. Price flew the other two Meteors. A full account of this sortie is contained in the CFS Aerobatic Teams chapter.

'High level conversations'

In May, Punch reporter Mr B.A. Young wrote of his experience of flying as a passenger in a close formation of Meteors following a visit to Little Rissington. The three-ship team was led by Sqn Ldr G.A. Brabyn AFC RNZAF, and Flt Lt Titmus DFC, while Flt Lt D. James flew Mr C.C.H. Cole (of the Air Ministry Information Dept.) in the back seat of the number two aircraft. Mr Young occupied the rear seat of the third Meteor which was flown by Flt Lt J.D. Price. Called 'High Level Conversations', this is the account of his trip at the CFS.

"It takes sixteen weeks for the RAF's Central Flying School to turn its scrupulously-seeded students into qualified instructors. For eight weeks they learn leadership, how to speak and instruct in the air, and such elementary background as Navigation, Meteorology, Engines, Instruments, Jet Handling and Aviation Medicine. Then, swapping their Prentices for Harvards or Meteor T.7s, they move on to the advanced stuff - still devoting alternate days to Navigation, Meteorology, Engines, etc.

Owing to prior engagements, I had only twenty-four hours in which to cover all this. Clearly I could not master the whole syllabus in that time, so I decided to concentrate on something simple. I would learn, I thought, to speak in the air.

During the early fifties, the Meteor T.7 was the sole advanced jet trainer in RAF service and was utilised by many display teams. Three instructors from CFS performed this daring manoeuvre on 28 March, 1952, when Sqn Ldr George Brabyn flew his aircraft inverted as two colleagues formated either side of him. The photograph was taken by Mike Chase from a Meteor T.7 flown by Flt Lt John Severne. (*Mike Chase, via John Severne*)

Civilians who think that you can pick up flying as you can cycling may not understand the importance of speaking in the air. But one of the RAF manuals puts it strongly: *'The instructor should spare no effort to find out whether he can be heard,' it says, 'and to choose the most suitable words and phrases.'*

All good instruction starts at an altitude where errors will not lead to irreparable damage (*'the increased complexity of modern aircraft to-day requires that much of the instruction must be done on the ground'*). I could, I thought, hear some clever airborne speaking without myself soaring into the blue (*'pupil and instructor should be in reasonably warm and comfortable surroundings'*). The Control Tower seemed a sensible starting-point.

The RAF offered to demonstrate a rapid controlled jet descent. A Meteor pilot twenty thousand feet up spoke to the Flying Control Officer through a loudspeaker. '*Love Five*,' he said '*Testing*.'

The Flying Control Officer said '*Descend now to ten thousand feet*.'

'*Roger*,' said the Meteor.

'*Love Five*,' said the Flying Control Officer, '*steer zero-one-zero*.'

'*Roger*,' said the Meteor.

'*Love Five*,' said the Flying Control Officer, '*you are now overhead. Turn port two-nine-five*.' '*Roger*,' said the Meteor.

'*Love Five, rapid descent to two thousand feet*,' '*Roger*.'

'*I am bringing you in on one-zero-zero*.' '*Roger*.'

I felt certain that in the same circumstances I should be able to choose equally suitable words and phrases. But at twenty thousand I might not find it so warm and comfortable. The Station Medical Officer offered to reproduce on me the effects of being four miles up. If he did it to someone else, I said, I should be able to see the effects better; so he collected four guinea-pigs from among his medical orderlies.

They all climbed into a small sealed chamber and donned flying helmets and oxygen-masks. The SMO left his mask disconnected; he would demonstrate, he said, the effects of 'anoxia,' which could be quite amusing. '*I got myself really blue in the face the other day,' he said, 'and my finger-nails were bright purple*.'

I watched through a glass spy-hole while another doctor, grinning happily, turned on the taps that exhausted the air in the chamber. The guinea-pigs seemed quite unaffected by the decompression, but the SMO soon began to suffer from anoxia and smilingly went blue in the face. '*All your aeroplanes have plenty of oxygen in them?*' I asked anxiously. They said yes, plenty.

By the time lunch was over I was fully confident of being able to speak in the air, and they proposed that I should go up in a Meteor and try. It just happened that a formation of Meteors was about to take off with the object of practising close-formation flying with the middle aeroplane upside-down, '*But I'm afraid,' they said, 'you can't go in the middle one. The pilot wants someone to count*.'

'*Count?*' I said.

'*Well, you see*,' they said, '*a Meteor can only fly upside down for fifteen seconds and after that the engines cut out*.'

Snow swept across the runway.

I sat in the after cockpit of the Meteor while the pilot told me exactly what to do if I had to jump. '*Of course I shall keep talking to you all the time*,' he soothed me. It occurred to me that in my clumsy efforts to get out of the cockpit I might disconnect the intercom-thing of my helmet, but it seemed churlish to raise the point.

The two jet-engines whined like dentists' drills, and we sauntered gently round the perimeter-track and formed up at the end of the runway. The air was full of voices – the Control Tower's, the formation leader's, my pilot's. I badly wanted to say something myself to show I could, but could think of nothing to say.

Then with astonishing smoothness we rolled down the runway, our wingtip far closer to the leader's wing than I should have advised. I watched the leader with the eye of a hawk, determined that if we did touch him I should tell my pilot right away, so that he could open out a little.

Quite suddenly the runway dropped away below and the untidy bottom of the clouds rushed down on us. The three Meteors moved as if riveted together with (very short) invisible ties. '*All right?*' asked my pilot over the intercom. Here at last was a chance to put my learning into practice. Speaking in the air for the first time, I said '*Yes, thanks.*'

In a couple of minutes we were through the clouds, three stationary silver Meteors shining, like flying saucers at eight thousand feet while the world went slipping by. The sky was immaculately blue. My pilot edged in a little towards the leader, and the leader's voice came sharp over the air. '*Our wingtip was getting in his jet exhaust,*' said my pilot apologetically. The leader spoke again. '*Red Formation, open-out!*'

We swung abruptly away to port. When next I looked at the leader he was flying belly-upwards. We edged in as close as possible while his passenger counted out the fatal fifteen seconds.

Then – '*Red Formation,*' came the leader's voice, '*open-out!*'

We turned away again and the leader made a half-roll to resume his normal attitude. We closed in once more. There was an oval hatchway in the leader's fuselage, just at the roundel, on which I could read stencilled Desert Equipment. To practise my speaking technique I decided to ask what it was. My inquiry should be modest, yet urbane and well-enunciated. But the leader was on the air before me and we were giving him elbow-room for another handstand.

Finally it was time to go home. '*You want to make sure your ears aren't bunged up as we come down,*' my pilot said. '*Yes,*' I said. It was my last airborne remark of the day; below the clouds the air was a little bumpy...

Doubtless if I had raised the point someone at the School would have taught me how to get round that difficulty too. Here at nought feet, my parachute replaced by an armchair, my oxygen-mask by a cup of coffee, I can speak without restraint—speak of the skill and charm of those hand-picked pilots, of the merits of the Meteor 7 as an air-yacht, of the joy of jet flight under a sky of uninterrupted blue. Possibly it all looks a bit sentimental reduced to cold print. You can, if you like, put it down to a mild degree of anoxia but it's not that really."

40th anniversary

To mark the 40th anniversary of CFS, an event held in front of the national press on 13 May included, as a highlight, three Prentice aircraft flying a formation display with their wings tied together with 12 ft lengths of strapping. With Flt Lts Unwin, Wood and Pedder at the controls, the team completed their performance with a heartily applauded loop. An impeccable composite formation of an Anson with a Harvard and Vampire FB.5 in echelon starboard in Nos. 2 and 4 positions and a Spitfire LF.XVI and Meteor T.7 in echelon port in Nos. 3 and 5 positions was also flown.

The Commandant at this anniversary was Air Cdre A D Selway DFC (known universally as 'Mark' because his name was Anthony) with Gp Capt W E 'Bill' Coles DSO DFC AFC as Chief Instructor

The interesting mixed-type formation flown to mark the 40th anniversary of CFS comprised: Anson C.19, TX191, Harvard T.2b, FT213, Spitfire LF.XVIe, SL721, Vampire FB.5, WE830, and Meteor T.7, WH245. (*David Watkins*)

with Wg Cdr 'Pop' Sewell as CFI South Cerney and Wg Cdr Don Willis, Little Rissington, with Wg Cdr Russell Bell as OC Examining Wing and Wg Cdr Tony Trumble as Station Commander.

Anniversary dinner

At the 40th Anniversary Reunion Dinner on 18 July, founding members of CFS, MRAF The Viscount Trenchard, ACM Sir Arthur Longmore GCB DSO and Air Cdre Louis Gerrard CMG DSO were present, in 1912 respectively a Major, Lieutenant RN and a RMLI Captain. Sir Arthur Longmore and Air Cdre Gerrard were two of the first four officers allowed by the Admiralty to draw pay while learning to fly. Among the 220 diners were MRAF Sir John Slessor, ACM the Hon Sir Ralph Cochrane plus Air Marshals Sir John Baldwin, Sir Hugh Walmsley and Sir Thomas Williams and nine Air Vice-Marshals, The Earl of Bandon, Sir Paul Maltby, C. McC Vincent, F.W. Long, L.F. Pendred, D.A. Boyle, F.H.M. Maynard, W.A.B. Bowen-Buscarlet and G.D. Harvey, among many other senior ranks, also celebrating the success of the recently formed CFS Association, whose formation had been accelerated by the help of ACM Sir James Robb GCB KBE DSO DFC AFC who had been Commandant between 1937 and 1940. Membership of the CFS Association was nearly 900 and Sir James said he hoped that the others eligible would shortly join.

The Guest of Honour, 'Boom' Trenchard, told how the post of Assistant Commandant was kept open for ten days for him to qualify and that it was Sir Arthur Longmore, who had taught him to fly. Lord Trenchard said that when he was appointed as Instructor he had to examine and pass himself as qualified by the simple expedient of setting the papers and passing himself. He paid high tribute to Captain Godfrey Paine RN, the Central Flying School's first Commandant and how he was able to withstand pressures from both the Navy and the Army and stand up for the interests of both CFS and the RFC. Many had been those after WW1 who had tried to break up the infant Royal Air Force but he remained proud of the achievements of those who had died for the roundels on the blue sky background and was as determined that these roundels would remain as for the Royal Air Force to commemorate those lives through its continued existence.

Sir John Slessor in both a humble and grave mood said that "*we must move out of the old idea of armies and navies, we have passed into a completely new era*". Sir Arthur Longmore reminded the assembled company of the beginnings of instructional flying with some stories of warping wings and the early days of CFS.

Harvard collisions

On June 26, Harvards FS890 and FT337 collided at Moreton-in-Marsh, with only minor injuries being sustained by both the QFI pilots. However, tragedy struck on 28 July when two Harvards, FS822 and KF948, were involved in a collision near Calmsden, four miles from South Cerney, killing all the occupants on board. The funerals took place on the 31st.

More Harvard mishaps

Flt Sgt Tomczak and a student were flying dual in a Harvard of Refresher Squadron on 25 August when engine trouble developed near RAF Brize Norton. As the runway was obstructed by trucks and construction personnel, the aircraft was landed with wheels retracted on very rough ground parallel to the runway. Although both pilots were unhurt, considerable damage was suffered by the aeroplane.

On the following day, during a practice formation sortie by No. 1 Squadron at RAF Fairford, two Prentice aircraft piloted by Flt Lts Bain and Christopherson collided. Flt Lt Bain managed to bale out at low altitude and was fortunate to escape with only a sprained ankle on landing as his aircraft, VS394, crashed into the runway close by. Flt Lt Christopherson managed to get his damaged aircraft safely back to South Cerney.

New RLG for Rissy

On 29 August, RAF Enstone became operational for use as a Relief Landing Ground for No. 5 Squadron's Little Rissington-based jets following rehabilitation of the main runway, peri-track and control tower. Relevant personnel were transported to and from the airfield from Little Rissington on a daily basis. As fire trucks and airfield service vehicles were driven to Enstone on a Monday morning and remained there until the Friday evening, a two-man guard was mounted overnight on the airfield from Monday through Thursday.

Led astray!

Sqn Ldr T.S. Syme was a 'creamed-off' instructor who passed out with Distinction and as a B1 QFI on No. 146 Course, completing this in November 1952.

> *"The students were a mixture of 'creamies' like me and a bunch of WW2 reservists, recalled to do their bit during the Korean conflict. I went from being a clean-living innocent to a confirmed rabble-rouser/drunk almost overnight, such was the influence of our wartime buddies!! I remember little from my CFS course of interest and I would imagine that most of those involved have now gone strato-AWOL. There were still a fair number of NCO instructors in those days. However, I do clearly recall that the top guy on our course, a wartime recall, was an heir to some big business in Yorkshire. He achieved the top honours in spite of never studying – the latter was not on the cards as he was in the bar every night. I believe he was killed rather tragically at some later date. We found him and a buddy in the streets of Cheltenham one Saturday when the bars had closed after the lunchtime session, which was the custom in those days, they were stopping all the locals and begging for a shop where they might find nylons (a scarcity then) for their wives!! On our Course Dining Out night our senior pilot, a handsome Scot, made some unpopular remarks about the staff during his farewell speech. Someone managed to pull his shirt tail out, which was promptly set alight. With great aplomb and never missing a beat in his spiel, he calmly patted out the flames with his hands. Later, after his second demob, I believe he went on to achieve some considerable success in the City.*

That year I went to the Farnborough Air Show with David Craig, a future Chief of the Air Staff. It was the year of the John Derry tragedy and we were on the hill, which was in direct line with one of the engines of his DH110, which came out after the aircraft broke up. Fortunately the engine went over our heads, but besides John Derry and his observer, Tony Richards, 29 spectators were also killed."

Over at South Cerney

Number 28 Refresher Course consisting of 36 students arrived and were allocated to: J Flight – sixteen students and K Flight – twenty students. A special course for fourteen Burmese Air Force students was divided equally between the two flights. The training included formation flying and back seat landings before moving on to the Spitfire conversion course.

Following receipt of an order cancelling formation aerobatics by piston-engined aircraft, synchronised aerobatics was introduced in its place. Practice formations of the letters 'C', 'F' (Prentices) and 'S', and 'R', 'A', and 'F' (all Harvards), were flown in preparation for the forthcoming Battle of Britain day.

Battle of Britain Day – South Cerney

Over 10,000 spectators turned-up for the BoB day which was held on 20 September. The weather was reasonable and the flying display highlights included:

- Formation of Prentices and Harvards depicting the letters 'CFS' and 'RAF'.
- Solo aerobatics by Flt Lt Byrne in a Harvard.
- Formation flying and synchronised aerobatics by the students of K Flight flying Harvards.
- Tied together formation flying by the three Prentices of A Flight, No. 1 Squadron.
- Formation drill display by Prentices of B Flight.

CFS Harvards capture the spirit of the 1952 Battle of Britain celebrations with this formation flypast. (*Les Lane*)

CFS instructor to teach Duke to fly

The following extracts are taken from various press cuttings in 1952.

Shortly before completing his tour as Flight Commander at CFS, Flt Lt Caryl Gordon was selected by the Air Council to teach The Duke of Edinburgh to fly and on 5 November he was invited to Buckingham Palace to be introduced to the Duke. They talked for half an hour. Flt Lt Gordon explained to the Duke that the training course he would undergo would start with 60 hours dual and solo on a brand new De Havilland Chipmunk primary trainer, and would take place at RAF White Waltham, the headquarters of Home Command. An advanced course would follow after this primary training. The Duke and his tutor also discussed a series of dates for the start of the training and it was agreed that it should begin on 12 November.

Flt Lt Gordon almost missed the honour of being selected to teach the Duke to fly as he had been nominated for an Aide-de-Camp (ADC) post overseas. Caryl joined the RAF in 1942 and operated with Bomber and Transport Commands and had logged 2,500 hours, 640 of them in Meteor jet trainers. He had recently been awarded the Queen's Commendation for his work at the Central Flying School, at Little Rissington.

The Duke goes solo

The date was 20 December 1952 and for 15 minutes the sky suddenly brightened and the Duke of Edinburgh made his first solo flight, which looked impossible almost up to take-off time. It drizzled all the time he was in the air – and then it poured again. But the Duke flew well enough to please his instructor and himself, and he came in with a good three-point landing. Two questions about his flight were answered in an official announcement:

The announcement said that the Duke was in the air 15 minutes, a little longer than average as he flew strictly to RAF rules – making a wider-than-civilian circuit of the airfield to give himself time for radio 'drill' with flight control. The announcement also said that the Duke flew solo after about the normal period of dual training, which was about eight hours. The Duke had taken ten because many of his training flights had been in bad weather.

As the first solo was about to take place at White Waltham airfield, all other aircraft on the airfield were grounded and a general 'keep clear' warning was radioed to all airborne planes. Just before 11:00 cloud-base was down to 1,000 ft, with visibility of less than a mile, but by 11:00, the clouds had lifted slightly and visibility had increased to two to three miles.

Flt Lt Gordon, the Duke's instructor, taxied the Chipmunk trainer to the offices of RAF Home Command without stopping the engine and got out. Standing on the wing, he gave the Duke a few final hints, before stepping back and waving the Duke away. The Duke taxied to the east side of the airfield and turned into wind for final check of instruments and controls. He then asked the control tower for permission to take off and this was granted. The engine opened up and the Chipmunk began to gather speed. In a few seconds the tail

lifted, followed by the main wheels – and off into the drizzle he went.

After calling the control tower for permission to land he began his glide-in and, according to his instructor, "*made a very good three-point landing*." The Duke taxied the Chipmunk back to the offices and, as he stepped out smiling broadly, his instructor and other RAF officers shook his hand. Flt Lt Gordon climbed into the instructor's seat and took the Duke up for a few minutes' dual instruction. The Duke still had 40 to 50 hours' instruction ahead of him before he would be able to graduate to more powerful planes.

When Caryl Gordon read this published account fifty–one years later, it evoked a few more memories from his time as an instructor. "*In July 1952 the Headmaster of Cheltenham College – the Reverend. Pentreath – visited CFS and asked to be flown over the college to inspect the roof of the chapel! It was necessary to fly over very low and inverted to get a proper view. The Headmaster said he enjoyed it! From my logbooks, when not otherwise occupied, I seem to have spent many happy hours flying a variety of aircraft in a variety of attitudes with one Flt Lt John Severne.*"

King's Cup Air Race

The King's Cup Air Race is a handicap race with everyone competing on equal terms with all the others. In 1952 the CFS had its own entry in the King's Cup Air Race when Flt Lt John Severne flew a Vega Gull loaned to him by Lady Sherborne. Although competing against a Vampire FB.9, WR211, flown by DH test pilot John Wilson, Flt Lt Severne finished a creditable eleventh.

"It all began at a cocktail party at the Officers' Mess in 1951 to celebrate the Battle of Britain. There I met Lady Sherborne who, with her one-armed husband, were both ATA pilots during the war. She was telling me about her Percival Vega Gull which was a well known pre-war aircraft. She was complaining about the high hangarage costs at Kidlington and so I said that I would be delighted to hangar it free at Little Rissington as she only lived a few miles away. RAF officers at that time could do this provided the space was available.

After a few months, in return for my offer of free hangarage, Joan Sherborne asked if I would like to enter the Vega Gull in the King's Cup. You can imagine my reaction. CFS agreed to enter it in the name of CFS, but I had very little money at that time so I managed to bounce Shell into sponsoring me for all the fuel I would be using in practice and the race, and I bounced De Havilland into giving the Gipsy Queen engine a top overhaul. I consulted Air Cdre Allen Wheeler (a well known sporting pilot who was Commandant at Boscombe Down at the time) who gave me some invaluable advice:

- *Navigation must be spot on; if you wander off course you will lose time.*
- *Turns must be as close as possible to the pylons, but if you clip the corner you will be disqualified.*
- *Fly as low as possible into wind (I went down to 10 ft or so!). Climb to 200 ft downwind to get the advantage of a stronger wind behind.*
- *The handicappers will examine the aircraft in detail to make sure there are no unauthorised modifications. They will assume the aircraft has the performance as if it was new. Therefore prepare it very carefully.*

I did several practice laps the week before in an Anson from Little Rissington. This was invaluable in helping me to memorise the course in case the visibility was not good. We were given our handicap times shortly before the race and I thought mine was very fair. The race was around four laps from Newcastle Airport, each lap being about 32 miles.

I glanced at my watch; eight minutes to go before we were to be flagged away. Already two Tiger Moths and the Avro Club Cadet had passed overhead and were already on the second lap and still there were six others to take off before us (why couldn't I fly a nice slow aeroplane, I thought, and avoid all this waste of nervous energy!).

'Can you start up now, please?' shouted one of the Marshals, 'Can I stay another couple of minutes, I have no oil cooler and she gets a bit hot?' – 'No?' – 'Oh very well!' The next worry is, will she start? One push of the button and she fired first go and I saw satisfied smiles from Ian Scott and Dick, my brother, who were standing by my wing tips. A moment or two later we were trundling forward to fill up the gaps of the last chaps off.

With engine at part throttle, Flt Lt John Severne eagerly awaits the marshal to drop the flag and enable his participation in the 1952 Kings Cup Air Race to begin. (*John Severne*)

The starter held up two fingers, which I hope meant that we had two minutes to go, (this I checked with my watch and found to be so!) and at the same time we were marshalled on to the starting line, on a dusty old runway, which could only take two abreast. The last Proctor had just been flagged away and beside me was the beautifully polished 'Falcon Speed 6' which was not due off for some time.

Whilst I was noting all this, I suddenly realised that the starter's flag was up, which meant I had ten seconds to go, so I opened up the throttle as far as I could against the brakes (no point in checking the magnetos for fear of frightening myself), and as the flag whipped down: 'Throttle wide open, brakes off, tail up' and the event had really arrived which we had been awaiting for many months.

Only a few hundred yards from the airfield lay the first turning point of nearly 180 degrees to set us on the first leg towards St. Mary's Lighthouse – this safely negotiated we settled down on our first lap. We flew at about 200 ft to catch the best of a tail wind on this leg and there were no problems in keeping on course as one just kept an enormous slag heap slightly to the left of track and one found the lighthouse dead ahead. It was interesting to watch the turning technique of the experts. It certainly didn't pay to vary one's height in the turn and one wasn't supposed to in any case. Some rolled rapidly into the turn and hauled the aircraft round the corner and rolled rapidly out. This looked most impressive. Another school of thought was to roll more gently, thus avoiding excessive drag during the roll from the ailerons, turn tightly as you saw the turning point below and roll out gently. Not such fun to see, but I think this resulted in less loss of speed after the turn than the other method. We had no alternative as the Vega's ailerons were fantastically heavy at full speed and it was very hard work to roll at all!

The second leg was a straightforward low level run over the sea as low as one dare, and the third was more difficult, being a climb of some 500 ft of coal mining country. This was into wind which meant flying as low as possible to avoid the bad wind effect. The fourth leg led straight towards the airfield and again meant a few more minutes of glorious legal low flying!

All the legs were about eight miles long, and took some three minutes to complete, but the Vampire would complete a whole lap in 4 minutes! As the handicappers had tried to arrange for us all to cross the line together there was not much excitement until about the third lap when we began to bunch up a little and we realised that it was going to be an excellent finish. By the time we had started the last lap the Vampire was only starting up. He later overtook us four times and finished three places in front of me.

It was on the third lap that I hit one of the biggest bumps I had ever known as I came round the leeward side of a large wood. My head came into violent contact with the roof and there was a most alarming noise from the wing – rather like a revolver shot. However, we were all in one piece so we pressed on. Inspection later revealed a very flabby piece of canvas which seems to have taken most of the shock but I now felt confident to fly the Vega through the most violent of storms (or do I?).

The last leg was incredibly exciting, we had already been overtaken by several others but we, on the other hand, had passed even more. As the finishing line loomed up I saw a Miles Messenger just ahead of me and I just failed to catch him by the end of the race. We started 16th and were to finish 11th out of a field of 23."

Marshal of the RAF remembers Little Rissington

Marshal of the RAF Lord Craig of Radley GCB OBE RAF passed through Little Rissington as a student on Meteor T.7s from 7 October 1952 to 12 January 1953.

"I was 'creamed-off' as potential QFI material after completing my Wings course at No. 7 FTS RAF Cottesmore on Harvards and 47 Course at No. 203 AFS, RAF Driffield flying Meteor F.4s and T.7s. I completed that course in August 1952.

On 29 July 1952, I flew solo in a Meteor 4 from Driffield to Little Rissington for an interview (I cannot remember with whom – possibly it included a brief meeting with the Commandant) and flew back later that day to Driffield. I had given myself a good scare on landing at Rissy with its considerably shorter runway than I was used to at Driffield. Arriving a couple of knots fast at the threshold, the far end of the runway over the hump approached all too quickly. I just managed to stop without burning out my brakes or running off into the soft grass at the far end. I don't think it was spotted, but the fright it gave me (and the passage of 50 years) seems to have sapped my memory of anything else that happened to me at Little Rissington that day.

A tragedy during my course was that one of my fellow students practising for the 'Brabyn Aerobatic Trophy' on the day of the 1952 Christmas Ball crashed and killed himself during his display. The weather was not particularly good at the time. The Ball was cancelled. After returning in the New Year the weather was still unfit for low level aerobatics. So the rest of us who were competing for the Trophy had to fly our display above cloud with OC Flying Wing, Wg Cdr T.D. W. Willis in the back seat. It happened on 2 January 1953, and to my surprise I won the Trophy.

I left Rissington on 7 January, still a Flying Officer, to start my one 2¼ year QFI tour at RAF Weston Zoyland (No. 209 AFS) on Meteors. I had less than 500 hours total flying and not even 100 hours on Meteors. Not exactly a great depth of experience, which was more than brought home to me at Weston Zoyland where some of my students had hundreds more hours than me in their log books, all on piston engines and with many WWII sorties to their credit. They came to Weston Zoyland to get their first experience of jet engine flying. I still think that I learnt more from them than they ever did from me! It made me realise that the RAF was not just a flying school."

Trophies and Awards

At the end of each course at Little Rissington, two trophies were competed for; the CFS Trophy for the best all-round student on the course and the Clarkson Trophy for individual aerobatics. To this a third was added in 1952, the Brabyn Trophy for Meteor aerobatics. Consisting of a Silver Meteor mounted on an ebony base, it was presented to CFS by Sqn Ldr George Brabyn who was a New

Zealander and had just completed a tour as an instructor on an exchange posting. (See Appendix 1 for a list and description of trophies.)

Former Polish Air Force pilot Flt Lt Dolicher flew his Harvard to perfection and claimed the prestigious Clarkson Trophy. Air Cdre Selway's second presentation was made to Fg Off G.G. Farley who became the first recipient of the 'Brabyn' Trophy for the best aerobatic pilot on his Meteor course. Geoff writes,

"After serving on Nos. 26(AC) and 94 Squadrons in Germany on Vampires, I was posted to South Cerney to do a Harvard Refresher course in November 1951. My own No. 139 Instructors Course at CFS began with 40 hours of Basic Flying on the Prentice at South Cerney from 11 January 1952. Over seven weeks later on 25 February 1952, the course transferred to Little Rissington where we were then split into two flights, one of which was to fly Harvards and the other, which I joined, to fly Meteors. At the end of the course two pilots were chosen to compete for the aerobatics trophies, one for each aircraft type. Each pilot was required to perform a number of set piece aerobatics at low level but in those days with no minimum height restriction! The routine had to include at least a mandatory loop, slow roll, roll off the top and stall turn, plus one voluntary additional manoeuvre. The sequence could be of your own choosing but ended with a 'dead stick' forced landing from 2,500 ft. Marks were awarded with 30 points for each manoeuvre, 20 points for the forced landing and a further 30 points for overall impression, totalling maximum points of 200. Marks could be deducted for poor positioning such as 'into sun manoeuvres' or continuity lapses within the chosen aerobatic sequence, etc.

The Harvard prize was the Clarkson Trophy, won by Flt Lt. Dolicher, an ex-Polish Air Force wartime pilot. The new Meteor prize was the Brabyn Trophy, recently donated by Sqn Ldr G.R. Brabyn AFC, a RNZAF officer on exchange with the staff at CFS, who had just returned to New Zealand. This was the first time that the Brabyn Trophy was to be competed for and presented, with my being lucky enough to win this competition. The prizes were presented by the Commandant, Air Cdre A.D. Selway DFC (who had been at CFS between 1932-34 after No. 1(F) Squadron Siskins at Tangmere). The day of our aerobatics competition coincided with the 40th Anniversary of CFS on 13 May 1952, four decades after being formed on 13 May 1912, as part of the Royal Flying Corps to train all pilots. Since 1920 CFS had only trained flying instructors and is unique in being the only 1912 air unit to have retained the same unit title since its formation – one could suggest that until 1976 and at Little Rissington, certainly on the fixed wing side, the 'Central' adjective did stay a fairly true description in CFS's title!

With this particular day being the Fortieth Anniversary, a large number of journalists had been invited to Little Rissington for the day. Our aerobatic fly-off efforts were watched and judged first, before CFS then put on its own mini air display for the benefit of our visitors. These items included a team of three Prentices, with wing tips tied together by 12 ft. lengths of webbing straps, which flew a flat formation display before finishing with a loop. This was followed by a composite formation of Meteor Mk.7, Spitfire Mk.16, Anson, Harvard Mk.2b and Vampire Mk.5, all flying at 145 kts. Finally 20 Harvards in formation formed the letters 'ER', as a rehearsal for a flypast salute to our new Queen later in the year.

Because of the large increase in pilot requirements at this time, several Meteor and Vampire Advanced Flying Schools (AFS) were formed. Both these aircraft were popular at air displays, with many instructors trying their hand at aerobatic sequences. However the lack of a minimum safety height did result in a number of pilots killing themselves, so a minimum height of 300 ft. was introduced for rolling and turning manoeuvres, with a 500 ft. base for vertical manoeuvres. This took some of the challenge out of performing but display flying was still good fun. Similarly the previous Meteor engine off 'dead stick' landings, a single engine landing with the other Derwent shut completely down rather than merely throttled back, were also stopped at about the same time because of accidents."

Farewell message from the Chief of Air Staff

On completion of his time as Chief of Air Staff, MRAF Sir John Slessor GCB DSO MC was invited by the Commandant to send a farewell message to all past and present members of the Central Flying School.

"It is nearly 34 years since I was posted to CFS as Assistant Commandant to Jack Scott in the spring of 1918 – I had of course been there before to be passed for my Wings in 1915. Ever since then CFS has, to me, stood for all that is best in the RAF, for brilliant flying, for discipline and pride in the Service and the unequalled comradeship of the Air. To anyone – of any rank or trade – it is a source of pride to be able to shoot a line beginning with the words 'When I was at CFS'.

The old CFS tradition, founded by Godfrey Paine and the early pioneers 40 years ago, is still alive to-day and will be going strong when I and others of my generation come down in our bath-chairs and CFS ties to future re-unions, when some Cadet now at Cranwell is Commandant.

All good wishes and a Happy Christmas to you all."

Fg Off Geoff Farley receives the prestigious Brabyn Trophy from Air Cdre Selway. (*Graham Pitchfork collection*)

1953

Duke's instructor sets poser

An extract from 'The Evening News', 2 January 1953:

"Flt Lt Caryl Gordon, the 29-year-old instructor who is teaching the Duke of Edinburgh to fly, has astounded fellow-pilots and aviation medical experts by performing a remarkable aerobatic manoeuvre without showing the slightest ill-effects. According to the generally accepted view he should have experienced a 'red-out' and been blind for several days. This, he was told, could be expected for certain if he flew his plane above a certain speed at the critical moment of the manoeuvre. But there were no such effects and Flt Lt Gordon has set pilots talking in RAF messes about his remarkable flying skill and judgment and medical officers thinking of his high physical qualities.

The whole manoeuvre was worked out carefully beforehand at the Central Flying School which has a world-wide reputation for precise and accurate flying. It was decided that the School should have a Christmas card that was different by having a photograph between the covers that would make even the Chief of Air Staff exclaim: "*How on earth did they take that?*" It was to be a photograph of four Meteor jet trainers, flown, by the school's Meteor aerobatic team making a formation half loop. But here was the trick – the leader, Flt Lt Gordon, was to fly in a different attitude from his three team-mates.

The photograph, taken from a fifth Meteor trainer flown by Flt Lt John Severne, showed that Caryl Gordon's aircraft was inverted in relation to the other three, so while the three were performing a standard inside loop, he was doing what was technically known as a half bunt: outside loop in modern parlance.

Such a manoeuvre imposes terrific strain on pilot and machine. At the first attempt Caryl completed his part of the manoeuvre before the rest of his team had time to see which way he went as he 'blacked them out.' During subsequent attempts his team complained that it was difficult to keep their position because 'he looked so different upside down.' The Christmas card complete with picture went out with the season's greetings."

The Spinning test

This interesting snippet about three CFS students appeared in the February 1953 edition of the *'Aeroplane'* magazine:

"Three of the 'coming-on-nicely' pupils started an argument about who could do the most spins from 5,000 ft. for a side bet of 2s. 6d. Number 1 spun to within 500 ft. or so of the ground and pulled out. No. 2 went a lot closer before he pulled out, but No. 3 only pulled out as he hit the ground and completely disintegrated his aircraft. Fire engines and a blood wagon raced out to the wreck with the other two competitors standing on the running boards. As they reached it, the putative corpse stood up, stepped out and started pulling splinters from himself. The other two grabbed him by the arms and shouted at him: '*What the hell did you do that for, you B.F.?*", to which he replied: "*Well! As a matter of fact, I was thinking of doing another turn, but I thought, after all, for half-a-crown, is it worth it?*"

A Thomas Deehan on the other hand was not so lucky as he was sucked into a Meteor engine intake on 19 February 1953 and died from his injuries.

Aircraft incidents

The early part of the year witnessed several minor accidents involving aircraft, the most notable being the overshoot of a Prentice T.1 which ended up in the airfield boundary hedge, a wheels-up landing by the crew of Meteor T.7, WL359, an overshoot on beam approach by Harvard T.2b, KF698, that nosed-over, and the disintegration of the hood on Meteor T.7, VW434. Another Harvard T.2b, FX434, had an engine failure shortly after taking off from South Cerney and was badly damaged during the subsequent forced landing. All crews were reported to have escaped injury.

The crew of Harvard T.2b, KF211, were however, killed when their aircraft was seen to lose control during a spin at about 1,500 ft and it crashed a few miles from Naunton village.

Flood Relief Fund

Flt Lt Caryl Gordon performing his half-bunt manoeuvre with his three colleagues in close attendance. This unique formation was flown specifically for the 1952 CFS Christmas Card photograph. (*John Severne*)

As the extent of the damage caused by the flood disaster on the North Sea coasts of England and the Netherlands became known, no time was lost in launching relief funds at RAF stations across Britain. At South Cerney, the Station Commander set a target of £250 but so great was the sympathy felt by all ranks for those that had suffered, that a grand total of £544-11s-11d was contributed. A cheque for 150 guineas of this was presented to HM Queen Juliana and HRH Prince Bernhard of the Netherlands by the Station CO when they arrived at RAF Hendon for a state visit on 26 February.

Trappers go overseas

A number of Examining Wing staff left Little Rissington on 27 April to begin a four-week tour of the Middle East Air Force to:

- Examine standards of instruction techniques
- Re-cat instructors
- Discuss and make recommendations on instrument and pilot techniques
- Recommend appointment of Command instrument rating examiners
- Undertake Instrument Rating checks

Airfields visited included Luqa, Takali, Hal Far, Fayid, Kabrit, Nicosia, Habbaniya, Abu-Sueir, Deversoir and Khormaksar. On 3 June, another team spent three weeks in Rhodesia assessing instruction in the Air Training Group.

First Piston Provosts

At 17:00 on 28 May 1953, Wg Cdr K.J. Sewell AFC DFM, the CFI, flew the first CFS Piston Provost, WV432, into South Cerney having collected it directly from the manufacturer, Percival at Luton. This was an event eagerly awaited by CFS pilots and by 21:15 on the same day, Wg Cdr Sewell had checked-out Sqn Ldr Gartrell, Flt Lts Bain and Wrigley, and Fg Off Evans. Its flying time on that first day was 3.2 hours to which was added another 4.1 hours on the 29th. On 26 June, four Provosts departed for static display at RAF Odiham just as three more were flown in from Percival, bringing the total on strength to ten machines.

Piston Provost: Intensive flying trials

At South Cerney, pilots of the Central Flying School (Basic) began subjecting a number of Percival Provosts to the most gruelling treatment ever undergone by a new RAF basic trainer. The object of intensive flying trials, which had been introduced for all RAF quantity-production aircraft some two years before, was to identify the inevitable 'bugs' which appear in any new type early in its Service career. Any modifications would then be embodied on the production line. The trials also enabled the Equipment Branch to produce a list of the type and quantity of spares required. In addition, pilots taking part in the trials completed questionnaires designed to identify any potential causes of accidents in the new type.

Wg Cdrs Sewell (CFI) and A.W. Lindley (CTO), directed the trials, phase 1 of which began soon after the arrival of the first Provost on 28 May. Within five days it had flown 100 hours and had doubled this figure within 11 days. By 25 June, when phase 1 ended, four Provosts had flown 631 hours, and with seven aircraft on board, the total passed the 1,000 hour mark on 17 July.

The first phase of trials consisted of flying the aircraft at maximum intensity (one Provost flew 21 hr 5 min in one 24 hour period) while familiarising instructors and groundcrews with its characteristics. During this four-week period 101 pilots were converted to the type, and a visit was paid to Valley, where Provost and Vampire T.11 instructors discussed details of the proposed Provost-Vampire training sequence and flew each other's aircraft.

During the second phase, which began on 27 June and included pilots of several nationalities, the rate of utilisation was lower – but still well above the normal figure. The Provosts were now being used in their intended CFS role in the training of experienced pilots as flying instructors. Half the students on the first course were trained on the Provost and half on the earlier and less agile Prentice. This enabled instructors to assess the new aircraft's merits as a trainer and to adjust the syllabus to match its improved performance. An Air Ministry observer wrote, "*The Provost has performed well during the trials and the good impression given by the prototype has been confirmed. It has no 'vices' and is easy to fly, but not so easy that the inept pupil remains un-detected.*"

The side-by-side seating arrangement was deemed comfortable and convenient, and cockpit layout evoked particularly favourable comment. Several of the Provost's performance characteristics resembled those of the more powerful types which pupils would fly later in their training: in aerobatics, for example, it had much in common with the Vampire trainer, and instructors described the aircraft as very suitable for performing simulated jet QGHs (controlled descents through cloud). They emphasised that although pleasant and straightforward to fly, the Provost should be flown accurately, and that it showed up pupils' faults better than its predecessor. Despite its comparatively high output, the 550 hp Alvis Leonides was reported to be both smooth and reasonably quiet.

In a preliminary report on the trials in August, the principal items noted as requiring attention were the Artificial Horizon and Accumulator Mounting Tray securing device. The former was not very robust and had given a high incidence of failure and was deemed very sensitive by pilots. On two occasions the battery mounting tray had broken loose in the aircraft, fortunately without serious mishap. The Provost Trial was concluded on 16 September 1953.

The first Provost course

Thirty-four students of No. 157 Course arrived at South Cerney in time to start the first Basic Training Course to be run on the Provost on 5 August.

Coronation Review

As a prelude to the forthcoming Coronation Review, celebrations took place at Little Rissington on Tuesday 2 June, commencing with a ceremonial parade, followed by prayers of thanksgiving and dedication. From 10:15 to 11:15 television sets were provided for personnel and their families in the station Cinema, NAAFI and individual messes. Coronation mugs were presented to the children of all service personnel culminating in an open air tea party for them in front of the Officers' Mess. A Coronation Carnival and fun fair on the sports field began at 21:00 and a fireworks display at 22:00 concluded an exciting day.

The day of the Coronation Review of the Royal Air Force by Her Majesty the Queen was held at RAF Odiham on 15 July 1953. Participation by CFS was minimal, four Prentices being flown in the flypast by CFS pilots and a further six aircraft with pilots lined-up for the static display. Sqn Ldr Gartrell led the CFS formation while the Station Commander, Gp Capt Lucas, flew as an observer in one of the aircraft.

From heavy to light!

Most of the students on No. 153 Course were 'Heavies' from Transport Command or pilots with limited recent flying experience and, considering their backgrounds the results attained were very gratifying. The course was not without incident, the most notable being when a student in the rear seat of a Meteor T.7 raised the undercarriage too early and aircraft sank back on to the runway causing Cat.3 damage to its port engine nacelle. Fortunately the alert student in the front seat took over and completed the circuit before landing safely.

Many of the students on the next course, No. 154, also arrived with 'Heavy' backgrounds which probably accounted for the disappointing standard of aerobatics. On the other hand, their final handling tests were very encouraging and the course was described by instructors as above average.

Parrot's Progress

Sqn Ldr J.R. Goodman DFC AFC was the Chief Ground Instructor at Little Rissington until the summer of 1953 and gave his impressions of life in the Ground School in the June edition of the CFS magazine.

"If you have ever been to the Parrot House at the Zoo you will have a good idea of what life is like in an RAF Ground School. On relinquishing my grip as Chief Parrot at Little Rissington I have been asked, or dared, to give my impressions of life in the Ground School at CFS, which is of course like any other ground school only more so.

Examinations, reports, and arguments have now gone by the board together with the endless duty of trying to persuade those unfortunates who insist on gaining bottom place, that they weren't as bad as they had been painted. In many cases they were of course far worse.

A flying instructor has a distinct advantage over his counter part in the hot air department, in that he can easily gain ascendancy over his student. This can be done by ignoring the chap, who promptly feels that he is a rotten pilot and comes to heel. The ground instructor however, is under a constant barrage from up to thirty savages at a time, all of whom are determined to disprove everything he says. The best he can hope for is that he will be able to make someone look a fool in which case, human nature being what it is, attention will be diverted and he will 'get by'. At worst he must out-bellow everyone until saved by the bell at the end of the lecture period.

The ground instructor is essentially in the position of trying to sell something which nobody wants to buy and it is a sine qua non that a lecturer should be persuasive, something of a soap box orator, and an expert in unarmed combat. A Chief Ground Instructor is of course a complete nonentity who says Yes to everyone that matters and No to everybody else.

Students are essentially little boys who refuse to grow up. Every trick known to the schoolboy is practised by his grown up version at CFS. Rude messages about teacher's parentage are apt to appear on the blackboard, demonstration equipment is liable to be 'fixed' so that it does something quite different from that which the instructor had said it would do. This applies in particular to the smoke tunnel, which can be made to backfire and scare the living daylights out of everyone present. Howlers such as, 'An iceberg doesn't have a centre of gravity, otherwise it would sink,' come up with monotonous regularity and, intentional or not, gain the students no marks. If the examiner feels particularly vicious it may lead him to deduct large lumps of marks along with large lumps of his own hair.

This leads imperceptibly to the problem of length of ground instructional tours. Headquarters staffs are always so satisfied at trapping someone into a Ground School job that they invariably leave him to think it over for years. Is it any wonder that eventually the poor fish goes completely grey, and ends up by believing that the highest ratio CL max./CD min. is the same as best L/D ratio. Come to think of it, I'm not so sure that it isn't."

Early Meteor experiences

With the Meteor T.7 firmly established as the RAF's advanced jet trainer, the CFS formed a four-ship display team called "The Meteorites". Publicity photographs for the team were taken by Russell Adams, Gloster's chief photographer, from the back seat of a fifth T.7 flown by Flt Lt John Severne who recalls two flights he made with Russell on 24 July 1953.

> *"My aim was for the photographs to show each of the four formating aircraft without any part being covered by another aircraft. I flew a further five sorties with Russell on 10 August, but this was to make a film of formation aerobatics for The Gloster Aircraft Company. It was a good film (for that period), but I have no idea if any copies exist."*

Over the summer months of 1953, John Severne also explored inverted spinning in the Meteor.

> *"We used to do single-engined loops which was a good co-ordination exercise as the rudder loads increased significantly when the speed reduced on the way up, and then decreased as the speed increased on the way down. However, we thought someone might let the speed get dangerously*

slow at the top of a single-engined loop and fail to reduce power sufficiently to prevent a violent yaw with the possibility of then entering into an inverted spin. So, on 11 August, I found myself as captain of a Meteor 7 with the CFI, Frank Dodd, as co-pilot or whatever. My log book simply says 'Inv Spins'! Frank Dodd and I thought we had better find out what happens if a Meteor was so badly mishandled that it then entered an inverted spin. In fact the Meteor was very reluctant to enter such a spin, and even if it did so, it recovered easily - provided you remembered to move the stick in the right direction! I don't recall this exercise being repeated by anyone, although no doubt some idiots might have stuck their necks out!"

CFS 41st Anniversary reunion

The ensuing report of the Central Flying School 41st Anniversary reunion dinner which was held at Little Rissington on 24 July 1953, was published in Flight magazine. The guest of honour at the reunion was Marshal of the RAF Sir John M. Salmond, and the president of the CFS Association, Air Chief Marshal Sir James M. Robb, was also present.

"Giving the customary brief review of the CFS's work, the Commandant, Air Cdre A.D. Selway, mentioned that the courses had been much the same as in the previous year, entailing six weeks on Prentices at South Cerney and twelve weeks on Harvards or Meteors at Little Rissington. Both types of instructors had still to be trained so long as Advanced Flying Schools had only jets and Flying Training Schools only piston-engined types.

During the past year there had been thirteen courses, and 541 instructors had passed out successfully, 310 on piston engines and 231 on jets. The instructors had been "*rather a mixed bag*"; average wastage had been 17 per cent, ranging from $6\frac{1}{2}$ per cent on one course to 40 per cent on another. Thirty-one officers of foreign air forces had passed through, comprising two from Italy, two from Malaya, one from Thailand, one from Syria, six from Burma, three from Lebanon one from Iraq, and fifteen from Pakistan. In equal and open competition with RAF officers, some of them did very well indeed. The Clarkson Trophy for aerobatics had twice been won by foreign students: once by a Syrian and once by a Pakistani.

An analysis of ages indicated that those qualifying as piston-engine instructors average nearly 30, and those for jets 28. This was too high. CFS believed that the instructor's age should be such that, after his instructional tour, he would still be acceptable in an operational squadron.

Flying intensity had been high, and during the summer months there had been a lot of night flying. Some local residents who complained accepted the Commandant's explanation and apology; a few wrote to their M.P. To CFS these were known as "*the local Mau Mau,*" but fortunately they were far outnumbered by "*the loyal Kikuyu.*"

In his conclusion, the Commandant referred to the CFS Association; to the departure after three years of the station commander, Wg Cdr Trumble, who had received the customary silver

The 'Meteorites' immaculate displays are exemplified in this view taken by Russell Adams over the Cotswold countryside, 24 July, 1953. Flt Lt John Severne flew the camera-ship T.7. (*Russell Adams, via John Severne*)

'Pelican' memento on leaving for the Air Ministry; and welcomed Wg Cdr Rogers, who was taking over his post at Little Rissington.

ACM Sir James Robb proposed the toast of 'The Guests' which included the Secretary of State for Air, Lord De L'Isle and Dudley, Chief of Air Staff, ACM Sir William Dickson, MRAF Sir John Slessor, AM Sir Hugh Walmsley and AOC-in-C Flying Training Command. Covering Sir John Salmond's remarkable record as one of the original members of CFS at Upavon in 1912, Sir John Robb went on to say how much that foundation of the Central Flying School and its traditions had affected the lives of so many of those present and now in every part of the world.

In reply for the guests, Sir John Salmond said it had not been really heroic or hazardous to fly in those early days and recalled one occasion when he had a slight fire in the cockpit of his aircraft – he had "*ballooned down and landed in a field using a run of exactly six yards. The only real hazard was of breakage and that this very seldom occurred.*"

VC bales out

On 10 August, New Zealander Wg Cdr Leonard Trent VC DFC, recently posted from CFS where he was OC No. 3 Squadron, had to bale out of a Meteor F.Mk.4 over Cambridgeshire. He had spun off an upward roll at about 19,000 ft, first into an inverted spin and then flicking into a normal spin, which developed extreme pitching and yawing. Wg Cdr Trent had taken over as CFI at RAF Oakington but his wife, Ursula, was still at Little Rissington with their two girls and a boy. She heard the news over the telephone that he was quite all right and noted that this was two days after their 13th wedding anniversary.

Provosts pose!

One of the best known aviation photographers during this period was Mike Chase of the Air Ministry Photographic Reproduction Branch and he visited South Cerney on 6 August specifically to take photographs of the Provost in action. A five-ship formation was put up for him by No. 1 Squadron and Flt Lt Byrne flew solo presenting his aircraft in various aerobatic poses.

Green endorsements

It did not take long for serious incidents to arise on the first Cerney Provost course. On 13 August Flt Lt Chapple found that after a slow roll executed by the student, the elevator control became virtually inoperable and the trimming gear completely so. By considerable effort the elevators could be moved but only in jerks. He effected a safe landing in considerable difficulties. On the 26th of the month, while giving aerobatic instruction to his student, Flt Lt Beddoes experienced severe jamming of the elevator control following an inverted turn. This was a result of the accumulator breaking free from its mounting and coming to rest on the elevator cables. Considerable force was required to operate the elevators and a safe landing was effected. Both instructors were awarded Green Endorsements.

More problems with the Provost

A civilian working party from Alvis Ltd was called in during September to carry out modifications to the engines on WV430, 432 and 476 to prevent venting and to make them fully aerobatic. Problems of a more serious nature were detected by the Percival Aircraft Co. on its production line in the form of cracks in some longerons. As it was feared that some of them might have been built into the CFS Provosts, spinning, aerobatics and flying at speeds in excess of 160 kts was forbidden until Modification 141 had been embodied.

Visit to 2nd TAF

On 28 September a team of Trappers departed for a three-week tour of RAF stations in 2nd TAF, Germany, spending time at Wahn, Geilenkirchen, Wildenrath, Celle, Gütersloh, Ahlhorn, Jever and Sylt. The opportunity was taken to hold conferences at Wahn, Celle, Gütersloh, Sylt and Bückeburg.

The final overseas visit of the year began with the departure of Trappers to the Far East Air Force and Royal Pakistan Air Force on 26 October, and returning on 7 December 1953. The trip included stopovers at HQ FEAF, AHQ Hong Kong, Kai Tak and Sek Kong, Tengah, Changi and Seletar in Singapore, Butterworth, AHQ and Kuala Lumpur in Malaya. On their way back the team paid visits to RPAF bases at Risalpur and Mauripur.

Exercise

Being a flying training station, Little Rissington was involved with fewer exercises than those housing front line units, so it probably came as a bit of a shock to the system when Exercise 'Blackbird Jaunt' was held there over the weekend beginning 17:00 on Friday 16 October. The Evaders consisted of all available aircrew including students of Flying Wing. The Defence Force comprised the County police forces of Gloucestershire, Oxfordshire and Warwickshire, the Oxfordshire Home Guard and such airmen as were available from Little Rissington.

Harvard's rasping noise passes into history

On returning from a three-and-half year 2nd TAF tour in 1953, mostly on Vampire fighters with No. 16 Sqn, Flt Lt James Shelley was offered a choice between three different recruit training establishments. Responding that this was not exactly what he had hoped for, he was grudgingly offered CFS if that was a more preferable alternative. James remembers well the horse trading that went on right up to C-in-C level.

"2nd TAF wanted better standards in trained first tourist pilots than they were getting from the OCUs, so Flying Training promised in return that, given a greater flow back of ex-Fighter QFIs, they would limit the QFI commitment to single tours in Flying Training.

Before finally graduating from No. 163 Course, I had almost completed the last ever Harvard QFI course before being whisked into

RAF Hospital Wroughton to have my tonsils removed. When I returned to Rissington in 1954, the place was strangely quiet – no Harvards! The Harvard had been replaced by the Meteor but a couple of Vampires signalled an intended, alternate type of QFI course. Already an experienced Vampire FB5 pilot, I was selected for the first course on the Vampire. Experienced or not, when my farewell interview with the Commandant came, he indicated that, although I had scraped a 'B2', there was no danger of my ever returning to CFS on the staff. Imagine my surprise and amusement to be posted back as Chief Instructor some 17 years later!"

Examining Wing: The task

The following item is an extract from the 1953 CFS Association magazine. It explores key aspects of the important role and duties carried out by the Examiners, affecting both the wider life of units and individual pilots being tested as well as 'trappers' themselves:

"CFS are coming." How often does this phrase completely disorganise the Flying Wing on a station, albeit for a short period of time, but it is doubtful if any other body has such an impact on the flying on a unit than does Examining Wing. Has it occurred to you what really goes on behind the scenes when a visit from Examining Wing is imminent, not so much from the Station's point of view, but from the Examining Wing angle?

When a team of officers from the Wing visit a Station, the Station is naturally more preoccupied with the visit of the team as a whole than with any particular individual. But what about the impact of those visits on the individual examiner, how does he feel about visiting a strange station and being confronted with many strange and occasionally unfriendly faces? Fortunately, the unfriendly types are in the minority and the officers are generally well received, a programme of tests is made out, and the job begins.

Contrary to many pilots' ideas, Examining Wing does not arrive with the idea of creating turmoil within a unit. They have a set and exacting job to do within the Charter of the Central Flying School. They are, above all else, a normal crowd of individuals who are there to help. They assess the standard of Flying on the unit, categorise flying instructors, and are responsible for implementing the Instrument Rating Scheme by testing suitable candidates for appointment as Instrument Rating Examiners.

The conduct of these tests, poses problems for both the pilot being tested, and the examining officers. From the latters' point of view consider how difficult it sometimes must be to be pleasant when one does not feel pleasant; how difficult to be civil when occasionally the individual being tested is feeling far from civil towards oneself. Any test must be at all times fairly and impartially conducted, and it is the problem of impartiality divorced from personal prejudice, that is one of the more difficult tasks confronting the examiner.

A certain amount of natural sympathy always lies with the person being tested, but relatively little thought is ever given to the exacting task of the Examiner. Consider the position. The Examiner is confronted by an individual a stranger, quite often of senior rank to himself, of whose background he has only a limited knowledge. Sometimes the Examiner may have to give a decision that may adversely affect a person's career. It takes a fair amount of moral courage combined with understanding to make such a decision. Let it not be thought that Examining Wing officers are automatons, concerned only with theory; they deal more with human beings than with books, and their outlook is mainly practical and by and large sympathetic.

The tests also pose problems from the more practical angle. How, it might be asked, is it possible to differentiate between the below average, above average, and exceptional. It is not a simple question to answer. Primarily it depends upon the experience and integrity of the examining officer, and officers posted to the Wing are chosen for these, as well as other qualities. Secondly the problem depends largely upon the attitude of the person being tested. It is fairly true to say that an Examiner never fails anyone; it is the person who fails himself. To pick out the mediocre is fairly easy, but to pick out the above average, irrespective of 'testitis,' one looks for those qualities that 'testitis' cannot hide, a certain polish, knowledge and self-confidence that overcomes nerves. The exceptional is again a quality that leaves absolutely no doubt in the Examiners' mind that the individual being tested can fly, teach and possesses a background of knowledge that enhances his overall ability as an instructor and as a pilot.

To break away from the personal, and get back to the general, the Officers of Examining Wing do quite a big job. In 1953 a total of some 3,000 tests were carried out, consisting of recategorisation, standardisation and Instrument Rating Examiners' tests. These were done all over the world, Britain, Germany, the Middle East, Africa, Pakistan, Ceylon, Malaya and Hong Kong. This year's itinerary includes all the above and more. The job is interesting if somewhat expensive. Its biggest asset is that it gives the junior members of the Wing an opportunity to see the Air Force as a whole, and to gain insight into the problems connected with training in all commands, an opportunity that few other jobs in the Air Force presents.

The many different types of aircraft flown by members of Examining Wing, twenty-five in one year by one member, broadens the flying experience of the Wing pilots. There are relatively few problems connected with instructional technique or pure flying on any type of aircraft in current use that cannot be answered by at least one or more of the Wing Officers. The difficulty in keeping up-to-date on various types, is circumvented by having two training periods per year, where newly joined members are converted to types they have not flown, and experience is gained by other members on later types of aircraft.

Finally, Examining Wing is, as has been shown, a group of experienced individuals who strive to raise and maintain the highest standard of flying throughout the Royal Air Force. The members of the Wing carry out their duties extremely well and with a remarkable amount of spirit and teamwork, considering their tedious and exacting job."

1954

Lost days

Number 158 Course commenced in September 1953 and progressed as scheduled until January of the following year when bad weather caused the loss of 26 out of 50 flying days. At one stage a request for a two-week extension was requested but fortunately the weather cleared in the last 3 weeks and the course completed without the need to extend.

Christopher Paul: 'My Story'

Sometime after his retirement from the RAF, Air Cdre Christopher Paul wrote a personal account of his service career especially for his family and closest friends. Called 'My Story', one complete chapter was devoted to his time as Commandant of the CFS and a few extracts are included here thanks to the kind permission of Christopher Paul's widow Mollie.

The chapter begins at the completion of a year long course Christopher had undertaken at the Imperial Defence College (later renamed The Royal College of Defence Studies). 'My Story' gives a fascinating insight into the lifestyle and the responsibilities of a Commandant of the CFS.

"And so we dispersed, with almost the last of the announcements being my own appointment, which included promotion to Air Cdre, to become, on 1 January 1954, the twenty-seventh Commandant of the Central Flying School, with Headquarters at Little Rissington.

When I joined the Service in 1929, the highest achievement possible as a pilot was to attain the difficult 'A1' category as a CFS qualified instructor, and the staff of CFS, then at Wittering, included such famous people as Dick Atcherley, George Stainforth, Willy Watt and Dermot Boyle. My own contacts with CFS, through Willy Watt, were confined to visits which always confirmed my opinion that CFS was my ultimate ambition which, until 1954, remained unsatisfied. In 1954 the posting filled me with astonished delight. My first duty was to visit my new Commander-in-Chief at HQ Flying Training Command. This was Sir Lawrence Pendred who, as an Air Vice-Marshal, had been my Chief when I first went to Intelligence duties. I left this interview with the heart-warming knowledge that my C-in-C had specifically asked for me, and that I would have his full support in what, he made quite clear, was to be a difficult and challenging task. And so it proved.

To describe two years at CFS as a catalogue of events as they occurred would be disjointed and tedious, so I intend to describe various aspects of the job, not in sequence, but each separately. First, because it was one of the happiest two years we had in any RAF appointment, I must describe our house.

House and Garden

The Commandant's house at CFS was built before the war as the largest and newest type of married quarter for a Group Captain Station Commander. The reason for this was that Little Rissington was designed as the home of a large Flying Training School. The Officers' Mess was a particularly commodious three storey building. There were four big pre-war pattern hangars, workshops, stores, barrack blocks and married quarters; the whole capable of accommodating a peacetime population, including families of between one thousand five hundred and two thousand souls. The first Station Commander was Group Captain ap Ellis, who moved in to watch over the final completion of his new station. Being wise in the ways of authority and a keen gardener, he noted that the Group Captain's garden had been marked out at slightly less than one acre in extent. He also knew that the official establishment for gardens of over one acre included a full-time gardener; so, he moved the marking out pegs and kept quiet. In due course the attractive stone walled garden was completed, lawns made and shrubs planted, and ap Ellis applied for his official gardener. The application was duly refused as he expected, so he followed up his first application by quoting regulations concerning gardens over one acre, adding, if you don't believe me, come and measure it. In due course an unbelieving works and building committee arrived and proceeded to measure up, and were so startled by the result that they remeasured again, not once but several times. There was no doubt about its size; moreover it was too late to make alterations because the semicircle of senior married quarters, with their south east facing gardens, now formed part of an interlocking pattern and had all been carefully made, planted and defined with Cotswold stone walls. So ap Ellis got his gardener and, ever since, the Commandant's house at Little Rissington has been blessed with one. Thus, on our arrival, we found Mr. King, competently caring for a beautiful pleasure garden, facing south east, and sloping down towards a wooded valley with a little stream at the bottom; and in the field beyond the garden, a second vegetable patch beside the well stocked one in the garden itself. Thus, during the whole of our two years, we never had to buy vegetables. This was a great boon for, in 1954, rationing was still severe and we had a great deal of official entertaining to do. There was a constant stream from all over the world, as well as home, of important visitors, many of whom stayed in our house. For this reason, our meagre meat ration was supplemented by what was officially known as 'the entertainment joint' usually a sirloin of beef supplied to us by the camp butcher. It arrived once a week, and was free.

When we arrived on 1 January 1954, the freezing east wind had been sweeping across the Cotswolds for several days and Little Rissington which at 730 ft above sea level, was the highest occupied RAF aerodrome in the British Isles, got it all. Our house, empty since the departure of my predecessor two months earlier, like any uninhabited building, had cooled down so that coming in through the front door was not to enter any warm cosy atmosphere but more like coming into a cold store. Our first night we sat in the frozen drawing room in great coats and fur boots; it took nearly a week to warm up the house, and in the first two months of our stay we consumed the whole of our fuel ration for the next twelve months. This was a financial disaster because we had to pay for our heating; however, we paid no rent for the quarter so, unlike present day when every increase in Service pay tends to be swallowed up by increased charges for rent, we were spared that. Everything else came

out of our pay and we found that, over two years, our very small entertainments allowance hardly ever dented the costs of looking after the many Official guests who came to us, and in the winter months keeping them and ourselves warm. However, in the spring and summer the house and gardens were delightful.

1954 Reunion and Guests

Mr. Streatfield was the major domo who presided over our house. Starting as a boy entrant into the Royal Marines he had served in China and taken part in the fighting during the Boxer uprising in 1900. He refused to mention his age, but when we came to CFS in 1954, he cannot have been less than seventy. He had served his time to a pension in the Royal Marines, and then rejoined again during the Hitler war when, to his intense fury, he was considered too old to serve afloat. After the war he came to CFS and took charge of the Commandant's house. I was the sixth and, as it turned out, the last Commandant he looked after.

The great Lord Trenchard was our guest of honour at the CFS Reunion of 1954. He arrived by air in particularly foul weather, when Little Rissington was in and out of cloud. Another guest at the same dinner was Jack Baldwin who was Commandant of CFS in 1929/30 at Wittering and responsible for the coat of arms granted to the CFS by the College of Heralds. We sent a two-seat Vampire to fetch him. During the war he had, as the AOC of No. 3 Group, taken part in the first of Bomber Command's mass assaults on Germany, the famous thousand bomber raid on Cologne. Lord Trenchard had asked for the old Royal Flying Corps songs to be sung, so after dinner in the ante room, we recreated for him, as best we could with piano, beer and songs, some of the tunes that he must have been thinking about when, as Major Trenchard, he was the Deputy Commandant of CFS at Upavon in 1912. He listened often with eyes closed and sometimes a faint smile. Just what were his thoughts one can only guess, but when he returned to the house a little early for the evening had tired him, he thanked me very kindly, and then added, 'They're really very much the same'. During the dinner he made one of the most stirring speeches of its kind that I recollect. It wasn't so much that it was a particularly clever speech, or that it was full of novel ideas. Rather the contrary, for he spoke in simple words of the old virtues which had stood the test in his own vast experience, but with a forceful vigour of conviction that held his whole audience spellbound. His authority was absolute; and when he sat down there was a little silence, until the spell was broken by an explosion of cheering such as I have seldom heard. One sentence was this, 'Always remember that quality will cut through quantity like a hot knife through cheese'. This was one of the last visits made by Lord Trenchard, for he died in 1956. I like to think that we made it a very happy visit for him, and I believe that we did.

Trenchard: quality versus quantity

Lord Trenchard's reminder about quality versus quantity might have been an apt introduction to the first major problem that I had to tackle on taking over CFS. This was the indifferent quality of many of the candidates to become flying instructors. The system was that every Monday morning the Commandant interviewed candidates. These were the result of every Command being required to provide a given number, and in this way to keep up the continuous flow of trained instructors into the flying training organisation. Normally, the RAF did not keep anybody on instructional duties for too long a period in one spell; two to two and a half years was the desired maximum, after which the pilot concerned would be posted to other duties, perhaps to return to a further spell of instructing later. In this it was intended that the flying instructors should never become out of touch with the main purpose of the Service, which is to fight in the air; and the instruction they gave would have as its aim, the production of a pilot fit to take his place in a front line squadron. In this respect, RAF requirements differ notably from civilian flying training. In clubs and similar places, instructors can spend a lifetime, solely on basic flying instruction. Moreover, the pupils they teach are, for the most part, paying customers who can, if not satisfied, take their custom elsewhere. Thus, although the methods of basic flying instruction may be very similar in the early stages, the conditions are different and the ultimate aim so totally apart, that the two cannot really be compared; for example, when considering the RAF flying instructors, whose task is advanced instruction in the handling of fast jets capable of very high speeds and of imposing stresses on its pilots which are unknown in civil operation. Similarly, the infusion of experienced flying instructors into both staff and front line squadrons, served to keep everybody aware of the needs of the training organisation, both for skilled pilots for training, and for the continuing need for close liaison between the two. It is worth noting that, in 1943, for every pilot in a front line bomber squadron, it was necessary to have about thirty pilots, either instructing or coming up as trained replacements, to keep the front line going.

Conscripts versus volunteers

It is this very thing which created the first difficulty which I encountered at CFS in 1954. During the war, the demand for instructors could not be satisfied by returning enough front line tour expired pilots to the training machine. By the time the demands of the fighting Commands for experienced men to lead Squadrons and Flights on a second tour and to man their own operational training units had been satisfied, there were simply not enough left. In consequence, the basic training organisation was operated with a multitude of civilian instructors back in uniform, and these were supplemented by a system which 'creamed off' the best pupils, and kept them back in the flying training schools as instructors. The full story of the truly magnificent work of the numerous Elementary Flying Training Schools has never been properly told; without them, the supply of pilots to the front line could not have been maintained. However, the result of the system upon young men who had volunteered for aircrew in order to fight, was that the role of flying instructor not only became exceedingly unpopular but, even in 1954, was still regarded as a second rate job. This feeling persisted in the front line squadrons of the time, for although we were now under the vastly different peacetime regimes, the RAF was going through the very exciting stage of its re-equipment with aircraft which were the equal, or ahead of, anything else in the world. We were still reaping the benefits of Frank Whittle's pioneering work on jet engines. So who, when he might be going to fly Hunters, wanted to leave his squadron and teach on Chipmunks in a strictly disciplined Flying Training School. Most of the candidates at my first interviews reflected this outlook, and they were mostly conscripts. They were also the type of pilot I wanted, who would, I knew, instil in any pupil, the same enthusiasm for big performance flying that burned in them. The ones I did not want were mostly the few volunteers. They tended to be heavily married, often too young, and clock watchers who left for home when the whistle blew. The sort of pilot once described to me who added ten knots to the recommended approach speed for himself, and another ten for the wife and child. These seldom did well on the course, and most of them I turned down anyway as unsuitable. In the end we resorted to a severe remedy, and in this I must pay great tribute to my Commander-in-Chief, Sir Lawrence Pendred who gave me the support without which it would have been impossible. For a month, or a little over, I rejected all conscripts out of hand. Naturally they were delighted, but I explained to each, for which I hope I may be forgiven, that they did not meet the exacting standards which CFS required. The volunteers mostly eliminated themselves. When, after this slaughter, we were left with no suitable candidates and future courses likely to be empty, my Commander-in-Chief wrote to the other Commands suggesting that the quality of Pilots who were sent to CFS would, in the end, directly affect the quality of the newly trained products who would come to their squadrons so would they please cease to send to CFS, candidates who were clearly unsuited for the task. At the same time, the buzz went round that it was by no means easy to gain acceptance for training at CFS; and to do so was evidently something of an achievement. This also had its effect and very soon we began to get candidates coming to us who were genuine volunteers, and regarded becoming a flying instructor as something well worthwhile. From then on, the quality improved until, before long, we could pick and choose from candidates of very high quality indeed.

Return to "all-through" QFIs

My second important task concerned the re-organisation of CFS courses, and the content of them. The war, which resulted in many short cuts, was, as I have already indicated, responsible for the specialised flying instructor such as the creamed off pupil who remained on at his basic flying training School to instruct subsequent pupils. When I arrived at CFS, we still made two types of instructor designated 'Instructors (Piston)' and 'Instructors (Jet)'. The former were trained at South Cerney which was, in effect, a self-contained half of CFS; the latter were trained at Little Rissington the other half, and the place at which the Commandant had his abode. Until 1939, there was only one kind of instructor, and they were expected to cope with whatever aircraft came their way. It was my responsibility to preside over the restoration of the old system, and to initiate the production once more, of the all-through instructor. To put this into effect, South Cerney became the Basic half of the full course, and Little Rissington the Advanced, with students moving on from Basic to Advanced after a half term break.

Eligibility and Ratings

To be eligible for the CFS course, pilots had to have at least five hundred hours flying as Captain or First Pilot, a current instrument rating, and to have completed not less than eighteen months in a front line squadron. Sometimes a pilot would be accepted who, for no fault of his own, had allowed his instrument rating to lapse; the Army Air Corps pilots at this time seldom had ratings. As instrument flying was essential in order to take part in the course, one of the first tasks of the staff at South Cerney was to ensure that all pilots were rated, and those who were not were required a week or so early for instrument work. The flying units at South Cerney comprised two squadrons of piston-engined Provosts, and two flights of miscellaneous aircraft for communications and use by pilots requiring practice on other types on which they might later have to instruct. These included some Austers for the Army Air Corps pilots. When I arrived at CFS the Commanding Officer was Group Captain Sam Lucas.

A course normally comprised about thirty students. Most, of course, were RAF, but we always had, in addition to the soldiers, some Royal Navy and a few from the Commonwealth Air Forces. There were students from time to time from foreign countries. I remember the Israeli Air Force as sending many very able and skilled pilots to qualify at CFS and the Indonesian Air Force at one time sent a fair number. Not all from some other air forces were up to the standards required, and these created diplomatic difficulties. I found it hard to write 'this pilot is unsuitable for training as a flying instructor, and is unable to absorb the tuition given' when the British government had already accepted large sums of money from some newly emergent state to have its pilots trained by us! Fortunately, these cases were infrequent, and we solved the problem, sometimes at considerable cost to the patience of my devoted staff, by persisting with the teaching of doubtful cases, and awarding them, on completion, not with the certificate to say that so and so had qualified as a flying instructor at CFS, but that so and so had attended a flying instructors course at CFS. In this way, we maintained standards and, one hopes, satisfied the consciences of the officials in government and treasury who had taken the fees. Never did we award the 'Qualified' certificate to anybody who did not deserve it, even though there was sometimes intense pressure to do so. Again, in this, as in so much else, we were given wonderful backing from our Commander-in-Chief.

Having completed his ten weeks at South Cerney, the student had a week's leave, and then moved to Little Rissington for the Advanced half of his course, which lasted another ten weeks. By this time, numbers had always fallen below the original thirty, partly because of the departure of soldiers who were not required to fly and instruct on advanced types, and partly because of an unpredictable number of failures. Usually we made up the numbers to thirty again by bringing in suitable instructors already qualified on piston-engined aircraft so as to add their qualification or others returning to instructing after a spell away on other duties. In 1954, the two flying squadrons at Little Rissington, now termed 'CFS Advanced', used the Meteor T.7. In addition we had a flight of Vampire T.11s and, like Cerney, a variety of other aircraft for communication and other purposes. These included a Vickers Valetta transport in which the Examining Wing used to travel. Like the Basic course, the Advanced also took ten weeks, although sometimes when persistently foul weather delayed training, it was necessary to seek an extension. The normal duration of the whole course, however, including the mid-term break of one week, was twenty one weeks.

At any one time, South Cerney and Little Rissington each had two overlapping resident courses necessitating a new intake of thirty every five or six weeks, and resulting in a normal student population of one hundred and twenty. At the end of each course, they dined out at a formal guest night, when the top pupil of the course sat on the Commandant's right, and the Chief Instructor from either Cerney or Rissington gave, not his formal report (that had been done already), but his informal and often very amusing one. For example, on the student who perfected a method of letting off a thunderflash placed under a dustbin lid outside his office. This particular instrument of noise was taken up by the examiners, of whom more later. It was whilst several Israelis were at CFS as students that we also had a number of Iraqis, including a Major A.L. Mahmood. Mahmood's party trick was to give a perfect imitation of an Egyptian gulli-gulli man, such as the production of chickens from everywhere, including apparently empty space and other people's heads. He had a wicked sense of humour, very blue eyes and fair hair. He always declared that the Scots were one of the lost tribes of Israel, and that his real name was McMood. This, he said, proved that Arabs, Scots and Israelis were all related. It was during a visit of General Moshe Dayan, then Israeli Minister of Defence, accompanied by several members of his Air Force staff, that McMood was heard expounding this outrageous theory in the bar. Standing between Moshe Dayan and his team on one side of me and the Iraqis on the other, I felt a trifle exposed.

By the end of his course, a student would have flown about one hundred to one hundred and ten hours, roughly equally divided between Basic and Advanced, and, of course, by night as well as day. Later, we always endeavoured to include some extras like a few new types and, in due course, when we acquired three Hawker Hunters, this became an accepted part of the course.

Student feedback and Hunters arrive

I have spoken of students. In fact, courses of instruction at CFS were very much a two-way exchange of knowledge, and we always expected to learn a good deal from them as well as to teach. Students were encouraged to question accepted ideas and methods, and in the course of justifying them the CFS staff not only increased their own skills, often by demonstration in the air, but sometimes found that our ideas were due for a change. This kept everybody on their toes, and gave students a sense of participation in the life of CFS which the term 'pupil' would have denied.

The arrival of our first Hunter produced problems at Rissington. On its somewhat short runway, it soon ended up with burned out brakes and tyres, so we deemed it wiser to locate the Hunters elsewhere and for this purpose they became a detached flight at the more suitable location at Kemble, the home of No. 5 Maintenance Unit who looked after their day to day needs. The remainder of the Advanced instructor training organisation at Rissington resembled that at Cerney. The whole was commanded by Group Captain Philip Heal, with Wing Commander Frank Dodd as his Chief Instructor. But we had other things at Rissington which were important parts of CFS. Most important was the Examining Wing.

Examining Wing

When I arrived, the Examining Wing was commanded by Wing Commander Dennis Lyster, an old hand at instructing, and formerly a much decorated Bomber Command pilot. I can best explain the functions of the Examining Wing by quoting the charter for it, written by Air Chief Marshal Sir Ralph Cochrane when he was the Commander-in-Chief of Flying Training Command. It was to:

a) Provide an inspectorate of Flying Training for all Commands

b) Undertake the examination and re-categorisation of flying instructors of 'B' Category and above

c) Appoint examiners under the RAF Instrument Rating Scheme

d) Ensure that the latest instructional technique is being used by qualified Flying Instructors (QFI's)

e) Provide liaison between units employing QFI's and CFS

f) Feed back to CFS the latest ideas on operational flying which may affect instructional technique

g) Provide Examiners as and when necessary to visit Commands overseas

Item (g) was, in practice, extended to include visits to Commonwealth and Allied Air Forces and, during my time at CFS, visits were paid to India, Singapore, Pakistan, Canada and the United States. In addition to the Examining Wing, commonly known as 'The Trappers', there was one further, though smaller, organisation within CFS. This was the Link Trainer Instructor School, commanded by Squadron Leader Bill Veseley. It had no aircraft of its own, but operated a battery of Link trainers. Finally, CFS had the use of two large airfields in addition to Cerney and Rissington. To the south was Blakehill Farm, with concrete runways but little else except one disused hangar and lots of hard standings. It had been one of the airfields from which the Airborne Forces in gliders were launched on D-Day for the invasion of Normandy. It was used by Cerney's Provosts, who had to take some care to keep out of the way of the four-jet bombers of the USAF based, at that time, at nearby Fairford. To the north we had the use of Enstone, whose long runway we found useful, especially when we had one of the many types of aircraft which were borrowed by Examining Wing from time to time, in preparation for their visits to operational conversion units, and organisations using types which we did not possess at CFS itself. It was from Enstone that I did my first Canberra flying. Examiners who were expected to fly anything that came their way did not often get dual instruction. Thus my introduction to the Canberra was not unlike my first introduction some years earlier, to the Mosquito. I spent some time learning 'the taps' and reading the pilot's notes, after which the Trapper, who was the current Canberra expert, gave me a thirty minute demonstration with myself in the navigator's seat; we then changed seats and I flew it; and that was that. My log book records that it was a Canberra B.2, WE112, borrowed from the Operational Training Unit then at Bassingbourn and that this was in preparation for a visit by the Examining Wing to that unit. The Trapper was Flight Lieutenant Paddy Gilmer, and I afterwards went with them to Bassingbourn to observe how their work there went. I note that my personal call sign at this time was 'Reflex One', in rather similar fashion I experienced a number of new types including the Percival Pembroke, the four-engined Miles Marathon, and a Fairchild C.117 'Packet' belonging to the 15th Wing of the Tactical Command of the Belgian Air Force. When it arrived from Belgium, it brought with it my old Gunner, Mich Jansen, who insisted on sitting alongside me whilst I flew it, and in banishing everybody else on board somewhere into the vast interior at the back.

Command structure

The organisation of CFS on two separate, both large, stations, each commanded by a Group Captain created some interesting problems. Not least of the causes were the directions contained in the relevant Air Ministry Order (No. A.74/50) which made the two Group Captains responsible to the Commandant for everything on their Stations to do with flying; and to the AOC of No. 23 Group for everything else, which in broad terms meant engineering, accounting and administration. Each Group Captain thus had two masters, the Commandant and the AOC 23 Group. In turn, the Commandant, with direct responsibility for everything to do with the Examining Wing, was responsible, himself, not to the AOC 23 Group, but directly to the Commander in Chief of Flying Training Command. The AOC of 23 Group was Air Vice-Marshal George Harvey, himself a subordinate to the C-in-C Flying Training Command, and having full responsibility for all the RAF Flying Training Schools in the UK. The advantage to me of this system was that I was free of administrative problems and able to devote my attention to the affairs of the Flying Wings at Cerney and Rissington, to the Link Trainer School, and to the Examining Wing. The system would not have worked as well as it did had not each of the four Group Captains there during my time been easy to get on with, and always helpful and co-operative. At Rissington, Philip Heal was there when I arrived, and later was succeeded by Colin Scragg. At Cerney, Sam Lucas was succeeded by Giles Gilson, my old shipmate from my Fleet Air Arm days in HMS Furious. I relied especially on Giles Gilson, and knowing each other as well as we did, soon realised that he had no reservations about telling me when he thought my ideas were wrong. Usually these sorts of discussions took place in his house at Cerney where Rosemary and I often paid visits to Giles and Sylvia. Naturally I did not always agree with him, but when I persisted in my point of view, and when it required action in CFS, Giles invariably adopted my point of view as his own, and I could not possibly have had more loyal support.

Frank Dodd arrives

Not long after my arrival, Dennis Lyster was succeeded in command of the Examining Wing by Bob Radley in whose house I had been a guest when, during the IDC tour, we had visited Aden. This, with Frank Dodd as the Chief Instructor at Little Rissington, completed a very happy team. Frank had already served twice at CFS, twice as an Instructor when CFS was 'The Empire CFS' at Hullavington during the war. When he was not at CFS, Frank was flying in front line units, and made his name as a Photographic Reconnaissance pilot flying Mosquitos. He made not only what turned out to be one of the longest reconnaissance flights made by Mosquitos but also secured the photographs which were ultimately responsible for the location of the German battleship Tirpitz and her subsequent destruction in Tromso Fjord. On his fourth and final return to CFS in 1965, Frank Dodd was the Commandant.

In order to emphasize the equal status of the two halves of CFS, I moved out of the building which was rightfully the Station HQ at Rissington, so that the Group Captain could run his command in exactly the same circumstances as his opposite number at Cerney. I then established my own Commandant's HQ in some wooden buildings which had been put up during the war and which also housed the Link Trainer School. My own office looked out onto the very pleasant rugger field onto which we sometimes put the helicopter which I later used. To help me I had John Gale, described originally as 'Personal Assistant' and, later, more formally as the ADC, and Keith Panter, a former Mosquito pilot who had been a POW in the last days of the war in Germany. Both were Flight Lieutenants, and were joined later by Squadron Leader James Short. From this small HQ I presided for two years over CFS. Two or three years later, the split in responsibilities was eliminated by giving the Commandant Air Officer Commanding status, and overall responsibility for everything, it also meant that his married quarter was officially re-designated as his 'residence' and was accordingly furnished to an altogether more luxurious scale by the Office of Works instead of Air Ministry stores. But that came after my time.

Helicopters and convention

During the summer of 1954, we became increasingly interested in the training of helicopter instructors. At this time there were no CFS trained helicopter instructors; the Navy, who were at that time the biggest rotary wing users, trained their own and had, in fact, taught numbers of RAF pilots to fly rotary winged aircraft as well. Accordingly, Giles Gilson and I decided that, as a first move, we would organise a helicopter convention to take place, over a period of two days, at Cerney. For this convention we acquired two very experienced RAF helicopter pilots, both of whom were already CFS qualified instructors on fixed wing aircraft. These were Flt Lt Bartlett, who gave me four days introductory instruction flying a Sikorsky S.51, which we also borrowed, so that I would know a little more about it; and Sqn Ldr John Dowling, probably one of the most experienced and knowledgeable rotary wing pilots, until his retirement, that the RAF has possessed. To this conference we invited about fifty people, all specially qualified in various ways to discuss the problem of setting up a helicopter instructors element in CFS. They included designers, test pilots, operational pilots from the Navy and RAF, instructors from the Navy's school squadron, and staff officers from Flying Training Command and the training branch of the Air Ministry. We modelled proceedings broadly on the periodical instructors conferences which CFS was accustomed to hold each year for fixed wing instructors.

As usual in meetings of this kind, we found that the more formal parts of the convention were supplemented in important aspects by discussion, occasionally developing into animated arguments in the bar and after dinner. We did our best to stimulate this informal side of the convention and, in consequence, the participants not only enjoyed themselves and, as subsequent thank you letters showed, derived much value from the meeting, but we at CFS learned more in the two days than could have been remotely possible in any other way. Moreover, the higher staff who controlled establishments were equally convinced that the time was ripe to provide CFS with the means to get into the helicopter business. Our first move was to acquire John Dowling to take charge of a new unit to be based at Cerney, and to comprise a small ground school and a flying instructional flight, equipped with the Sikorsky S.51, built by Westland's and named 'Dragonfly' by the RAF. We then recruited a small team of CFS instructors who had become helicopter pilots, and collected a guinea pig course of students for them to instruct, not to become helicopter instructors, but on whom they could practise and develop the art of instructing and, with it, incorporate the standards that CFS has always demanded.

It was also in the summer of 1954 that I accompanied the Examining Wing team on their visit to the RAF in Germany, travelling in a Vampire T.11. On arrival at Jever, the Vampire was smartly appropriated for check flights, and I found myself dependent upon a borrowed Anson. In this I paid a visit to the BAFO HQ at Bad Eilsen, where I had been before, and managed to work in a long weekend at Scharfoldendorf to fly a Weihe. Sadly, my own beautiful blue Weihe, which I had flown in the BAFO Gliding Contests, had been crashed and written off."

Ice brings down Provost

On 13 January, while flying a Provost and executing a Controlled Descent Through Cloud (CDTC), Flt Lt Thomas experienced an engine failure and was able to land the aircraft in a ploughed field. Both crew escaped uninjured although the aircraft sustained Cat. 2 damage. Subsequent ground runs could find no problem and the failure was assumed to have been caused by icing, prompting a recommendation that an air temperature gauge should be fitted to the induction system on all Provosts.

During February there were no fewer than five incidents of Provost carrying out emergency landings as a result of surging and loss of power from the Leonides engine. The symptoms of each incident pointed towards ice forming on the fuel vents and interfering with the flow of fuel to the engine.

Prentice disposals

Having been superseded by the Provost, twenty Prentices departed South Cerney during January for Nos. 9 and 29 MUs, leaving just three of the type on strength. Two of these, VR209 and VR293, were despatched in February leaving the final machine, VR270, awaiting AOG parts. It remained on strength until 7 September 1954, bringing to end the type's six-year association with CFS.

Air Cdre Chirstopher Paul flying the Weihe glider during his visit to Germany. (*CFS magazine*)

Helicopters arrive

The Helicopter Development Flight was formed as a lodger unit at RAF Middle Wallop on 8 March 1954 with two Dragonfly HC.Mk.4s, XF260 and XF261. On 14 June the two aircraft and three instructors, together with one SNCO, and twelve corporals and airmen, moved from Middle Wallop to take up residence at South Cerney. The unit's mission was to train helicopter pilots and then enlarge its scope by training helicopter pilots as instructors. The first course, which began on 16 August, consisted of Air Cdr G.J.C. Paul, Gp Capt O.I. Gilson, Sqn Ldr R.S. Bradley and Flt Lt K,V. Panter.

Examining Wing: a first incarnation

In March 1954, Flt Lt Mike Vickers arrived back at Little Rissington for his first tour on Examining Wing. At that time, the Wing was divided into three squadrons – Basic under Sqn Ldr Hugh Forth, Multi-engine where Sqn Ldr Freddie Hazlewood was CO, and Jet under Sqn Ldr 'Farmer' Steele.

"Allocated to Basic Squadron, our job was to look after basic FTSs with their Prentices, advanced FTSs operating Harvards and Piston Provosts, University Air Squadrons flying Tiger Moths and Chipmunks, Army Training on Austers and civilian schools with contracts for RAF training such as the RAFVR bases. The Jet Squadron looked after all the jet AFSs and operational squadrons of which there were a great number in the early 50s, civilian CAACUs and RN training bases. The Multi Squadron was responsible for those bases carrying out multi-engined pilot training, navigation and air gunners' schools, etc. The Wing was commanded by Wg Cdr Dennis Lyster ('Teacher').

The RAF in those days was an extremely large organisation, resulting in a huge number of visits to make as well as tests to do back at base. We went to all the training establishments at least once every year and

Forerunner of a long helicopter association with CFS, one of the first Dragonflies lifts-off from Rissy in the summer of 1954. (*Bert Brand*)

made lots of visits to operational units both at home and overseas, so it was a very busy time for the wing. During my time at Tern Hill I had become qualified on the Meteor at RAF Middleton St. George. In addition, Examining Wing held a three-week training period twice a year when all the aircraft types for which we were responsible were assembled for us to fly. This was a great opportunity to amass hours on many types of aircraft. I became instrument and QFI rated on jets and also had the opportunity to fly naval types such as the Sea Fury, Firefly and Sea Hawk. With this experience, I was able to join a few of the Jet Squadron's visits – two to Germany and one to the Middle East. It was while we were on the Middle East visit that Terry Fennell and I learned that two Vampire FB.9s needed ferrying back to the UK from Kasfareet in Egypt to Benson. We volunteered and got the job. On a visit to Exeter with Jim Corbishley, we managed to scrounge a flight in a Spitfire Mark 16.

Being away on visits much of the time, any decent social life was a rare experience. Dining out nights for the end of courses tended to be lively affairs. On one well known occasion the 'Top hat' student tipped a barrow load of steaming horse manure in front of the CGI's table. At another the then Commandant (who was very keen on fireworks) threw one, which exploded close to his Adjutant's ear rupturing his ear drum! My first tour at Rissington was by now drawing to a close. I had enjoyed myself immensely and the variety of experience stood me in good stead for my next posting on the NATO Air Training Advisory Group Squadron based at Villacoublay near Paris in February 1956."

To Africa in a T.11

In order to assist pilots of the Southern Rhodesian Air Force to convert to the Vampire, Flt Lt J.D. Upton accompanied by Flt Lt E. Richards (a QFI with 229 OCU), flew Vampire T.11, XD454, in formation with four Vampire F.B.9s on a ferry flight to Salisbury Air Base on 10 May. Training was completed on 5 August and the T.11 left N'Dola for Nairobi on the 9th to await an escort back to the UK. On the following day, the captain of a Central African Airways Viking agreed to accompany the Vampire as far as Marseilles from where it could continue solo to RAF Benson for customs checks.

Vampire Flight

Not long after the arrival of the first Vampire trainers, a Vampire Flight was formed on 1 July and operated within 1 Squadron until November when it was absorbed into 4 Squadron.

Awards

The following awards were presented in June:

Flt Lt W.G. Myatt	AFC
Flt Lt J.H. Liversidge	AFC
Flt Sgt J.F. McCorkle	AFM
Flt Lt G. Wrigley	QCVSA

First all-through Course

Number 163 Course was the first to pass through CFS after the change-over to all-through training on the Provost and Vampire, although owing to a general shortage of Vampire T.11 aircraft, it was only possible to train eight students using the new syllabus. The remainder had to finish their training on the Meteor T.7. However, the opportunity to evaluate the T.11 syllabus before the full complement of aircraft arrived proved invaluable. At the end of the course, it was perhaps ironic that the Brabyn Trophy should be won by a Vampire student.

CFS Reorganisation

In June 1954, CFS began a re-organisation to form what practically amounted to a two-station group; henceforth all piston-engined training would be undertaken at South Cerney while Little Rissington provided the jet-powered training. One of the major changes was the reformation of 2 Squadron and the enlarging of E Flight.

The 42nd CFS Reunion dinner

The date was 16 July 1954. All arrangements had been made and a distinguished gathering of guests assembled at Little Rissington. The Annual General Meeting was held in the Officers' Mess, with the President-Elect, Sir John Baldwin, in the chair. After the AGM there was to have been a flying display but the English summer refused to be co-operative and the weather stayed firmly 'clamped'.

Undeterred by this the guests assembled for sherry at 19:30 and at 20:00 dinner was served, the company filing in to the strains of "The Roast Beef of Old England" rendered with great gusto by the Station Band. After a sumptuous meal coffee was served, the port went on its rounds, cigars were lit and the assembly sat back, replete and comfortable, for the feast of words which was to follow.

Nor were they disappointed. Sir John Baldwin introduced the Commandant, Air Cdre G.J.C. Paul, who gave a succinct and impressive report upon the activities of Central Flying School during the past year. He made particular mention of Examining Wing and the way in which it had carried out its large and frequently irksome task. After thanking the Commandant, the President then introduced "The Chief", Lord Trenchard, who was warmly greeted by the company.

Lord Trenchard treated us to a scintillating and witty speech. Delving into his vast store of memories he recalled his initial posting to CFS. The day after he arrived on the Unit, the Commandant sent for him and told him that he was to be Station Staff Officer. Major Trenchard, as he then was, went away and looked into the duties of the Station Staff Officer. He found that they were to set all examination papers, examine the students, mark the examination papers and assess the results. Amidst laughter, Lord Trenchard remarked, "*I set my own examination papers, sat the papers, examined myself, marked my papers, passed myself and have maintained the same high standard ever since.*"

Going on to deal with the present state of international tension, Lord Trenchard said that there was far too much pessimism about today. All that people could talk about was the number of divisions and aircraft and pilots possessed by certain unfriendly powers. Since when, he asked, had quantity counted for more than quality? "*I would remind you, gentlemen,*" he remarked, "*that there are a lot more useless people in the world than useful ones!*" On the subject of instruction, Lord Trenchard was of the opinion that in this jet age we were trying to do everything in too much of a hurry. He advocated a return to the more leisurely days before and after World War I, "*which I would remind you, gentlemen, it only took US four years to win!*" The President thanked 'The Chief' for his good advice and paid him a pretty compliment when he said: "*The Navy has its hero in Nelson. The Army has its hero in Wellington. The Royal Air Force is luckier, gentlemen. We still have our hero with us.*"

On that note the dinner came to an end and the company repaired to the ante-rooms where the musical tradition of CFS was upheld in no uncertain fashion; songs ranging over a period of forty years being flung at the pianist, who refused to be beaten throughout the entire evening.

The next day our guests departed, the verdict on everyone's lips being, "*Jolly good show, chaps.*"

From Meteor type flying to Meteor as Applied Stage

An illuminating article on the introduction of wider Meteor instruction between 1952 and 1954, written by Flt Lt Brown OC 'M' Flight No. 5 Squadron for the Central Flying School Magazine, is reproduced in full as a fitting tribute for the achievements of both CFS ground technicians and aircrew in implementing this important step transition stage into the jet era.

"All-through instructor training has returned to CFS. In consequence the old No. 5 Squadron as we all knew it has ceased to exist. As Little Rissington has gone over solely to jet instruction, the two Meteor flights have been expanded to form the new Nos. 3 and 4 Squadrons. In view of all these developments, now seems an appropriate time to review progress since the advent of jet instruction at CFS.

In 1951 there was one Meteor Flight situated in the accommodation now occupied by the Vampire Flight. It was their task, with four aircraft, to get each student up to solo standard on the Meteor before leaving Little Rissington. This flight was moved to Kemble during the winter of 1951-52 while the runways at Rissington were repaired. On its return to Rissington in March 1952 plans were soon laid to expand this flight into No. 5 Squadron consisting of 'M' and 'L' Flights so that a fully qualified jet instructor would be produced. Sqn Ldr J. Hutton moved from South Cerney to form the squadron and the first Flight Commanders were Flt Lt Highet and Flt Lt Gordon respectively. Some instructors from the Harvard squadrons were soon converted to the Meteor and by July 1952 everything was ready to accept this first course, No. 144.

The Meteor course was planned to last eight weeks: in that time the students were required to complete just under thirty hours flying. The courses invariably consisted of students from South Cerney, who had passed basic instructor training on the Prentice. These were then joined by ex-piston QFIs bringing the total student strength up to about 16 per flight. Very few of these students had ever flown a jet aircraft and a considerable amount of the 30 hour course inevitably had to be spent in pure conversion flying on to the aircraft.

Soon it was realised that if the necessary time was to be spent on instructional sequences the length of the course would have to be increased. By February 1953, Sqn Ldr A.E. Harkness had arrived from No. 205 AFS RAF Middleton-St.-George to replace Sqn Ldr Hutton, who had left to take over an appointment in Brussels. Steps were soon taken to have the course extended to twelve weeks and each student was required to complete 50 hours. Number 156 course was the first to complete this new syllabus in August 1953. This course also had the advantage of a set of instructional sequence notes, which had been produced by the Squadron Commander. These two factors contributed to a marked improvement in the quality of jet instruction produced thereafter. During the past year each flight on No. 5 Squadron has been operating with eight aircraft and approximately eight instructors. Their task has been to pass a course of about 20 students out every three months, with each student having completed 50 hours flying.

While carrying this out during the months of April, June and July 1954, 'M' Flight flew 412, 417 and 413 aircraft flying hours respectively. These hours were flown with an average of six aircraft in use, which represents an intensity figure of 69 hours per aircraft. The magnitude of this effort is realised when one considers that the average AFS works to only half this intensity. It is probably safe to say that few other units in the Air Force have achieved this intensity over a three monthly period, which reflects great credit to No. 5 Squadron's servicing personnel.

In the two years since No. 5 Squadron was first formed many changes in personnel have occurred. On the instructional staff, Fg Off Bell is the only original member still with us, although Fg Off Bart and Flt Lt Brown joined after the squadron had only been operating a few months. Among the ground crew, Flt Sgt Harvey, Sgt Lucas, Cpl Bufton, Cpl Forrest and SAC Walker are original squadron members who are still with us today.

The month of August would seem to be a decisive one in our 5 Squadron calendar. In 1952 the first course of jet instructors was completed in August. In August 1953 the first course to take the extended 50 hour syllabus was completed. This year, even more decisively, the first course on all-through instruction is beginning at Little Rissington on 25 August, when No. 5 Squadron will cease to exist, having been expanded and re-numbered as Nos. 3 and 4 Squadrons."

PA to the Commandant

From August 1954 to January 1956, Sqn Ldr John Gale served as Personal Assistant to Air Cdre Christopher Paul, then Commandant at CFS. He remembers the CFS HQ which was located in a wooden hut alongside the Officers' Mess at RAF Little Rissington.

"Both the Air Commodore and his PSO, Keith Panter, had distinguished wartime service records – almost five decades on, I can see the Edmund Miller painting of a 98 Squadron B-25 formation, led by Wg Cdr Christopher Paul into Europe out of Dunsfold airfield. In such company and this desk job, I was very much the office boy and not so good at that but felt most fortunate to have such excellent and understanding bosses!

The Air Commodore believed that, since CFS represented the undoubted centre of flying/handling excellence within the RAF, the unit deserved more support and its staff merited more appreciation than was generally forthcoming from Flying Training Command. I gained the impression that he carried his wholehearted loyalty to CFS to a point, which sometimes made him a little unpopular higher up.

He recognised a need to ensure that Flying Instruction did not become a rarefied activity apart from mainstream RAF flying, while seeing the quality control of QFI selection and recycling as a means of achieving this objective. In an era when the Operational Commands were well stocked and the UK air defences boasted numerous Meteor Wings, he made a point of vetting each individual potential candidate passed down for CFS training. Before long in each interview the question would arise 'Why do you want to be an Instructor?' Where the answer was a great deal of flannel about 'passing on experience' or 'moulding a new generation' he was unsympathetic and often turned the volunteer away. Where the answer was a heartfelt cry of 'I don't want to be a QFI, I'm here under duress and want to get back to Squadron life', then he would smile knowingly and say 'Quite right too and you are just the sort of fellow we are looking for!'

Of course this approach to QFI selection was controversial and, even though other individual factors were certainly not ignored, it looks risky. However, I have never seen any evidence that instructional standards were adversely affected in practice and the spirit of FTC units benefited greatly. Moreover the attitudes towards the Service and service life, which instructors naturally pass on to their trainees, were kept both up-to-date and appropriate. Air Cdre Paul was surely right in all this rather unorthodox approach. As a QFI, who later became unhappily and inextricably trapped in the Flying Training web, I think the associated policy the Air Commodore advocated, of bringing new young QFIs into the role for one tour only before releasing them back to the front line, was farsighted.

Helicopters were still something of a novelty at this time and the CFS Helicopter outfit over at RAF South Cerney was breaking new ground. The CO, Flt Lt John Dowling, was an acknowledged expert and he and his team were not just training new helicopter pilots but at the same time developing the most suitable schedules for both ab initio and QHI instruction. The Air Commodore was quite excited by the pioneering aspect of this work and supported this new arm of service flying fully in every way he could.

Life in the CFS HQ wooden hut was humdrum: I was only there 1½ years with nothing much happening to break routines. I do recall some considerable excitement one day when a new pilot flew in from South Cerney, bringing some papers or perhaps even for interview. His helicopter touched down outside on the grass just before he encountered ground resonance, a rare phenomenon, not perfectly understood in 1955. The aircraft bounced sideways across the soccer pitch and finally lurched into the air, when he had opened the throttle, missing the roof of the Air Commodore's office by mere inches only. Also recalled was the Air Commodore's deep interest in gliding which saw both of us under canvas at Lasham one summer, where I helped run the camp domestic arrangements for the RAFGSA Team in the National Championships. I managed to get quite a lot of time off for flying, including a Hunter Conversion on the Type-Flight at RAF Kemble, playing rugby, maintaining an active social life, and, above all, the sheer pleasure of working for such a splendid man with such a charming wife and family."

Derwent blows!

On 27 October, Sqn Ldr A.E. Harkness was carrying out a dual night check with student Fg Off P.D. Stoneham in a Meteor T.7. Two circuits had been completed when there was a loud explosion coupled with a bright flash as the aircraft became airborne for the third circuit. The aircraft speed was only 105 knots, 55 knots below the safety speed for asymmetric flying. It yawed to port and full starboard rudder was applied. While holding the aircraft at 50 ft, Sqn Ldr Harkness told the student to raise the undercarriage and flaps. The aircraft yawed slowly through 90° until further directional control was attained at 140 knots. The port fire extinguisher was operated and the high and low pressure cocks closed. At 160 knots, Sqn Ldr Harkness was able to gain height and complete the circuit for a safe landing.

Subsequent inspection of the Meteor revealed that the port turbine disc had broken in two and burst through the nacelle. The turbine blades had ricocheted off the runway causing major damage to the ventral tank and starboard wing. The aircraft was declared Cat. 4.

Jet conversion and No. 169 Course

After three and a half years as a basic instructor on pistons at RAF Moreton-in-Marsh, Flt Lt Peter Crouch applied for a jet instructors course.

"In October 1954 there I was back at RAF Little Rissington learning

the instructional patter but this time it was to be from the back seat of a Meteor. By now I was thirty-one years old and some of my fellow students looked awfully young. They obviously knew a lot more about jet flying than me but I had three and a half thousand hours under my belt, so I felt I could keep my end up.

I passed the course on 31 December 1954, and the day after I learned that I had been awarded the Air Force Medal for Instructional Duties. I continued to instruct on both the Meteor T.7 and the Vampire T.11 for five years, enjoying every minute of it. In 1958 I was offered a week's course on the Hunter F.4 and I flew this beautiful aircraft for eight hours that week, which was the pinnacle of my jet experience. By this time I had served for twelve years in Training Command with only a three months' break during 1957 at the Officers Training Unit.

One further vivid recollection of Rissy remains. We were walking down to the flights one morning and one of our party, a Naval Lieutenant, was walking on the grass. The Station Adjutant's window flew open, as a red-faced Flt Lt bawled out: 'You are walking on the grass, get off it!' The said Naval Officer was not amused. He strolled over quietly and enquired if the Adjutant had ever served on an aircraft carrier. The answer was, of course, No. 'There is no grass anywhere on aircraft carriers and anyone serving on them is allowed to walk on any grass that is available for the first year he is ashore', our Naval Person told the open-mouthed Adj, 'and I have just come ashore from a two year tour!' With that, he walked smartly off. We didn't like the Station Adjutant very much and we were delighted with this wonderful 'Students 5, Staff Nil' putdown … not that we believed him of course!"

Staff Continuation Training (SCT)

Records show that at about this time, Staff Continuation Training and Navigation exercises were introduced in between courses for the benefit of QFIs. The first of these took place between 8 and 12 November when two Vampire T.11s departed for a visit to operational units at RAF Wahn in 2 TAF, West Germany. Major Richard Emmons USAF was assigned to lead the pair in XD393 with Flt Lt F. Franklin acting as his navigator. The second aircraft, XD590, was piloted by Flt Lt A.K Ibbett with navigation provided by Flt Lt A. Sunderland-Cooper. The trip got off to an ignominious start when it was discovered that both aircraft were due Primary inspections soon after their arrival in Germany. They remained on the ground until the appropriate servicing schedules arrived from the UK two days later.

Despite the setback, much valuable experience was gained in the use of radio facilities for navigation and the various procedures at different airfields, and the stations visited seemed genuinely happy to see CFS keeping in contact with operational units.

A second SCT exercise commenced on 9 November when five Meteor T.7s departed for a five-day trip to RAF Idris in Libya. Again the crews were assigned roles as pilot and navigator, the tasks being reversed for the flight home. Sqn Ldr Harkness and Wg Cdr Pye in WL357 led the formation which comprised Flt Lt Ferguson and Fg Off Bell (VW472), Flt Lt Houser and Fg Off Wardell (WL481), Plt Off Spurr and Flt Lt Allum (WL370), and Flt Lts Robinson and Horn in WL364.

Shortly after overflying Dijon, Flt Lt Ferguson found that his drop tanks were not feeding and he was given directions to land at Lyons. The aircraft was refuelled before continuing on to join the others at Istres. Following the discovery of a faulty voltage regulator on WL370 the aircraft was repaired by swapping the regulator with that from VW472 which was despatched back to Rissy via Dijon.

In his report dated 17 November, Sqn Ldr Harkness wrote: Two new points became evident on this trip:

a) That the French Fixer Services though most efficient in operation, were sometimes extremely inaccurate. With good weather over France and the Mediterranean many fixes were double-checked visually and the following inaccuracies highlighted;

i.	Bando Fixer	80 miles out
ii.	Cantal Fixer	25 miles out
iii.	Cite Fixer	45 miles out

b) That the Meteorological Forecasting in the Central Mediterranean was vague and inaccurate. The forecast at Tunis and Idris of weather conditions en-route and on landing at each of these bases was extremely poor and bore little relation to actual conditions.

Trappers visit the Far East

In the course of its annual visit to the Far East Air Force, Examining Wing was invited to visit the Commonwealth Air Forces in that region. The broad purpose of the visit was to exchange ideas of flying training and to assess the standard of flying instruction. A team of eleven officers led by Wg Cdr D.G. Lyster left Little Rissington on 4 October in Valetta C.1, VW843 and 64 stations were visited before their return on 9 December. One hundred and eighty hours were flown in the Valetta while a further 237 hours were flown by the team in eighteen different aircraft types.

CHAPTER 3

All-through Training

1955

Last Auster departs

The last Auster T.Mk.7 to be operated by CFS, WE569, departed South Cerney on 26 January and was flown to 19 MU.

Trophy winner of distinction

In February, at the conclusion of No. 165 Course, Fg Off Patrick Hine, originally a National Serviceman who came to the course from No. 1(F) Squadron at Tangmere, gained a Distinguished Pass after first winning the coveted Clarkson Trophy at the end of the Basic stage. Awarded the CFS Trophy for the best all round student, Fg Off Hine would return to the CFS staff and eventually become AOC-in-C Strike Command 1988-91 and Joint Commander British Forces in the first Gulf War.

That yawing feeling! A Green Endorsement

Flt Lt M.G. Tomkins, a student on No. 168 Course at South Cerney, was carrying out a solo aerobatic detail in a Piston Provost on 14 March when the port rudder pedal broke, trapping his foot in the fully forward position. Unable to free his foot, Flt Lt Tomkins managed to return to the airfield and carry out a landing with full left rudder on. The aircraft executed one and a half ground loops but fortunately no further damage was sustained, leading to a Green Endorsement award. When retired, Air Cdre Mark Tomkins MBE became RAFA Secretary General 1986-93.

Administrative affairs

The testimony of Flt Lt George Lau, a GD/Nav, illustrates the importance of the third prong of the standard three wing RAF station organisation, the Administrative Wing, which in 1955 was commanded by Wg Cdr R.O. Buskell. George arrived at the station in June 1954 on his first non-flying ground tour as Station Adjutant reporting to the Stn Cdr, Gp Capt C. Scragg. *"At that time our Admin Wing's main functions were:*

> *a. to provide full Admin Support Services to all units based at Little Rissington and especially to HQ CFS, CFS(A) plus HQ Sqn and Examining Wing, these units all undergoing major role changes involved in conversion to and re-equipment with Meteors and Vampires.*
>
> *b. to complete the take-over of a large new development of badly needed married quarters and the furnishing and allocation of these MQs.*

Group photograph of the Administrative Wing in 1955. (*back row, l to r*) Sgts P. De Naeyer, S. Vose, A. Tucker, Flt Sgt G. Baxter, Sgts D. Owen, M. Partridge, Flt Sgt K. Brooke. (*third row, l to r*) Flt Sgt S. Williams, M/P H. Rogers, W Os G. Squires, A. Bell, M/P J. Connon, W O F. Davidson, Flt Sgt A. Maskell. (*second row, l to r*) Fg Offs C. Purser, N. Walton, C. Marshall, Plt Off C. King, Fg Off N. Robertson, Plt Offs J. Cartright, D. Broadhurst. (*front row, l to r*) Flt Lts J. Stannis, V. Vesely, Sqn Ldr I. Evans, Wg Cdr R. Buskell, Sqn Ldr M. Dyer, Flt Lt G. Lau, Fg Off N. Jones. (*Graham Pitchfork collection*)

c. to develop, repair and maintain all station buildings and infrastructure with particular attention to the many old wartime wooden buildings which housed HQ CFS, CFS(A), Examining Wing and Air Traffic Control.

d. to foster and maintain good neighbourhood relations with local towns and villages such as Bourton-on-the-Water and Cheltenham.

e. to arrange itineraries for frequent inbound VIP visits and social functions like Guest Nights and the end of course Dining Out nights.

f. to plan and carry out annual Escape and Evasion exercises.

The Administration Wing was successful in its role, which inevitably entailed much hard work, diplomacy and determined efforts but was often reliant on the goodwill, understanding and co-operation of these CFS Units.

One memorable Escape and Evasion exercise ended with an unexpectedly exciting and hilarious 'treat' after a surprise night attack on the Escapees' 'safe house', a pub on the River Windrush. A group of QFIs, enjoying their refuge, complete with pints and cosy fire, had suddenly to take to dinghies, promptly sunk by the use of pyrotechnics and fireworks, leaving our escapees adrift in the icy cold waters of the Windrush, leading to their capture.

During my time at Rissy, I managed to get in quite a few flying hours at the HQ Comms Flight and even with the Meteor display team once on a weekend visit to the French Air Force near Bordeaux. Concerning Station Parades, perhaps the least said the better – QFIs might have been brilliant in the air but definitely did not appear bred to display with equal effect on terra firma manoeuvres around a parade square. In summary I made many fine friendships in an unforgettable tour being posted out in November 1956, with my inscribed mounted Pelican in hand, on promotion to Squadron Leader and return to flying duties."

Long Range Navex

Based on the experience gained on the continuation training exercises conducted in the previous year, it was decided to continue with the programme in 1955 under the guise of Long Range Navigation exercises. The crews were paired-up and designated pilot and navigator for the outward flight, the roles being reversed for the return flight. The exercises continued throughout the year and the first three are outlined below.

Nicosia

Four Vampire T.11 aircraft departed Little Rissington on 24 March on the first leg of a long range training exercise to RAF Nicosia in Cyprus. Under the Command of Sqn Ldr C.A. Browne, the nominal role of aircrew and aircraft were as follows:

XE891	Sqn Ldr Browne (pilot), Flt Lt Cartwright (nav)
WZ551	Flt Lts Robinson (pilot), Lunn (nav)
XE831	Flt Lt Meldrum (pilot), Fg Off Back (nav)
WZ510	Flt Lts Rowden (pilot), Glover (nav)

The aircraft were fitted with external wing tanks and flew in pairs up until the final stages of the return journey when one aircraft underwent an engine change at RAF Luqa in Malta, after metal filings were found in the oil filter.

Wahn

The second Navex of the year began on 29 April when four Vampire T.11s set out from Little Rissington for RAF Wahn in West Germany. Under the Command of Flt Lt D. Allum, the nominal roll and aircraft allocated for this five-day trip were:

XD600	Flt Lts D. Allum (pilot), R. Levente (nav)
XD436	Flt Lt R. Tavanyar (pilot), Mtr Plt L. Gapper (nav)
XD448	Plt Off C. Roper (pilot), plus navigator
XD527	Flt Lts A. Ibbett (pilot), Markwell (nav)

Luqa

One month later, on 10 June, the next Navex saw four Vampire T.11s depart on a four-day trip to RAF Luqa in Malta. Under the Command of Flt Lt T.J. Meldrum, the aircraft and crews for this trip comprised:

XD381	Flt Lts T.J. Meldrum (pilot), L.J. Russell (nav)
XD531	Flt Lt Cartwright (pilot), Fg Off Johnson (nav)
WZ551	Flt Lts P.E.G. Bell (pilot), Roe (nav)
WZ510	Flt Lt Rowden (pilot), Fg Off Pollitt (nav)

Liaison visits and 'Trapper' activities

The activities of the Examining Wing 'Trappers' were a continuous routine of visits to military establishments at home and overseas to ensure the standardisation of instructional methods throughout the RAF and to re-categorise instructors. A team of six to eight Staff would pile into an ageing Anson and set off for a stay of up to three days at each unit on their list of annual visits, and those of 1955 offer an insight as to some of the tasks they were expected to perform.

Several staff liaison visits were also made to civilian establishments and contractors. The first of these occurred as early as February when a team visited Rolls-Royce at Derby, Bristol Aero Co Ltd at Bristol, Gloster Aircraft Co at Hucclecote and Hawker Aircraft Ltd at Dunsfold and Kingston-upon-Thames.

Examining Wing teams also made a quick start with visits to 2 ANS at Thorney Island, 5 FTS at Oakington and the Cambridge University Air Squadron, the total of tests being as follows:

	1 Sqn	2 Sqn	3 Sqn	Totals
Instructor re-cat.	14	2	14	30
Instrument rating	14	8	15	37
Standardisation	23	49	83	155

A month later the Air Ministry arranged a liaison visit to Ministry of Supply contractor Redifon Ltd of Crawley, Sussex, to enable the OC Examining Wing and a team of five officers to discuss with Managing Director, Mr Norman Hill, the merits of flight simulation and its use in flying training and to witness a demonstration of a working simulator.

The eight Primary visits made by 'Trappers' during March, provide a good illustration of the heavy workload and wide range of flying skills and knowledge these professionals required in order to carry out their everyday tasks, from Shackletons at Kinloss to Canberras at Bassingbourn and Wyton, from navigation trainers at Hullavington to Hunter fighters at Pembrey. The number of tests completed during these visits amounted to:

	1 Sqn	2 Sqn	3 Sqn	Totals
Instructor re-cat.	27	14	11	52
Instrument rating	10	7	16	33
Standardisation	97	71	90	258

In addition, OC 3 Squadron led a team of six 'Trappers' to the Central Fighter Establishment at RAF West Raynham.

The pattern continued throughout the summer, the highlight being a visit by 'Trappers' to the USA and Canada in May.

Training the Examiners

In preparation for the trip, Flt Lt Agnew spent a day with Hunting Percival at Luton learning to fly the Jet Provost. Flt Lt Finnimore was detached to Melsbroek Air Base at the request of the Belgian Air Force, and Sqn Ldr Hazlewood spent four days at RAF Gaydon flying the Valiant in preparation for testing Bomber Command pilots. A few weeks later, Wg Cdr Radley travelled to Gaydon for a three-day Valiant conversion course, while all Examining Wing pilots underwent continuation training on the Piston Provost, Valetta, Vampire and Meteor.

Training continued apace during July 1955, with 670 hours day and night flying achieved over an eighteen day period; this represents 35 hours per examiner. The following aircraft types were made available from various resources: Sea Hawk, Auster, Chipmunk, Balliol, Meteor F.8, Hunter, Canberra, Lincoln, Shackleton, Gannet, Firefly, Marathon, Pembroke, Mosquito and Varsity, plus home-based Harvard, Provost, Meteor T.7, Vampire T.11 and Valetta.

With training over, it was back to the everyday routine, commencing with an urgent request for three Command Instrument Rating Examiner (CIRE), four Instrument Rating Examiner (IRE) tests and three re-cats, followed by examination of the personal pilots assigned to HRH The Duke of Edinburgh and AOC Flying Training Command in the Devon and Vampire T.11 respectively. 'Trapper' visits were also made to HMS Bulwark, RNAS Ford, and RAF Stations Benson, Boscombe Down, Farnborough, Bassingbourn, and several Flying Training Schools.

The teamwork environment in which Examining Wing functioned dictated that individuals could not necessarily take their main leave at will but had to take it en bloc. The first three weeks of August being assigned for block leave in 1955. Nevertheless, they were able to squeeze in visits to 229 OCU at RAF Chivenor, 230 OCU Flight at RAF Upwood, 1 FTS at RAF Syerston, the Instrument Training Squadron at the Central Fighter Establishment, the Flying Boat Training Squadron at RAF Pembroke Dock and the RAF College Cranwell. The number of tests completed during these visits amounted to:

	1 Sqn	2 Sqn	3 Sqn	Totals
Instructor re-cat.	18	3	14	35
Instrument rating	7	8	11	26
Standardisation	101	13	71	185

On 19 September a 'Trapper' team departed for the annual visit to the Far East Air Force. Led by Wg Cdr Radley and Gp Capt Gilson, the South Cerney Station Commander, the eleven man team flew in a Valetta which CFS had acquired for longer flights. The CO at Little Rissington, Gp Capt Scragg, led members of another 'Trapper' team to examine the pilots of 2nd Tactical Air Force, while other teams visited RAF Binbrook and the RAF Flying College at Manby. The opportunity was also taken by the examiners to carry out further continuation training on the Sabre, Hunter, Canberra, Valetta, Pembroke, Buckmaster, Meteor, Brigand, Balliol and Beaufighter. The total number of tests amounted to 504. Continuation training was extended to include the Anson and Shackleton in November, when further visits were made to 238 OCU at RAF Colerne, RNAS Lossiemouth, 236 OCU at RAF Kinloss, 5 FTS at RAF Oakington, the Central Navigation School at RAF Shawbury, Manchester UAS and 2 ANS at RAF Thorney Island, the Wing undertaking a further 520 tests during the process.

It was universally acknowledged throughout the three services, at home and overseas, that the 'Trappers' played a major role in maintaining the high standards of flying instruction taught at the CFS.

More from the Commandant

Towards the end of 1954, Air Cdre Paul was informed that one of CFS's tasks in 1955 would be to assess the suitability of the Jet Provost for flying training.

"It was very much with this in mind that we planned our visit to Canada and the United States for May 1955. The other two important things were to see as much as possible of the way in which helicopter pilots were trained in the United States Services, and to pay a visit to Pensacola in return for the visit to CFS by Admiral Doyle and his staff.

For this visit, we picked a strong team. The trappers were led by Bob Radley, and we added to his pilots Alec Harkness, commanding the Meteor Squadron at Rissington, and Jock Agnew from the Vampire Squadron. Jock Agnew loved spinning, and when there had been some queries about the certainty of the Vampire T.11 recovering from a fully developed spin, Jock took up the challenge enthusiastically. One day we counted him to do no less than thirty full turns, and then recover normally. In addition, there was John Dowling for helicopters and myself, making eight in all. Our first visit was to the Royal Canadian Air Force HQ in Ottawa, thence to their Training Command HQ and Central Flying School at Trenton. From there, Jock Agnew, John Dowling and myself were to go on into the USA, leaving the rest of the team to continue work at Trenton and other RCAF stations, and to join up with us again on our return north for the flight back to England. We flew up to Heathrow in the 'Trappers' Varsity and there transferred as ordinary passengers into a BOAC Boeing Stratocruiser.

We arrived back at CFS in the 'Trappers' Varsity after 13,000 miles and twenty nine days, landing at thirty two overseas airfields. The Cotswolds, Bourton-on-the-Water and English beer were very welcome.

Later in the summer of 1955, the BBC did a live broadcast from CFS. This took up a good deal of time and I was by no means convinced that the final result was satisfactory. As Commandant it was my task to make the opening statement, and this I did in an empty hangar, facing microphone and camera, with nobody in sight except the camera crew. I found the lights very hot, but the most difficult thing was to talk convincingly, as though to a room full of people, into the wall eye of a TV camera. This was something I had never done before, and do not ever wish to do again. Further scenes were broadcast from the museum, from briefing rooms and cubicles, and some from the air.

It was also in the summer of 1955 that we got our first Jet Provost. This was described as a modified Provost. In fact the alterations were considerable, for the piston engine, the Alvis Leonides, was removed and a small jet engine, the Armstrong Siddeley Viper, substituted in a central position in the fuselage, much further aft. Wing, undercarriage and tail unit remained the same, and as much as possible of the Piston Provost airframe was used in this first version of the new trainer. The use of the old main undercarriage in conjunction with a long-legged nose wheel to make it a tricycle, resulted in a rather giraffe appearance, and an aircraft very different from the compact and shapely products like the British Aerospace later developments of it. We did a lot of flying on this first version and, in spite of its appearance, it was well liked. It did, however, seem to me to introduce a number of new problems.

The intention of the Air Ministry was that the Jet Provost, like the Piston Provost before it, should be the RAF's ab initio trainer, and that the pupil pilot should do as much training on this jet as possible; in fact right up to the stage of getting his wings. But it was very soon apparent that, with a performance approximating to the earlier marks of Spitfire, the Jet Provost was capable of getting very rapidly into situations which earlier piston engine trainers could not attain, and that its performance not only enabled it to use much more of the sky including the upper air

To be chosen as the subject of a television programme in the mid-fifties was indeed an honour and much of Little Rissington's airfield had the air of a TV studio for several days. *(left inset)* Air Cdre Paul rehearses his lines for the BBC director, while various sets are in place (*top inset and above*) for some of the action sequences. One of the old 'tin' hangars and what looks like a pill box can be seen in the background. (*Bert Brand*)

space, but that to exploit it to best advantage, this ability had to be used to the full. My own feeling, after some experience with it, was that the RAF might very well find that the Jet Provost was too much of an aeroplane for a pilot's first flight when beginning to learn. This was the last major task during my two years at CFS, and I get some satisfaction from knowing that the Jet Provost which finally resulted has served the RAF very well.

It is, of course, impossible in only a few pages to recount all that took place in my two years as Commandant of CFS. Here I have confined myself to events which, for various reasons, stand out in memory or importance. Although there was plenty of routine work, every day provided something of absorbing interest. For Rosemary, as well as for myself, it was, I think, the best two years of our life in the Service. We shared it with a great many wonderful friends, who were also some of the most brilliant pilots and instructors of their day. When, in the New Year's Honours of January 1956 it was announced that I had been awarded the honour of appointment as Commander of the Order of the Bath, a rare distinction for an Air Cdre, I did truly feel that this was something earned by the whole of CFS."

All-through training

Returning from a visit to the USA and Canada, Air Cdre Christopher Paul voiced strong reservations about certain aspects of altering the RAF training policy of an all-jet syllabus then being advocated. He was sure that the best way for pupils to gain confidence was to begin their training on a basic piston-engined trainer before moving on to the Jet Provost.

Air Cdre Paul's ideas were put into practice on 1 July 1955 when the first stage of the new all-through Piston Provost/Vampire syllabus came into effect. From that date, Little Rissington became CFS (Advanced), with South Cerney CFS (Basic) and the previous practice of training instructors who were qualified to teach on piston-engined or jet types only, but not both, came to an end. Numbers 3 and 4 Squadrons began exchanging their Harvards for Meteor T.7 trainers, pending the arrival of the Vampire T.11, while the Meteors of No.5 Squadron, which was disbanded, were shared out between 3 and 4 Squadrons.

Once the School's aircraft re-equipment programme was completed, the process of converting its own piston-engined instructors commenced under the No. 23 Group Special Jet Conversion Course. This began on 14 July and ended on 24 September and gave the Meteor Squadrons a breathing space of five days before they took on the first batch of Provost Students from No. 164 Course from South Cerney.

To accommodate the change to a jet-only unit, the Flying Wing of CFS (A) was reorganised, with Nos. 3 and 4 Squadrons operating Meteors and an HQ Squadron consisting of a Communications Flight and a Vampire Flight. As soon as new Vampires were released from the production lines, they replaced the Meteors allowing the CFS to establish a training model that remained standard until the advent of the Jet Provost T.3 and the all-through jet training syllabus in 1959.

Meteor Team displays at Le Mans

One of the highlights of the French National Air Meet which was held at Le Mans on 3 July 1955, was a display by the CFS Meteor Aerobatic Team, "The Pelicans". Four T.7s plus one reserve departed Little Rissington on the 2nd accompanied by the unit's Anson C.12 carrying a servicing team. The aircraft and personnel comprised:

WL367	Wg Cdr P.M. Dobree-Bell, Cpl Trigg
WA668	Flt Lt Harrison, Sgt Edwards
WL373	Flt Lt D.R.J. Hall, SAC McCartney
WH192	Flt Lt T.J. Doe, Fg Off A.H. Back
WL370	Flt Lt D.G.T. Franklin, LAC Penzer
PH810	Flt Lts J.F.M. Widmer, G. Lau (nav), Sgt Wharrier, J/T McKay, Cpl Snook, Cpl Betts, LAC Tromans, LAC Sams

Bird of a feather

One amusing incident recorded in the CFS magazine, tells of a young barn owl that perched behind the rear cockpit instrument panel and completed three sorties in a Meteor 7. During the flights the bird experienced aerobatics, instrument flying and asymmetric flying exercises. When it was discovered, it was found to be suffering from severe anoxia and air-sickness, and was declared sick and unfit to continue jet training.

Jet Provost T.Mk.1

Sqn Ldr W.G. Drinkell and Flt Lts J. Morrice, G.D. Walker and Houser were appointed to carry out an initial evaluation of the Jet Provost Mark 1, the first two of which arrived on 22 July. This was completed on 25 August by which time the team had produced notes for a Basic syllabus. The aircraft then moved to RAF Hullavington to join three other production aircraft, XD679, 680, 692 for a full trial. Flying a programme which lasted 111 hours, investigations were implemented to assess the behaviour of the type as a potential ab initio trainer, to formulate a possible training syllabus, and to convert the first ten instructors.

At Home Day

Preparations for the station's fourth successive At Home Day reached a climax at 13:00 on Saturday 17 September. Distinguished visitors included the Mayor and Mayoress of Cheltenham, who arrived in a Comms Flight Anson from Staverton, the C-in-C Flying Training Command and the AOC No. 23 Group.

Early visitors were able to experience pleasure flights in a Rapide or Auster or wander round the static displays which included a representative mix of aircraft from most RAF Commands and other services and included Chipmunk, Hastings, Provost, Shackleton, Hunter, Canberra and Gannet.

"Nellie of Oyster Creek Bay" (a decorated tractor and trailer set equipped for carrying passengers) in the capable hands of Cpl Burns,

'Nellie of Oyster Creek Bay', with Cpl Burns at the controls, on its circuit of the camp during Battle of Britain day. (*CFS Magazine*)

gave over 1,600 rides around the hangar area for spectators and their children. The flying display commenced at 14:00 with the arrival of four naval aircraft from Boscombe Down, and displays by Gladiator, Sunderland, Valiant, Hunter and Jet Provost were interspersed with displays by CFS Basic and Advanced, the highlights being:

- A dive-bomb attack by four Vampire T.11s led by Major Emmons (USAF) against a fort on the airfield, the illusion of live bombs cleverly effected by members of the Station Armoury.
- Solo aerobatic displays of the Provost, Vampire and Meteor by Flt Lt G. Armitage and Fg Offs Clayton and Henderson respectively.
- A daring display, spiced with comedy, of aerial gymnastics by Cpl Bennett suspended from a Dragonfly helicopter skilfully flown by Flt Lt Pinner.
- Impeccable formation drill by nine Provosts led by Sqn Ldr Buckley and precision aerobatics by "The Pelicans" Meteor Aerobatic Team led by Flt Lt Harrison brought the show to a close.

The Sunday was devoted to restoring the station to normal. Over 12,000 people had passed through the camp gates resulting in a cheque for £332. 1s. 10d. being sent to the FTC Central Fund for sharing between the RAFBF and RAFA.

A young spectator's impression

The following article was sent to the CFS Magazine in the spring of 1956 by the previous Commandant, Air Cdre G.J.C. Paul. It was written by a Miss Pauline Drake, a schoolgirl of Churchdown, near Gloucester, and was originally published in her school magazine.

"On September 17th, my father took my younger brother, sister and me to the Central Flying School at Little Rissington in Gloucestershire for the Battle of Britain Week Display. After following numerous cars through the tiny Cotswold villages, we eventually arrived at the Station. We drove past the barracks, which were surrounded by beautifully kept gardens and soon obtained our first view of the aerodrome. We parked the car and bought a programme from one of the many Royal Air Force officials.

We then went to see a representative section of Service aircraft in the static aircraft park. The show included a helicopter, a light bomber and various types of jet aircraft. For a small charge people had their photographs taken in the cockpit of one of the aircraft. Passenger-carrying aircraft were available for part of the afternoon giving joy rides. A picturesque miniature train, Nellie of Oyster Creek Bay, gave rides to children.

In order to obtain a clear view of the runway we waited behind the barriers provided and were fortunate enough to be in the front row. The airfield was enormous and on the far side was an imitation fortress, which later was attacked. Immediately in front of us were nine Percival Provosts, the standard basic trainer in the Royal Air Force to-day, which, later on, took off and demonstrated formation drill. The display began with a parachute-dropping display by a Hastings. We were told that the aeroplane had dropped supplies for the men in the fortress.

There were various individual aerobatic displays performed by pilots in Vampires, Meteors, and other jet aircraft; these were very interesting to watch. Between these displays were formation fly-pasts of Valettas, Hunters and F-84s of the United States Air Force. There was an individual fly-past of a Sunderland flying boat, which dominated the sky with its majestic structure. The most exciting feature of the proceedings was a helicopter display. A man who had arrived in the helicopter swung himself to the ground by means of a rope. He then put one arm through the loop of one rope and one leg through another rope, both of which were attached to the helicopter. The machine rose and circled the airfield with the man suspended from it.

During the afternoon the Mayor of Cheltenham arrived by aeroplane and was welcomed by the Commandant, Air Cdre G.J.C. Paul DFC.

As the afternoon drew to a close, the fortress was attacked by four Vampire T.11s. The defenders offered no resistance and the fortress soon collapsed, a smoking ruin. The show was terminated by a fly-past of the Station's emblem, five Gloster Meteors in formation, the leader flying the wrong way up.

We went home from Little Rissington after a most enjoyable afternoon. From Central Flying School came a number of 'The Few' who fought in the Battle of Britain in 1940. It was to commemorate their heroic deeds that the Royal Air Force was holding this static and flying display. We must never forget those brave men or allow the remembrance of their deeds to pass from us. Sir Winston Churchill said:- 'Never in the field of human conflict was so much owed by so many to so few.'"

De Havilland liaison

It was during this period that the De Havilland Aircraft Company commenced in depth investigations into the spinning characteristics of the Vampire T.11, for not only was the aircraft entering RAF service in large numbers but many overseas orders depended to some extent on the performance of the trainer in home use. Flt Lt Fennell visited the manufacturer in November 1955 for initial discussions on the subject, and in December, De Havilland invited him to Hurn Airport to carry out inverted spinning trials in a specially equipped T.11. 'Hussenot' recordings, films and wire recordings were taken during a series of tests.

Hunter Flight

The establishment of a CFS Hunter Flight under the direct command of OC Flying, Sqn Ldr B.L Partridge with Flt Lt D.R.J. Hall as Flight Commander, occurred on 8 November. The Flight was based at RAF Kemble because the runway at Little Rissington was too short for Hunter conversions (1,600 yards) and the circuit too congested to allow for another type of aircraft; Kemble also had servicing facilities available. Equipped with a trio of Hunter F.Mk.4s, WV319, WV325 and WV331, the Flight's purpose was to give Hunter experience to QFIs on CFS Basic and Advanced, and staff on Examining Wing. A conversion course was prepared and commencing on 12 November, four instructors were converted every two days. Motor transport conveyed six pilots and their kit from Flying Wing HQ each Monday to Friday at 08:00.

Trappers wind down

As the year drew to a close, continuation training commenced on the Lincoln and Jet Provost T.1 and the 'Trappers' made visits to 228 OCU at RAF Leeming, 2 FTS at RAF Hullavington, the London UAS and 42, 206, 220 and 228 Squadrons at RAF St Eval, a total of 299 tests being carried out.

New C-in-C for Flying Training Command

In December 1955, Air Vice-Marshal Richard Atcherley took over as C-in-C, Flying Training Command.

1956

More liaison work

The Vampire spinning focus continued into 1956 when Flt Lts Fennell and Fellows entered into discussions with De Havilland's at RAF Middleton St George. Down at the HQ Flight at RAF Hullavington, Sqn Ldr Jacobs and Flt Lt Swart discussed training methods on the Jet Provost T.1. This was followed by a conference on cockpit standardisation of the Jet Provost held at the Hunting Percival works in Luton, with Sqn Ldr Edelsten in attendance.

Helicopter Squadron

Meanwhile, the Helicopter Development Flight disbanded on 1 January 1956 at South Cerney to be reformed as the CFS Helicopter Squadron (Dragonfly HR.4, Skeeter Mk.6, T.11 and T.12, Sycamore HC.14 and Whirlwind HAR.2).

Hunter mishap

A few miles away at Kemble, the pilot of Hunter F.4, WV319, was unable to stop his aircraft after touching down and it overran the runway before crashing into a stone wall bordering the airfield. This occurred on 13 January and there were no casualties.

This Category Business

A send-up on Instructor classifications from Flt Lt R. Crouch:

The B2 Instructor:-

1. Flies all day, all night, all weathers. No time to sleep (or drink).
2. Tries to teach four students and has to fly with most of the others as well.
3. Everybody asks him all the questions.
4. Is really an A1 who is having an amazing run of bad luck.

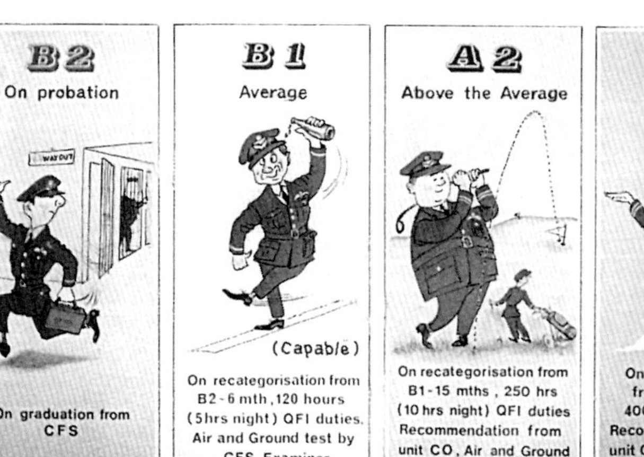

A light hearted interpretation of the QFI categories. (*CFS Magazine*)

The B1 Instructor

1. Flies all day and sleeps (drinks) at night.
2. Manages four students and runs the Flight.
3. Could answer most of the questions if he weren't so awfully busy.
4. Had better apply for the A2 just before the next CFS standardisation team comes round.

The A2 Instructor

1. Flies when the weather's poor and sleeps (drinks) when it isn't.
2. Just copes with one or two students, but interferes with everyone else's.
3. Far too experienced to be asked silly questions.
4. No need to re-cat as he already knows more than the A1 blokes.

The A1 Instructor

1. No time to fly. Sleeps and drinks.
2. Avoids all students.
3. Evades all questions.
4. A B2 really having an amazing run of good luck.

Air Chief Marshal Sir Patrick Hine GCB GBE ADC FRAeS

"My association with RAF Little Rissington began in November 1954 as a member of the CFS's No. 165 Course which, having completed the Basic Phase on the Piston Provost at RAF South Cerney, moved to 'Rissy' for the Advanced Phase on either the Meteor T.7 or the Vampire T.11. Having just completed my first tour on the Meteor F.8 with No. 1(F) Squadron at RAF Tangmere, it was logical for me to instruct on the Meteor, and I graduated in February 1955 with a B1 QFI category and as winner of the CFS and Clarkson Trophies.

After almost a year's instructing at Weston Zoyland and Strubby, and with A2 and IRE qualifications, I returned to Little Rissington as a CFS staff instructor on the Meteor Flight (as it had become by then), which was a small independent unit commanded by Flt Lt 'Frank' Franklin and reporting to the OC Headquarters Squadron, Sqn Ldr Brian Partridge (nicknamed 'Bright Eyes'). The Meteor Flight had five QFIs and about twelve students at any one time. It also provided the CFS formation aerobatic team (that year the 'Pelicans') comprising: Flt Lt D.G.T. Franklin (leader), Fg Off Paddy Hine (No.2), Flt Lt Matt Kemp (No.3) and Flt Lt John McArthur (No.4). I thoroughly enjoyed my 18 months on the Meteor Flight as the job was most rewarding and there was plenty of flying – up to 7-8 sorties per day when we were night flying and on average about 40 hours per month. Normal sortie lengths were 40-45 minutes with the ventral tank empty and 60-65 minutes when full. By the time I left CFS, my pure flying and instructional skills had reached their pinnacle, and they stood me in great stead for my subsequent flying career on the Hunter, Lightning, Phantom and Harrier. Above all, CFS taught me to fly really accurately and smoothly; fighter pilots really don't need to fly as if they had St Vitus's dance!

During my first couple of weeks on the staff, I was involved in the 'acquisition' of the CFS 'Top Hat' which ever since has been awarded to the course student coming bottom in groundschool. I was in London with a party of students on No. 174 Course who were celebrating their pending graduation in what turned out to be a major manifestation of joy. When we were finally evicted from the West End pubs and clubs, I suggested that we might relieve the Commissionaire at the Dorchester Hotel of his ornate gold and black 'topper'. The plot was to drive up to the hotel forecourt (there was no drink/drive problem then) when one of the backseat passengers would wind down the window and say to the commissionaire 'My good man, would you be kind enough to give us directions to the Tower of London', and then when this worthy bent forwards to oblige, whip off his hat, shut the window and speed off pronto. With any luck the bareheaded victim would be so surprised (principle of war!) and startled that he would not even get the number of the car which belonged, I might add, to one of the students – I was after all on the staff!. The plan worked a treat and by the Sunday night the 'Hat' was safely at 'Rissy' and was duly presented to the 'dunce' on 174 at their farewell guest night later in the week. The recipient was, I believe, one of the perpetrators – poetic justice indeed. Thus began a new CFS tradition that has lasted 50 years, although the original hat is no longer in a fit state to present (it is now in the CFS museum) and has recently been replaced.

I loved the life at Little Rissington, living in comfort in the spacious Officers' Mess. We flew hard and we played hard, with most courses having a very lively core of socially-minded students who in the main had just come from squadrons based in UK, Germany, or the Near, Middle and Far East Commands. They all had their 'old' songs and a repertoire of stories that were most certainly not suitable for mixed company.

The Commandant, then Air Cdre 'Hetty' Hyde who as well as being a real character was also an incorrigible pyromaniac, regularly held sway in the bar in the early evening and on Saturday nights. He enjoyed a party and had a great sense of humour and fun. On one occasion this was carried a bit too far when he blew up a squadron leader's wife by mistake with a thunderflash that was intended for a rather deadbeat member of staff but went off instead between this lady's feet, in the process blackening her legs and virtually destroying her dress and shoes. Mayhem ensued as one angry lady physically assaulted the Commandant who eventually managed to calm her down with a large gin and tonic and the promise of a new outfit.

'Hetty' Hyde's daughter was a 'chip off the old block' and certainly a character in her own right. He called her 'Wintry Day' – as she was 'short, dark and dirty' – which was perhaps a bit unkind but she was undoubtedly attractive to many of the students. Whatever, Mess profits, and those of attractive nearby pubs (the Old New Inn in Bourton being our local), soared when the Eden Government awarded the Armed Forces a very substantial pay-rise in the spring of 1956 (flying pay too received a real boost). As a lowly Fg Off, I was about £1 per day better off which was a fortune at a time when Mess charges were minimal and a pint of beer cost around one shilling. While this welcome windfall played havoc with our livers, we were young and a good dose of 'high flow' oxygen the following morning usually assisted a rapid recovery!

Slightly to my surprise, I got real satisfaction from my task of teaching relatively experienced pilots to instruct on the Meteor. It was a challenging aircraft to fly accurately, particularly on one engine when it was quite easy to get into difficulty. Any significant yaw with the airbrakes extended could lead rapidly to loss of control and accounted for a number of fatalities on the T.7 which had no ejection seats. Apart from the normal course flying with students, there was a generous allowance for Staff Continuation Training (SCT) and, with the Meteor Flight providing the aerobatic team, there were added opportunities to hone one's flying skills and keep the adrenalin flowing. I see from my logbook that in 1956 I flew some 450 hours and 650 sorties, 30 of which were on the Type Flight's Hunter F.4s at Kemble.

Among my many students was a certain Fg Off Peter Harding who had just returned from an exchange tour flying Canberras with the RAAF. He and I later served together as station commanders in RAF Germany and then eventually as fellow Members of the Air Force Board. By then Sir Peter Harding and Chief of the Air Staff, he went on to be Chief of Defence Staff in the early 1990s. I sometimes wish ruefully, for career reasons, that I had scrubbed him at 'Rissy'! But that would have been difficult because he was an above average student.

Despite the busy flying regimen and active Mess life, I still found time to court a young trainee nurse in London, to persuade her to marry me (difficult!) and then, before she could change her mind, to set a date for our wedding in Harrogate. This meant taking a couple of weeks off flying for the honeymoon and Christmas, but c'est la vie - you can't have everything! Having moved into part of a lovely old Cotswold house in Bourton before the end of December, I introduced my wife to 'Rissy' by escorting her to the New Year's Eve ball in the Officers' Mess. It was a fancy dress do and she came in a splendidly sartorial gypsy regalia, via the Commandant's residence for pre-ball drinks. My wife was understandably a little apprehensive but progressively relaxed until at the end of the drinks 'Hetty' Hyde's mother said to her "Are you going home dear to get changed into fancy dress"! By now completely unnerved, my wife took a lot of persuading to move to the Mess but eventually a good time was had by all. However, it was really not our day because on the way down the hill to Bourton we suffered one of our regular punctures in our old 1934 Morris Cowley saloon which I had bought off one of the Vampire T.11 staff members, Master Pilot Laurie Gapper, for the princely sum of £50. Fortunately, a week or so later my wife received a small nursing gratuity through the post which was rapidly converted into payment for 4 new remould tyres from 'Pop' Lake's garage in Bourton.

Life at 'Rissy' continued through the first part of 1957 in much the same vein, my liver recovered somewhat from the ministrations of the nurse, and I settled happily into married routine. Then, out of the blue, I received an invitation from Sqn Ldr Roger Topp to join the 'Black Arrows' aerobatic team of 'Treble One' Squadron. This meant being short toured at Rissy but the Commandant was indulgent of my passion for formation aeros and kindly agreed to my request to leave. I left Little Rissington (and Bourton-on-the-Water) in the May with very mixed feelings because I had had a very happy time at CFS. The station had a wonderful feel to it with everyone serving there, in whatever capacity, being very much part of a team. CFS was particularly well supported by every unit on the station, without which they could not have fulfilled their many commitments. I shall never forget my time there and my subsequent attendances at the annual CFS Association Dinners, and it was a very sad day indeed when the station came to close as a result of the 1975 Defence Review. I do not believe that CFS has ever been quite the same since."

Trapper training

For Examining Wing, the month of March was set aside for training on aircraft types not currently established at CFS. Commencing on 27 February, the first of many non-CFS establishment aircraft, including Shackleton, Canberra, Prentice, Chipmunk, Pembroke, Marathon, Varsity and Lincoln, began arriving at Little Rissington. By the end of the month, the Trappers had amassed 640 hours in seventeen different types of aircraft.

Provost fatality

On 28 March, Flt Lt C.A. Coatesworth was flying with his instructor, Flt Lt K.J. Evans, on a normal instructional detail in Piston Provost T.1, WV423 when the engine caught fire. The instructor gave the order to abandon the aircraft and although the student made a successful parachute landing without injury, Flt Lt Evan's parachute failed to fully deploy and he was killed.

Aircraft establishment

At the beginning of June, the number of aircraft allotted to CFS was as follows:

Vampire T.11	-	22
Meteor T.7	-	4
Provost T.1	-	2
Anson C.19	-	3
Valetta C.1	-	1
Hunter F.4	-	3

Examining Wing visits Middle East

This account of an Examining Wing visit to units in the Middle East was written by Sqn Ldr B.L. Partridge and published in Air Clues. During the visit, the Commandant took the opportunity to visit HQ Middle East Air Force at Nicosia, Cyprus, and to see the Examiners at work (and play) at Nicosia and Habbaniya in Iraq.

Via Istres to Malta

"The section of two Meteor T.7s, led by the Commandant, left Little Rissington on the sunny morning of 12 June and rapidly climbed to 30,000 ft in the direction of the South Coast. Twelve minutes later they passed over Selsey Bill cruising at 30,000 ft, heading for Istres near Marseilles in the South of France. For once, a deep depression was depressing most of France and the ground was invisible. However, the French fixer service kept the pilots happy without recourse to the multilingual talents of the Flying Wing Engineer who rode in the

Displaying individual CFS squadron codes of the period are Piston Provost T.1, WV508/XE, *(above)* and Vampire T.11, XD605/IU *(below)*. *(David Watkins)*

Wing aircraft. As the two aircraft approached the Rhone Valley, the weather began to improve and the snow-capped symmetry of Mont Blanc could be seen in the distance. By then, the very efficient Kiwi controller with the delectable callsign 'Cassis' took over and shepherded the aircraft past the border at Avignon and the bull-rings at Arles to land in warm sunshine on the immense runway at Istres.

In the afternoon the pilots tackled the longest leg of the whole trip, the six hundred and twenty-five miles to RAF Luqa, Malta. This was made unpleasant by opaque dust-laden cirrus cloud, which forced the section up to 36,000 ft for an hour to make it possible for the wing aircraft to stay in formation with the leader. To a physical discomfort similar to that experienced when sitting in a tent on top of Mount Everest was added anxious uncertainty as the fuel gauge readings dropped inexorably and still nothing but cloud could be seen below. Then, suddenly, all was blue below; in the middle of the blue was a strangely golden island, Gozo, and beyond lay Malta.

Malta, El Adem, Nicosia

Malta offered a pleasant interlude and next morning the section set off in perfect weather for El Adem in Libya. The North African coast was discernible at a range of 150 miles and the navigators sat back, at ease but relishing the bright Mediterranean sunshine. Just after take-off from El Adem the crews caught a glimpse of vividly coloured arab robes as the two aircraft swept low over a group of camels on whose dignified progress the roar of Derwents had no discernible effect. An hour later the section cruised down over the forest-clad Troodos mountains into the sun-scorched plains of Nicosia to land at the busy little International Airport. Here the familiar processes and bane of all travellers, Customs, Immigration, Security and Currency Exchange, delayed the party but by early evening they were established in a hotel in the outskirts of Nicosia. By now dressed in crumpled lightweight suits redolent of Avtag (for they had been packed into the entrails of the Meteors) our foursome was ready to step into long cool brandy sours.

However, once the arrangements for the next stage to Habbaniya had been completed the section lost no time in leaving the heat and oppressiveness of Nicosia for the cool breezes and crystalline waters of Kyrenia.

Nicosia to Habbaniya

The blast of hot air, which greeted the travellers when they opened the Meteor canopies after landing at Habbaniya Plateau Airfield on 18 June, was a reminder that service in the Middle East is not all roses. How strange it was to see the lawns and trees of the main aerodrome, a green oasis in a howling desert and a slowly decaying monument to the Royal Air Force. It was here that the Examining Wing team, which had visited the remote units on the Persian Gulf, received from the Meteor crews their first mail since leaving the United Kingdom. Fg Off Patrick Hine recalls this part of the trip,

"This visit in fact took place in June 1956 with 'Hetty' Hyde and Sqn Ldr Brian Partridge being in the lead aircraft, and myself and engineer Flt Lt Dick Levente in the other. I remember this trip well for a wild party in the Officers' Mess bar at RAF Habbaniya, at the end of which I tried to ride back on a bicycle to my quarters, rounded a hedge and promptly rode into the swimming pool. It was by this time dark and I thought the end of the world had come; I have never sobered up so quickly in my life!

Next day, the Meteors began their return flight against headwinds all the way. After Cyprus and El Adem, they stuck to the North African coast and flew via Idris (another monument called Castel Benito) to Tunis for a comfortable overnight stay.

The last stage on 21 June, from Tunis to Istres, Dijon, Tangmere and then base, was made in four hops because of prevailing headwinds and the usual poor weather forecast from the South of England. The sheet of cloud began twenty miles south of Tangmere and grew thicker as the aircraft flew north to Little Rissington, where they landed at half-past five in the gathering gloom of an English summer's evening.

One final word must be to pay a tribute to the sound, efficient work of the Meteor Flight ground crews at CFS (A), who prepared these aircraft for the six thousand mile journey, throughout which they performed flawlessly in every respect."

Second tour, but now on CFS Staff

Shortly after obtaining his A1 Instructor category rating at Oakington, Flt Sgt Maurice Biggs, known as Biggles to his friends, was posted back to Little Rissington on 18 July, joining 4 Squadron then equipped with Vampire T.11s.

"A good family friend, Nibby Fellows, known to me at Oakington, helped with my introduction to the Squadron's routine. After the first month the Squadron CO became Major A.J. Chesser, USAF, on an exchange posting. There was only one other NCO pilot on the staff at this time, Master Pilot Laurie Gapper. Once established in married quarters, life became quite pleasant. My flying now was altogether a different task, training experienced pilots often with as much if not more pure flying experience than myself, often on diverse aircraft types. Differences in rank did not seem to exist and all Laurie and I missed out on were the social activities in the Officers' Mess. One of the first parties I experienced was the 'going away' party for the outgoing CO, Major Emmons. Little about this function is remembered except a local hostelry and the large consumption of alcoholic beverages.

At Rissy I was able to obtain several flights in the Meteor to keep my hand in – it was always a pleasant aircraft to fly and without a student to teach this was even more enjoyable. There were no vast concrete parking areas for aircraft then, now so evident at training schools. Our aircraft were parked outside the far end of the hangar. Weather always played an important part in our flying, since, pre-DME fit, we had no radar aids nor cockpit navigational and landing aids, just our reliance on mental Dead Reckoning and the Mark 1 eyeball. Approach lighting was minimal and on some night flying details because of the height of the airfield, we would see the fog at low levels slowly creeping up the side of the hill. As a matter of honour circuit flying was only called to a halt when the fog was really lapping at the edges of the airfield.

During this CFS tour, I experienced a peculiar fault with a Vampire T.11 aircraft, XD457 coded IW. When gently pushing over at the top of a climb, there had been a loud bang from the rear of the aircraft. After increasing height once again, I tried the same procedure, once more with an identical result. My return to base quickly followed with an expectation that there had been a flash fire in the fuel collector box. Some explanation was required for any early return, so, after discussions, the Flight Commander, Flt Lt Allum, and myself went up to see if the fault could be repeated. The dreaded noise certainly was still there, if not now louder than ever. Before long this aircraft had to be inspected by De Havilland, who eventually diagnosed that the problem was caused by some oversize holes on this particular aircraft's wing attachment points! The aircraft never flew again and was confined to the museum in Airmanship Hall.

One of my own highlights was the existence of the Hunter 4 Flight over at Kemble. Mainly used for student experience, it was nice to be able to fly the aircraft myself. The first day I went over to Kemble the weather was not exactly the day for any first solo on type. However I had forgotten I was now on the staff and weather was only a minor consideration. This is not to say safety factors were ignored completely but soon I did find myself climbing up to height through cloud faster than I ever usually achieved in level flight. That day I had three Hunter flights including my supersonic 'boom run' flight down the Bristol Channel or at least that was where I thought I was. At lower speed I switched my powered controls over into the heavy manual standby system but did not persist very long that day before my reversion to powered control.

For the Royal Visit when HRH Princess Margaret visited the station we had the expected flying display and our Vampires were a full part of this occasion. After nearly an hour in formation including the fly past, as ever, both the cockpit and personal temperatures were quite high. Those organising the show were fully aware of this fact. After landing and before being presented to Her Royal Highness in a marquee, certain arrangements had been made! At the entrance to the marquee we were issued with brand new flying gloves and our Presentation followed. Within a minute as we left, these brand new gloves were taken from us to be returned to stores. As far as I am aware, the only photographic record of this event is one of Princess Margaret talking to my twins during a visit to the station school.

One of the warnings given to me during my Instructors' Course was that a student would always find a way of catching you unawares. For many years I had instructed on Meteors and thought I knew all the tricks that any student could use to catch you out. In the early days of Meteor instruction the way to demonstrate asymmetric flying was to shut one engine completely down. The instructor closed one throttle and the student went through the engine shut down drill. The instructor's trick, a life-saving precaution at times, was to keep the appropriate hand firmly on the LP cock of the remaining engine to ensure this remained turning. Students did have a tendency in moments of stress to get port and starboard mixed up.

CFS shortly obtained a few Canberra T.4s to give air experience on type to the students. I was fortunate to be chosen to be an instructor together with Sqn Ldr Adams, who was OC of this flight. To me the Canberra seemed just like an overgrown Meteor but with side-by-side seating. I was very impressed and looked forward to the next flight, strangely not to be, as my posting to Officer Training School at Jurby was announced and all hope of a further flight was gone. I had enjoyed my stay at Little Rissington and was sad to leave but the advantages this gave me for my future flying career were great. In the event I only managed to get out of the instructor role once in my remaining 27 years of flying when on a tour on VC10s. Instruction was certainly not the worst job in flying as I had once thought."

RAF Little Rissington Wives' Club

The Wives' Club was re-opened on 20 January 1956 and continued with their meetings on alternate Tuesdays at 19:45. At the general meeting Mrs Jenkins handed over the secretaryship of the club after a very successful year. Mrs S.S. Kemp was voted as the new Secretary. The committee for the next six months was elected and is as follows:

- Mrs Cassels as President
- Mrs Zala as Chairman
- Mrs Radley remained as Treasurer

There was an interesting programme arranged for the next few months which included lectures by Major Cunningham on Care and Devotion shown to the children of Dr Barnardo's Homes. In an effort

to attract new members an open house was kept on alternate Tuesdays.

CFS Hunter and Javelin collide

Having completed tours as a flight commander both on Sabres in Germany and on Balliols and Vampires at RAF Cranwell, Flt Lt Peter Hicks embarked on his first posting to CFS as a 'Trapper' on the Advanced Examining Wing in 1956.

"As has been mentioned already, a Type Flight was established at Kemble to give CFS instructors the opportunity to be familiar with current first line aircraft. In 1956 and for years after, this meant the Hunter F.Mk.4. A fine aircraft, though I would have preferred a Sabre with an Avon engine and a Martin Baker seat (but not a Mk.2H seat as you will see!).

On 24 August 1956, I was happily detailed for a day on the Hunter at Kemble, having left my wife and three children in the old cottage we were renting in Chedworth, and drove to Kemble in our first car, a 1932 Austin 7, bought for £35. It was a bright day but with the sky obscured by 8/8 altocumulus at about 10,000 ft. My intention on the first trip of the day was to climb to 35,000 ft heading out to the Bristol Channel, make a sonic bang (still a novelty 50 years ago!), followed by stalling, aerobatics, perhaps a spin, and return to Kemble. 'Twas not to be.

The medium cloud presented no problem as far as Air Traffic Control was concerned. In those days there were very few regulations compared with those needed in the much more crowded airspace we now have. If you wanted to climb through cloud you did so; there was thought to be no requirement in uncontrolled airspace, nor were there allocated facilities to be monitored for collision avoidance. An accident was about to occur which would help to provide ammunition to bring about change!

I took off heading west and commenced to climb at the recommended 430 knots. Almost immediately after clearing the thin cloud there was an indescribable impact. All that followed is very clear and occupied split seconds, totalling less than about 30 seconds, I would say. 'Must have been another aircraft. We're tumbling. This is where we eject. Can't find canopy ejection handle. Go straight up to the seat ejection handle and pull'. In the wind outside (400-500 mph initially – very rough). So rough that as though someone else watching I decided that that was that. Noticed that my right leg was trailing behind at an impossible angle but felt nothing. Then – objectivity failed – the safety harness box was rotating – a moment's panic (very illogical). Look up, whichever way, and happiness! The parachute canopy. But with a missing segment. And what have we here? The seat is attached to the apex of the chute and is dangling over the side above my head. 'Better climb up the rigging and try to release it, otherwise it will hit me on landing'. I raised my right hand to start climbing and at that point the delayed shock of a very severe bang on the head finally took effect – and I came too in Gloucester Hospital (before being transferred to RAF Hospital Wroughton).

The bone dome ended up in the Black Museum of the Institute of Aviation Medicine at Farnborough entitled 'The wearer lived'. A good design, well produced. Thanks to that, and above all to the Martin Baker seat which functioned in spite of considerable damage, the tale can be told. The collision was between myself in Hunter F.Mk.4, XF980, (barely a month old) and Javelin FAW.Mk.4, XA644, flown by a Gloster test pilot with an RAF navigator on loan to the company. The Javelin must have broken in two laterally for the navigator saw the floor opening beneath his feet. Apparently part of the wreckage must have operated his ejection seat and he was safely ejected. The pilot ejected but sadly his parachute was damaged in contact with wreckage and he did not survive.

The Hunter broke in two somewhere between the wing and the tailplane and crashed near farm buildings at Wotton-under-Edge. Part of the Javelin smashed the Hunter's canopy (and my bonedome), and part, probably the pitot head, made a 3 inch hole in the side of the seat about 10 inches behind my left ear. More significantly it cut the drogue-withdrawal line. The results were potentially unpleasant for the drogue remained throughout in the seat, unable to develop ½ second after ejection, slow and stabilise the seat, and at 10,000 ft to release the wearer from the seat, and finally to pull the ripcord and open the chute. Since none of this happened except the automatic release of the seat harness, one was lucky that only one leg went up over the thigh guard and broke at the hip (no leg restraints on the Mk.2 seat). And even more lucky that since the drogue could not open the main parachute, one fell out of the seat so that the pull of the seat against me opened the chute, and it developed without wrapping round either the seat or me.

Finally, the Board of Inquiry found that in view of the closing speeds of the two aircraft and the very short time available between possible visual contact and impact no blame could be allocated to either pilot."

Accident report

The following extract was taken from the report produced at the conclusion of the inquiry into the accident and was written by Wg Cdr J. Jewell.

Hunter Pilot's Seat

On the 28 August at Little Rissington we examined the Mark 2H Ejection Seat, Serial No.55917, which was used by Flt Lt Hicks, the pilot of the Hunter, who fired himself out immediately after the collision. On this seat the drogue gun had fired but the drogues were not extracted from their container and the reason for this non-extraction was that the drogue withdrawal line had been severed, having been cut by impact with aircraft structure. The blow which had been received on the port side of the headrest was by impact with aircraft structure and not by impact with the ground. Crystallised perspex and perspex dust had accumulated in crevices in the top region of the port seat beam, particularly in the drogue gun top mounting bracket and this was indicative of a shattering blow on the aircraft hood before ejection.

The drogue line top stowage clip on the port seat beam was broken, also by structure impact damage, and this broken clip acted as a cutter, cutting the withdrawal line completely through about 3 inches from its attachment to the drogue gun piston. Also, the 'neoprene' sleeved automatic line was badly cut at the same position, evidently by the same means. This damage to the top portside of the headrest area indicated that the blow was sustained by impact with aircraft structure and not by the seat penetrating through the perspex aircraft hood and, it seemed from the marks, that the impacting object came from a forward port direction. It was noted that severe damage to the pilot's protective flying helmet had occurred in a co-incidental area and not on the top of the helmet which would be expected from contact with a closed perspex hood.

The main time release mechanism had correctly operated and opened the harness thus freeing the pilot from the seat. The pilot then separated from the seat, and, as the automatic line was still connected to the automatic rip cord, this separation opened the parachute. Evidently, the parachute developed, with the ejection seat still fastened to the parachute apex, as it was when we examined it. The pilot's descent would have been made in this condition. This would have a two-fold deleterious effect on the descent.

First, the drop speed would be increased by the additional weight of the ejection seat and, secondly, the ejection seat would continually obstruct the full development of the parachute. This second factor was substantiated by black dye marks on the parachute canopy, made by the ejection seat rubbing on it during the descent. The only other damage to the parachute is that No. 14 panel rip-cord had its 'V' strengthening gusset torn away from the periphery hem.

Pilot's Leg Injuries

As the stabilising drogues had not developed on this seat and because of the absence of leg restraining harness, the leg injury to the pilot is not surprising. (Note: Leg restraining harness will be retrospectively fitted on Mark 2H seat by Modification No. 272).

General

From the examination of the ejection equipment in this accident and a study of the location and distribution of aircraft wreckage, it seems that the collision occurred at about 10,000 ft and that the intercepting speed of the two aircraft, at the time of collision, was over 1,000 m.p.h.

In summarising his findings, Wg Cdr Jewell stated that the safe escape of these two airmen, in the exceptionally difficult environmental circumstances, was noted to be remarkable. A replacement Hunter F.4, XF999, arrived on 9 September and Peter Hicks was able to return to flying duties on 25 February 1957.

Russian Pot-Pourri

The Central Flying School had for some time past been one of the 'shop windows' of the Royal Air Force, so it came as no great surprise when the staff were informed that the Soviet Chief of Air Staff and a party of Russian Staff Officers were to visit CFS. An article in Air Clues summarised the event as follows:

"The original plan was for them to arrive at CFS (A) for lunch on Friday, 7 September. After lunch there was to be a tour of the Station, finishing with a flying demonstration of the new Jet Provost and the usual impeccable aerobatic display by "The Pelicans". The party was to stay the night in the Officers' Mess after having been taken to Stratford-upon-Avon to see a performance of 'Othello' at the Memorial Theatre. Things finally turned out rather differently but this was the basis on which planning for the visit commenced some weeks before the actual date.

For any visit of this description a mass of small details always has to be finalised and we then became involved in such things as arranging for cars, seats for the theatre, Guards of Honour, menus for supper in Stratford, interpreters, times of arrival and departure, bands, photographers, press publicity and of course the sordid question of finance. The latter is always a source of trouble on these occasions and negotiations with the finance divisions at Air Ministry became somewhat acrimonious before we finally convinced them of the fact that you could not give a Russian General a good 'blow out' with all the wines and trimmings that he would expect for a mere three shillings and sixpence.

The inevitable alterations to the planned programme started a few days before the visit. First of all the stop overnight and the visit to Stratford were put off. This cancelled a large number of special arrangements, which had only been made by the courtesy of various organisations and individuals in Stratford and we almost ran out of apologies by the time we had cancelled them all. Then we were told that the party would not travel by air but by road and this of course changed all the times of travel. We had hardly started thinking how to cope with that when we were told that they would travel by air after all! Half an hour before the actual arrival the news was passed that they would leave at 15:30 instead of 16:30.

To the casual observer it might of course appear to have been just as inconsequential as that but in fact the visit bore fruit in a number of ways. This was inevitable when you consider the personalities present. Among the Soviet Visitors there was Chief Marshal of Aviation Zhigarev, equivalent to our Chief of Air Staff; Marshal Sudets who holds a position equal to a C-in-C in the RAF; Lt Gen

The CO, QFIs, Staff and ground crews from one of the Vampire squadrons pose in front of one of their aircraft, circa 1956. (*Graham Pitchfork collection*)

Ponomarev who is a technical officer; Lt Gen Blagoveshehenski, a Soviet pilot of considerable experience and repute and who flew the dual Hunter at Farnborough; and Lt Gen Sinyakov, a navigation specialist. Four Senior Staff Officers of varying ranks and trades completed the party which also included Col Konstantinov, the Soviet Air Attaché in London. Accompanying the Party was Air Cdre MacDonell, our Air Attaché in Moscow and members of his staff. Air Marshal Sir Richard Atcherley was here to greet the party in his capacity as Air Officer Commanding-in-Chief Flying Training Command and he was accompanied by the AOC of No. 23 Group, Air Vice-Marshal Graham.

Thus, although the visit was finally a very short and hurried affair, we did in fact have an entertaining and instructive exchange of views and there is no doubt that our visitors left feeling very impressed by the standard of flying that we showed them and also by our meticulous attention to the details which go to make up a happy and efficient service."

Final Meteor Course

The final Meteor instructors Course concluded in September when three students on No. 179 Course completed their training. Two of them, Flt Lts Ray Hanna and Peter Evans, were to make their names with "The Red Arrows" a decade later. "The Pelicans" Meteor aerobatic team also disbanded at this time due to the posting of its leader Flt Lt Franklin and the reduction in establishment of Meteors at CFS to three. During the month three displays were given, one for a group of senior Soviet Air Force officers plus another at RAF Thorney Island and culminating with a display at Little Rissington. Students on subsequent courses were given a two-week proficiency period on the Meteor after completing the Vampire T.11 syllabus, prior to posting to Meteor or Canberra units.

At Home Day

The Battle of Britain At Home day saw the station open its doors to the public from 13:00 to 18:00 hours and approximately 10,000 people visited the base in 1,600 cars and 19 coaches, and on 301 motor cycles and 176 bicycles. Specially invited guests for the occasion were a number of staff comprising a Soviet Air Force delegation, headed by Marshal Zhigarev, Soviet Chief of Air Staff. After lunch in the Officers' Mess they were given a brief tour of Flying Wing before settling down to watch the air display.

Aircraft incidents

Two incidents incurring damage to aircraft occurred in October, the first involving Hunter F.4, WV325 which suffered a partial engine failure due to a broken turbine blade; Cat. 3 damage was caused to the air intake boundary layer ducts. In the second, the brakes were applied on Vampire T.11, XE893/IS just prior to take off, causing damage to both mainwheel tyres. On landing, the port tyre disintegrated causing major damage to the undercarriage.

1957

New years Honours

Four Little Rissington personnel were recognised in the 1957 New Year's Honours list:

Sqn Ldr D.L. Hughes, 3 Squadron – AFC
Flt Lt J. Stanley, 3 Squadron – AFC
Flt Lt Allum, 4 Squadron – Queen's Commendation
W O A. Randell – MBE.

Unscheduled engine change!

As the result of improperly refitting a voltage regulator cover, the cover entered the air intake on Vampire T11, XD590 and the engine had to be changed. Charges were brought against both the NCO and airman responsible.

Those were the days, my friend

Former aviation medicine specialist, Doctor and later Squadron Leader, N.C. 'Nick' Lee flew Venoms in Germany before undertaking his QFI course and moving on to Oxford UAS.

"The after effects of Rissy are still engraved on both my heart and liver – there was much more I could have put in. Firstly, there were experiences in 'The Bay Tree' at Burford, where nubile young maidens were trained into dealing with the vagaries and temptations of the hotel and catering trade, not to mention the amorous attentions of hot-blooded young jet jockeys. Secondly, not revealed here for public consumption was that slice of my misspent youth at 'The Shaven Crown' in Shipton-under-Wychwood, thankfully still going strong today.

My arrival at Little Rissington to partake in No. 184 course was a trifle unusual. I was on my way there from London but happened to bump into some old friends in Oxford, so a somewhat beery impromptu reunion ensued. This was of course long before the days of breathalysers and threats to your driving licence. I remember being in the Mitre (Bishop's titfer), the Eagle and Child (Bird and Baby), the Golden Ball (Lacquered Knacker) and a few other well-known hostelries in the Oxford area, so I was feeling no pain at all when I set out from Oxford at about 9 pm to find Rissy. Unfortunately, I only had a venerable AA map which didn't show where it was. Without my trusty 1 in 500,000 flying chart with me, I knew roughly where the airfield was but not how to get to it by road. A little innovation was called for. According to my slightly fuddled reckoning, Rissy was about 285° True from Oxford, so as there was a moonless clear sky that night, I set off across country using the Pole star as a reference point. It was an interesting journey involving ploughed fields, farmyards, muddy cul-de-sacs, barking dogs and lights being switched on in upstairs bedrooms, but I got there eventually. I was jolting along in the midst of nowhere, just about to give up and doss down in the back of the car for the rest of the night when I saw a set of approach lights looming up ahead. Sure enough, they were those of Rissy's main runway. Eureka!

I had been looking forward to seeing what Little Rissington was like, as most of our instructors at South Cerney had taken great delight in telling us that South Cerney was 'Happy Valley', so we had better enjoy it, while we could, before going to 'Hell on the Hill'. In retrospect, I found it quite the other way around. Perhaps my opinion of Cerney was coloured by an unwelcome episode in which the OC Flying caught two of us in the local Cinema one Wednesday afternoon when we should have been playing sport. Our explanation that we had been beagling but couldn't keep up with the dogs didn't wash. Ah well, can't win them all.

Most of us on the CFS course were ex-2nd TAF, so were haughtily aware that we were pretty hot stuff in the air and that there wasn't much more that anyone could teach us about flying. How very wrong we were! I never knew that the dear old Vampire T.11 was capable of such things as we did to it. At that time, there had been a scare that there were some rogue T.11s around in Training Command, which would not recover from a spin. A doughty team from the Trappers went around, put every single T.11 into at least an 8-turn spin and recovered without incident. One of these airborne warriors, George Beaton, was my instructor, so we spent more time in unusual positions (unusual to me at least) than average. Then of course there was the big bonus – going over to Kemble to fly the Hunter F.4. At that time, the Hunter was looked upon with awe. Not only was it a beautiful looking aircraft but its performance after the humdrum T.11 was little short of spectacular. In fact, a young JP at Oldenburg had been heard to mourn into his beer: 'Man has at last built a machine that he cannot master…'. The Hunter had a few unexpected foibles like, for instance, doing a loop and not being able to check the wings against the horizon while going through the vertical. Oops! No wings! They were swept back too far to be seen – old stuff now but somewhat startling at the time.

The big boss at Rissy at the time was Air Cdre 'Hetty' Hyde, a most engaging, urbane man who called everyone (whether singular or plural) 'Chaps'. He always had a quizzical look about him as though he was nursing some private joke that he wasn't quite ready to share with you. At one of the cocktail parties, he said that he had just heard that he had been posted to (the then) Malaya as the AOC there, and asked me whether I'd like to come along as his PSO. 'Of course, chaps', he mused, 'you'll have to wear a funny hat and a robe'. He never repeated the offer and, from that day to this, I've never been quite sure whether he was joking or not.

Sadly, my flying instructional career did not last that long. This was the time of the 1957 Sandys Defence White Paper, which prognosticated that 'the day of the manned aircraft was over', and from here on in the future was going to be all missiles. This meant that although most of us recognised it for the horse manure that it was, there were clearly going to be massive redundancies in the RAF. All the eggheads pushed off to Burbank to learn about missiles and things, while the rest of us, who had difficulty in totting up the figures in our logbooks each month, started looking for something else to do, which is how I came to study medicine. One thing that Rissy did for me, apart from giving me a hugely enjoyable experience, was to provide me with a conversational gambit that not many medical officers could come out with – 'When I was on the QFI course at Little Rissington ….'."

New aerobatic team

In the early spring of 1957, HQ Flying Training Command decided that it would be desirable to contribute a formation aerobatic team from CFS for the SBAC show at Farnborough in the September. Suggestions that the team should be formed of Hunter F.4s were dismissed because of lack of aircraft and it was felt that the Vampire T.11 was not suitable, so the onus fell on Basic Squadron and the Piston Provost. A four-ship team was formed with Flt Lts Charlie Kingsbury, Les Howes, Bert Lane and Mike Bradley with Flt Lt Black as reserve. The team worked-up with appearances at a number of air shows culminating with impressive performances at Farnborough and a brace of Battle of Britain open days.

Getting in some practice for the start of the 1957 air show season, the four Piston Provosts in echelon formation. (*David Watkins*)

The Sandys White paper

April 1957 will be remembered by military historians for the infamous White Paper published by the Minister of Defence, Duncan Sandys, as it called into question the very need for the Royal Air Force. Claiming to be the greatest change ever made to the country's defence system in peace-time, it mistakenly established that manned aircraft would soon be superseded completely by guided missiles for both attack and defence and, as pilots would no longer be needed, production contracts for aircraft such as the Hunter were to be cancelled. Production of the Lightning the RAF's first true supersonic fighter would proceed however.

With no need to teach men how to fly fighters and bombers, the effect on flying training schools would have been catastrophic and a bleak future lay ahead for CFS had the Paper been implemented in full. And Little Rissington would probably have closed much sooner than it did. A dark shadow hung over the RAF for some time before gradual recognition that Sandys had made a huge gaff became clear and projects for new piloted-aircraft were given the go-ahead. In anticipation, the RAF revised its training policy, making known its intent to become the first air force in the world to introduce all-through jet training.

Four Vampire T.11 aircraft XD621/IO, XD541/IT, XD605/IU and XD436/IB, shimmer in the sun during a high level formation photo sortie in 1957, the pilots enjoying the relative comfort of a spacious cockpit prior to the fitting of ejection seats in the trainer. (*David Watkins*)

Faulty Goblin and a lucky escape

Flt Lt Keith Rice left Cranwell to join the CFS 'Waterfront' in April 1956, already with Harvard, Chipmunk, Provost, Balliol and Vampire instructional experience under his belt after the rapid changes in RAF College trainer aircraft in the previous two years. Keith stayed at Rissy until August 1957 before his promotional posting to take over Bristol UAS.

"The comparatively short time I spent at 'Hell on the Hill' was both busy and most enjoyable – Rissy was a happy place to be and getting paid as well was the icing on the cake. I was lucky on this tour too. An engine failure immediately after take off in a Vampire T.11 happened just high enough for me to do a full 180 degree 'turnback' for real to land back safely on the reciprocal runway with no one taking off behind me. At Kemble, where each of us could do a day's Hunter flying every six months, an undercarriage leg snapped on landing after metal fatigue, promptly leaving me staring at a line of parked Javelins before coming to a grateful halt about 200 yds from them.

My most vivid memory was the social life at that time, in particular our Guest nights and the CFSA reunions. Our Commandant, Air Cdre 'Hetty' Hyde, was a noted firework enthusiast and it would be an unusual Guest night when, soon after dinner, it was still possible to see through the smoke to the other side of the anteroom. On one occasion our Commandant chose to lob a thunderflash into the crowd around the temporary bar just at the moment when the collapsible table collapsed, taking with it several chaps who were leaning against it. The left ear of one such chap arrived in neat formation with the exact time and place as the thunderflash, with the result that the AOC's PA was able to listen most attentively to the explosion, which punctured an eardrum. Because his aircrew medical category was at stake and compensation might be involved if he had lost it, a formal enquiry was now needed. With a major witness an Air Cdre, the Board would need an Air Vice-Marshal in charge. Fortunately it was not too long before the eardrum healed itself with no other ramifications so this splendidly senior Inquiry never saw the light of day.

Another occasion, either at a formal VIP lunch or CFSA reunion, may not have involved Hetty but his spirit did certainly live on. The guest of honour that day was Duncan Sandys. As Defence Minister he had recently brought out his infamous 1957 White Paper introducing missiles in place of many front line aircraft and was now about to take his seat at the top table. He cannot have failed to see, about three feet above him and slightly to his front, a paper notice proclaiming 'The Sandys of time are running out'. This streamer was suspended by some rough, 'hairy' binder twine from a large balloon, floating and bobbing against the Mess Dining Room's glass panelled ceiling. I remember thinking what cheap and nasty string – surely, if we expected him to hang himself, we ought at least to have supplied a decent silken rope. An ex-Etonian Territorial artilleryman, Sandys had been the Chairman of the War Cabinet committee for defence against V-weapons, so just may or may not have noticed the single strand of wire also in front and above him, sloping gradually upwards and away from left to right.

At the appropriate time after the meal, probably after the president's welcoming speech, a little model aircraft appeared and slid slowly down the wire. As this neared the centre of the top table a model missile also appeared and rapidly followed the aircraft so that it overtook and intercepted it, producing a most impressive explosion, complete with a shower of sparks over our said guest of honour. A hand then reached up with a cigarette lighter and set fire to the 'Sandys of time' notice. The flame from this rapidly travelled up the 'hairy' string to the balloon, demonstrating some method in our meanness. There then followed the most enormous bang, which shook the building, yet did not even crack the glass – one missile, one aircraft and one hydrogen bomb! I think the only casualties were a dinner suit or two, which suffered collateral incendiary damage from sparks, but the message certainly did reach its intended target at high level".

Amalgamation

Beginning on 16 May 1957, the first contingent of CFS (Basic) moved from South Cerney to Little Rissington as part of a planned amalgamation with CFS (Advanced). This involved the transfer of 12 Officers, 2 Flight Sergeants, 4 Sergeants, 7 Corporals and 37 Airmen from South Cerney to Little Rissington. Included with this element was the "Sparrows" formation aerobatic team.

South Cerney remained home to the CFS Helicopter Squadron with a secondary role of Relief Landing Ground (RLG) for the Piston Provosts. At Little Rissington, the amalgamation effected changes within the Squadrons, No. 1 being reorganised into three Piston Provost Flights and No. 2 into two Flights of Vampires. The Vampires operated from the surfaced runways and when conditions allowed, the Provosts from the grass. To lighten the load on the circuit and the nerves of controllers and instructors, Kemble was used for circuit-bashing by the jets and heavier piston-engined aircraft.

Following the amalgamation a semi-specialised course structure was introduced and intakes now comprised 42 students every 9 weeks. During the first half of the sixteen week course, all students received 51 hours' basic Provost instruction after which the intake was split in two. Twenty students continued on the Provost with 27 hours' applied instruction before completing their course flying aircraft operated by Type Flight. These students were then posted as QFIs on piston-powered units. The remaining 22 students moved on to the Vampire where they received 40 hours' instruction plus a short spell on Type Flight, before being posted as QFIs on jet-powered units. All students undertook a common ground school syllabus.

Type flexibility: all part of a CFS QFI's job

Flt Lt Don McClen was on No. 175 course at South Cerney and Little Rissington from November 1955 until late March 1956 when he was posted as a flying instructor to Aberdeen University Air Squadron, despite never having flown, let alone instructed on, a Chipmunk before!

"CFS was planning to move the Piston Provosts from South Cerney to Little Rissington at the beginning of July 1957, only two months after my arrival, so that all the QFI training (principally on the Piston Provost and Vampire T.11) could be done from one location. The first professional problem, which occupied my own mind, however, was that I had not taught anyone to fly the Piston Provost. Neither had I even flown the Piston Provost since being at South Cerney on the CFS course sixteen months previously. Flying instructors at CFS had distinguished themselves in many ways over the years. My first thoughts were, therefore, how the hell could I be expected to live up to their standards!

After a few hours of revision flying on the Piston Provost and avuncular advice from my betters and elders, I was let loose. As expected, my first few students took some convincing that I knew what I was talking about, especially as it was common knowledge that my experience as an instructor was limited to a year on Chipmunks. Although the basic patter for ab initio flying instruction was similar for all training aircraft, it would have helped had I known from first hand experience what kind of faults might be expected in a raw student being taught on a Piston Provost, with its more sophisticated systems and quite different handling characteristics. Furthermore, the instructor sat behind the student in a tandem arrangement in the Chipmunk, whereas in the Provost the seating arrangement was side by side. Inevitably, of course, when I was demonstrating a particular manoeuvre, it took a few sorties before my handling of the aircraft matched, as accurately as it should have, my line in patter.

As if that introduction wasn't testing enough, I was next asked to complete a refresher course on the Vampire so that I could help out in training students to instruct on Vampires – not that I had ever instructed on Vampires either! I was getting used to such demands by now so this time I was quite unperturbed! Flexibility and variety were the hallmarks of my predecessors at CFS; it seemed appropriate that I should accept the tradition.

A much easier request was to join the CFS Examining Wing for a visit to Oxford University Air Squadron to carry out standardisation tests on their instructors and students in the Chipmunk. I felt confident that I knew what to look for!"

Hunter familiarisation

In June, the opportunity was taken by 28 members of CFS staff to refresh their skills on the Hunter with a programme of flying the aircraft of the Type Flight at Kemble.

Honours and awards

The following personnel on the station were recognised in the Queens' birthday Honours list:

Flt Sgt Terry	–	AOC's commendation.
Flt Sgt Hurdle	–	AOC's commendation
Sgt Cobb	–	Long service medal
W O Taylor	–	Certificate of merit

Flt Sgt Lucas received an AOC's commendation with effect from 1 January 1957.

Sports day

The station sports day was held and resulted in a win for Flying Wing with 165 points, with Admin Wing taking the runners-up slot with 124 points and Tech. Wing 3rd with 91 points. A team of ten of the best athletes was selected and sent to compete in the Command sports competition held at RAF Cranwell.

Type Squadron forms

On 10 July, a Type Squadron was formed by merging CFS Headquarters Flight and the Type Flight, operating Canberra, Meteor, Vampire and Communication Flights at Little Rissington and a Hunter Flight at Kemble under the command of Sqn Ldr M. Adams. The new Squadron compositions and establishments are summarised below:

1 Squadron Three Flights operating 22 Piston Provost T.Mk.1.

2 Squadron One Flight with 15 Vampire T.Mk.11.

Type Squadron Divided into four Flights:

Meteor/Canberra	3 Meteor T.Mk.7, 3 Canberra T.Mk.4
Hunter	5 Hunter F.Mk.4 (based at Kemble)
Vampire	4 Vampire T.Mk.11 (under 2 Squadron for servicing)
Communications	1 Valetta C.Mk.1, 3 Anson C.Mk.19, 2 Piston Provost T.Mk.1

Flt Lt Roy Davis was placed in charge of the Hunter Flight assisted by Flt Lt Denis Witham, and with ground support provided by the civilian staff of 5 MU under the management of Mr Phillips. The unit was housed in a wooden hut near the north end of Kemble's main runway 27. The Meteor Flight was commanded by Flt Lt 'Mac' McArthur in collaboration with Flt Lt 'Denny' Beard.

The first Canberra T.4, WD944, had arrived in June and the

(*left*), Judging by the position of the steps, Canberra T.4, WJ991-CB, is about to receive a new starter cartridge in the starboard engine, outside Type Flight's crewrooms. Meanwhile over at Kemble (*below*), the presence of a generator and hydraulic rig indicate rectification work is in progress on Type Flight's Hunter F.4, XF935-D. (*MAP*)

Canberra Flight placed under the command of Flt Lt George Beaton. With no Canberra towing arm on site at the time, the aircraft had to be manhandled into 1 Hangar for the Aircraft Servicing Flight (ASF) to carry out acceptance checks. Flt Sgt Coates then scoured the unit for ex-Canberra tradesmen for assignment to a servicing team led by Sgt Parker. A second T.4 which, like the first, was painted all-over silver with yellow training bands arrived in the autumn.

Revised hangar allocations were as follows:

1 Hangar	Aircraft Servicing Flight (ASF)
2 Hangar	1 Squadron C+B Flights, Comms Flight
3 Hangar	1 Squadron A Flight, Type Squadron HQ (Canberras)
4 Hangar	2 Squadron Vampires and Vampire Type Flight
5 Hangar	MT Repair Section
6 Hangar	Meteor Type Flight

Number 6 Hangar, which was located on the apron to the south of 4 Hangar, was demolished in about 1958 and the Meteors moved into 4 Hangar.

Two Hangars, Nos. 3 and 5, were placed under the control of Technical Wing which was divided into three Squadrons; Engineering, Signals and Armament. Hangar 3 was assigned for aircraft servicing, 5 Hangar for the servicing of mechanical transport. The Electrical and Instrument Flights were accommodated in the annexe of 2 Hangar and the Radio/Radar Servicing Flight was housed in the annexe to 3 Hangar. The Station Armoury was housed in a separate building, the main task of the armourers being the servicing of revolvers, rifles and ejection seats. Also housed in a separate building were the Station Workshops, its responsibility being to maintain Station facilities at a high level of efficiency.

Provost/Vampire training – initial assessment

An early assessment of progress on the second phase of the Piston Provost/Vampire training format was acquired during a visit to 5 FTS at RAF Oakington by CFS staff on 3 June. They learned that having completed Phase 1, students moved on to 5 FTS for the Vampire phase and that the average course comprised 16 students and had a duration of 42 weeks.

Two weeks later a team of CFS 'Trappers' visited the Maritime Operational Training Unit (MOTU) at RAF Kinloss to test instructors converting Neptune pilots onto the Shackleton.

At Home Day

The CFS At Home day display lasted three hours and included displays by a variety of aircraft types ranging from the Folland Gnat Fighter to the V-Force. Included in the show was a 'savage' attack by six Piston Provosts on an armoured car and formation aerobatics by "The Sparrows" and a CFS team called "The Helicans", a Hunter F.4 leading two Meteor T.7s. For the set piece, a large guided missile and its site was dramatically destroyed by six Vampire T.11s for the 'loss' of one aircraft. A crowd of several thousand enjoyed the spectacle.

Royal visit

July 1957 was a busy month the highlight of which was a visit by HRH Princess Margaret on the 23rd, the first official royal visit since that of her grandmother, Queen Mary, to the ECFS at Hullavington in 1945. Her Royal Highness arrived at 11:30 in a gleaming silver Viking of The Queen's Flight to be greeted by a small contingent of senior officers in ceremonial dress headed by the Deputy Lieutenant for the County of Gloucestershire, Lord Ashton of Hyde, who presented Air Marshal Sir Richard Atcherley (known as 'Batchy' by fellow officers) and the Commandant, Air Cdre N. C. Hyde (who was known as 'Hetty'). Following an inspection of the Guard of Honour, the Princess was escorted to 2 Hangar, where a collection of historical aircraft had been lined up for her to review. These included an Avro 504K, a Bristol Fighter F.2B, Caudron biplane, Sopwith Camel, S.E.5A, Tiger Moth, Harvard, Vampire T.11 and Hunter F.4. Her Royal Highness then inspected the WRAF quarters, before taking lunch in the Officers' Mess. An air display in the afternoon commenced with a flypast by a Hunter, two Vampires and a Meteor. Further displays by a solo Hunter, two Vampires and four Piston Provosts were performed before a finale of twelve Piston Provosts and twelve Vampire T.11s appearing from opposite directions and crossing in front of the Royal Enclosure. Shortly before her departure, Her Royal Highness presented the Wright Jubilee Trophy to the winner of the competition, Fg Off Rorison.

Princess Margaret and the Sopwith Camel

Flt Lt McClen was given the task of briefing the Princess on the Sopwith Camel, one of the most famous fighter of the First World War.

"I described the aircraft's history and fighting characteristics as elegantly and succinctly as I could, with the AOC Flying Training Command, Air Marshal Sir Richard 'Batchy' Atcherley (a committed bachelor, one of the great characters in CFS folklore, and the first serving officer to win the King's Cup Air Race, in 1929) looking on, together with the Commandant, Air Cdre 'Hetty' Hyde, and visiting dignitaries. A photograph of that event shows Princess Margaret regarding me with a slightly mocking, if not downright supercilious, smile. I was probably being compared unfavourably with the love of her life, Gp Capt Peter Townsend."

Instructor qualities

A memorandum at about this time notes that "CFS demands high qualities for pilots selected for instructor training:

1. He must already be both an experienced and skilful pilot, who has served a tour of duty with a front line squadron.
2. He must have a good technical knowledge because a modern flying instructor is required not only to be able to demonstrate what an aeroplane can do in the air but has to be able to understand and explain the aerodynamic principles of flight which govern its behaviour.
3. He must be something of a meteorologist and an engineer with a sound grasp of radio, radar and gyroscopic instruments.
4. He must be able to impart knowledge and skill patiently, clearly and interestingly to a pupil.
5. Finally he must be something of a leader – a man who keeps fit, lives cleanly, has high ideals and lives up to them.

A flying instructor has a great influence on his pupils, who have to develop into men of skill and courage to fly and fight in any weather and against any odds as members of our first line of defence."

Cerney transfer completed

The move from South Cerney was completed in August by which time most of the Piston Provosts operated by Comms. Flight had been transferred to 1 Squadron, just two Provosts, a Valetta and three Ansons remaining for the Communications function.

During her visit to Little Rissington, HRH Princess Margaret was given a tour of static aircraft paraded in one of the hangars and is seen here accompanied by Flt Lt Norman Giffin, senior officers and various dignitaries. (*Norman Giffin*)

CFS Staff recruitment

The task of recruiting qualified instructors for positions on the Staff at the CFS was a continual process, and appointments were often made by chance meetings. One such encounter was when Flt Lt Norman Giffin, who was instructing at RAF Syerston at the time, met one of his instructors from his initial training days at Cranwell during a visit by CFS Examiners. *"On successfully completing my A2 recategorisation, the Examiner asked me if I would consider a Staff position at the CFS. 'Yes I would', I replied without hesitation and following an interview with Air Cdre Paul, I moved down to Rissy a few weeks later as a Piston Provost instructor."*

Jet Provost trial concludes

Coinciding with Norman's posting, the evaluation of the Jet Provost T.Mk.1 as a basic jet trainer for the RAF at 2 FTS, RAF Hullavington was winding down and Hunting Percival was given the green light to produce a developed version for full scale production. Students would soon be flying jet aircraft from their first day in the air.

With the completion of the experimental courses at Hullavington, seven T.ls, XD675-680 and 693, were transferred to CFS with the first aircraft arriving on 19 November 1957. This enabled CFS staff to familiarise themselves with the aircraft. Over the next two years, these aircraft were used to train 141 RAF, 4 Royal Navy, 10 Army Air Corps and 6 overseas air force pilots to QFI standard.

The turning point in Don McClen's tour at Little Rissington occurred with the arrival of the Jet Provosts from Hullavington. *"My first flight in the JP was on 2 December, 1957 with a fellow instructor, Freddy Packer, who had flown it at Hullavington. The JP Mk 1 had an Armstrong Siddeley Viper engine producing 1,750 lb of thrust, with a maximum speed of 330 mph at 20,000 ft. In performance terms it could reach 20,000 ft in 11½ minutes and 30,000 ft in 23 minutes, and with Martin Baker lightweight ejection seats, it was a far cry from the Tiger Moth, on which I had done my own basic training in Southern Rhodesia."*

AM Sir John Kemball KCB CBE

Sir John Kemball, who was Commandant of the Central Flying School between 1983 and 1985 before appointments as Commander British Forces Falkland Islands and Chief of Staff and Deputy to C-in-C Strike Command, recalls, through Plt Off R.J. Kemball's eyes, some unusual events surrounding the return of the first 'creamed off' students for some time on No. 189 Course.

"At Hornchurch and South Cerney on my National Service, I had been pre-selected for pilot training – I was half way through Feltwell and the Provost stage, when I was told that I would not be able to finish the course unless I stayed in the service for 3 years. On completing my Wings at Oakington I was off on leave late in 1957, expecting to be posted as Assistant Adjutant at Booker. Six of us, all from Oakington, were then posted as trainee first tour instructors to No. 189 Course at Little Rissington. Harry Gill and the late Mike Morrissey (ex-FAA), went with me. QFIs I particularly remember were two South Africans, Mike Langley and Mike Holmes. After the Provost stage at Rissy all the other five were allocated to the Vampire, with myself being the sole exception on basic instruction. An unusual aspect of my own time was having a good instructor, 'Mo' Ahmed, who was a Pakistani exchange officer.

As with others before and afterwards I had been promised my first choice of a flying posting at the end of my QFI tour. However, I could be streamed for Lightnings or Hunters later only if I remained 5 years: this sounded worthwhile, although I was still intending to go to Trinity at close of play. All five others progressed right the way through the whole course and had even taken their Final Handling Tests before their being scrubbed all in one fell swoop. Whatever explained these strange circumstances still puzzles me today. On one final personal side, a further exception occurred – I was 'specially picked', so they said, for the urgent filling of an ADC's position with AM Sir Maurice Heath, Chief of Staff to Paddy Bandon, then COMAIRCENT, definitely not how I had understood my promise of a choice flying tour but I suppose that my next tour in Aden on No. 8 Squadron was worth some of that extra waiting.

For both students and instructors as an ab initio trainer the Provost was good from every point of view. The Tucano might be economical and the Jet Provost had certain other virtues but for a first stage military trainer surely both of these were too easy to fly to be outstanding training aircraft.

One obvious change, which I noted over the 26 years between my CFS involvements, was how under ever increasing budgetary constraints, the academic psychologists and education specialists seemed to have had a stranglehold on flying training 'by Objectives'. Their emphasis was for everyone to simply soldier through to the required minimum standards for squadron service than the total potential of the really good pilots being particularly stretched as far as possible. Looking back there did seem also to be a different mix of background in the Training world. When I began my own flying training, at least half the instructors seemed to have come off Hunters or Venoms, whereas later it appeared that a combination of V-Force and Hercules backgrounds affected the overall ethos and training philosophies in the Command."

Jet Provost Mark 2

The solitary Jet Provost T.Mk.2 (XD694, a conversion of a Mark 1 airframe) to serve with the RAF was used for a period by the CFS, after trials at Boscombe Down, for QFI training before it was flown to 27 MU at RAF Shawbury where it was scrapped in 1960.

The 'Trappers' return and disband

The Examining Wing returned to Little Rissington earlier in the year and in addition to carrying out visits to several UK establishments, its Staff made overseas visits to the air forces of Ceylon, FEAF, Pakistan, Canada and the USA. Their stay, however, was short-lived as the Wing was disbanded in November and divided to become the Directing Staff and the Standards Squadron.

1958

Sandys Axe triggers 100% volunteers

The disbandment of nine Hunter and six Venom Squadrons in 2nd TAF in 1957, and many others elsewhere, was the direct result of defence cuts introduced by Duncan Sandys. Flt Lt Peter Frame, who was flying Sabres and Hunters with No. 112 Squadron at RAF Brüggen at the time, recalls the more positive knock-on effects of these cutbacks for the CFS and FTC.

"Regrettably I do not have a host of funny stories to tell and would be sued if I quoted some of them. I was on No. 191 Course from 9 December 1957 to 18 April 1958, which was the first split (Piston) Provost/Vampire course. My own course flying amounted to 56 hours dual and 56 hours solo and mutual flying, almost equally split between the basic Provost and Applied Vampire stages. In those days Rissy was full of real volunteers, since we had all been made redundant from our Squadrons in Germany, courtesy of Duncan Sandys. The only way to keep flying was to volunteer for CFS. Consequently most of us knew each other already, which made for a more enjoyable course than otherwise. In fact there was a waiting list to get on the course; I had to wait five months for mine.

I didn't enjoy the Piston Provost phase because I couldn't get the hang of these funny three point landings, although I had originally been trained ab initio on the mighty Harvard in Canada and without any pre-grading on Tigers. When I greased it in on the main wheels, I was told off and when, occasionally, I performed a three pointer I was praised. Didn't make sense to me! The Vampire phase was more to my liking and my instructor was Pete Phillips, well known for his aerobatic prowess, so we got along fine. The only thing I knew about patter was gleaned from fellow course members on mutual sorties. Nevertheless I somehow managed to graduate as a B1 rather than a B2."

Formation of fast jets specially flown for the 1957 CFS Christmas card photograph. (*Michael Bradley*)

Jet powered aerobatic team

In January 'Batchy' Atcherley decided that the Jet Provosts should form a new CFS display team, "The CFS Jet Aerobatic Team", and volunteers were invited to apply. Flt Lts Freddy Packer, Don McClen and Peter Millington put their names forward and their applications were approved. Flt Lt Norman Giffin, a more experienced instructor, was selected as formation leader. Between them they agreed that Don would fly in the number two position, with Freddy in three, and Peter in four. *"Unfortunately"*, recalls Flt Lt 'Curly' Hirst, *"because of the difficulties in maintaining this additional fleet of aircraft (which amongst other undesirable characteristics employed a pneumatic system for raising and lowering the undercarriage!) the CFS engineers could only guarantee to provide a maximum of five aircraft for the new team – four plus one spare."*

The five Jet Provosts were despatched to RAF St Athan early in the year for repainting in a special red and white colour scheme. Being the first of its kind the aircraft had several characteristics that would limit the complexity of manoeuvres the team could pursue, and the most important of these are outlined by Norman Giffin.

"Because Hunting Aviation had been instructed to utilise as many Piston Provost T.1 parts in the Jet Provost T.1, (I think about 45% was achieved) the end result was an aircraft which although it had a jet engine, the wings, tail assembly etc, and ancillaries were not really suited to a jet aircraft. The top speed was therefore not as high as it could have been, but the handling characteristics were first class. The very long undercarriage legs were a characteristic of the JP1 which had been designed to try to give a safe clearance at the tail pipe when landing – this clearance was reduced greatly in later marks of JP. The engine was a Viper which was designed for use by a guided weapon and adapted for the JP. Because there was so little thrust from the engine, the JP1 was often referred to as 'a constant thrust, variable noise' aircraft.

After several close formation flights to explore the performance and flying characteristics of our aircraft, we discussed what sequences we

Flt Lt Norman Giffin leads his newly formed team of four Jet Provost T.1s, XD680, 676, 677 and 678, for a photo-shoot with an accompanying Meteor T.7. (*Norman Giffin*)

should practise. We agreed that one approach I should investigate with Freddy Packer was the pre-war CFS tradition of performing formation aerobatics with the aircraft connected by coloured streamers. So we attached a long piece of stout string to his cockpit and fed this into my cockpit, allowing about twenty feet of slack. Having agreed to test the limits in formation aerobatics while keeping the string from snapping, we took off in close formation. After a few tentative turns to gain confidence, Freddy flew some barrel rolls and loops. I kept my position without too much difficulty but we quickly realised that we would be severely constrained in the variety of manoeuvres we could perform, if all four of us were attached to each other in this way. So, having concluded that there was no particular merit in further trials, we turned towards base and lost interest in the string.

When the string snapped, I was not particularly perturbed until I became aware that the engine revolutions were reducing with a corresponding dramatic rise in the jet engine temperature towards the upper limit. I was incredulous at what was happening but I had no choice than to close down the engine and make a forced landing on the airfield. When the engineers removed the engine panels they discovered that the string had been ingested through the engine intake, and wound itself around the axis of the compressor. The string had inhibited normal rotation of the compressor and effectively caused engine failure. We all registered astonishment, engineers and pilots alike, and agreed that this particular CFS pre-war tradition was no longer appropriate!

Our formation practice thereafter proceeded along more conventional lines. We embraced a variety of formation changes during the aerobatic manoeuvres, including an inverted loop performed by the leader (another CFS tradition from pre-war years) while the rest formated on him in the normal way. The negative g throughout the loop put quite a physical strain on me. Finishing our display with a formation landing put quite a different sort of strain on Peter Millington; he had to formate below the jet pipe of the leading aircraft while judging his round-out for landing on the runway before the leader touched down.

To generate even greater interest we asked the engineers to design a smoke container, which could be attached to the underside of each of the wings, and triggered off by a switch in the cockpit. This could only be operated once but it did allow us to finish our programme with a flourish."

Standards Wing

The Examining Wing had undertaken the testing of instructors on every operational aircraft type in service with the RAF for decades, but the growing complexity of aircraft entering service made it progressively more difficult for the 'Trappers' to be proficient on each type. The formation of the CFS Type Flight with its Hunter fighters and Meteor and Canberra trainers had provided limited access to operational types, but this was no longer acceptable in a fast changing air force. In consequence, Air Marshal Sir Richard Atcherley, C-in-C Flying Training Command, announced in March 1958 the formation of the Standards Wing as successor to the Examining Wing, and that in future it would be responsible for testing aircraft types that were available solely within Flying Training Command.

Agency scheme

To ensure the capacity of CFS instructors to remain fully conversant with the operation of every type of front-line aircraft, and the standards of training, recategorisation and upgrading of CFS qualified instructors, along with testing the instrument rating examiners at operational units and certain OCUs, an Agency scheme was devised. Under this scheme, which was administered by Standards Wing, the agents were selected from QFIs serving on units flying the operational types. Their Agency commitment was small and involved liaison with CFS personnel during visits to their units, and attending the annual Agents Convention at Little Rissington. Eventually, each flying training school formed a small Standards Squadron, under the control of the Station Commander.

Return to Ris as Meteor QFI

After instructing at 7 FTS Cottesmore and converting a future Commandant, Sqn Ldr Ivor Broom, to the Meteor, Flt Lt Mike Dobson undertook a three and a half year tour at Valley as an A2 instructor before returning to Little Rissington as a trapper in March 1958.

"At the time I was up at Woodford on the initial ground side for Vulcan conversion for briefing by Roly Falk on how easy the Vulcan was to fly – so I had mixed feelings about re-deployment back to CFS. I remember flying AOC No.1 Group, Gus Walker, later AOC-in-C Flying Training, Charles Whitworth and wives to and from a boxing match at Bassingbourn with a late night flight return to Finningley in Gus's VIP Anson. As many others can testify, Gus Walker was able to fly the Canberra more accurately with one arm than most two-handed pilots.

Mostly on Meteors and presumably recruited for my specialist Canberra background, after my Command IRE qualification in November 1958, I was encouraged to take my re-categorisation to A1 standard on the Canberra T.4. This took the form of all my ground knowledge examination over one full day taken by OC Multi Standards, Sqn Ldr Norwood. Ironically the specialist topic given me to thoroughly research and lecture on was 'Early Propeller Developments', from underpowered single to high powered multi-bladers, in the morning before a wide-ranging but fairly relaxed formal coverage of the instructor's job in the afternoon. My airborne instruction flying test was done on one Canberra T.4 sortie with Flt Lt 'Nibby' Fellows, as ever at CFS being examined on asymmetric flying after demonstrating Canberra aerobatics in both looping and rolling planes. My Multi Standards work required conversion on to the Valetta and Varsity, besides examining occasionally on other multi-engined aircraft such as the Devon at Northolt.

On 1 April 1959, I again flew with the Commandant, Air Cdre Whitworth, in Canberra T.4, WT480, on a visit to Rhodesia routeing via Luqa and El Adem. Flt Lt Preston was our navigator and the CI and Sqn Ldr M. 'Bill' Adams flew in a second Canberra. Luqa as usual was a three-hour leg, with 1hr 20min on to El Adem for night stop. The next day was a 2hr 50min flight down to Khartoum and just over two and a half hours down to Nairobi, having to stay above 40,000 ft to clear Inter Tropical Front cumulonimbus clouds. On 3 April a 2hr 35min flight took us from Eastleigh to Salisbury. Our Royal Rhodesian Air Force hosts were most interested in every aspect of the Canberra and part of the visit's aim was to explore the possibility of the RAF renewing an overseas flying training school there. The Canberras performed well from every point of view. On our 8/9 April return flight with favourable winds, I experimented with the newish 'cruise climb' technique, slowly reaching 48,000 ft on our final, homeward north-westerly leg from Luqa. Although we had taken off from Rissy we had to land back at Kemble for customs clearance.

Seven weeks later, on 1 June, I was off again, this time in Valetta C.1, WJ496, to Madrid and Lisbon with the CI, Wg Cdr Peter Gilpin, and six passengers. This was my last overseas trip as a trapper for in the following month I was posted and promoted as OC 2 Squadron at Manby and Strubby. For me, from the course, through instructing and examining at Little Rissington and under the agency scheme, CFS was a large part of my flying life. My only regret now at my 80th birthday is how few of those early Cotswold QFI stalwarts are still around for our CFS Reunions."

New aircraft paint scheme

Throughout the 1950s, training aircraft in all RAF Commands were painted in all-over silver with yellow bands, but on 24 January 1958 the CFS received instructions from HQ FTC to carry out trials on a new colour scheme to make training aircraft more conspicuous in all weather conditions. The project was called 'Marking of FTC aircraft with fluorescent paint', and was headed by Flt Lt A.J. Fellows with Sqn Ldr G.N. Buckle co-opted to assist with the design arrangements.

To be effective the scheme had to fulfil certain objectives:

1. Large areas of aircraft must be painted 'Fluolac' fluorescent orange.
2. The flight path of the aircraft must be immediately apparent.

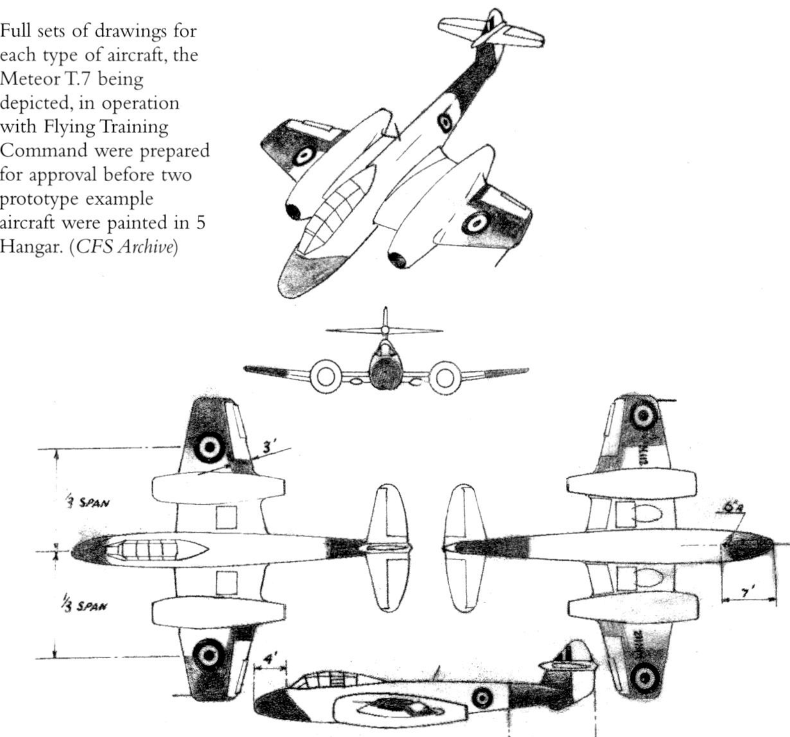

Full sets of drawings for each type of aircraft, the Meteor T.7 being depicted, in operation with Flying Training Command were prepared for approval before two prototype example aircraft were painted in 5 Hangar. (*CFS Archive*)

Piston Provost T.1, XF607/PE (*above*) and Vampire T.11, XK633/VA (*right*), were selected as the trial aircraft for the new colours and photographs were taken from the ground and in the air to assess the effectiveness of the new scheme. (*CFS Archive*)

3. There was not to be any confusion between head on and tail views.
4. The scheme should not cause any distractions during formation or night flying.

At one point, HQ FTC suggested that the complete airframe should be painted all-over fluorescent but this was rejected on the grounds of cost and because it would not fully meet the objectives. Two sets of drawings were produced for the Vampire T.11 and Piston Provost T.1, on which areas of the airframe were shaded to illustrate where the 'Fluolac' paint should be applied. On one set of drawings the painted area extended along the full leading edge of the wing to a depth of four inches, while the second showed the trailing edge of the wing painted to a depth of two feet.

Two aircraft were selected for trials; Vampire T.11 XK633/VA and Piston Provost T.1 XF607/PE. Work on the T.11, which commenced on 10 April and was completed on the 15th when attention turned to the Provost. With the painting completed, test flights where carried out on both aircraft between 18 April and 14 May 1958 in all kinds of weather conditions. Photographs were taken by Flt Lt S.T.F. Webb MBE, from the ground and in the air to aid the final assessment. The trial concluded after 47 sorties had been flown on the Vampire and 26 on the Provost. An excessive amount of stripping on the aircraft leading edges was apparent.

Pilots were unanimous in their belief that the aircraft were more discernible and clearly visible on flight paths and ranges far in excess of non-painted aircraft of the same type. Perhaps of more significance, they stood out more clearly in poor visibility due to smoke haze, drizzle or low cloud. On the ground, the benefits to ground crews

during ground handling and marshalling, especially at night, were much improved.

In his final report, Flt Lt Fellows made four recommendations:

- Air Ministry authority should be sought to introduce similar aircraft markings on all FTC aircraft: Piston Provost T.1, Jet Provost T.1,Vampire FB.5, 9 and T.11, Meteor T.7 and Canberra T.4.
- Fluorescent orange paint, which became known as 'day-glo', should be used for the markings.
- An investigation should be instigated to determine the wear qualities and best method of application of 'Fluolac' paint.
- Docker Brothers (the agents for 'Fluolac' paint) should be requested to provide technical assistance and liaison during the investigation.

By the end of the following year, nearly all aircraft operated by FTC units had been repainted in fluorescent day-glo markings.

First Jet Provost students

Students on No. 191 Course were the first to commence training on the Jet Provost T.1. Later Fg Off I.A.L. Sheppard was the first all-through jet trained pilot to undergo an instructors' course (No. 196) at CFS having had no previous piston-engined flying experience.

Restraining the vocals

Flt Lt Tom Lecky-Thompson became famous for winning the London-New York Air Race from the PO Tower in 1967. Flying a Harrier, he took off from a coal yard in clouds of dust at St Pancras station and reached the top of the Empire State Building 6 hours 11 minutes 57 seconds later. Here, he recalls an amusing incident that occurred in 1958 and involved the Commandant.

"Air Cdre 'Hetty' Hyde's wife had told us that she wished she could stop him singing in the bath. Near the end of the course a group of us went round and waited until we heard him, stuffed a FEW explosives up the drainpipe, bunged it up with clods of earth and stood back. The result was amazing.

The singing stopped abruptly; we ran back to the safety of the bar and started telling every one the story, to be interrupted a few minutes later by one purple-faced earth-spattered Commandant, clad only in a 'sarong' style bath towel, bursting into the bar pointing at US innocent looking chaps, saying he KNEW it was us!! To which we all shouted back in unison: 'Improperly dressed, Sir, drinks all round!' Which he did, immediately. Can you imagine any of that happening now?"

Graduation dinners

By way of celebration, a graduation dinner, or 'dining-in' night, was held in the Officers' Mess at the end of each Course. They were renowned for the antics of both Staff and Students and one of the most memorable is retold here by Flt Lts Norman Giffin, Ces Crook and 'Jock' Colston.

"'Hetty's' Farewell Guest Night went off with more than just a bang and was certainly the most memorable Guest Night we ever attended, anywhere. The pre-dinner drinks session was fairly uneventful but Hetty had with him the Admiral in charge of flying training for the Fleet Air Arm as a guest, who was portly and sported a splendidly bushy, ginger beard. We had a naval student instructor called Dickie Wren, who had to go formally and say good evening to the Admiral. Before dinner we were all very couth. All the table lamps were on, plugged into sockets in the tables. There was a great big flower arrangement on the top table right in front of the Air Commodore. The ginger bearded Admiral sat on his left.

The Dining Hall at Rissy had a high glass ceiling with the lighting behind. Several met. balloons floated up against the ceiling and each balloon had a long length of string dangling from it. Assuming that the balloons were filled with hydrogen, it was only later realised that these string cords had been soaked in saltpetre and were in fact fuses. As the room warmed up, the balloons started moving around and the long bits of string drifted closer to the diners. Before long someone lit the end of one and soon all the others were smoking away. As these little spluttering fires crept up the strings, it became obvious that the balloons would almost inevitably explode and, as they were rubbing against the glass ceiling, the chances were that the roof would come down on top of us. The mess stewards became apprehensive, not only because it was clear that the balloon hazard would affect them as well but also because the room was by now gradually filling with smoke.

Sensibly before long all stewards had retreated into the kitchen and bar. Everyone stopped eating and waited for the explosions. An uncanny silence led up to the moment when, with the sudden whoosh and sheet of flame across the ceiling, the gasps of relief when the glass did not fall down on top of us, and the sudden click, click, click of cutlery on plates as we all started eating again.

Dickie Wren or Keith Williamson noted with admiration that the band up in the Minstrels' Gallery kept playing right through the whole balloon episode. The formal service and dining resumed, with the stewards having regained their confidence but little knowing what was to come. There was a lull in dangerous activity for a while, as it was clear to all (including our future MRAF and Chief of Air Staff, the then Sqn Ldr K.A. Williamson) that it would be bad form not to finish dinner, when the mess staff had gone to so much trouble to provide the meal. After all, it was the Commandant's Dining-Out Night and we had to Pass the Port, attend to the Loyal Toast and have some speeches.

The first thunderflash went off and gradually this thick toxic cloud descended, lower and lower, and to such an extent that, at one point, someone, who had stood up and was making a speech on the floor (he was not even standing on the Mess table!) gradually went totally IMC and could only be seen by the two or three on either side of him. We moved our chairs away from the tables so we were sitting backs to the wall. The stewards sensibly all ran away and even the band now stopped playing when there was an explosion in the Minstrels' Gallery. It sounded as though a missile had dropped into the mouth of some brass instrument just before the music stopped; however it was not long before the music slowly spluttered back into life again to the rousing cheers of the discordant 'mob' below.

The most amazing thing happened at this particular juncture. The gathering was chanting 'UP ... UP ... UP', wanting Hetty to stand on the table to make his farewell speech. Politely our Commandant obliged, thus standing on the table and right in front of the big flower arrangement. No sooner had he started to speak, when, literally bang on cue, the flower arrangement exploded. The charge placed in the flowers had been detonated electrically from a table lamp socket. The Commandant was covered in debris but appeared not unduly concerned. Quite calmly in measured tones he said: 'Thank you chaps, but I do believe I may even have the last laugh yet'. And he did.

He had put what looked like chocolate Smarties all over the pudding, which was delicious and gobbled up by all. But they were not Smarties! They were full of a medical dye called methylene blue, a so called biological stain. Nearly everyone at that dining-out peed green for a couple of months after munching that pudding and the jape was not appreciated by our ladies. Vivid memories remain of Hetty's Admiral guest with his ginger beard dyed very, very green because he liked his pud too much.

After dinner the Admiral was invited to meet staff and students in the Anteroom. That already shell-shocked naval person had put his coffee cup on the mantelpiece while his host went to get him a brandy. The Admiral was standing by the fireplace all by himself when a thunderflash came down the chimney and exploded, soot all over him. A remarkably concerned Air Commodore rushed up with the brandy, patted the Admiral all over and said, 'Oh, my dear chaps, there's been an explosion down the chimney'. The Admiral downed his brandy in one gulp and had a few more. Flt Lt 'Bunny' Austin had been told to climb on the roof and launch the thunderflash but he never owned up to it. Clearly, that last jape had to have been carefully planned – it was so beautifully timed and thoroughly effective.

Norman Giffin also remembers returning to his room much later in the evening and passing with someone else along the corridor past Hetty's room (he was staying in the mess that night) when he burst out of his room with an evil glint in his eye and accused us of planning to plant a bomb in or near his room! Norman believed that the pyromaniacal Hetty had only returned to his room to stock up with yet more explosives."

The following day many, including Flt Lt 'Curly' Hirst, could not remember much about the night before, *"It must have been something I ate"*, says Curly. Flt Lt Terry Gasson is not able to recall much either, *"but peeing green is something that one does NOT ever forget! Interesting wasn't it, though, how Hetty Hyde always called people 'chaps' regardless of whether he was talking to one person or many?"*

Learning to be a Naval QFI

Lt Michael Doust was one of the first Royal Navy instructors to complete the QFI's course at Little Rissington in the latter half of 1958. He remembers his time at CFS and imparts a few of his experiences.

"My QFI's course was scheduled to commence on 21 July 1958, but before I left RNAS Yeovilton I was interviewed by Lt Cdr Ray Rawbone, who had been the CO of 897 Seahawk Squadron during the Suez crisis. There was a perfectly good reason for the interview; there had been several RN aviators who had gone to Little Rissington and had failed the course quite early on. These aviators were totally unsuitable for being instructors and had they been interviewed in the first instance and their weaknesses exposed, they may have saved the Navy a great deal of embarrassment. Ray considered me good enough to go on the QFI course and I passed the interview.

To Royal Navy pilots, the RAF's Central Flying School was the Air Force University of Flying. It was the Air Force's task to produce flying instructors as laid down by an Act of Parliament for all three armed forces. Each course consisted of officers from all three services and from foreign nations. My course, No. 194, consisted of British officers only from the navy, army and air force. I had a naval companion with me, Lt Martin Packhard, who had been back classed to my course due to a car accident. There are usually two naval aviators on each course so that they can keep each other company. The same routine was followed as at other RAF Training Schools, the course was divided into two watches, with Martin in 'A' Watch and myself in 'B' Watch, with the watches alternating between flying and ground school.

Probably, the most important aspect of teaching is the ability of being able to stand up in front of a group of students and teach a subject. There is nothing more soul destroying than standing on a platform looking out on to a sea of faces all looking up and expecting something profound from you. My course had an excellent tutor, a RAF Flight Lieutenant, RAFVR, who also lectured at Bristol University on Aerodynamics. He was hard on us, and when he had torn you to pieces in front of the course, I felt as if I was never going to be an instructor. However, he taught me and others on the course several important aspects about teaching: be thoroughly prepared; know your subject; speak with authority and purpose; above all remember that you are better and know more about your subject than those out front! From then on, I never felt afraid of standing up front of any group of people to speak or lecture about any subject whatsoever.

Our course started on 21 July and finished on 15 November 1958 and was divided into basic and advanced instructional training plus ground school. A third was given over to ground school. After six weeks' tuition in the Provost trainer you either stayed for the remainder of the course on this aircraft learning how to teach basic flying, or were moved across to another squadron/flight to be taught advanced flying on Vampire T.11 jet trainers. Martin would stay on Provost aircraft while I went onto Vampires. All the officers on course were very experienced aviators and many had come from front line tours where they had seen action. Not one of the course failed in any respect, and I would eventually meet many of them later on during my flying career. Our instructors were of the best and I had a Flt Sgt John Webster as my basic flying instructor. He was thorough and taught me a great deal about how to handle students and how to teach them. He was of the breed of teachers whom I call 'Old Dads', who know instinctively how to encourage you, praise you and extract the best from your capabilities and abilities.

It was during one of my dual instructional rides with John, I had noticed that our Provost's engine was gradually losing power as indicated by the boost gauge. He said quite casually, 'Oh don't worry, it will get us back on the ground!' It was a final landing, and was probably one of my

As airborne photographs of RAF stations tend to focus on the airfield, tower and hangars, it was a pleasant change to find this late-fifties view of Little Rissington looking across the senior officers' married quarters, Officers' Mess, other ranks' quarters and administration buildings. (*Rod Brown*)

best in the aircraft. At the end of the landing I closed the throttle, then turned to clear the runway and 'gunned' the engine to get the plane moving again, but the engine stopped dead! John informed the tower, we climbed out and walked back to the training flight and a while later the aircraft was towed into the hangar. The engine was a write-off; one of the piston rods had broken and gone through the casing, so it had to be returned for rebuild or salvage.

On another occasion flying a Vampire with Flt Lt Marsh, another student on course with me, we experienced a very dangerous incident. We were scheduled to do mutual tuition in which we 'pattered' to each other the aspects of clean and 'dirty' stalling. It was decided between us that I would go through the tuition sequence first. I covered the preliminaries of going through the aircraft and flying area checks, then commenced the 'patter' sequence for a clean stall, that is a stall with undercarriage and flaps retracted. I brought the throttle back slowly, raising the aircraft's nose as the speed fell off to remain in level flight until the stall was reached. Suddenly, without any warning at about 160 knots airspeed, the aircraft pitched nose up and rolled violently to the right and entered a spin. I quickly recovered and climbed back up to 25,000 ft. We both looked at each other and said in unison 'What happened there?' Marsh then had a go and exactly the same happen to him. Then I went into a 'dirty' stall with undercarriage and flaps fully down; exactly the same happened with the aircraft going into a right-handed spin at 130 knots. There was no doubt now that we had a dangerous aircraft on our hands. The tower was informed of our problem and we decided to make a fast flapless approach, closing the throttle immediately the wheels touched the runway. The landing went as planned, then we taxied the aircraft back to the hangar to establish what was wrong with it.

This particular Vampire trainer had been in the maintenance hangar for major overhaul. Apart from the engine and airframe inspections, both wings were stripped of all cellulose and fillers and cleaned down to bare metal. However, when the wings were refurbished their original shapes were not restored to the correct aerofoil cross sections. Consequently, the right wing had a different shape to that of the left wing, causing it to stall earlier at a much higher speed than normal. This serious blunder on the part of maintenance could have led to a landing accident in which one or both pilots might have been killed! The evidence would have been lost in any fire and it would have been blamed on the pilots as 'Pilot Error'. The Flight Commander had the aircraft returned to the maintenance hangar to restore the wings to their correct shape.

On my graduation from CFS, a combined Mess dinner was held both for my course and the retiring Commandant of the School. Now it was known that the Commandant was somewhat of a pyrotechnic maniac in his early days, so the organisers of the dinner decided to give the retiring officer something to remember CFS. They called in an ordnance expert from RAF Valley and he 'mined' both the huge flower bowl in front of the guest of honour and the flower bowl suspended below the orchestra pit. It was arranged that he would operate a switch and set off a tiny amount of explosive, which would throw the flowers into the air without causing any injuries.

The dinner was a most sumptuous affair with the station band playing away high up in the orchestra pit some wonderful melodies and tunes. Once the 'Loyal Toast' had been made, the speeches began and finally the retiring Commandant was invited to stand and make his outgoing speech. As he stood up, everybody in the mess roared 'UP, UP, UP!' until he finally climbed and stood on the table with the bowl of flowers just in front of him. As he started his speech, a nod was given to the ordnance man and he pressed the switch. There was a dull thud and the flowers rose in the air to fall over our gallant Commandant. He almost collapsed with laughter at such a prank, and when he had recovered, he went on to make a splendid farewell speech which, when he had finished, brought everybody to their feet with cheering, whistles and clapping. This was an officer and gentleman who was so well liked that he was going to be a great loss to the RAF. Why he was not selected for higher rank I will never know but he was the sort of leader any service could ill afford to lose.

At the same time of dining out the old retiring Commandant, the new Commandant was also dined into the mess. His name was Air Cdre Whitworth. He did not like what he had witnessed and cleared the 'upper deck' of all officers the following day and mustered them in the anteroom of the Officers' Mess. He gave us all hell for what he called outrageous behaviour at the previous night's mess dinner. He was referring to the flower prank, which he considered most inappropriate and unbecoming of officers. The next day he addressed my course and made 'no bones' about the fact that he could not understand why there were two naval officers on course at CFS. Both Martin and I were extremely incensed by his outrageous remark, as were our course chums, and we were nearly on the point of walking out of the room. None of us could understand why he had made such a remark and could only put it down to the fact that something must have happened to sour his opinion of the Navy. Our course chums, especially the RAF officers, apologised profusely and asked us to forget about it. Martin graduated with a QFI category of B1 and was appointed to basic flying tuition at RAF Linton-on-Ouse. I managed to obtain a B2 category and was appointed to 738 Squadron at Lossiemouth, equipped with Sea Venoms, Vampire and Meteor trainers."

Question of the Queen's Colour

The new Commandant asked the AOA in a letter dated 1 August 1958, if the question of the award of the Queen's Colour to the Central Flying School had ever been raised. He felt that the claims of CFS for the award of a colour could hardly be disputed and suggested that a suitable occasion for the presentation would be when CFS reached its half century in 1962.

The SPSO sent a reply on behalf of the AOA on 14 August, to the effect that the proposal had been put to the Air Ministry twice, once in 1952 and again in 1955, and had been rejected on both occasions. One of the grounds for its rejection had been that CFS would be unable to mount appropriate ceremonial parades of the type and frequency as those held at Cranwell or Halton at which the Colour could be carried.

Despite these earlier rejections the Commandant informed the SPSO on 20 August, that he still felt inclined to mention the matter to the Commander-in-Chief, who together with the Chief of Air Staff, had strong ties with the Central Flying School and may be prepared to re-open the matter.

Busy month for aeros

The CFS Jet Provost Aerobatic team participated in the SBAC Air Display at Farnborough each day from the 1st to 7th of September. They then flew across to the Channel Islands to give a display in Jersey on the 18th before returning to the mainland for Battle of Britain displays at RAF Tern Hill, RAF Cosford, and finally the RAF "At Home" at Little Rissington, all three on the 20th. CFS staff instructors were also kept busy flying individual displays in the Piston Provost, Vampire and Canberra at eleven other RAF bases.

With the learned Provost 'Provosts'

Flt Lt Richard Bates arrived at CFS from No. 256 Sqn, RAF Geilenkirchen, 2nd TAF in September 1958 to join No. 196 Course, having flown Meteor NF.11s and the T.7 two-seat trainer for three years, both at Geilenkirchen and at Ahlhorn.

"My logbook reminds me that Norman Giffin gave me my 'famil' on the Piston Provost on 1 October 1958 and, four months later, my Final Handling Test. Surely, I felt on arrival, as an experienced pilot and Instrument Rating Examiner, I could look forward to the CFS course as a straightforward and undemanding conversion. Wrong!

Soon it became apparent that there was a great deal to learn. One of the keys to being an instructor was the 'ability to impart knowledge' to that long-suffering student, 'Bloggs'. 'If you are flying straight and level, You may know this … but does He?' were the memorable words from Arthur Sunderland-Cooper on an early trip. Lookout, 'learning plateaux', reference points on the distant horizon and instrument checks to confirm aircraft attitude while 'pattering' the exercises – these were all vital, and hammered home by the likes of Norman, Arthur, Fred Packer

Bearing the brunt of long range trips by the Trappers was Valetta C.1, WJ496-MF, until 1960 when these duties were undertaken by the Varsity. (*David Watkins*)

and 'Ces' Crook, another memorable character and his close colleague, 'Curly' Hirst.

Another recollection from Rissy is of John Charlesworth and Mike Neil at the pinnacle of the CFS operation in Examining Wing. I knew Mike as a Chipmunk expert in later years at RAF Gatow, Berlin and No. 6 AEF, Benson. He completed his half-century in 'blue uniform', well lapping my own 40-year association with the Chipmunk. At Little Rissington I did two trips in the Vampire T.11 with Chick Hemsley. The objective was to achieve twelve jet hours before launching forth in a Hunter – probably not a great factor in my forthcoming posting to the Oxford UAS but nevertheless a great privilege. In the event, poor weather and another look at the policy meant that we did not get our Hunter trip. Indeed, the winter weather of 1958/59 was so bad that Little Rissington was isolated with snowdrifts deep enough to obliterate nine-foot bus stop signs on the narrow road down to Bourton-on-the-Water!"

CFS Organisation

In reply to a reminder from Command Headquarters, the Commandant stated in letter dated 8 October that proposals for the re-organisation of CFS courses were still receiving careful consideration. The present course organisation was working very well and he was loath to make precipitate changes which might be regretted later. He asked that a realistic idea of future tasks for CFS be obtained from the Air Ministry so that proposals could be formulated on a sound basis. On the subject of the organisation of CFS itself, he expressed his entire satisfaction, likening it to that which was obtained at class one stations in Bomber Command.

Jet Provost Mark 3

In a letter dated 20 October to Headquarters Flying Training Command, the Chief Flying Instructor asked that a Jet Provost Mark 3 be made available to CFS for the purpose of completing the Instructor's Handbook on the type. A previous proposal that experience should be gained on the aircraft loaned to the Handling Squadron at Boscombe Down was considered unsatisfactory as it appeared unlikely that more than ten hours could be made available and this was with a Handling Squadron pilot on board, performing his normal flying tasks. He considered that at least forty hours flying by two instructors was necessary.

In its reply dated 29 October, HQ Flying Training Command stated that with careful programming twenty hours flying experience was all that was required and it enclosed a copy of a letter to Air Ministry requesting confirmation that this amount of flying would be made available.

Visits to CFS

On 4 October, personnel from the Gas Turbine Engine Works at Birmingham visited CFS where they were shown around Technical Wing, Air Traffic Control and the Ground Instructional block. They were then given a short flying display.

From the 13th to 16th the Commandant of the German Air Force Advanced Flying Training School at Fürstenfeldbruck, Oberst Heinrich Hrabak and three of his staff paid a liaison visit to CFS.

On the 16th of the month Wg Cdr N.K. Shitoley and Flt Lt R.D. Sahni, of the Indian Air Force Examining Wing Board, visited CFS to discuss matters of mutual interest.

From the 23rd to 31st, 'World Wide Films Ltd.' shot film sequences for three flight safety flashes at CFS.

Examining Wing responsibilities

An Air Ministry letter dated 5 November affirmed that the role and examining responsibilities of the CFS and Command examining units for recategorisation, standardisation and instrument rating examining tests were to be revised. CFS would continue to be responsible for recategorisation and standardisation of QFIs outside Flying Training Command, but where types of aircraft were involved which were different from those available within FTC, QFIs in the commands would be appointed for CFS on the appropriate aircraft type. Similarly CIRE tests on types of aircraft not available to FTC would be carried out as appropriate by the Bomber Command Standardisation Unit, the Transport Command Examining Unit, the Coastal Command Categorisation Board or the Fighter Command Instrument Rating Squadron.

An Air Ministry order entitled "The CFS and Flying Instructor Policy" was published on 19 November. It explained the changes in the examining role and changes in the function and organisation of CFS. Revisions to the selection process for CFS courses, the length of flying instructional tours of duty and flying instructor categories were also defined.

First all-through jet student

On 27 November the Commandant interviewed and accepted Fg Off I.A.L. Sheppard as a student for No. 196 Course. As mentioned earlier Fg Off Sheppard was the first all-through jet trained pilot to undergo a CFS instructor's course with no first-pilot time whatsoever on piston-engined aircraft.

Tragic loss

After morning ground school on 4 December 1958, Flt Lt Richard Bates completed a formation dual-trip with Fred Packer in Provost XF542. *"We handed the aircraft over to instructor Flt Lt Pete Millington, who took off with my fellow student, 22 year old, Fg Off Dave Hough. They did not return. Wreckage was soon discovered near Kingham and this tragic loss contrasted with three fortunately accident-free years of 2nd TAF squadron flying in Germany."*

The tragic accident referred to by Richard occurred when Peter Millington, box-man in the JP display team, and his student Fg Off David Hough, were killed while carrying out low flying instruction in Piston Provost, XF542. They were flying as leader of a pair in a tailchase when the aircraft seemed to stall at about 500 ft. The port wing dropped and the aircraft struck a tree and dived into the ground.

Peter left a widow with two young children, and two months pregnant with a third who was to become Don McClen's godson, Peter, the following July.

The working week

Early in December, the Commandant submitted in a letter to the AOA stating that it would be more economical and efficient for CFS to work a five day week rather than a five and a half day week with Wednesday afternoon devoted to recreation. The main thrust of his contention is outlined below:

a. That CFS has a large and increasing civilian complement whose conditions of employment are based on a five day week. Under the present system many of them have next to nothing to do on Wednesday afternoons yet have to be brought in on Saturday mornings and paid overtime. With a five day working week the overtime saved could be allotted to holding the various functions in the Officers' Mess which the C-in-C considers desirable.

b. Meteorological statistics show that over a period of a year Wednesday afternoons provide 15% better chance of flying than on Saturday mornings, this percentage could be as high as 30% for the months of November to February.

c. Night rectification teams presently work Monday to Friday nights preparing for the following day's flying. Saturday morning flying however often produces a crop of unserviceabilities, quite disproportionate to the amount of flying achieved and this prevents a good start the following Monday morning.

In his response, SASO wrote on 22 December to all formations of Group status within the command stating that he propounded the view that Wednesday afternoons were an integral and necessary part of service life and should not be sacrificed for other considerations. He thought the time was ripe for the C-in-C to issue a clear directive on the subject and he invited the views of addressees.

Radio Compass

On 19 December, approval was received for the fitting of the Marconi Radio Compass into two CFS Canberra T.4 aircraft. The fixed installation was to be completed as soon as possible, but the Black Boxes would have to be borrowed until sufficient units became available for issue to CFS.

Work on repainting CFS aircraft in the new day-glo training colours continued through late 1958 and all of 1959, until images such as these portraying (*below*), Vampire T.11, XD523/ND, and (*inset*) Piston Provost T.1, XF895/PA, in the silver and yellow colour scheme were just a memory. (*Graham Pitchfork collection and Rod Brown*)

1959

The working week issue

On New Year's day, in replying to the Commandant's letter of 11 December 1958, the AOA agreed that on a strictly economic basis the civilian five-day working week and the service five and a half day week, with Wednesday afternoons devoted to sport, were incompatible. However, because of the C-in-C's and SASO's strong views on Wednesday afternoon sport, he felt unable to act upon the Commandant's recommendations at this juncture, but he would bear them in mind when the subject came up for review in April.

On 9 January, in response to SASO's letter of 22 December 1958, the Commandant agreed entirely with SASO's view on the value of Wednesday afternoon games, but re-emphasised that CFS had special problems and thought that the best solution might be to work a five-day week with longer working hours, with Wednesday afternoons still allocated for sport.

University Air Squadrons

A Headquarters Flying Training Command instruction on the transfer of University Air Squadrons from Home Command to Flying Training Command, was issued on 8 January 1959. The major responsibilities transferred to CFS were:

a. The general supervision of UAS flying and associated activities, and the air staff facets of pre-AOC's annual inspections

b. Administrative matters normally undertaken by a Group HQ

CFS participation in air displays

By 15 January the CFS had already received requests for CFS participation at air displays. Requested items included the CFS Jet Provost Aerobatic Team, a demonstration by the unit's helicopters and an aerobatic display by the Wright Jubilee Trophy winner. The latter two items presented no great difficulty but the Jet Provost Aerobatic Team raised a point of principle. Jet Provost commitments for the year included the conversion to type of QFIs from RAF Syerston and the training of CFS students, commitments that would absorb all the resources of aircraft and manpower. The formation of an aerobatic team, though highly desirable, would therefore have required a separate establishment and the Commandant requested Command HQ to give a quick ruling on the subject.

Correspondence between the Commandant and SASO on the possibility of forming a CFS Aerobatic Team for 1959 continued through February. Following a suggestion by the Commandant on 13 February that it may be easier to form a team of Piston Provosts rather than Jet Provosts, SASO put forward an alternative suggestion to Air Ministry on 23 February, that six Mark 3 Jet Provosts be released to CFS for QFI training so that existing Mark 1s could be allotted for a team this year.

Since there seemed little hope of obtaining the additional aircraft and manpower to form and maintain a four-ship team at CFS, SASO suggested in a letter dated 19 March, that it might be possible to work up from existing resources a programme of synchronised aerobatics using two JPs only. The proposition was accepted by CFS and preparations begun to form a team.

Manpower shortages

Referring to a letter from the Chief of the Air Staff to the Commander-in-Chief, the AOA stated in letter dated 16 January 1959, that manning problems were likely to arise during the next few years, particularly in the radio engineering, ground signalling, radar operating, accounting and secretarial trades. CAS suggested that the situation might be alleviated by keeping demands for establishment increases to a minimum by the reduction, amalgamation or even disbandment of existing units by civilianisation and by making use of work study. He also issued a request for further suggestions that might help solve the problem.

In his reply dated 23 January, the Commandant expressed the view that the RAF flying training organisation was fundamentally inefficient, in that it was split into so many penny packets in a country increasingly subject to air traffic control and congestion. One basic and one advanced FTS in say, Rhodesia or Canada he continued, would probably be able to train the annual requirement of about 350 pilots. However, failing a re-organisation of this sort the following suggestions might help:

a. Further civilianisation could be effected at CFS in Type Squadron servicing, Motor Transport servicing and in the Ground Equipment Flight

b. Serious undermanning in key trades should be avoided as servicing is geared to the tempo of these men and under manning results in enforced idleness among other trades

c. The few officers at CFS who have undergone short work study courses could study different aspects of station activity

Student selection

On 22 January the Commandant wrote to HQ Flying Training Command outlining a recent application for a CFS course that had satisfied the condition of serving eighteen months on an operational squadron, but mainly as a second pilot on Beverley aircraft. The Commandant felt sure that the intention was that eighteen months should be spent as first pilot and he recommended that the relevant AMO should be amended accordingly.

In a letter dated 3 February to HQ FTC, the Commandant referred to his previous letter dated 22 January on the conditions of eligibility for CFS courses and recommended that candidates should possess an absolute minimum of 500 hours first pilot experience. He recognised that second pilots in Bomber and Transport Command may have difficulty in accumulating this total so he further suggested that those who were clearly potential QFI material might be posted back to operational squadrons where they could gain the required experience, possibly replacing pilots who would never make QFIs. These views were put to the Secretary of State for Air during his informal visit to CFS on 6 February.

Jet Provost conversion

The conversion of QFIs from RAF Syerston on to the Jet Provost began during February and continued throughout the month.

Visits and visitors

A QFI from Basic Standards was detached to Boscombe Down from 16 to 27 February and flew 22 hours' intensive flying trials on the Jet Provost T. Mk.3 to assist in the composition of instructor's notes for the aircraft. On 26 February, a Squadron Leader from Advanced Standards and a Staff instructor paid a visit to Hawker Siddeley at Dunsfold Aerodrome to gain spinning experience in a manufacturer's Hunter T.7.

At the Commandant's invitation, one officer and eighteen cadets from the Royal Military Academy Sandhurst visited Little Rissington on 7 and 8 March. They were shown various aspects of CFS activities and were given flights in Anson and Piston Provost aircraft. The new AOC-in-C FTC, Air Marshal Sir Hugh Constantine KBE CB DSO, paid his first visit to CFS on 13 March. A guard of honour and the station pipe band were paraded for his arrival.

'Batchy's' portrait

The Commandant, Chief Flying Instructor and three Wing Commanders made a visit to HQ Flying Training Command on 18 February to witness the presentation to Air Marshal Sir Richard Atcherley of his portrait to mark his retirement from the Royal Air Force.

Runway Maintenance

To facilitate runway resurfacing at Little Rissington between 14 April and 26 June 1959, 2 Squadron and Type Squadron were detached to RAF Aston Down and RAF Kemble respectively. Three Canberra T.4s, two Meteor T.7s and the Valetta were operated out of Kemble, although two Meteors, WL403 and WL460, were later redeployed to RAF Thorney Island. Nine Vampire T.11s and four Jet Provost T.1s were flown from Aston Down. The Jet Provosts, however, remained at Rissington for as long as the grassed landing area remained practical for use.

The Kemble detachment shared the Hunter Flight's accommodation with the addition of a tent for use on the dispersal. More spacious accommodation was available at Aston Down, where the detachment made use of building No. 68, Hangar No. 2, two tents and a marquee.

The groundcrews were transported to and from each airfield by road on a daily basis which was not possible for those on the Thorney Island detachment. A team of technicians led by Sgt Barraclough and including Cpls Taylor and Crooke, J/T Grubis, and SACs Samson, Milstead, Allen and Edwards, was allocated billeted accommodation and offered flights back to Rissy at weekends if they so desired.

A USAF perspective on CFS!

Reminiscences from former Capt John A Smitherman USAF who served on a two year exchange posting at CFS in 1958-60.

"In 1958 I checked in with No. 2 Squadron down in 4 Hangar, as a USAF Captain and flight instructor. Sqn Ldr Archie Dick was the CO at the time, with Flt Lt Gerry Coles becoming my 'check out' instructor. Who would ever have dreamed of doing high level aeros, stall turns, eight turn spins and other death defying 'stunts' that we didn't teach back in the Colonies? Well, I learned how to teach such manoeuvres and even later became a member of Advanced Standards: i.e. 'The Trappers'.

Before that, however, on 7 April I made a low level training mission in Vampire T.11, XK631, which did not include a landing. My student for the occasion was Flt Lt Dennis Allison, who later became Commandant CFS, now a retired Air Vice-Marshal. Well, we had engine failure with a fire warning light and all the bad signs, ending up ejecting from a zoom pull up at perhaps 100 ft or so. Somehow my chute became split almost in half and the stony Cotswold Hills made for a damaging impact to my legs. Dennis came running from across the ridge with only a cut lip, as I recall. Our Vampire managed to kill two cows on the Oxhall Farm; we were recovered by chopper from Rissy. I had no permanent injuries and was back on flying duty in a couple of weeks."

This was certified as Martin Baker's safe ejection No. 276, the 26th carried out from a Vampire.

"All in all, what a superb bunch of guys across the board in 2 Squadron at Rissy. Just think, Air Cdre J.N.H. 'Charlie' Whitworth was Commandant back then, Gp Capt 'Jimmy' James was Chief Instructor and Wg Cdr Peter Gilpin Chief Flying Instructor, all WW2 veterans, yep, and I met 'Batchy' Atcherley, ACM Sir Thomas Pike et al.

The unfortunate Vampire T.11, XK631-ND, from which Capt Smitherman and his student, Flt Lt Allison, were forced to eject when the engine failed. (*MAP*)

One helluva posting! I guess it helped save my ass on 186 F4 Phantom missions in Vietnam with three hits on my aircraft on three separate missions. I was also very lucky as I lost so many priceless friends out there."

Type Squadron

On Type Squadron, the Meteor detachment continued throughout May but due to very poor serviceability no QFI flying was possible. The Hunter Flight flew five QFIs from other stations in addition to fourteen from CFS. Completion of resurfacing work on the main runway at Little Rissington mid-way through June enabled the Meteor Flight to return from Thorney Island. No students were able to fly the Canberras during June, owing to aircraft unserviceability but nineteen students, plus ten QFIs from other stations, flew the Hunters.

Exercises

CFS aircraft participated in an exercise involving the Royal Observer Corps on 23 June. Various CFS aircraft and pilots took part in a second exercise between the 18th and 25th for the benefit of No. 42 AGRA (TA). Brigadier Sykes, OC No. 42 AGRA, flew in a Vampire to assess the progress of the exercise on the final day.

Birthday Honours

Two people were recognised in the June Birthday Honours:

Flt Lt N H Giffin	–	Queen's Commendation
Sgt Sishton	–	AOC's Commendation

Course Progress

When No. 198 Course completed its Basic stage on 1 July, the Advanced and Applied Flying stages commenced on the following day. Suspensions from courses were a common occurrence but six was considered high. Four students were suspended for failing ground school and two for lack of instructional aptitude. A further six were also suspended from the next course, No. 199.

New Aerobatic team

The new CFS aerobatic team was soon working up to display standard and went on to entertain the crowds at air shows throughout the summer of 1959. Flying a pair of the 1958 team's Jet Provost T.1s, Flt Lts P.J. 'Curly' Hirst and J.R. Rhind produced a programme that extended the range of manoeuvres usually performed by a 'duo' at the time. The team's first public appearance was at Hucknall on 18 May and subsequent performances included the Coventry Air Pageant, RAF Coltishall, The Imperial Defence College, RNAS Culdrose and RAF College Cranwell in July, and RAF Middleton St. George, RAF Leuchars, RAF Swinderby, Colwyn Bay and Wolverhampton (for RAFA) in August.

'Trappers' visits

The heavy workload of the Standards Wing 'Trappers' continued as normal throughout 1959 with team visits to RAF and RNAS bases at home and overseas, and to a number of foreign air forces. The first long distance trip of the year took place between 1 to 10 April when a party of QFIs under the command of the Commandant flew on a liaison visit to the Royal Rhodesian Air Force in two Canberra aircraft. Their schedule for the second half of the year provides a good general representation of the type of activities undertaken on these visits.

June

- Visit by 'Trappers' to the Spanish and Portuguese Air Forces for an exchange of views and noting of procedures on flying training.
- No. 2 FTS at RAF Syerston for routine Standardisation visit during which 46 instructors were tested.
- Visit to RAF Watton to assess the standard of flying on Lincoln, Canberra and Meteor aircraft.
- Visit to RAF Swinderby for Standardisation checks on Vampire T.11 instructors and students of No. 8 FTS.
- Standardisation checks on a number of instructors of the Ferry Wing at RAF Benson.
- RAF Lindholme for Standardisation tests on Lincoln and Varsity instructors.
- Standardisation checks on eleven instructors and students of 229 OCU at RAF Chivenor.
- RAF College at Cranwell for Standardisation tests on 31 instructors and students.
- No. 6 FTS at RAF Tern Hill for Standardisation checks. At the time of the visit there were 45 instructors and 110 students of whom twelve were from the Sudanese Air Force, three from the Lebanese Air Force and six from the Jordanian Air Force.
- At the request of Flag Officer Flying Training, 'Trappers' visited RNAS Brawdy to carry out Standardisation checks on twelve Sea Balliol T.21, Sea Vampire T.22 and Sea Prince instructors.

July

- RAF Tangmere for Standardisation tests on Canberra B.2 and Varsity T.1 instructors.
- Following request from Fighter Command, CFS team visited RAF Middleton St George to liaise with 33 Squadron on operational and training aspects of flying training aircraft – seven instructors tested.
- Eight 'Trappers' to RAF College at Barkston Heath to examine 38 instructors.
- Central Fighter Establishment at RAF West Raynham to test

three members of the Fighter Command Instrument Rating Flight in Meteor T.7s.

September

- RAF Coltishall to examine Meteor T.7, Hunter F.6 and T.7 instructors on 23 and 74 Squadrons.
- RAF Leeming to examine Meteor T.7 and NF.14 instructors with 228 OCU. CFS staff also flew with pilots in Javelin T.3s.
- By Varsity to FEAF and the Air Forces of Pakistan and Ceylon.

October

- RAF Stradishall to examine seven Meteor T.7 target tug instructors on 54 Squadron.
- 'Trappers' visit to FEAF stations at Tengah, Seletar, Kai Tak and Kuala Lumpur for Standardisation checks on 47 instructors, including those on helicopter units in the area.
- Arabian Peninsula for CFS Standardisation tests on:
  - a) Nine Vampire T.11 instructors on 208 Squadron at RAF Eastleig
  - b) Two Meteor T.7 instructors on Recce Flight at RAF Khormaksar
  - c) One Meteor T.7 and one Canberra T.4 instructor on Station Flight at RAF Khormaksar

November/December

- RAF Valley for Standardisation checks on 21 instructors and students of No. 7 FTS.
- 231 OCU at RAF Bassingbourn for Standardisation tests on eleven Canberra instructors and students.
- RNAS Lossiemouth to observe and report on flying standards of students and instructors on the Operational Fighter School. Eight checks were completed flying Hunter T.8s and a further ten in Vampire T.22s.
- Flying in two CFS Canberra T.4s, WJ991 and WT480, a CFS team led by the Commandant and CFI Wg Cdr Peter Gilpin, made liaison visits to several Commonwealth and Foreign air forces to exchange views and note procedures used in flying training. This was the longest overseas tour in the history of the School. After a session with staff at the Australian Central Flying School at RAAF East Sale, they flew on to meet officers of the New Zealand CFS at RNZAF Wigram. The aircraft routed back through Indonesia, Thailand, Burma, India and Pakistan, to allow the team to renew acquaintances with many former students, some of whom had achieved high rank in their national air forces by then. On arrival back at Little Rissington on 9 December, the Commandant was interviewed about the trip by the BBC and two days later, he visited HQ FTC to brief the AOC-in-C on the visit.

Peter Gilpin shares his memory of that Commonwealth trip.

"When I was CFI in 1958-60 we carried out a number of visits to overseas Air Forces. The longest was one full month to the Far East, predominantly to cover our CFS visits to Australia, New Zealand, Thailand, Burma, India and Pakistan. We used two Canberras with the Commandant, Air Cdre Charles Whitworth, in the other one. In Australia the Commandant took the opportunity to deliver a formal letter of greetings from the Mayor of Cheltenham to the Mayor of Cheltenham, near Melbourne, and I was present at this personal handover to our local mayor's down under equivalent.

In addition to that trip there was one to the Royal Rhodesian Air Force, which the Commandant also undertook, when again we used two of our Canberras. For the teams I took to Turkey and separately to Spain and Portugal, we flew in the Valetta."

London – Paris air race

The Daily Mail sponsored an Air Race which took place between 13 and 23 July and several aircraft from the CFS Helicopter Squadron participated. Two Sycamores operated between Biggin Hill and the Thames foreshore at Chelsea at low tide, while another two Sycamores and a Dragonfly provided a link between Villacoublay airfield and Issy heliport in Paris. Following several unfortunate setbacks, the RAF team eventually put up an unbeatable time of 40 minutes 40 seconds, and it is fair to say that the CFS Helicopter Squadron played no small part in this success.

The team did not escape completely unscathed, however, as the tail rotor of Sycamore HC.Mk.14, XG540, being flown by Flt Lt R.W. Smith, struck the ground at Villacoublay airfield causing the aircraft to yaw and roll over. Flt Lt Smith escaped without injury and the aircraft was declared Cat.4.

Vampire replacement!

During this period the RAF began seeking a replacement for the Vampire T.11 in the advanced training role, and Hawker Aircraft Ltd was invited to fly a Hunter T.7 into Little Rissington for the Commandant, Air Cdre Whitworth to fly in. Flown by Hawker Test Pilot Bill Bedford, the aircraft arrived in typical Bedford style with a high speed roar across the airfield and a landing so short he was able to turn off the main runway at the intersection. Intent on selling the aircraft to CFS, Hawker's had sent a trainer equipped with a nosewheel brake to demonstrate the aircraft's capability to operate out of the airfield. On exiting the cockpit, Bedford and the high ranking CFS staff waiting to receive him, made use of 1 Squadron 'B' Flight Commander, Flt Lt Norman Giffin's office. "*While his aircraft was refuelled and turned-round*", Norman continues, *"Bedford and the Commandant discussed the merits of the Hunter as a Vampire replacement over a cup of coffee before going off together for a short demonstration flight. After a couple of touch-and-goes, they landed and returned to Norman's office, where Bedford stressed the Hunter's short landing run. Air Cdre Whitworth*

responded by stressing Bill's experience of test flying against that of trainee instructors."

An interesting addendum to this episode was that following his retirement, former C-in-C Flying Training Command, Air Marshal Sir Richard Atcherley, was on the management team at the Folland Aircraft Company and the Gnat was subsequently selected as the Vampire replacement.

To mark the 47th anniversary of the formation of the Central Flying School, Air Chief Marshal Sir James Robb visited Little Rissington in July accompanied by seventeen officers of Air rank.

Jet Provost Mark 3

On 31 July 1959, Flt Lt Norman Giffin and two of his colleagues were flown to RAF Lyneham to collect the first three of six pre-production Jet Provost T.Mk.3 trainers destined for the CFS, XM355, 356, 357, 359, 360 and 361. None of the pilots had flown the Mark 3 before, so after familiarising themselves with the new cockpit layout, they took off and flew to Little Rissington. *"This one flight was deemed sufficient to check us out on type"*, says Norman.

In August, a team from CFS visited the Empire Test Pilots School at RAE Farnborough to assist with the provisional instructional sequence for the Hunter T.7 spinning trials.

In the same month, the CFS was invited to the US Embassy in London to advise on the establishment of a helicopter ferry service from Regents Park to Chequers for use by Embassy VIPs. A letter of thanks was received from Rt. Hon. George Ward M.P., Secretary of State for Air.

Hunter spinning

With the recent introduction of the Hunter T.Mk.7 into squadron use, and with no trainer version of its own, CFS staff requested early access to an aircraft in particular to learn of its spinning characteristics. Consequently two staff from Advanced Standards, Sqn Ldr R.W. Jordan and Flt Lt J.H. Hardaker spent 17, 18 and 19 August with ETPS tutorial staff at Farnborough where they flew five spinning sorties each, comprising 53 spins and seven stalls in all. Sadly, Flt Lt Hardaker was fatally injured on 23 August near RAF Chivenor after ejecting from a Hunter T.7 which would not recover from a spin. He was buried at Little Rissington Church on 29 August.

Visit of the President of the USA

During a visit to the UK by USA President, Dwight Eisenhower, over the last weekend of August, CFS provided two helicopters for operations out of Chequers and two more at the American Ambassador's residence in Regents Park. These aircraft operated an hourly shuttle between the two locations from 07:30 to 19:30. A letter of appreciation from the US Ambassador was sent to the MoD. Four CFS Staff pilots were seconded for the detachment; Sqn Ldr A.J. Lee and Fg Off Chase to RAF Hendon for the US Ambassador's residence, and Flt Lt R.W. Smith and Flt Lt N.H. Fuller to RAF Halton for Chequers.

Battle of Britain

Held on 19 September, no fewer than 22 Little Rissington-based aircraft of varying types were employed on Battle of Britain displays throughout the country. "The Redskins" Aerobatic Team was kept busy, giving displays at the SBAC Farnborough, Jersey Airport, RAF Tangmere and RAF Biggin Hill, having warmed up with a show for over 700 ROC members at Little Rissington the day before. The 'Pair' remained active throughout October, performing at RAF stations West Malling, Chivenor and Stradishall, before winding down for their final performance at RAF Shawbury for HRH The Duchess of Gloucester on 22 October.

Deployment of CFS

The continued occupation of Little Rissington by CFS was confirmed in a letter from Flying Training Command dated 22

Three brand new Jet Provost T.Mk.3 aircraft lined up on the pan alongside a single Mark 1 in 1959, heralds the beginning of an era in which the Mark 3 operated from Little Rissington through to the airfield's closure seventeen years later. (*Norman Giffin*)

September 1959, which stated that "for the foreseeable future, the CFS would remain at RAF Little Rissington until a suitable alternative airfield becomes available" and concluded by confirming "that in the meantime there would be no development of the airfield."

ROC Day

The Royal Observer Corps open day was held on 13 October and was attended by a large contingent of members. Special demonstrations and exhibits were laid out in the hangars and a flying display provided the highlight of the afternoon.

Farewell Snowdrops – Welcome AMC!

Having a low security rating, the policing requirements at Little Rissington were quite small. Cpl Norman Ratcliffe spent three years as an RAF Policeman on camp, much of that time in the Guardroom; *"The change-over to Air Ministry Constabulary was a strange affair and I had no idea it was afoot. It was around the autumn of 1959. I went home on two weeks leave, leaving two RAF Policemen and some RAF Regiment Guardroom Assistants in the Guardroom. On my return two weeks later and much to my surprise, I was greeted by a constable of the AMC. He told me that during my absence all the other RAF security guys had been posted out, the AMC had taken over guardroom duties and that in order to maintain RAF discipline I would remain as the solitary MP. Until I left Little Rissington and the RAF in July 1960, I usually worked a 9 – 5 day, the exceptions being when I was called out by the AMC to deal with situations involving RAF personnel. A cushy little number."*

No. 250 Maintenance Unit closes

No. 250 MU had been a lodger unit based on the south side of the airfield for some time but it was closed with effect from 1 November 1959. The facilities then remained unused for several months until agreement was reached with the Triumph motor manufacturer for the storage of new vehicles in the hangars. The sight of car transporters crossing the far side of the airfield became a common occurrence.

Surprise, Surprise!

The C-in-C Flying Training Command, Air Marshal Atcherley, was not a regular visitor to Little Rissington, but on those rare occasions he would announce his arrival with a high speed run over the airfield in his Meteor at 07:30, when the airfield was still closed. A mad panic would ensue as Air Traffic rushed to the Tower to open up. 'Batchy's' opposition to Standards Wing was well known and Staff would quickly pack everything up and close their offices to delude him into thinking the building was closed, and join the 'Waterfront' guys on the lines and if possible, get airborne to give him the impression the Wing no longer existed. As soon as he left, the 'Trappers' re-opened their accommodation.

Boxing Tournament

Two other high ranking visitors to the station were Air Marshal Sir Hugh Constantine, AOC-in-C FTC, and Air Marshal Sir Arthur McDonald, specifically to attend an inter-command boxing tournament, held on 15 December. The result could not have pleased them as Technical Training Command beat Flying Training Command.

Santa Specials

As Christmas approached, two CFS helicopters from South Cerney were used to take Father Christmas to American air bases in the area – one to Brize Norton and the other to Fairford. A third chopper was used to bring Santa to the children's Christmas party at Little Rissington.

Three instructors waste no time in getting to grips with flying their new mounts in formation, Jet Provost T.3s, XM355/RA, XM360/RE and XM361/RF, soon after their entry into service at CFS. (*Norman Giffin*)

CHAPTER 4

Evolution Within The Fleet

1960

The year began with high pressure over the Continent and depressions moving northeast over the UK. As per normal the month of January was very dull, wet and windy, with up to 5 inches of snow laying on the ground from the 9th to 17th inclusive and again from the 21st to 28th. Personnel were employed on snow clearing tasks for much of the month until torrential rainfall washed it all away. Temperatures dropped to 20° F (17° F on the ground).

RLG

A letter from FTC HQ dated 15 February 1960, gave authority for CFS to start using RAF Aston Down as a Relief Landing Ground.

The Varsity arrives

With the arrival of the first two Varsity T.Mk.1s at Little Rissington, the Varsity Flight was established within Type Squadron on 22 February, under the command of Flt Lt Noonan. The full complement of four aircraft was reached in the early summer.

Multi-stream training

Early in 1960, the RAF adopted a multi-stream training system whereby all pilots qualified on Jet Provosts. Those destined to serve in fast jets moved on to complete their advanced training on Vampires, while pilots considered more suitable for flying propeller-driven types such as the Shackleton and Britannia, undertook their advanced training on Varsities. To cater for this revised syllabus, a small Varsity Flight was established at Little Rissington, operating from the pan adjacent to 1 Hangar.

One of the most interesting overseas visits by the Standards Wing occurred in March 1960 when the Trappers flew out to Ankara for an exchange of views and discussions on respective methods of flying with staff from the Turkish Air Force. On 5 July, they departed for a week's study of flying training techniques in the Royal Norwegian and Danish Air Forces.

Squadron dispersal

In the spring of 1960, No. 2 Squadron was operating twenty Vampire T.Mk.11s from the eastern end of 4 Hangar, the other end being home to 3 Squadron with three Meteor T.Mk.7s and three Canberra T.Mk.4s. Number 3 Hangar was allocated to Rectification Flight, while 1 Squadron occupied No. 2 Hangar with thirty-plus Piston Provosts and the six pre-production Jet Provost T.Mk.3s. The Handling Squadron's twin-engined Valetta, Varsities and Ansons, were usually parked outside with air and ground crew facilities provided at the western end of hangar number 2.

Two Pelican aerobatic teams!

Throughout the 1950s, nominations for title of the official RAF aerobatic team were limited to units from within Fighter Command, the most famous of these being the glossy black Hunters of 111 Squadron, the 'Black Arrows', while several Fighter and FTC units maintained teams that were invited to display at venues that could not justify the appearance of 'Treble-one'. In 1960, CFS flew two four-ship teams out of Little Rissington, one comprising Vampire T.11s and the other Jet Provost T.3s. They performed at various air shows throughout the summer, the Vampires as "Pelican Red" and Jet Provosts as "The Pelicans", which must have caused some confusion among air show organisers. Being faster, the Vampires could give a more thrusting performance than the under-powered JP3s, which seemed to struggle to reach the top of a loop.

WF412 was one of the first Varsity T.1s to serve at Little Rissington, arriving in July 1960. Initially coded MG it was re-coded 17 in 1961. (*Ray Deacon*)

Air Chief Marshal Sir Michael Graydon GCB CBE FRAeS

"Racking my brains for anything useful to add to a tome on CFS made me recall that I was a scaly Pilot Officer back in 1960, when attending No. 202 course between February and June. There were only two first tour instructors on our course, Andy Jones and myself. Andy later became a Hawker test pilot and did sterling work on the Hawk's initial development. Hugh Rigg, another test pilot, was also on this course with Ian Bashall, who had married Hugh's wife Sue's sister, when we were all at Linton, before Ian returned to the waterfront and led the Pelicans. Allan 'Kiwi' Williams was another, who subsequently married one of my then girlfriend's flatmates and packed a lot else into his dozen years in 'light blue'.

CFS was undoubtedly a good course and many memories linger of that early hot summer at Rissy, with some great flying and much hard work for a sprog Pilot Officer's eventual qualification as a B2 on Vampire T.11s. One story comes to mind which still amuses me. As usual, and even with several dozen aircrew, our RAF contingent carried its quota of a few rough diamonds. On 202 there was an Army Air Corps officer, a Captain Pike, who did attempt to add some tone and refinement to our course. One particular night our carefully spruced up Army officer was off to do his worst or best with the ladies at one of the nearby hotels – remember that there were trainee hoteliers in the Cotswolds and rather nice some of these were too. As the gallant Captain passed directly under the stairwell on his way out of the Mess for this particular evening's foray, a cry from above suddenly caught his attention. He looked up only to receive a french letter full of water (and they hold a serious amount) 'DH', a straight direct hit onto his head. Drenched by the water bomb, his fine suit now ruined and with all thoughts of his evening's dalliance vanished in that single instant, this incident confirmed once again for him and our other Army brethren that essentially we, the RAF, were all mere peasants!"

Hunter Courses

The five Hunter F.4s of the Hunter Type Flight over at Kemble were kept extremely busy running short familiarisation courses for Flying Training Command pilots. In April, for example, 13 pilots from various FTC bases undertook type flights while 5 students from courses at Little Rissington took the opportunity to experience the joys of supersonic travel. In May the number increased to 10 CFS instructors, 2 students, 11 FTC pilots and 1 pilot from Maintenance Command.

Throughout the remainder of the year, no fewer than 52 FTC pilots, 60 CFS Staff and 49 CFS students passed through the hands of the Hunter Type Flight, a creditable achievement and testimony to the high serviceability rates able to be maintained by the civilian staff of 5 MU.

Varsity Courses

The imminent delivery of the third and fourth of the allocation of Varsities to Little Rissington enabled the first course to get underway and the first three students began their instructor training on 27 April. One month later, the sole Valetta C.1, WJ496, was flown out to an MU.

Practice engine failure after take off (EFATO)

Flt Lt Peter Frame returned to Little Rissington as a QFI on the staff at CFS from 21 April 1960 until 12 June 1962, and became Flight Commander of the combined Vampire/Meteor Squadron in July 1961. Here he recalls one unnerving exercise in the Vampire training syllabus.

"One part of the course, which caused some members to be rather unhappy, was the practice of 'turn backs', following a simulated engine failure after take off. One ended up quite close to the ground and the stall with a Goblin engine that took an awfully long time to wind up (or so it seemed at the time through those long nine seconds). I remember that a few QFIs actually lost their category through apparent Low Moral Fibre (LMF) caused by this manoeuvre. The 'turn back' manoeuvre was quite fun, as long as you kept your nerve, although I do not recollect anyone having done it for 'real'. If I remember correctly, the minimum

A mixed formation over the Cotswold countryside on 2 July, 1960, comprises a selection of fixed-wing types operated by CFS. Trying to maintain station behind Anson C.19, TX225, are Canberra T.4, WD944, Varsity T.1, XD366, Jet Provost T.3, XM361, Piston Provost T.1, WW439, Meteor T.7, WL403 and Vampire T.11, XK582, flanked by Kemble-based Hunter F.4s, XF935 and XF944. (*Ron Dunn*)

speed to initiate the manoeuvre was 160 knots, and involved a steep wingover into the wind, keeping the speed about 140 knots and then hoping that you could make the threshold for the ensuing low overshoot or downwind roller. Doing the turn back yourself was fun but sitting there, whilst some pimply faced student at an AFS/FTS got into the buffet during the wingover was different. The biggest difficulty was getting Air Traffic's approval with a busy circuit.

Vampire turn backs were finally banned because simulating this as a practice emergency was resulting in more accidents than actual EFATOs would have caused. This story perhaps also highlights how good the Jet Provost's Viper was in this respect for being both faster on the wind up and more forgiving of rough throttle handling at any altitude. Earlier on piston-engined aircraft there also had been a fair number of real EFATOs on re-applying the power, after practising forced landings, without and even with those plug-clearing bursts to minimise this risk.

Our first child was born at the Cottage Hospital in Moreton-in-Marsh. On the day in question I had to rush back to Rissington after visiting Betty and new daughter because we were night flying. After consuming a few beers en-route (naughty) I got airborne with a student QFI to carry out his final night test. His patter for the night landing I will always remember because I had been doing it for years but had not put it into words: 'We keep coming down until the lights are up around our ears and then brace ourselves'.

The thing that caused problems for visiting QFIs on recats was that the field elevation of 730 ft was on average 500 ft higher than the recat's home base so that they very often fouled up their PFLs by being too low. That was when we used QNH of course. Interestingly, Mike Graydon, who had earlier been in my Flight at Cranwell, was my first student back at CFS. On leaving CFS I went on an exchange posting to the RCAF CFS for two years."

First of the new breed

Having completed his instructor training on Course No. 199, Flt Lt Chris Wilmot recalls an occasion when he was aircraft captain carrying out a mutual sortie over Chedworth,

"By the time I had suggested that my fellow and older student, later a test pilot, should put more power on and abort his forced landing, we were sufficiently low and to prove the fact handsomely - we came back to Little Rissington with decorative arboreal foliage hanging from the undercarriage, a distinctive appearance somewhat to the surprise of the airman marshalling us in.

I was one of half a dozen pilots selected at Intermediate Handling Test (IHT) on ability and background to form the first half dozen new Jet Provost instructor cadre at RAF Syerston. Five other QFIs off No. 199 Course who went to Syerston as pioneer Jet Provost instructors were Flt Lts Barry Dale, Brian Stephens, Andrew Whitaker and two creamed off QFI graduates, Jim Watts-Phillips and Alec Reid."

At that time the Intermediate Handling Test took place after 45 flying hours, during which time the stress was placed on familiarisation with type and the development of an accurate flying technique.

Creamy's persistence beats the system

Flt Lt Alasdair Liddle, after half a century in both military and civil aviation, reminisces on his determination to fly the Hunter Mark 4 at Kemble, with an affectionate memory of a welcome intervention by the Commandant, Air Cdre Whitworth.

"Like many youths in the early 1950s, I fell in love with the Hunter at first sight. In fact, I joined the RAF in October 1958 to fly that beautiful aeroplane. Approaching 'Wings' at Oakington a year and a half later, I had to complete a list of preferences: I wrote, '111 Squadron', '43 Squadron' and another Hunter outfit, which also appealed. Shortly afterwards, I was ordered into the Flight Commander's office, to be told that I was a b..... fool and that I should have nominated Fighters, Light Bombers and CFS. However, he added, it did not matter as I was going to CFS anyway! Not what I wanted but, he said, I could choose my posting after the instructional tour. As almost all my course seemed to be going to Hastings, Shackletons and Beverleys, I acquiesced with 'Hobson's Choice'!

Thus on 9 May 1960, I joined No. 203 Course at 'Hell on the Hill', as some called it, although I actually enjoyed both the place and the course. Basically I was doing the same as I had been doing for the previous year and a half, on the Piston Provost and Vampire, albeit now in the other seat – so maybe I knew no better. The big improvement was that I was now being treated more like an adult and an officer, rather than just another dim student! The great attraction of the course was to fly the Hunter – or the Canberra: both lovely aircraft which I wanted to fly. When the 'type flying' started, the Hunter was naturally my top priority, so I opted for that. 'No!' I was told, 'you'll have to fly in the Canberra, not the Hunter'. 'Why?' I asked. 'First tourists fly in the Canberra' was the curt reply. 'Why?' I repeated. 'Not enough first pilot jet hours'. 'What then is the minimum number of hours for the Hunter?' '70 hours' (if I recollect correctly) was the answer. So I rushed off to Shawbury, at every opportunity, and shot about a million QGH/GCAs, for the training of new controllers. Eventually I announced at Rissy that I now had the requisite number of hours and that I should like to fly the Hunter. To my immense disappointment, I was yet again told that I could not. 'Why?' Answer: 'Policy – first tourist!' End of conversation! To spite myself, I declined to fly the Canberra: in some ways I regret that decision, so please ask me now!

Late in the evening of our final dining-out night, my boss, Squadron Leader Peter Hicks, asked me if I had enjoyed the course. I answered, honestly, that I had but added that I was very disappointed that I had been unable to fly the Hunter. I think that there was a non-committal reply – but it was late at night! The following morning, the Commandant, while presenting me with my QFI certificate, mentioned that he had heard that I regretted not being allowed to fly the Hunter. I agreed. Air Cdre Whitworth then said, 'Well! Get a b..... move on. Pete Frame is in a Vampire T.11, waiting to take you to Kemble, which shuts today at 13:00 hours!' I cannot remember how I answered. I suspect that I spluttered thanks as I exited his office – supersonically! Ever since that remarkable order, I have hoped, fervently, that I had expressed my gratitude properly: if not, excitement must excuse any lack of decorum.

Within milliseconds, I was leaping into the T.11, the Goblin already being wound up by Pete Frame, as I continued strapping in as we taxied out. I really cannot remember the short trip to Kemble. Etched forever in my mind though, was the thrill of climbing into this gorgeous Hunter F.Mk.4. Strapping in, while 'Sharky' Hastings was on the ladder, he fixed an emergency checklist to my thigh and asked if I knew how to start it. 'No!' I apologised with a grin. Sharky leaned down and pressed something in front of the 'stick' … 'Bang!' went a cartridge … the Avon 122 engine slowly wound-up … the ladder was whipped away in a trice … and he was gone. 'Now, what the hell do I do next?' I wondered briefly.

After a simple taxi round the perimeter track, in my excitement I scarcely noticed the high pressure nosewheel tyre and oleo beneath me, before calling for take-off, lining up and then catapulting down the centre-line of Runway 27. Needless to say, I twitched my way into the blue sky – as most of you will know, the Hunter's powered ailerons were considerably lighter than the Vampire's manual ones. Then followed 30 minutes of sheer bliss, rolling and looping in that 8/8ths clear, mainly Gloucestershire sky. What joy! J.G. Magee's poem 'High Flight' recalls the ecstasy. All too soon, as fuel and curfew dictated, the short flight ended in a surprisingly smooth landing on those high pressure tyres and that lovely wide track. This was, by far, the most exciting and memorable flight in my whole 50 years' career with 20,000 hours on a wide variety of aircraft types. Days later, I arrived at Cranwell as a brand new instructor, allegedly the youngest"

Royal appointment – Commandant-in-Chief

On 29 June 1960, Her Majesty Queen Elizabeth the Queen Mother was appointed Commandant-in-Chief of the Central Flying School, making this only the second RAF unit to have links with a member of the Royal Family, the RAF College at Cranwell being the other. Her Majesty made the first of several visits to Little Rissington when she arrived in a Heron of the Queen's Flight on 16 November. That she took her appointment seriously was conveyed by the warmth and genuine interest she expounded as she toured the base.

Arriving at 11:40 Her Majesty was received by Air Marshal Sir Hugh Constantine C-in-C Flying Training Command, Lady Constantine, Air Cdre Whitworth Commandant CFS and Mrs Whitworth. A formation of Type Squadron Hunters saluted her arrival with a flypast over the airfield. Luncheon was taken in the Officers' Mess with grace being said by the Reverend Pickthorn the officiating chaplain. Her Majesty and the invited guests were treated to music played by the Salon Orchestra of Central Band of the Royal Air Force.

Following the luncheon and official photographs including invited guests, Her Majesty was taken to the Airmanship Hall, where NCOs and civilian staff were presented to her. Among them were; WO Randall the longest serving airman who had seen some 35 years service since joining the RAF in 1925, Ch Tech Salmon the second longest serving airman with 34 years service and WO Cullen the third longest serving airman who joined the RAF in 1929. Two civilian staff presented were Mr Pearce, a Clerical Officer with 30 years service for the RAF, and Mr Peachy, a Charge Hand who was the longest serving civilian at Little Rissington having joined the station in 1938 on its opening.

Her Majesty was then invited back to the Officers' Mess where seated at the entrance hall she was treated to music by the Station's Pipe Band. The day ended with a flying display by CFS aircraft before Her Majesty boarded her Queen's Flight Heron and departed at 15:30.

Ground Training

Ground training was completed in the first twelve weeks of the Instructors course. The syllabus was aimed at refreshing the student's knowledge of basic subjects and developing his interest and knowledge of the more advanced subjects such as high speed flight.

Before departing Little Rissington in the Queen's Flight Heron at the conclusion of her first visit to CFS as Commandant-in-Chief, HRH The Queen Mother greets pilots from the unit's display teams - Pelican Red (Lt R. Wren, and Flt Lts P. Broughton, P. Frame and J. Mayes) on the left, and The Pelicans (Flt Lts R. Langstaff, F. Brambley, J. Nicklin and Plt Off B. McDonald) on the right. Sandwiched in between is Meteor solo pilot Flt Lt D. Goodsir. Flt Sgt Tucker, background left in white, heads up the ground support team while the Commandant, Air Cdre J. Whitworth, would appear to be signalling an instruction to someone. (*Simon Watson*)

Examinations were set at the completion of a subject in the Ground School and Progress Checks were included throughout the Flying syllabus. To graduate, all students must have attained the standard required for the award of B2 Instructor category.

Flying Training Sequence

During his speech at the CFS annual conference, Air Cdre Whitworth stated that, "Despite reductions of aircraft in recent years the front line service is expanding once more and is now seven times the size of the 1935 Air Force."

The Instructors' Course lasted sixteen weeks with each intake of 42 students spaced at nine-week intervals. During the first eight weeks, all students undertook 51 hours of training on the principles of Basic instruction on the Piston Provost T.1. On completion of this stage, students were provisionally streamed as either Basic or Advanced Instructors.

During the final eight weeks, twenty students moved on to 27.5 hours learning the applied stages of the Provost course plus a twelve hour familiarisation course on the Vampire T.11. The remaining 22 students selected for the Advanced Course were taught the advanced principles of instruction with 40 hours flying on the T.11. In addition, during the second half of the course all students were given a limited amount of flying in the Hunter (2 hours) and Canberra (3 hours).

Flying Instructional Exercise Numbers

To make things easier for instructors to authorise, or students to be authorised for, the main exercise elements of their instructional sorties in the Jet Provost T.Mk.3, Alan Pollock outlines the exercises and numbering system that was used over several years. *"The relevant Exercise Numbers would be entered into the appropriate column space of each Flight's large daily Authorisation Sheets (the 'legalising' RAF Form 1575B system) before each training flight.*

Ex.1 Familiarisation with the Aircraft
Ex.2 Preparation for Flight and Action after Flight
Ex.3 Air Experience
Ex.4 Effects of controls
Ex.5 Taxiing
Ex.6 Straight and Level Flight
Ex.7 Climbing
Ex.8 Descending
Ex.9 Medium Turns
Ex.10 Stalling
Ex.11 Spinning
Ex.12 Take-Off and Climb
Ex.13 Approach and Landing
Ex.14 First Solo
Ex.15 Advanced Turning
Ex.16 Low Flying
Ex.17 Forced Landing
Ex.18 Aerobatics
Ex.19 Instrument Flying
Ex.20 Night Flying
Ex.21 Pilot Navigation
Ex.22 Formation Flying
Ex.23 High Level Familiarisation

Once a QFI, an instructor would almost invariably be self-authorising of his own and his students' flights and sortie objectives. A pilot's last job before aircraft final inspection and flying would be to inspect the Form 700 technical serviceability log of his aircraft and sign for its acceptance against the NCO i/c Servicing's aircraft 'readiness to fly' signature.

After landing and leaving his aircraft, the pilot's first task was to fill in the Form 700 in the Line Hut, thereby formally handing back his aircraft to the care of the ground crew technicians. In the Captain's after flight certificate and change of serviceability log, the aircraft, if no problems had been encountered in flight, would be certified by him as 'Serviceable'. If problems had occurred, the unserviceable items found in flight for that aircraft would be carefully recorded, often after discussion with the relevant tradesmen.

Next, in the Ops Room, the after flight F1575B 'Authorisation Sheet' would be completed for those actual exercises, which had been carried out (DCO = Duty Carried Out, DPCO for Partly or DNCO for Not Carried Out) and the length of time spent airborne entered to the nearest five minutes. Also recorded, if applicable, would be the time of 'simulated', in clear air, instrument flying with a safety pilot/instructor ('under the hood', i.e., effectively flying 'blind' with a blue goggles and amber screen system or later the helmet visor preventing external vision) or/and minutes flown 'actual'. 'Actual' Instrument Flying meant time in cloud, totally on instruments and without any external reference possible. Lastly the total number of landings, roller and final, would be entered before finally initialling for all these figures recorded in the 'Authorisation Sheets'.

At the end of each month, all aircrew would copy out their month's flying from the filed copies of the Auth Sheets in a standard fashion for their monthly, annual or course totals to be signed by flight and squadron commanders. Many thousands of logbooks are filled with the above exercise numbers, which changed little over the years, particularly on the basic stages of flying, and I feel that the above example of the numbers used half way through the period in question would be of interest to the vast majority of pilots without their relevant key to the exercise numbers.

Because of a different requirement to cover a given number of course exercises with some, such as Basic, Intermediate and Final Handling Tests, Instrument Rating Tests or High, Low, High Navigation and Diversion exercises, containing a whole menu of different elements, there was a move, particularly on later more demanding sorties and aircraft, to switch towards a more closely planned Flying Syllabus Sortie Number basis.

AP3225, the CFS Instructional Guide, developed as soon as possible for each aircraft type, would include three to ten pages of Aim, Sequence and Observations in summary for each of these major flying exercise areas. This Guide would also assist standardisation for all instructors to cover the most important aspects of each major element in the flying training syllabus."

Air/Sea search

Two Helicopters from the CFS Helicopter Squadron at South Cerney assisted in search for the crews of two tankers which sank after collision on the River Severn in October. One body was recovered.

ROC Day

On 28 August the station played host to over 1,000 guests from the Royal Observer Corps (ROC), the highlight of which was the afternoon's flying display. Home-based participants included the two "Pelican" aerobatic teams (Vampire and Jet Provost) supported by various solo displays. An interesting array of visiting aircraft included Hart, Hurricane, Spitfire, Mosquito, Shackleton, Beverley, Hunter and Javelin. For the finale, the sixteen glossy black Hunters of 111 Squadron gave an exhilarating performance, one of the Black Arrows final displays before the unit's conversion to Lightnings.

By JP to West Africa

In September, the Jet Provost "Pelican" team departed for Nigeria to help the country celebrate its independence. Having given displays at various venues, the main highlights of the tour were; a formation flypast as part of the Commonwealth Air Forces parade at Lagos racecourse on 29 September and full aerobatic displays over Lagos harbour on 2 October and before President Nkrumah at Accra Airport on the 6th in Ghana.

Examining Wing

That the 'Trappers' had another busy year would be an understatement as a glance at the table below will verify. Visits to home and overseas establishments continued at a regular pace with well over 1,200 tests and checks carried out (April to December shown):

	Basic	Advanced	Multi	Totals
Instructor re-cat.	100	46	1	147
Instrument Rating	74	67	41	182
Standardisation	605	155	164	924
Totals	779	268	206	1253

In addition to checking instructors at 19 RAF bases in the UK plus several more in 2 TAF, Staff also carried out tests at 26 University Air Squadrons, two Royal Navy Air Stations, one Army Air Corps unit and no less than 15 civilian aero clubs, such was the high esteem in which the Wing was held outside of the RAF.

Overseas visits were made to several air forces including those in Denmark and Norway, led by Gp Capt E. James, and to RAF units in the FEAF from 17 September to 19 October. A further visit to the MEAF took place in November.

Liaison visits were also arranged to give Staff the opportunity to exchange information, impart new methodologies and to study different techniques employed elsewhere. On one such occasion, a Multi Standards team visited 231 OCU at RAF Bassingbourn.

Vampire spins into trouble

In the first half of 1960 a number of inexplicable difficulties in Vampire T.11 spin recoveries were reported. In some cases eventual recovery had been achieved in others the crew ejected and there were fatalities. Surviving 'rogue' aircraft were flown to CFS and after thorough re-checks of rigging, were spun and recovered repeatedly at various loadings and centre-of-gravity positions. Cpl Malcolm Thomas was responsible for carrying out some of these rigging checks and he reported that *"No problems were identified and no conclusions reached except that the subject aircraft were serviceable."* Nevertheless the official view was that perhaps spinning instruction in the advanced trainer had become too expensive and might have to be deleted from the syllabus. HQ Flying Training Command put the problem to the then Commandant of CFS, Air Cdre 'Pat' Connolly (a pre-war ex-Halton Apprentice). He called a meeting attended by the CFI, the CI and the Squadron Commanders to consider the situation and the advice to be given to HQ FTC. The Commandant convinced all that if spinning the Vampire were to be abandoned the effect would be to compromise handling and operational efficiency because of the lack of confidence which would be instilled. More investigation into the causes of delayed spin recovery was required, and the results widely disseminated to restore confidence.

Sqn Ldr Peter Hicks was tasked with this, being OC the Advanced Squadron and having already carried out some appropriate investigation as President of Boards of Inquiry into spinning accidents. He selected Flt Lt Don Sly of 2 Squadron to make up a team to carry out the task.

> *"We formulated a plan of approach",* writes Peter Hicks, *"and commenced by identifying and then consulting as many authorities on the theory of spinning as possible. Perhaps the greatest of these was a Mr. Bisgood of Cranfield. Finally it was agreed that the most likely cause of the difficulties was in the case following spin initiation, or unintentional spin entry, when the aircraft entered an unrecognised inverted spin and normal erect-spin recovery action was taken, this then being pro-inverted spin.*
>
> *A single suitable series of actions to effect recovery in all types of spin was decided upon and agreed by all. From 13 October to 15 November, Don and I visited the RAF College Cranwell, the FTSs at Oakington, Valley, Swinderby, Linton-on-Ouse, and the School of Air Traffic Control. At each place we explained the new theory and the actions to be taken to ensure recovery before briefing and flying with the CFIs, Squadron and Flight Commanders and the Standards Flight members. Each sortie involved a climb to 35,000 ft and normally about four spins to get the message across and practised. It says much for the 'victims', none of whom had spun for at least six months during the suspension, that they evinced keen interest throughout! Each of the two team members carried out 20 sorties involving a total of approximately 160 spins.*
>
> *Confidence having been restored (it was felt!) each establishment visited was cleared to resume spinning instruction."*

CFS Vampires visit the Italian Air Force

Vampire T.11s, XK586 and WZ416, taxi out on the first leg to Italy. (*Ray Deacon*); (*below*), Sqn Ldr Peter Hicks, Flt Lt 'Bertie' Cann and Lt 'Dickie' Wren with Italian Air Force personnel shortly after arriving in Turin. (*Peter Hicks*)

For many years CFS attached great importance to visits to the flying training establishments of foreign air forces. These visits were always welcomed by other air forces in view of the established CFS position in the forefront of flying training throughout the world since the year 1912.

On November 21 1960, two 2 Sqn Vampire T.11s (XK586 and WZ416), fitted with drop tanks and crewed by Sqn Ldr Peter Hicks with Lt Gene Rohr USAF and Lt 'Dickie' Wren RN with Flt Lt 'Bertie' Cann, left Little Rissington to visit the Flying Training Organisation of the Italian Air Force (IAF).

"The first leg was to have been to Turin direct", recalls Peter, *"but due to a little confusion with the French Air Traffic Control and doubtful weather at Turin, a diversion was made to Orange in France and the aircraft were refuelled before continuing to Turin. The aim here was to tour the Fiat Aircraft Factory to see the Fiat G-91T, to be the first IAF swept wing transonic advanced trainer. At this time the RAF was well advanced with the introduction of the Gnat Trainer. Of course, the team was shown all over the car factory willy-nilly!*

The next day the team left Turin for Pratica di Mare the HQ of IAF Flying Training Command to be met with an official and very warm welcome which set the tone for the entire visit. At the end of a mutually informative day the team enjoyed its first taste of warm IAF hospitality, but managed to have clear heads to depart to their Central Flying School at Amendola for more presentations and exchanges of facts and ideas. During the four days here the team members were driven to Grottaglie for flights in the G-91T, but these were early days to make any really useful comparisons with the Gnat. The team was then driven to Lecce to gather information on the IAF's Basic Flying Training programme.

On the sixth day, we returned to the HQ at Pratica di Mare for final 'wash up' discussions and sincere mutual exchanges of appreciation and goodwill. Our return flight was made via Orange (planned this time – one learns!), and Lyneham for Customs Clearance. It was as well that declarations were made, for the IAF, bless'em, nil dubitare to show that all work and no play makes Jack a dull boy, had crammed the hydraulic bays of both aircraft with – bottles of Chianti! An interesting and happy visit."

Not all liaison visits were external to CFS. Senior personnel were invited to come to Little Rissington as was the case in November when Gp Capt Hunderson of the RAAF arrived to study CFS Training Methods.

Hunter trainers allocated to the Kemble Type Flight

Late in 1960, the first of two Hunter T.Mk.7 aircraft (WV318) arrived as replacements for two Hunter Mark 4s, the second machine (XL611) being delivered in May of the following year. At this time, the Flight had an establishment of three instructors, all ex-Hunter squadron pilots who had completed a tour of instruction at a Flying Training School.

Weather hampers training

The second half of 1960 was most notable for prolonged periods of heavy rain and strong winds, the worst on record, causing major disruption to the course schedules, many of which had to be extended.

1961

New aprons

In January 1961, work commenced on the construction of the first of two new Aircraft Servicing Pans (ASP), to the south of No. 2 Hangar. Large areas of grass by the flight line were dug out and the first sections of concrete laid. The project was programmed to take six months to completion.

Staffing levels

The number of Staff and Airmen allocated to RAF Little Rissington fluctuated from month to month, as people were posted out and either gaps or overlaps occurred with the arrival of their replacements. In early 1961, 148 Staff officers and 100 Students, supported by 590 Airmen and 72 Airwomen, were assigned to CFS but, following an Air Ministry Sub-Committee review on 6-8 February, these figures increased slightly over the ensuing twelve months. An additional 300 or so civilian workers were employed as tractor and bowser drivers and on ancillary tasks on the various flights and messes across the station.

Wheels up at Aston Down

With the steady increase in Jet Provost training, nearby RAF Aston Down saw increasing use for roller landing practice and in one unfortunate incident involving T.3, XM355, a student's glove caught the HP cock causing it to partially close and flame out the engine. The quick witted instructor managed to relight the engine but, with insufficient power available, the aircraft made a wheels-up landing.

Little Rissington was a popular destination for cadets of the Air Training Corps with visits and summer camps commencing from late spring onwards. A full programme of activities, which included range practice, Link Trainer exercises and visits to the Control Tower were arranged for them, but the highlight was a trip in a Piston Provost at the end of their stay.

Royal Navy to the rescue

Having been a B2 category instructor on the Hunter T.Mk.8 since its introduction at RNAS Lossiemouth, Lt Michael Doust decided that, together with one of his colleagues, Arthur Stewart, it was time for them to go south to CFS and be examined for their A2 category.

"Over the next six weeks or so, we sat down together in Arthur's married quarter dining room studying the RAF Instructional Manual, and everything to do with the Hunter T.8 jet trainer. By the time we arrived at CFS, we knew every rivet, nut, bolt and piece of piping in the aircraft. In addition, we had 764 Squadron's home made instructional manual for the T.8 (there was at that time no RAF Instructional Manual for the Hunter trainer). This manual was to stand us in good stead, because the CFS examiners could not believe that we had gone to such lengths to produce it. They were so intrigued with it that we left a copy with them, and it would eventually become the standard RAF manual after some modifications and re-writing.

We arrived at RAF Kemble where the school kept its Hunters. Arthur went for his flight test first, while I stayed on the ground being thoroughly quizzed on all aspects of flight, aeronautics and weather. When Arthur had finished his flight, I was briefed and up I went and was back on the ground in time for lunch. We both passed the flying examination, and the examiners were extremely pleased at our standard of airmanship and handling ability in an aircraft, which was not used too much for advanced flying training. When lunch was over, they quizzed both Arthur and I even further about our academic flying knowledge, until 18:00. We both thought that the examiners were not going to stop, and then suddenly

One of the first conversions from Hunter fighter to two-seat trainer, Type Flight's Kemble-based WV318 is seen on static display at the CFS 50th anniversary celebrations at Little Rissington, 7 July, 1962. Coincidentally, the aircraft is still flying out of Kemble airfield as the flagship of Delta Jets. *(Rod Brown)*

they stood up, said, 'Thank you, well done both of you, you have passed with flying colours!' We looked at each other, with great big smiles all over our faces and shook hands with each other and the examiners, we had done it! As it was now so late, and the airfield personnel had secured for the day, we stayed overnight at the CFS Officers' Mess and celebrated somewhat. Early the next day we were on our way back to Lossiemouth, where congratulations all round were waiting for us. Arthur and I were chuffed to the core, we felt like two little suns glowing with success!"

Aircraft movements

To say that Rissy was a busy airfield would be an understatement. Movements of jet aircraft for the month of April 1961, for example, were 2,191 during the day and 250 at night, to which can be added a further 919 piston aircraft movements, producing a total of 3,360. Three months later, when better weather allowed for a more concentrated flying programme, jet movements amounted to 3,504 of which 694 occurred at night, while piston aircraft increased the figure by 1,394, giving a total for July of 4,898. In August the total exceeded 6,000 movements.

Aircraft inventory

The number of aircraft on the CFS inventory in 1961 totalled 84 and it was during this year that individual aircraft codes began to change from the two-letter alphabetical system loosely based on aircraft type, V=Vampire, P=Piston Provost, C=Canberra, etc., to a numerical system, 01-84. By comparison with other FTC establishments, the numerals applied to the CFS aircraft were small and applied to areas on the airframe that were difficult to see.

Flying Wing reorganisation

A major reorganisation of the Flying Wing came into force on 4 May, the main changes being as follows:

1 Squadron

A Flight. Role changed from Basic Jet Provost and all through Piston Provost and Chipmunk flight to Basic Jet Provost flight.

B Flight. Became responsible for Piston Provost and Chipmunk.

2 Squadron

A and B Flights. Reformed from a single squadron of Vampires.

C Flight. Comprised remnants of Vampire squadron plus the Meteors from 3 Squadron.

D Flight. Became the Jet Provost Applied Flight.

3 Squadron

Originally known as the Type Squadron, its mission was unchanged but it was reorganised into three flights: Varsity, Canberra and Hunter (the latter flight remaining at Kemble).

Revised colour scheme

By the turn of the decade, when most aircraft in Flying Training Command had received the silver and day-glo livery, it was found that the 'Fluolac' paint tended to peel back from the nose and wing leading edges within a few months of application. As the Maintenance Units did not have the capacity to trial new designs and materials, CFS was called upon by HQ, FTC to resolve the issue and to produce standard designs suitable for all aircraft types operated by the Command.

Seven aircraft were allocated to the project and the work was carried out in No. 5 Hangar throughout the summer of 1961. Vampire T.11, XK633/VA was the first aircraft to be treated, followed by examples from the Jet Provost (XM355), Varsity (XD366), Piston Provost (XF900), Canberra (WD944) and Chipmunk fleets, plus one of the two Ansons (VP517). The new styling comprised narrow strips of 'Scotchal Fluatape' tape applied to the nose, tail and wing surfaces over a silver base. On the Vampire, Jet Provost, Canberra and Varsity, the strips were initially applied to the fuselage sides forward of the wing and were difficult to see head-on. The best solution was found

In 1961, several aircraft were used to trial a new day-glo red-striped paint scheme including Vampire T.11, XK633, which carries both old and new codes VA and 30. *(Ray Deacon)*

Apart from the arrangement of the stripes on the forward fuselage on Jet Provost T.3, XM355/RA, the design was perpetuated on all Flying Training Command aircraft over the ensuing years. *(Ray Deacon)*

by applying the strips in a radial pattern from the centre of the nose, as in a starburst, and all FTC aircraft adapted variations of this scheme over the next few years. Strangely, no Meteors were involved in the re-styling at CFS but the design was perpetuated on most FTC 'Meatboxes' by MUs.

New terms and responsibilities

Under the terms of a new Air Ministry Order, Central Flying School took over responsibility for the re-categorisation and standardisation of Hunter QFIs and pilots. At that time Flying Training Command used the Vampire T.11, Meteor T.7, Jet Provost T.3, Provost T.1, Chipmunk T.10 and Varsity T.1 as training aircraft. Swept-wing aircraft differed from all of these aircraft in such aspects as stalling and transonic characteristics, take-off and landing techniques, control, trim, brake, oxygen and anti-g systems. With the introduction into the services of such aircraft as the Lightning, Victor, Comet, Sea Vixen and Buccaneer it became of paramount importance to acquaint instructors of Flying Training Command with the characteristics of swept wing aircraft. Thus they would be better equipped to discuss knowledgeably with their students all the important differences of swept wing flying.

CFS Helicopters move to Ternhill

After four years based at South Cerney, the CFS Helicopter Squadron was reformed as part of a Helicopter Wing and departed for its new home at RAF Ternhill on 10 August 1961. It arrived with all its 14 aircraft flying in formation, having first overflown Little Rissington on the flight north to Shropshire. The Wing comprised No. 1 Squadron (Pilot and Instructor Courses), 2 Squadron (Operational Training Courses) and 3 Squadron (Helicopter Examining Unit). The Search and Rescue Training Squadron (later to become 3 Squadron) formed on 23 April 1962, at RAF Valley.

Safe ejections from Jet Provost

While on a navigation exercise on 30 August, the Viper on Jet Provost T.3, XM423 failed and the crew ejected safely. The aircraft crashed into a national grid pylon and was totally destroyed. No mention was made in the records as to the effect on power supplies in the area.

"All right, provided one does not inhale!"

No. 208 course was held in the middle year of post-war Rissy CFS. Flt Lt Alan Pollock describes some course memories, a lost toss and (for him) an expensive line hut refuelling mistake, nearly leading to a bricked up ground school:

"After a 36 hour Provost Refresher Course at Manby, No. 208 course began for me on 8 May 1961. The Provosts had now gone at Rissy: for two thirds of us we were an early straight through course on the Jet Provost Mark 3. Our syllabus was 96 hours: for the Applied stage our remaining third split between Chipmunk, Vampire or Varsity.

Rissy course photos were in front of the Mess portico, below that impressive balcony, with its imposing stonework coat of arms and behind that the VIP room's three windows. This route for a tiny irreverent 208 band was a midnight rite of passage into the Mess, in tailchase line astern formation, shinning up the convenient drainpipe on the left, pull up and swing over on to the sacred balcony, pause to reconnoitre before stealthily

(*left*) Snapped by Ray Deacon from his Baldwin block window, thirteen of the sixteen CFS helicopters overfly Little Rissington on their way from South Cerney to Ternhill on 10 August, 1961. (*inset*) XL826/A leads eight Bristol Sycamores into RAF Ternhill. (*MP*) *climbing through the sash windows quietly across this darkened room to open its door. Within that room, two out of three times, a sonorous Chief Instructor would lay dreaming or even making less intelligible snore-patter, perhaps why career-minded colleagues chickened out and I never led more than a pair through this, our own sobering up 208 Course 'Exercise 99'.*

Thirty-five QFIs completed our course including three RN pilots and one of our two starting Army Air Corps pilots. Also on course was Sulie Sulaiman bin Sujak, who subsequently helped start the Royal Malaysian Air Force: from Flt Lt to AV-M in six or seven years was not bad going. Our fast chat watchword riposte to take on the CFS staff, as we swiftly had to learn to fly accurately and talk over our strange patter techniques to an imaginary student 'Bloggs' was: 'Look, maestro, if I'd really wanted to become an actor, I'd have gone off to RADA six years ago.' The second 'knowledge' response was that the height of Little Riss airfield was really only 600 ft asl, with the top 130 ft being pure compounded bullshit. In a week less than four months, my logbook notes that I flew 53.45 dual and 41.50 mutual and solo hrs, our 96 hr entitlement then".

Clarkson Trophy – "How not to compete"

Al Pollock was just off a ground tour and pleased enough to have reached the Clarkson final stage, and for what Kiwi Snowy McKee, Bob Jennings and others had taught him in order to smarten up the basics.

"It paid to finish off one's Final Handling Test early, so thank you, Boss Peter Hicks, for that - one gash Hunter T.7 flight at Kemble with M/Plt Trigg and a further nine enjoyable, mostly low level, aerobatic sorties were more fun than our surfeit diet of 'patter patter, our brains to scatter' exercises. For the work up and pre-qualification in 1961, one had one's instructor but flew solo for the first fly-off competition to reduce the field for the final. There were eight of us left as pre-qualified for the low level aerobatics competition final on the last day of our 208 course, after previous day fly-offs on 31 August. The four of us flying JP Mark 3s (Pete Jennings, Brian Stead and Ed Stein) had all flown mutual with each other on those last three days. In earlier Meteor CFS course eras we knew there were no height limits and for some time Meteors landed on one engine. To our surprise there was no realistic lower rolling limit differential of, say, 200 ft as opposed to looping recoveries safely by 500 ft. My instructor, Bob Jennings, had managed to see the dress rehearsal markings and pre-briefed me for my final solo competitive slot on the following day. Told that I had come top on the laid down set piece textbook aerobatic markings in the fly off, I was advised that I would need to improve my voluntary additional manoeuvres and add some continuity polish and pizzazz in order to impress the judges to decisively beat my friend Pete Jennings.

By coincidence Don Cameron, also off a ground tour, was separately disqualified for using flick manoeuvres in the Chipmunk. Events were not, as subsequent rumours had them, some planned Spartacus and the Slaves Revolt conspiracy, which precipitated my low level inverted arrival up the Rissington Hill in the 05 Runway direction. A groundcrew or line-hut cock up meant that the three aircraft allocated to Pete, Brian Stead and myself were each differently fuelled, one two thirds internals, one full internals and one mistakenly with full tiptanks, which on losing the toss was the only one available for yours truly. Brian wanted the full

Course No. 208 had a typical joint service content, with students from the RAF, the Royal Navy and Army. (*back row, l to r*): Plt Off T. Thornton, Fg Offs E. Stein, J. Barker, Flt Lts J. Timms, B. Stead, W. Norton, J. McCluney, W. Mills, A. Pollock, Sulaiman-Bin-Sujak, T. Watson and Fg Offs E. Hall and G. Thorneycroft. (*centre row, l to r*); Capt J. Coles, Flt Lts E. Lance, P. Jennings, J. Hickmott, R. Chambers, P. Cash, D. Brett, C. Beckwith, N. Bacon, R. Blockey, D. Cameron, A. Chambers, M. Hardy, A. Holbourn, J. Laing. (*front row, l to r*); Lt P. Fish, Flt Lt T. Gill, Sqn Ldr G. Burleigh, Flt Lt A. Dodson, Sqn Ldrs A. Trowbridge, P. Hicks, Wg Cdr C. Gray, Gp Capt R. de Burgh, Wg Cdrs K. Tapper, J. Lee, Sqn Ldrs D. Franklin, J. Woods and P. Peters, Lts G. Harris, C. McClelland. (*CFS via Alan Pollock*)

internals and Pete sensibly took the lightest aircraft. With full tiptanks, available 'g' was reduced from 6 to 5 with tip fuel and aerobatics prohibited – what a circus! My race to get airborne and burn off at high throttle with airbrakes out was a vain attempt to be light enough for an absolutely silent roll off the top arrival and relight.

Stop-cocked with its donk out, the Viper's two JP cheek intakes had this disquieting, excessively noisy popping and banging, previously practised with my opposition and present helper in recall, Peter Jennings, the deserved Clarkson winner. The JP's spilling intakes with increasing drag and speed from 180 to 280 kts caused compression flatulence and this noise if heard from the ground would spoil the pure windmilling glide flamed out loop and relight. The sheer volume of sky over Aston Down used in a flamed out loop higher up at that weight and my imminent premature call-in time meant an immediate plan B .... to arrive quietly from nowhere up the hill inverted, the only spur of the moment manoeuvre for the required distinctive panache. My careful inverted extra low level arrival up the Runway 05 approach hill from Great Rissington meant that I must avoid either skying or skylining for the 'different' voluntary surprise arrival. To look smooth, since inverted, I had, so obvious in retrospect, to pull down around the hilltop to follow the airfield's contours, a literal learning curve, as I had never flown up a hill inverted before. My very public disqualification, three seconds into my pull up, after my safe slow roll out from my inverted arrival next to the tower, in my book was not cricket, as I had not really even begun my Clarkson aerobatic routine – in the little JP, with the donk going, one could easily gain height on every manoeuvre. For ever I regretted not being 'current' enough to have immediately pulled my R/T connector out 'by mistake' and got on with my so carefully practised Clarkson routine – the apoplectic Group Captain bellowing expletives through the air waves into my headset, was more than upsetting – was CFS teaching not also those three letters emphasised for every recruit in the RAF … Resolution, Audacity and Fortitude?"

The Gnat Project

The decision to establish a project team at CFS to prepare for the introduction of a new trainer into service followed precedent. The appointment of Flt Lt Derek Bryant to lead the project was unusual in that he was not a CFS instructor. Nonetheless he received a warm welcome and was attached to Standards (the Trappers) in March 1961 to await the delivery of the first aircraft. On 2 February 1962 he flew in the rear seat of XM709 on the delivery flight from Dunsfold to Little Rissington.

"The intervening eleven months had not been idled away. The end product of the project was to be the publication of the Gnat Instructor's Handbook, the creation of various syllabi for instructor conversion and for ab initio students, and help (to the extent possible) Handling Squadron, Boscombe Down to produce Pilot's Notes for the aircraft. Current publications and syllabi, particularly those for the Vampire, were therefore studied with greater than usual diligence to ensure an evolutionary approach to our task. I also made several visits to Dunsfold where Folland's testing and development programme was taking place on pre-production, i.e. sub-standard, aircraft. The purpose of these brief visits was to gain a pilot understanding of this technically complex little aircraft sufficient to devise adequate conversion and emergency handling advice. Two of the Folland test pilots, Mike Oliver and Dick Whittington, were unfailingly helpful in this context. Better still, on the rare occasions that the rear cockpit could be made habitable I accompanied them or Ted Tennant, the Chief Test Pilot, on their test flights. . . . mainly on routine profiles. Continuity was appalling and 'hands on' time extremely limited although I did fly XM705 on a burst of six sorties in two days (28/29 September 1961) . . . my first solo on type.

Here a brief diversion is appropriate. The merits or de-merits of an unproven tandem seat Gnat trainer versus the side-by-side version of the proven Hunter was not a project issue. The team was all ex-Hunter, but our energies were not wasted in pointless comparisons. Others argued the topic endlessly. However, after nearly 1,000 hours on Vampires my preference was for tandem seating at the advanced training stage. Whatever the Gnat's idiosyncrasies (more of which later), it undoubtedly commanded attention and respect. Old fashioned pilots like myself still hold this to be no bad thing in a trainer, whilst accepting that in combat aircraft there should be minimum distraction from weapons system operation. But I digress.

Seared in my memory of Phase 1 of the project, i.e. pre-first aircraft delivery, was the need to make monthly progress reports to HQFTC. The combination of my less than gifted pen and a CI (through whom my reports went) who was both highly literate and pedantic (a true textual pervert!) led to a record of sixteen rejected drafts in one month. But of course he was right, the importance of concise and accurate writing being brought home time and again during the rest of my career."

Early experience on the Gnat

As a young teenager and keen aircraft modeller, one very exciting and beautifully streamlined model which took Cpl Tom Thomas's fancy was the Folland Midge. *"Later as I passed through my RAF Apprenticeship I was always drawing Hunters and Gnats, so I could not have been more excited when in June 1961, along with a Flight Sergeant whose name I forget, I was sent on a three-week course to the Folland Apprentices School at Hamble to learn about the new training aircraft for the RAF – the Folland Gnat. During our time with Folland's we also visited the test sites at Chilbolton and Dunsfold. The course was comprehensive and I loved this little aeroplane from day one. I thought that its control system, hydraulics and clever design were exceptional. When the course ended we returned to Little Rissington only to find that the Flt Sgt had been posted to RAF Bicester to work on Gliders!"*

A Naval perspective

Lt Peter G. de Souza joined No. 209 Course in July 1961 and shares some of his recollections about his course with the 'crabfat', 'fishhead' slang for fliers and the Royal Air Force.

"With Mike Mumford, I was one of two Royal Navy representatives on my course, which was predominantly RAF Officers of varying experience

ranging from a DFC to postgraduates, and included one officer from the Yugoslav Air Force. My selection was solely on a voluntary basis, as I needed to specialise, after I had recently been granted a permanent commission on the General List. In 1957 I had graduated from Valley, initially specialising in the anti-submarine role, flying Gannet AS.Mk.1s and 4s. After two front-line tours, I escaped to the fighter world at Naval Air Station Lossiemouth on Seahawks and was fortunate to be given a slot on the second Scimitar squadron for tours in HMS Ark Royal and Centaur.

Life at Rissington was most comfortable and relaxed after the enhanced discipline and rigours of shipborne life. RAF Messes were a relative luxury after the Nissen hut complexes of our FAA shore establishments of that period. The food and service were also superior and there were fewer duties, with less regimentation and ceremonial about one's daily life. The course was enjoyable and generally stress-free. There were no conflicts of character or unhealthy one-upmanship evident. Each student seemed genuinely eager to help others in whatever way their particular experience or expertise could be applied. The major benefit I took away from the course was the realisation that I was basically pretty average and that if I was ever going to keep ahead of the rest I would need to constantly polish my flying and keep in the books. This awareness was something I carried through to my later civilian career as a trainer and examiner in civil aviation.

We graduated in November 1961 after completing the course on Jet Provost Mk.3s and Vampire T.11s. Since I physically loathed the Vampire due to its claustrophobic cockpit ergonomics, I was fortunate to be appointed directly back to Lossiemouth to carry out conversion courses for the Scimitar, thus successfully avoiding a conventional QFI's role in basic or advanced flying training duties.

In retrospect, the CFS Course did me and my general attitude to the flying profession a lot of good; that added discipline which I applied to my flying helped me survive through my subsequent 43 years and 20,000 plus hours."

Technical Examination – Jet Provost

Many students did not take kindly to the ground training part of their course, but a thorough grasp of the internal workings of their aircraft was an essential ingredient for attaining a high grade from the school. As an example, this was one of the half-a-dozen or so of the second batch of Ground School Exams taken by Alan Pollock and his fellow students on No. 208 Course in August 1961.

Time allowed – 2 Hours Total marks – 100

1. AIRFRAME FUEL SYSTEM

(a) Sketch the Jet Provost airframe fuel system, giving tank capacities and booster pump pressure.
(b) Two test buttons are installed in the cockpit for checking the correct functioning of the collector tank float switches. A cage is fitted over the buttons so that both cannot be pressed together. Why is this necessary?
(c) The airframe fuel system is pressurised by air. State:-
 (i) The sources of pressurising air
 (ii) The purpose of pressurising the system
 (iii) The amount of pressure in PSI

(15)

2. BASIC GAS TURBINES

(a) It is stated that the maximum static thrust of the Viper 5 ECU is 1,750lb. When is this condition obtained?
(b) What effect, if any, will a change in
 (i) Ambient air pressure,
 (ii) Ambient air temperature, have on the thrust of an engine?
(c) A propelling nozzle is fitted to most gas turbine engines. What is the reason for its inclusion?

(10)

3. LUBRICATION SYSTEM

(a) Three bearings support the main shaft of the Viper engine. State:-
 (i) The name and type of each bearing
 (ii) How each bearing is lubricated
(b) Why is there an air space in the oil tank?
(c) What provision is made in the lubrication system for inverted flight?

(10)

4. ENGINE FUEL SYSTEM

(a) A Jet Provost aircraft is flying straight and level at a given RPM and climbs to a new altitude. Describe how the fuel system will compensate for this change in conditions.
(b) Explain why it is necessary to have a Rate Reset Valve in the engine fuel system.
(c) Why is it necessary to fit an Air Fuel Ratio Control?
(d) The main half ball valve in the BFCU becomes stuck open during flight. What effect would this have on the engine?

(20)

5. ELECTRICAL SYSTEM

(a) State the cycle of operations from pressing the starter button until the engine reaches idling RPM.
(b) The relight button is pressed after a 'Flame Out'. What main components are brought into action?
(c) What causes the starter button to 'throw out' if the engine reaches idling RPM before the end of the normal starting cycle?

(15)

6. HYDRAULIC SYSTEM

(a) There is an electrical failure of the aircraft. The undercarriage must be lowered using emergency air. Briefly describe the operation from selecting until the undercarriage is locked down.
(b) How would a pilot check for correct accumulator air pressure on his pre-flight inspection?

(c) Give an example when it could be necessary for a pilot to use the hydraulic hand pump.
(d) Is it necessary for the pilot to select 'UP' if using the undercarriage override switch?

(15)

7. FIRE DETECTION AND SUPPRESSION

(a) Where on the engine is the spray ring situated? What extinguishant is used?
(b) Which warning devices are switched off on pressing the cancel button?
(c) How does the pilot test the fire warning system, described in Pilot's Notes

(5)

8. ENGINE CONSTRUCTION

(a) What is the purpose of:-
  (i) Primary Air Tubes?
  (ii) Nozzle Guide Vanes?
  (iii) The Turbine?
(b) What is the purpose of:-
  (i) Primary Air?
  (ii) Secondary Air?
  (iii) Tertiary Air?
(c) List the main components of the Viper Engine.

(10)

Farewell prank

Flt Lt Ralph Chambers earlier of the Royal Canadian Air Force was also a student on No. 208 course and he recollects, *"I went to Rissy in the spring of 1961 and of all the courses a pilot takes in a long career this was by far the best. I still use the fundamentals learned there. After the graduation dinner in the Officers' Mess that evening, Alan Pollock, myself and some of our colleagues decided to bow out in style by bricking-up the entrance to the Ground School in the early hours. We were hauled in front of very senior officers the next day and it cost us money!"*

Dropping yet more bricks!

Flt Lt Alan Pollock exposes more of what happened on that memorable last night of No. 208 Course.

"After my friend Pete Jennings won the Clarkson, and my other ex-26(AC) Sqn compatriot, Gil McCluney, was awarded the Brabyn Trophy for his Vampire aerobatics, while walking back to the Mess, I noticed bags of quick drying cement and a cement mixer. Thus swiftly evolved the extra 208 project that night. Our great and glorious gift, not only to Rissy but for every future course, had flawless logic – with a bricked up Ground School, instant and massive Treasury and establishment savings for the Ministry, faster course turnover and a more enjoyable course, only pure flying for succeeding students, for ever and ever, amen. Little inspiration was needed from me to quickly persuade a quorum working party of the less career minded on the course in the Mess that night – my libellous recall of those mainly involved, now 45 years on is of Jim Timms, Mike Hardy, Tony Chambers, Gil McCluney, Dave Brett, Sulie Sulaiman, Ralph Chambers and those spurious, inebriated and late-arriving skills of our other Canadian, Lofty Lance. We were working well, undiscovered for at least 90 minutes. Pete Jennings was i/c our 'bar diversion tactics': the main problem was to keep the bar adequately manned to allay suspicions of any separate nefarious activity. Lofty Lance, one of our three ex-RCAF transfers insisted on our taking down to re-lay 'more Rissy expertly', when nearly at eye level, the last six or seven brick top courses. This commotion and vital delay brought a police posse, shortly followed by a decidedly crinkly SDO. How sad that, thus in Mess jackets, early on Saturday, 1 September, after high level negotiations to please our ex-WW2 avuncular Course Leader, Sqn Ldr Chippy Woods, we had to carefully dismantle our permanent, step quality, syllabus improvement for HM Treasury – the Ground School door never was wholly bricked up solid by next morning – two DPCO failures within 12 hours.

Gp Capt Mike Hardy painfully reminds me: 'Racking my brains on CFS, all I recall at the moment is being pattered to by a lunatic fellow student on the subject of how (not to) fly close line astern – hanging in our straps inverted above the other guy's fin! That and having bricks and mortar £6 added on my final mess bill as a result of being talked into helping brick up the front door of ground school with materials from the site of the new ATC Tower in the early hours following 208 Course's final dining in night.' What I never had the brass to tell Mike Hardy or the others was that hidden elsewhere on their mess bills was his or their own, as indeed the staff's, fractional contribution to the Mess's presentation silver cigarette box for my wedding that month! Our course ended, unforgettably, on Friday, 31 August, three weeks before my being spliced by a CFS Association member, Rev Sqn Ldr E.K. Peter Ince DFC, a wartime No. 7 FIS QFI!"

Aircraft Noise

Although most of the local inhabitants were tolerant of aircraft noise, the high number of hours being flown at Little Rissington generated an increase in the number of complaints from some communities which could not be ignored. And so, on 27 September, local parish councillors were invited for a tour of the airfield and its facilities and treated to a display by "The Pelicans" aerobatic team, a grand lunch followed by a presentation of various CFS functions. Several people subsequently wrote to the Commandant thanking him for putting them in the picture and the local press gave the event and the CFS good write-ups.

New Visitors Pan

In October, preliminary work commenced on construction of the second new ASP to the west of the control tower while work on the other ASP continued although way behind schedule. No. 5004 Airfield Construction Squadron from RAF Wellesbourne Mountford was assigned to the task and, on account of trails left by their muddy boots, they soon became known as 'Clay Kickers' by airmen.

Winter arrives

December was noted for a whole range of bad weather which included hail, freezing rain, gales, fog and, to cap it all, ten inches of snow. Only eight days of significant flying were achieved causing the end dates of all courses to be put back. Inclement weather due in part to its exposed position, was probably the major drawback with operating an intense flying programme from Little Rissington.

On days when visibility was poor yet safe enough for the Jet Provosts to fly locally, their Piston-engined brethren flew out to South Cerney to practise their circuits and bumps. On the occasions when the weather clamped in quickly the Provosts made a mad dash back to Rissy at 'zero' feet over Northleach, using the A429 as a reference.

First Jet Provost Mark 4s

Initial deliveries of the T.Mk.4 version of the Jet Provost, powered by the larger Viper 202 engine, occurred on 23 November 1961, with the arrival of XP549 and XP550.

'Flying Doctor'

Dr Peter Saundby, whose father, Sir Robert, had been SASO and then Deputy C-in-C Bomber Command between 1941 and 1945, was at Rissington for three and a half years and had 37 years of commissioned service, before retiring as an Air Cdre. Many will remember him as a 'flying doc' and he remains active in both gliding and powered aviation. Here he reveals his CFS role in the early 1960s.

"At one time the RAF selected small numbers of officers from the specialist branches for flying training, these being employed subsequently in posts requiring both skills. One such Flying Personnel Medical Officer (FPMO) post was established at Little Rissington on the CFS Headquarters staff and I was fortunate enough to fill that post from July 1961 until November 1964.

The Flying Training Command Aeromedical Centre was located at RAF South Cerney, a unit established for both QHI training and initial aircrew entry training. This Centre was also my responsibility. Programmed aeromedical work included courses of ground school lectures followed by practical demonstrations in the decompression chamber for those on CFS courses, the hypoxia training of aircrew cadets, with additional refresher training and special courses as requested by HQ FTC. The latter included the few females trained at that time and destined for aeromed crews. In total, many hundreds of personnel each year passed through the South Cerney chambers. Despite Air Ministry concern we seldom suffered problems with decompression sickness but when a high pressure chamber was installed in the RAF Hospital Wroughton as a precaution, this gave me another task for which I was trained by the Royal Navy.

My Little Rissington office was in the old control tower and, while I attempted to run a morning clinic, this was not a great success. The absence of records and support equipment meant that we often had to transfer to the Station Medical Centre. More interesting were the tasks that arose. Some students found the course stressful and their problems had to be addressed. CFS also received pilots referred from elsewhere for assessment, often following failure at an OCU. Sometimes these had been formally labelled under the Air Ministry letter as having lost the

The first Jet Provost T.4s for CFS, XP549 and XP550, shortly after arriving from Percivals, Luton, on 23 November, 1961. (*Ray Deacon*)

confidence of their Commanding Officer. Diagnosis of the cause is always an essential preliminary to management and cases ranged from inadequacies of their original training to early mental illness. While at Little Rissington we initiated medically controlled remedial flying, which remains to-day as an established procedure. A special sub section of this was the referral to CFS of student pilots suffering from air sickness. Following de-conditioning they then flew graduated exercises before returning to their FTS.

A great treat was to be a member of the CFS team visiting RAF overseas Commands and foreign air forces. A trip around Africa in a Varsity will never be forgotten. My log book records that I flew some 480 hours during my tour at Rissington, over 400 of which were as captain. Aircraft types included Vampire, Chipmunk, Piston Provost, Jet Provost, Anson, Varsity, Gnat, Sycamore and Whirlwind."

The CFS Hunter Flight

The following article, written by the OC CFS Hunter Flight, Flt Lt T.A. 'Sharky' Hastings, was originally published in Air Clues:

"As one of the newest additions to the oldest established flying school in the world, the Hunter Flight of Central Flying School gives pilots air experience of an operational type of aircraft without the need of a lengthy simulator or instruction course. The method by which hundreds of pilots in Flying Training Command have completed a Hunter conversion course at CFS is described in this article.

The Flight, still part of CFS Type Squadron, recently re-designated No. 3 Squadron (under Sqn Ldr D.G.T. Franklin), has three instructors on the staff, all ex-Hunter squadron pilots who have done a tour of instruction at an FTS.

The aim of the Hunter Flight is incorporated in the directive to No. 3 Squadron of Central Flying School: "No. 3 Squadron at CFS is responsible for giving students flying experience of representative service aircraft of an advanced type, so that they may appreciate better the problem their own students will have to face."

Under the terms of a more recent AMO, CFS is now also responsible for the re-categorisation and standardisation of Hunter QFIs and pilots. At present Flying Training Command uses the Vampire, Meteor, Jet Provost, Piston Provost, Chipmunk and Varsity as training aircraft. Modern swept-wing aircraft differ from all of these aircraft in such aspects as stalling and transonic characteristics, take-off and landing techniques, control, trim, brake, oxygen and anti-g systems. With the introduction into the services of such aircraft as the Lightning, Victor, Comet, Sea Vixen and Buccaneer it becomes of paramount importance to acquaint FTC instructors with the characteristics of swept wing aircraft. Thus they will be better equipped to discuss knowledgeably with their students all the important differences of swept wing flying.

The comparatively viceless Hunter is ideally suited for swept-wing familiarisation and the aircraft in this role provides one of the major tasks of Hunter Flight. The other major commitment of the Flight is the provision of support for the Advanced Standardisation Flight of CFS which re-categorises and standardises Hunter QFIs and pilots. Aircraft are provided for their continuation flying and the development and evaluation of new techniques. Hunter Flight instructors help in this work and often complete standardisation teams when visits are made.

Pilots in Flying Training Command who come to the Hunter Flight for flying can be divided into three categories. Firstly, there are those pilots passing through on CFS instructor courses. They do a conversion course of three sorties making a total of two hours on type. Secondly, Flying Instructors from the RAF College, Cranwell and the other Flying Training Schools come to the Hunter Flight for a one-week course. This course consists of nine sorties, giving a total of six hours' flying. Three sorties are for conversion, three for consolidation in general handling and three for formation flying. The third category includes the instructors on the staff of CFS who come to Kemble at frequent intervals to keep in current practice on the Hunter.

The aircrew bus leaves Little Rissington at 08:30 but by this time the driver has collected the official mail for the Flight and any safety equipment which has been in for inspection. The journey to Kemble takes about an hour, and this time is often used for a quiz on the aircraft systems and emergencies. In the meantime the groundcrew, who started work at 07:30, are completing their daily inspection on the aircraft. On arrival at Kemble, a Met. briefing is held, pilots are briefed for their appropriate exercises and the first detail is airborne at 10:00 hrs. After Met. briefing, one instructor starts the three-hour technical briefing if there are pilots requiring it. The day's programme is planned for three to four aircraft each flying three 40-minute sorties in the morning and two in the afternoon. This is fitted into the airfield opening times, which, being a Maintenance Unit, are 09:00-12:30 and 13:30-16:00 from Monday to Friday. During this time the QFIs are briefing for exercises, supervising starts, leading formations, de-briefing and in the tower as duty QFI. The staff QFIs obtain their flying from air tests, weather checks, leading formations, night flying and SCT. After flying has finished, the inevitable 'paper work' is completed and the bus leaves for Little Rissington, arriving there between 17:00 and 17:30. The groundcrew after-flight the aircraft and 'clock-off' at 16:30.

All pilots who fly with the Hunter Flight attend a lecture which lasts about three hours, covering the systems and emergencies. The student instructors are briefed by courses, while visiting instructors are briefed on the first morning of their attachment. After the lecture a comprehensive questionnaire is given to the pilot to complete. Before flight all pilots receive a further briefing on the handling of the aircraft and local procedures, and they have time in the cockpit to familiarise themselves with its layout.

The three familiarisation flights are:

Familiarisation 1 Take off; climb to 35,000 ft; effect of controls and turning; descent to 27,000 feet; incipient stall; CDTC; circuits.

Familiarisation 2 Climb to 42,000 ft; sonic dive under radar control; return to Kemble for circuits.

Familiarisation 3 Climb to 10,000 ft; practise manual flying; aerobatics; GCA.

The first familiarisation exercise is usually given dual in the Mark 7 but pilots who have recently flown the Hunter and are attending for re-familiarisation will often be sent off solo in the Mark 4 at once.

All pilots carry a knee pad covering all checks, vital actions, limitations and emergencies. In addition, a card outlining emergency procedures is fitted to the aircraft in place of the gunsight. All the starting, after-start checks and vital actions are closely supervised by a Hunter QFI for the first two flights, and a Hunter Flight QFI is on duty in the control tower for the first solo. All pilots are de-briefed after each flight. After three familiarisation sorties, the initial conversion or re-familiarisation is complete. This, therefore, constitutes the CFS student instructor's Hunter flying syllabus.

Instructors from the FTSs and CFS Staff use these exercises as a basis for their Hunter flying and continue with aerobatics, practice forced landings, manual landings and formation flying. Although the aircrew travel the 60-miles return journey from Little Rissington daily by bus, the servicing of the aircraft is carried out by civilians who are part of No. 5 MU Kemble. The Foreman of Trades, Mr J. Phillips, has twelve men to maintain the five aircraft. One aircraft is usually undergoing minor servicing and four aircraft are available for flying.

The groundcrew all live locally and have been associated with the MU for many years; most of them have been with the Hunter Flight since it was formed and they have become an efficient servicing team. They know their aircraft and are extremely conscientious – as a result the serviceability of the flight is very high. No. 5 MU also provides Hunter Flight with Air Traffic Control, crash facilities, fuel and midday meals at the Officers' Mess. The co-operation between Kemble and CFS has always been very close, and the Station Commander, Wg Cdr P.A.S. Thompson, and the Senior Technical Officer, Sqn Ldr W.W. Suckling, have been responsible for first-class backing to all the Hunter Flight operations. It will no doubt be of interest to readers to know that No. 5 MU Kemble, has the function of preparing many types of aircraft for Royal Air Force Units and foreign Air Forces, and is also used as a relief landing ground by CFS jet aircraft. Far from being a quiet MU, there are up to 2,000 aircraft movements a month.

By the end of 1961 the CFS Hunter Flight has successfully completed hundreds of initial conversions and re-familiarisations. In spite of the fact that the flying programme must be arranged to fit the airfield opening times and that most of the flying consists of 40-minute conversion sorties with a necessarily restrictive weather minima, the Flight has logged a total of more than 6,000 hours since November 1955. During 1961 alone, 204 pilots were converted, all of whom had a minimum of three trips and some considerably more. While achieving this, the Hunter Flight flew 1,260 hours which was also the best-ever total by some 23 per cent above the previous highest in 1959. There were no incidents of any description in 1961 with the exception of a heavy landing in a Mark 7. The CFS Hunter Flight can therefore look back with some pride on its achievements over the past years and at the same time anticipate sending many more pilots on their first swept-wing ride both safely and efficiently."

Flt Lt Alex Wickham about to climb aboard Hunter F.4, XF944/A at Kemble for a familiarisation flight. (*Alex Wickham*)

Aircraft Inventory

The aircraft inventory at Little Rissington at the end of the year comprised: Vampire T.11, Meteor T.7, Canberra T.4, Hunter F.4 and T.7, Jet Provost T.3 and T.4, Piston Provost T.1, Varsity T.1, Anson C.19 and Chipmunk T.10. In anticipation of the arrival of the first Gnats, the rundown of Vampire fleet saw the number reduced to ten aircraft and only seven Piston Provosts remained, the type having been superseded by new JP.3s and 4s. A new control tower and purpose-built visitors pan were also commissioned during the year.

1962

Kemble detachment

To facilitate the installation of Category 2 lighting, the main runway was closed in January 1962. As the Jet Provosts and all other piston engine aircraft could operate from the other two runways, they remained at Rissington. However, the Vampires, Meteors and Canberras of Nos. 2 and 3 Squadrons were detached to RAF Kemble, some 24 miles to the south west for the first six months of 1962, to allow flying of the fast jets to continue. Here they shared a D-site hangar with the three Hunter F.Mk.4s and two T.7s of the CFS Type-Flight. Each day the flying and technical personnel were transported to and from Kemble in the 'luxury' of RAF Bedford coaches. Crewroom facilities for the airmen were provided in a Nissen hut and the crescent-shaped pan nearby was adopted for use as a flight line, a converted runway controller's van and portakabin providing cover for the 1st line servicing team.

First Gnat arrives

On 2 February, the first Folland Gnat T.Mk.1, XM709/95, was flown to Little Rissington from Dunsfold where it was greeted by the AOC-in-C Flying Training Command, Air Marshal Sir Augustus Walker. By virtue of his appointment as project leader, Flt Lt Derek Bryant became the first Gnat QFI/CIRE.

"My first task was to convert Dennis Yeardley (whose DFC had been awarded for shooting down an Me 262, I believe the first jet kill of WWII) and John Young. On the 9 February Dennis and I took off on his first conversion sortie and landed at Kemble where early conversion flying took place. Thanks to our ground crew, backed by a first class Folland rep, the project made a great start. I flew 25 sorties in the first ten flying days, concentrating on team conversion but with two familiarisation sorties for our Commandant, Air Cdre Pat Connolly. The 26th sortie on the afternoon of 28 February was to practise close formation on a Jet Provost whilst it took Public Relations photographs of our aircraft.

This sortie attracts particular attention because it ended in a two wheel landing, the starboard undercarriage being unlocked. The cause was no mystery. . . pilot error. I had retracted the undercarriage too soon after take off. A co-incident wing wobble caused the retracting starboard undercarriage to strike the ground; the impact sheared the datum shift link. A 'starboard red' confirmed that we had a problem as did some pitch control problems caused by unpredictable datum shift inputs (the mechanism was an ingenious solution to a stability problem introduced by stretching the Gnat fighter to create the trainer). Dennis (in the rear cockpit) and I discussed the control problem and decided to revert to manual, thus regaining positive control of the tailplane. Consequently we sought advice from Folland test pilots via ATC but, in the limited time available and given the uncertain nature of the damage, there was little they could do to help.

We therefore burnt off fuel and prepared for an emergency landing. I would carry out the approach and touchdown; Dennis would then help me to keep the aircraft straight and the wing up for as long as possible. We had a nasty moment on finals when selection of full flap gave us a momentarily uncontrollable pitch problem which I instinctively countered by turning and Dennis intuitively re-selected power controls. The eventual touchdown was uneventful and luck was with me when, on two wheels and a wing tip, we slid between two prominent runway lights and came to rest on the grass."

XM709 suffered Category 2 damage and was repaired on-site by a Hawker-Siddeley Civilian Working Party (CWP) from Dunsfold. It was two months before the second Gnat (XM706/92) was delivered and three months before the damaged aircraft took to the skies once again.

"There was no excuse for my error", Derek continues, *"but 'it is an ill wind that blows no good'. Cpl Tom Thomas remembers the subsequent introduction of a 140 knot minimum speed retraction switch; and the*

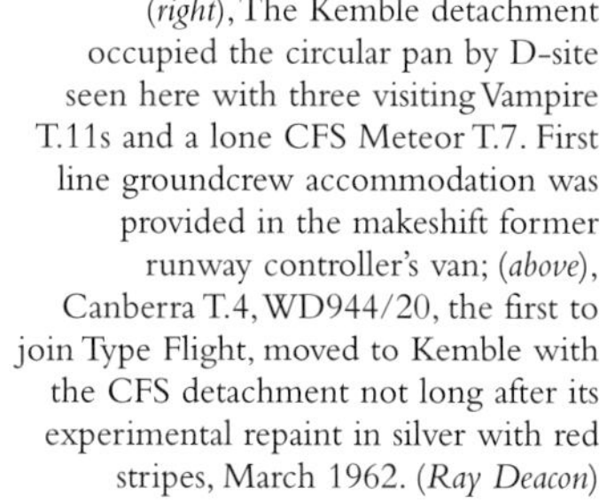

(*right*), The Kemble detachment occupied the circular pan by D-site seen here with three visiting Vampire T.11s and a lone CFS Meteor T.7. First line groundcrew accommodation was provided in the makeshift former runway controller's van; (*above*), Canberra T.4, WD944/20, the first to join Type Flight, moved to Kemble with the CFS detachment not long after its experimental repaint in silver with red stripes, March 1962. (*Ray Deacon*)

With Flt Lt Dennis Yeardley in the back seat, Flt Lt Derek Bryant taxies XM709 back to the flight line at Kemble in mid-February, 1962. (*Ray Deacon*)

control problems experienced on 'finals' heightened my enthusiasm for a modification which transferred tailplane control to the stick mounted trim switches when in manual. Follands were already promoting the modification at a cost. In my opinion it should have been part of the into service acceptance standard. In October I flew with Sqn Ldr (later Air Marshal Sir Donald) Hall of 'A' Squadron Boscombe Down (who was the RAF test pilot for the Gnat) on an informal evaluation of the need for the modification. Later still, my final sortie on the project was to return to Dunsfold to fly a solo evaluation sortie on a pre-production aircraft (XM694) with the modification incorporated. Thus my project flying neatly came full circle; but more importantly, the modification was accepted by the RAF.

The pre-modification standby trim system required considerable manual dexterity which has prompted another recollection. Our C-in-C was the then Air Marshal (later Air Chief Marshal) Sir Augustus Walker. As many will know he lost his right arm in WWII in circumstances which reflect his bravery; and his determination thereafter to lead a 'normal' life included re-learning to fly with an artificial limb strapped to the control column. In May 1961 he undertook a brief conversion course on the Gnat and went solo without difficulty. To watch his 'good' hand dart about the cockpit was an object lesson in manual dexterity. He did not need the modification

Although arguably not part of the history of the Gnat project, the aftermath of my accident provides an interesting insight into the attitudes then prevalent in the HQFTC/CFS hierarchy. The Commandant had arrived swiftly at Kemble to witness our landing, with which he was impressed. He was less impressed to learn from me that it was my fault. Quite properly a Board of Inquiry was assembled with a view to taking Court Martial action. Having considered the evidence I believe the Commandant took the view that my admission of gross negligence clearly established culpability, but that the overriding Service interest was the swift introduction of the Gnat. The C-in-C must have agreed because the outcome was a formal interview before him. Thereafter, during later appointments with increasing command responsibility, I never forgot that loyalty is a two way street.

(*above*), The stricken Gnat, with the damaged starboard undercarriage swinging limply, as seen from the accompanying Jet Provost, shortly before making a two-wheel landing at Kemble, 28 February, 1962. (*David Watkins*). (*below*), Having filed his initial incident report, Flt Lt Derek Bryant (in greatcoat) walks across to inspect the damage to his aircraft. (*Ray Deacon*)

But I get ahead of myself. Another interesting incident occurred on 28 June. John Young and I were working up an 'unusual attitude' sequence for inclusion in training syllabi. As a matter of principle I believed that we should explore recoveries from more extreme attitudes than we would include in the syllabi. It was during an 'unload' from a slightly overcooked low speed vertical recovery that the aircraft fell over backwards, picked up dramatic yaw without significant roll, and we sensed a hint of negative 'g'. We sat still and allowed the airspeed to increase before recovering. The aforementioned Don Hall was informed and the following day he and I attempted to reproduce the symptoms but without success. The upshot was that we curbed our enthusiasm for the esoteric and concentrated more on recovery from those unusual attitudes more

likely to occur in real life. That said, John Young devised an absolutely brain scrambling entry into an unusual attitude taking full advantage of the Gnat's extraordinary lateral agility. In fact he used to hand over for us to complete a recovery on instruments alone with the aircraft more or less in straight and level flight but still rolling. Much to his amusement I (and others) then developed our own unusual attitude whilst trying to unscramble our physiological confusion. I hasten to add this was a staff only 'treat'.

My Log Book reminds me that quite early in our internal work-up we converted a Trapper (Freddie Latham): and Bill Croydon who, halfway through his conversion, was promoted and posted elsewhere. What a waste of precious Gnat hours at that stage - an example of Air Staff/'P' Staff disconnect which was not unusual in those days. On 7 July I performed a modest low level display in front of HM The Queen Mother as part of CFS Golden Jubilee celebrations. It was a typical English summer day. Sunshine and showers with some well developed cumulus clouds around. My display finished with a high speed run followed by an 'upward Charlie' (vertical continuous roll). On about the second twizzle I entered a dark cumulus cloud. Soon thereafter, rapidly running out of airspeed and still in cloud, I was grateful for the aforementioned practice I had with John Young.

July also saw the arrival of the first batch of advanced instructors who had been selected to start the student training programme at Valley. Thus they were all competent and well regarded instructors. I suspect that at times our 'instruction' (perhaps 'guidance' would be a better word) was based on the principle that 'In the land of the blind the one eyed man is king'. That said, I do not recall any serious disharmony between us either with the content of their own conversion syllabus or that proposed for their students; nor any disagreement with the advice on one's approach to Advanced instruction which was to be included in the Instruction Handbook. Indeed some of the course 'helped' us in our evaluation of training profiles. A low level profile flown with Al Pollock largely in Northern Ireland was one such sortie which I will not readily forget.

By this time the Project had returned to Little Rissington. I had been asked by the Commandant if I would be happy with the arrangement and I assured him that I would. The main runway at Rissy was entirely adequate for Gnat operations if the aircraft was flown accurately. As accurate flying is the foundation stone of credible instruction, I could see no good reason for not moving back. I had but one reservation. One of the Gnat's less endearing characteristics is 'earholing' down the runway in a cross-wind. This lateral tilt, a feature of the undercarriage geometry, felt most uncomfortable and detracted from efficient braking. But it only became a serious concern if the runway was wet. There was little margin for error at Rissy in those conditions.

My reports to HQFTC forecast possible student problems with fine pitch control in close formation as we on the team had experienced some early difficulties. In fact the aforementioned instructors on the first course did not seem to have much of a problem; and successive improvements to the seals and valves in the Hobson Unit (tailplane motor) much improved the break-out response. The 'Yellowjacks', led by Flt Lt Lee Jones, put to rest any lingering concerns we may have had, although his penchant for misreading his altimeter during low level formation aerobatic displays did cause me concern in my post-project appointment on the Air Staff at HQFTC!

The Gnat was particularly well equipped (to partial OR 946 standard as I recall) with up-to-date instrument/navigation systems. Offset DME and ILS provided useful freedom and a sense of confidence when flying and recovering in marginal weather conditions. It also made the Gnat particularly well suited as a lead-in to Lightning conversion. One of the privileges I greatly enjoyed in April 1963 was a brief Command sponsored detachment to Middleton St George to fly the Lightning T.4 and to discuss with the instructors what they felt should be emphasised during advanced training. Received wisdom is that ex-Gnat students usually performed well in the Lightning world.

As Martin Baker ejectee No. 256 I am second to none in my appreciation of Sir James' achievements. But it would be remiss not to mention the revolutionary lightweight seat fitted to the Gnat trainer. Although, fortunately, its operational performance was not tested during the project, we were involved with IAM Farnborough's efforts to further improve user friendliness and comfort. Amongst other things a Wg Cdr Tony Barwood (I think) was trying to create a plastic seat mould compatible with the average male bum (known colloquially as 'the Barwood bum') upon which would be fitted a slim cushion with appropriate compression characteristics. Anyone who has had a communal shower after a rugby/football match will know that an average male bum does not exist. Undeterred, and assisted by our 'sensitive' comments, the Wing Commander eventually perfected a compromise profile. Thus, to the brilliant simplicity of the Gnat seat was added a user friendly harness and comfortable seat. Wonderful, especially on the third instructional sortie of the day!

Thus far I have scarcely mentioned the engineering element of the team. Others will cover that from a more involved and better informed perspective. Suffice to say that, in my opinion, the set up was ideal. A small, hand picked team of enthusiastic young NCOs and airmen given some pre-training at the firms and supported in the field by representatives of those firms. Of course it was in everyone's interests that Gnat serviceability was high and we took full advantage of this privileged support. However, thinking about the groundcrew sparks another recollection. As already mentioned, I caused serious damage to an aircraft through pilot error. My engine Corporal made a similar (in context) error. He left a glove in the engine intake, and then conducted an engine run, thus damaging the engine. Inevitably he was charged; equally inevitably as his Flight Commander I had to hear the charge. I recall receiving advice that, in career terms, the least damaging punishment would be a fine. This I imposed. But the unfairness of the punishment compared to my own treatment still rankles. Worse, I still have no answer to the vexed question of balance between punishment for aircrew and groundcrew error.

There was no clearly defined end to the project. I suppose it could be said to have ended when we submitted the final version of the various publications and syllabi we had been tasked to produce. I then took over the Gnat Air Staff desk at HQFTC and was thus 'hoist with my own petard'. Actually, the transition from project to routine at CFS was seamless. We had already converted additional CFS and Valley

instructors during the validation process and that process continued, albeit with excitements and disruptions ably described elsewhere by Messrs Young, East and others. Conversely, student training at Valley got off to a less than ideal start as maintenance and logistic difficulties severely reduced aircraft availability. One of my early staff tasks was to re-write our carefully structured ab initio student syllabus which had been based to some extent on short endurance high intensity sorties. Instead, we had to resort to fewer, longer sorties in order to take full advantage of any serviceable aircraft. But that, as they say, is another story.

On reflection

Forty years on one tends to remember high and low points of the project and forget the solid and continuous effort by all involved. But looking back on our success, if that is what it was, considerable credit must go to the HQFTC/CFS hierarchy. They gave a 27 year old Flight Lieutenant command of a small hand picked team and, within the broad guidelines of probable training resources, also gave the team a remarkably free hand and very full support. We were trusted to liaise direct with all involved in the development and acceptance into Service of the Gnat trainer and encouraged to consult widely with, amongst others, users of the end product. Moreover, we had the well tested Vampire training system as a sound foundation for our work. But above all we were fortunate to be introducing into the service an aircraft which, whilst commanding respect, had the performance and capability to stimulate the sheer joy of flying."

The Gnat Project – a technician's perspective

Ch Tech 'Tom' Thomas sums up his early experience when, as a Corporal, he was one of those selected for the Gnat Project Team.

"When XM709 arrived at Rissy I thought it looked really beautiful as it flew over but more like a knock-kneed Rhode Island Red once on the ground. The 'Gnat Project' commenced straight away. Our boss was Flt Lt Derek Bryant with Flt Lts Dennis Yeardley and John Young completing the aircrew team. Flt Sgt Jimmy Gallagher was posted onto the project but unfortunately he had not even seen a Gnat until the day it flew in. Sgt "Pip" Piper was assigned as the senior airframe NCO but promptly terminated his service to take over as licensee of "The Inn for all Seasons" on the A40. It soon became our favourite 'watering hole'. So I was the sole airframe fitter for a while until two Junior Technicians, Pete Durdin and Jack Foley, arrived. Pete was a very quiet, likeable lad straight from his fitters course, while Jack was a 're-tread' who had served in the RAF then left but as he could not settle in civvy street he rejoined and had to start over again as a J/T. He was a star, liked by everyone and always had stories to tell.

Referring to the landing accident to XM709 on 28 February, very little damage was sustained by the aircraft in what was a skilfully handled landing – turning the aircraft onto the grass just as the wing gently lowered prevented a more serious outcome. On inspection the starboard main undercarriage radius rod was found to have fractured which allowed the undercarriage leg to swing freely until pushed back into the bay on touch down. As a result of this accident, the Speed Selection Switch was modified on all Gnats to prevent the undercarriage being raised below 140 knots. Dan Parker was the Folland representative on the project team at the time and although we had only been together for three weeks, he imparted so much information about the aeroplane and the Folland Aircraft Company that he fired our interest and enthusiasm for the task ahead.

The RAF has a great variety of specialist equipment to call on when retrieving aircraft after crash landings but the Gnat, being so tiny, required a simple sling and a crane to lift it. To keep the aircraft straight and level while hanging on the sling required myself and Sgt Pip Western to sit one on each tail plane as the crane began a long and slow crawl back to the 'D'-site hangar to await inspection.

Folland's, or Hawker Siddeley as it had become, soon assembled a repair team and they duly arrived at Kemble. My job was to liaise with them and supply any equipment they needed such as hydraulic test rigs, pitot static equipment and inclinometers, etc. Together, we soon removed the complete starboard undercarriage unit. Now, part of the pivot assembly on which the undercarriage rotates houses a small cam plate which, when the airbrakes are selected, operates a hydraulic valve that locks the undercarriage at 35°. This plate was given to me for safe keeping while new doors, seals, hydraulic lines, etc., were fitted to the undercarriage leg. Re-fitting the leg to the aircraft was a time consuming operation requiring the trimming and shimming of the doors with many undercarriage retractions to ensure a good flush fit once the gear is up. When we eventually completed the job, the new doors were resprayed, before final testing with the cam plate fitted in place. Alas no cam plate! I had lost it – how embarrassing!! So Dan obtained another from Dunsfold but my colour still reddens when I recall the loss.

The loss of '709 brought the Project to an abrupt halt but it was able to re-start in earnest with the arrival of XM708 on 9 May and XM706 a day later."

Feathered Pelican

Purchased by CFS staff officers and given into the safe keeping of Mr Len Hill of Bourton-on-the-Water's Birdland, "Patrick" the Pelican was the Central Flying School's first official mascot and was presented to CFS at the graduation dinner of No. 210 course in the Officers' Mess on 2nd February 1962. Patrick was named after the Commandant, Air Cdre Pat Connolly, and brought on to the strength of CFS as Pelican 1st Class, Branch GD/Pel.

Patrick caused considerable interest from the press and was kept busy for several weeks posing for their cameras; the BBC even made a short film of him. The Commandant always escorted Patrick on these occasions. Despite being photogenic Patrick did not like being too much in the public eye and consequently it required considerable time and patience to get a good shot of him. However, it did not take too long for him to get accepted into the social circle and on 10 May 1962, the then Minister of Defence presented him with a CFS bow tie which he wore with pride at the Central Flying School Association Reunions and other formal functions.

Unfortunately the life of a social jet setter was too much for him and Patrick left for the great Birdland in the sky in 1969.

The extra power available from the Jet Provost T.4 encouraged the Red Pelicans to add a fifth aircraft to their display for the 1962 season. Following a practice sortie, the team perform a formation touch down on the Rissy runway. (*Ian Bashall*)

All change on "The Pelicans"

In March 1962, the new season's CFS Jet Provost aerobatic team was formed and the number of aircraft in its display increased from four to five to enable an increase in the number of formation changes during their displays. New formations and a new mount as the team also exchanged their JP T.3s for the T.Mk.4 which was powered by a 2,500 lb. Viper turbojet, 750 lb. more power than the engine of its predecessor.

The pilots, all drawn from No. 1 Squadron, were Flt Lts I.K. McKee (team leader), a New Zealander and an instructor with the CFS since July 1960, I. Bashall, R.G. Fox, K.F. Beck, J.E.S. Rolfe and A.J.R. Doyle. Apart from their duties with the aerobatic team they continued with their primary job of training future flying instructors.

First of three!

Flt Lt 'Cas' Maynard spent three periods at Little Rissington. The first was in 1962 as a member of No. 212 Course on the Jet Provost T.3 and 4, preparing to become a Basic QFI for all-through jet training.

"The CFS training was intensive, the standards demanded were high but at the same time there was a great deal of fun and challenge in the flying. The groundschool, I recall, was rather more of a challenge.

I can remember taking part in the flypast for the freedom of Cheltenham, watching my instructor, Flt Lt Jock Byrne hold position as Pelican Red 2. Later in the course there was a tragic event when one of my colleagues, Henry Carter and his instructor, Trevor Doe, died in a Meteor T.7 following an engine failure on take-off; the Meteor was unforgiving between unstick 120/130kt and safety speed 165kt.

After completing my Final Handling Test I spent a couple of days at Kemble where, after a short dual check in the Hunter T.7 (a first for me as there had been no T.7 when I flew Hunters before), I managed to do three nostalgic trips in the Hunter F.4. What a Joy! Apart from training me as a QFI, the CFS Course provided an introduction to display flying through competing for the Clarkson Trophy; my mentor was Flt Lt Bryan Nice, later a Red Pelican in 1963/4."

Freedom of Cheltenham

Her Majesty The Queen Mother and Commandant-in-Chief, arrived on 5 May to accept the Freedom of the Borough of Cheltenham on behalf of the Central Flying School. The ceremony commenced at the Pittville Pump Room in Cheltenham where the Queen Mother accepted a scroll declaring the freedom of the borough upon CFS and gift of a sword from the Mayor of Cheltenham, Alderman F.L. Carter. The sword was then presented to the CFS Commandant, Air Cdre H.P. Connolly.

Having inspected the parade, The Queen Mother watched a flypast of sixteen Jet Provost in boxes of four. Personnel from the School then exercised their new Freedom with a march-past from Pittville towards the Promenade in true tradition with colours flying, drums beating and bayonets fixed. The Queen Mother and all the dignitaries, which included Sir Dermot Boyle, Sir James Robb, Sir Richard Atcherley, the Air Officer Commanding-in-Chief of Flying Training Command Air Marshal Sir Augustus Walker, and the air attachés of the United States of America, France, Germany, the USSR, Egypt and India, were assembled in the Promenade where the parade gave a swift eyes right and presented arms in salute of their Commandant-in-Chief. The contingent then assembled in Montpelier Gardens where they were treated to a magnificent buffet luncheon laid on by the borough.

New Control Tower

The new control tower was located a couple of hundred yards out on the airfield, directly to the south of the original tower. It was completed by the spring and became fully operational on 14 May.

On the flying side "The Pelicans" team were over in France performing at air shows at Valenciennes and Denain. By June the team's programme had become more concentrated as it carried out several more displays in France and in Belgium and Denmark.

With the main runway lighting upgrade completed, the detachment of aircraft and personnel returned from RAF Kemble.

From the front-line to instructing

Having successfully completed a Canberra Conversion Course Flt Lt Tony Featherstone joined 16 Squadron at Laarbruch in December 1958, where for three years he flew some 700 hours on the Canberra B(I)8, mostly at low level!

"Alarmed that most of my fellow first-tourists were moving to co-pilot seats in V-bombers, I made full use of a six month extension and an undeserved 'above average' assessment to volunteer for CFS. I joined 212 Course at Little Rissington on 5 March 1962. Many of my fellow students were at least second or third tourists and I felt somewhat daunted by my relative lack of experience. How the 'creamed-off' course

members felt, I cannot imagine – these included Henry Crone, Bob Morris and John Wilkinson, a Conservative MP for almost 30 years.

The day after starting the course, I was airborne in a Jet Provost Mk.3. This aircraft aptly deserved the epithet 'constant thrust, variable noise machine' – it lacked oomph and the controls were lumpy and uncoordinated. Groundschool was a steady grind and I wondered if I would ever master the intricacies of aerodynamics and meteorology. Heavy workload apart, the course progressed through to the specialisation phase without incident. I found myself selected for basic flying training on the JP4, a distinct improvement on the Mark 3. Close to the end of our course and looking forward to posting, a fellow Canberra first tourist, Henry Carter, and I found ourselves suddenly switched back to the half-way point, when re-selected for the Meteor. My Meteor instructor was Bill Loverseed, who went on to lead the Red Arrows, and later still, to slightly overdo a short landing demo at Farnborough in the Caribou."

Meteor fatalities

June 26 was a very sad day for the base when the starboard engine on Meteor T.7, WG962 suffered a compressor failure at the critical point on take-off. The aircraft turned over before the crew could take corrective action and it crashed upside down on the runway killing both pilots, Flt Lt T.J. Doe, an experienced instructor, and his student pilot Flt Lt H.W. Carter.

There for the grace of god...

Tony Featherstone again.

"Compared with the JP, the Meteor had quite a bit of punch. Although poling the T.7 from the back seat was a bit like flying from the wrong end of a tunnel, the job was all quite exhilarating. Training continued apace with between two and four sorties a day – being taught a sequence, doing a mutual practice and then returning it. On the fateful day, 26 June, I was programmed for a dual circuit detail immediately after Met. briefing but Bill was delayed by a need to complete some urgent admin task. The aircraft, WG962, we were programmed to fly was ready first, so my fellow student Henry Carter and his instructor, Trevor Doe, took this instead. Just as they took off, a fatigue fracture in the engine compressor caused it to disintegrate, resulting in loss of control and both pilots being killed. Not only was this a near miss for me but this brought to six the number of friends and colleagues who had died in less than two years. For a week or two, I wondered whether I was in the right job. Three more weeks, which passed in something of a blur, took me to graduation and a posting to No. 3 Sqn of the School of Refresher Flying at Strubby, a satellite of the College of Air Warfare at Manby. In those three weeks it was hard to ignore the scar left by '962 in the grass beside the runway, visible on every sortie. Thus I remember my time at 'Rissy' more with sadness than anything else."

A clash of experiences

Flt Lt Terry Kingsley's first involvement with Little Rissington was an unexpected posting as a student on No. 214 Course in 1962.

The ill-fated WG962 taxies in at the end of another sortie, circa late 1961. (*Ray Deacon*)

We were a large and very experienced Course; in fact the last Course before the full impact of 'Creamed Off' candidates was felt. Number 214 was not about to be messed with by the imperious 'waterfront' instructors, and conflict quickly arose over teaching attitudes. I was very glad that people far senior to me took issue with these attitudes before I became isolated. The crux of the matter was that we were not allowed to differ from our instructor's delivery, as they differed from themselves. Simple you might say, but not in the hallowed halls of aviation. The conflict reached quite high up the food chain and was never really resolved, just quieted. The net result was that we were told what to buy for the Mess on our departure, and the senior people took issue with that and said that we would determine what, if anything, we bought. Hence, the 214 Course photo was never put on the Wall in the Officers' Mess, giving us far more notoriety than we hoped for. It has not been corrected at the new home of CFS the last time I checked."

Another student on 213 Course was Flt Lt Brian Waters flying JPs and Meteors. *"This course was marred by compressor failure in a Meteor's Derwent on take-off, which killed Flt Lt Trevor Doe and his student. Lt R.J.A. 'Lou' Moverley, one of our four naval officers, and I were the only ones to get away with wearing our service issue sunglasses on those stilted photos, which lined the Mess corridors. Like our forebears we used to frequent the local pub, 'The Old New Inn' at Bourton-on-the-Water, run by 'Bo' Morris and his family. His lovely Labrador bitch was got-at by the village mongrel and 'Bo' was having a struggle getting rid of the resulting seven puppies. With great astuteness, he advertised them in the 'Horse and Hound' as 'genuine Cotswold Gundogs'. The pups then sold like hot cakes and funded several days at the Cheltenham races.*

The 'Trappers' coffee bar at Rissy had all the welcoming ambience of a wartime dentist's waiting room. A mate of mine had just flown in from RAF Strubby and was sitting there nervously sipping his coffee. In rushed Freddie Latham, asking 'What's the wheel track of a Meteor?'. 'Ten foot six', snapped our erudite would-be A2. 'You landed in the undershoot then', came the smug response. Love-Fifteen and this particular match had not even started! A cynical view at the time was that you had to have a 'sound grasp of the inessential' to graduate!"

50th anniversary visit by the Commandant-in-Chief

Saturday 7 July was cause for more excitement when the Queen Mother arrived in a helicopter of the Queen's Flight to participate in the celebrations marking the 50th anniversary of CFS. Lined-up on the apron in a horseshoe formation were examples of the many aircraft types used by the School over the years. In front of each aircraft stood an officer, airman and airwoman in the period dress of the day for the particular aircraft. The centre of the horseshoe was occupied by a parade of station personnel who were duly inspected by her majesty.

Wg Cdr John Langer, who returned to CFS as Chief Instructor in April 1962, taking over from Wg Cdr Tapper, recalls an amusing incident that occurred during the celebrations.

> *"After her inspection of the line up of most of the aircraft that CFS had ever operated, many borrowed from the Shuttleworth Collection and the manufacturers, there was a formal lunch in the Officers' Mess. Mr Gray, the Mess Manager, had the Mess looking splendid and, in particular, the CFS silver on the dining table was absolutely sparkling. The meal proceeded uneventfully until the main course, when the Commandant handed the condiment 'bandstand' to the Queen Mum. When she used the pepper pot, the silver top, loosened by the cleaning, fell off, covering her plate with the contents. Quick as a flash, the Commandant exchanged his plate for hers and very few people noticed what had happened. Only Air Cdre 'Pat' Connolly could have turned a potential disaster into the big joke that the Queen Mother thereafter was fond of relating – with much mirth."*

Following the luncheon in the Officers' Mess, the Queen Mother was treated to a flying display, which included many of the aircraft used over the years by the CFS and culminated with a display by "The Pelicans". The day concluded with a garden party and the Queen Mother left by helicopter at 16:15.

At the evening celebrations a number of airmen were called upon to assist with serving drinks. One of them was assigned to the Gentlemen's only bar to support the normal Officers' Mess bar staff. Four elderly officers dressed in civilian clothes arrived and after ordering their drinks requested the airman and members of staff to join them. The drinks order for the officers was three shorts and a half-pint of bitter, and two shorts and a half-pint of bitter for the airman and bar staff. Without concentrating on what he was doing, the airman picked up a half-pint of bitter and had hardly taken a sip when one of the officers said, *"Where's my beer?"* The airman, realising he had picked up the wrong glass, offered his humble apologies to

Every effort was made to ensure that 50th anniversary of the Central Flying School was celebrated in true fashion. (*right*), A selection of vintage aircraft were flown into Little Rissington especially for the event and presented in this evocative line up (*Graham Pitchfork collection*). (*Below*), Officers and other ranks appeared in uniforms representative of a bygone age. Sqn Ldr Peter Hicks is second from the right and SACs Dave Lee and Taff Langdon second and seventh from the left. (*CFS Archive*)

which an officer replied *"Do you know what you have just done?" "No, sir"* came the reply, to which the officer retorted, *"You have just drunk the beer of a Marshal of the Royal Air Force"*. The poor chap was never allowed to forget this momentary lapse.

The Air League Founders' Medal

During the 50th Jubilee celebrations, the President of The Air League, The Duke of Hamilton and Brandon, presented Her Majesty The Queen Mother, Commandant-in-Chief of the Central Flying School, with 'The 1961 Air League Founders' Medal of the British Empire'. Awarded annually the citation reads, "For the most meritorious achievement in the whole field of British aviation on reaching its culmination during the calendar year under review." Other notable recipients of aviation interest include Dr Barnes Wallis, Mr W.A. 'Bill' Bedford, Mr Brian Trubshaw, "The Red Arrows" in 1973, and Gp Capt John Cunningham.

One of three!

Having successfully completed his instructor training with No. 194 Course through the summer and autumn of 1958, Flt Lt John Young undertook a two-year tour of Vampire flying instruction at RAF College Cranwell before returning to CFS staff on 28 December 1960 as a Vampire instructor. He remained at Little Rissington for the next four and quarter years and transferred to the fledgling Gnat Flight as one of the first three instructors on Gnats from 9 February 1962. Here he recalls the first of several interesting and amusing incidents from his time on the Gnat. *"On 19 September 1962, during a Gnat high level air test and high speed run at 0.96M, the Orpheus gave a series of explosions and had to be shut down. All tail control was lost and we had to ride the aircraft until our Mach number dropped below 0·9M, before unlocking the tail to restore the emergency manual elevator control. The engine was re-started and a normal manual landing followed. The faults were attributed to engine stalling and a split in the tail hydraulic accumulator."*

Migrating to the Gnat

Having completed a 3-year tour on No. 3(F) Squadron in 2 TAF, Germany, on Sabres and Hunters; and a two-year tour at the Central Air Traffic Control School, Shawbury flying Ansons and Vampires, Flt Lt Alan East was accepted for No. 200 Course at CFS, over the winter of 1959/60.

> *"Everybody did the first half of the course on the Piston Provost. Then, according to our ultimate destination – which may not have been what we had chosen! – we either stayed on Piston Provost or Chipmunk for the basic phase or moved to the Vampire or Varsity if we were to be advanced instructors. From there, I was posted to Swinderby as a QFI on Vampires before moving on to teach on Jet Provosts with No. 3 FTS at Leeming.*
>
> *When the opportunity arose, I volunteered for a tour on the Gnat, which was being introduced as the advanced trainer to replace the Vampire at 4 FTS, Valley. There was already the Gnat Evaluation Team at CFS: three QFIs, Derek Bryant, John Young and Dennis Yeardley, and three pre-production aircraft, XM706, 708 and 709. In July 1962 myself and a few others formed the first conversion course and, including the CFS staff, I became the 7th Gnat QFI in the service. By the time we had finished, the first aircraft had still not arrived at Valley, so we stayed on to help with the conversion of the next batch. Eventually, the first production aircraft were ready for delivery. On 12 November 1962, I flew with Derek Bryant in XP501 to combine an acceptance Air Test with my Instrument Rating Test (IRT) on type. Later that month, I made my first flight at Valley, in XP502. Our families were pleased to see us home after so long at Little Rissington!"*

Hunter swansong

In the spring of 1962, Flt Lt John Hawtin assumed command of the CFS Hunter Flight at Kemble.

> *"Having read through the comprehensive article written by my predecessor, Sharky Hastings, there is little I can add about the rationale for the flight or its daily routine and procedures. All I would add is that it was perhaps my most enjoyable tour. It was the first time I was given full responsibility for a team of instructors, ground crew and six aircraft with little supervision. At one stage my boss at Rissy was not even checked out on the Hunter! Moreover, all the instructors who came to fly with us treated the opportunity with quite obvious pleasure. The flight office was simply a prefab-type married quarter and this added to the atmosphere of a friendly, homely environment devoted to the sheer pleasure of flying one of the best aircraft ever produced by the British aircraft industry. It could have been described as a Supersonic Flying Club but this would be to deny the very real purpose and value of the flight over its years of operation.*
>
> *Within the Hunter fraternity the idea of selecting the Gnat in preference to the Hunter as an advanced trainer seemed inexplicable but this topic has been covered elsewhere. When I took over the Hunter Flight the selection of the Gnat was well advanced and, therefore, I knew that my time would be limited. The Gnat Project team even shared our meagre quarters and as far as I remember it went very smoothly. Derek Bryant was particularly sensitive to the potential for resentment or intrusion and made every effort to minimise any interruption to our normal operations. He even made sure that we got the chance to have a ride in the Gnat at a time when there was considerable pressure to devote every available hour to the principal task of developing the Gnat training syllabus.*
>
> *Night flying was never a very popular occupation with Hunter pilots and even when forced to participate the tentative activity was generally limited to circuits, a practice diversion and a few GCAs. Admittedly my previous tour instructing students on the Vampire necessitated a certain amount of night flying but I remained convinced that flying after dark should be left to the professionals in the field (those flying Javelins, V Bombers, Shackletons and various Transport aircraft). Since our civilian ground crew on the Hunter flight operated limited hours, and Kemble airfield was only open during the day, I assumed that my antipathy for night flying would be allowed to continue during my tour on the CFS*

Hunter Flight. Imagine my surprise, therefore, when soon after my arrival I received a deputation from my loyal ground crew with a request to arrange a session of night flying. This request was further supported by Kemble ATC staff. Of course it was not difficult to determine the motive behind this irrational desire: in a word it was overtime. Naturally I acquiesced to the request and invited all my 'waterfront' colleagues to join in the fun while I felt obliged to locate myself in the tower to perform the vital function of duty instructor.

While on the Hunter flight I owned a rather large Boxer dog that went by the name of 'Tiny'. For many people associated with the Flight, Tiny was considered the real boss. As Sharky Hastings explained in a previous section, the daily bus to Kemble would leave Rissy at 08:30 and would pick me up in Bourton as it went through the village. It was a small twelve-seater bus which had a single seat in front alongside the driver. If anybody attempted to sit in this seat the driver would point out that it was reserved for the Boss. On one occasion one of the students embarking at the Officers' Mess decided to ignore the driver's advice muttering something about free world and democracy. What the luckless student did not realise was that the seat was actually Tiny's preserve. On arrival at my house the dog clambered aboard the bus, leapt onto the seat beside the student and spent the entire journey leaning heavily against him while thanking him for his company with copious licks and much drooling. Tiny was very disappointed that his friend did not join him for the return journey.

Tiny would accompany me out to the flight line whenever I went out to fly. As I departed I could see him sitting patiently on the edge of dispersal, or so I assumed because he was always in the same position when I taxied in. But I would later discover that the moment I took off so did Tiny on a tour of his friends round the airfield. This discovery was made when instead of entering the airfield by the back gate, the one closest to the Hunter Flight accommodation, I had to go in via the main gate where Ministry of Defence Security was much more in evidence. As I opened my window to show my ID card Tiny poked his head out of the back window. The guard took one look at the dog, declined my ID card, and declared 'That's all right, Sir, I recognise your dog'.

The team's Varsity, WJ908/29, at RAF Khormaksar, Aden, with 105 Sqn Argosies in the background. (*Ray Deacon*)

During the handover, Sharky Hastings casually mentioned that, as OC Hunter Flight, I was expected to demonstrate the Hunter at various airshows during the summer season. So as the summer approached I started to work up a simple aerobatic sequence and was eventually cleared by the Commandant to perform this sequence down to 500 ft. In retrospect I should have consulted with a few experts in the field before embarking on the enterprise, because there were a couple of occasions when I frightened myself, and presumably the people in the tower who were given a very close look into the cockpit, as I swerved past at 400 knots and considerably below 500 ft while completing a Derry Turn. At the first show (Imperial Defence College at Cottesmore 11 July 1962) I met up with an old friend, Bugs Bendell, who was demonstrating the Lightning. In conversation I mentioned my close encounter with the tower and he immediately identified the problem. He explained that although flap helped to increase the rate of turn it should never be left down while completing the roll-under because too much yaw was induced. After that I never got to see the whites of the ATC controller's eyes again.

In November 1962 a team from Advanced Standards was scheduled

Trapper team about to depart for the Middle East and Southern Rhodesia; (*l to r*): Flt Lts John Hawtin, Jim Halliday, Fg Off Chick Kirkham, Sqn Ldr Pete Watson, Flt Lts Ian Brimson, Peter Saundby, (the Navigator - christened Persil for obvious reasons), and Gp Capt de Burgh, (*John Hawtin*).

to complete a tour of Hunter Squadrons in the Middle East and to visit Southern Rhodesia to advise on Hunter operations." Flt Lt Hawtin had never entertained any aspirations to become a Trapper so it was with some trepidation that he received the news that he was to be included in the team. *"Before we embarked Chick Kirkham (a real Trapper) coached me as to the procedures to follow and helped me to understand that even with a rusty recollection of essential ground school topics (meteorology, aerodynamics, aircraft systems, etc.) it is possible to give an impression of great erudition by simply asking the right questions. On the trip my time with the various operational squadrons was most refreshing. I thoroughly enjoyed myself flying with so many old friends on 43 Squadron in Cyprus and in Aden on 8 and 208 Squadrons. As Peter Saundby explained earlier our mode of transport for this trip was a Varsity and we all took it in turn to fly the aircraft on its laborious traverse into the southern hemisphere - a traverse that included many of the furthest flung outposts of the empire such as Malta, El Adem , Wadi Halfa, Port Sudan, Aden, Mogadishu, Dar-es-Salaam, and Salisbury. The flying alone was an experience in itself especially as I had never flown anything so cumbersome and slow. In addition to the flying the trip was filled with so many memorable images: the desert conditions in Sudan, the herds of game as we flew low across Kenya, the dominating image of Kilimanjaro, the beauty of the Victoria Falls in Rhodesia, and the vast artificial lake formed by the Kariba Dam project. But perhaps the most unusual image for me occurred while at a urinal in the Officers' Mess at Bulawayo. I noticed that every member of the CFS Team was peeing bright orange. Moreover several of us had shown evidence of some form of allergic reaction. Our tame Doctor (Peter Saundby) soon diagnosed the cause. Since the beginning of the trip he had been feeding us some experimental pills designed to minimise the risk of Gippy Tummy for personnel on temporary detachments. Soon after discontinuing the treatment our colourful symptoms disappeared. Ever since then I have harboured a suspicion of Doctors bearing strange looking pills particularly brightly coloured ones – pills, I mean, not Doctors.*

My main regret is that the last few months of the CFS Hunter flight ended rather unceremoniously. There was no final parade or ceremony. I cannot even recall whether I received a farewell interview though I do remember my dining out night. Soon after returning from the Trappers tour of Africa, a particularly harsh winter set in. Rissy was cut off and for several weeks travel down to Kemble was impractical. Moreover, I personally was kept very busy travelling three times a week to London to brush up my French and getting checked out in T.33s with the USAF at Wethersfield in preparation for my next tour at SHAPE in Paris. I was particularly sorry to leave the superb civilian ground crew whose contribution to the success of the Hunter Flight could never be exaggerated. The aircraft were always in immaculate condition as witnessed by the very low incidence of any failures and the serviceability rate was exceptional."

In August, the Jet Provost Aerobatic team was kept busy with displays at several air shows in the UK, interspersed with another visit to Belgium.

A further honour bestowed on the School was the appointment of Flt Lt D.S.J. Homer as flying instructor to Their Royal Highnesses the Duke of Kent and Prince William of Gloucester.

New Group

On 1 September 1962, the attainment of Group Status caused a certain amount of restructuring at CFS. The new formation consisted of a headquarters with two stations, RAF Little Rissington and RAF Ternhill, and three University Air Squadrons; Bristol, Oxford and Southampton.

First CFS instructor wins Brabyn trophy

Little Rissington was again a focus for the aviation press when on 7 September 1962, Flt Lt Barry Dale of CFS 'D' Flight, flying a Jet Provost T.4, won the 'Brabyn Trophy for Aerobatics'. This was the first time that the trophy had been competed for by CFS staff instructors as they had been excluded from the competition until then.

Gnat simulator arrives

A significant advance in the training of students on the Gnat arrived at Rissy on 5 October in the shape of a new Gnat Simulator. Built by Link Miles it was mounted on a standard lorry chassis and was small enough to be moved around without too much effort, a benefit fully realised as the Gnat fleet moved between various airfields.

During the month, No. 3 Squadron was disbanded when the Hunter Type Flight was incorporated into No. 1 Squadron, although its aircraft remained at RAF Kemble, and the Varsity Flight was incorporated into No. 2 Squadron. The Canberras were retired at about the same time.

In the same month, project No. 25 'Evaluation of the Gnat Trainer' began commensurate with transfer to RAF Kemble of the Gnats for night flying trials.

Command Hockey honour

WRAF Cpl Hall was chosen to represent Flying Training Command in the forthcoming inter command WRAF competition at Hockey.

Snowed in – again!

The weather deteriorated somewhat as December progressed as Little Rissington was once again engulfed in a Cotswold winter wonderland. The average depth of snow only reached four to five inches, however, due to the high winds, drifting snow of up to fifteen feet became common. To help everyone recover from their Christmas festivities, a snow digging operation was instigated to clear the camp and the road to Bourton. It was said that this road was cleared not just for the benefit of moving traffic but to enable RAF personnel to reach their natural watering holes at the 'Old New Inn' and 'The Mousetrap'. Joining in with the spirit of things, the CO resorted to skiing round the unit to ensure all was as well as could be expected.

1963

Appalling weather deteriorates

The winter of 1962/3 was the worst on record since 1947 with high winds, heavy snow and freezing temperatures, and Little Rissington was covered by several feet of snow for many weeks recalls CI Wg Cdr Langer.

"The RAF and Council snowploughs did their best to clear the roads but the station was completely cut off. Some enterprising officers, living off-station, even managed to get in on skis. Eventually, when the road to the bottom of Stow Hill was opened, the snow banks either side were in excess of ten feet high.

There had been no flying since 21 December and by mid-January the CFS flying task was way behind schedule. I flew several weather and runway checks but it was not until 22 January when, under pressure from the Commandant, I declared the airfield fit for Chipmunk and Piston Provost flying only. The immediate priority was for staff continuation training. On one such flight with one of my QFIs on 22 January, I flew a dusk sortie. After much circuit work I made the final approach in the dark. Shortly after landing my port wing tip caught the snow bank lining the runway and we spun off. Luckily there was no damage, other than to my pride: sportingly the Commandant, Air Cdre Bird-Wilson took the blame for pressing us to fly before the runway was fully fit. During a short lull, the opportunity was taken to fly a few Piston Provosts and Chipmunks out to snow-free airfields to allow flying training to resume."

Provost stranded

Towards the end of February, as the thaw began to set in, the decision was taken to try and complete the night flying phase of the current Piston Provost course. The runway still had patches of ice and layers of snow along its surface with steep snow banks on either side. On 21 February, the pilot of Piston Provost T.1, XF895/01, turned off at what he thought was the runway intersection and ran into a runway light hidden in a snow bank. The port undercarriage leg collapsed and the aircraft remained stranded on the airfield until conditions eased sufficiently for it to be retrieved. Damage to the aircraft was assessed at Cat. 5 and both the instructor and student were fortunate to escape without injury.

Hunter Flight disbands

A change in policy brought about the demise of the Hunter Type Flight at Kemble on 28 February, the swept wing commitment being transferred to the Gnats. The unit's two remaining Hunter F.4s, XF944 and XF973 were the last of the Mark in regular service with the RAF and were placed in long term storage with 5 MU. Ten years later both were converted to F.58A standard and sold to the Swiss Air Force, while one of the T.7s, WV318, is still airworthy and flying at Kemble albeit under the auspices of Delta Jets.

From Lightnings to JP3s

Wg Cdr E.J. 'Ted' Nance recalls his time when, as a Flt Lt, he made the transition from fighter pilot to QFI:

"Reportedly, I was the first front line Lightning pilot posted to Flying Training Command to become a QFI, commencing with No. 217 Course at Little Rissington in March 1963. Believe it or not, I was a volunteer! I had spent over five years on No. 74(F) Sqn, firstly on Hunters before Lightning Mark 1s and three seasons as a member of the Lightning RAF display team. While tremendously rewarding for the lucky ones on the team, the squadron inevitably became somewhat divided, with morale not always at its highest among our non members

The sleek lines of Hunter F.4, XF973/W, taxiing in at Kemble in April 1962. After more than decade in storage with 5 MU on the same base, it was converted to F.58A standard and sold to the Swiss Air Force. (*Ray Deacon*)

for whom one had to feel concern. Since I wanted a change, CFS seemed to be the correct way forward for me. At Rissy I found there were many interesting staff and students including my previous Station Commander at RAF Coltishall, the first Lightning base, Air Cdre Bird-Wilson, by then Commandant. Ray Hanna was on my course and Lee Jones was one ahead of us. With our various convictions, we lobbied 'Birdy' and Henry Chinnery, expressing the view that the RAF display team logically belonged in FTC. It was not long before 'The Yellowjacks' were formed, followed in turn by 'The Red Arrows'. Maybe our voices were heard in high places, who knows?

*Convinced that at the end of my course, I would be posted to Valley on the Gnat, it was a surprise to be earmarked for RAF College Cranwell on Jet Provosts. I well remember my first right hand seat conversion ride in the Jet Provost at Little Rissington. Somewhere stuck at the back of my mind was the minimum JPT (jet pipe temperature) for take off of 560 degrees. I opened the power lever on the take off roll. After the Lightning, the acceleration of the JP3 appeared non-existent. The JPT was barely 560 degrees, so intuitively I closed the throttle and aborted the take off. My instructor, Mike Ware, went off the wall and told me in no uncertain terms that the performance on take off was completely normal and for me not to be such a smart ****. As one says … I learned from that … but it was not me who had dubbed the JP3 as the 'variable noise, constant (lack of) thrust machine'."*

Embarrassing moment

A delicate situation arose in April when several high-ranking German Air Force personnel visited the Station. The Noratlas transport aircraft in which they were about to depart had started-up and was preparing to taxi away when it mounted a chock jamming it between the wheels. The Rissy groundcrew were able to dislodge it but only after a great deal of manual effort.

'New' Aerobatic Team

In April the CFS announced the formation of an expanded "Red Pelican" aerobatic team for the 1963 season, comprising six Jet Provost Mark 4s painted in an all-over day-glo colour scheme. Flt Lt Ian Bashall took over as team leader with positions 2 to 6 flown by:

No. 2 Flt Lt K.F. Beck
No. 3 Flt Lt A. J. Hawkes
No. 4 Flt Lt N.T. Raffin RAAF
No. 5 Flt Lt B. A. Nice
No. 6 Flt Lt T. E. L. Lloyd

Fired up and fireless - a scorching Clarkson sortie

Flt Lt Charles Sturt joined his course at Little Rissington late in 1962 after a tour on Shackletons in the Far East, and recalls that it was uneventful until 2 May 1963, in what proved to be his last sortie there.

"Flying in Jet Provost T.Mk.4, XP588, this was a practice aerobatic trip flown in the morning over the disused airfield at Chedworth for the Clarkson Trophy competition to be held that afternoon. Half way through the first practice run and while inverted in a slow roll, the fire warning attention getters illuminated as simultaneously the audio warning went off noisily, an event which tends to freeze the thought processes at that particular altitude. Continuing the manoeuvre and now the right way up, I then shut down the engine, whereupon the cancelled attention getters and audio warning went off once again. With what appeared to be a smell of burning in the cockpit (subsequently thought to be oil fumes), I was convinced of fire so, as per Pilot's Notes, I gave out my Mayday call and pulled the overhead ejection handle.

After that expected big boot up the backside on departure, I experienced a tumbling sensation, after which the drogue pulled out the main parachute. I found myself suspended over the woods at Chedworth, watching my empty aircraft nose-diving towards the trees but with no signs of fire. The JP eventually crashed but nothing ignited, so I had obviously departed from a perfectly serviceable aircraft, which dismayed me considerably. I continued on down on my 'chute and landed in a tree, not far from the wreckage, ending unhurt apart from a few scratches and only about two feet off the ground. Having undone my harness and dropped to terra firma, I walked downhill through the wood until reaching a road. This I followed to the left, eventually coming across a row of six houses. Knocking on the first door, with my bone dome tucked under my arm, I explained my predicament to the lady who answered. Asking if I could use her telephone to contact the Station, she invited me to come in and sit down. Next she disappeared into the kitchen and came back with a glass and a bottle of scotch. Since it would have been churlish to refuse I watched her pour, with a trembling hand, a good measure. 'I think I am more nervous than you', she said. Next my hostess explained that she had no telephone but could drive me up to the Roman Villa at Chedworth, which had the only one in that area. When I had duly drained the glass, she kindly drove me to the Villa, during which journey she confided that she had wondered on my arrival whether I was not from 'Candid Camera', a TV show popular at the time which hoaxed members of the public. The call to Little Rissington was made without further ado and I was told that the Commandant of the day, Air Commodore Bird-Wilson no less, was already on his way to pick me up! He arrived shortly afterwards and I then had to retrace my steps as best

For the 1963 season, the Red Pelicans, now led by Flt Lt Ian Bashall, increased the formation to six Jet Provost T.4s painted in a new all-over day-glo red colour scheme. (*Ian Bashall*)

I could to the wreckage area and explain what had happened. Thankfully he was very relaxed about the whole affair but did comment later on that evening at my dining-out night that I had indeed left the course on a sufficiently high note. Needless to say, I never did take part in the Clarkson Trophy.

The cause of the spurious warning was subsequently found to be a kink in the fire detection wire, as a result of which all Jet Provosts with the system were modified, as also were the drills for a fire warning. This seemed to avoid future repetitions of my incident within Flying Training Command."

That seasick feeling!

Soon after the "Gnat Project" was completed the 'Gnat Course Line' was formed and the first course for Gnat student QFIs commenced. Cpl Tech Malcolm Thomas moved from the Project Team to the Line and remembers a close call that occurred during that first course.

"On 16 May, QFI Flt Lt Bill Loverseed had nearly completed a training sortie with a student on board XM705 when on the approach to Little Rissington, the undercarriage failed to lock down; moreover the undercarriage selector was jammed and could not be moved. With the aircraft very low on fuel WO Barber called the Gnat course line for any help or suggestions but no help was forthcoming in the time available.

Although not apparent to either instructor or student, the Undercarriage Emergency Down lever had been inadvertently selected. In this situation, the shuttle valves controlling the undercarriage have hydraulic pressure at 3,000 psi and compressed air at 3,000 psi acting in opposing directions, causing them to stall in the midway position. Neither hydraulic or air pressure could feed the undercarriage operating cylinders and a lock had engaged preventing any further selection of the undercarriage. Under these conditions, the undercarriage is left to swing freely under the aircraft, leaving Bill with the task of putting the aircraft on the runway with the undercarriage unlocked. Unfortunately, as no one had experience of landing a Gnat with the undercarriage swinging freely, no advice was forthcoming!!

The Gnat had some very clever features, one of which was a system known as 'Datum Shift' which counteracted the drag caused when the undercarriage was lowered. This drag tended to pull the nose down as the undercarriage came down or lift as the wheels went up into the wheel bays. Mr Petter (Folland's Chief Designer) had devised a system that connected the undercarriage to the all moving tailplane so it moved about 4° to keep the aeroplane steady.

So Bill was about to 'chase the tailplane'. As the undercarriage moved so the tail moved and as Bill fought to counter the motion the aircraft porpoised down the runway, with bits flying off it in showers of sparks every time it touched the tarmac, a very alarming spectacle to watch but much more alarming for the crew. Fortunately the only damage was to the aircraft and after an investigation into the problem at Little Rissington, '705 was shipped back to Hawker Siddeley Aviation at Dunsfold for repair. Bill suffered a sore back for a while but he was otherwise OK as was his student.

The investigation concluded that if hydraulic power to the flying control had been manually turned off when the problem first occurred, the 'Datum Shift' mechanism would not have operated. More significantly, the undercarriage would have locked down due to the compressed air being automatically reduced below 2,000 psi when the hydraulics were switched off to the tailplane and ailerons, and the 3,000 psi hydraulic pressure would then have powered the undercarriage operating cylinders.

Soon after this incident, a modification was issued in which the cross-sectional area of the operating surface of the shuttle valves on all Gnats were re-profiled to prevent equal and opposing forces causing a repetition of the occurrence."

Mosquito arrives

Having participated in the flying sequences of the film '633 Squadron', Mosquito B(TT).Mk.35, TA639, was acquired for the RAF Museum and flown to Little Rissington on 31 May for safe keeping with CFS. Air Cdre Bird-Wilson, was an accomplished Mosquito pilot and took great delight in displaying it at air shows during his term as Commandant.

After appearing in the film 633 Squadron, Mosquito B.35, TA639, was acquired for the RAF Museum and allocated to CFS where it continued to be flown at air shows. (*Ray Deacon*)

Awards

During the annual parade in June to mark the Queen's official birthday W O Cowdrey was presented with a Bar to add to his existing Long Service and Good Conduct medal.

Sport

The Flying Training Command athletics championships, held at RAF Cranwell on 10, 11 and 12 June, saw creditable performances by Rissy personnel, especially the WRAF contingent which performed magnificently to finish in 1st place overall. The following deserved special mention:

100 yds.	1st	Cpl Gray in 12.5 secs.
	4th	SACW Culling
220 yds.	1st	Cpl Gray in 27.5 secs. **
	4th	SACW Culling.
440 yds.	1st	Cpl Gray in 65.6 secs.
	5th	SACW Jones
4x110 yds.	1st	Little Rissington – Cpl Gray, SACWs Culling, Jones and Dempster
Discus	1st	SACW Dempster 89ft. 5in
	2nd	SACW Jones
	5th	Plt Off Pitcher
Long Jump	2nd	SACW Harris 14ft
High Jump	1st	SACW Harris 4ft. 9in **
	2nd	SACW Dempster 4ft.5in
Shot	1st	SACW Dempster 29 ft 9.5in
	3rd	SACW Jones 27ft. 9.5 in
	5th	SACW Watkins 25ft. 10in

** New Flying Training Command Records

The men's team finished a creditable 4th overall with the following returning notable performances:

800 yds.	4th	Cpl J. Hine 2min. 3.6secs
1 Mile	4th	Cpl A. Cobie
	6th	SAC Lovatt
3 Miles	1st	Cpl A. Cobie 15min. 0.2secs
3,000 metres Steeplechase		
	5th	J/T Wrigglesworth

CFS visit to German Air Force

One of several overseas visits by CI Wg Cdr Langer was at the request of the German Air Force.

"The GAF had started operating F-104s in the ground attack role and its accident rate had been far too high, resulting in this aircraft, the Starfighter, becoming known as the 'Widowmaker'. Both the RCAF and the Belgians also flew F-104s in Europe and their accident rates were low. In August 1963 the CFS was invited to send a team to the F-104 OCU at Norvenich. As CI and because I had been a fighter squadron commander, I carried out the visit accompanied by Flt Lt Derek Bryant, the Gnat Project Officer. It did not take us long to pinpoint the problems and to write a report for which the GAF was very grateful. The visit was a welcome diversion not least because it resulted in my joining the Mach Two Club when I flew a F-104 at twice the speed of sound, albeit in a fairly steep dive."

Life on the 'Waterfront'

Flt Lt M.A.F. 'Mick' Ryan, after *"being lucky enough to spend three years on my first tour with No.93 Squadron at Jever on Hunters in Germany"*, completed his Jet Provost QFI course at Little Rissington in February 1961. Having obtained his A2 instructor category while instructing at the RAF College, Cranwell, he was posted back to the 'Waterfront' at CFS in August 1963, during Air Commodore 'Birdie' Bird-Wilson's tenure as Commandant.

"The flying was great – lots of it. However, by the end of my three years we were being capped on the monthly hours we now could fly. My average for 1964 was 30 hrs 25 mins a month and we were capped at 40 hrs for any one single month. This was because of Flying Training Command's fear of pilot fatigue – what a way to go!

As others will recall, all the staff had to undertake secondary duties in addition to their QFI Instructor role, so I volunteered to be Station Flight Safety Officer. This was at a time when 'Flight Safety' was becoming a more universal and conscious consideration, perhaps linking into those new limits on our flying hours. The overhead of sheer paperwork for processing Special Occurrence Reports (SORs) was a great deterrent to submitting such reports. The CFS line was that we should set an example, so I became very active in promoting and speeding up the processing of SORs. I was not popular. When I introduced new wooden folders for circulating the reports up through the chain of command, these were deliberately made too big to fit into In or Pending trays. I was particularly impressed by the quality and attitude of the engineering staff. So often it was easy for the pilots to raise SORs for any problems which came up when flying. Nearly always there was a detailed engineering problem to be researched and written up by the technical staff. Driving up SOR reporting numbers pleased the chain of command but it was often at the expense of these hard working men on the engineering staff. Their co-operation and professional approach always impressed me.

Getting the aircrew to report their own pilot errors was a little more difficult but I think it was better at CFS than most places because the staff needed to set an example. Occasionally I could even be of direct help to the aviators. CFS was working up its JP formation aerobatic team, the Red Pelicans. Returning after one practice session, the team had to land after a heavy rainstorm. The leader skidded on a very wet runway: embarrassment all round ensued as he went off the end of the runway into the crash barrier. Immediately it was assumed that this must be pilot error from a staff QFI, who ought to have known better. However, I remembered reading an Air Clues article a few months earlier from the Royal Canadian Air Force about aquaplaning. This phenomenon was little known or understood in the RAF at that time. Basically, when landing on puddles, the physics of aquaplaning causes the tyre to spin down (assisted by pilot braking, of course), to become stationary and then to slide on any standing water. The small bow wave set up ahead of the stationary tyre was subject to such buffeting that the water boiled and caused distinctive bubbling of the tyre rubber. Taking the article down to the hangar, I was able to find the exact same marks on the leader's JP tyres as in the article's photographs. This was greatly appreciated by CFS as this was one of the first recognised examples of this little known phenomenon and got the Red Pelican team leader 'off the hook'".

ROC Open Day

Once again Little Rissington played host to the ROC for their annual reunion 15 September 1963. During the day almost 400 members were given trips in a Hastings. The afternoon saw fly-pasts by several aircraft including, Mosquito, Spitfire and Fouga Magister. The flying display was closed by "The Red Pelicans", a fitting tribute to a team giving its final performance of a year in which it had put on over thirty displays at home and overseas.

Forbidden fruit: first Gnat formation aeros

Posted to Valley in January after Gnat conversion, Al Pollock reveals how strictly forbidden Gnat formation aerobatics led to a debt owed by the "Yellowjacks" and "Red Arrows" to then Wg Cdr W Edwards and a visiting matelot:

> *"Flying Training Command was proud of its new Gnat simulator. When a Bristol Siddeley ex-RN photographer, Bob Lomax, came to Valley to photograph the simulator in September 1963, four of us decided Bob should take photographs of real Gnats flying in formation. Boscombe Down had issued a strict instruction forbidding anyone to fly the Gnat in formation aerobatics, with rumours of soft option courts martial. On 10 September I flew two sorties with Bob Lomax on board. Next day, with Flt Lts Lee Jones as leader (02), Roger Hymans No. 2 (04) and myself No. 3 (08), superbly aided and abetted by Tony Doyle flying Bob in his 'camera-ship', we flew the first formation aerobatic sequences.*
>
> *As No. 3, I saw roving Tony Doyle suddenly snap half roll inwards as we passed each vertical. Bob took the photo from the port side. On the ground Roger and Lee charmingly suggested that I was to chat the CI up – he was not in his office and I left this identical shot with a brief note on his desk. That 'blue touch paper' photo launched thousands of displays, since ex-Rissy Waterfront 'Bill' Edwards was quick to appreciate that increasing Gnats and QFIs meant 4 FTS could work up a formation team – in 1964 this evolved into the 'Yellowjacks' under Lee's leadership. On 29 April after three No. 3 sorties, I was offered the No. 3 slot but by then I was Command singleton display pilot and flight commander heavily involved with the new Gnat Squadron and syllabus.*

One of several exceller photographs taken during prohibited formation sorti flown by No. 4 FT instructors at RAF Valley *(Bob Lomax via Alan Pollock*

Later this massively enlarged photograph became the Ops Block's stairway mural."

CFS Examining Wing visit down under

One of the highlights of Wg Cdr Langer's tour as CI was the CFS visit to the Royal Australian Air Force and Royal New Zealand Air Force in November and December 1963.

"The team was led by Air Cdre 'Birdy'-Wilson, while I led the fixed wing element and Wg Cdr 'Jim' Corbishley, CI at CFS Shawbury, looked after the helicopter aspects. We had been asked specifically by the Australian and New Zealand HQs to talk about the reasons for the RAF adopting all-through jet flying training, the advantages and disadvantages of so doing and our experience to date with the system. Although warmly welcomed by the Aussie CFS at East Sale, with whom we had useful discussions, our receptions at No. 4 FTS at Pearce Base near Perth and the Mirage Base at Laverton were positively cool. Many elements of the RAAF thought they knew it all and did not want the 'bloody Poms' giving them advice. By comparison the RNZAF went out of their way to make us welcome wherever we went. In particular they were extremely keen to hear what we had to say and to learn everything, which they could use to improve the effectiveness of their training."

Aircraft availability

The average aircraft availability at Little Rissington during 1963 is listed below.

	January	**December**
Aircraft Type	No.	No.
Vampire T.11	6	1
Piston Provost T.1	5	5
Jet Provost T.3/T.4	25	26
Varsity T.1	5	5
Meteor T.7	3	1
Anson C.19	2	1
Chipmunk T.10	4	4
Gnat T/T.1	5	12
Hunter F.4 (Kemble)	2	-
Hunter T.7 (Kemble)	2	-
Totals	**59**	**55**

Station strength

The average station strength for the year stood at Officers 120, Airmen 530 and Airwomen 55. These figures do not include student pilots or attached personnel.

1964

New Year's Honours

Several names from personnel based at Little Rissington were contained in the New Year's Honours list. Top of the list was the Queen's Commendation for services in the air to Flt Lt M.H. Hoare, Air Officer Commanding-in-Chief Commendations went to WO D.J. Barber and J/T C. Lambert, and Air Officer Commanding Commendations were presented to Mr J. Wright, Ch Tech P.J. Pearce, Cpls M. Brewer and P.P. Adlem, and J/T M.E. Goddard.

Gnat raid on Rissy

Although the Gnat trainer carried no weapons there was ample space for leaflets and 4" 50mm bog-rolls in the brake-chute housing as Flt Lt Al Pollock divulges with this story of his first day as a flight commander at 4 FTS Valley: *"With my deputy flight commander, Dennis Hazell (we still had no real OC), and both Flt Lts Perry Edwards and Mike Kelson with first sortie students for the baptism of our new squadron, we arranged a Bodenplatte style 'weapons' strike on Rissy on New Year's Day, 1964. By 09:45 on day one, relieved of my first 'squadron command', I had to hand over for two days to Dennis, which was a bit rich when he was on board this flight with me!"*

Flu!

The early months of the year were notable for an unusually high number of influenza cases, caused mainly by the very damp weather conditions prevalent at the time.

Aircraft On Ground

Eight Jet Provost T.3s were placed on AOG for the whole of January due to the shortage of Viper 10201 engines. Increasing rates of compressor disc failure led to a reduction in the operational life of the engines and the lack of replacement units being returned from overhaul.

1964 Aerobatic Team

"The Red Pelicans" aerobatic team reformed as a six aircraft formation for the 1964 season, with Flt Lt T.E.L. Lloyd as team leader and Flt Lts H.R. Lane, W.A. Langworthy, B.A. Nice, R.S.S. Cox and D.F. Southern occupying the remaining slots.

Flying the Gnat

Flt Lt Alex Wickham first experienced life at Little Rissington as a student on the Piston Provost in December 1959. Then at the end of February 1960, he moved on to the advanced phase of the course flying Vampire T.11s on No. 2 Squadron and, having qualified as an instructor on 27 April 1960, embarked on a tour as a QFI with 5 FTS at RAF Oakington. After three years instructing on the T.11, Alex returned to CFS as a staff QFI.

"When I arrived at Little Rissington in February 1963 the Gnat Project was still ongoing so I was assigned as the last instructor on the Vampire T.11s of C Flight, 3 Squadron. In July, the Gnat Project came to an end and all but one of the remaining Vampires were flown out to the MUs, enabling me to concentrate on converting to the Gnat.

In 1964 the Commandant signed me off as the CFS solo display pilot in the Gnat and I was privileged to display the aircraft at RAF air shows all over the UK and Germany. On occasions I also went down to Dunsfold to ferry new-build Gnats back to Rissy. Later in the year I was appointed Flight Commander of C Flight, 3 Squadron, and one of my first tasks was to organise and execute the smooth relocation of C Flight to Fairford.

An interesting incident that occurred in October 1964, involved a photographic company making an instructional film for the RAF. The producer wanted a shot looking out of the front cockpit of a Gnat when breaking cloud in bad weather on an ILS approach to Valley. Being concerned that it was a bit of a risk to put a non-qualified person in the front seat carrying a bulky 16mm hand-held camera, I decided to put a student instructor in the back seat to do the flying while I sat in the front with the camera. As we waited for the weather to play ball we heard that Valley had deteriorated so we took off and headed for Anglesey. On arrival we lined up for an approach down the glide path and by the time we reached break-off height I couldn't see a thing, so, as we could not film the required shot we climbed away and headed off back to Fairford. The next day I decided to try it again but this time on my own with the camera in the front seat. This time the filming was achieved but on the way home I was advised that the Fairford weather, like most of Southern England, had deteriorated and I was to divert to Gaydon. I didn't see a thing on an initial ILS into Gaydon and went round for a second attempt, at which point, Gaydon, probably very conscious that it was an operational V-bomber base, prohibited any further attempts to land and advised me to contact the emergency services for an alternative airfield. By now fuel was getting on the low side so I climbed steeply to altitude and headed back towards the Fairford area while the emergency services struggled to find a suitable diversion airfield within range. I declared a Security alert state followed by a Mayday call as the fuel situation became critical. With discussion centring on where to direct the aircraft before ejection, I decided, as a last resort, to attempt a landing at Brize Norton, only to be informed that it too was clamped in. Nevertheless I'd just had a lot of recent ILS practice at Brize and knew the powerful approach lights and the wide runway well, so I decided to give it a go. I had just enough of a visual picture at break-off height to put the Gnat on the ground and flamed-out the engine on the runway before it ran dry. At the time Brize Norton was also US nuclear reflex base and later I thanked the Commander for helping out.

Another close call occurred when turning finals at Rissy. I called 'Final landing, streaming' to the tower which was acknowledged by a young WRAF on her first day as a controller. The normal procedure was that as soon as we touched down and the brake chute deployed, the controller would transmit 'Chute streamed'. On this occasion I touched down and pulled the brake chute lever but there was no instant deceleration. 'Chute gone' said the young lady, and as there was no sign of the chute in the mirror, I quickly opened up to go round again. Being so far down the runway we just managed to get airborne as the tarmac ran out but flew through the hedge by the Great Rissington road. I warned the student that we might not make it and prepare to eject. Superficial damage was inflicted on the airframe and I suspected that the pitot head had been damaged and the airspeed indicator was giving false readings, but it remained airworthy and we headed off for the long runway at Brize,

When Flt Lt Alex Wickham was the Gnat Flight Commander he photographed many of its activities. Typical of these was the view taken of Gnat T.1s, XP535/102 (*above*) taxiing out at Little Rissington and (*right*), XM704/95 lifting off the Rissy runway in 1964. (*Alex Wickham*)

accompanied by a second Gnat to lead me in for a safe landing.

One early problem with the Gnat was a tendency for an aileron cable to jump a pulley and lock the ailerons, a situation which should have resulted in the loss of the aeroplane. On one occasion when this happened to Flt Lt John Young's aircraft he found he was able to move the stick from centre to the fully left position only and thus fly a left hand circuit. After several practice approaches he managed to put it down safely on the short runway, an amazing feat."

Night flying the Gnat

The relatively short main runaway length of 1,600 yds was a major shortcoming for the safe operation of high speed aircraft at Little Rissington. Considered too short for night flying instruction on the Gnat, the decision was taken to make use of the runway at RAF Gaydon which at 2,000 yds was considered a safer and more effective alternative. Six Gnats, plus supporting ground equipment, air and groundcrews moved to Gaydon on the 24 February to enable six students of No. 220 Course and two staff members on conversion training to complete the night flying phase of their training.

"Pelicans" collide

On 12 March, while practising their new formation routines for the coming season ten miles north-north-west of the airfield, two Jet Provosts of the "Red Pelicans" touched, causing sufficient damage to Flt Lt Cox's aircraft to force him to eject. Although he sustained minor back injuries from which he duly recovered, his place in the team was taken by Flt Lt E.C.F. Tilsley.

Waterfront QFI

After a short tour at No. 7 FTS at Church Fenton, Flt Lt 'Cas' Maynard returned to Rissy in April 1964 to join the CFS 'Waterfront'.

"We were kept pretty busy with course flying and I was lucky to get involved in low level aerobatics for Brabyn and Clarkson contenders. In May 1965 I started to train as No.4 in the Pelicans, coached by Dennis Southern who had flown with the 1964 'Red Pelicans'. The leader was Bill Langworthy, No.2 Derek (Dinger) Bell and No.3 Roy Booth. All three joined the 'Red Arrows' in 1966 while I stayed on the Waterfront and flew No.4 in the 1966 Pelican team, led by Eddie Edmonds with No.2 Don McClen and No.3 Colin Thomas. Chas Sturt replaced me when I was posted at the end of June on promotion to run the Standards squadron at No. 2 FTS Syerston. Besides the Pelicans, highlights for me were flying displays and sales demonstrations for potential customers of BAC (British Aircraft Corporation) at Wisley and Warton. At Warton, which was for a Jordanian mission, my JP4 shared the programme exclusively with a Lightning flown by 'Bee' Beamont.

Another highlight was a week in RAF Germany during November 1965 in a small CFS team with the aim of making the CFS Course a worthwhile posting option. I shared a JP4 with Bill Langworthy and we flew 'famils' with Squadron pilots at Wildenrath, Brüggen, Geilenkirchen and Gütersloh. This type of detachment was an excellent way to engage with operational units and the benefit was two-way. For example, I managed to get famils in the Canberra and Wessex, neither of which I had flown before."

Anniversary dinner

The 52nd Anniversary Reunion Dinner of the CFS, held in the Officers' Mess on 10 July, was toasted by Marshal of the Royal Air Force Sir Dermot A. Boyle. Reminiscences were given by Air Chief Marshal Sir Arthur Longmore and the Band of the RAF Salon Orchestra, led by Sen Tech T.P. Holmes, played a varied programme of music which included 'Swan Lake', 'Gilbert and Sullivan Memories' and many other pieces.

RAF Organisational changes

At the end of the Second World War, the RAF was operating no fewer than 55,469 aircraft, of which 9,200 were in first-line service. By 1964, when this number had progressively shrunk to a little over 2,000, this combined with the need to keep abreast of the continual advances in military hardware, meant the time had come for a radical reorganisation. As the same issues affected the Royal Navy and the Army, a resolution was found by reorganising all three services and placing them under the direct control of the Ministry of Defence. Later, in 1968, Fighter, Bomber and Coastal Commands disappeared, their units being combined within Strike Command, and a restructured Transport Command would be absorbed along with Training and Maintenance Commands under the umbrella Support Command.

In 1964 the future of Little Rissington seemed assured as the Central Flying School had maintained its role without any loss of identity or change of purpose. However, the Commandant, Air Cdre H.A.C. Bird-Wilson, believed that the School's authority on matters of flying training was threatened by a lack of operational awareness due to shortcomings on the airfield preventing the operation of advanced, high performance aircraft from the relatively short main runway. In his view, the greatest single limitation to the realisation of the CFS objective was the unsuitability of the airfield which not only limited Gnat operations but prevented visits by front line high-performance aircraft. The airfield would most certainly be more inadequate for the next generation of advanced trainers and a continued stay at Little Rissington might well result in CFS becoming a 'bit of a joke'.

First day gaff!

A tale submitted anonymously, tells of a young officer arriving to join the CFS Staff in June 1964 and before attending his interview with the Station Commander in the afternoon, goes to the Officers' Mess Barber for a quick short back and sides. While waiting for his turn he stood at an open window watching "The Red Pelicans" practising their display.

A gentleman, dressed in civvies, who was sitting in the barber's chair says, *"You'll be with them this year, I suppose." "They'll have to get a lot better than that before I join"*, says the over-confident young man. Imagine his surprise and horror on marching in for his interview later that day, when he discovers that the Station Commander has just had his haircut!

Birthday Honours

'Queen's Commendations for Services in the Air' were awarded to Flt Lts I. Bashall and K.F. Beck, the leader and No. 2 respectively in the 1963 "Red Pelicans" aerobatic team.

Sir Augustus Walker bids farewell

On 12 June, the Air Officer Commanding-in-Chief, Flying Training Command, Air Marshal Sir Augustus Walker, paid his final visit to Little Rissington. After inspecting a Guard of Honour, he partook of a farewell luncheon in the Officers' Mess.

From Canberras to Gnats

Flt Lt Nick Ireland arrived at Little Rissington from a Canberra tour in Cyprus and without a UK car licence.

> *"I had bought a long stroke Panther 650cc motor bike with a double adult sidecar to be my personal transport. Clear memories swim back of being invited never to park this at the front of the Officers' Mess – strangely I have little recall of coping with this conundrum – perhaps it was parked in front at times anyway, which could just partly explain my longevity as a Flight Lieutenant!*
>
> *As many others, my recall swings back to that pair of 10-minute lectures during the course groundschool. We were warned off home brewing, car maintenance, etc., as they had already been done to the point of boredom. My second lecture was a practical one, complete with Gaz cooker and necessary utensils, on how to cook an omelette. Went down quite well!*
>
> *I did some Gnat flying at LR, characterised by hectic arrangements in the circuit where many a/c types of highly varying performance were all in and 'mixing it' at the same time! You could be Number 4 downwind in a Gnat but then swiftly become Number 1 on finals! We also spent a lot of our time diverting to Fairford as the LR runway was a pain when wet. The Gnat was hard to control in a crosswind and the runway had been resurfaced with something, which I think we called 'slick slurry'. Whatever, when it was wet it had the braking action of wet oily glass. One very old pilot (Wg Cdr Arthur Turner, OC 4 FTS designate) was teamed up with Flt Lt Doug McGregor (very young QFI designate) for their mutual sorties and they once stopped their Gnat with the pitot head stuck through the overrun barrier!*
>
> *My Gnat flying skills were not helped, in my view, by an exchange instructor called Benny Raffin who was an Australian and whose instructional technique involved a lot of shouting when things weren't going well, which they often were not, but I did get through!"*

Farnborough rehearsals

The task of providing the RAF's official aerobatic team was taken seriously by Flying Training Command, which took the opportunity to demonstrate to the aviation world how training aircraft could fill the void left by the more potent jets of Fighter Command. "The Red Pelicans" were dispatched to RAF Valley on 6 August in order to work up a joint presentation with the Gnat-mounted "Yellowjacks" aerobatic team of No. 4 FTS, in readiness for the SBAC air show at Farnborough. A captivating synchronised display was devised and was well received by spectators and commentators when performed at the event.

As preparation for the 1964 Farnborough Air Show, the Red Pelicans moved up to Valley to rehearse a synchronised display with the Yellowjacks, devised specifically for that event. *(Ray Deacon)*

Battle of Britain Day

After a long gap, Little Rissington opened its doors to the public for a Battle of Britain Day in September. The Ground School Museum and Airmanship Hall were both opened and on display were a number of splendid model aircraft on loan from RAF Hendon. The flying started at 14:00 with a variety of demonstrations by a Swordfish, SE5, Spitfire, Mosquito, Hurricane, Hunter and Lightning. Interspersed were displays by a team of Canberras from RAF Bassingbourn and another with Meteors from RAF Strubby. The final airborne display of the afternoon was a demonstration of synchronised aerobatics by the "Yellowjacks" Gnat team from 4 FTS, RAF Valley and the "Red Pelicans" in their Jet Provosts. This was also the final display by the "Pellies" as the official RAF aerobatic team. The day was brought to a conclusion by the massed pipes and drums of No. 1 School of Technical Training RAF Halton playing 'Beat the Retreat'.

During the summer, while Gate Guardian Spitfire, LA226, was away being refurbished at one of the Maintenance Units, probably 5 MU at Kemble, No. 5003 Airfield Construction Squadron was tasked with building a plinth on which to mount it on its return. This occurred during the autumn.

Shiftless datum porpoise arrival

On 14 August 1964 Flt Lt John Young was flying with Master Pilot Evans, a Jet Provost instructor on a Gnat familiarisation flight, and they were about to land back at Little Rissington.

"I had briefed him to fly the approach but that I would take over for the landing, when he would deploy the brake chute after touchdown. All was normal until after our touchdown, when I closed the throttle and he streamed the 'chute – suddenly we were 50 ft above the runway and there followed a series of three porpoise-like impacts with said runway until the nose undercarriage strut failed and we slid to a graceless halt. On inspection, our technicians found that the datum shift had stuck and not operated when the gear was lowered. Master Pilot Evans was unaware of this malfunction, not having been briefed on this possibility, but was certainly far more intimately concerned about the broken end of the undercarriage strut, which had pierced the nosewheel dome between his legs, stopping just inches short of his marriage prospects.

A month later, on 19 September, one of the groundcrew and I flew to RAF Waddington to take part in the static aircraft display for the Battle of Britain. Unfortunately, at the end of the show my Gnat was allocated the first departure slot immediately following the flying display. Start up was normal and the RAF police kept the crowd back to allow me to taxi out. We came over the brow of a hill on the taxiway to find it jammed with motor cars as the great British public, all with the same idea, departed the central parking area. I therefore joined the queue, without ever knowing how the paintwork on the cars of those behind us fared. What I did note was how excited the little old lady in the Morris Minor ahead of me got, when she looked back to see the tip of that very long pitot probe menacingly close to her rear window. All this ground traffic was eventually sorted out and it was the airborne return to base that proved to be the most normal part of the sortie.

By October 1963 we were no longer using Kemble for weather diversions but used RAF Brize Norton instead. Because of the frequency of these and the assistance of our USAF exchange officer, Capt Tom Narbles, we were offered the use of their Officers' Club – what a way to live! Everything was subsidised and at weekends the floorshow was filled with top London artistes, who gave their performances gratis in exchange for a weekend of free accommodation. I gather that this arrangement continued right up to the departure of the USAF and the return of the Brize base to the RAF, when further offers of free British entertainment were thereafter refused!

When it was finally accepted that Little Rissington's runway was too short, coupled with plentiful other slower traffic for continuous Gnat operations, the Flight moved to RAF Fairford after the USAF departed. The changeover had been co-ordinated by Capt Narbles along with the station commanders of Fairford and Little Rissington, but nothing goes smoothly once bureaucracy takes over. HM Customs & Excise ruled that all equipment brought in by the Americans and subsequently left behind was liable for import duty, which the RAF would have to pay if it wanted to keep it. Not unexpectedly the opportunity was declined and the USAF removed much of their valuable equipment, from entire Air Traffic Control consoles and Instrument Landing System down to anything moveable such as light fittings and electrical appliances. Everything was ruthlessly stripped, removed and buried by bulldozers on the far side of the airfield, but I did hear that the local community soon possessed some extremely well equipped homes."

Spitfire diversion

Air Marshal Sir Ronald Stuart-Paul KBE, never a QFI, recalls here how, when a Flight Lieutenant, he paid a brief visit to Little Rissington and an encounter with an unexpectedly crafty, 44 year-old, ex-Battle of Britain Commandant, the first never to have been a QFI and anxious to get his hands once more on a Spitfire!

"On Saturday 22 August 1964, I deployed to RAF Kemble to take part in their Air Display. I was flying a Spitfire PR.Mk.19, PM631, and was No. 2 to a Hurricane 11C, LF363, piloted by the then Sqn Ldr Dave Seward. We refuelled at Kemble and on completion of our display, without landing back on, we set course on the return flight to RAF Coltishall.

In transit at 2,000 ft we were flying on a track, which took us close to Little Rissington. Shortly after passing Rissy, a routine check round the cockpit revealed the drastic news that the engine oil pressure was falling rapidly. Without a reasonably normal oil supply, the Rolls-Royce Griffon engine life is measured in seconds rather than minutes. I needed to land, and quickly.

We did not know if Rissy was open, as it had not been given as a diversion for display aircraft but, as the oil pressure was by now just above zero, it was Rissy or an unthinkable potential loss of the aircraft,. Throttling back as much as possible, I turned back towards Little Rissington by then fortunately a mere five miles behind us. Dave was still accompanying me to give moral support, as I called Rissy blind on

NATO Common. To my considerable relief, they replied and, informed of my predicament, cleared me for an immediate emergency landing on their main Runway 23.

So far so good, even though any straight in approach from 5 miles out by then and at some 1,000 ft is not an easy task in a Spitfire, in particular for the Griffon-engined Marks, as forward visibility in a shallow descent is virtually nil! Thankfully my engine continued to run smoothly, despite the oil pressure having fallen to zero, allowing me to make a normal landing at about 16:00 hrs.

Unfortunately, this was my first ever visit, let alone landing, at Rissy. From the little I could see ahead there appeared to be very little runway remaining, so I naturally commenced to brake as heavily as I could without tipping the aircraft onto its nose. Just as the aircraft came to a stop, we reached the top of what I soon knew as that inverted "soup bowl" of a runway, to reveal that still much more than half of the runway length still remained!

As soon as the aircraft was stationary, I switched off the engine. Dave, having seen me land safely, continued back to Coltishall. After being towed to dispersal, I was met by a Sqn Ldr Engineering Officer and the ground crew supporting those CFS-based aircraft taking part in RAF Kemble's Display. After some discussion, we came to a consensus – since the engine had run without any distress for some 3 - 4 minutes with zero indicated oil pressure, there was a good chance that the fault was a failing pressure transmitter and not the oil pump, so the engine might still be undamaged.

By some miracle, a replacement transmitter was found in Stores and a qualified fitter volunteered to fit it immediately. At this point in the proceedings the CFS Commandant, Air Cdre Bird-Wilson, turned up. He deftly tried to convince me that it was now too late to fix the aircraft that day and I should accept his offer of a flight back to Coltishall in a CFS aircraft. He would then air test the Spitfire when it was ready and deliver it back to Coltishall. As a mere Flt Lt, it was difficult to oppose Birdie's blandishments but I stood my ground. I insisted it was my duty to stay with the aircraft until it was serviceable and then recover it to Coltishall. Foiled in his naked attempt to fly a Spitfire once again, Birdie accepted the situation with good grace and gave me his full support in the efforts made to get me quickly on my way.

The pressure transmitter was changed and a speedy engine run-up proved that this new part had cured the oil pressure problem. The aircraft was buttoned up and I took off at 18:10 hrs to land my Mark XIX safely back at Coltishall at 19:00 hrs.

... And that, dear reader, is the tale of the first and the last time I ever operated an aircraft into and out of Little Rissington."

Gnats move away

As mentioned by Flt Lt Young, continuing concerns over the operation of the Gnat trainer in the busy, mixed Rissy circuit and relatively short runway, led to the decision to relocate the Gnat Flight to RAF Fairford on a permanent detachment basis. Located some twenty miles to the south it had recently been vacated by the B-47s and B-52s of the USAF, and would provide an ideal base for the Gnats. The Flight moved to Fairford on 2 November 1964, together with a detachment of technical and air traffic personnel who, although working at Fairford, commuted in RAF buses from Little Rissington every day. With its extra long runways and fewer aircraft movements, Fairford proved to be a more efficient and safer environment for the operation of the Gnat, and the use of a spacious modern hangar was much appreciated by the crews.

New NAAFI facilities at Rissy

In October work commenced on re-furbishing the old Corporals and other ranks NAAFI building, a project that was expected to take six months to complete. When finished the building became more of a sports and social club.

With the objective of improving shopping facilities for unaccompanied personnel and married families, a new NAAFI shop was opened on 17 November. The original shop had been managed for many years by a former German POW and located in a wartime Nissen hut close to the Cinema. When opened, it was intended to cater for fifty families instead of the 276 now living in married quarters. The new facility introduced self-service to the Station.

From the Sudan to CFS

One fine day in 1964 in Khartoum, Flt Lt Danny Lavender was coming to the end of an exciting two years with the Sudan Air Force and over 500 hours flying armed Piston and Jet Provosts, Pembrokes, Dornier 27s and Dakotas, when the Air Adviser summoned him to his office.

"He announced my next posting - promotion to Squadron Leader to command 3 Squadron of the Central Flying School at RAF Little Rissington, with a Flight each of Gnats, Varsities and Chipmunks. Whoopee! Not having flown any of them before, conversion onto all three – not only as Captain but then to supervise the training of flying instructors – was going to be a bit of a challenge. However, I had an A2 instructor's category and within two months had qualified as an instructor on all three, so I settled down to a busy couple of years.

While I tried to share my time and effort equally among the three Flights, the attractions of that tiny, sleek, fast jet, which one literally strapped on one's back, did result in a certain bias! Bill Petter and the Folland Aircraft Company had done a magnificent job with the Gnat: it was no wonder that in 1962 it entered service as the RAF's advanced trainer, with single seat fighter version deliveries already to the Indian and Finnish Air Forces. This trainer's pretty economical Bristol Siddeley Orpheus 101 ensured a super performance enabling 40,000 ft (12,192m) to be reached in 7 minutes, Mach 0.9 in level flight, and Mach 1·15 or more in a shallow dive.

The aircraft handled like a dream but some of the emergencies associated with the longitudinal control system raised one's pulse a bit. Twice it was my sad duty to appear on Boards of Inquiry at RAF Valley when students/instructors were killed while practising forced landings. Instructing from the rear seat at night was also challenging and we used to pray for a cross-wind so that the runway could be seen up to the closing stages.

In 1965 I flew to Warton with Sqn Ldr Derek Bryant (known as 'Dr Death' because he used to turn white and then green after a few beers!) to discuss visibility and other factors concerning the back seat: I hope Jaguar instructors appreciate the work that we did for them so long ago. At times Air Marshal Sir Richard 'Batchy' Atcherley is credited with the foresight to recognise that the Gnat would make a good formation aerobatics aircraft. As a result, Flt Lt Lee Jones, to whom we owe so much, formed 'The Yellowjacks' by sheer drive and persistence. After a successful first season in 1964, he was sent to CFS to learn a bit of discipline and to start afresh under the team's new title of 'The Red Arrows'.

These were heady days for me because, with little else to do at the weekends, I would sometimes fly 'the Red Arrows' spare aircraft, invariably staging through Chateauroux, to exotic places on the Continent for the team's shows. I used to hide my Squadron Leader tapes, not because I wouldn't have been pleased to be mistaken for the leader of the team but because of the 'blacks' invariably put up at the parties afterwards! It was enormous fun to share some of their experiences with the great characters on the teams – I remember entertaining a restaurant full of Italians in Ravenna with a rendition of '0 Sole Mio', which brought rapturous applause!

The runway at Little Rissington was a bit short for the Gnat, if flooded or at night, so Flt Lt Alex Wickham, my outstanding Gnat Flight Commander, made arrangements to move us to Fairford where the Gnat could almost land across the runway! No sooner had we settled there than our hangar was required for use by the Concorde trials team. Thus began the CFS's long association with Kemble where we were welcomed with open arms. Apart from the routine training of flying instructors, for which the Gnat proved to be an excellent platform, we had other distractions. The diminutive aircraft gave a radar paint quite similar to a missile, and so we were sometimes tasked to go on exercise with the Royal Navy. These sorties were great fun as one needed to simulate a sea-skimming missile at 600 kts, aimed at the waterline of destroyers and carriers – the lower you got, the more you were praised, quite unlike our RAF in certain places and at times!

One of my most memorable sorties was flying the late King Hussain of Jordan on his State Visit to the United Kingdom in 1967. Since it was an official visit to CFS, we had to deploy the Gnat into Little Rissington. All sizes of flying gear were assembled for HRH's arrival, including long johns, which were donned with alacrity. While I was looking discreetly at his head, I recognised that this particular crowned head was unusually large. The bone dome fitting started close to the largest size and soon we ended up having to ram the RAF's biggest size made onto his head. Anyway, he did not complain too much and proved to be an excellent fast jet pilot in our 40-minute flight around the Cotswolds, including a high-speed run low over the Kemble runway. As other RAF aircrew, I had always avoided those purple 'Royal Flights' like the plague but now I found that I was one! After a slightly fraught final landing, which he insisted on making – the runway was a bit short, particularly for a king – he emerged from the cockpit sounding excited and enthusiastic, also having called me 'Sir' about 40 times!

During my time at Kemble, life was always interesting, with frequent practices and displays from 'The Red Arrows' led by Sqn Ldr Ray Hanna. Occasionally observed would be the odd Gnat 'kangarooing' down the runway when student instructors had become a bit 'ham' with the sensitive control system – even the late Bill Loverseed could not prevent a collapsed nosewheel once. How delightfully nostalgic that the 40th anniversary of the Gnat's arrival at Little Rissington was celebrated by the Delta Jets team at Kemble Airfield in February 2002!"

Command Change

The command of RAF Little Rissington was relinquished by Gp Capt H.M. Chinnery in December and handed over to Gp Capt J.F.J. Dewhurst.

Sport

More sporting recognition for Rissy came when SACs Dawkins, Williams and J/T Elwick represented Flying Training Command against Fighter Command in the 'Cochrane Cup' boxing competition. Both men were successful in winning their particular weight divisions.

The small contingent of WRAF on the station continued in the footsteps of their predecessors on the sports field with three players, SACW Taylor, ACW McLaren and Cpl(W) Edgell, being selected for the inter-command netball team. Cpl Edgell was further honoured by being selected for WRAF inter-services team.

Liaison visit to USA

A team of four officers from CFS accompanied by a staff officer from HQ FTC made a liaison visit to the USA from 4 to 15 December 1964. The team was led by the Commandant, Air Cdre H. Bird-Wilson who was accompanied by Wg Cdr D.G.F. Palmer – OC Standards, CFS; Sqn Ldr D.T. Bryant – Air Staff, HQ FTC; Sqn Ldr D.T. McCann – OC Basic Standards, CFS; Flt Lt A.D. Yeardley – Advanced Standards, CFS.

The aim of the visit was to study flying training methods in the US Air Force and Navy, and to discuss and compare problems of mutual interest.

Fatal accident

December 14 was a black day for the base when Jet Provost Mark.3, XM460 was involved in a major accident. It was being flown by the Flight Line Controller and Deputy Unit Test Pilot, Flt Lt E. Roberts, who managed to eject clear of the aircraft but suffered severe burns and was taken to the Princess Mary hospital at RAF Halton. The aircraft sustained Cat. 5 damage and was transported to Farnborough for further investigation into the cause of the accident.

1964 turned out to be the driest year on record with an average rainfall of 18.9 in, compared with the normal average of 29.6 in.

CHAPTER 5

The Queen's Colour

1965

The beginning of 1965 was marked by the death of Flt Lt E. Roberts, who was badly injured in the Jet Provost T.3 accident on 14 December. He died on 26 January as a result of injuries sustained in the accident.

A QFI returns

In December 1964 Flt Lt Alan East was posted back to CFS as an instructor on the Gnat Detachment at Fairford.

"The Flight Commander there was Alex Wickham and our Squadron Commander at Little Rissington was Danny Lavender, who also commanded the Chipmunk and Varsity Flights there. What splendid variety! The Gnat Flight occupied a building which had been one of the B.47 operations rooms, complete with comfortable crew rooms, etc., which we shared with the newly formed 'Red Arrows'.

The flying programme comprised not only the second half of the course for the QFIs under training, but also the conversion of pilots posted in to 'The Red Arrows' to augment the nucleus provided by the founding-members of 'The Yellowjacks', who had moved down from Valley. During this phase, I flew with Ray Hanna, Bryan Nice and Eric Tilsley as part of their conversion to the Gnat.

At that time the late Freddie Latham was the main Gnat examiner at CFS, so he was a frequent visitor to Fairford. Freddie had seen service at the end of WWII and had taken part in the Victory Flypast over London, flying Tempest Vs on 3(F) Squadron. He was one of the service's 'characters'. It was the custom at CFS for members of staff to make a small contribution towards a silver Pelican which was presented when they were dined out. Freddie objected to this unnecessary expense, but he still wanted a Pelican. So he borrowed someone else's and made a mould. Then he cast his own in some cheap metal. Finally, he rigged up a plating tank and used a pre-1920 two-shilling piece, the silver content of which was high enough to be an effective anode.

He had an inquisitive mind and his list of interests was endless. Many a candidate down to gain his A2 QFI Cat, has complained that in the middle of his ground test Freddie had put him off by throwing in some obscure question which had nothing to do with the subject under discussion. At one time he became fascinated by honey bees and decided that the best way to study them was to build a glass-sided hive on the dining room window sill of their married quarter. One day they escaped into the dining room and, knowing no way into the hive other than from outside through the hole in the window frame, they were still there when Ann entered the room. So Freddie received a frantic phone request to go home and rescue his wife.

At around the same time, another wife caused a little consternation. One Saturday evening she left the Mess to take the baby-sitter home in their Standard Vanguard Estate, but did not return. Her husband assumed that she had gone to bed. Eventually he walked the short distance home to their married quarter and found that she had. In the morning he went to their garage. There was a Vanguard Estate in there, but on the bonnet was the unmistakable chrome mast provided for the Station Commander's pennant. His official car was also a Vanguard Estate and the wife had taken the wrong one. No doubt by then the MT

With the end of instructor training on the Vampire and Meteor in 1963, one of each type was retained at CFS for continuation training and Examining Wing use. Meteor T.7, WH166/27, performed this task for over four years from January 1965, while Vampire T.11, XD550/32 was on strength for eight years from July 1959. *(Ray Deacon)*

Section had received an interesting call from the Group Captain enquiring into the whereabouts of his car!

In June 1964, Freddie Latham left Examining Wing and I was transferred to replace him. Very soon I was renewing my acquaintance with the Vampire T.11, one on which at that time I had the most hours, having flown it on two tours; and with the Meteor T.7, on which I had done my advanced jet training twelve years previously. Soon, I and the family settled into the routine of my occasional absence for a week away on 'trapping' visits, conducting annual standardisation tests and IRTs. Places visited included CATCS at Shawbury, which was now manned by civilian pilots under contract, although several of them were there from my tour six years before; they were still flying Vampires. The CAACUs at Exeter and Woodvale, providing target facilities for Army and Navy gunners, flew Meteors and Vampires, so their test could be conducted in either type. My log book also records a visit to No. 85 Squadron at Binbrook, where over three days I did two tests in their Meteor T.7, but also two sorties of Practice Interceptions in their Meteor F.8s. Surprisingly, I have no recollection of that at all.

Another aspect of CFS's role is to visit other air forces in order to compare notes on flying training standards and techniques. These are definitely more memorable! On a visit to Jever, I was given a very instructive 45 minutes in a German Air Force 2-seat TF.104F, the Starfighter with that impossibly small wing. A week earlier, I had been given a 35-minute trip in a Lightning T.5 in order to compare the two. I am not sure how valid were my conclusions after two such short flights, but the experience was much appreciated.

On another trip, to Kauhava, I had a trip in the back seat of a Finnish Air Force Fouga Magister. One engine flamed out during a stall demonstration, so the remaining one was working hard at some unheard of rpm while we relit. We spent five days in Finland, flying from base to base in a Varsity piloted by Danny Lavender. One evening we were invited to join our hosts in the sauna, a first for me. This was not in some hotel fitness centre, but in a traditional lakeside chalet. There was snow on the ground and this was matched by the temperature of the water in the lake. As you dived in it took your breath away. Back to the sauna for another ten minutes, then – into the lake again. This was much more difficult because now you knew exactly how cold it was! But it set us up for another evening of hospitality.

At that time the Finns were still very much under the shadow of Russia, but they were very proud of the fact that since before WWII they had always had at least one British aircraft type in service. Then it was the Gnat Fighter. Finland and India were the only two countries to buy the fighter version. India went on to build more under licence and they now provided the spares for Finland. This Gnat squadron shared a base with a Mig.21 unit. We were allowed close enough to see the round-headed rivets and rather agricultural undercarriage. I had also heard that the time between engine inspections was quite short. We were escorted everywhere by an air force officer-cum-interpreter. In the bus en route to our accommodation I commented how many more German and Swedish cars there were on the streets than Russian models. He explained that they were more reliable and that the Russian engines often gave trouble. 'Oh, much like their aircraft!' I ventured. To which he grinned and replied, 'You're as bad as Wg Cdr Peters!' He was the Air Attaché at the time and I imagine that our guide was used to his probing!"

Rather sooner than expected and at quite short notice, Alan was posted – from one CFS to another, that of the RAAF at East Sale in Victoria where he and his family arrived in July 1967. For the first four months it was back to Vampires, but by November the first of their Macchi 326H trainers had arrived.

New official RAF Aerobatic Team forms

Following on from the success of "The Red Pelicans", Flying Training Command decided to continue utilising CFS instructors for the official 1965 RAF aerobatic team. Earlier concern as to whether the Folland Gnat T.1 was a suitable aircraft for formation aerobatics had been dispelled by the Valley-based "Yellowjacks". The new team's nine aircraft, XR540/986/7/991-996, were repainted brilliant red by 5 MU at Kemble and all but XR996 had been flown to Little Rissington by the end of February. XR540 was used for handling trials on the smoke generating system at Boscombe Down for a short period before being released to the team and a tenth aircraft, XS111, the last production Gnat trainer, was delivered to Little Rissington on 14 May, completing the team's allocation of ten aircraft.

XR987 had only been on-site for a couple of weeks when it was dispatched to Hawker Siddeley Aviation Ltd at Dunsfold on 15 May for Category 4 repairs, where it was joined by XR996 a week later, this aircraft having been classified as a rogue.

During February, final selection of pilots for the team, christened "The Red Arrows", was announced. Flt Lt Lee Jones was nominated

A new phenomenon in the world of aerobatic teams - The Red Arrows. Formed out of the Yellowjacks late in 1964, the team gave its first display in May 1965, and it continues to entertain the crowds over forty years later. A rare photograph of the initial team pilots posing for the camera at Little Rissington with Team Leader Flt Lt Lee Jones (*kneeling*), with (*l to r*); Flt Lts Gerry Ranscombe, Bryan Nice, Eric Tilsley (reserve), Bill Loverseed, Henry Prince, Ray Hanna and Fg Off Peter Hay. (*Tony Gannon*)

leader with Flt Lt B. Nice as deputy leader, and Flt Lts R.G. Hanna, R.E.W. Loverseed, H.J.D. Prince, G.L. Ranscombe and Fg Off P.G. Hay completing the team. Flt Lt E. Tilsley was nominated as Reserve pilot. Four of these, Flt Lts Jones, Prince, Ranscombe and Fg Off Hay, were previously with the "Yellowjacks" and were initially on detachment from 4 FTS but their status was quickly revised to permanent. In March, the initial "Red Arrows" Team Manager, Sqn Ldr W.E. Kelly, was posted out following his promotion and his replacement, Sqn Ldr R.A.E. Storer, was appointed in his place.

Henry Prince has fond memories of his flying days with the team.

"In 1964, the official RAF aerobatic team was 'The Red Pelicans', flying Jet Provosts from Little Rissington. At Farnborough in that year the 'Yellowjacks', already formed from Gnat instructors at No. 4 FTS Valley, were invited to fly in a synchronised display sequence with the Pelicans. The JPs actually closed the show, but so many people said the Gnats looked better, faster and slicker, that a changeover was ordered.

There were just two problems. One was our colour – yellow looked fantastic on a gin clear day but not so wonderful against grey skies. The other was our name – the air marshal in charge couldn't stand the title Yellowjacks because he said it was Australian slang for yellow fever. So the Yellowjacks kept their Gnats but acquired the Pelicans colour. Our numbers were boosted from five to seven and we were renamed 'The Red Arrows'.

It was tremendous fun in those days. We were able to try almost everything we wanted. There were regulations, of course, but they weren't fantastically rigid, as they are today. For instance, we'd arrive at displays from behind the crowd at 100 ft and roar over their heads – much lower clearance than would be allowed nowadays."

Chipmunks multiply

The number of Chipmunks doubled to eight to accommodate an amended all-through jet training programme incorporating the reintroduction of these diminutive piston-engined trainers to provide ab initio experience for pupil pilots moving on to the Jet Provost. Already being used by CFS to train University Air Squadron instructors, they took on an additional commitment to train instructors for the RAF's new Primary Flying Squadron.

Weather records broken

The Station's reputation for weather extremes struck with vengeance in March when two records were broken; the lowest night temperature of -7.5°C (18.5°F) on the 3rd, and the highest daytime temperature 20.4° (68.7°F) on the 29th. A heavy snowstorm early in the month caused 2 ft snow drifts and stopped flying while fog curtailed flying on several mornings.

Jet Provost hits the undershoot

On 10 March, Fg Off R.W. Godfrey of 226 Course, stalled into the undershoot while attempting to land Jet Provost T.3, XN591 at Kemble, causing Cat. 4 damage to his aircraft.

Service and Civilian awards

The 20 March was a special day for a number of personnel when, during pouring rain and with the whole Station on parade in front of the hangars, the Commandant, Air Cdre Bird-Wilson presented them with awards. Flt Lt S. Hitchen received the Queen's Commendation for services as Beverley Captain flying on operations over Borneo, and no fewer than five awards were made to civilian staff. Mr Bernard Day of Bourton received the Imperial Service Medal for 25 years' work in the Officers' Mess; Mr George Beacham of Bledington was presented with the AOC-in-C's Commendation, for his 25 years' service on the Station, and similar commendations were presented to Mr C.J. Clifton of Stow, who was responsible for the documentation of all officers passing through CFS; Mr W.E. Foster of Witney who maintained the radio equipment on the airfield and in the control tower, and Mr G.F. Pratley of Stow for his work as a charge-hand paint sprayer on the Jet Provosts of "The Red Pelicans".

Although "The Red Arrows" had had little time to practise their routines, the C-in-C Flying Training Command, Air Marshal Sir Patrick Dunn, made a short visit to Little Rissington on the morning of the 26th before flying over to Fairford to watch the team practise. Suitably impressed with their progress, he gave clearance for them to fly down to 500 ft.

Chipmunk T.10, WG348, one of several to arrive at Little Rissington during the mid-sixties to handle the expanded mission taken on by CFS. (*David Watkins*)

Strapping yarns and bra stories

During Flt Lt Mick Ryan's time at CFS, the MoD made 20 to 30 brief flight safety film clips, each only a few minutes long. These were to be added to the front of all RAF training films as a constant flight safety plug. Filmed by a private film contractor and starring the comedian Stanley Unwin, famous for mixing up his words, most of the clips were shot at Little Rissington.

"During early 1965 I was appointed as liaison officer for both film crew and the director. The scripts were already written and agreed – our role was simply to film them. My job, although fun, was purely as a 'Gopher'

link to harness whichever station resources were necessary.

One of the clips was aimed at emphasising the need for aircrew to be strapped in tightly to an ejection seat. The script called for a female tightening her bra strap, with the female's hands slowly fading accurately into the pilot's hands as he carefully adjusted his own ejection seat shoulder straps. The film director promised this would be a discreetly filmed close up of the shoulder and strap with no faces on show. He asked me if I knew a female who would pose for the bra strap shots as he was anxious to film as much as possible at Little Rissington without incurring the extra costs of a studio. I knew a lively young WRAF Officer and asked her if she would like to take the role. She gamely agreed and the shot was duly taken late after work with no one else around. We thought we were home and dry but were thwarted the next morning. Her boyfriend, in on the secret plan, shot off his mouth at the breakfast table in front of, among all people, the 'Queen Bee' Squadron Officer, head of all the WRAF at Little Rissington. The next thing I knew I had to report to the Station Commander, Gp Capt Henry Chinnery, with all the offending footage. He confiscated the film and explained my foolishness in the most direct and simple terms. The director ended up with a dent in his budget for a professional model to finish that particular clip.

On taking one's A1, I was unaware of any particular 'Waterfront' policy at that time but certainly there was some degree of animosity between the CFS 'Waterfront' staff instructors and the Jet Provost 'Trappers'. The feeling appeared so strong that no one from the 'Waterfront' had been prepared to present themselves for re-categorisation up to A1 for a long time. Naïvely, I could not see the point of all this and I thought I'd have a shot at it. I was given excellent support by my colleagues on the 'Waterfront', who flew with me and tried to educate me ready for this the first A1 test the 'Waterfront' had taken for a couple of years. By the time I wound up for the test, I had been promoted to Squadron Leader and my test was taken on by OC JP Examining Squadron, Sqn Ldr Dave McCann.

The test was completed over two separate days. Surprisingly the flying test was only one extended 90-minute sortie on Wednesday 14 July 1965, in a JP3. The two halves were firstly 'pattering' a full instructional lesson, that gruelling standards and staple fare 'Effects of Controls Part 1'. Circuits then followed before the pure flying ability check part of the test. The ground examination was similar with the usual ground briefing for the lesson to be taught in the air, plus a detailed technical grilling on the aircraft and the theory of flight. The pure flying air test was daunting but I had volunteered to be one of the CFS JP Display pilots for the seasons of 1964/5, and so I thrashed through a demonstration of my aerobatic display routine. After that Dave was happy to give me a flame out practice for a bit of peace!

For the A1 ground test I also had to present a lecture to all the A1s who could be assembled. That was a real challenge. I chose to lecture on the principle of the hovercraft. The CFS station workshops made me a marvellous rig to illustrate the hover skirt principle, powered by my wife's vacuum cleaner. I cannot understand why the engineers ever helped me after I had caused them so much extra work as Station Flight Safety Officer.

When awarded my A1 (and in hindsight view of the political situation, I would have had to work very hard to fail), I was immediately posted to the Jet Provost Trials Unit Far East in Singapore and Malaysia for five months – but that is another story. In January 1965 I took over as OC University of Wales Air Squadron at RAF St Athan. Never once would I extricate myself from the Training machine again. My flying job as a Wing Commander was OC Examining Wing, Central Flying School. I have no complaints about that job which was marvellous but I never did fly operationally again. There must be a lesson from that experience.

As an aside I would like to tell a story about the excellent CFS Chief Instructor at the time, the late Gp Capt DL 'Eddie' Edmonds CVO AFC. Eddie, then Wg Cdr, had to fly with me to check out my routine to be one of the low level aerobatic pilots for external displays at other airfields and events during the 'silly season'. It was Thursday 8 October 1964, when I demonstrated to Eddie my wonderful inability to do low level aeros. I pulled out frighteningly too low from some daft manoeuvre. Eddie sat there silent and did not try to take over. I promptly assumed I had failed my check out but he was kind enough to 'put it down to nerves'. He gave me my official authorisation, which I did not deserve. Always personally grateful for that act of faith, I could readily understand how popular and successful he had been as boss."*

Second Aero team

Not satisfied with operating the RAF's premier aerobatic team, the CFS received authorisation to form a second display team. Flown by four enthusiastic, volunteer CFS instructors, and known as "The CFS Jet Provost Aerobatic Team" they flew the red Jet Provost T.4s previously used by "The Red Pelicans". Their first display was at RAF Shawbury on 1 May, only three weeks after forming, and there soon followed performances at RAF Hullavington and at Little Rissington in support of the Hack Trophy competition.

Led by Flt Lt Bill Langworthy, other members of the team included Flt Lts Roy Booth at No. 3 and 'Cas' Maynard at No. 4. Flying at No. 2 in the team was Flt Lt Derek Bell who remembers that,

"Long before I joined the Air Force I had watched aerobatic teams and had convinced myself that the pilots must be something really special. Little did I think that I would ever be able to follow in their footsteps.

During Farnborough 1958, by now a junior pilot on a Hunter squadron, I watched with awe and admiration as 'The Black Arrows' stunned the crowds and became the first team in the world to loop 22 aircraft. Fabulous, amazing! After the display I realised that one of these 'aces' had been on the same OCU as myself and I knew I could 'wax his ass' any day of the week!! So what's to stop me?

In those far off days there were opportunities to fly formation aeros as most Squadrons had some sort of display team but of course they were a closed shop for junior pilots. Always you bumped up against the old adage 'You can't go night flying until you have flown in the dark'

Things took a turn for the better when I joined my next Squadron and the boss decided we should have a 4-ship display team. The boss would lead the team and the other three pilots would be from 'A' Flt. I

was on 'B' Flt. Fortunately for me and some others our Flight Commander had been on "The Black Arrows" and he convinced the boss that we needed a back up team. By luck and a bit of bullshit I made it and for the rest of that tour did several displays - well two or three!

Next chance followed soon afterwards at FTS on the JP4. This time when they asked for volunteers. I could claim that 'I have flown in the dark!' and so I got one of the two slots going. Harder work in the JP than with the Hunter but what fun, morning practice before met briefing and numerous Saturday shows during the summer, even managed to wangle one weekend away as long as we were back for 08:00 on the Monday!"

"Arrows" Press Day

In an atmosphere of great excitement and with the C-in-C Flying Training Command in attendance, "The Red Arrows" put on their first public display over the airfield on 6 May, in front of TV, film and Press cameramen and reporters. With the Press day over, the team settled into a routine of practice and more practice before embarking on a full programme of displays in the UK and on the Continent, commencing with Clermont-Ferrand in France on the 9th.

Wright Jubilee

The competition for the Wright Jubilee Trophy was held on 11 May 1965. The trophy was presented by Air Chief Marshal Sir Theodore McEvoy at the Guest Night following the competition. Among the distinguished guests was Hawker Siddeley test pilot Bill Bedford, who had arrived in spectacular fashion in Hurricane IIC, PZ865. Before departing, he let the Commandant, who had flown Hurricanes with 17 Squadron in 1940, put in a little refresher flying.

(*Above*) In a spirit of controlled excitement, the Red Arrows pilots walk out to their aircraft before giving their first Press Day display, 6 May, 1965. (*Tony Gannon*)

(*Left*) Many personnel were still struggling to work when this view of the 1965 Jet Provost display team approaching the airfield was taken. Three of the team pilots, Flt Lts Derek Bell, Roy Booth and Bill Langworthy, joined the Red Arrows in 1966. (*Michael Rigby via Derek Bell*)

Keeping them flying

With the initial requirement for Gnat instructors fulfilled, seven Gnats, XP515/30/31/34-37, were re-allocated to Valley during 1965, leaving ten for the Course line, XM704-709/XP501/XR534/69/XS101. At Fairford the main priority was getting "The Red Arrows" ready for the new season, a requirement for which Course aircraft were regularly loaned to the team, putting pressure on everyone to maintain high serviceability rates. The responsibility for providing a full line of serviceable aircraft was that of the Flight Commander, Flt Lt Alex Wickham.

> *"As the throughput of instructors began to reduce, so my allocation establishment of Course Gnats decreased. By mid-year it was down to ten aircraft plus the ten from the aerobatic team. Innocuous snags were sometimes signed-off as 'ground tested and found serviceable' which, dependent on the type of snag was OK up to a point but, when something as serious as a rumbling engine occurred, I couldn't let that go. Hence my 'invitation' on 24 June to Cpl Chadburn to don some flying gear and come listen to the noise for himself. As a result we lost another aircraft, XR534, for a few days for the engine change. I note that I also air-tested this aircraft on 16 and 17 June, first with Cpl Bailey, then Cpl Linz; this latter flight was just 10 minutes so we must have experienced something serious! So the flight with Pete Chadburn must have been quite a nail-biter for him."*

The Standards Squadron became the Standards Wing from April and the Primary Flying Squadron formed on 1 July at South Cerney with Chipmunks. It subsequently disbanded on 1 January 1970 at RAF Church Fenton to become No. 2 Flying Training School.

Honours and Awards

Several officers and airmen from the station were included in the Queen's Birthday Honours List:

Sqn Ldr P.M. Worthington	OBE
Flt Lt T.E.L. Lloyd	AFC
Ch. Tech. Leggat	BEM
Flt Lt I.G. Douglas	Queen's Commendation
Flt Lt B. Nice	C-in-C's Commendation
Flt Sgt C.F.J. Hutson	C-in-C's Commendation
Ch. Tech. W.R. Wright	AOC's Commendation
Sgt K.C. Fisk	AOC's Commendation
Sgt P.C. Pashley	AOC's Commendation
SAC L.D. Lawrence	AOC's Commendation
Mr H.W.J. Butt	AOC's Commendation

Air Traffic Control Movements

Movements of jet aircraft for the month of June 1965 were 5,384 during the day and 1,762 at night, plus a further 1,508 daytime piston-engined, giving a total of 8,654 movements. Approximately one quarter of these were accumulated by CFS aircraft operating to and from Fairford and aircraft of the Gnat detachment.

Displays gain momentum

For one week during the month, "The Red Arrows" operated out of RAF Wattisham, practising for their combined show in Paris with the Lightnings of 111 Squadron. While at Wattisham, they gave performances at RAF Church Fenton and North Weald before flying off to Besançon and Paris for the Air Show. The Commandant and other officers from the CFS flew to Paris to watch the display.

Back in the UK, the "CFS Jet Provost Aerobatic Team" gave displays at RAF Tern Hill and Wolverhampton, proving that Flt Lt Langworthy and his men were also capable of stimulating the public with precision formation aerobatics.

Sport

WRAF personnel distinguished themselves at the Flying Training Command Athletic Championships at RAF Cranwell, where Cpl(W). Gray won the 100, 220 and 440 yards outright and SACW. Higgins won the Shot Put. At the combined RAF and Flying Training Command Small Arms Championships at Bisley, Little Rissington won three team events and came second in three more. Flt Lt R. Wood won the first stage of the FTC Individual Championships and was awarded a shield for reaching the highest score in the Command's 'A' team.

Fairford Detachment

July was an extremely busy month for the Central Flying School, both operationally and socially. Flying Wing, with the exception of the Chipmunk Flight, moved to RAF Fairford for six weeks while the Rissington runway was resurfaced. This resulted in a substantial loss of flying hours. Sixteen civilians living or working in the Fairford area were entertained to lunch to explain the purpose and possible effects of increased aircraft activity in the hope that they would pass on the information to other residents. The detachment concluded on 7 September, although it took four days to complete the transition. Despite all the interruptions, all courses managed to complete on time.

'Windrush Club'

Air Vice-Marshal R.B. Thomson CB DSO DFC RAF, AOA of Flying Training Command, visited CFS to open officially the former NAAFI building which had been converted to an Airmen's Club, called the 'Windrush Club'. Facilities included a Tavern Bar, Lounge Bar, Restaurant, Social Activities Room and Games Room, providing an attractive social centre where airmen and airwoman could entertain their wives, relatives and friends.

New Married Quarters

Meanwhile, on the northern extremity, work continued apace on the construction of eleven Officers', six Warrant Officers' and seventy-eight Airmen's married quarters, with the first of the Officers' homes due for completion in December. The final Airmen's quarter was scheduled for hand-over in July 1966.

Senior Service enjoys the spirit of Rissy!

"Having been the first all-through jet pilot to join The Fleet (JP3 with Swas Wackett plus Vampire with Mike Graydon/Barney Bullocke on 93 course), it was natural that I would then be sent to Gannets." So says Lt Len Townsend RN who, following a tour in Ark Royal, had to spend some years fighting his way out via a Pilot Navigation Instructor job in Malta on Venoms/Pembrokes – lovely. *"My final exit (I thought) was on No. 232 Course on JPs at Rissy, where I was lucky to have Cully Earlendsen RCAF as my tutor.*

As we all know, the first one airborne at Ris was allowed a few impromptu aeros. Cully and I plotted and schemed, and finally made it. Cully was so pleased that he climbed to about 1,500 ft, inverted AND PULLED THROUGH. It all went very quiet while I screamed inwardly. I actually said 'I don't think so, Cully'. Thank God for the Hill, with our pull out below airfield level. The Tower confined itself to the usual 'Station Commander on Landing' and poor Cully went to the Dew Line pretty smartish. An utter gentleman and a fine poker player – but never after midnight during the week.

Having survived Cully, and a marvellous batch of V-Bomber pilots (e.g. Ced Hughes and Al McDonald) it was time to pass out, saying 'goodbye' to Groupie en passant. His reply was riveting: 'Townsend, there's been a terrible mistake, and you should have been on Chipmunks'. And there was no way out. Two happy years at Linton in 1966/67 were followed by command of RNEFTS at Church Fenton/Leeming/Topcliffe on the brand new Bulldog in 1975/76. Of course there was my Bulldog conversion at Rissy – well remembered because of the amazing social life engendered by 'The Mad Doctor'.

However, a sharp-eyed staff officer (and you lot are good at that) might spot that I haven't actually qualified for the CFS Association. Well, actually, it was decided that all dual aircraft, of any Service, would come under the aegis of Examining Wing, and that the senior instructor would be examined by OC Exam Wing and become an Agent and a member of his staff. I duly made an appointment with my new (part-time) CO and flew a T.5 Gannet from Lossie to Rissy. Knowing Pat Lewis and the Mad Doctor, I planned to be away for the whole week.

The first challenge was to ensure that I passed the course. I issued a challenge that, if Pat failed to climb into the (open) cockpit without external ladders, I would pass out. He duly failed, and I became a CFS Agent and thus am allowed to haunt you at re-unions. By the way ... if you put your hand in the first footstep in the Gannet fuselage (shoulder level), a ladder swings down and you can climb up ... simple really."

ROC Day

On 3 October 1965, members of No.3 Group of the Royal Observer Corps and invited guests visited the station for their open day. The morning was occupied with a training programme in 3 Hangar while the afternoon's entertainment included an air display and air experience flights in a visiting Hastings transport. Participating in the display were both CFS aerobatic teams, a Victor tanker, Hunter, Javelin, Canberra, plus a number of vintage aircraft including a 'Battle of Britain Flight' Spitfire and Hurricane. A Jet Provost flew a 'Judge the Height and Speed' competition which was won by ROC member Graham Beard who recalls the excitement of collecting his prize. *"I won the height and speed competition the prize for which was a 30-minute flight in the Jet Provost. Piloted by Flt Lt D. Bell, we spent much of the time doing aerobatics over Pershore airfield, a wonderful experience."*

Flt Lt Bell was also the Station's Flight Safety Officer and he gave a most instructive and illuminating talk to members of the Special Constabulary of the Warwickshire Division on the matter of rescuing crews from crashed service aircraft.

Return to CFS

Sqn Ldr Don McClen returned to CFS in May, 1965 to command the squadron of Jet Provosts, consisting of 22 flying instructors and a total of some 25 aircraft, which were serviced by Engineering Wing, technically responsible for all the other aircraft at CFS as well.

"The Marks 3 and 4 Jet Provost had a much improved performance over the Mark 1 which I had flown six years previously. By the time I assumed command, CFS had enjoyed several consecutive years' providing 'The Red Pelican' Jet Provost aerobatic team for public displays.

In the autumn of 1965 when the display season had nearly finished, one of the team pilots, Derek Bell, was transferred urgently to fill a slot in 'The Red Arrows'. Rather than cancel the three remaining engagements, I offered to step into the breach after a few practices to confirm that I was up to scratch, with Bill Langworthy remaining as the competent formation leader until the end of the season when he, too, was selected for 'The Red Arrows'.

The Commandant of CFS in 1965 Air Cdre 'Birdie' Bird-Wilson, to my and others' surprise, was not a QFI. He was a fighter pilot through and through, with a flying career straight out of Boy's Own. His face had been smashed in a pre-war crash in an aircraft, which was being flown by another RAF pilot. He received a new nose (of his choice!) from New Zealand born Archie McIndoe at East Grinstead, becoming only the second official 'Guinea Pig'. He fought in the Battle of Britain and was shot down by Adolf Galland in the Thames estuary (Galland's 40th kill). Burnt and battered about the face again as a result, he quickly recovered and went on to greater glories as a Spitfire and Mustang Wing Leader during the war, to be rewarded with a DSO and two DFCs. He was closely involved in fighter development and tactics in the late 40s and early 50s, again narrowly escaping death when a Meteor he was testing (before the advent of ejector seats) disintegrated around him. He was awarded two AFCs for this work, first in 1946 and then in 1955. Although not a QFI he had been selected as Commandant, ostensibly to bring his vast fighter experience to bear on influencing flying instruction.

One entertaining diversion was a visit to the German Air Force to advise them of our approach to basic jet instruction. The Luftwaffe had been disbanded in 1945 at the end of the war, and had not reformed until 1956, as the German Air Force. RAF flying instructors had been seconded to provide the initial backbone to get things going again, and the inventory of front line aircraft was now dominated by the US F-104 Starfighter, a fighter aircraft with an unenviable accident record in Germany. A ten year hiatus between 1945 and 1956 obviously did not help but the F-104 had attracted the sobriquet 'widow maker' and morale was said to be low.

Our first stop was Jever, where I was given a dual flight in a F-104. The pilot, Captain Liedke, was a Bavarian who handled the aircraft with panache in aerobatics and in a high speed low level run; I assessed he would have made a formidable adversary in time of war. We then spent two days at Landsberg, the principal flying training base, where I flew the basic jet trainer, a Fouga Magister, and discussed flying instructional techniques."

Winter servicing for the Arrows

At the end of a successful first season the Gnats of "The Red Arrows" aerobatic team were flown from Fairford to Little Rissington to undergo a period of servicing and modifications. While the pilots took a well earned break the groundcrew returned to their home base to work alongside their Rissy-based colleagues on the aircraft. By January of the following year, the first of the rebuilt Gnats was ready for flight test and all were back at Fairford by March.

New AOC

On 4 November, Air Cdre H.A.C. Bird-Wilson CBE DSO DFC AFC handed over his command as CFS Commandant to Air Cdre F.L. Dodd DSO DFC AFC.

'Flag Wave'

In an effort to recruit more volunteer pilots for the CFS Course, a team of five aircraft comprising two Gnats, two Jet Provosts and a Varsity flew to RAF Germany to show the flag and project the CFS image over a six day period from 8 November. Many flying details were carried out, giving pilots first hand experience on the main aircraft types.

'Follow me through'

The following item is a summarised extract from an Air Clues article written in 1965 by Flt Lt Mike Doherty.

"Every ten weeks, pilots from all RAF Commands, the Royal Navy, the Army, and sometimes from foreign air forces, make their way up the hill as another course assembles. From the moment of the Commandant's welcoming address to the graduation dinner 18 weeks later, they will be busy learning a new skill – how to pass on their own flying ability to the younger generation of pilots. The graduate

At the end of the first season, the Red Arrows Gnats were flown into Little Rissington for winter servicing which involved a complete strip down and rebuild. XR994, 993, 996 and XS111 are ready for final checks in 5 Hangar prior to air test while much work is still to be done on the remaining aircraft, January 1966. (*Ray Deacon*)

emerges with that special tag – Qualified Flying Instructor (QFI).

What do 18 weeks at CFS hold in store for the pilots on course? The training includes nearly a hundred hours of flying and a detailed syllabus of ground instruction. Flying initially takes place in the Jet Provost or the Chipmunk. The Chipmunk element is small, consisting of Army pilots and those RAF officers who have been chosen for service with University Air Squadrons. Everyone else completes the first half of the course on the Jet Provost before specialising as a basic or advanced instructor. The majority continue on the Jet Provost and become basic instructors, the rest converting either to the Gnat or Varsity. Their selection depends partly on personal preference, partly on aptitude and Service background.

This course 'split' coincides with the end of the ground instructional phase, which up to this point has been running concurrently with air-work. Thereafter, the whole working day is devoted to flying, which is carried out from the Little Rissington 'Waterfront' for Jet Provosts and Varsity aircraft, while Gnat trainees fly from Fairford, appearing to pay their respects to the parent station by making early morning noises in the sky. Ground instruction, completed in the first ten weeks of the course, is standard for all, regardless of types flown.

Naturally, tests are frequent both in the air and on the ground. The first progress test takes place after 13 flying hours, during which time the stress is placed on familiarisation with type and the development of an accurate flying technique The reasons for this are, first, that a man, who is to teach others how to fly effectively, must set an example by demonstrating perfectly every manoeuvre and procedure in the book; second, an aspiring flying instructor must be confident of his professional prowess before he becomes capable of combining lesson patter with his manual dexterity of flying.

After the progress check, pilots on course start the patter sequences, which cover every airborne exercise from the effects of controls to formation station-keeping. They undergo two more tests, the Intermediate Handling Test after 45 hours, and the Final Handling Test at the end of the course.

Airborne instruction

In the air, the emphasis is placed on the development of instructional technique. The sequences, starting with the simplest exercises, are all dealt with in the same way. Before strapping in to the Jet Provost, Chipmunk or Varsity, or 'putting on' the diminutive Gnat, there is a briefing on the aim, execution and any special matters relating to airmanship entailed in the exercise. The instructor, with the student following through every control movement, then demonstrates what to do in the air. He also indicates common faults. This is followed by a post-flight discussion.

For the next stage, the student accompanies another member of the course who, in turn, gives the patter and acts as student for each other. Finally, a dual exercise is flown, the pilot on course acting as instructor and his instructor being the student who occasionally commits errors. So all the qualities expected of the flying instructor – flying ability, cogent demonstration and fault analysis – are developed simultaneously.

Ground instruction

In the Ground Training Squadron, the subjects taught are Principles of Flight, Navigation, Airmanship, Meteorology, Engines and Aircraft Systems, together with Aviation Medicine. The aim of the Ground Instruction is to provide members of the course with a working knowledge of subjects associated with flying, and preparing them for teaching pupils. As such, instructional technique is considered as important as academic knowledge. Hence there are not only ground examinations, but, after several lectures on the learning process, each student delivers two 20-minute practice lessons, and also gives oral answers to questions put by the ground instructors who act as average students. It is sometimes said that the instructors act as 'well below average' students, if indeed they are acting at all! However, the justification is that the questions, which seem more absurd, often penetrate right to the foundation of knowledge.

Proven techniques

The CFS patter system has its origins in the earliest methods of instruction employed at the school. Over the years it has been refined and re-energised by successive generations of QFIs, to be adapted for particular training aircraft. It is the means whereby our service pilots have been trained for the entire period of our country's military aviation history. Having stood the tests of time and war, the CFS standard patter is inherently flexible and will be as relevant to the future as it has always been in the past.

Maintaining the aim

Standards Wing's main task is to ensure that the standard of instruction, laid down by CFS, is maintained at the Flying Training Schools. The staff of the Standards Wing does this by touring flying training establishments throughout the country and testing both students and instructors in the air and on the ground. The history of the Standards Wing dates back to 1927, when a team of flying instructors from CFS flew to No.1 FTS Netheravon to examine the general ability of pupils and to ascertain whether the CFS system of training was being maintained. This was the first of a series of informal visits. However, in 1938 it became obvious that the new monoplanes were not being handled uniformly or correctly. Air Ministry accordingly made CFS an official inspectorate. It was to be the final authority on the flying techniques of all aircraft, and one aircraft of each new type was sent to the school. From this arrangement the first set of Pilot's Notes was produced by CFS and a team of examiners was added to the establishment to make frequent visits to training units. Now their successors also carry the CFS message overseas to the Commonwealth and foreign countries. In the operational Commands and the Royal Navy, the supervisory authority is delegated to 'CFS Agents', officers from within those commands who have vast instructional experience."

Mainstay of CFS (Advanced) over the decade beginning 1953, was the Vampire T.Mk.11. XK627/VC seen here in the early silver and yellow training colours, awaits an air test outside No. 1 Hangar in 1958. (*Rod Brown*)

Central Flying School crest

Prime type on CFS (Basic) over the same period was the Piston Provost T.Mk.1. Also carrying the silver and yellow colour scheme is XF892/PB, out to undergo an engine run outside No. 1 Hangar, 1958. (*Rod Brown*)

CFS badge and markings applied to the unit's aircraft

Displaying the ultimate Flying Training Command livery from the early 1960s until the type's retirement from service in 1971, Vampire T.Mk.11, XK624/32, operated with CFS for nearly five years, having replaced XD550 (*below*) in 1967. (*Adrian Balch*)

Vampire T.Mk.11, XD550/VL, has just been issued to 2 Squadron after receipt checks by Rectification Flight, following refurbishment and repainting at an MU, 1960. (*Malcolm Thomas*)

Early morning condensation clouds the canopies in this 1960 view of No. 4 Hangar, packed with 2 Squadron Vampire T.Mk.11s and 3 Squadron Canberra T.Mk.4s and Meteor T.Mk.7s. (*Malcolm Thomas*)

An excellent portrayal of fourteen Vampire T.Mk.11s lined up on the 2 Squadron pan in 1960 depicting aircraft bearing several variations of the day-glo livery. (*Malcolm Thomas*)

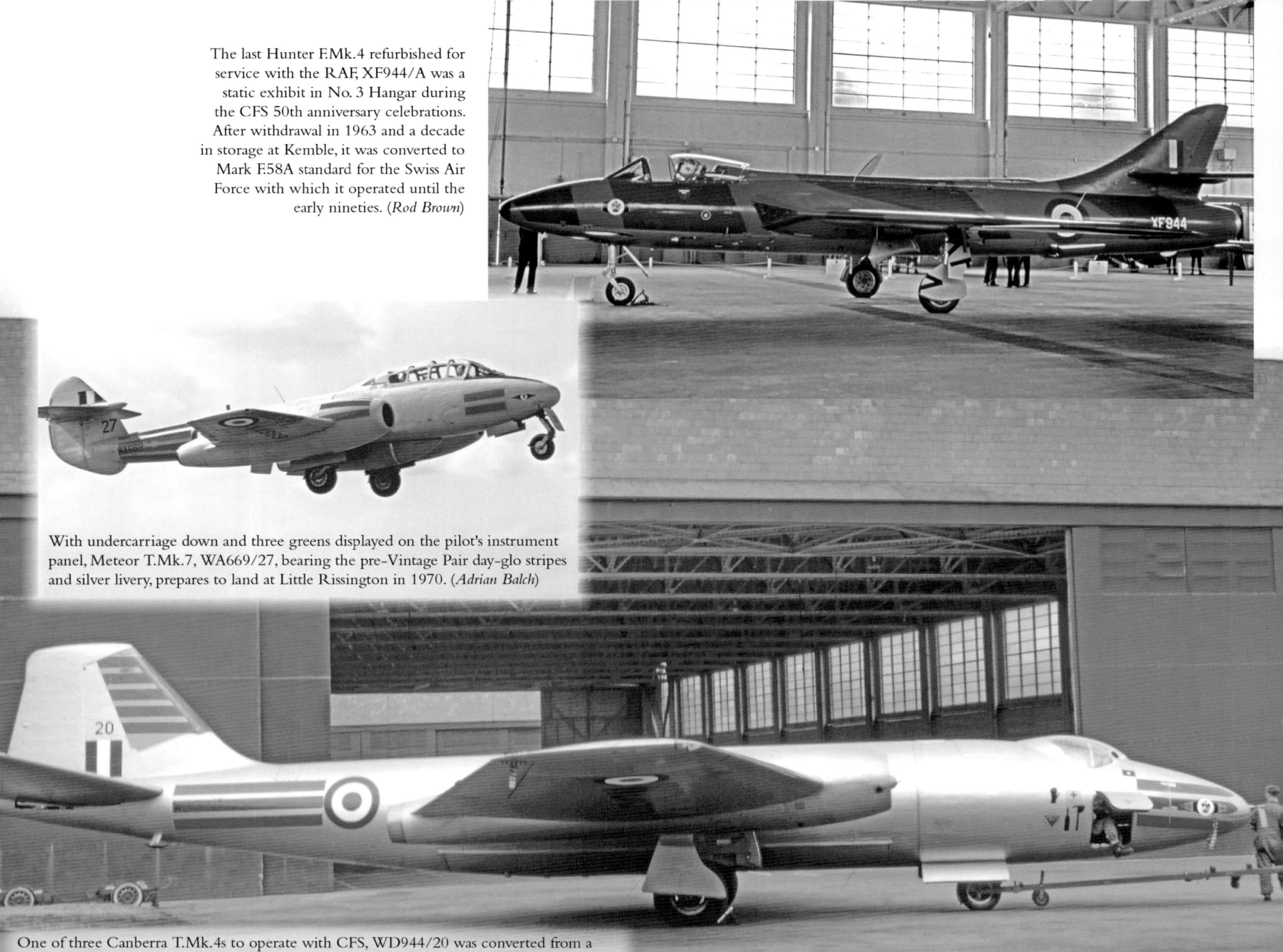

The last Hunter F.Mk.4 refurbished for service with the RAF, XF944/A was a static exhibit in No. 3 Hangar during the CFS 50th anniversary celebrations. After withdrawal in 1963 and a decade in storage at Kemble, it was converted to Mark F.58A standard for the Swiss Air Force with which it operated until the early nineties. (*Rod Brown*)

With undercarriage down and three greens displayed on the pilot's instrument panel, Meteor T.Mk.7, WA669/27, bearing the pre-Vintage Pair day-glo stripes and silver livery, prepares to land at Little Rissington in 1970. (*Adrian Balch*)

One of three Canberra T.Mk.4s to operate with CFS, WD944/20 was converted from a B.Mk.2 bomber in the late fifties. It is pictured here between Nos. 2 and 3 Hangars, in the experimental striped livery, applied in 1961, on the occasion of the 50th anniversary of the founding of CFS, 7 July, 1962. (*Rod Brown*)

The Piston Provost served with CFS continuously from 1953 until 1964 and there the association ended until T.Mk.1, WW397, (*above*) returned to Little Rissington for a short duration in 1968 (*Keith Watson*). The Anson too had a long association with CFS, with several examples on strength from 1946 until their withdrawal eighteen years later. C.Mk.19, VP517/11 (*below*), was assigned as Commandant's aircraft and is seen on 7 July, 1962. (*Rod Brown*)

After a gap of nine years, the Varsity reintroduced piston-powered, twin-engined QFI training to CFS in 1960. One of the first to arrive was T.Mk.1, XD366/16, the final production aircraft, pictured on the 2 Squadron pan six years later. (*Ray Deacon*)

Both aircraft carry standard CFS markings and the colour scheme used on the type through most of the sixties, a significant change from the prototype livery applied to '366 in 1961 and depicted in Appendix 4.

Lining up on finals to Little Rissington on 9 March, 1970 is T.Mk.1, WJ949/19. (*Adrian Balch*)

Towards the end of the 1960s, Flying Training Command began repainting its aircraft in the red, white and light grey colour scheme exemplified here on Varsity T.Mk.1, WJ949/19. The photograph was taken at Little Rissington on 1 December, 1970. (*Adrian Balch*)

Replacement for the Chipmunk, the Bulldog T.Mk.1 was first allocated to CFS in May 1973. XX539/46 was one of the early arrivals and is seen taxiing in past the old control tower on 12 September, 1973. (*Adrian Balch*)

The first replacement for the Varsity, the Jetstream, began arriving at CFS in late 1973. Boscombe Down's T.Mk.1, XX475, paid a visit to Little Rissington in the summer of that year and is seen on the 2 Squadron pan. (*Dennis Barber*)

First issued to CFS for a short spell in 1950, the Chipmunk returned to Little Rissington in the late fifties where it remained until the closure of the airfield. Typical of this venerable trainer is WP848/06 which was photographed when allocated to the Skylarks. (*Keith Watson*)

On display in the 50th anniversary static display was Bristol Sycamore HC.Mk.14, XF269/G, of the CFS Helicopter Squadron which at this time was operating from RAF Tern Hill. (*Rod Brown*)

Saro Skeeter AOP.Mk.12 helicopter XM556 appeared in the static park assembled in No. 3 Hangar for the 50th anniversary of CFS. (*Rod Brown*)

The Bell Sioux AH.Mk.1 was perhaps one of the lesser known types operated by CFS. Depicted here alongside a Boscombe Down Whirlwind is XT146/Z. (*Keith Watson*)

The Helicopter Squadron flew various types into Little Rissington for special occasions such as here where Westland Whirlwind HAR.Mk.10, XR485/WQ, is included in the static park line up for an AOC's inspection. (*Keith Watson*)

The Jet Provost, in the form of the Mark 3, began to replace Piston Provosts in earnest at Little Rissington in March 1960 and nearly sixty were taken on charge over the ensuing years. In this early 1961 view, No. 1 Squadron's XN472/RV and XN137/RS are lined up with several others around the patch of land that once provided the base for a hangar and was subsequently resurfaced for use as a JP pan. (*Malcolm Thomas*)

Externally indistinguishable from the Mark 3, the first Mark 4 Jet Provosts arrived at Little Rissington towards the end of 1961 and some thirty-eight eventually served with CFS. XP588/51 (*below*), was almost new when photographed in the static line up marking the unit's 50th anniversary in July 1962. Less than a year later the aircraft was abandoned over Chedworth when a spurious fire warning caused the crew to eject. (*Rod Brown*)

Unlike its earlier sister, the higher power available from the Viper 201 engine increased the stresses on the Mark 4 airframe, shortening the aircraft's fatigue life. By the spring of 1970 all but one had departed CFS. After four years with the Red Pelicans, XS217/50 remained as the sole T.Mk.4 at Little Rissington for some time and is shown here, still bearing the aerobatic team's colours, on 17 November, 1970. (*Adrian Balch*)

Both prototype Jet Provost T.Mk.4s spent some time at Little Rissington, XN468/41, from 1966 with the Red Pelicans in whose colours it is seen here. (*Keith Watson*)

As replacements for the Mark 4, the first Jet Provost T.Mk.5s started to arrive at Little Rissington in September 1969 and the type was soon assigned to the Red Pelicans aerobatic team. Unlike most earlier Pelican team aircraft, the Mark 5s retained the standard training colour scheme, albeit with the addition of the team's name along the fuselage sides and Pelican badge on the fin as depicted here on XW295/88. (*Keith Watson*)

(*left*) Pictured on the Visitors pan at Little Rissington, from where the Folland Gnats were initially operated, during its first week of service, Gnat T.Mk.1, XP530/97 has yet to receive the CFS crest on the forward fuselage. Note the deeper red of the day-glo colour compared to the lighter shade on XM709/95 in the background, April 1963. (*Ray Deacon*)

(*below left*) Another of the pre-production Gnats, XM708/99, stands alongside XS101/101 on Kemble's short runway which was utilised as an operating pan for the first few months of the Gnat Flight's tenure. (*Adrian Balch*)

(*below*) XM704/95, the last of the pre-production Gnats, known as T.Mk.185D, to join CFS was captured on 27 September, 1966, on the short runway at Kemble, one day after the Flight's move from Fairford. Sadly, the aircraft made a two-wheeled landing on the following day, sustaining Cat 5 damage in the process. (*Ray Deacon*)

Its day-glo paint beginning to fade, Gnat T.Mk.1, XR534/93 taxies out for another sortie from Kemble, 29 March, 1967. (*Adrian Balch*)

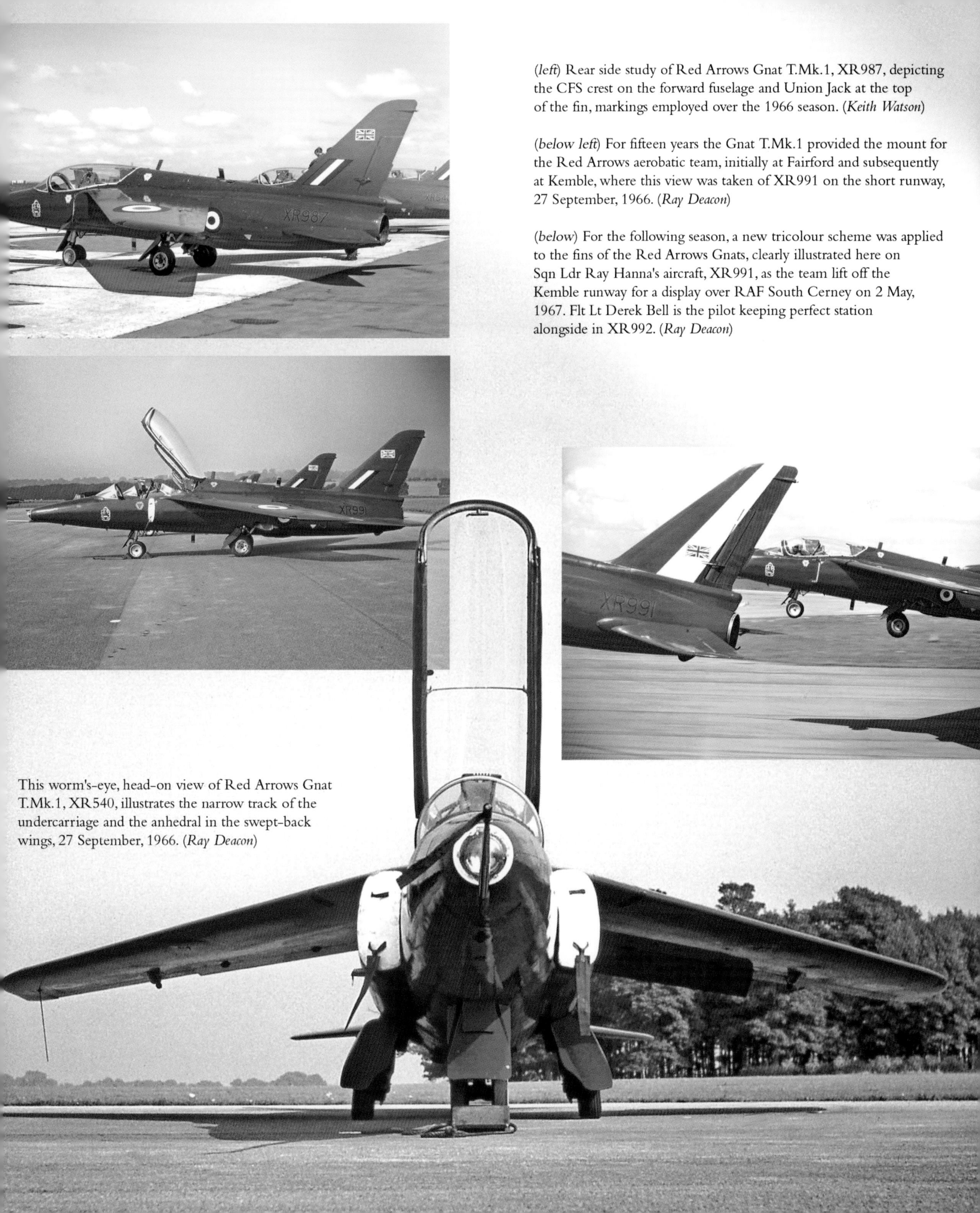

(*left*) Rear side study of Red Arrows Gnat T.Mk.1, XR987, depicting the CFS crest on the forward fuselage and Union Jack at the top of the fin, markings employed over the 1966 season. (*Keith Watson*)

(*below left*) For fifteen years the Gnat T.Mk.1 provided the mount for the Red Arrows aerobatic team, initially at Fairford and subsequently at Kemble, where this view was taken of XR991 on the short runway, 27 September, 1966. (*Ray Deacon*)

(*below*) For the following season, a new tricolour scheme was applied to the fins of the Red Arrows Gnats, clearly illustrated here on Sqn Ldr Ray Hanna's aircraft, XR991, as the team lift off the Kemble runway for a display over RAF South Cerney on 2 May, 1967. Flt Lt Derek Bell is the pilot keeping perfect station alongside in XR992. (*Ray Deacon*)

This worm's-eye, head-on view of Red Arrows Gnat T.Mk.1, XR540, illustrates the narrow track of the undercarriage and the anhedral in the swept-back wings, 27 September, 1966. (*Ray Deacon*)

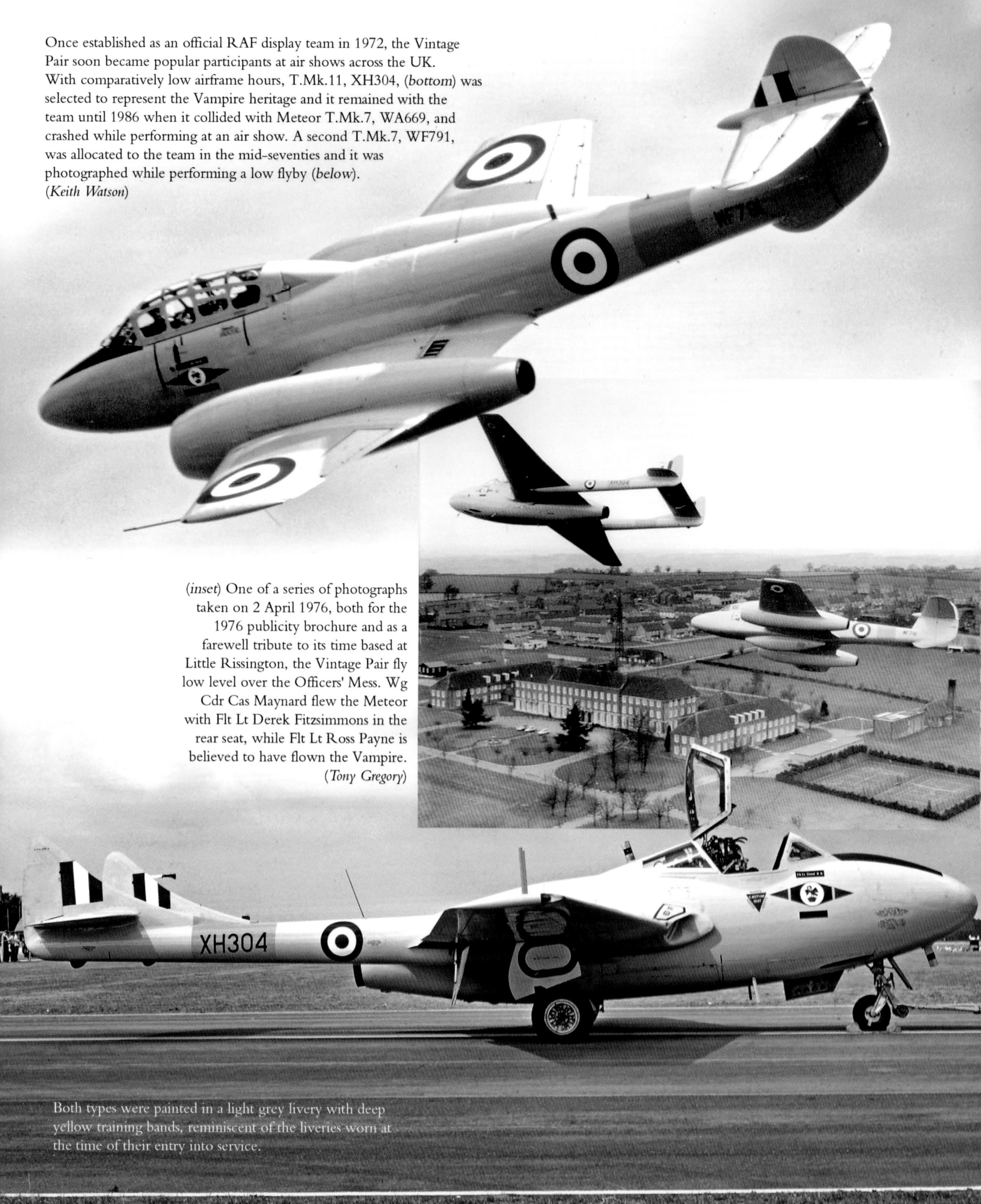

Once established as an official RAF display team in 1972, the Vintage Pair soon became popular participants at air shows across the UK. With comparatively low airframe hours, T.Mk.11, XH304, (*bottom*) was selected to represent the Vampire heritage and it remained with the team until 1986 when it collided with Meteor T.Mk.7, WA669, and crashed while performing at an air show. A second T.Mk.7, WF791, was allocated to the team in the mid-seventies and it was photographed while performing a low flyby (*below*). (*Keith Watson*)

(*inset*) One of a series of photographs taken on 2 April 1976, both for the 1976 publicity brochure and as a farewell tribute to its time based at Little Rissington, the Vintage Pair fly low level over the Officers' Mess. Wg Cdr Cas Maynard flew the Meteor with Flt Lt Derek Fitzsimmons in the rear seat, while Flt Lt Ross Payne is believed to have flown the Vampire. (*Tony Gregory*)

Both types were painted in a light grey livery with deep yellow training bands, reminiscent of the liveries worn at the time of their entry into service.

Government cuts in funding saw the responsibility of providing official RAF aerobatic teams move from Fighter Command to Flying Training Command. The Central Flying School was selected to form the new RAF team and in 1964 the Red Pelicans took up the chalice. Painted in an all-over bright red livery the team's six T.Mk.4 Jet Provosts are shown reaching the top of a loop. (*Ian Bashall*)

By 1970, the Mark 4 Jet Provost had been superseded by the Mark 5 at Little Rissington and the type was utilised in a four-ship Red Pelican team for four seasons. No special livery was adopted, the aircraft appearing in standard Flying Training Command colours. (*Keith Watson*)

With Flt Lt Norman Giffin as its leader, the CFS Jet Aerobatic Team was formed in 1958 at the behest of A M Sir Richard Atcherley and it represented CFS at air shows across the UK throughout the year. Its four Jet Provost T.Mk.1 aircraft were painted in a special red and white livery depicted here during a photographic sortie. (*Alex Wickham*)

Of the plethora of photographs published of the Red Arrows over the years, the majority would have been taken by professionals. On this page we portray the team as seen through the lenses of the groundcrew. (*above*) Closing in at 800 mph, the synchro pair cross half way round the Roulette manoeuvre. (*top right*) Sqn Ldr Ray Hanna flying low and fast between the hangars at Fairford. (*right*) Heading straight down in Diamond formation, the team have a split second to judge a perfectly executed loop by the shadow in the clear blue sea. (*Malcolm Thomas*)

Sqn Ldr Ray Hanna leads the team in a right turn in preparation for the initial run-in, low over the RAF South Cerney hangars, 2 May, 1967. (*Ray Deacon*)

(*inset*) The Red Arrows in line abreast formation in 1971 (*Tony Gannon*) and on the pan at Kemble in 1968 (*below*). The aircraft carry the full aerobatic team livery devised by Sqn Ldr Ray Hanna and introduced at the beginning of the 1968 season. (*Malcolm Thomas*)

(*left*) Spitfire F.Mk.21, LA226/DLE, was positioned outside Little Rissington Station HQ as Gate Guardian in 1958 and it remained 'on duty' there for nine years, until removal and stardom as a static airframe in the film Battle of Britain. This photograph was taken soon after its repaint for the CFS 50th anniversary, 7 July, 1962. (*Rod Brown*)

(*above*) Harvard T.Mk.2b, FS890, joined the Spitfire near the gate in the same year and remained there until the early seventies. In this April 1963 view, LA226 can be clearly seen in the background. (*Ray Deacon*)

(*left*) Last of Rissy's Gate Guardians, Spitfire LF.Mk.16e, TE356, was mounted on a pole in flying attitude, directly outside Station HQ in an attractive setting among the flower beds depicted in this 1974 scene. The aircraft is now flying on the civil register in the United States. (*Alex Wickham*)

Allocated to the RAF Museum collection after appearing in the flying sequences of the film 633 Squadron, Mosquito B.Mk.35, TA639, flew into Little Rissington in 1963. It was displayed at various UK air shows over the next few years until grounded by cracking in the glue joints and it now resides with the RAF Museum collection at RAF Cosford. In this 1966 view, it is parked outside No. 4 Hangar. (*Ray Deacon*)

1966

Squadron changes

In January 1966, the Jet Provost element of the CFS was re-organised into two squadrons with Sqn Ldr P.J. 'Curly' Hirst taking charge of No. 1 Squadron and Sqn Ldr Don McClen commanding No. 2 Squadron. The existing No. 2 squadron, with its Varsities and Chipmunks, was re-numbered 3 Squadron and placed under the command of Sqn Ldr B.W. Lavender

"Red Pelicans" reform

Having finished with the name "Red Pelicans" in 1964, it once again embellished a CFS aerobatic team when the four-ship formation of Jet Provost T.4s, painted in a new deep red colour scheme, was formed in February 1966. To minimize interference with their roles as instructors, team practices were limited to between 08:00 and 08:30, weather permitting.

There remained the question of who would lead the CFS Jet Provost aerobatic team for the 1966 season. In discussion with the CFI, Wg Cdr Eddie Edmonds and knowing that he had experience of leading a formation aerobatic team, Don McClen suggested that Eddie should lead and that he would be happy to continue in the number two position. *"To Eddie, this was an offer he couldn't refuse. And so the training began with Flt Lts Chas Sturt, Colin Thomas, and Cas Maynard sharing the other two places during the season, outstanding and exceptionally reliable pilots all. We gave 25 displays throughout the summer and early autumn, including two in Germany."*

New "Arrows" line-up

The line-up in "The Red Arrows" team cockpits saw significant revision for the 1966 season. Sqn Ldr Ray Hanna took over as Team Leader with Flt Lts W. Langworthy, R. Booth, D.A. Bell, H.J.D. Prince, T.J. Nelson, and P.R. Evans flying the six aircraft behind him. Flt Lt F.J. Hoare and Fg Off D.R.H. McGregor were assigned as reserve pilots while Sqn Ldr R.A.E. Storer continued as Team Manager.

Onward, upward but slower

Air Cdre John Delafield MRAeS, who won No. 231 course's CFS and Hopewell trophies, recalls joining the course in the winter of 1965/66 as a Flt Lt.

"My logbook shows that I last flew the Hunter, T.7, XL 573, with DFCS at Binbrook on 26 October 1965, with Sqn Ldr Dave Goodwin from the Central Fighter Establishment. The culture shock came on 16 November that year with my first flight in a CFS Jet Provost T.Mk.3 with Flt Lt Colin Thomas for the 'left seat famil'. How well I remember that cold, clear, frosty morning (global warming was not too evident then) and this JP 3, with its hugely powerful engine delivering 1,750 lbs of thrust, crept up the hill of Rissy's SW runway with not much more than a trundle but the aircraft did indeed eventually fly. The sensation and contrast with the Hunter could not have been more marked as we inched skywards with a sewing machine noise behind and making so little progress over the ground that the machine gave the sensation of being near stationary!

For me the JP quickly became a fun aeroplane, so much that I decided to opt to stay on the type as a QFI as a change from rushing everywhere at 420 knots or more. Conversion to the JP 4 in mid-February (with its 2,500 lbs of thrust) further persuaded me that its aerobatic potential meant that this really was to be an enjoyable aircraft to fly. Alas, the Clarkson Competition on 29 March saw my efforts eclipsed by an impressive performance by the Gnat; but I think I may have had more fun!

That winter at Rissy was one of the most memorable I have had. A rented cottage, Rose Cottage in Blockley, was home from December to March 1966 – like most houses in those days, ours was unheated but perhaps we were then hardier creatures than now. Frost and snow were frequent visitors and the daily car pool drive to the airfield proved an added excitement in itself. Graduation for No. 231 Course at the end of March was the highlight of those years."

Flying Programme

Student flying training was badly affected by the weather in April as it turned out to be one of the worst on record for that month. The first three weeks saw only 25.3 hours of sunshine with 3.11inches of rain falling against the 1.8 inch average for April. Snow fell on four occasions even settling on the 14th and 15th to a depth of 4–6 cm. Jet aircraft managed only 972 flying hours and piston aircraft 267 hours, most of this being achieved in the last nine days of the month when the weather improved. The year's monthly average flying hours would otherwise have been higher than the 1,624 recorded.

Chipmunk down!

On 21 February, a Chipmunk from Little Rissington suffered an engine failure and force landed near Northleach. The aircraft was being flown by Sqn Ldr Butcher on a mutual detail with Lt Forrest. No injuries were sustained by the crew and no damage was done to the aircraft. The following day the 'Chippie' was airlifted back to Rissington, slung under a Wessex helicopter.

Thespian interlude

Social life on the station was enhanced with the formation of the 'Rissington Drama Group' which, after many arduous hours of rehearsal, put on its first production in March. Called "My Three Angels", it was a rousing success and fired the group with so much enthusiasm they went back to work on a second production.

'Trappers' revert to original name

In March 1966, the Standards Wing title reverted to the original name of Examining Wing. Its role was unchanged and the Staff continued to be known as 'Trappers', but one sometimes wondered what life was like for their families. One view is vividly portrayed in the anonymous exposé reproduced below:

Trapped in the life of a 'Trapper's' wife!

"'So your husband is a trapper?' The query is usually accompanied by respectful or envious looks from other officers and sympathetic condolences from their wives! The times for basking in the reflected glory of Examining Wing-ites are limited, for their wives, to the odd Ball, Cocktail Party or Dinner that may be their lot during their husbands' sojourns at Base. For the rest they must play a waiting game, to the tune of howling winds and in the shadow of the dark clouds that usually envelop CFS in a damp and perpetual mist. The poets who write so blithely of 'living in the clouds' should come to Little Rissington and try it.

A recent article told of all the idyllic splendid qualities needed by an Examiner, such as 'moral courage' and the 'ability to be practical'. Their wives need to have all these qualities – and more – (even if they were not chosen for them!) if they are to survive – and remain sane! The brief interlude of connubial bliss comes to an abrupt end on the day of their husbands' departure on one of the all too-frequent visits. The day before is usually reserved for a final 'fling', chores go by the board and the family rush en masse to Cheltenham for haircuts (which will have to last indefinitely), plus a 'slap-up' tea for the kids. Later perhaps, if lucky, we have a few drinks with friends, followed by last-minute packing and the usual frantic searching for those cuff links that are so essential – and so elusive!

The morning dawns grey and misty. The wife wakes with a sensation of approaching doom and a heavy feeling in her stomach – this turns out to be a large suitcase dumped unceremoniously on her unconscious diaphragm! From then onwards, events move quickly and, with a final wave, she finds herself once again a 'grass widow'. A peculiar phenomenon usually occurs when the wife, Mrs Murphy, is left to 'keep the home fires burning' – everything goes wrong! After a brief survey of the chaos of neglected chores, she may retire to the kitchen fortified by a cup of tea while she contemplates the prospect of loneliness for the next few weeks or months. Vague thoughts of spring-cleaning the house or catching up on neglected correspondence usually vanish when one or more of the children develop all the signs and symptoms of mumps or measles! Or maybe break an arm or leg – or the neighbour's window!

The wireless immediately develops a persistent cough and finally dies on them. The cat has kittens in the wardrobe or the clothesline will break on washing day! It is necessary to be equipped with information on the art of mending a blown fuse, the alternative being to sit in darkness and eat sandwiches for weeks. Wives also learn to chop wood and carry coal – or freeze! The advantages a lone husband has over a Grass Widow are innumerable. He is an asset at a party. She is an embarrassing extra for whom it is necessary to find a partner – usually only an elderly relative is considered 'safe' for this job. Anything in trousers, under the age of sixty, may cause a scandal. He can go to a 'pub' or to the Mess for congenial companionship and the odd drink. She, doing exactly the same, would be considered 'beyond the pale' or 'obviously making hay while the sun shines'.

This being so, she confines herself to the occasional coffee party or shared television evening with other wives. The results of this enforced confinement are usually confined to … Socks … knitted by the yard, while she longs for a good book to stimulate a mind, fast becoming dull and cow-like. But, of course, that so 'practical' Trapper husband forgot to change the library books. Small wonder that the bright and inspiring letters her husband looks for become a monotonous discourse on the children's latest sayings!

'You poor thing' is a condolence, which can be taken literally by these wives, since their husbands' expenses, like the proverbial fisherman's tale, get longer and bigger with the telling. Usually."

Britannia Trophy

"The Red Arrows" received this prestigious award at the Royal Aero Club on 27 April, Air Cdre F.L. Dodds accepting the trophy from Lady Hilda Brabazon on behalf of the Arrows. The trophy is an annual award given by the Club for what it judges to be the most meritorious British performance in the air during the preceding year.

CFS Fleet changes

At this time only one Vampire and one Meteor remained active on the station while the Canberras, Piston Provosts, Ansons, and Kemble-based Hunters had all gone. A large fleet of Jet Provost Marks 3 and 4 together with an increased number of Varsities and Chipmunks, were in evidence, but perhaps the most significant change over the preceding five years was the establishment of a 20-strong fleet of Gnats on permanent detachment at RAF Fairford – ten for instructor training and ten assigned to "The Red Arrows".

The lost spirits

The intake of one course included a Royal Navy pilot. He and Alex Wickham were standing outside the Reflex building at Fairford watching 'The Red Arrows' arrive back from one of their first overseas trips of the year:

"What baffled us was why they taxied back so slowly with canopies half open, so we walked across the pan to greet them. Ray Hanna jumped out and walked over to me with a deep frown on his face. 'How did it go then Ray, good trip?' I enquired. 'Yeh, yeh' replied Ray, 'what do you want us to do?' he said directing his request to the navy chap. 'I don't want you to do anything, why do you ask?' 'Well you are Customs aren't you?' said Ray. What transpired was that someone in the tower had spotted our naval student and mistaking him for a Customs inspector, warned the team that Customs were waiting for them. Fearing the worst they had ditched their excess spirits and cigarettes on to the grass beside the runway as they crawled back to the pan. Of course everyone but the team pilots thought this was hilarious and they wasted no time commandeering a vehicle to take them out to collect their booty.

Course instructors and students were housed in the Reflex building which was located to the side of the apron and afforded a good view across the airfield. One of the most dominant features of the building was 'the world's largest safe' access to which was gained by a huge door with tumblers on the front. Inside the vault was a large room lined with shelving and with the marks from where the top secret Nuclear Release Procedures Plans once laid. We used it for storing our flying helmets. Flt Lt Bill Loverseed, one of the 'Red Arrows' pilots, was intrigued by anything mechanical and he decided that he was going to hack the system, spending hours with his ear to the dials trying to work out the combination. One day after a few weeks of getting nowhere, he rushed into my office in uninhibited excitement and dragged me down to the safe to show me how he'd broken the code. To prove it he swung the door closed spun the dials and tried to reopen it. 'Nineteen left, sixty four right, twenty three left' he muttered to himself, but to no avail, it refused to budge.

Now this was a busy time, the weather was fine and we had lots of aeroplanes on the line. I was half way back to my office when I suddenly realised that none of us would be able to fly because all our helmets were locked in the safe. A few choice expletives later and we were back by the safe but Bill could not get it open. As the helmets were tailored to fit individuals, I placed an urgent call to Rissy for a team of flight safety fitters to bring twenty helmets over to Fairford as soon as possible; it would have been seriously embarrassing if all of a sudden Fairford stopped flying. Wg Co Flying would have been after my blood. Fortunately little flying time was lost and at the end of the day, we sat down to discuss how we were going to retrieve the helmets. 'OK it was my fault, I'll get them out' said Bill.

We arrived next morning to the sound of banging in the vicinity of the room containing the safe. Bill had come in early, knocked a false wall down and was on the roof of the vault hammering his way through the reinforced concrete with a cold chisel. As he progressed he used a small saw to cut through the metal bars. He was covered in white dust and had made a hole some four or five inches deep – we subsequently found that the concrete was three feet thick. I said, 'Bill for Christ's sake you'll never get through that and we need to get on with the flying programme.' In between sorties Bill nipped back to have another session with his chisel. During the day a couple of Gnat examiners came down from Ris to do some flying and as their helmets were also in the safe, they had to be fitted up with new helmets. Flt Lt Freddie Latham was one of them and he went to see if he could help Bill who was still banging away.

Freddie had friends in both the Army Air Corps and SAS and the following day an AAC helicopter arrived. An Army chap stepped out and asked me where I wanted the explosive. When Bill and Freddie saw him they came rushing out and whisked him into the building before anyone else could see him. They filled the hole that Bill had gouged out with plastic explosives and covered it with something heavy. As the charge exploded there was cloud of smoke and dust which once cleared, exposed a neat hole into the vault. It was not big enough for someone to climb through but we could see why the lock had failed to open – Bill had forgotten to fit the back plate to the tumblers. Poking a long pole through the hole he managed to slip the plate back on the mechanism and release the door, much to everyone's relief. The helmets, however, had sustained some damage by the blast and had to go back to Rissy for attention.

The explosion had also damaged the roof of the building so I had a quiet word with Works & Bricks, who owed me a favour, about getting it repaired with no fuss. Despite their shock on seeing the damage and a bullshit tale as to how it happened, they agreed to put it right. When finished it was as good as new, which was just as well because 'Birdie'-Wilson was on his way down to carry out his AOC's inspection. Thundering in with a serious frown on his face, he uttered the immortal words, 'I'm going to give this place a thorough going over'. When he entered the safe room his first concern was for the ceiling which revealed that he knew something. So when he asked me why the roof had been repaired I told him what the Works guy had advised – 'Bird damage Sir' hoping he wouldn't think I was taking the mickey. He didn't."

Three course Gnat T.1s, XS101, XP501 and XR569 on the Fairford pan in August 1966. (*Ray Deacon*)

Go-Karting

Go-Karting became an increasingly popular sport at Little Rissington and a competition between British and French karters, held on behalf of the Royal Automobile Club on 3 April, attracted one of the largest crowds ever seen on the airfield. A special track was laid out utilising the taxi-ways around the MU site on the south side of the airfield. It was the first in a series of three seven-man international team events to be held during the year and was attended by Sir George Dowty, who presented the teams with souvenir pennants before racing commenced and awards to the winners at the end of the final race.

Athletics

RAF Little Rissington played host to a relay race involving fourteen teams from the surrounding area and one comprised of station personnel. The event was won by St. Paul's College Cheltenham with Little Rissington finishing a disappointing thirteenth.

Royal Flush

On 2 June 1966, Her Royal Highness the Duchess of Gloucester visited Rissington in her capacity as Air Chief Commandant of the WRAF. During her stay she toured the WRAF domestic accommodation, Airmen/Airwomen's Mess and Windrush Club. After luncheon in the Officers' Mess she was entertained to an aerobatic display by "The Red Arrows". A second royal visitor, HRH The Duke of Edinburgh, arrived on 9 July and during his stay, was treated to an aerial view of the School from a Sioux helicopter. Three days later King Hussein of Jordan flew in for a visit to the CFS during which he experienced flights in a Gnat trainer and in one of the new twin-jet Dominie navigation trainers then entering RAF service.

Before the King could undertake his flight in the Gnat he had to be kitted-out and the responsibility for this befell Flying Clothing specialist SAC Ivan Hogarth.

> *"My boss was a Sergeant WRAF of the old school called Anne Cuthbert who, every Tuesday, used to come to work with a fistful of 10 bob notes to lend to the lads so that we could go for a drink; it was deducted from our pay on the Thursday. She told me I had to go with her and assist her to fit King Hussein with flying suit, anti g-suit and if my memory serves me right, a Mk.2a helmet and mask. The station MO was also present. Anyway the King arrived, and I don't recall whether it was protocol or what, but Sgt Cuthbert was not allowed to fit him up and I got the job. HRH had rather a large head and after a struggle I managed after loosening all the cords, to let the inner harness go to its fullest extent to get the helmet on. He went away for his trip but the biggest shock for me was when he came back. He thought all the equipment was a gift and walked away with the lot. Sgt Cuthbert smiled at me and muttered very quietly, 'And how are you going to write that lot off, Geordie?'. I always remember that. I had a great time at Rissy, it was about the nicest camp I ever worked on, the locals were always very friendly and we got on well with lads from Bourton."*

King Hussein's Scottish strawberries

In early 1966 Don McClen was appointed President of the Officers' Mess Committee.

> *"When I heard that King Hussein of Jordan was coming in July for a formal lunch I was confident that I could supervise that with the required panache. 'Not so', the staff at HQ Training Command informed me, 'we are responsible for the programme and catering arrangements for royal visits. You don't need to do anything.' So I stepped back and concentrated on my primary duties as squadron commander and aerobatic team pilot – that is until the Command catering officer sought me out in a state of agitation. He explained that the menus had been printed showing strawberries for dessert – alas! no strawberries could be found in local markets at this time of year and were now only available in Scotland. Could I arrange for an aircraft to fly to RAF Leuchars to collect some strawberries which he knew were still growing in the Carse o' Gowrie west of Dundee? So I did to save the day – and his bacon."*

Flying manuals!

One unusual 'near miss' is retold by Flt Lt Vic Dabin from his time as a staff QFI on Varsities in 1966. *"One dark evening I was walking up to the Mess from my married quarter for some thrash or other. As I approached that big front door, a window was suddenly thrown open on the top floor with that characteristic 'bouncing wood' noise, as the sash was unable to match the said window's terminal velocity. That same instant, a tortured voice shattered the Cotswold tranquillity: 'I hate this f****** place!' The expletive's veracity was promptly reinforced as a spread-eagled AP129 fluttered down, more in aerodynamic uncertainty than incipient spin, to crash forlornly at my feet."*

The Top Hat award

Alan Pollock recalls,

> *"Earlier Sir Patrick Hine describes No. 174 Course's and his involvement in the 1956 requisition of the Dorchester Commissionaire's top hat for the CFS inventory. The Top Hat award went to the Student 'gaining' the lowest marks in the final Ground School exams without actually failing the course. Overnight a Top Hatter would become a bit of a star ahead of the traditional final Course Dining Out and Graduation Dinner. This was each fledgling QFI's convivial rite of passage away from the Pelican's tender(?) pecking to meet his first real life student 'Bloggs' a couple of weeks later at FTS or AFS.*
>
> *Almost without exception, every course produced an interesting character, who, sometimes by the skin of his teeth, managed the flying OK and survived all the continual mid-course assessments, right the way through but then found himself bottom of the course in the final ground school examinations.*
>
> *In extended tradition over many years, the winner of the prized Top Hat was viewed by each course as receiving an honorific award in his own right, with no shame attached, indeed quite the reverse. Usually the*

Top Hat winner would have had to be a determined, mature and press on bloke, not easily dismayed by the inevitable adversities encountered en-route to his final objective. Besides the Commandant's comments on each course, the Top Hatter's celebrity status over the last couple of days and his continuing role in CFS traditions at this juncture, meant that his speech would also be eagerly anticipated by the rest of CFS at every Course's Graduation Night. Sitting on the Commandant's right at the top table for the award and final Course formalities would be the overall CFS Trophy winner; on the Commandant's left or by tradition close to him, would be the equally esteemed and distinguished winner of the Course's 'Top Hat', often only there by dint of much persistence, hard work, sweat and sheer guts.

The approach of different winners in their speeches varied in content and originality, as they temporarily wore the said item in the latter 1950s and the 1960s. One constant did remain over time: it was the Top Hatter's proud privilege on behalf of all his course, with a complete degree of inebriated carte blanche, mercilessly to lampoon all the staff and CFS, in order to reverse any imbalance to the assumption that CFS did sometimes know best. Chris Wilmot on No. 199 Course and others as later AV-M B. L. 'Boz' Robinson (who for almost five decades would stay flying aircraft types which would become 'Classic Jets': the Meteor, Vampire, Hunter and Gnat) remember a different tack from 199's Top Hatter, Edinburgh-born Flt Lt W.R. 'Bill' Thomas, sadly killed in a car crash shortly afterwards when both were QFIs at Oxford UAS. Bill stood up, paused for some long time, then quietly said 'All I have to say about CFS is ...' with a further extended pause ...followed by one extremely loud and much attenuated scream."

Goodbye Sir!

One particular Top Hatter's speech took place when the Commandant's namesake, Knotty Ash's very own Ken Dodd, was a well known TV comedian and personality and the story is retold by Vic Dabin.

*"By this time, the Top Hat had been formally modified and lovingly adorned with the McMurdo Light off a Mae West, which was no longer now just worn but would be lit up for the Top Hatter's speech, which as usual was well received at the end of this course. This particular Top Hatter, not unusually also fairly inebriated for the occasion, received even more applause for his delivery, chutzpah and timing, as, gazing down soulfully at the deep, distinguished and charming Commandant, Air Cdre Frank Dodd CBE DSO DFC AFC** RAF, right next to him, he drew his speech to a close with this totally unexpected Ken Dodd punchline: 'Finally and to summarise, fellow students and instructors, I really now only have one simple briefing to impart, one last clear message to transmit for all the lovely staff and Diddy Men at our magnificent Central Flying School: 'Tatty Bye, Doddy Boy!' ... and promptly sat down. Our well respected Commandment, who, from all his earlier examining years at Rissy, knew a thing or two more than the average Commandant, took this whole speech better than anyone else, enjoying that typical and mildly frenetic atmosphere of every Course's final Dining Out Night."*

Tay Bridge opening

The new Tay road bridge was opened by HRH Queen Elizabeth on 18 August and twelve Jet Provosts provided by CFS Little Rissington carried out a fly past to commemorate the occasion.

Gnats move again

By the summer of 1966, the decision had been taken to redevelop RAF Fairford as an interim Transport Command base while the reconstruction at RAF Brize Norton progressed. Number 10 Squadron's VC10s and 53 Squadron's Belfasts were already being seen in increasing numbers at Fairford and when the hangar housing the CFS contingent was nominated as the test centre for Concorde trials, both Gnat Flights were transferred to G-site at RAF Kemble on 26 September 1966. Both air and ground crews remained accommodated at Little Rissington, however, and were bussed over to Kemble each morning. Where Kemble had previously been designated as the Gnat Relief Landing Ground, this role was taken over by RAF Aston Down.

Back to Ris and life as a Trapper

In the middle of 1965, Sqn Ldr Brian Ashley had been earmarked for the TSR2 but no one told that to the government of the day and they cancelled the programme. That left him high and dry until his boss told him that he was posted as OC Advanced Standards at Little Rissington.

"I had been away from Rissington for 13 years and my response was 'What on earth is that?' My boss said it was something like the old Examining Wing and that I would have a magnificent fleet of aeroplanes consisting of a Meteor T.7, a Vampire T.11 and a Mosquito. Somewhat deflated, I decided to wait and see.

Arriving at CFS I found that Advanced Standards was indeed the best bit of Examining Wing and that I would have the use of most aircraft in use throughout the RAF and other air forces. Unfortunately the Mosquito had been grounded. I had a splendid, but rather disrespectful, team of advanced examiners and the job turned out to be a pilot's dream. My first task was to get myself qualified as an A1 QFI on the Gnat, the Meteor and the Varsity and also took instrument rating tests on all four categories of fixed wing aircraft to prepare myself for anything. Then began a period when I spent more time away from Rissington than at home. We flew with the best and the worst of pilots and learned a great deal from both.

During every test I tried to do some flying because I believed that pilots would accept criticism or praise better if they knew you could do your stuff. Every flight was one's best performance and there were no relaxed flights. A flight with an A1 QFI such as Mike Vickers, who was then the doyen of Gnat QFIs, was a great challenge - this might include a practice fire in the air at high level followed by a practice forced landing in manual control through scattered cloud into Mona airfield. My adrenaline was maintained at high flow.

On a typical weekend I would arrive back at Rissington on Friday evening and go into my office to dump my draft report for the week's visit and pick up the contents of my in-tray and the Pilot's Notes and Operating Data Manual for next week's aircraft. A lot of time was spent sitting on the edge of my bed doing emergency drills and flying let downs and circuits. My bed became the flight simulator for about 30 different types of aircraft.

In June 1966 the team flew to Iraq to examine the Iraqi Air Force after an absence of 10 years. They wished to set up an Instrument Rating System for their transport pilots and they had designated their most experienced pilot as their first Command Instrument Rating Examiner. The aircraft selected for the first test was the Bristol Freighter, which seemed as if it had been rescued from a museum for the purpose. With Major Mohammed Adham I drafted a suitable test for the aircraft and then I found myself making my first flight in the Bristol Freighter, or Frightener, in the left seat with a blind flying visor on my head and attempting to fly the first Instrument Rating Test in the Iraqi Air Force. By hook or by crook I survived and was awarded a pass. Then we swapped seats and Major Adham showed his ability. Fortunately he was the pick of the Iraqi pilots and passed his test. I was dreading that he might fail and thereby create a diplomatic incident and precipitate the Iraqi War 25 years ahead of schedule.

Such a high workload also had its brighter times. In 1967 Vic Stanton of Multi Engine Flight and I were involved in the introduction of the Dominie into the RAF. To enable us to keep our hands in we were allocated 6 hours per month at Stradishall and Strubby. We accumulated our hours and before going to examine Stradishall we would have a concentrated flying session at Strubby and vice versa. The Dominie at that time was probably better equipped than any other squadron aircraft and we delighted in getting up to speed on the systems. During testing our biggest problem was encouraging the pilots to use the new whistles and bells. We thought the ability to fly an autopilot-coupled ILS approach better than sliced bread but most pilots preferred to fly manual ILSs. During this time we had to introduce an Instrument Rating Test for the Dominie and when ready we had to prove it. As the boss I claimed the right to have first attempt in the left seat with Vic's eagle eyes glinting from the right. I managed to struggle through the test and Vic gave me the nod. We then changed seats so that Vic could demonstrate his usual prowess. Unfortunately during the latter stages of an approach he slipped out of the limits and I failed him. Bosses can be vicious! If I had tried to pass Vic he would not have accepted it.

On overseas examining tasks we normally flew in one of Rissington's Varsities. The team usually comprised fast jet, basic and helicopter examiners and for the Iraq visit I was the only Varsity-qualified pilot on board. We had to take a navigator and an engineer plus some spare parts, which might be needed during the flights. Transport Command would have had a fit if they had seen our flight planning. We worked out the fuel required for each leg and then the take off weight. We then knew how much we were overweight and we were prepared for anything. On the first leg to Istres we could not avoid the usual severe thunderstorms over the Massif Central and the noise in the Varsity was unbelievable. Huge hailstones and heavy rain were noisier than the 1812 Overture. Frequent lightning and St Elmo's fire on the wings were quite spectacular.

Once settled in at Kemble, the CFS Gnat Flight operated from the taxi-ways while construction of a new pan continued. Depicted (*above*) is XM707/91 about to taxi out while (*below*), having made a two-wheeled landing two days after the move from Fairford, XM704/95 is about to be lifted from the Kemble grass: (*bottom*) Six months later another casualty. This time XM705/98 awaits retrieval from the fields beyond the end of the runway after suffering power loss during take-off and crashing through the runway approach light masts. Amazingly, '705 was rebuilt and returned to service while '704 was struck off charge. (*Ray Deacon*)

To ease the piloting load each of the examiners took their turn to fly from the left hand seat, while I looked after all the boring stuff such as engine starting, checks and radio contact from the right hand side. A Jet Provost examiner made his first Varsity landing at Luqa followed by our Wessex helicopter examiner at El Adem, a Royal Navy Hunter examiner at Nicosia and an RAF Hunter examiner at Habbaniya. They were much more entertaining than a boring old auto pilot.

On the day before we were due to leave Habbaniya a group of Iraqi Air Force officers mounted an attempted coup d'etat from Mosul and we were surprised to see a continuous patrol of a pair of rocket armed Hunters over Habbaniya. Our Varsity was the only aircraft on the tarmac and we were worried that they might use it for target practice. The Station Commander asked us to cancel our planned reception at the Ministry of Defence and then he was arrested by some of his junior officers. We returned to our house, destroyed any compromising documents and packed our kit and stood by to make a hasty departure. Next morning the Station Commander was free again. He thought the coup was collapsing and advised us to get airborne as quickly as possible with radio silence and head for the nearest RAF base at Nicosia. Our navigator was with the British Air Attaché in Baghdad but they promised to send him on when the coast was clear. We made all speed to the Varsity and I did the outside checks while all the team piled on board. Syd Taylor, a Hunter pilot, went in the left seat and Keith Rawlinson RN took station on the navigator's table. I started one engine and Syd started taxiing out. The second engine came on line while taxiing and I managed to complete all the essential checks before we turned on the runway and started the take off. By the time we reached our cruising height of 1,000 ft we were all ship shape and Bristol fashion. We cantered along to Nicosia much better than when we had to continuously check our navigator. However, when we returned to the tender loving care of the RAF we then had to sit and wait for our navigator to arrive. I took great pleasure in sending a Trans Delay signal, which included as the reason for the delay 'Waiting for navigator to catch up with the aircraft'.

A high spot of my tour was the opportunity to renew my 15-year-old friendship with the Meteor. Life at Rissington included frequent air displays, some of them for our highly popular Commandant-in-Chief, HM The Queen Mother, and I was able to resume a series of solo aerobatic displays begun in 1952. The Meteor T.7 was underpowered by contemporary standards but because it was big it was easily seen by the audience. By keeping very tight control on airspeed and height it was possible to fly an aerobatic sequence in a small area before the crowd. It had manual controls and every tremble from the airframe could be felt through the control column as if the aircraft was talking to you. In return I talked to it all the time. The conversation during a good stall turn was always lively.

Life on the Trappers also had its domestic high spots. Our wives compensated for our frequent absences by being a close family. Keith Rawlinson, our Naval examiner, had a notorious reputation for never taking his wife, Pat, out for a meal. One day he and I were due to spend a day trapping at Exeter and about six of our wives had planned a coffee party at Pat's house. Before he left the house Keith told Pat that he had left a gallon of sherry for them and jokingly promised that if they finished it he would take her out for dinner. Keith and I disappeared towards Exeter but Syd Taylor was in the office for the day. At lunchtime he found his house empty but before he returned to work he left a note to tell his wife, Kay, that her lunch was in the oven. When he returned home in the evening the house was still empty and the note remained on the table. He wandered round to Keith's house and found it in darkness. He entered through the back door and eventually found Pat and Kay comatose side by side on the bed. When I returned to Rissington with Keith my house was also dark and, of course, my wife, Marlies was on the bed imitating a bloodhound with a hangover. I subsequently discovered that Marlies had driven Pat's batwoman home before becoming very tired and full of stress. The wives had demolished the sherry and thus Pat got her night out.

Life on the Trappers at that time was hard work but any pilot's paradise. Where else could a pilot in one tour lay his hands on Antonov AN-2s, Shackletons, De Havilland Herons or BAC Lightnings, etc., etc? All the aircraft had a fascinating collection of pilots to go with them. If they openly referred to you as 'the Trappers', you were doing well. If they were careful never to use the name, you could be in danger of becoming a real trapper."

Trapping from a Tent

In August 1968 Alan East had two week's leave and took the family camping on the Cardigan coast. He picks up the story:

"The following week I was to be one of the team of Trappers making their annual visit to No 229 OCU at Chivenor. This seemed an ideal opportunity to extend the family's camping holiday.

Our only car at the time was a 1930 Alvis 4-seater tourer, which we still have. Having packed all the gear in and on the car – the tent frame was wedged between the bonnet side and the front mudguard – I left Thelma and our two young daughters with her parents in South Wales and drove back to Rissy. After a couple of SCT trips in the Meteor, I packed my uniform and flying gear and drove to Croyde Bay, where we had booked a pitch for the tent. Having set up camp again, I then drove to Ilfracombe to collect Thelma and the girls, who had sailed over from Swansea on the White Funnel paddle steamer.

For the remainder of that week, those in neighbouring tents were intrigued by this strange chap emerging from our tent in uniform and driving off to work in his funny old car. Trappers did not always make a profit from their Rate 1 allowances, but I think I must have done that week!"

Chipmunk assault!

Flt Lt Roy Clee returned to the CFS in 1963 for the Gnat conversion course and, following a tour instructing students at 4 FTS, found himself back at Rissy working on the Gnat Detachment at Fairford.

"Our flight commander, one Alex Wickham, led two of us on a very early flight to Rissy, and woke up the eight o'clock met briefing with a low fly past. Next day, a flight of Chipmunks appeared to try a form of retaliation. However, our fifth column at Rissy forewarned us and we broke up the formation with a shower of Very lights. Not the sort of fun

Flt Sgt Gordon Hutson receives his BEM from the Commandant, Air Cdre F.L. Dodd. *(Gordon Hutson)*

that would be approved of now!

When we moved to Kemble in 1966, I often flew the 'Arrows' spare aircraft and the team manager. As well as flying, I had charge of the Gnat simulator."

Gnat loss

Two days after moving to Kemble, Gnat T.1, XM704, touched down just short of the runway, the main undercarriage wheels striking the end of the tarmac surface as the pilot accelerated to get airborne. Close inspection by controllers in the tower revealed a problem with the port leg and the aircraft eventually made a two-wheeled landing. The aircraft was lifted by crane and taken back to G-site where provisional damage was estimated as Cat. 4, but this was altered to Cat. 5 (scrap) when it was discovered that the main undercarriage casting was cracked. It was impossible to replace that casting.

More awards

The British Empire Medal was awarded to Flt Sgt G.F.J. 'Jock' Hutson in recognition of his excellent work with the Gnat Project and Rectification teams and as the first Senior NCO in charge of "The Red Arrows" groundcrew.

Other awards where made to Flt Lt J. Holmes, who received the MBE, and Wg Cdr D.L. Edmonds and Sqn Ldr Ray Hanna added a Bar to their AFCs.

1967

CFS function and organisation

This extract from the CFS Handbook outlined the basic function and organisation of the unit: "The Central Flying School is a formation of Group status within Training Command with an Air Commodore as Air Officer Commanding. There are two stations in the Group, Little Rissington and Ternhill, which is near Market Drayton in Shropshire.

The primary function of Little Rissington is to train flying instructors for the Royal Air Force on fixed wing aircraft. Students also attend the courses from various Commonwealth and foreign Air Forces. The training is given on Jet Provost, Varsity, Chipmunk and Gnat aircraft. The Gnat Flight is permanently detached to Kemble (some 20 miles south of Little Rissington), which is also the base of the Royal Air Force Aerobatic team – the Red Arrows.

Little Rissington is organised on the usual three Wing basis of Flying Wing, Engineering Wing and Administrative Wing, with the addition of Examining Wing whose function is to check and maintain flying standards throughout the Royal Air Force.

Royal Air Force Ternhill has the same responsibilities for rotary wing instruction as Little Rissington has for fixed wing aircraft. It also has responsibility for training all ab initio helicopter pilots for the Royal Air Force. Similarly, students attend both courses from various Commonwealth and foreign Air Forces. There is also a rotary wing element of the Central Flying School permanently detached to Royal Air Force Valley where helicopter mountain flying and air sea rescue techniques are taught and practised.

The reluctant flying instructor

There were many reasons why pilots found themselves on a CFS course: Flt Lt John Preece's was to escape from a ground tour that was becoming increasingly unpleasant.

"In 1965, after three fighter tours on the beautiful Hawker Hunter, I had been posted to RAF Chivenor as OC General Duties flight, once known as station adjutant. Command requests for CFS volunteers regularly came through, so, thinking an instructor qualification would be a useful career add-on, I put my name forward. Much to my chagrin, the acceptance came through OK but only on my ground tour's completion.

At the end of March 1967, Audrey and I packed our belongings with two small boys into one elderly Jaguar and an even older A30 Countryman to head ENE for RAF Little Rissington. We rented the Old School House in the pleasant little village of Salford near Chipping Norton and thus I joined No. 238 Course. At the welcome thrash in the bar, I bumped into Bob Johnson, an old rugby-playing mate from RAF Germany days, by now flight commander on the Varsity squadron. He asked me which aircraft did I wish to instruct on. My background suggested the Gnat advanced jet trainer but many younger course members revealed the majority would opt for that. Having sampled the Jet Provost's 'sparkling' performance, I did not fancy spending two years flying JPs, so when Bob suggested that I apply for the Varsity, suddenly

I got all excited. A totally new experience, this could open the door to extra options at tour-ex but would anyone take my bid seriously? Bob said he would recommend me and cross fertilisation would be good for the Varsity flight too, with few on my course likely to apply for the two student slots available. So on 31 May 1967, I climbed into this huge machine, with its twin Bristol Hercules radial engines, to convince Flt Lt Vic Dabin all this was not a huge mistake and that I could fly this machine, even teach others to do the same.

The initial handling work went well enough, as earlier Meteor asymmetric training was useful and I soon got used to climbing in the back door for the route march up to the cockpit. The fun began when we went on the airways navigation exercise to Gütersloh in Germany. Paired with a senior instructor, one Flt Lt Coombes, he was to be acting student captain on the outbound flight, co-pilot on the return, while I was to carry out co-pilot duties as well as instruct him on captaincy outbound, reversing our roles on the return. 'Make your airways joining call', he says, once we are airborne. Now for one who had studiously avoided contact with airways for all his flying life, this was a challenge I failed to meet. Shortly after this embarrassment, he asks me for my fuel log. Fuel planning in a Hunter is fairly straightforward: you keep the throttle in the far left hand corner until the 'Bingo' lights come on and then you find somewhere to land fairly quickly. A fuel log? This was more foreign language. 'OK' says my rather terse instructor, 'just sit there, watch and we will talk about this, once we get on the ground'. A somewhat ominous comment, I thought, and so it proved to be. He proceeded to dissect my performance as potential Varsity instructor with lethal precision, telling me that, unless something dramatic happened, I would be looking for a different role in life. After a much more thorough briefing, the return journey demonstrated some improvement and I was given an extra navigation flight. This turned out to be a real 'jolly', as the Commandant of CFS was going on an official visit to the French Air Force helicopter training school in the French Alps. He probably had not bargained for having an incompetent like me to get him there but Master Pilot Edwards was aboard to referee and keep us on track.

At the end of July I graduated, not at all surprised that I failed to win any trophies and we headed off to No. 5 FTS at RAF Oakington."

A Gross change of mindset

Flt Lt Keith Piggott went through an early Gnat course at No. 4 FTS at Valley as a student, before joining No.1(F) Squadron on Hunters. He remembers his unusual 'doubled course' period at CFS and some memorable incidents at Rissy:

"Like many others I had not expected to take a liking to CFS, nor instructing. Seen as a 'punishment tour' after digging my heels in, when my Pilot Attack Instructor (PAI) course was diverted to a RNAS Buccaneer posting on Rhodesia's UDI, MoD(Air) offered me Sultan of Oman's Air Force before finally posting me to No. 238 Course at CFS. To my surprise both CFS and instructing afterwards were great value. Re-coursed on medical grounds, after a sojourn in RAF Wroughton Hospital, I completed the advanced stage, with my Applied flying carried over from 238 on to 239 Course.

Both CFS course involvements were brilliant, bringing home to me all I had missed as a student pilot or forgotten about on my first Hunter tour. My 'seat-of-the-pants' skills were finally joined-up more to the 'grey matter' – surprisingly I discovered I could apply myself to ground school and win the Gross Trophy with a 96% average. Held back after my Jet Provost basic stage for the advanced stage on Gnats after my unplanned absence, I was detached daily over to RAF Kemble, the home of the Red Arrows, which was magic. Maybe I did miss all the '50 feet' clearance flying, deployments and low level combat stuff of No. 1(F) Sqn but, as an early Gnat student, I quickly realised that this aircraft was my true alter ego. Although I felt the Gnat would do (almost) anything for me, I did not impress Dennis Hazell with my aerobatic sequence's inclusion of some low-speed wheels-down variations: 'Ground-breaking stuff, Keith!' he quipped.

Later I did persevere with these for two display seasons at Valley, where the CFI was Dave Moffatt (earlier my Flt Cdr at Cranwell), who fully supported my wish to aerobat. My own preferred display was completed with a 220 kt dirty-u/c loop into landing until Valley's CO, Gp Capt Colahan, put a stop to that – some manoeuvres in the Gnat did look much more dangerous than they really were.

At CFS Kemble at that time, there was an excellently relaxed but professional spirit engendered by Dennis, Bill Loverseed, Roy Cope-Lewis, John Lloyd and the other Gnat QFIs. To my utter confusion, at 239 Course's graduation dinner, suddenly I heard my name being called out to receive the CFS Trophy, an event when, for me, the expression 'gobsmacked' was first coined. That's all I recall at this distance of years, except one non-scheduled night landing at Kemble with the Gnat's right brake locking fully on, when first applied after touchdown with John Lloyd. We sharply departed the runway for a high speed dash across the airfield … not in the brief! In summary the No. 4 FTS Valley job after my CFS course was certainly worth doing and both places were most thoroughly enjoyed."

Il Comandante di volo britannico: il Piaggio allegro non adagio

On 1 October 1967, Vic Dabin flew the Commandant and his team over to Italy for a week's visit to the Italian Air Force's training facilities, through Roma Ciampino and on to Grottaglie, Lecce and Amendola before returning via Napoli and out again via Rome. *"At Amendola, the Italians were not a little surprised when the Commandant, Air Cdre Frank Dodd, invited to take the controls to fly one of their general purpose, light transport trainers, the rear pusher-propped, twin-engined Piaggio P166M, simply could not resist (certainly con brio if not even sforzando) rolling the aircraft quickly 'to see how it handled'. When 'i passeggeri' emerged haltingly from the cabin, one at a time down onto the sunny tarmac, most of them looked more shaken than stirred, with complexions also more to match Italy's 'tricolori' national colours, red, white and green!"*

By J2 to Kemble

When Flt Lt Terry Kingsley returned to Little Rissington in 1967, it was to join "The Red Arrows". *"Almost all of our flying was done at*

Kemble. That venerable piece of British engineering, the J2, used to collect the pilots each morning and at valve bounce, proceed to Kemble" recalls Terry, *"whoever was driving, being insulted as to his abilities for the whole trip. Pete Evans would come past on his 'crotch rocket' leaning over and wearing out the sides of his flying boots as he cornered. Stores never did understand this strange wear pattern."*

Foggy landings

Sqn Ldr Eric Evers was on the staff at Rissy, first as OC 2 Squadron with Jet Provosts and then DCI Flying.

"I well remember my next door neighbour, Roy Booth, then in 'The Red Arrows', as I moved into my married quarter in that freezing cold, foggy January remarking, 'Welcome to Little Rissington, where the wind from the Andes hits nothing until it reaches us up here!' On reflection there was considerable truth in that remark!

That typical winter weather brings me to my first vivid memory of Rissy. Firstly, a reminder that it was a long standing joke that Rissy, as an airfield where future flying instructors were being taught the 'patter' for basic flying training, was about as non-standard an airfield as you could choose. For example, the runway was shaped like a banana so that lining up for take-off you could not see the other end of the runway and this only came into view about halfway down the runway. Likewise, on landing, the second half of the runway would suddenly disappear on approaching touch down, which, at night in particular, made for most entertaining variations and intermissions in the standard 'patter' for judging height above the runway for landing.

The second non-standard feature of the airfield was the layout of the runway approach lighting when landing East to West. The approach crossed the Burford to Stow-on-the-Wold road and then traversed a little valley before reaching the threshold of the runway on the far lip of this valley. The problem was that there were no poles long enough to maintain the approach lighting through the valley so, in fact, two full crossbars of lighting were missing, something you never noticed on normal flying but would prove significant on the particular day, or maybe those few key stretched seconds of it, etched permanently into my sharpest recall.

The CFI, Wg Cdr Dave Moffat, and I were trying to fly to RAF Leeming in a JP for a visit. The weather was typically bad, with fog and low cloud over the whole country. An attempt to fly up to Leeming the previous day had been abandoned because of the weather and so on this particular day the pressure was on us to take off and get the job done. Rissy was just about on the limits with poor visibility in fog, with Leeming a little better but forecast to stay that way, so we decided to go. About fifteen minutes after take-off, we got an urgent call from Ris that Leeming was now out for landing, that the weather at base was getting worse and for us to get back quick! Dave Moffat said that he would fly the GCA and I was to look ahead and, just as soon as I saw the approach lights, I was to yell, take over the controls and land. Dave flew an immaculate GCA down to 200 ft, still in cloud/fog and no sign of the ground and then suddenly....... lights! I yelled 'I have control' as I saw what turned out to be the crossbar lights just before the Burford to Stow road. No sooner had I taken control than we were straight back into fog, as we flew over the little valley, devoid of approach lights and still descending. Quick decision....... overshoot or continue the steady well trimmed descent that I had inherited from Dave Moffat........ decision....... continue! Suddenly, once again, lights..... and this time the threshold lights and, we crossed them, that unique flier's twinge of both relief and fear, then sight of the first painted white line marker on the centre of the runway, so I was able to keep the aircraft going straight with no more than one visible at any one time.

The man in the caravan on the end of the runway reported to the tower that he had heard the noise of an aircraft passing but no sighting and the tower only saw us as we taxied into dispersal and shut down. Needless to say, the Commandant and Station Commander were not amused!"

Former Chief of Air Staff, ACM Sir Richard Johns GCB CBE LVO FRAeS

Having almost completed an exhilarating tour flying Hunter FR.Mk.10s with 1417 Flight in Aden, Flt Lt Richard Johns began to look forward to his next posting, either No. 2 or No. 4 Squadron in Germany, or so he hoped.

"Tough', they said, 'there aren't any slots available, you're going to CFS.' 'I don't want to go to CFS, what else is there?' I retorted. 'THOR missiles or Tech Training,' came the reply, to which I said I would love to go to Little Rissington!

On arrival at Rissy I joined No. 239 Course. The one part of the course I was nervous about was the Ground School phase but it turned out to be OK. During this phase we had to give two presentations, one on a civilian topic of your choice and one on a service topic of your choice to demonstrate your teaching skills. One of the students, Martin Molloy, got up and gave an outstanding presentation on how to iron a civilian shirt. The instructors were over the moon about this and thought it was superb. However, when he came to do his service topic, all his credibility was blown when he gave a presentation on how to iron a service shirt. One thing you quickly learned was that there was a love-hate relationship between instructors and students and 'Thou should not take the p... out of the Staff,' which is what he'd done.

I remember my very first trip in a Jet Provost. I walked into the changing room and got changed into my flying gear, which included the desert boots I wore in Aden. Wg Cdr Flying came in and gave me a ferocious bollocking: 'You don't wear those bloody things here,' he said, 'you wear proper flying boots.' So I changed my boots and went outside to be introduced to this horrid little aeroplane called the Jet Provost. Once airborne, my instructor told me to just fly it around to get used to it and enjoy myself. So I did a few rather incompetent aerobatics and so on and so forth and he didn't say very much. Then he told me to take us back to Ris. On arrival back at the airfield, I tried to see what the horrid little machine could do, winding it up and yanking it into the circuit. I said 'How was that then?' Still not a word from the other seat until we got back to the crew room. 'I have never seen such a disgraceful exhibition of undisciplined flying in my life. You did not pay any attention to departure

CENTRAL FLYING SCHOOL

This is to Certify that

Flt. Lt. R. E. Johns.

has successfully graduated from the Central Flying School as a Qualified Flying Instructor

DATE 5th Oct. 1967.

J Trotman A/ Gp Capt COMMANDANT

Certificates were presented to successful students on graduation. The certificate shown above was presented to Flt Lt Richard Johns at the end of his course in 1967, signed by Gp Capt D. A. Trotman for the Commandant. (*Sir Richard Johns*)

procedures, climb-out procedures, you were not in the general handling area until I nudged you into it, and we do not recover at Rissington with a corkscrew.' It brought home to me how many bad habits I'd picked up in Aden.

Another incident that sticks in my mind involved another sortie in a JP3. My aircraft was parked facing the upward slope on the Rissy JP pan and I opened up the power to 90%. The aircraft didn't budge an inch, so I got out of the aeroplane and put it u/s for lack of thrust, only to be informed by my Flight Commander that this lack of forward motion was quite normal on the JP. I soon had enough of this so, when volunteers were called for to move on to the Gnat, I jumped at it.

Dennis Hazell was my Flight Commander at Kemble and he had an air of always being in control. The only occasion on which I saw him flustered was while we were flying mutuals for the first time at night. Kemble wasn't the best lit airfield and it took some getting used to, which made it quite exciting. I went off with a Navy guy and, having successfully completed our sortie, got down after a fashion. As we taxied in, dismounted and walked back to the hangar, we could still hear Carver in another Gnat doing overshoot after overshoot after overshoot. Dennis by this time was concerned that they would run out of fuel but they eventually managed to get it down with not much to spare.

Several years later when I was a Squadron Commander at Cranwell, I was privileged to be selected to train HRH Prince Charles to fly jets, having previously flown with him on several occasions in a Basset of the Queen's Flight. Two custom-built Mark 5 Jet Provosts were provided especially for his course."

Brabyn success

Held on the 6 June 1967, the leader of "The Skylarks" team, Flt Lt John Merry, was entered for the Brabyn Trophy. *"It was competed for by Gnats, Jet Provosts and Chipmunks (the Varsity not being suited to low level aerobatics) and was won on this occasion by yours truly, in a Chipmunk. I don't think this was expected – certainly not by me – though I regarded it as justification for my CAAT (Chipmunks Are Aeroplanes Too) campaign".*

From 'Creamy' to Clarkson

This edited extract from the recollections of Wg Cdr John L Bishop give an insight into one young student's course journey and flying development from fledgling pilot to full QFI status:

"In 1967 RAF Little Rissington was where we learned to instruct. After advanced flying on the Gnat at No. 4 FTS RAF Valley, I had hoped to be posted on to day fighter/ground attack or fighter reconnaissance Hunters. However, Flying Training Command had a curious, continuing system of posting a few selected graduates to CFS to become 'Creamed off' flying instructors. QFIs might have been revered by

A scene familiar throughout Flying Training Command for many years, a briefing by an instructor to students about to fly a formation sortie. (*David Newham*)

student pilots but were somewhat pitied by their fighter pilot contemporaries, certainly until these in turn received their own call to become instructors.

The life of a bachelor in any 1960s Officers' Mess was pleasant. RAF Little Rissington, a fairly small station with a cosy atmosphere in the Cotswolds, basked in CFS's long tradition. Even as a 22-year old I shared a batman who kept my room tidy, pressed uniforms and clothes, polished my shoes and so on. In the dining room there was waiter service with hotel-style food. The ante-room (sitting room) had large comfortable chairs and the mess staff laid out a full range of newspapers and magazines in perfect order, while the nearby bar formed one focal centre of station life.

Every month we had a Dining In Night, a formal dinner in special Mess Kit uniform dress, afterwards drinking socially into the small hours. Add to that a live band, impressive mess silver, the tables beautifully decked out, waiters dressed up, our passing of the port hand to hand only to the left before the Loyal toast, speeches formally introduced by The President, with mess games afterwards and even the odd thunderflash. On special occasions, there were Ladies Dining In Nights, when wing collars and white waistcoats were worn and married officers brought their wives to the Mess.

My personal instructor was an American, a USAF pilot called Major Snow. He told me that on his arrival at Little Rissington he had been extremely surprised at the comparative freedoms we enjoyed in the Royal Air Force. Not only could we fly almost anywhere but we apparently undertook manoeuvres in our aeroplanes either unknown or banned in the USAF. The RAF also seemed to love (very) low flying and formation aerobatics. My fellow students, Doug Marr, Dickie Duckett and Jonnie Haddock were on their way to join 'The Red Arrows', to be turned into instructors as all members then were QFIs.

Major Snow took a deep interest in every advanced manoeuvre he had been shown and was pleased to find me equally keen to extend my flying skills into such areas. Between more boring, set piece instructional patter exercises, we would practise these additional aerobatic variations, often not too far from the ground.

Towards the end of the instructor's course those CFS students who wished could participate in the low level aerobatics competition. We were 'authorised' to fly down to 1,500 ft solo or mutual (with another course student) to practise at one of the many nearby disused airfields. I decided to 'go for gold' by stringing together a mix of these crazy manoeuvres which Major Snow had taught me among the set piece aerobatics. The sixth and final practice was over Rissington airfield itself, on a typical March day with a strong wind under partial cover of puffy cumulus clouds.

Unlike my practice with my heart rate pounding near the 200 mark, I was able to fly the competition with a calm air of detached, mechanical precision. The pleasing result was that this 'Creamy' won the prestigious Clarkson Solo Aerobatic Trophy, the only cup from my entire RAF service, presented to me that evening by the Commandant of the CFS at our Course's glittering final 'dining out night' in the Officers' Mess. Today the miniature silver cup award still adorns my desk.

The following day our postings were pinned to the notice board. Ian Mackenzie, a fellow graduate, looked a bit glum. 'I see you're going to Linton-on-Ouse, lucky devil', he said, 'whereas I'm going to the dreaded Leeming'. 'Where's Linton-on-Ouse?' I said. He stared at me in disbelief at my ignorance: I had not given a single thought to where I might be going next."

Naked lady!

Flt Lt Peter Bouch first passed through Little Rissington as a student on No. 240 Course which ran from August to December 1967. *"Our course was famous mainly for a Stripper at the Graduation Guest Night. Permission was not requested, so the WRAF Officers were escorted out and entertained by junior course members. A very attractive girl appeared from a giant Top Hat towed in on a bomb trolley and did a dance of the seven veils amongst the tables. The Commandant enjoyed it but the Station Commander did not and tried to have a Board of Inquiry the next day – and failed, phew! The lady and her 'manager' were hired in Brum and they also showed 'blue films' in the Ante Room after the meal. The Station Commander retired hurt!"*

Back to base!

Making a return to Little Rissington nearly twenty years after he served as a Flight Commander at CFS, Gp Capt B.P. Mugford took up his new post as Officer Commanding the Station. In 1946, he had served with 7 FIS at Upavon and moved with the unit to Rissy in the May of that year.

Aircraft loses part of canopy

While flying on a standard training sortie, a 3 ft metal section from a Jet Provost canopy came off and fell to earth somewhere north of Cirencester. The aircraft returned safely to base and an air search was launched to try and locate the missing object in order to determine what caused it to come adrift. As the search failed the police appealed to the public to help try and find it.

Instructions to Aircrew

As the year drew to a close, a number of instructions were issued which became mandatory for all QFI and student pilots, the most important of which are outlined below:

Instruction No. 8 – Maximum Flying Hours

Introduction

> Flying personnel become inefficient if they fly too much and rest too little. Insufficient flying to keep in full practice also leads to inefficiency.

Rest Periods

> Whilst engaged in flying duties all personnel are to have a period of eight hours uninterrupted in any twenty-four hours.

Night Flying

When engaged in night flying they are to stand down from the preceding lunchtime.

During night flying after two sorties a rest of one hour is to be taken before a third sortie.

Subsequent to night flying all personnel are to be stood down for a minimum period of eight hours from the time of release.

Maximum Hours for Flying Personnel

Advanced Jet Trainers

The following maximum flying hours apply.

Annually	500 hours
Monthly	50 hours
Twenty Four and Twelve	4 hours*

*Note that in either twenty-four or twelve hour periods, students are limited to three sorties or four hours maximum flying unless permission is granted by the Chief Flying Instructor.

Instruction No. 23, Part H – Pilot Continuation Training

Introduction

All pilots are to carry out the required continuation training on the types of aircraft in which they fly. Continuation training is to take precedence over all other flying training commitments. Every effort is to be made to ensure that the flying hours allocated for this training are used to the best advantage.

Flying Practices

Single Engine Aircraft

Practice flame out and forced landings
Instrument flying
Instrument letdowns and approaches using GCA and other aids fitted to the aircraft
Aerobatics (on aircraft where aerobatics are permitted)
Circuits

Night Flying

Night flying continuation training on all types is to be carried out at least once every three months. In addition, if a QFI has not instructed by night within the last three months he is to carry out at least one night Staff Continuation Training (SCT) exercise, covering instruction sequences just prior to the night instrument phase.

Emergency Drills

When a member of the QFI staff or a student has not flown for a period in excess of fourteen days, supervisory staffs are to ensure that they carry out, emergency and drill practices in aircraft cockpit procedures or simulator where available.

1968

RAF Little Rissington's reputation for unpredictable weather was said to comprise four seasons in a day and January 1968 was no exception. In the space of seven days from the 6th to the 13th temperatures were consistently below freezing and fell to –7.4° Celsius on the night of the 9th. Snow started to fall at midday on the 8th and by 09:00 on the 9th it was some 10 inches deep. By the 12th it had melted down to 5 inches and had completely vanished by the following day. Frost occurred on 14 nights during the month and on the 16th, 17th and 18th winds of up to 60 knots were recorded. The highest wind previously recorded at Rissy was 63 knots. Coupled with a very low cloud base of between 200 and 800 ft and dense hill fog, flying was severely restricted. The only aircraft to leave the ground during the four and half days of deep snow were the Chipmunks, but these had to be grounded during the period of high winds.

Jet Provosts collide

While carrying out a practice display on 26 February, two Jet Provost T.4s of "The Red Pelicans", the leader's aircraft, XS229, being flown by Flt Lt D.J. Smith and the No. 4, XP675, by Flt Lt J.D. Blake, suffered a mid-air collision. Flt Lt Smith and his student pilot, Fg Off J. Tye both ejected and landed safely, while Flt Lt Blake managed to fly his badly damaged aircraft back to Rissington, escorted by another team member. XP675 was declared Cat 4. Despite this setback, the team had recovered sufficiently by 31 March when it participated at the Staverton air show.

The unfortunate XS229/49, the last production T.4 in Red Pelican colours at Little Rissington. (*David Watkins*)

New "Skylark" team announced

Approval for the formation of a four-ship Chipmunk team for 1968 was announced in the February of that year, under the leadership of Sqn Ldr B.A. Owens. Flt Lts J.S Hindle, P.J. Dummer and G.S Webb completed the line up. Sqn Ldr R.B. Nelson took over as leader in May following Sqn Ldr Owen's posting out.

Cracked tails

In the spring of 1968, the RAF Gnat fleet was grounded following the discovery of cracks in the base of the tailplanes of two "Red Arrows" aircraft. As both aircraft were returned to Hawker Siddeley for repairs, a silver and day-glo Gnat was quickly obtained on loan from 4 FTS and flown as the lead-ship at Biggin Hill Air Fair by Sqn Ldr Ray Hanna. Checks on the remaining Gnats revealed no signs of cracking.

'Big crowds attend RAF Kart races'

This was the headline in the Gloucester Echo reporting on the RAF Karting championships which were held at Little Rissington over the weekend 4/5 May. Competitors from RAF units based in the UK and from afar as Germany and Cyprus participated. Ch Tech Bryan Boyce from RAF Finningley was the most outstanding competitor, winning nearly all the races in which he competed and taking two of the class championships. The CFS Kart Club was assisted by Dowty and the Bromsgrove Kart Clubs who used the circuit at Little Rissington, and who provided many officials, marshals and stewards for the meeting.

Supplying my own store of recollections

Wg Cdr Tony Howells was OC Supply at Little Rissington from 1966 to 1968 before escaping to Staff College. He recalls:

"A happy tour with a sound working relationship between my Squadron and the Engineers, serving a bunch of dedicated and professional pilots, acknowledged to be the best instructors in the world. Occasionally I felt that these played the Prima Donna but only rarely … and were in retrospect usually right (but not always).

Little Rissington, as we all knew or soon found out, was 730 feet above sea level and the highest RAF airfield in the UK. All the other Cotswold villages nestle in protected valleys but Rissy's Married Quarters sat on top of the hill, like the airfield itself. This encouraged the wind to enter by the front door and sweep out through the back. Our first MQ at Rissy had three doors, front, back and one in the sitting room, facing the front, which, if opened, led you straight into a rose-bed. Some residents had converted these extra doorways into bookcases by fitting shelves. As a place to live, Rissy was great if you had a car but not so good if you had to rely on public transport. A bit like today really!

Down in Bourton-on-the-Water lived a Mr Hill, who ran Birdland, an excellent place to take the children if you wanted a quiet morning after a Guest Night. He said that he had originally made his money by being contracted to build a dry-stone wall around the airfield. True enough there the wall stands to this day, including beautiful curved sections around the trees, which grew alongside the road running past the entrance to the base. He owned a number of Hyacinthine Macaws, which flew loose over the village. Our family and possibly others called them the Red Arrows

Dodd Drive was a road built by the Royal Engineers as a field exercise. It ran from the MQs to the back of the Officers' Mess. The 'Drive' had a dogleg in it, said to be a realistic representation of the Air Commodore's typical golf shot – probably a foul libel but I am no golfer.

During Frank Dodd's tenure as Commandant there was a Guest Night for the departing CFS course. It was the practice for the course to make a presentation, such as a port decanter or something like. This course provided a stripper, who, as part of her routine, hung her bra on Mr Vice. This officer was one of my staff, a bit straight-laced and was not entirely sure what to do with this surplus to requirements item. The Commandant was not deeply amused as there had been some recent bad RAF tabloid publicity over a Ball at Halton, which had entailed Mess Staff being dressed in powdered wigs and embroidered tailcoats. You could see his point!

The visit of King Hussein of Jordan required, from memory, three practice lunches to get the silver-service up to speed because the waiters were from the RAF School of Catering and not familiar with either the process or our Rissington Mess – roast lamb three times and no choice as to either the menu or your attendance!

The wide mix of aircraft included the Vintage Pair of Meteor and Vampire, the last Mosquito (finally grounded because of adhesion problems), Chipmunks, Varsities and a multitude of JPs plus the real Red

Staff on the MT section pose for a photograph marking the retirement of Cecil Arthurs in 1968. (*l to r*); Tom Fitzsimons, Brian Close, Wilfred Lane, Bill French, Bill Lake, Reg Avery, Dickie Brain, Frank Hunt, Charley Stevens, Cyril Cambray, Cecil Arthurs, Don Davidson, Stan Taylor, Eric Saunders, Ted Connolly, Harry Minchin. (*Ken Cole*)

Arrows flying their Kemble-based Gnats but supported from Rissy. A visit to my Technical Spares store prompted the then OC Eng Wing to opine that 'about 50% of the spares were redundant and that they should be disposed of'. Our debate was over which 50%, as my experience told me that the surest way to ensure that an item was required was to dispose of it. At Rissington we were also the first flying station to go live on using the Hendon Supply Computer. This led to the strange experience of having to ask a remote computer whether you should use items, which you knew were in your own store, as we held no accounting stock record at Rissy, only a stock location system. The advantage we gained was that we now had access to stocks at other stations for priority requirements."

Chipmunk fatality

While performing low-level aerobatics over Moreton-in-Marsh airfield in Chipmunk T.10, WZ874, on 2 May, in preparation for the end of course trophy, the engine cut at the top of a loop and the aircraft crashed heavily on the runway before slithering onto waste land and was completely wrecked. Sqn Ldr Brian A. Owens was killed instantly but his student pilot, Flt Lt Robin K.C. Melville, escaped with moderate injuries. The airfield was home to the Home Office Fire Training Centre and firemen from the Centre helped ambulance men extricate the crew from the wreckage.

Thirty years a civilian at Little Rissington

After thirty years working as a civilian at Little Rissington, 69-year old Mr Walter Mathews was presented with a silver tray by Wg Cdr P.H.T. Lewis to mark his retirement in May 1968. Following service with Nos. 8 and 250 MUs between 1938 and 1957, Mr Mathews transferred to the Station Workshops and his long association with the RAF also earned him the Imperial Service Medal.

By minibus to Kemble

Still serving as a QFI, full time reservist, and back as a Flight Lieutenant on Cambridge University Air Squadron, former Gp Capt Tom Eeles recently celebrated 40 years' continuous service as a qualified military pilot. Tom first passed through CFS on No. 244 Course between August and December 1968 following earlier tours on 16 Squadron Canberras at RAF Laarbruch and a RN exchange on 801 Squadron, Buccaneers and Hunters at RNAS Lossiemouth and on HMS Victorious.

"I don't really have much to offer about the Gnat conversion course as such", says Tom, *"apart from that prolonged agony of travelling from Rissy to Kemble for our flying each day in the ancient Morris J2 minibus, driven by a civilian driver called Charlie. He claimed, each and every day, that he had never had an accident in 30 years of driving for the RAF, which was unlikely given his lack of driving skills. The return journey, after four hard trips, was just as bad.*

One day, whilst outward bound and as we were going down the hill into Bourton-on-the-Water, the offside rear wheel came off and rolled quickly past us into a field. The J2 ground to a juddering halt, as Charlie broke down in tears. Out we all got to look for the said wheel, just as Dennis Hazell, the Boss, squealed to a halt in our squadron mini. He just roared with laughter in his typically unrestrained way but then sped off, which now upset Charlie even more. We decided to take Charlie down to the Old New Inn, where we knocked on the door to ask for an emergency out of hours, restorative brandy to sort him out. We were all admitted, Charlie for his brandy, us for a coffee........ then we realised we too now must also be shocked, so could we also all have a brandy as well. We never did get to Kemble that day!"

Film – The Battle of Britain

As production of the film depicting the "Battle of Britain" gained momentum, the search began for RAF pilots with Spitfire and Hurricane experience. Advertisements were placed in RAF stations across the country and two CFS Officers, Flt Lts R.D. Cole and R.G. Lloyd were selected. Several other pilots who had experience on these aircraft volunteered but were rejected because they looked too old!

Awards

Awards announced in June included a CBE for the Commandant, Air Cdr F.L. Dodd DSO DFC AFC, the MBE for Flt Lt J.C. Hemsley and an AFC for Wg Cdr B.A. Ashley. The Queen's Commendation for Valuable Services in the Air were presented to Sqn Ldr P.J. Hirst and Flt Lts D.A. Bell, R. Booth and P.R. Evans, the latter three in their third year with "The Red Arrows".

Gnat Flight becomes squadron

The Gnat Flight, which had been operating as C Flight, 3 Squadron over at Kemble for some time, received its autonomy on 16 July when it was classified 4 Squadron, with Sqn Ldr D.G. Hazell appointed as its first OC.

Examining Wing and a second tour

The second tour of Sqn Ldr Mike Vickers on Examining Wing began in October 1968 after a seven-year spell at No. 4 FTS Valley, initially flying Vampire T.11s and then the Gnat T.1 and Hunter F.6 and T.7. During that time he accumulated some 2,500 hours on the Gnat.

"My arrival back at Rissy followed a 6-month secondment to the Battle of Britain film company, to fly Spitfires, Hurricanes and Messerschmitts. In the 1950s the Wing was housed in a fairly large wooden building adjacent to the eastern hangar. By the 60s, when the task had begun to shrink, the number of examiners was also reduced and the Wing was given one of the permanent buildings not far from the main gate.

The number of squadrons at CFS was now down to two – Basic and Advanced. Wg Cdr 'Charlie' Slade was the Basic boss and the Advanced Squadron, of which I was a member, was commanded by Sqn Ldr Holdway. The task was very similar to that of my first tour – the most notable difference being that it had shrunk considerably. The Jet side now consisted of Colin Holman, 'Jock' Byrne and myself. As the main runway at Rissy was pretty short (1,600 yds) and unsuitable for Gnat operations, 4 Squadron was based at Kemble nearly 30 miles distant. Transport to Kemble was by bus at 07:30 each day returning at 16:30. 'The Red Arrows' also operated from Kemble. This required us to make frequent trips down there to fly Continuation Training and test students and staff on 4 Squadron. Fortunately we rarely used the bus as the Meteor T.7 and a Vampire T.11 were on our charge and we used these to commute. From this Colin Holman and I began 'the Vintage Pair' and displayed at a few air shows. The Vampire was retained as we were still responsible for the testing and training pilots operating the type at Exeter, Hurn (RN) and Shawbury. As the Hunter was no longer operated by CFS we frequently travelled to Valley either by road or air. Overseas visits to both the Middle and the Far East were still a common occurrence and one liaison and testing trip took in Pakistan and Malaya.

So again, I enjoyed my second tour with the Trappers – many types of aircraft flown, many units and countries visited, and many types and abilities of pilot and student tested. The job was interesting and fulfilling – lots of advice to give and lots to learn from others. In November 1970 I left CFS to join the Empire Test Pilots School as the QFI.

Looking back over my two tours at CFS, I made many friends, learnt a lot and hopefully passed on some worthwhile information. It is impossible to remember them all but all these years later I still meet people who say 'I remember you – you trapped me in such and such'. On one occasion at the 2001 CFSA reunion, when the then CAS (now Air Chief Marshal Sir Peter Squire GCB DFC AFC) was guest of honour, he was singing the praises of Examining Wing and mentioned a Wing visit to No. 20 Sqn at Tengah in 1969, when he said, 'I flew a standardisation flight in a Hunter with one Mike Vickers, who is here tonight' much to my surprise!"

Argosy trainer!!!

On 20 November, the Commandant visited RAF Thorney Island where he flew the Argosy. The purpose of the visit was to assess the suitability of the aircraft as an advanced trainer.

London – Sydney Marathon

The adrenalin buzz produced when flying their high speed Gnats a few feet off the ground was not enough to satisfy three "Red Arrows" pilots, Flt Lts Terry Kingsley, Derek Bell and Pete Evans. At the end of 1968, they were entered in the London-Sydney Marathon in a BMC 1800. Terry continues, *"There was a very strong following from the Station and our position was broadcast each day. On the day we were to drive down to Crystal Palace for the start, I had the car at home in my married quarters. I checked the oil, to find that the end of the dipstick, which had been newly calibrated and etched, had dropped into the sump. So we commandeered a three-tonner with much illicit help, and somehow got the heavy 1800 onto the truck for the drive to Abingdon. Much work was required to get the Sump Guard off, and get at the offending piece of spring steel. Do not forget that they had to replace all the dipsticks on all the team cars".*

1969

New Year's Honours

The following personnel were recognised in the New Year's Honours list:

Air Cdre I. Broom	–	CBE
Flt Lt N.M. Shorter	–	MBE
Flt Sgt R. Ashton	–	BEM

During the early part of January, Air Cdre Ivor Broom completed his Varsity conversion making him current on all CFS types, including the helicopters at RAF Tern Hill.

A bad year!

The year was about to turn into one that CFS would wish to forget, as it was to witness a number of fatal incidents. The first occurred on 24 January when Jet Provost T.3, XM360, of No. 2 Squadron crashed into Abdon Hill north east of Ludlow, while on a low level exercise. Both pilots Flt Lt J.S. Watson and Fg Off I.S. Primrose were killed and their funeral services were held in the Station Chapel on the 28th.

Trapper visits

Several visits were carried out by CFS Staff during the month. These included London UAS, Liverpool UAS, Northampton UAS and RAF Linton-on-Ouse. Overseas trips were made to the Kenyan Air Force and Hong Kong Auxiliary Air Force.

Despite restrictions on flying due to bad weather, CFS still somehow managed to return a high number of flying hours for January. How was this achieved? Although a backlog of flying hours had built up the situation was relieved by detaching five Jet Provosts to Pershore for five days and three Varsities to RAF Manston for four days. Circuits and bumps training was concentrated at RAF Aston Down and weekend flying took place over the weekend 18 and 19 January.

Fuelled up and ready to go!

Flt Lt Peter Blake was OC 3 Squadron from January 1968 until July 1969.

"I do know that the very sociable 3 Squadron was visited by the Donnington Brewery delivery lorry, almost as often as the Chipmunk refueller. Whether that had any effect on the decision that flight commanders would benefit from flying each other's aircraft, I'm not sure, but after years on Canberras, Victors and Chipmunks, I was launched solo in a Gnat from Kemble, with the manual reversion checklist written large on my kneepad. Thinking about that flight, it wasn't so much the marginally greater acceleration than the Chipmunk on take off but that I was outside the recognisable Chipmunk operating area at about the time the undercarriage was up. This was an exhilarating experience and one, sadly, never repeated."

Aerobatic team replacement

Capt G. Rich, the number three in "The Red Pelicans" aerobatic team, was medically repatriated to the USA. The remaining members continued practising until a new member, Flt Lt Mackenzie-Crooks, arrived on 3 February.

Awards

Three noteworthy awards to be made in February occurred on the 11th, when Air Cdre Broom and Mrs Broom attended an Investature at Buckingham Palace where the Commandant received his CBE, and on the 14th when the Commandant presented AOC-in-C Commendations to WO Summers and SAC Barrett.

Meteor crash

While test flying a Meteor T.7 from Tarrant Rushton airfield CFS pilot Flt Lt Robert Patchett was killed when his aircraft crashed near Hurn on 13 February.

Lucky escape!

When "The Red Arrows" undertook one of their visits to Europe, the Commandant decided to accompany them, flying in 4 Squadron Gnat, XP501/96. Flying as the eleventh aircraft, and with SAC Robin Williams in the back seat, the aircraft suffered an hydraulic failure forcing the Commandant to return, choosing to land at Fairford as it had a longer runway. The aircraft rapidly lost height during the approach and struck a pile of manure which had been heaped in a field outside the airfield boundary, before leapfrogging over a road and perimeter fence and coming to a halt in the undershoot. Air Cdre Ivor Broom suffered two broken feet on impact. Although the aircraft caught fire, the airman managed to clamber out and assist with the Commandant's escape from the cockpit, despite having to struggle to disconnect him from the dinghy pack in the ejection seat!! Fire and ambulance crews arrived in time to dowse the flames; however, the aircraft suffered Cat. 5 damage and was struck-off-charge. A week later both casualties were still in hospital, the Commandant with both feet in plaster and the airman with facial burns bearing the outline of his oxygen mask.

Fraternising with the 'Arrows'

Fg Off Maggie Pleasant (née Dawson) served at Little Rissington as the Accounts Officer from June 1967 until September 1969. *"I was one of only two or three WRAF Officers to be there at any one time"* writes Maggie, *"and for a period of about six months I was the only WRAF officer on site."*

Maggie recalls how fortunate she was to go abroad with "The Red Arrows" on two occasions.

> *"The first time I went with them to the Ravenna Air Display and the second trip was to Calais. Nobody ever wanted to take the imprest so when I volunteered to do so they were always grateful!! In those days the aircrew had no funds to enable them to return the hospitality they received when they were away and of course in those days their own income was reduced every time they were away from Rissy because they lost ration allowance – all except the single ones of course. So, having experienced the generous hospitality they received I was reasonably sympathetic when Terry Kingsley came back from one trip and said that he had paid for 12 bottles of champagne from the imprest and he had no intention of repaying the money because the wine had been for returning hospitality – it took me almost two years to persuade Command HQ to fork out the money!*
>
> *On one occasion I attended a 'Red Arrows' dining in night in the Mess and it was the first time they showed everyone the film that Arthur Gibson had made of the team. In its day it was quite innovative as he had set the aeros sequences to modern jazz. We were all very impressed with it and there was a natural pause of appreciation afterwards during which, Plt Off Anne Burt turned to Euan Perreaux, whom she was sitting next to at the dinner table, and said in a very loud whisper 'Cor Euan – that doesn't half bring out the sex in flying!'. This comment reverberated round the dining room causing great hilarity.*
>
> *We had a twin tub washing machine in the batting room which was always going wrong. I was there one day when the repair man came and he showed me why it wasn't working when he pulled a rugby boot out of the mechanism – some guy had put it there to try and dry it out and it had spun out of the top of the spinner into the works. The machine was really quite ferocious in the way it worked and when Terry Kingsley was living in the Mess for a short time before his wife Betti joined him, I offered to wash his few items of underwear for him when I was using*

Gnat T.1, XP501/96, at Fairford in August 1966. Some three years later, Air Cdre Ivor Broom and SAC Robin Williams were fortunate to survive a crash landing on the airfield boundary in this aircraft. (*Ray Deacon*)

Little Rissington regularly hosted visits by members of the royal family. (*middle right*) Having disembarked from the Queen's Flight Andover, HM The Queen Mother is greeted by the Commandant and Station Commander. (*above and below right*) Two views taken on the occasion of the presentation of the Queen's Colour to CFS on 26 June 1969. Miss Tracy Robinson presents a bouquet of flowers to HM The Queen and Miss Wendy Dennis a bouquet of flowers to HM The Queen Mother as HRH Prince Charles looks on. The Royal Family pose with the Commandant, Station Commander and CFS staff for the official photograph. (*CFS Archive*)

the machine one day. Unfortunately his 'shreddies' really did come out of the machine 'shredded' and he subsequently introduced me to his wife as the woman who shredded his underwear – fortunately we became good friends!

One final anecdote concerns the 4 Squadron Gnats at Kemble. Being low to the ground, the aircraft scorched large swathes of grass beside their operating pan, so it was decided that DOE would tarmac an area of hardstanding which would include a small access ramp. Unfortunately the ramp was angled too steeply causing the OC 4 Sqn, Sqn Ldr Dennis Hazell to reject it on the grounds that the aircraft would 'scrape their arses on the ground'. So the DOE had to return and redo the whole thing."

"Red Arrow" fatality

The first fatal accident suffered by "The Red Arrows" occurred in the morning of 26 June 1969, when Flt Lt Jerry Bowler's Gnat T.1, XR573, struck the trees surrounding the B-site hangars at Kemble and crashed in the field adjacent to the G-site hangars occupied by the CFS. Jerry was rushed to Cirencester hospital but pronounced dead on arrival. In the afternoon, the rest of the team, including the rear-seat groundcrew, flew their aircraft to ensure there were no psychological repercussions in the team, watched by the lonely figure of Sgt John Stuart, Jerry's rear-seat man. He had only been with the team since 31 January and was replaced by Sqn Ldr P. Dunn RAAF.

The Queen's Colour

June 26, 1969, marked a significant achievement for CFS when it became only the seventh RAF establishment to be presented with the "Queen's Colour". Her Majesty arrived at 11:15 in an aircraft of the Queen's Flight, accompanied by HRH the Duke of Edinburgh, the Queen Mother the Commandant-in-Chief of CFS, and HRH the Prince of Wales.

Upon her arrival and after the formal greetings HM was escorted by the Duke of Beaufort to the assembled parade where she presented the colour to Flt Lt A.C.R. Ingoldby, the colour bearer. The Royal party then moved on to No. 3 Hangar where they were shown static

displays depicting the evolution, functions and current activities of CFS. These included:

- An Avro 504, Harvard, Vampire, Gnat and Sioux helicopter
- A stand showing the origins of CFS in 1912
- Ground and Air training
- Aerobatic team members
- The work of RAF Ternhill
- The world wide influence of CFS
- Community activities
- Ground crew at work on a Gnat

The Duke of Edinburgh then departed for another royal engagement while HM Queen Elizabeth, The Queen Mother and Prince of Wales were entertained to luncheon in the Officers' Mess. In the afternoon the royal party returned to the airfield where they were treated to a flying display by CFS aircraft, including both aerobatic teams and a visiting Jaguar, before departing at 15:00.

In 1962, having been granted the Freedom of Cheltenham, personnel from RAF Little Rissington were allowed to march through the town with 'flags flying, drums beating and bayonets fixed'. Every year since then the Station exercised that privilege, only this year it had the additional pride of flying the newly presented "Queen's Colour" for the first time to the people of Cheltenham.

Build-up to Royal visit

Maggie Pleasant had an important role to play during the build up to the royal visit and on the day itself.

"We had numerous practice parades and I was stand-in 'Queen' for many of them – they even went to the extent of erecting aircraft steps on the runway and telling me to dress in civilian clothes to make it as realistic as possible. That will be the only occasion that someone of my standing and rank I suspect has ever received the General Salute as the whole thing was played out as per the day. On the final parade rehearsal – much to my chagrin, the CO's PA took over as stand-in 'Queen' and had her photo in the papers. I was relegated to being myself – which was chief 'lavatory attendant' as the CO so charmingly put it. There were two WRAF Officers there at the time and Bridget (Waller I think) and I had to take the Queen and Queen Mum respectively to the loo when they arrived at the Mess. Cavendish House in Cheltenham had been invited to furnish a retiring room for them but the CO (Gp Capt Blaize Mugford – a man with little sense of humour) said, when it was done that it looked 'like a tart's boudoir', so all the lovely furniture was taken back to Cavendish House and replaced with the new RAF G plan furniture – you may recall – it was hard and square and with dull grey covers. Bridget and I thought they made the room look like a railway carriage and the first thing we heard the Queen say when she walked in was that there was nowhere for her to hang her coat. Fortunately the day before she arrived, Bridget and I decided we would try out the newly refurbished Ladies Loo and it was a good job we did as we nearly fell flat on our backs. They had forgotten to fix the carpets down properly. We also had at least three practice lunches although I think we only had the full menu on one of them – Saddle of Lamb followed by fresh local strawberries.

As I remember the day, the Commandant, Air Cdre Broom, greeted the Royals sitting in a wheel chair with his legs in plaster following his accident in a Gnat a few days beforehand. I was seated at the most lowly place near to the kitchen door and it was very obvious as the stewards filed out with the fruit in the individual serving bowls that the strawberries were getting smaller and smaller!"

London – Sydney Air Race

Having succeeded in driving all the way to Sydney, Flt Lts Terry Kingsley and Pete Evans together with Arthur Gibson, a well respected civilian aviation photographer, decided to take on another daring challenge – the 1969-70 London-Sydney Air Race. A Siai Marchetti SF260 was kept at Little Rissington in preparation for the event and this was sometimes flown to Kemble by Terry, a quicker and more comfortable means of transport than the dreaded J2.

Departure for the start at Gatwick Airport was very traumatic as all aircraft had to assemble at Biggin Hill before being called forward to Gatwick. The weather was terrible and Terry made two attempts to get to Biggin, being forced back to Little Ris on each occasion. Finally, on the last day, Rissy was still frozen in, covered in ice, making taxiing almost impossible. So the hangar doors were opened, the aircraft pushed onto the frozen grass, and he took off straight into wind across the airfield.

SF260

For display purposes, Terry kept the SF260 at Rissy after the race. The AOC had opened up a line of communication throughout the Xmas period to be able to follow their progress on the way to Australia. The trials and tribulations of that race are documented in Terry's fascinating book, 'In the Red' (see Reference sources for details). Terry continues with the story,

"I made strong efforts to get CFS and Handling Squadron to consider the SF260 as a Chipmunk replacement. It did actually replace much of the Jet Provost's training capability, and would have been much cheaper. In the end the Bulldog was 'chosen' when the 260 would have done it all.

The first test flight for the 260 at Little Rissington was done to evaluate its ability to complete the training schedule of the JP, or part of it. Monday morning, at 08:00, we took off and encountered trouble immediately. I retracted the gear and there was a loud 'bang' followed by an inability to speak on the radio. The Screw Jack gear retraction mechanism, sits between the seats, with the manual control knob on the top. This was flailing around and pulling out wires from the console. I thought that the main spar was broken or damaged, such was the bang.

Further flight seemed inappropriate, and so I decided to put it back down on the grass after completing a 150 degree turn. I could not stop the flailing of the retraction system, as the circuit breaker was on the end of that mechanism. Knowing that I had less than '3 Greens', I attempted to cut the throttle and switch off the magnetos at touch down. The prop gave just too many turns before stopping, and so there was a minor contact with the grass, as we settled onto the underside of the aircraft, a belly landing.

The Crash Rescue people appeared and in double quick time, the 260 was hoisted onto its wheels. Even though the wheels had been partially extended at touch down, the damage was minimal; a new propeller, complete nosewheel assembly, antenna and straighten the fuel drain on one tip tank. 'Tommy' Thomas, my ever available 'Red Arrows' back-seater and mechanic, also a contributor to this book, fixed the aircraft in time for its display at the World Aerobatic Championship at RAF Hullavington that weekend.

For the record, the SF260 has an electric gear system, the Screw Jack being in the cockpit. The nosewheel retracts into a slot under the engine, and is prevented from retracting sideways by a small metal plate which engages on retraction and corrects any alignment problems. This plate 'was' painted and is part of the before flight check. In my case, it was cracked under the paint and separated on retraction allowing the nosewheel to miss the slot. There is a 'weak link' on the jack, there to prevent the situation we faced. It did not fail, but the main jack eventually did. These guider plates are no longer painted!"

Aero teams in demand

Both "The Skylarks" and "Red Arrows" aerobatic teams were in demand through the middle of September with displays at home and overseas. In the afternoon of the 16th the Chipmunk team performed at RAF Biggin Hill and returned again on the 19th to prepare for a second appearance at the airfield in the Battle of Britain air show on the following day.

Spreading their wings farther afield, "The Red Arrows" gave displays at Monaco on the 13th, Cannes and Nice on the 14th, Biggin Hill on the 16th, Guernsey and Jersey on the 17th and 18th respectively, and Benson and Biggin Hill again on the 20th. Asking a lot of the pilots, groundcrew and supporting Hercules teams perhaps – not to mention the aeroplanes – but all went smoothly apart from one hitch on arrival at Biggin Hill when Sqn Ldr Phil Dunn's aircraft experienced a brake failure.

Team leader elect, Sqn Ldr Dennis Hazell flew with Ray Hanna to gain experience prior to taking over at the end of the 1969 season.

New version of the Jet Provost arrives

The first of a new fleet of the Jet Provost T.Mk.5, XW287, was delivered on 4 September and was joined by the second aircraft, XW288, on the 20th.

Jet Provost double ejection

On the 29 September, Staff QFI Flt Lt Francis of No. 2 Squadron and Flt Lt Foster a student on No. 250 Course, were forced to eject from Jet Provost T.3, XN576/79, following engine failure. Neither sustained injury.

Two "Arrows" Gnats abandoned!

During a practice session involving four "Red Arrows" Gnats over Kemble on 16 December 1969, two of the team's aircraft were abandoned in extraordinary circumstances. A description of the incident, published in the July edition of the 'Air Clues' magazine, is replicated below:

"This month's story relates the circumstances leading to the ejection of two pilots during a working up session of a rather famous aerobatic team.

No sooner had the latest version of the Jet Provost arrived at CFS, the pressurised Mark 5, than they were allocated to the Red Pelicans. The standard red and white FTC colour scheme was retained albeit with the addition of the team name on the fuselage and Pelican badge on the fin. (*Dave Newham*)

In order to fully understand and appreciate the cause of the accident it is essential to have certain background knowledge. Briefly, the team comprises nine members who fly in a basic 'Diamond 9' formation. Each member has a specific position within this basic pattern and is given a callsign which relates to his position. Once allocated, a callsign remains unchanged no matter what variations are played on the 'Diamond 9' theme. If, for example, a pilot is tasked to fly in the No. 3 position at the beginning of the season, he will assume the callsign 'Red 3' and retain this throughout the season. It will be used on every formation sortie he flies, be it practice or an actual display. There is good reason for this. The team performs a number of rapidly changing formation patterns and this calls for an acute awareness of everyone else's position within the formation at all times. It is achieved by constant practice and the association of a particular voice with a particular callsign. Having made this aspect clear, the story can be told.

Four pilots were briefed for a formation aerobatic flight in their Gnat aircraft. The aim of the exercise was to give a new team member some practice in flying his basic position in the 'Diamond 9' pattern. The pilot had been allotted the No. 8 position for the season and consequently his callsign was 'Red 8'. Because there were only four aircraft available for the practice, the full Diamond could not be flown, However this did not detract from the value of the exercise. The No. 8 occupies a position in the right hand side of the Diamond and so for the purpose of training this one man, only the right hand half need be flown. In consequence, on the particular day in question, the other three members of the formation were briefed to fill the remaining right hand slots although these were not necessarily their normal positions. The make up of the formation was as follows:

Red 1 flew in the No 1 position

Red 4 flew in the No 2 position

Red 7 flew in the No 6 position

Red 8 flew in the No 8 position.

The formation sequence went without a hitch and was completed with a 'bomb burst' over the airfield. The four aircraft then rejoined in line astern for a tail chase in the order Red 1, Red 7, Red 4 and Red 8. It was during the tail chase, while the aircraft were pulling over the top of a loop that a large flame suddenly spurted from the tail of the third aircraft (Red 4). The flame was 30 to 40 yds in length and spread almost back to the fourth aircraft. Red 8 was compelled to take avoiding action and he gave a warning over the R/T. In his urgency he said 'You're on fire last aircraft No. 7'. This he followed with a further message advising the pilot of the burning aircraft to shut down the engine.

Almost simultaneously with the warning the third aircraft (Red 4) realised that he was on fire. The warning system operated, there was a bang, and the engine lost power. At this stage he was inverted. As he rolled the right way up, the cockpit filled with smoke which obscured the instrument panel, and the controls became ineffective. He was at about 3,000 ft and had no alternative but to eject – and quickly. Unfortunately he did not have the time to make an R/T call before leaving his stricken aircraft.

The leader at this time, being ahead of the line astern formation, was unable to see what was happening but on hearing the warning pulled his aircraft round in order to view the situation. As he did so, the fourth aircraft (Red 8) reported that the rear seat of the burning aircraft had been ejected. This was in fact Red 4 ejecting in the front seat. The leader then saw the blazing Gnat, the flames having now reached alarming proportions. Believing that it was Red 7 who was on fire, and having been informed that only the rear ejection seat had gone, the leader called Red 7 and advised him of the seriousness of the fire.

Meanwhile, Red 7 had left the formation and checked his aircraft for signs of fire. He could find nothing amiss. However, having heard the original fire warning call which indicated that No. 7 was on fire, and subsequently being advised by his leader that the fire was serious, he became convinced that his aircraft was in a perilous state. This conviction was strengthened by a further call from the leader ordering him to eject. This he did.

Both the ejections were successful and the pilots were soon collected and returned to base. One was completely unharmed and the other had bruising of the legs which was not serious. The two aircraft were destroyed of course, but fortunately fell into open ground and did not inflict any damage to buildings or people."

In his response, Wg Cdr Spry said:

"There is little that I want to say about the accident to the fully serviceable Gnat (Red 7). It was caused by Red 8 misidentifying the aircraft ahead of him in the tail chase. Unfortunately, he had not remembered the briefed order of join up for line astern and in the urgency of the situation called out the wrong number. This was excusable because, as a new member in the team, the pressure was on him all the time in order to achieve the very high standard required. He had a lot to remember and was operating under very exacting conditions. I doubt if any of us can recall every word of the pre-flight brief once we are airborne and in the case of formation aerobatics this brief can be pretty comprehensive.

It is a pity that Red 4 did not have time to make an emergency call because, with the team's ability to associate voices and callsigns, the situation might have been retrieved. However he cannot be held to blame because it is obvious that he had to abandon his aircraft without delay."

After the two pilots ejected their aircraft (XR992 and XR995) crashed in fields near the village of Latton. Both crew were able to return to flying duties with the team.

1970

Instruction syllabus

Flt Lt Peter Bouch returned to Rissy as a 'Waterfront' QFI in January 1970. *"There was a good crowd on the Staff at the time, treating us as intelligent grown ups and allowing us to make our own decisions. Flying instruction comprised a Briefing followed by a Dual sortie (instructor/student), Mutual sortie (student/student), back again to Dual, and so on. The system seemed to work very well. We had three Marks of Jet Provost at our disposal: T.3, popularly known as variable noise – constant thrust; T.4, a lot better and could be good fun; T.5, more sophisticated but no better than the T.4."*

Back to Ris one last time

Having completed his exchange posting with the RAAF, Flt Lt Alan East returned to the UK and, having decided this was to be his last tour, he requested to return to Little Rissington.

"There was no immediate vacancy on the Gnats, which by now had moved to Kemble, so I spent five months instructing on the Jet Provost at Rissy. In mid-January 1970, I transferred to the Gnat Squadron, where my Boss was Malcolm Webber, one of my students on a UAS course at Leeming. Again, 'The Red Arrows' were at the other end of the corridor. In early June the Commandant, Air Cdre Hazlewood, came across for a few sorties on the Gnat and I was detailed to fly with him. This culminated in us flying as Red 11 to RAF Wildenrath, where the team were to display during the Open Day there. We flew XM708, the second Gnat that I had ever flown, and now the team's second spare aircraft which, although not modified to make smoke, etc., was painted as a Red Arrow. The rest of that summer was devoted to the routine of helping course members become competent instructors on the Gnat. I assumed that would continue until my 38th birthday in April 1972, the day I planned to retire from the RAF. Until Friday 13th November that is.

*'The Red Arrows' were practising over the airfield with four or five aircraft when the lead aircraft suffered an engine failure. Sqn Ldr Dennis Hazell immediately turned towards the runway, but on base leg it was obvious that he was too low to make it, so he ejected. Unfortunately, due to a malfunction of one leg restraining strap, he broke his thigh rather badly. In fact, so badly that he had to hug his flailing leg to his chest for fear of losing it, while sorting out how he was going to land on the good leg (*an account can be found at the end of the chapter*).*

Obviously he would not fly again for several months. Bill Loverseed was chosen from within the team as the new leader, but how to make the number up to nine again at short notice? I was asked if I was interested, but had to explain that it was too late for me because I had less than eighteen months still to serve. However, in the event my service was extended to the end of the year, which allowed me to complete two seasons."

One stoned Gnat

On 13 May, Gnat T.1, XR534, sustained Cat. 4 damage when it was struck by large hailstones. The pilot Flt Lt W. Tait managed to fly the aircraft safely back to Little Rissington, but it was several months before the aircraft was able to fly again.

Chipmunks and Varsities split

On 18 May the Chipmunks of 'A' Flight, No. 3 Squadron, were separated from the Varsity Flight and reformed as No. 5 Squadron. Flt Lt J. Sprackling was promoted to acting Squadron Leader and took command of the new Squadron.

Queen's Birthday Honours

The Queen's Birthday Honours List for 1970 included the award of the prestigious Air Force Cross to Flt Lt Peter Evans, a member of "The Red Arrows" from 1966 to 1969, and Flt Lt J.B. Robinson of Flying Wing.

The CFS story...my version

Flt Lt Bob Osborne joined the RAF in 1960 and was trained on Jet Provost, Vampire and Varsity aircraft. He was initially employed mainly in the transport fleet flying first Hastings and then Hercules aircraft after a spell as a student at Little Rissington.

"I arrived at RAF Little Rissington in 1970 following a tour flying Hercules in the Far East. I had neither volunteered to become an instructor neither had I refused; I was therefore as motivated for the CFS experience as anyone else on my course including one young flight lieutenant who later became Chief of the Air Staff. It might come as a surprise to some, but the students were nearly all conscripted into the system. There was no attempt to select those best qualified by ability or temperament and the idea of calling for volunteers had long since been discarded as the small supply always failed to meet the large demand. These randomly selected pilots were then given a course by instructor pilots, many of whom would have much preferred to be elsewhere.

At various points in the course the students were examined on their ability to impart information and techniques to the same persons who had conveyed the information to them in the first place. This rather incestuous system gave rise to the unofficial motto of the Central Flying School, 'Shut up! I explained.' In fairness the attitudes had improved since the Second World War where the average student pilot felt that the Germans were really rather nice people in comparison to the screaming psychopaths employed as instructors by the Royal Air Force.

There was then, an atmosphere of constrained animosity between the staff and the students. The traditional policy of giving any officer who failed the course his own choice of a posting had been ditched, so the normal service courtesies were still observed lest the alternative to instruction proved worse. Observed that is, at least until the final Dining Out night where the student who had come bottom of the course was awarded the 'Top Hat' prize and called upon for a speech. My course was well aware that the previous 'Top Hat' speech had resulted in the speaker being collected the next morning in the Commandant's car and taken for a rather heated career interview. We therefore chose the text with care; just

enough insolence to get noticed but not enough to give them an excuse for more verbal brutality. One course had cringingly thanked everyone for all their help, feeling constrained to mention one name, who, above all others, had contributed most to the success of their course. As certain egos were being polished around the room the speaker then continued: 'And in thanking SAC Fillingham of the battery charging section…'

Another course had been told that the Mess was planting a rose garden in the front flower bed and…hint hint, they might like to contribute. The speaker agreed with this idea and emphasised that the presentation would certainly indicate the respect that they all had for the concept of CFS. The gift arrived in the back of a lorry and several tons of prime horse manure was dumped on to the waiting ground.

It would be unfair not to acknowledge the small number of staff who were only too aware of the shortcomings of the system and who were constantly looking for ways in which to help their students. If only these critics had been listened to. I had the temerity to question the ground syllabus that covered Venetian-blind flaps and travel at Mach 5 in some detail; yet imparted no information on turbo-props; despite the Service owning some one hundred and fifty such aircraft. I later heard that the policy in Flying Training Command changed from one where the student was always at fault to the equally ridiculous concept that there are no bad students, only bad instructors. What should have been tried is some form of psychological assessment of the pilots under consideration for instructor duties.

The historical aspect of CFS was always of great interest to me, having started one of the few Museums in the Service. I was busy one day, surreptitiously typing an advert for my house on the ground school typewriter. One of the clerks commented how they were fed up with the students using that machine for their own personal work and showed me a framed letter that had also been typed in the ground school. It was a patent application for a new type of Aerial Propulsion by some chap called Flying Officer F. Whittle. I often wonder if they framed my letter as well.

I did achieve some recognition when I plotted to kill the then Commandant, Air Cdre Fred Hazlewood. It all started, when at my home near Bath, I saw and heard a hot air balloon pass overhead. Latching on to the idea with the enthusiasm of a certain Toad, I followed the device until it landed and then assisted with its recovery into a trailer. The balloonist turned out to be Mr Don Cameron who went on to find fame and success in that field. I soon found out that he had flown Chipmunks in the University Air Squadron and would welcome another such flight. Sensing that a deal could be cut, I approached the Commandant and he agreed to swapping a Chipmunk ride for Mr Cameron with a balloon ride for himself. With luck, I might be included.

It was late afternoon on 3 September 1970 when, having received dual instruction on a Chipmunk, Don felt obligated to erect his equipment. It was a warm sunny day but the North Westerly breeze failed to abate and caused him a little concern. Having accepted the largesse of CFS he felt that he must reciprocate despite frequent Scottish mumblings about unsuitable conditions. The Air Commodore arrived dressed in his blue flying suit and SD hat. We were briefed as the propane burner slowly inflated the bag and the basket was held fast to the ground by a bunch of Air Commodore groupies who had arrived on the scene. Don briefed that he would stand in the basket with one of us and when the balloon started to lift the other would run alongside and jump in. At this point the Commandant tapped me on the shoulder and muttered 'Good luck Osborne'.

There followed much roaring from the burner and grunts of efforts from the assembled sycophants. Then, with a final scream of 'Now' from Mr Cameron, the basket was released and the whole device drifted across the airfield at a prodigious and increasing pace with me running, skipping and clutching the basket. As it lifted from the ground I managed to pull myself over the edge of the basket and find a relatively safe position under the feet of the Commandant and what appeared to be a Scottish clog dancer. After a short while I struggled to my feet and started to enjoy the view. I had been given a primitive two way radio, and the other set,

(above) Superb view of Red Pelican Jet Provost T.5, XW293/86, gently rising over the Great Rissington road, (*David Newham*). *(below)* Red Pelican team pilots for the 1970 season with (*l to r*); Flt Lts Terry Francis, Ken Tait, Sqn Ldr Eric Evers and Flt Lt John Davy. (*John Davy*)

clutched in some squadron leader's sticky hands, could be seen disappearing behind us as the balloon climbed to around three hundred feet. Those left behind, but still desirous of impressing the Commandant with their general enthusiasm, followed us in a convoy headed by an ambulance and tailed by a staff car.

The three balloonists travelled some ten nautical miles across Oxfordshire in what must have been the first ascent of an Air Officer in a free balloon since the Service was formed. After 40 minutes airborne we descended rapidly into a large field and with considerable forward momentum hit the ground. Try as I might I was unable to stand on the Commandant and again became trapped under both him and the pilot as the balloon fell on its side and was dragged for some distance. Hoping that I had impressed the man with my general usefulness and uncomplaining attitude, I scrounged a lift back in his car.

It was difficult to ignore the fact that CFS was also home to the Red Arrows and the members were frequently seen hanging around the Mess even though their Gnats were safely locked away at Kemble. I found them a very pleasant bunch and felt rather irritated by some of the underhand remarks from certain CFS staff instructors who seemed to resent them taking time off in the week, despite their regular weekend commitments. With hindsight, I suppose that a certain amount of petty jealousy was to be expected.

Watching their practice displays, which occasionally took place at Rissington, was always good value. Even for the sluggards like me who were by now flying the Varsity. I was even roped in to crew one Varsity when it was deployed as the Air Commodore's barge to convey him back from Farnborough during the week of the air display. Rumour had it that the Arrows' performance had ruffled a few feathers at air rank and the Commandant was ordered to watch each Farnborough display so that he would be on hand to reprimand the pilots for over enthusiasm.

I eventually graduated and departed to the Hercules Operational Conversion Unit to start my life as an instructor. This was against the wishes of a couple of Squadron Leaders who felt that I should suffer the exposure to Flying Training Command like everyone else. I left one office with a benediction ringing in my ears that he would guarantee I would never return as an instructor on the staff. I was sorely tempted to ask that he put the promise in writing. Fortunately the Commandant, having himself been posted directly from CFS to the Lancaster OCU, took a more realistic attitude. I have to confess that I later sent several postcards to my good friends that I had made on the course and were now completing their stint in the system. With training flights to South America, the Caribbean and the Far East, the temptation was too great."

Near Russia with love

On 25 September, "The Red Arrows" departed their temporary base at RAF Gaydon, the runway at Kemble being resurfaced and updated, for a four-day visit to Finland. After re-fuelling at Aalborg in Denmark, the team flew on to Helsinki where it was due to give a display the following day. Because the powers that be decided that it was a hazardous flight, due to the unfriendly terrain and temperature, and the individual pilots should decide whether or not to take their backseaters, only two pilots felt confident about this – Flt Lts Dickie Duckett and Bill Loverseed. So only Ch Tech 'Tom' Thomas and Sgt John Stuart flew in the back seats on the outward and return flights. No sooner was the first display over than they were off again with a full 'Circus' crew in the back seats, for a second show at Turku, before re-fuelling and returning to Helsinki before dusk. On the 27th the team departed to display at Tampere accompanied by the Hercules which gave an unofficial display before bursting a number of tyres on landing. Spare wheels had to be flown out from the UK which generated a few questions! On the final day the team departed Helsinki for Gaydon, staging through Aalborg en-route. The Station Commander, Gp Capt Adams, accompanied the team on the trip.

"Red Arrow" ejection

On Friday 13 November 1970, Sqn Ldr Dennis Hazell was leading a formation of four or five aircraft in a practice session as part of the preparation for the 1971 season. As the formation approached Kemble Airfield the lead aircraft's engine suddenly and dramatically blew up and debris spewed out the back end. Sqn Ldr Hazell, his aircraft now without power, realised he was too low to reach the airfield and managed to eject. Although he landed in Kemble churchyard, Sqn Ldr Hazell sustained a badly broken leg due to the failure of one of the attachment points of one of the leg restraint straps during the initial stage of the ejection.

The cause of the engine failure was attributed to salt corrosion of the roots of the compressor blades. The solution was to wash the engines with clean water during a ground run followed by a mixture of paraffin and oil (OMD11) on a monthly basis. No. 4 Sqn aircraft seemed to be immune to the problem as it only occurred on the "Red Arrows" and 4 FTS aircraft. The deputy team leader, Flt Lt R.E.W. 'Bill' Loverseed assumed the role of team leader and Flt Lt Alan East was transferred from his duties as a QFI on No. 4 Squadron (Gnats) to fill the gap.

CHAPTER 6

Rundown and Closure

1971

Synchro-pair collide over Kemble

Some pilots on "The Red Arrows" had become concerned about the speed of response and power output at different throttle settings on the Orpheus engine when performing certain manoeuvres. A request was made to Rolls-Royce for checks to be carried out, but as the company maintained there was nothing wrong with the engines, the Team decided to fly the standard Synchro sequence with a couple of tradesmen in the rear seats, monitoring the settings and responses from the instruments and writing the data onto knee pads. The date was 20 January 1971 and with winter servicing still in full swing back at Rissy, no airmen were available, so two of the new team pilots, Flt Lts Colin Armstrong and John Lewis were installed in the seats behind Flt Lts Euan Perreaux and John Haddock. The aircraft, XR545 and XR986, collided while performing the Roulette manoeuvre and crashed onto the airfield, killing all four crew. Having just recovered from the loss of Dennis Hazell, this was worst accident rate endured by the team.

Station Photographer

Dave Newham has every reason to remember his eighteen-month tour at Little Rissington which began towards the end of 1969, not only for his promotion to Sergeant ten days after his arrival, but for the variety of events he attended in his capacity as Station Photographer. On one occasion Dave recollects,

"A USAF exchange officer, Captain Lord, was presented with a Vietnam medal during a Station parade that turned into a bit of a farce. The weather was foggy and soggy and nobody in the ranks could see the dais from the flights and Lord had trouble finding it through the murk. Not a good thing to do as Gp Capt Adams had a reputation of not being

Sgt Dave Newham, left, and Flt Lt Ken Tait disembark from their Army Scout in the grounds of the Weymouth convent. (*David Newham*)

the most tolerant of Station Commanders.

On another occasion, I was over at Kemble with the 'Red Arrows' when I met John Rigby (a civilian photographer known as Eleanor by the Team), who was doing a piece on the 'Arrows' for Cosmopolitan magazine. That morning, Sqn Ldr Dougie Marr, the solo pilot, was flying over to Ris to demonstrate the undercarriage roll to the AOC for display clearance. He told John that he would do some low passes for him on his return but when he realised that Rigby was going to shoot the take-off, he told me to get behind Rigby and stay prone if I wanted to get a good shot. So I took up my position deep in the dandelions and daisies and snapped away. As Dougie's height was estimated at four feet, it was no surprise to see Rigby diving to the ground as the Gnat's spear-like pitot head zoomed in at a high rate of knots."

Dave also went on a few displays with the "Reds". On one occasion, he flew to Hurn in an Argosy where the Gnats were refuelled and 'derved-up'. He then flew on to Weymouth for the display in an Army Scout together with Flt Lt Ken Tait. The landing site was to be in the grounds of a convent. The Army pilot was first to spot the site. *"I can see it, look down there, they're all outside...I can see their habits,"* he asserted. Ken peered down, *"They look like a lot of bloody penguins!"* he quipped. They duly landed and Mother Superior walked across the lawn to greet them. *"I'm so pleased you found us,"* she remarked brightly. *"Quite easy maam,"* Ken replied politely. *"We saw your habits from the air."* The Mother Superior laughed, *"Oh dear, we must have looked like a lot of penguins,"* to which Ken could only manage an uncomfortable smile.

Red Pelican team announced

During February the second CFS aerobatic team for the 1971 season, "The Red Pelicans", was formed. Flying the Jet Provost T.Mk.5, the team pilots were:

Flt Lt T. Francis	–	Team Leader
Flt Lt B. Donnelly	–	No. 2
Flt Lt M. Langham	–	No. 3
Flt Lt R. Lewis	–	No. 4

Sqn Ldr B.L. Woods, Officer Commanding No. 2 Squadron, was assigned as Team Manager.

Spitfire gets airborne

The area outside Station HQ previously occupied by Spitfire LA226, looked distinctly barren after it was removed to participate in the film, The Battle of Britain. This was remedied on 4 December 1970, when refurbished Spitfire LF.Mk.XVIe, TE356, was delivered to the station and mounted on a plinth by Station HQ. This aircraft also played a part in the film, albeit in a taxiing role only as it was not airworthy at the time.

New Waterfront 'customer' changes attitudes

Having been informed at the end of his course in 1954 that he would not find himself back at CFS, Wg Cdr James Shelley confounded that prediction and returned to Little Rissington as Chief Instructor in 1971.

"Since, on returning to Rissington and having to complete a QFI Refresher Course, there was ample opportunity to observe the 'Waterfront' at ground level, so to speak, before moving my kit over to Flying Wing HQ. One of the mildly disconcerting things was that, after so long an interval, there still remained something of a 'them' and 'us' complex. Since most of the student QFIs were experienced pilots with a lot to offer from their varied operational backgrounds, I felt that this experience should be given better recognition and took steps to encourage more integration within the squadrons. Fortunately in this I had the full support of the Squadron Commanders. Furthermore it did seem desirable for course members and their families to take a fuller part in the social life of the station. Therefore I augmented the barrel of beer, normally put on after completion of the handling phase, with a Flying Wing cocktail party for the staff, students and their wives, to which heads of sections from the other wings were also invited. This coincided with significant improvements to arrangements in the bar on a Saturday night, when there was good food and wine available. Taken together, I hope that student QFIs and their families were made to feel more welcome as members of our CFS Mess.

At the time when I was doing my own refresher, Pat Lewis became the new OC Examining Wing. We hit it off immediately and as I got to know more about the role and became aware of the helpful attitude of the examiners, I felt that CFS Instructors probably had something useful to learn from the Trappers. So, when it was decided to examine the Waterfront QFIs, I gave my full support and encouraged everyone to take it all in good part and to deliver a worthy result. Of course I had to put myself up first – what more natural than that I should opt to be tested by OC Examining Wing, a touch of the blind leading the blind!

My role as CI also embraced that of OC Flying Wing, with control of flying at Little Rissington and, subsequently, airfield services such as fire fighting and air traffic control. 'The Red Arrows' were detached to Kemble and, together with the Gnat element of CFS, came under the jurisdiction of Wing Commander Ops who travelled to Kemble daily.

Although 'The Red Arrows' came under the aegis of CFS, there was also a 'domestic' formation aerobatic team of four Jet Provosts – 'The Red Pelicans'. As a former team leader on a fighter squadron, I much enjoyed my supervisory flights with them and when the time came for official photographs, I was able to fly as a fifth member of the team, with the photographer talking me through some near impossible formation changes!

While the team produced an excellent standard of formation flying, the same could not be said for the staff as a whole. At this time we had quite a few who had come from large multi-engined aircraft and who had not had the opportunity to practise much formation flying in their previous operational roles. In order to remedy this situation, I established a programme of continuation training as a Friday afternoon 'treat'. Finding some convenient chinks in Air Staff Instructions, I was able to build these sessions up into formation drill for larger numbers of aircraft and eventually we were even ready to tackle battle formation as well. In due course we could now participate comfortably in successful fly-pasts, including a large letter 'A' for the departure of Station Commander Bill Adams. This new found enthusiasm was heartening, although I did have some difficulty persuading some QFIs to break and land in pairs!

The main change in training policy was the experimental introduction of a 'tutorial' system of training on the Jet Provost, conceived by Air Cdre Freddie Hazlewood, Commandant CFS at the time. Traditional procedure had been for an initial ground briefing of any instructional sequence by a Staff QFI, followed by a demonstration in the air and repetition by the Student QFI. Mutual practice with a fellow student followed before the 'give back' to the Staff instructor on a subsequent sortie before receiving the demonstration of the next lesson on the syllabus.

The Tutorial system was introduced with the idea of getting the student QFI to think more deeply about the requirements of the exercise rather than repeat each exercise more or less by parrot rote. At the same time it offered the attractive prospect of saving expensive flying hours. The essence was that, with some of the less demanding sequences, the student QFI was required first to discuss the principles with his staff instructor and next devise a way of presenting a particular exercise before carrying it out it in the air, without the benefit of a prior demonstration by the instructor. Although there were some weird and wonderful ideas at times, the system did make for a more thoughtful approach rather than an attempt at producing an exact repetition of the instructor's demonstration. Some of the simpler exercises, such as High Speed Flight in Jet Provosts, were not taught at all since the sequence was so straightforward.

Initially some significant savings were made in flying hours but gradually there was a reversion to the more traditional method for an increasing number of exercises, partly due to a 'belt and braces' attitude and some deep-rooted resistance to new ideas. Nevertheless, a compromise system was able to continue with some success until a student pilot at one of the Flying Training Schools got into difficulties and ejected during a solo High Speed Flight exercise. When it was discovered that his flying instructor had not been taught this particular sequence at CFS, it virtually sounded the death knell of what had started out as an imaginative innovation.

One thing I do remember about those most enjoyable dinners was the arrival of our Pelican mascot who was led up to the top table where the Commandant would take a tray of herrings and throw them one at a time for the Pelican to catch and store in his pouch. My tour as Chief Instructor came to an end all too quickly, lasting two years to the very day. My successor was already on the station poised to take over, whilst I found a little office tucked out of the way to finish all those annual confidential reports (F1369) for the staff officers of Flying Wing!"

Reunion Dinner receives special guest

The CFS Association held its 59th annual reunion dinner on 9 July in the Officers' Mess. HRH Prince Charles was the principal guest and during the evening he was invited to unveil a portrait of Sir Richard Atcherley, the late president of the association. *"By the time Prince Charles arrived at the ante-room for pre-dinner drinks we were all assembled,"* recalls Flt Lt Alan East, *"Noticing that we were all wearing name tags, he whispered something to his Equerry, who promptly disappeared.*

Guest of Honour at the 59th anniversary of CFS, HRH Prince Charles, flanked by Air Cdre Freddie Hazlewood to his left and MRAF Sir Dermot Boyle on his right. (*David Newham*)

He returned a few minutes later and pinned a medal ribbon bar to Prince Charles's lapel. On it was a strip of dymo-tape which read, 'Watch this space'".

New Mascot

On 7 January 1971, the newly graduated instructors of 254 Course revealed their well-kept secret, Patrick's replacement. At the graduation dinner a pink breasted pelican, named Frederick sporting a CFS bow tie waddled up to meet his new boss, Air Cdre Freddy Hazlewood.

Flt Lt Sierwald, a graduate of 254 course said *"We wanted to present a living memory of course 254 and not something which, like a piece of silver could be put in a drawer and forgotten. Fred seemed the ideal answer since a pelican forms part of the School's crest".*

Frederick, a South African Pink Breasted Pelican, was born near Lake Barigo, Kenya in 1968. Educated at the Birdland Institute of Zoology, Bourton-on-the-Water, he commenced his service in the General Duties Branch in the rank of Senior Under Pelican. After a 4-month probationary period, which included attendance at the Freedom of Cheltenham Parade, he was promoted to Plt Off on 1 May 1971. Plt Off Frederick was presented to HRH The Prince of Wales at the 59th Annual Reunion Dinner of the Central Flying School Association. Air Cdre F.S. Hazlewood, AOC and Commandant of CFS carried out the annual AOC's inspection on the 13 July. Normally parades such as these followed a standard format but this one included the presentation to all ranks of the School's new mascot, 'Frederick the Pelican', by the Commandant.

Frederick completed his first tour at Central Flying School on 6 May 1972, however, in view of his exemplary conduct and performance in duties he was promoted to Fg Off and re-posted to CFS. He continued to give good service, establishing healthy relations with the local community, attending parades, providing publicity for the RAF and so on until 1 May 1974, when he was promoted to Flt Lt.

Frederick enjoyed a long and active service as the CFS mascot and

A rare presentation indeed! Gp Capt Adams presents Long Service Medals to three Ch Techs, M. King, J. Ramsey and M. Thomas, all three of whom joined the service with the 75th Entry Apprentices at RAF Halton in 1953. (*Malcolm Thomas*)

died in December 1986 of 'natural causes'. A self-confessed career officer Frederick was once heard to say that his ambition was to become Commandant of the Central Flying School.

Triple presentation

In a rare presentation ceremony held on 1 November by Gp Capt M. Adams, Officer Commanding Little Rissington, long service medals were awarded to three SNCOs who joined the RAF on the same day in 1953 with 75th Entry Apprentices at RAF Halton. The proud recipients were; M. J. King, J. Ramsay and Malcolm Thomas (co-author of this book).

Rules of the Hunt

Many QFI primary memories record aspects of air instruction, so in a change of tempo an experienced QFI and former Hunter and Venom pilot, Flt Lt Mike Telford, recalls a ground-related incident, albeit in his words, 'rather more snide and gossipy than normal'.

"Once upon a time Gp Capt Adams, our stationmaster, allowed the local hunt the right of pursuit across the airfield, were the fox to decide to go that particular way. The day in question, with its 'normal' full flying programme, had quite specific orders issued to cover this exciting possibility. Most agreed that these directions in practice boiled down to: 'The hunt – with or without fox – has overall right of way'. That our said stationmaster was within months of retiring to live locally, as did most hunt members, is, it must be stressed, an entirely unrelated fact!"

Arrows gear up for next season

It was announced on 19 November that Sqn Ldr Ian Dick would take over as team leader of "The Red Arrows" from Sqn Ldr Bill Loverseed and that the 1972 display team would return to a nine aircraft formation.

'Tiger Squadron'

Sqn Ldr Michael Sparrow was posted to CFS on 1 February 1971, as OC 4 Squadron over at Kemble. Prior to CFS, he had completed a tour on 2 Sqn at RAF Valley.

"Here I had been mindful that our students would soon be in the front line, and that the next best thing to actual experience was to talk to someone who had had that actual experience, in this case the USAF with several bases in the UK, they were at war in Vietnam and they welcomed us with open arms. And so it was that on the last sortie of a Friday afternoon, 2 Sqn Gnats would land at any of the USAF bases, stay overnight and land back at Valley the next morning with students full of modern fighter tactics.

RAF Upper Heyford was home to the 20th Fighter Wing USAF and was but a short distance from Little Rissington. Soon it was quite usual for 4 Sqn CFS members to be seen at Upper Heyford whilst USAF members attended all our Kemble parties. It was at one of the parties at Upper Heyford that I was introduced to squadron commanders from many different nations. Enquiries of my host informed me that this was the Tiger Association, it met once per year and each squadron had a tiger in its badge. At this time all flew fighter aircraft. This seemed a good way to cement relations with our NATO allies, so I agreed to forward a copy of our tiger badge. Our Gnat aircraft was accepted as a fighter, modified for the training role.

Next morning my two senior students, Dave Roome and Mike Rigg, were 'asked' to design a 4 Sqn CFS Tiger badge which, as I recall, was ready by lunchtime. It showed a tiger leaping through a figure 4 and on its arrival at Upper Heyford assured our associate membership of the Tiger Association.

To record the occasion, we decided to take an airborne photograph of our 'Tiger' Gnat, XS109/A, and this occurred on Thursday, 9 December 1971. It is the only photo to my knowledge of a 4 Sqn Gnat with the unofficial 4 Sqn badge on the tail fin. Flt Lt Bill Blair-Hickman was in the front seat and Flt Lt Des Sheen in the rear. The photo aircraft pilots were myself in the front seat with camera and fellow QFI Flt Lt Dave Longden in the rear."

A regular sight around Little Rissington during the winter months, the Heythrop Hunt is seen assembled outside the Officers' Mess. It was not unknown for flying to be curtailed as the fox was chased across the airfield. (*Ron Dunn*)

Gnat crashes at USAF base

On the following Monday, 13 December, Mike Sparrow briefed and led a formation of four Gnats on an SCT formation practice. *"A fly past over RAF Upper Heyford was carried out at 1,000 ft followed by a break where individual aircraft were to overfly at 500 ft prior to rejoining the formation. Dave Longden was flying XR567 as No. 4 with Dick Storr as his student, when the fin of the aircraft suddenly detached from the fuselage and both pilots were killed when the aircraft crashed on the runway."*

Inspection of the fin on XR981/J revealed serious cracking and all Gnats, including those on "The Red Arrows", were grounded for inspection. Both pilots were interred at Little Rissington village churchyard.

Flt Lt Bill Blair-Hickman holds Gnat T.1, XS109, in the vertical while Sqn Ldr Mike Sparrow takes the photograph. The unofficial 4 Sqn 'Tiger' badge can be seen on the tail fin. (*Mike Sparrow*)

Station Strength

	Staff Off'rs	WOs	SNCOs	Cpls & Below
RAF	137	12	139	397
WRAF	4	—	2	51

Over the year this was an unusually high increase in male numbers with Staff Officers rising by 19% and Airmen by 14%.

Air Traffic Movements

Daytime

	Jets	Piston
January	3924	1560
February	5888	3166
March	4564	2478
April	2294	2496
May	4640	2712
June	3322	2632
July	2372	1960
August	4972	2678
September	3298	2078
October	2912	3414
November	7011 (combined totals)	
December	3545 (combined totals)	

Night time

	Jets	Piston
January	842	0
February	106	748
March	110	114
April	878	0
May	28	544
June	56	398
July	552	0
August	2	728
September	58	276
October	778	32
November	1262 (combined totals)	
December	415 (combined totals)	

1972

New Year's Honours

The year began on a high note with an announcement of New Year's Honours.

Sqn Ldr D.S.B. Marr	-	AFC
Sqn Ldr M.J. Webber	-	AFC
Sqn Ldr N.R.W. Whitling	-	Queen's Commendation
Flt Lt J.E. Stuart	-	MBE
Flt Lt M.J. Hannam	-	AOC-in-C's Commendation
Ch Tech K.J. Mayo	-	AOC-in-C's Commendation
WO L.C. Ludlow	-	AOC's Commendation
Sgt D.B. Sampson	-	AOC's Commendation
Cpl W.A. Hay	-	AOC's Commendation
Cpl P.A. Laslett	-	AOC's Commendation
Cpl O.M. Scammell	-	AOC's Commendation
Mr L.J. Coventry	-	AOC's Commendation
Mr W.R Dixon	-	AOC's Commendation

30 years' service at Little Rissington

After completing 30 years of service as a civilian employee, Mr Day of the Officers' Mess staff retired on 5 January. On behalf of his colleagues, the Station Commander presented him with a handsome wall barometer.

Change of Commandant

On 7 January, the Commandant, Air Cdre F.S. Hazlewood, was dined out at the Officers' Mess. Four days later, senior officers held a welcoming party for the new Commandant, Air Cdre R.H. Crompton.

Flying hours by type

Despite the usual battle with the January weather and a grounding of the entire Gnat fleet for most of the period, a creditable number of flying hours was achieved for the month:

Aircraft Type	Hours	Landings
Vampire T.11	0	0
Meteor T.7	0	0
Jet Provost T.3	309.00	978
Jet Provost T.4	19.20	36
Jet Provost T.5	186.50	578
Gnat T.1 – Course	15.35	72
Gnat T.1 – Team	51.30	132
Varsity T.1	135.20	308
Chipmunk T.10	316.55	1177

Gnat fin modification

As soon as the failure of the fin was confirmed as the cause of the crash of XR567 in December 1971, the CFS Gnats were despatched to Hawker Siddeley's base at Bitteswell for modification. The first aircraft to return to Little Rissington arrived on 19 January and Staff flying began using this aircraft on 25th. At the conclusion of this, the aircraft was flown over to Kemble to enable course flying to recommence.

Aircraft movements

	Little Ris	Aston Down
Day	5603	526
Night	428	0
Total	6031	526

Jet Provost aerobatic team

HQ Training Command authorised the re-formation of the "Red Pelicans" aerobatic team for another year, under the managership of Sqn Ldr J.R. Johnson. Team pilots comprised:

Flt Lt C. Mitchell	-	Leader
Flt Lt R. Lewis	-	No. 2
Capt R.F. Lord, USAF	-	No. 3
Flt Lt P. Tait	-	No. 4

Got to keep them flying

With poor weather having prevailed throughout February, it became necessary to send six Jet Provosts north to RAF Kinloss on the 29th to allow at least some flying to proceed. CFS Varsities acted as support aircraft, ferrying up the remaining instructors and students. Three instructors and six students remained behind just in case the local weather improved. The JPs managed to fly non-stop to Kinloss but were forced to stage through RAF Leeming on the return flight due to strong headwinds.

The Tutorial System

In March 1972, Flt Lt Peter Bouch helped pioneer what became known as 'The Tutorial System' of instruction. *"Each particular session of the course began with a ground tutorial and this was followed by both the Mutual Flight and Dual sortie (give back, correct and polish where needed). It worked reasonably well and was adopted as the norm. I must admit that I didn't like it particularly and preferred the 'old system'! Coupled with this, the Educators insisted that air testing and assessments should be objective, which caused big, long arguments. We said things could never be wholly objective but must inevitably be partly subjective."*

Aero teams gear-up

As the weather improved so did aircraft serviceability and this enabled both "The Red Arrows" and "The Red Pelicans" to sustain a high level of training and display practice. No fewer than 569 sorties were completed by the "Arrows" during the month, mostly at Kemble but also at RAF Manston and RAF Valley when the weather closed in. The "Pelicans" were content to consolidate their manoeuvres down to 5,000 ft over some eleven practice sessions, some of which were also flown from Valley.

RAF Benevolent Fund

On 13 April, Air Marshal Sir William Coles, Controller of the RAF Benevolent Fund, presented the Fund's poignard (dagger) to the Station Commander who received it on behalf of the Station. The presentation was made in recognition of the Station's donation of £12,394 to the Fund from the previous year's Open Day. Until then it was the highest donation ever made to the Fund.

This was to be one of the last yet most pleasurable duties for Gp Capt Adams as he handed over command of Little Rissington to Gp Capt R.J. Barnden four days later.

Aerobatic team activities

One of the new Station Commander's first tasks was to attend "The Red Arrows" Press Day on 25 April, during which the RAF Regiment Band played the first public performance of the aerobatic team's new march, composed by Flt Lt E. Banks. Meanwhile, "The Red Pelicans", having completed thirty practice sessions during the month, were cleared down to 500 ft by the Station Commander. Sixteen public displays were booked for the team, the first of these taking place on 20/21 May at Spangdahlem and Oerlinghausen in Germany and Shaffen in Belgium. And the two vintage jets were not forgotten, both the Vampire and Meteor having returned from a winter repaint by 5 MU at Kemble in their original silver and yellow training colours to undertake a secondary role on the airshow circuit.

Ups and downs on the "Arrows"

"The Red Arrows" seldom cancelled public displays, and it was uncommon for show organisers to cancel at short notice, but one such cancellation occurred on 6 May when their scheduled display at Glasgow was stopped by a local turkey farmer who obtained a Court Order banishing the team from the area. The disappointment was short lived, however, as the team departed for a month-long tour of the United States on 15 May. Support was provided by two Hercules transports. Displays were given at many venues, the most prominent of which included Goose Bay, St Catharines, Trenton, plus two photo sorties over the Niagara Falls, another over Washington DC, and culminating with eight displays during ten days at Dulles International Airport in front of audiences of 160,000, and a further two at Reading.

Queens' Birthday Honours

Mr J.D. Stevens	-	MBE
Flt Sgt J.H. Millar	-	BEM
Ch Tech D.G. Dicker	-	BEM
Sgt A.P. Bryant	-	AOC's Commendation
Sgt D.N.M. Crowe	-	AOC's Commendation
Sgt A.H.L. Fisher	-	AOC's Commendation
Sgt H.E.B. Hood	-	AOC's Commendation
J/T S. Toone	-	AOC's Commendation

One hungry bird!

As the AOC's inspection of the Station was about to conclude with a march-past in front of the dais, Fg Off Frederick showed a complete lack of discipline, not in keeping with his recent promotion, by attempting to bite the Commandant while being congratulated on his turnout.

Catching Concorde

In May 1972, Sqn Ldr Mike Sparrow received a priority signal from the MoD stating that approval had been given for a Gnat to fly a photographer to film Concorde as part of a normal training sortie. Arthur Gibson had become a good friend of Mike's over the years, and of course was famous for his films of "The Red Arrows" and his thousands of photos depicting all sorts of air activity.

> *"The idea of getting photos of Concorde was entirely his and took a great deal of perseverance. The briefing with John Cochrane, who was to fly Concorde during our photo shoot, was fairly short, covering mainly the R/T frequencies and emergencies. 'Flown formation, have you?' he asked. 'Since I was knee high to Pontius,' I replied. 'Ok, don't hit me' – and that was that.*
>
> *By 18 May I had positioned two Gnats at Little Rissington. Once the initial checks had been carried out on Concorde (ATC Fairford to ATC Little Rissington), Arthur and I lashed ourselves into 'H' (XS101) with Arthur in the front seat. When word came that Concorde was taxiing we started and got airborne. At full throttle we caught Concorde on take off and stayed with her for an initial climb to around 30,000 ft, taking many photos. Overhead Valley we left and Concorde went into the Irish Sea supersonic area. We hurried back to Little Rissington where we leapt at once into the other Gnat, got airborne and caught Concorde coming back to Fairford. Again many photos were taken, including one from the ground of Concorde in company with a Gnat passing through the overhead of Little Rissington.*

Two flashbacks stand out in my memories of that day:

> *Arthur – 'Ask John to put reheat in so that I can catch the flame in the shot.' Me – 'Okay.' Press R/T. 'John, could you engage reheat?' John – "Yes, but I'll have to stabilise JPTs first on these prototype engines.' Me – 'Roger.' What we had not understood was that to stabilise JPTs John*

had to go to full throttle, sit there for about 10 seconds, then engage reheat. By the time flame appeared, Concorde was about 5 miles away. Arthur – 'Think we'll give that a miss.'

Coming into land at Fairford Concorde increased its angle of attack and condensation was formed as a cloud over its wing, making a fantastic sight from our position. On landing I asked Arthur what settings he'd used on his cameras to catch the wing cloud. His reply was unprintable as he'd been in the middle of changing magazines!"

Royal High Flyer

In July 1972, Mike Sparrow was informed that he was to fly HRH Prince Michael of Kent in a Gnat during his visit to CFS. On the 17th a Gnat was flown into Little Rissington from Kemble ready for the Prince's visit on the following day.

"The ground crew and I were in spanking new overalls, the aircraft positively gleaming. Dawn revealed a dank, drizzly, low cloud day. HRH arrived in his purple Triumph Stag and was whisked off to meet VIPs and carry out the bad weather programme. By 11:00 the portents were good for an afternoon sortie – and so to the official lunch. Now, one thing Little Rissington did extremely well was to look after visiting dignitaries, especially the Royal Family. After all, the Queen Mother was our Commandant-in-Chief. However, it was with some trepidation that I watched HRH consume his strawberries and good Devonshire clotted cream!

We got airborne shortly after 14:00 and climbed to around FL 150 for HRH to see the general handling he had requested. During the climb he remarked on how quiet it all was, so I set off explaining how our new helmets kept most of the noise at bay. But no, that wasn't it – 'The radio is so quiet, nobody seems to be talking except when you want them to,' he said. I then explained about the purple area we were in, the strict radio silence in case of emergency and all the radar units watching us. He remarked sadly, 'Can't get away from them even up here.'

He appeared to genuinely enjoy the handling of the aircraft and flew it himself on a number of occasions. High g manoeuvres and aerobatics caused a momentary silence but an offset Tacan let down to Little Rissington soon got him buzzing with questions. He would have loved a low level navigation sortie but I was not authorised for that. However, we could do a low level fly past at Little Rissington at his special request so, after completing two circuits, we flew low over his entourage (not too low) and finally landed. As we completed our shut down checks I could see that the low fly past might have caused some consternation among some of the senior officers so, as I helped HRH from the cockpit, I asked him in a loud voice if he had enjoyed the REQUESTED low fly past. With a twinkle in his eye he replied in an equally loud voice, 'Splendid.'

The final twist in this tale came as I said goodbye to Prince Michael in the Officers' Mess car park. Number 4 Sqn CFS was a member of the Tiger Association and his beautiful purple Stag was now covered in yellow tiger paw marks! I mumbled something about sending me the bill, but he just laughed and said he thought he had got off rather lightly. I never did find out for sure who had done it."

No suspensions

When No. 260 Course graduated on 7 July, it became the first course on record to complete with no suspensions. Thirty-eight students started the course and thirty-eight graduated. Students on Course No. 262 witnessed two innovations: firstly, students selected for training on the Gnat joined 4 Squadron at the end of the Ground School phase without intermediate training on the Jet Provost; and secondly, the split system of Flying and Ground School was changed so that half the course were in Ground School for the whole day while the other half were flying.

Life-long servant

Another life-long member of the civilian staff to serve at RAF Little Rissington was Mr C.R.S. Arthurs who was presented with a CFS badge by Gp Capt Barnden in September to mark the completion of 34 years service in the MT section.

4 Squadron CFS Course Gnat T.1s on formation take-off from Kemble with XR981/J in the lead and XS109/A and XM706/D on either wing. (*Mike Sparrow*)

'Bo' Morris

On 4 July Sqn Ldr T.A. Warren attended the funeral of Mr 'Bo' Morris on behalf of the Commandant. The late Mr Morris was Landlord at the Old New Inn in Bourton-on-the-Water and had formed a close relationship with CFS over many years.

Supporting the Arrows

When former CFS student Flt Lt Bob Osborne was a pilot on the staff of the Hercules OCU, he and another instructor were detailed to fly the support aircraft for an overseas trip with "The Red Arrows" one weekend in July 1972.

"We were to collect the Arrows ground crew and equipment from Manston and basically chase the team around Europe. We met the team in the Officers' Mess just in time for their first briefing about the flight over to RAF Brüggen. We were totally impressed by the way the leader briefed from one armchair whilst the team paid rapt attention...to the Telegraph crosswords. The only interest they showed was in glancing in his direction when he mentioned something about playing bingo.

Following a night stop, the chase began. I seem to remember that we followed them to Gütersloh and then, en route to Friedrichshaven, which is close to the Swiss border, the trail went cold. We blundered on southwards asking all the air traffic centres within range if they had noticed ten red aircraft passing their way. Eventually, acting more on rumour than fact, we called up a place called Soellingen, near the French border. They rapidly admitted to hiding the team and we arrived in time to see them leave.

The night stop in Friedrichshaven, the home of the Zeppelin, was memorable. We found that the team, far from being prima donnas, always insisted on their ground crew and support crew being invited to functions. We were collected in police cars (nothing unusual there for a transport crew) taken down to a jetty and ferried across the lake to Constance. It was the night of the annual firework display and we were soon to find out that the locals used floats out on the lake from which to launch the fireworks. The police launches that were carrying the party decided that being military, we would appreciate a close look and took us through the display itself. At least we then knew how a thousand bomber raid had felt.

Dinner was in a former monastery and we were entertained by various local dignitaries and some charming young public relations ladies. Our navigator started the ball rolling by telling the mayor how delighted he was to be there as he had always wanted to visit Switzerland. The mayor leant over, fixed him with a very Germanic stare and told him 'Pity, mein freund, you are still in Germany!'

I meanwhile was receiving considerably more adulation than I was used to from one young lady, until she looked at one of the Arrows handouts and couldn't find me in the group photograph. (I can't imagine how the confusion came about). I managed to convince her that Bill Aspinall stood in for me in photo-calls on account of his extreme good looks, but I acted as his stunt double and did all the flying. Bill, bless him, nodded in agreement throughout the explanation.

The following morning we waited on the ramp as the Arrows departed. We were parked opposite the afore-mentioned dignitaries and as Red Ten passed upwind of them, he elected to check the smoke facility. We started our engines to the accompaniment of loud coughing from the crowd. The return to Kemble was via Wildenrath and we left the team at their base to return to RAF Thorney Island.

With the withdrawal of the last Meteors and Vampires from RAF service at Exeter and Shawbury, it was decided to retain single examples of each type at CFS. Repainted all-over grey with yellow training bands, Meteor T.7, WA669 and Vampire T.11, XH304, became popular participants as the Vintage Pair at air shows until they collided and crashed in 1986. *(Barry Jones)*

The collection of signed photographs that I brought back for my two young daughters greatly increased my status on the home front."

Busy month on Aeros

There were few, if any, units within the RAF that could equal CFS for the number of solo and formation display teams it provided in any one year. The climax to the season usually occurred in September and the organisation, intensity and sheer hard work involved in fulfilling its commitments, many of which were overseas, can be gauged from the 1972 September schedule (dates in brackets). They speak volumes for the personnel involved:

Red Arrows: The Gnat Team gave 14 displays during the month; Münster, Germany (3rd), Farnborough (4th - 10th), Guernsey and Jersey (14th), Finningley and Biggin Hill (16th), Schwenningen, Germany (23rd), and Schwenningen and Köln/Bonn (24th).

Red Pelicans: The Jet Provost Team gave two displays in Germany, at Münster (3rd) and Linkenheim near Karlsrühe (24th), at St Athan (14th), where Sqn Ldr Johnson flew as number No. 4 in the absence of Flt Lt P. Tait, St Mawgan and St Athan (16th), and finally at Linton-on-Ouse on the 20th for the Aerobatic Meet for all Training Command aerobatic teams and solos.

CFS Vintage Training Flight: Synchronised displays were flown in the Vampire T.11 and Meteor T.7 at Sibson, near Peterborough (10th), Biggin Hill (12th), and Abingdon, Biggin Hill and Wattisham (16th).

Jet Provost Solos: The JP Solo Display pilot performed at Sibson (10th), Biggin Hill (12th), Guernsey and Jersey (14th), Biggin Hill (16th), and Linton-on-Ouse (20th).

Chipmunk Solos: The Chipmunk Solo Display pilot gave displays at Finningley (16th) and Linton-on-Ouse (20th).

By November, consideration was being given to the composition of the teams for 1973 and Sqn Ldr I.C. Gibbs, OC No. 2 Squadron, was selected to lead a multi-service "Red Pelican" team. Capt R.F. Lord USAF was allocated the No. 2 position with Flt Lt W.B. Byron RAAF alongside at No. 3 and Lt M. Edwards RN in the Box. Meanwhile, over at Kemble a number of Gnats were borrowed from 4 FTS at Valley to enable continuation training on "The Red Arrows" and to bring on two new pilots; Flt Lts B. Donnelly (the previous year's Team Manager) and D.J. Sheen.

Awards

The Station Commander presented Long Service (LSM) and Good Conduct Medals (GCM) to Ch Tech G. Taylor and Sgts F. Bird and T. Smith, and General Service Medals (GSM) to Cpl R. Mitchell and J/T S.N. Faulkner. The SWO, G. Hobbs and WO R. Williams, the Servicing Controller, both of whom joined the RAF with 34th Entry at Halton, received clasps to their LSMs.

1973

New Aircraft Project Teams

It was quite unusual for one RAF unit to be entrusted with introducing two new and widely differing aircraft types into service simultaneously, but CFS was about to go through the experience with the Bulldog and the Jetstream. The former had been ordered in quantity to replace the RAF's ageing Chipmunks and the latter as a Varsity replacement.

Established on 1 January 1973, the Bulldog Project Team consisted of Flt Lts R.J. Hutcheson and I.C. Ray. In order to familiarise themselves with both the aircraft and its manufacturer, they spent the week beginning 8 January with Scottish Aviation at Prestwick and visited Pandeck Instrument Laboratories on 22nd of the month. A demonstration flight in a Bulldog lasted 25 minutes.

The Jetstream Project Team was assembled at the same time and consisted of Sqn Ldr R.C. McKinlay and Flt Lt A.J. Oldfield. They decided to commence their assignment by making visits to a number of RAF bases operating a variety of multi-engined aircraft types.

JP Squadrons reorganise

Shortly after Sqn Ldr R Johnson relinquished command of No. 1 Squadron, the two Jet Provost squadrons were combined into an enlarged No. 2 Squadron on 19 February under the command of Sqn Ldr I.C. Gibbs: the former 1 and 2 Squadrons becoming A and B Flights respectively.

An Examiner's lot

Having spent three years instructing on Jet Provosts at Ris, Flt Lt Peter Bouch was invited to become an Examiner on the Examining Wing and transferred in April 1973.

"In those days the Wing did its own thing selection-wise and I was invited to join a good team of blokes doing a good job. When checked out, you were classified Examiner on all appropriate types, even if you hadn't flown them before, and Command Instrument Rating Examiner (CIRE) on all types. I flew 27 different types during my three year tour on the Wing! I think Examining Wing did a good job (not trapping but examining) and were respected by the rest of the RAF as a genuine independent force – also by most foreign countries.

I found by far the most difficult part of the job came when one had to fail someone, luckily not too often. I made a point of never asking a question that I didn't know the answer to in case of having to explain it and I was told that when re-cating an instructor, if there was any doubt – then there was no doubt.

I also saw the arrival of the first Bulldogs – in fact collected two from Prestwick.

We had many students from everywhere and all ranges of experience, from 'creamies', who were usually very good if lacking in experience, to old hands with pretty variable skills. Interestingly, not all students were

volunteers and assessed as above average – in fact reading the F5000s, some were clearly 'got rid of' to CFS!

We did refresher courses, tailored to individual needs, experience and currency. I was presented with our first ever German student – 'Hello Gunter, tell me about your QFI course and experience'. 'Ja, I am off fighters and am PAI', he replied. So he got a 'one' off, very individual QFI course, went to Cranwell where he got more hours than anyone else and an A2 to boot, so all was well.

I felt it was a shame that Rissy closed – CFS was never the same again. I went back there in the late eighties as CFS Gliding Examiner – the place still looked the same, the quarters, the main station buildings and airfield were all in good nick, but by that time apart from the Gliding School, it was a reserve war hospital for the USAF. I got a tour of the hangars – full of operating theatres and intensive care units – enough goodies to cure the current shortfall in the NHS in one stroke!"

From V-bombers to the humble JP

Having trained on the Jet Provost and Vampire, Keith Wilson-Clark went on to fly Valiant tankers with 214 Sqn, Victors with 55 Sqn and Dominies with 1ANS at RAF Stradishall as a staff pilot. Flt Lt Wilson-Clark says,

"I finally escaped to Rissy to join No. 265 Course in April 1973. The summer that year was the hottest for a long time and Rissy in those conditions was six months of bliss. Flt Lt Colin Griffiths and myself narrowly avoided Victor OCU ground school postings so it was doubly wonderful. The first thing to do on hearing the news was to fly a Victor over there for a couple of visual circuits to have a look at our new home. First impressions, awfully small, awfully busy and they didn't really like tankers cluttering up their circuit. We thought we could fly but the JP conversion quickly disabused us of that idea, how we had stayed airborne for the past years without harm was a mystery. Then the first solo. All the original feelings coupled with, well I will never get back without a nav! The course was the most professional and hard working I had done, surrounded by some really seriously good people, no high adventure but satisfying to achieve."

Flt Lt Hutcheson approaching Little Rissington in XX515 accompanied by Rt Hon Anthony Lambton MP. (*CFS Archive*)

New Station Warrant Officer

Nearly thirty years after his first tour at Rissy, Gill Davies returned to take up his post as Station Warrant Officer. *"When I arrived it was obvious that both discipline and morale was very low and I was tasked by the CO to turn both around. To help achieve this I organised lectures by senior officers for all SNCOs and below in the main lecture hall. Subjects included the duties and tasks undertaken by various personnel, outlining their specific roles in the CFS organisation and their importance for the wellbeing of the station. Those ground personnel who wished to fly were offered the opportunity and arms and foot drill sessions were re-introduced to a number of NCOs and junior ranks for a reformed Guard of Honour which received the many Royal visitors and VIPs to the station."*

First Bulldog arrives

The Acting Station Commander, Wg Cdr J.V. Radice, accompanied by the Commandant, greeted the first Bulldog T.Mk.1, XX515, painted in RAF colours to arrive at Little Rissington on 23 March. The aircraft was flown in from 5 MU at Kemble by Wg Co I.D. Brimson, OC Examining Wing, and Flt Lt R.J. Hutcheson, Project Officer on the team responsible for the introduction of the Bulldog in the instructional role.

No sooner had XX515 landed at Little Rissington than its crew, Wg Cdr Ian Brimson and Flt Lt Hutcheson, were greeted by Air Cdre Crompton and CFS staff. (*CFS Archive*)

On the following day, The Parliamentary Under Secretary of State for the RAF, the Rt Hon Antony Lambton MP, visited Little Rissington and flew with Flt Lt Hutcheson in the Bulldog

Photo shoot

"The Red Arrows" rendezvoused with Concorde 002, piloted by Mr P. Cochrane, over the Bristol Channel and then flew in formation to RAF Fairford on 10 April. Team leader Sqn Ldr Ian Dick presented Mr Cochrane with a photograph of the formation taken by Arthur Gibson from a chase aircraft, and a Red Arrows tie as an honorary member of the Team during a Press Day held on 10 April at Little Rissington.

The number two team, "The Red Pelicans", had meanwhile perfected their formation aerobatics and were cleared down to 500 ft in time to give their first display of the season at Little Rissington on 13 April, for the Under Secretary of State for the RAF.

The CFS Historic Training Flight, which comprised the Vampire T.11 and Meteor T.7, was re-christened "The Vintage Pair" in time for the beginning of the display season.

Reorganisation

Changes to the organisation were introduced on 16 April by which the Operations Wing was disbanded and responsibility for Air Traffic Control, the Met Office and Fire Section was transferred to Flying Wing. As a result certain posts were renamed; Wg Cdr Ops became OC Kemble Detachment, Sqn Ldr Ops became Deputy Chief Instructor (Ops), and Sqn Ldr Training became Deputy Chief Instructor (Training).

Queen's Birthday Honours

Recipients for this year's Queen's Birthday Honours were:

Flt Sgt D.R Fisk	–	AOC-in-C's Commendation
Cpl W.A. Hay	–	AOC-in-C's Commendation
Cpl R. Hearfield	–	AOC-in-C's Commendation
Cpl D. Emerton	–	AOC's Commendation
Cpl C. Williams	–	AOC's Commendation
Mr A.T. Harris	–	AOC's Commendation

The Jetstream T.Mk.1

Originally conceived by Handley Page for the civilian market in the early sixties, it was 1972 before the RAF adopted a military version of the Jetstream as the T.Mk.1, to replace the elderly Varsity in the multi-engined navigation trainer role. An order was placed with Scottish Aviation Ltd for 26 aircraft. To speed up deliveries, the first two aircraft were conversions of civilian aircraft bought second-hand in the USA by SAL, and allocated the serial numbers XX475 and XX476. XX475 was delivered to the A&AEE at Boscombe Down on 26 July for acceptance trials, and it was flown into Little Rissington on at least one occasion before production Jetstream, XX477, arrived at Little Rissington on 30 September.

The Jetstream Project Team, which came together earlier in the year, could now get on with the task in hand. Part of the work-up involved cross-country trials, instrument and airways flying. One of the flights was to Malta and on the way back both engines began to run unevenly so the crew diverted to Nice. Once there the problem was attributed to the wrong fuel being used at Malta.

Standing in front of the first Jetstream, XX477, to arrive at Little Rissington are, (*l to r*); Sqn Ldr A. Gregory, Wg Cdr O. Corderey, A.N. Other, Air Cdre R. Crompton, CFS Commandant, John Blair, Jetstream Test Pilot, Scottish Aviation, Gp Capt R. Barnden, Station Commander, Sqn Ldr R. McKinlay, Jetstream Project Leader, A.N. Other, A.N. Other, Flt Lt A. Oldfield, Jetstream Project, Wg Cdr P. Harle, A.N. Other. (*Adrian Balch*)

World Helicopter Championships

The Commandant flew into Middle Wallop on the occasion of Air Day and World Helicopter Championships, held over the three days 26 to 28 July. The RAF was represented by a team from No. 3 Squadron CFS (H) from RAF Tern Hill comprising Sqn Ldr I.A.I. Smith (Team Manager) and Flt Lts N.R.W. Hibberd (pilot) and T.W. Eyre (crewman) flying in a Whirlwind Mark 10. The results for the first three individual places were:

Gold Medal	–	Russia	–	847 points
Silver Medal	–	RAF	–	828 points
Bronze Medal	–	Austria	–	822 points

For the team event, Flt Lts Hibberd and Eyre were joined by a Royal Navy crew flying a Wessex and an Army crew flying an Alouette Mark 2 to form a Combined British Services team. They came a creditable first equal with the team from Russia.

Accidents

On 26 November, a Bulldog of No. 1 Squadron, XX542, sustained Cat. 2 damage when it lost a nosewheel while carrying out a roller landing on the southern grass strip. It subsequently made a safe landing on runway 23. The crew, Flt Lt Bairstow and Fg Off Othman Tentku were both students who were flying a mutual sortie and were unhurt.

On the following day, Varsity WF411 of No. 3 Squadron sustained Cat. 5 damage when the take off was aborted. Although the aircraft left the runway and came to rest beyond the airfield perimeter, there were fortunately no casualties.

Mayhem in the circuit!

Flt Lt Sandy Sawyer (née Rummins), was posted to Little Rissington from RAF Linton-on-Ouse as an Air Traffic Control officer in 1973, together with her husband Sqn Ldr Peter Sawyer who took up his position as OC Operations. From their position in the control tower, one of the major everyday headaches encountered by the controllers was the very mixed circuit in operation, as Sandy explains. *"In effect, we operated two circuits at Rissy – an inner circuit from the grass for the slow moving Chipmunks and Bulldogs and an outer circuit from the main runway for heavier and faster aircraft such as the Varsities, Jet Provosts and the occasional Gnat. It was a nightmare!"*

Station Commander says Farewell

Little Rissington bade farewell to Gp Capt R.J. Barnden on 21 December 1973, his last official day as Station Commander. In true Rissy tradition, he was 'ceremoniously borne' from Station Headquarters to the Officers' Mess on the "Greasy Spoon" constructed on a surplus trolley by Engineering Wing. The origins of this rather odd mode of conveyance it seems began with the Group Captain's insistence that the Aircrew Buffet remained in No. 2 Hangar, the hot seat of Engineering Wing's power.

1974

Miners' strike and the fuel crisis

The nineteen seventies saw increasing use of the strike weapon as a means to bring government and business to its knees. By January 1974 the full effects of an ongoing Miners' Strike began to take its toll on the nation's power supplies, causing severe restrictions on the use of electricity, and ultimately cuts. And all in the middle of winter! The whole of Britain was put on a three-day working week to conserve energy, a rule that was also extended to the armed forces. An order defining the conservation of energy was implemented at Little Rissington, demanding a 10% saving of electricity by the Station and a number of restrictions were introduced.

'Reducing power' and the 3 Day Week …

Flt Lt Peter Moore was one who experienced the full effects of the power strikes and three day week.

"Number 267 Course started in October 1973 and heralded the move into a new custom built Operations Block, inevitably planting the certain

At the end of his tour as Station Commander, Gp Capt Barnden departs Little Rissington on the 'Greasy Spoon'. (*CFS Archive*)

Bulldogs over Northleach! The first two Chipmunk replacements to join CFS, XX515 and 516, fly low over the Cotswold village. (*Graham Pitchfork collection*)

kiss of death for the base, which duly closed within 3 years. Potentially, the course was no more significant than many others. However, Mr Heath and the coal miners meant that we completed our training as instructors during the infamous '3 day week'. To minimise national power consumption, full electricity was only available for 3 out of the 5 working days. As a gesture to the national effort, for 2 days a week we managed without domestic power, although power was still maintained to the airfield, which remained open. For the 3 days when power was deemed to be freely available, we worked a revised schedule. Only the RAF could have come up with a work plan that consumed even more electricity in a period of restraint than during normal times. On the days when full power was deemed available, we briefed at some ungodly winter hour and extended the flying day into night. The outcome was that, combined with our reduced operating days, more power was now consumed overall than would have been had we maintained our standard operational week. As often the way, this fact was glaringly obvious to a Flight Lieutenant, who had probably been briefed by a knowing Corporal, then just grazing the Squadron Leaders, went over the head of the CI and completely by-passed the Station Commander and Commandant.

The 3 day week was also followed by the 1974 'Who rules Britain?' General Election. No. 267 Course felt it appropriate to acknowledge the occasion with a little party in the Mess. The concept was simple. Having warmed up on beer, every time a Tory result was recorded, the ensemble was awarded a large glass of brandy. After a very short period, it was clear that this regime was not going to have the desired effect of total oblivion and so we reversed matters so that every Labour seat was to be marked with a large glass of brandy. For 'standardisation', we also retained the original rule and proceeded to eradicate numerous brain cells.

Perhaps because of personalities, the 3 day week or the atrocious weather, the Course was a remarkably boozy affair. Given half an opportunity, the flying was scrubbed so that we could repair to a local hostelry; this, we were told, was the advantage of having Kipper Fleet staff on the Waterfront. Night times became similarly indulgent. A prolonged spell of low cloud for Brize Norton or fog for Rissy meant that the flying programme became history. Of course, after a particularly wild night of excess in the bar, on the basis of an 8/8ths clag forecast, we were awoken by one of those wonderful retainers of yore, the Batman, to a breezy 'It's a grand day, sir – it'll be good for flying.' My next recollection, having landed after a formation sortie, was sitting on the loo wondering which end was going to be next. Looking at my watch I was greeted by 08:50: the day was young. Somewhere along the way someone had the notion of trying to drink in every pub along Burford High Street. I think this concept owed much to RAF Oakington and its then allegiance to the Cambridge University 'King's Street Run'. No matter the history, both course and staff were dispatched to Burford for this particular mission. This would have become a great tradition, had not some fool closed the station down a couple of years later.

Streaking was becoming fashionable and one of our number felt that we should keep up with the times. There was a dining-in taking place, while we were busy enhancing bar profits next door. Flt Lt 'Duck' Webb was the self-appointed expert on streaking and, as a former Lightning pilot, on all other matters. Duck reckoned he could streak through the dining room and not get caught, provided the exit door to the bar was clear. A deal was struck with his fellow imbibers, with Duck promptly removing every last stitch of his clothing. The door from the bar to the dining room was opened and Duck engaged reheat for his run through. As luck would have it, the door suddenly became stuck closed and Duck's escape route failed. Somehow, he negotiated his way back to the bar, to the interest of a few passing WRAF stewardesses, to find an added misfortune had befallen: his pile of clothes had disappeared without trace.

Such was our dismal progress because of weather and Mr Heath, rather than our own inabilities, we had to detach to St Mawgan for our final exercises and the dreaded Final Handling Test (FHT), possibly a first time CFS had taken such drastic action.

There are mixed memories of Rissy, with only a mere handful now left in the Service, who passed by and handed on its CFS ways. For many, it will always remain the spiritual home of a great CFS. Twelve years after I graduated in 1974, I became CI CFS at RAF Scampton. During my time there, I had the great privilege of twice meeting the late Queen Mother, our much loved Commandant-in-Chief. On the first occasion, she expressed delight to know that I had trained at Little Rissington. On the second occasion, two years later, she said 'I still think Little Rissington was better'. Who would argue with such a lady?"

New Commandant

Air Cdre Crompton's successor, Air Cdre J de M Severne, was posted in from the Royal College of Defence Studies on 4 February to take up his new post as Commandant CFS. At the same time, the command of CFS Little Rissington was delegated to the Air Officer Commanding No. 23 Group, Air Vice-Marshal J. Gingell CBE. Thereafter, RAF Little Rissington became a Station within 23 Group and the title "AOC and Commandant CFS" was changed to "Commandant CFS".

Fireman wins award

One of the new Commandant's first duties was to present fireman 19-year old Peter Kyte of Little Rissington village with the "Silver Axe" trophy. This award was presented to the best all round recruit on each initial fire-training course held at RAF Manston. Peter, who passed with flying colours, had only been an RAF fireman for six months and was previously a member of the local fire service at Stow-on-the-Wold.

Air Vice-Marshal Sir John Severne KCVO OBE AFC DL

"I suppose my main memory of Little Rissington" writes Air Vice-Marshal Sir John Severne, *"is one of the tremendous pride I felt when I was appointed Commandant of the oldest flying school in the world. I have to admit that it was always a cherished ambition that, one day, I might get that job – but I never told anyone!*

I have particularly happy memories when I was selected to do the course at Little Rissington in 1948 to learn how to become a flying instructor. All CFS students in those days had to fly solo, not just on the types on which they were going to instruct, but also on the Lancaster, Mosquito, Vampire and Spitfire. I suppose the theory was that we should be able to enthuse about the typical operational types our future students would be going to fly. This was a fantastic experience for a young Flying Officer. Needless to say the Treasury soon put an end to that!

I then returned to CFS Little Rissington as a staff instructor in 1950 and had three very happy years there. I used to fly the Meteor in aerobatic displays and there were no height limits laid down for CFS staff pilots at that time. What fun! Perhaps it is not surprising that some of us killed ourselves.

By the time I returned for the third time, "The Red Arrows" had been formed and were under the command of CFS. As Commandant I took a keen interest (for obvious reasons) and had great joy in being flown in the back seat of the Gnat with all "The Red Arrows" pilots on many occasions.

I was impressed with the high reputation with which CFS was held by other air forces throughout the world. I accompanied Examining Wing on several of these visits when most helpful exchanges of views for both sides took place. Notably to USA when we briefed the USAF on the introduction of the Hawk, to the Royal Swedish Air Force to discuss instrument flying training methods and to Jordan where their Chief of Air Staff asked us to report on their pilots by strict RAF standards, making no allowances at all."

Fireman Peter Kyte receives his Silver Axe from Air Cdre John Severne. (*CFS Archive*)

Silver Pelican

Traditionally at dining-out nights a small silver Pelican mounted on a wooden base was presented to departing QFIs who had been on the permanent flying staff as a memento of their tour at CFS. At some time in the seventies this award was extended to all officers of the permanent staff, whatever their role or branch. A special fund was used to procure the Pelicans, which officers paid into over the duration of their tours at CFS.

The Commandant's PA

Fg Off Cheryl Barber (née Cooper) was selected by Air Cdre John Severne as his Personal Assistant soon after taking up his post as CFS Commandant.

"Thanks to the generosity of the Commandant, who allowed me full use his house to prepare for my departure to the church at Chipping Camden for my wedding to Flt Lt Dennis Barber, the 23 November 1974, was an extra special day. Members of my family were invited to join us for lunch at the house after which we were driven off to the church in John's gleaming limousine with his personal chauffeur, Cpl Arthur Graham, at the wheel. Air Traffic Controller, Flt Lt Sandy Sawyer, was my Matron of Honour and the organ was played by OC Basic Squadron, Sqn Ldr Brian Russell, who also played the organ at Little Rissington village church on Sunday mornings. This wonderful day was rounded off with a reception in the Officers' Mess, one of the few occasions I believe that it was used for such a purpose.

I later found out that one of the main qualities Air Cdre Severne was looking for when interviewing applicants for the PA role was an enthusiasm for flying and I was very keen to fly. As I stepped out of the

Vintage Pair Vampire, having achieved my goal of flying in every type of aircraft operated by CFS, there was the Commandant and Station Commander waiting to present me with a CFS badge for my flying suit."

"The CFS version of the Squadron Badge or Patch seen on aircrew flying suits throughout the RAF", continues Dennis, *"was the Red Pelican on a purple background. While all fliers wear their badge with pride, the CFS QFIs considered theirs to have an additional cachet because of the role of the station. When Cheryl landed in the Vampire after completing the full house of nine CFS types, she was presented with the Red Pelican badge as an honorary award in recognition of this achievement."*

Ah, I haven't flown one of those!

"One of John's absolute aims in life while he was Commandant", resumes Cheryl, *"was to fly as many types as possible, to get as many types as he could on his log book. So as soon as anything unusual came in he would get a call from the tower informing him of the arrival of such-and-such a type and he would drop anything he was doing and head off to the airfield uttering the words 'Right, we're going flying' and off we'd go."*

New boss for Examining Wing

On leaving CFS in September 1966 Flt Lt Alex Wickham began a three-year posting with the MoD in London working on Advanced Flying Training Policy before moving to India on an exchange tour at the Staff College, a position that gave him the opportunity to regularly fly the Gnat Fighter. *"What a wonderful aeroplane that was"*, he recalls. After a further year as Station Commander at RAF Salalah, and newly promoted to Wing Commander, Alex returned to CFS in May 1974 where he took over as OC Examining Wing from Wg Cdr Ian Brimson. The total number of staff on the Wing at that time stood at eighteen and comprised: Wg Cdr A. Wickham, Sqn Ldrs B. McDonald, R. McKinlay, K. Pollard, B. Russell and Flt Lts D. Barber, P. Bouch, J. Brown, G. Foster, D. Gardner, A. Holyoake, R. Kennedy, J. Lloyd, R. Payne, B. Plummer, A. Oldfield, I. Ray and J. Willis.

62nd Annual Reunion

The 62nd Annual Reunion dinner of the CFS Association was held at the Officers' Mess at Little Rissington on 12 July. The Guest of Honour was ACM Sir Andrew Humphrey, Chief of the Air Staff. During the AGM of the Association, a proposal to allow WRAF officers to become members of the Association was accepted and the PA to the Commandant, Fg Off C.A. Cooper WRAF became the first female member.

Vintage Pair

July was a hectic month for the Meteor and Vampire crews of the Vintage Pair display team which gave displays at Greenham Common (twice), Little Rissington (Royal Visit), Plymouth, RAF Wattisham, Shobdon and RAF Locking.

That entrepreneurial spirit!

Air Traffic Controller Flt Lt Sandy Sawyer, alludes to the relaxed atmosphere that prevailed in the RAF in those days and at Little Ris in particular with a fascinating tale of entrepreneurial spirit.

"The wife of Sqn Ldr Tony Gregory, OC of one of the Jet Provost squadrons, was Dutch and had a reputation for making superb Pâtés. As word got about orders began to flow in from other RAF stations. Once sufficient orders had accumulated, Tony would fly one of his JPs on what became known as the 'Pâté Run', delivering Mrs Gregory's pâtés to the various air bases, either on the pretext of a Staff Continuation Training (SCT) sortie or a syllabus navigation exercise. Then there was the 'Fish Run'! This was a more unusual activity and strangely would often just precede a major function in either the Sergeants' or Officers' Mess. A Varsity would depart Little Rissington on a Friday morning and perform a stop-and-go at RAF Machrihanish in Scotland, where it would be loaded with boxes of fish to bring back to Ris."

Ah, those pâté runs

Sqn Ldr Tony Gregory took over 2 Squadron in August 1973, and the fact that the Squadron's 20-odd JPs were flying around the UK with empty panniers seemed somewhat unenterprising to him.

"By October that year my wife Biny's pâté business, supplying 30-40 pubs and Delis within about 25 miles of Rissington, had made a quantum leap in scale. Unsuspecting land-away cross country students delivered pannier-fulls of deep-frozen pâté 'bricks' to sub-agents in Wittering (Nigel Champness), Lossiemouth (Witney Griffiths) and Brawdy (Mike Shaw). Over 70 pubs nationwide(!) came onto the 'books' this way, regularly supplied with air-couriered Pelican Pâté. Mike, ever the entrepreneur, planned a mega-expansion (to Pembrokeshire . . and beyond . .) by way of Brawdy's Hunters, and we briefly researched with Mike Collins of 3 Sqn CFS how much pâté could be stacked in the back of a Jetstream without upsetting the C of G . . . The last 'brick' flew in October 1975, on my last day as OC 2 Sqn, marking two years of undiscovered crime."

Overseas in a Varsity

One of Dennis Barber's reminiscences concerns the navigation part of the Varsity course which required students to embark on an overseas training exercise.

"The aircraft departed on the Friday and flew to either Germany or Malta, depending on the season, and returned on the following Monday after the weekend layover. I suspect most of the station personnel regarded this as just a weekend jolly, and they may well have been correct! The freighting capacity of the Varsity was often utilised on return trips for shipping in supplies of sparkling wine from Germany for various functions.

Out with the old, in with the new! (*above*), The spacious cockpit and instrumentation of the Varsity, (*David Newham*), makes an interesting comparison with that of its replacement, the Jetstream. (*top right*) (*Alex Wickham*)

Flt Lt Mike Tinson, at the top of the steps, and groundcrew look on as Wg Cdr P. Harle hands the logbook for Varsity WJ945/21 to Sqn Ldr Mike Collins, shortly before the aircraft's departure for preservation at Duxford. (*CFS Archive*)

Another favoured perk in Flying Training Command was the 'Weekend Aeroplane', a scheme whereby staff could fly an aircraft away for a weekend somewhere. A Jet Provost for example, required a ten-shilling donation to the OC Flying Wing's slush fund. When Varsity instructor Flt Lt Ron Swann went to see the OC Flying about his Weekend Aeroplane, he was greeted with the words 'A Varsity, Swann, you want a Varsity? That's an airliner – you can't have an airliner for 10 bob', and he was sent on his way."

Varsity bows out

First flown in July 1949, the CFS took the opportunity to mark the Varsity's 25th anniversary with a gathering at Little Rissington on 17 July 1974 of Varsities from units still operating them. Highlights of the event were demonstration flights of the Varsity accompanied by displays from the "Vintage Pair" and "Red Arrows".

WJ949/19 departed for disposal to 5 MU at Kemble on 1 October followed one week later by WF424/17 which flew off to RAF Wyton for disposal. Finally, on 25 October 1974, the last Varsity to be operated by CFS, WJ945/21, was flown out for preservation at Duxford. Course No. 270 became the first to start their training on the Jetstream, but the honour was brought to an abrupt halt following a series of engine failures.

Two old timers made welcome

Two retired Royal Flying Corps personnel, Lt Lainchbury from Kingham and Cpl Selman from Swindon, visited the Central Flying School on 13 August 1974. After viewing course photographs, they were shown over a Bulldog aircraft and taken round Scheduled Servicing Flight aircraft in No. 1 Hangar. Following further visits to the Ground Instruction School and the museum, they were shown a film of "The Red Arrows", after which they were escorted to the Officers' Mess where they enjoyed drinks followed by lunch. They left CFS at 14:30.

The Jetstream saga

No sooner had the Jetstream established itself when it began to suffer a series of setbacks. On 18 October 1974, XX477/31 was on a routine training flight when it had to make an emergency landing at the RRE Pershore airfield due to engine failure.

"There were a number of unexplained engine shut-downs", recalls Sir John Severne, *"where no fault could be found after inspection on the ground and the crews were becoming apprehensive that, one day, both engines would fail. Consequently some of them even practised their forced landing techniques! Less than three weeks later, on 1 November, the same aircraft crashed through the boundary wall at the end of runway 23. This incident happened at Little Rissington when both engines failed at exactly the same time during overshoot from a roller landing. Witnesses on the ground confirmed the pilot's statement that, when the failure took place, there was no swing at all so the failure was definitely simultaneous. There was therefore no question that the pilot closed down the wrong engine after failure of one of them. Turboméca, the manufacturers, had been unhelpful over the previous investigations and said there was nothing wrong with the engines. In fact I seem to remember that the cause was the high pressure electrically activated fuel cocks slowly closing under the influence of a vibration at a certain frequency. In this case it was affecting both engines, where previously it affected only one. In the previous cases the pilot would have closed the cock after the engine failure while in the air, so, of course, everything would appear normal on the ground inspection."*

The two-man crew of XX477, Sqn Ldr Mike Collins and Flt Lt Tinson, suffered back injuries and were admitted to the RAF Hospital at Wroughton. The aircraft suffered Cat. 5 damage and was subsequently broken into sub-assemblies. The fuselage was moved to RAF Finningley in September 1976 where it was used for ground simulation.

Incredibly, on the same day, a second Jetstream, XX480/33, experienced a similar power loss on take off, but the crew managed to keep it airborne and return for a safe landing. All Jetstreams were grounded immediately pending investigation into the cause of the accident and Courses No. 270 and 271 did not fly after the 1 November. In order to trace the source of the problem and to maintain the aircraft at operational readiness, the nine remaining CFS Jetstreams were regularly taxied round the airfield. The fault was eventually traced to a fuel flow problem that was easily fixed, but events that would all but end its service with the RAF had already overtaken the Jetstream. The huge defence cutbacks introduced after the 1973 oil crisis brought with them the disbandment of many transport squadrons and the phasing out of their aircraft. With a surfeit of qualified multi-engined pilots, the RAF decided to end all multi-engined crew training for an indefinite period. The CFS and 5 FTS Jetstreams were flown to 19 MU at St Athan for storage in 1975.

In 1976, the Royal Navy opted to use the Jetstream as a replacement for its ageing Sea Prince trainers and fourteen of the stored aircraft were converted to T.Mk.2 standard. The remaining eleven machines were also reactivated, forming a new Multi Engined Training Squadron (METS) at RAF Leeming.

The broken remains of Jetstream T.1, XX477/31, lie in a field beyond the Rissy runway. (*Dennis Barber*)

1975

Frederick's moment of inspiration

AV-M Sir John Severne recollects an amusing incident during the press day at Kemble to launch the new "The Red Arrows" display season. *"Our pelican mascot, Flt Lt Frederick, was present. The press wanted a picture of Frederick briefing the pilots on their next practice. It was quite a windy day and Len Hill, his handler, warned us to ensure that there were people positioned in front of Frederick if he was facing into wind because his wings were not clipped and he would take off if he could. Needless to say, he found a gap and off he flew! It was a wonderful sight and we were all secretly delighted! Unfortunately for him, he was out of flying practice and did not have the strength to climb out of the ground cushion and, as a stone wall approached, he did the sensible thing and decided to do a precautionary landing. He then returned to his photographic duties."*

With the move to Cranwell, scheduled for the spring of 1976, the decision was taken to 'ground' Frederick after he had continued to give sterling service as CFS Mascot on many public occasions. He continued to live at Birdland and Mr Len Hill offered to take him up to Cranwell whenever he was required.

Chief Instructor-CFS-Fixed Wing

While at RAF Syerston Wg Cdr 'Cas' Maynard continued display flying – a synchro pair and in 1967 he led a four-ship JP4 team, "The Vipers".

"Then followed Staff College, the Gulf and MoD before returning to Little Rissington in October 1974 for refresher training on the Bulldog, which was new for me, and the familiar Jet Provost. The first trip was with Sqn Ldr Jack Hindle in the Bulldog and I well remember his chuckling as I inadvertently entered a high rotation spin during my first attempt and his calmly letting me sort it out.

I took over as Chief Instructor on 23 December 1974, looking forward with relish to a challenging and rewarding tour on familiar ground. I came to respect the staff both in the air and on the ground for their professionalism and enthusiasm. Before the end of January 1975 I had taken part in the first SPINEX of the year at Coltishall with No. 54 Squadron. Our task was to fly with each of the pilots to practise recoveries from full spins using the JP technique and then to do incipient recoveries using the Jaguar method. We used for briefing a record of a Jaguar in a full spin filmed from inside and outside the cockpit when the aircraft was being flown by a French Test Pilot. The film was quite dramatic and drove home the lesson to recover promptly as soon as the aircraft began to depart from controlled flight. SPINEX continued and I believe provided valuable dialogue between the Front Line and CFS.

I could not avoid getting involved with display aerobatics. It started when I had to adjudicate to decide the winner of the Clarkson Trophy, the two contenders being Flt Lts Dick Cole and Chris Rackham. The weather was quite unsuitable for low level aerobatics and there was no prospect of improvement, so we decided that I would fly with each of them to judge who flew the better sequence. This we did above cloud using the tops as simulated ground (not below 1,500 ft above ground level) and then had to return to the airfield using radar (PAR). Both performances were polished and enthusiastically flown but Dick Cole had the edge and was awarded the Trophy."

Bright idea

SAC Adams of the Station Armoury submitted a suggestion on how to improve a service pistol; his idea was accepted and subsequently implemented. The Air Officer Commanding No. 23 Group, Air Vice-Marshal Gingell, presented him with a cheque and Certificate of Merit as a reward for his design.

Air Chief Marshal Sir Brian Burridge KCB CBE ADC RAF

Later 2003 Gulf Commander and Commander-in-Chief Strike Command in 2005, Sir Brian here records a Flt Lt B.K. Burridge's first memories of Little Rissington. One of the last few dozen QFIs of a reputed total of 6,191 flying instructors produced at Rissy before the CFS's dispersal, he reminds most others before him of those special delights of bad weather Cotswold arrivals.

"I first 'arrived' at Little Rissington in a Varsity in March 1975, carrying the Commandant who had been on an Exam Wing liaison visit to Sweden (honestly!). I had heard about the bump in the first thousand feet of Runway 05 but that was the least of my problems given the stonking cross-wind and driving rain. Luckily, the oleos didn't quite go through the wings but they took a long time to reach their normal extension. The Commandant just looked ashen!

So, it was with some surprise that I found myself on No. 275 course some five months later as a potential JP QFI. I well remember the first day of the course because we had an arrival chat from a representative of every rank in the RAF from SAC to Air Cdre, a feat never equalled since. But the CFS course was a formative experience for me which has stayed with me throughout my career. In my view, I really learned to fly

Toasting the end of the very short Jetstream era along with Air Cdre John Severne (*left*) are; (*r to l*), Sqn Ldr John Winterbourne, Flt Lt Tony Oldfield, Gp Capt Mike Williams and two staff officers. XX480/33 was then flown to St Athan for storage. (*CFS Archive*)

at Little Rissington and I also learned to teach, both in the air and on the ground. My subsequent career as a JP QFI, Bulldog QFI, a Nimrod QFI (and boss of the OCU), as a university teacher and as Commandant of the Joint Service Command and Staff College has its roots in that six month period at CFS. Teaching has given me a lot of personal satisfaction over the years.

As for Little Rissington itself where we were the penultimate course, it had its own special charm. Lousy weather, isolation and that bump in runway 05 were more than compensated for by the great spirit that existed on that small but very focused station. So I have always counted myself fortunate to have been part of the Little Rissington era and I am proud of what CFS and being a QFI actually stand for."

Basketball success

The Little Rissington Basketball team had a big success by winning the 'Faville' Trophy on 26 March. The team consisted of: Flt Lt L. Palmer, Flt Lt C. Seirwald, Cpl I. Palmer, Sgt I. Snow, Ch Tech J. Rapley, Flt Lt P. Brightwell, Sgt P. Exon and Plt Off M. Faulkener.

Neat formation of four CFS Bulldog T.1s, lead by XX517/42 with XX539/46 and XX540/47 on the wings and XX514/44 filling in the box. (*MAP*)

Onward, upward but even slower

John Delafield, with his earlier A.1 category on Jet Provosts and newly promoted to Wing Commander at the Staff College, returned to the Cotswolds in 1975.

"Rissy became my short term home once more, this time thankfully in summer, when I was allowed out from the MoD to be given a Bulldog Conversion course, before assuming command of London University Air Squadron. Tom Sawyer was my tolerant instructor and put up with me remarkably well. Another enjoyable aeroplane, now even slower than the JP, but still a lot of fun! Little did I know in those early Bulldog months that I would amass well over 1,000 hours on the type, for not only did my UAS stint produce a satisfying total but later, having retired from full time service, I flew her again on No. 6 AEF, based then at Benson.

The Bulldog was an aircraft, which I came to treat with some caution when it came to spinning – I was the President of the Board of Enquiry into the first Bulldog loss through spinning in July 1976, when fortunately both survived. The initial Pilot's Notes gave a spin recovery that was virtually the same as the Chipmunk but we found in practice that the Bulldog was not always inclined to recover when requested! The recovery technique was amended at least twice to my recollection and the entry height increased to a typical 8,000 ft for a 4-turn spin, all to give one a chance to sort things out if the recovery all went to worms but we still keep losing aircraft this way.

On my part, I learnt from the one time Scottish Aviation test pilot, one Mr Blair, that it was not so much the amount of anti-spin control one applied that mattered but the rate at which it was applied that was the key to spin recovery in the Bulldog. This man should have known because he used to spin the Bulldog from low altitude at the SBAC shows in the early '70s and never had a problem! Sadly the RAF never embraced this rather rough technique officially but I know of many QFIs who always used it: I never had a problem thereafter as reluctant 'spinners' always snapped out promptly when given this robust Scottish Aviation recovery treatment! At nearly 67, I am still AEF-ing at Benson and have around 500 hours on the 'new' Tutor. An interesting parallel of note was that at CFS Wittering in the 1930s they used to climb their biplane Bulldogs to about 8,000 ft to spin, as it too created recovery problems at times, whereas their then Tutor was benign, a bit like our present one which normally will come out itself after two turns!

What is my only regret? Not having the chance to be Chief Instructor or Station Commander at that famous 'airfield on the hill' since, by the time my turn came for such command, it had long since closed. At least the Air Cadets still fly there but in turn, as readers will have guessed, their motor gliders are also even slower than those machines I had the pleasure of flying in from Little Rissington!"

Final Reunion

Little Rissington looked at her very best on 13 June, which was a lovely summer's day and fitting for the last CFS Reunion to be held on the Station. Sir George Edwards, Chairman of the British Aircraft Corporation, was the Principal Guest and he gave an extremely lively and witty speech in his own inimitable style. To celebrate a year of Women's lib, Air Cdre Molly Allott, Director of WRAF, attended the dinner.

The Random Memory Ledger of an OC Supply

Sqn Ldr David J. Powell arrived as a thirty-year-old OC Supply Squadron for a two year tour in 1973 and has committed to print some impressions and confessions of his job.

"My first recollection from being posted to Little Rissington was a reduction in status. As a Flying Officer on UK Mobile Air Movements

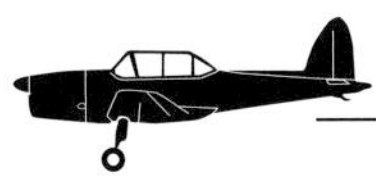

Squadron, I had a Land Rover and a driver at my disposal. As a Flight Lieutenant OC Gulf Mobile Air Movements Flight, I still had a Landrover but now I had to drive it. As a newly promoted Squadron Leader and despite the significant collection of storage buildings, fuel installations and customers at both Little Rissington and Kemble, all I was given was a rather ancient RAF blue bicycle! I did have my own office with a nice lady to make the tea. However, this too was a portent of things to come – when a Wing Commander at MoD, I had to both share an office and make the tea.

Our task at Rissy was to provide all the bits for a fleet of some 70 aircraft, which included Bulldogs, Jetstreams and Jet Provosts at Little Rissington, the Meteor and Vampire for the Vintage Pair display team and 'D' Squadron and 'The Red Arrows' with their Gnats across at Kemble. As well as the aircraft spares, tools and test equipment, my team of some 70 service and civilian personnel provided the full range of domestic spares support including mess and married quarters furniture, tools and test equipment, coal for the boiler house, etc., a total of some 26,000 different items. We also managed a raft of local contracts including window cleaning, the rat catcher, the undertaker and the tailor.

Being a training unit we had a high proportion of young airmen and airwomen, who came to us straight from training and for whom we had to provide a sort of finishing school. I remember going up onto the Receipt and Dispatch ramp one day to see a large crate addressed to RAF Jiberalterrer (Gibraltar) by a recently arrived lad who had only left Belfast for the first time a few months previously.

Unlike the 'sharp end', which still managed to exude a relaxed flying club atmosphere, many of the support areas had been cut back to the bare minimum. My own organisation comprised a Flight Lieutenant OC SCAF and deputy (the only other commissioned officer on the Supply Squadron) and two Warrant Officers – one looked after Tech stores, POL and Forward Delivery and the other looked after Domestic Support (Clothing and Barrack).

Tom, who had been there for years, was the civilian barrack warden and some civilians went back to when Little Rissington was an aircraft storage MU. WO Vince Culligan (Barrack and Clothing) looked as though he should be a RSM in the Irish Guards and was still playing veterans' badminton at senior level. Jenny, a Corporal, ran the clothing stores and was a keen sportswoman. Mrs Evans, who was the admin office, was another fixture from the year dot.

One inherited problem comprised several 45 gallon drums of concentrated red and blue biro ink. This had been obtained to mix with the Arrows' white smoke exhaust generators to produce the distinctive coloured smoke trails. Unfortunately (although not nearly as bad as the Royal Navy's acidic learning curve long decades earlier at Farnborough) they also left a trail of spotted residue across any parked cars and people etc underneath any display. The solution had been discovered on their travels with some special American-produced display 'goo', which did not leave any residue. The Treasury had been persuaded to cough up the money for the purchase of the new stuff: however, this was on the strict understanding that all the old biro ink would be used up first. What do you think actually happened? Correct first time – and I was the one stuck with several tired drums of ink. I could not pour it down the drains, as it would have finished up contaminating (and probably colouring) the Thames, as we were in the Thames water catchment area. Neither could I burn it without leaving great swathes of coloured stripes across the fields of Gloucestershire and nobody wanted to buy such a large quantity of ancient biro ink. What did I do? The resolution was the same as my predecessor's – so it was left for my successor, Duncan Grant, to sort out. For all I know he adopted a similar pragmatic approach and there still lurk a few old barrels of biro ink hidden in some unlit, dark, damp corner of the hangars on the South Side of the Airfield.

Rissington weather though could be very localised. We still recall the Saturday morning we awoke to find the Station under a thick layer of snow. This day was scheduled to be our essential monthly trip to the Witney supermarket, so the car was loaded up with shovel, old matting (to give the tyres grip if we slid off the road), spare warm clothes, thermos flask of hot drink, etc. Suitably wrapped up, we duly set off, only to discover on reaching the main Stow to Burford road, a journey of about 300 yards, that there was no sign of snow anywhere!

As OC Supply you had certain valuable and attractive items in your custody. These lived in a large ancient safe in stores, a typical example being spare aircrew watches. Interestingly one of the most attractive items kept in my safe were, in themselves, not particularly expensive – but were they attractive! These were the complex transfers of the Central Flying School Coat of Arms, which used to adorn the aircraft and were very attractive to aviation enthusiasts. Needless to say these were only handed over against a specific aircraft re-spraying task.

Another job, which went with the turf, was organising the annual visits to Austin Reed's in Cheltenham to sort out "The Red Arrows" blazers contract for their 'off duty' PR uniform. This and the associated fashion parade could take up far more time than the basics of Supply, such as keeping the aircraft in the air. I was also involved in arranging their red flying suits, made by a supplier who also provided kit for the F1 Racing Teams.

Supporting the Vampire and Meteor, our Vintage Pair, presented some challenges, not just engineering. Fortunately before I arrived, British Aerospace (or whatever it called itself then) had been rationalising its storage and with the demise of the Vampire and Meteor from front line service had shut down their spares support arrangements. Rather than just scrapping the residual items, they had offered the entire contents of the relevant warehouses to the Vintage pair. These spares were held in row upon row of racks and boxes in one of the hangars on the south side of the airfield. The Vintage Pair were 'official' RAF aircraft, to be managed and accounted for appropriately. 'Officially' within stores we should have gone through our entire ex-industry treasure trove to catalogue and list each and every spare – and there were thousands of them! We decided some more pragmatic process was needed. This was based on holding the items as a single local 'Not in vocabulary' (NIV) reference number for our 'Vintage Pair spares pack, quantity one' or some such generic title and then letting the Vintage Pair engineers rummage in the hangar when searching for a part. This meant a certain amount of subterfuge being required for any official visits by auditors or Command supply staffs. 'That hangar?' 'No, not ours – miscellaneous unit storage!' The 'official' spares record card was removed so that it would never be selected for any random stocktaking check!

Once a month, the OC Supply would go through the ceremony of the monthly dips. This involved going out to and standing on the top of each airfield's aviation fuel tanks, before dropping the dipping rods down their special tubes to register each tank's amount of fuel. In summer this was quite fun but such visits on a cold, wet, windy winter morning was not an experience to be given to your worst enemy.

Royal visit by HM Queen Mother, June 1975

For some unfathomable reason in 1975 I found myself with an additional task – Project Officer for a Royal Visit by our Commandant-in-Chief, HM Queen Elizabeth The Queen Mother. As a piece of 'one upmanship' we negotiated with Clarence House for Queen Mum's own Rolls-Royce to be used for the tour of the Station, although our Royal Visitor would arrive and depart by Royal Flight helicopter. The Royal route was for ever being chopped and changed, not helped by many interested parties or vested interests coming out of the woodwork! Rissington, being relatively old, had lots of narrow roads with restricted turning areas and the only vehicle on camp with the same turning circle as the regal Rolls was the station dustcart. So every time the Royal route was amended I had to pedal round to MT, sign out the dustcart and drive it round the route to check turning circles and ensuring the Royal visitor would be on the expected side of the car to alight for each successive event. The hassle was worth it when, on the morning of the actual visit, starting at about 08:30, with the camp looking immaculate, I travelled in the Royal Rolls to show the driver the route he would be taking later that day.

For the obligatory afternoon flying display, armchairs were provided for the VIPs. The normal drill is for blankets to be provided for additional warmth. However deciding to be a bit different for the visit, we raided the married quarters to provided warmth and colour with tartan travel rugs. Needless to say, as Project Officer, I made sure that it was our own travel rug, which became the 'Royal Rug'!

Another tip we picked up from somewhere was that Queen Mum liked to rest her feet at lunch. With her being petite, we provided a suitable footstool, a kneeler borrowed from the Station Church. At the Royal luncheon, it was rewarding to see our Royal Guest take her seat, within a few seconds, discover the footstool and smile with contentment. This was an added reason for the top table tablecloths to hang nearly to floor to give suitable privacy for our VIP guests' knees.

There were many organisations involved – the first complexity was that in addition to the Station Commander, Group Captain Mike Williams, the visit was very much the Commandant's baby, that of the excellent Air Cdre John Severne. Additionally we had to contend with a meddlesome No. 23 Group HQ and HQ Training Command and its specialist staffs wanting to have their say – or rather fire questions, not forgetting the protocol minders at MoD. Why can so-called specialist Command staff officers only ask questions, the answers to which are then questioned or rubbished without their ever volunteering specialist guidance at the outset? Thankfully, over the years CFS HQ had established an excellent working relationship with our Commandant-in-Chief's outer office at Clarence House, which tended to be the primary and most reliable 'How about, if we were to do this?' channel of communication.

Local Relationships

Local relationships could best be described as mixed. For some months my wife, Sue, worked for a mad inventor with an office in Bourton-on-the-Water – despite her daily afternoon visit to the Post Office with the office mail, it was ages before she was acknowledged as not being yet another day visitor. On the other hand the RAF were well received in the local pubs. Apparently, when the time came to close RAF Little Rissington, there was significant disquiet and apprehension at the visits by a 'liaison team' from the incoming Army unit. Their gist was for the pub please to contact the Duty Officer rather than the police when (and not 'if') the fights broke out.

Reportedly there were three prices in the local Stow-on-the-Wold antique shops – firstly, the advertised price for American tourists, next a 50% discount for British tourists and lastly a further 25% reduction for local Cotswold residents."

Frederick, the CFS Mascot, was a popular attraction with guests, none more so than with HM The Queen Mother, who is seen here admiring Frederick's CFS tie in the company of CFS Commandant, Air Cdre John Severne and keeper Len Hill. (*John Severne*)

Air Training Corps Cadets

Each summer Little Rissington, like many other RAF units, played host to ATC and CCF cadet units for summer camps. These normally lasted for one week. During the summer of 1975 seven such summer camps where held at Rissington with an average of 40 cadets each week. During their week on camp, cadets would:

a) Experience everyday life on an RAF base

b) Undertake outdoor fitness and initiative training

c) Have the opportunity to gain air experience flying

Each day was organised to ensure that cadets gained maximum benefit. While marching from point to point, cadets had to maintain marching discipline under a senior cadet, and had to keep to the specific routes and paths; grass plots could not be crossed. The Station's flying co-ordinator was responsible for the smooth running of the cadets' flying programme. He also had to notify all cadets who were due to fly where and when to report.

Vintage Pair

"The Vintage Pair", comprising a Meteor and a Vampire, completed their fourth successful display season. Training was delayed early in the season because of aircraft fatigue problems; however, these were overcome and the team of four pilots commenced display flying in June and flew a total of 29 displays during the season. This was the final season at Rissy for the pair as the CFS team and its aircraft moved to Cranwell in the spring of 1976.

Sqn Ldr Tony Gregory sums up his time with "The Vintage Pair". *"My recollection is of two great summers of the 'weekend job' in 1974 and 1975, flying the Vampire T.11, XH304, with Bill Shrubsole or Cas Maynard flying the Meteor T.7. We were much constrained by the engineers (300 kts, 3g, no negative g, as I recall it), but there was nevertheless a well-worn and graceful routine which showed the ancient jets very well – and all the better for their by then unique centrifugal compressor engine noise. 'Vintage' was forever threatened with closure on cost grounds, but survived for several more years thanks to the support of successive Commandants until the unfortunate accident at Mildenhall in 1986."*

A unique job

"Life as a Trapper was unique", says Alex Wickham, *"in that, like the Commandant, Examining Wing pilots were authorised to fly any aircraft, including those in foreign air forces when invited to. Overseas visits were of two types; CFS Liaison where the Commandant selected pilots to accompany him, and Examining Wing visits to check out instructors and training standards. We were tasked to fly any type of aircraft and examine the pure flying skills of pilots in their operational environment. One week we could be airborne in F-104s over Germany, the next in Mig-17s in Ceylon or hovering Mi-4 helicopters operating tourist flights in the Maldives.*

One of my most memorable Exam Wing visits was to Jordan at the end of October with a large fixed and rotary wing team. I also invited the Commandant, John Severne, along in return for the liaison visits he'd invited me to. I was a very keen amateur radio enthusiast and had

The Vintage Pair on a photo-shoot over a backdrop favoured by CFS, the Severn Bridge. (*Tony Gregory*)

conversed with King Hussein a few times, so I mentioned that we were coming out and that we were looking forward to the opportunity of meeting him. As we approached Amman a call came over the radio to say that the King was coming down to greet us. We hurriedly changed into best blue and as we taxied in we could see the figure of the King standing on the pan with his hands in his pockets. John went down the steps, shook his hand then came rushing back up exclaiming 'He's asking for Alex'. I climbed down to meet him and after a few minutes he invited me back to his palace, leaving the rest of the team to get on with the job for a couple of days."

The Tigers meet: literally!

Life as a Trapper was not all testing. Early in September, three Gnats attended the NATO Tiger Meet at the German Air Force base at Leck to represent the Royal Air Force, which did not have a Tiger Squadron at the time. The event was scheduled to take place from the 4th to the 8th and on the 3rd, the three diminutive trainers joined the tail-end of a practice balbo involving all the Tiger squadrons.

As they approached the airfield Gnat XS103 collided with an Italian F-104S, and although badly damaged, both pilots were able to land their aircraft safely. A multi-national Board of Inquiry, the first of its kind, was assembled on the 17th, chaired by the OC Examining Wing, Alex Wickham, who produced the following summary of the incident:

"The briefing was done in the Cinema. There were to be two sections of German Air Force Fiat G.91s, a USAF section comprising F-104s, followed by the Italian F-104s with the Gnats bringing up the rear. After take-off they formed up over the Schleswig countryside before turning back for Leck. Realising that the formation was too loose, the leader of the American section asked the formation leader to slow up a bit so that they could close in. So the G.91s lowered their airbrakes and as the F-104s closed up, they too lowered their airbrakes. The airbrake on an F-104 is very powerful and much more effective than that on the Gnat. As they were flying quite low the lead aircraft in the Gnat section had nowhere to go and flew right up the jet pipe of an Italian F-104. Damage to the aircraft's nose was substantial resulting in loss of airspeed indicator, battery power, radio and intercom, and there was a big hole in the front bulkhead. Fortunately the wheels came down with three greens and it landed without further incident. The Italian, who hadn't realised his '104 had been hit, said he felt a little bump but thought it was just a bit of turbulence reverberating through the airbrake."

Red Arrows intensive training

Despite it being the end of the display season, "The Red Arrows" carried out an intensive training programme during October, flying 64 SCT sorties and 75 practice formation sorties, all of which helped to bring the three new pilots up to speed within a short timescale. The two 'non-smoking' Gnats, XR572 and XR981, were flown to Hawker Siddeley at Bitteswell for conversion to full Red Arrows fit, including smoke generation equipment.

Training Summary

During the year, 96 students were trained on fixed-wing aircraft. Whereas the training of students for the Royal Navy and Army reduced from four to three, the number of foreign and Commonwealth students rose from 20 to 25. Included in the latter category, for the first time since 1950, was a student from the Egyptian Air Force. On a sadder note, due to the over-manning situation, the RAF temporarily halted ab initio pilot training on multi-engined aircraft, so the new Jetstreams were flown into storage at St Athan pending a decision on their future.

Examining Wing Activities

The Examining Wing continued its task of checking the standard of flying and flying instruction throughout the Royal Air Force, the Royal Navy, the Army and some foreign and Commonwealth air forces. During the year, teams of fixed-wing examiners from RAF Little Rissington visited 41 service units 10 civilian flying clubs, one civilian flying school and 6 foreign air forces (Jordan, Malaysia, Oman, Saudi Arabia, Singapore and Sri Lanka). In all 1,192 tests were conducted on many different types of aircraft.

"Examining Wing was a fascinating place, certainly during my time there", maintains Dennis Barber. *"One purpose of the Wing was to examine the flying and instructional standards at CFS, as well as those of all the flying schools. Dominie and Varsity staff pilot skills were also assessed at RAF Finningley where the Navigation, AEO and Air Engineering Schools were concentrated. Additionally, numerous examining visits were made to overseas air forces who sought the CFS imprimatur on their activities. The preparation and execution of all these visits provoked tremendous cross-fertilisation of ideas and trends in flying instruction amongst the wing staff.*

Under the command of Sqn Ldr Brian Russell, Basic Squadron was responsible for all the Jet Provosts and Bulldogs, and anything operated by civilian flying schools, whereas Advanced Squadron, under the leadership of Sqn Ldr Ken Pollard, had a High Speed Flight and Multi-engined Flight. Pilots on Advanced usually flew only the types associated with their respective Flights while all pilots on Basic flew all associated types."

Phantom spinners

Two QFIs, Flt Lts P.E. Rickard and I.D. Hill, were detached to No. 228 OCU at RAF Coningsby over 2 and 3 October together with two Jet Provost T.5As and Cpl Flaherty an aircraft fitter. Their mission was to carry out spin training with the Phantom pilots on the unit.

Jet Provost rundown

By the end of the year the rundown of the T.3 fleet was almost complete with eight aircraft having gone to 5 MU and two to BAC for T.Mk.3A conversion, although four T.3As arrived from BAC during the last quarter.

1976

Awards

On 12 January, Air Cdre Severne presided over his last award presentation as Commandant, CFS, the following personnel receiving recognition:

Flt Lt M.J. East	-	Distinguished Service in Northern Ireland
Cpl R. Johnson	-	Long Service and Good Conduct Medal
Ch Tech B. Eccleshare	-	Long Service and Good Conduct Medal
Cpl S.G. Gray	-	'Good Show' award for Air Traffic Control
WO W.H. Lumbard	-	CFS Silver Pelican on behalf of SHQ Staff

New Year's Honours

Little Rissington personnel were not overlooked in the New Year's Honours as outlined below:

Sqn Ldr P.G. Payne	-	MBE
Flt Lt G.M. Cullen	-	AFC
Sqn Ldr B.E. Russell	-	Queen's Commendation for Valuable Services in the Air
WO G. Bennett	-	AOC-in-C's Commendation
WO W.H. Lumbard	-	AOC-in-C's Commendation
SAC R. Homer	-	AOC's Commendation
Flt Lt M.J. East	-	Mention in Despatches
Flt Lt I.R. McLuskie	-	Mention in Despatches

Fledgling "Arrows"

Preparation for the forthcoming season had begun in earnest in the autumn of 1975 and the three new pilots, Flt Lts Dudley Carvell, Tim Curley and Nigel Champness, were settling in nicely. Bad weather in February severely limited formation practice but had improved sufficiently by March to allow the first nine-ship formation to be flown on the first of the month. However, two new formation manoeuvres – a seven-vic formation with the wingmen and the two adjacent to the leader inverted, and a seven-ship line-astern barrel roll - were excluded because they could not be flown consistently well.

Aircraft markings modified

In February 1976 most of the Bulldogs and some of the Provosts were repainted with new CFS markings. Previously the School coat of arms had been painted on the fuselage but now, following the style adopted by the "Vintage Pair", a red and blue chevron appeared on each side of the badge. After the closure of the airfield, these markings would become the only visible link between the separate units of the CFS.

New Commandant

Having bade farewell to the Mayor of Cheltenham, Councillor L.F.F. Gaylard, on 10 February, Air Cdre John Severne, handed over his long cherished role as CFS Commandant to Air Cdre John Sutton two days later. Air Cdre Severne was dined out during the 275 Course dining out night on the 12th when he had the pleasure of presenting the Course trophies.

Air Cdre Sutton's short tenure at Little Rissington commenced with him being presented to Her Majesty The Queen Mother at Clarence House on 17 February. His introduction to the Mayor of Cheltenham took place in the Mayor's Parlour on the 27th of the month.

New Station Commander

With the departure of Gp Capt M.R. Williams on 27 March and the imminent closure of the airfield not warranting a replacement of similar rank, Wg Cdr J.J. 'Cas' Maynard of Red Pelican renown took over command of the Station. He writes;

"During the summer of 1975 it was announced that the Station would close in 1976 as a result of a Defence Review. CFS had spent 30 years at Little Rissington and had become closely enmeshed with the Station though remaining a lodger unit, enjoying exclusive support from the Station. Communication was simple, not only with the Station but also between the various elements of the school – Basic and Advanced Instructors, Groundschool, Examining Wing, the CFS Headquarters, were within walking range or a short journey to Kemble. Everyone could

The final Red Arrows team to form while CFS reigned at Little Rissington pictured with attractive supporter are; (*back row, l to r*) Flt Lts Mike Phillips, Mel Cornwell, Nigel Champness, Sqn Ldr Dickie Duckett, Flt Lt Roy Barber; (*front row, l to r*) Flt Lts Bob Eccles, Tim Curley, Dudley Carvell, Sqn Ldr Adrian Wall (Manager), Flt Lt Alan Hunt (EO), Sqn Ldr Brian Hoskins. (*Nigel Champness*)

meet professionally and socially so there was a feeling of unity and cohesion; advice and opinion could easily be sought.

It was not until after the move in 1976 that the consequences of dispersal began to be felt and the Commandant, then Air Cdre John Sutton, started the formal process that would in September 1977 bring CFS Headquarters, Examining Wing, the Basic flying elements and Groundschool back together at Leeming. When I took command of the CFS Wing at RAF Leeming – the wheel had come full circle. I do remember that during the discussions while we were at Cranwell the phrase 'pool of expertise' came up. It seemed to sum up concisely the synergistic advantages of communication, control and, not least, of image with CFS under one roof. I guess that Robert Smith-Barry must have had a similar feeling in 1916 at Gosport as he assembled his staff from among those he had served with and trained when he commanded No. 60 Squadron in France. Those who knew their machines, knew their limits, were able to operate confidently up to the limits and had the communication and motivation to impart their skills to others. That seems to me to describe what The Central Flying School is all about.

'IMPRIMIS PRAECEPTA'. There are differing interpretations of the meaning. 'Our Teaching is Everlasting' so why do we run refresher courses? 'Follow these precepts specially' which is fine but I prefer one that I can more easily understand – 'Teaching is the First Principle'.

I remember competing with the early morning stratus during Red Pelican practices; a barrel roll in the middle of a 'flat show' giving very little margin for the recovery. There was Mrs Muriel Taylor, known to all as 'Mrs T', the Flying Wing Secretary who kept a succession of Chief Instructors out of trouble and who died suddenly only a few weeks after the departure of CFS. On a lighter note, a memorable Burns Night in 1976 with lots of fun and whiskey to the accompaniment of David Eastmond's rich baritone voice. The strong support of our Commandant-in-Chief, HM Queen Elizabeth The Queen Mother by her visit on 31 March. The farewell parade in Cheltenham; the warmth and friendship of the Mayor and Borough Council.

Finally, the last Course Graduation Dinner was on 7 April when MRAF Sir Thomas Pike was Guest of Honour and presented the Trophies to the Stars of No. 276 Course. Also present was our new Commander-in-Chief, Air Marshal Sir Rex Roe, who had previously served as a Staff QFI at CFS, had commanded the Central Flying School of the Royal New Zealand Air Force and had commanded RAF Syerston, a Jet Provost FTS.

Almost 30 years after Little Rissington closed I am still flying, now as a civilian instructor, and often pass Rissy on training sorties from Kidlington. The main runway (23/05) appears to be in good condition and the training area is still extensive. I was lucky enough to enjoy a long association with Little Rissington from the time I arrived to start the course in some awe at the reputation of CFS at 'Hell on the Hill' to the later time when I came to regard it with affection as my Alma Mater."

Total Flying Hours

The total number of flying hours, 1,384, achieved during the last full month showed the excellent utilisation figures, particularly by the Jet Provost T.5s, Bulldogs and Gnats, before their move to a new home:

Type	Hours	Landings
Jet Provost T.3A	140.00	432
Jet Provost T.5A	384.40	1068
Bulldog T.1	383.10	754
Vampire T.11	5.45	20
Meteor T.7	6.15	14
Gnat T.1	207.20	594
Red Arrows	227.40	481
Chipmunk T.10	29.10	109

Rissington residents, March 1976

As closure of Little Rissington drew ever nearer, only thirty-two of the fifty aircraft operated by CFS in March 1976 were based at Little Rissington:

Bulldog T.1	Jet Provost T.3	Jet Provost T.5
XX514/44	XM349/68	XW292/85
XX515/40	XM358/70	XW315/83
XX516/41	XM366/61	XW316/82
XX517/42	XM371/66	XW414/89
XX518/43	XM419/60	XW421/90
XX538/45	XN506/74	XW425/84
XX539/46	XN548/67	XW434/92
XX540/47	XN581/77	XW435/93
XX541/48	XN584/78	XW437/91
XX553/07		
XX554/09		
Vampire T.11	**Meteor T.7**	**Chipmunk T.10**
XH304	WF791	WZ879/14

The remaining CFS aircraft comprised the 4 Squadron and "Red Arrows" Gnats at Kemble and the Gate Guardian, Spitfire Mark 16, TE356. This was dismantled on the 13 April and transported by road to Cranwell.

Good Show!

One incident that sticks in the mind of Flt Lt Nigel Champness was an air test that he and Flt Lt Robert Eccles performed on a "Red Arrows" Gnat from Hawker Siddeley's Bitteswell airfield.

"The aircraft had just completed its winter overhaul and we were carrying out a series of aerobatic manoeuvres at 12,000 ft when the fuel caption lit and the engine suddenly began to lose power. I quickly rolled upright again, attempted a hot relight and although the rpm hesitated at 75%, the engine continued to run down. I handed over control to Bob in the back seat for him to set up a forced landing pattern into RAF Wittering while I carried out the drills and checked his actions against the Flight Reference Cards. We broke cloud at 7,000 ft ideally placed and I carried out a further two cold relight attempts while Bob continued to fly the forced landing pattern. The rpm increased to 30% only and had no throttle response, but between us we managed to get it down in

one piece. Subsequent investigation found that the inverted fuel trap had been fitted upside down which, as one can imagine, led to an interesting conversation between us and the chap responsible for fitting it." For their alertness and initiative and their valuable contribution to Flight Safety, Nigel and Robert were awarded 'Good Show' certificates by the AOC-in-C Training Command.

3,000 Hours

To mark the completion of 3,000 hours of airborne flying instruction with CFS at Little Rissington on 9 March, Sqn Ldr John Snell was given a Champagne reception on landing from the CFI and acting Station Commander, Wg Cdr J.J. Maynard. Sqn Ldr Snell had over 8,000 hours in his log book accrued on 56 different aircraft types and was a Bulldog QFI on 1 Squadron at the time of the reception.

Commandant-in-Chief makes one last visit

On 31 March, HM The Queen Mother arrived in Wessex HCC.4, XV733 of the Queen's Flight for her last visit to Little Rissington. Accompanying her were a number of VIPs who arrived in a pair of Devons, VP958 and WB534. A Canberra T.4, WE188 and Lancaster B.1, PA474, were parked on the hardstanding. Lined-up in one of the hangars were a Hunter FGA.9, XJ636, Varsity T.1, WJ948, Piston Provost T.1, WV499, a Spitfire and Harvard.

'It's an honour, Ma'am'

"During the Royal visits of 1972 and 1976," recalls Sandy Sawyer, *"I was given the dubious honour of being assigned as the Queen Mum's loo lady. Every so often HM would need a ten-minute break and it was my job to escort her into the retiring room where refreshments of her choosing were also provided. While she was in there, I stood outside chatting to her detective and learnt a lot about her fondness for CFS. As Commandant-in-Chief she maintained a close interest in the School and was very knowledgeable about its history and function. She looked forward with relish to her visits to Little Rissington."*

Permanent Staff award

When Cheryl Barber received her silver Pelican at the end of her CFS tour she was we believe one of the first permanent staff members to be awarded the memento and, as her husband Dennis, who was a Varsity pilot and Trapper at the time, already had his, they became the first married couple in service at CFS to each own the much coveted silver trophy.

During the last dining-out night, Sandy Sawyer received her silver Pelican and, being married to OC Operations, Sqn Ldr Peter Sawyer, they became only the second wedded couple to own individual silver Pelicans. Her final duty was to assist her ATC colleagues in seeing off the last aircraft to depart Little Rissington.

The CFS Helicopter Wing disbanded 31 March 1976 at Tern Hill and became 2 (Advanced) Flying Training School.

The final dining out night and Flt Lt Rob Lapraik receives the Clarkson Trophy from MRAF Sir Thomas Pike while AM Sir Rex Roe (seated) and Wg Cdr Cas Maynard offer their congratulations. (*Cas Maynard*)

Unit Strength

The gradual run down of RAF personnel at Little Rissington was already underway on 1 April as affirmed in the following table:

Staff	106
Airmen	372
WRAF	35
Airmen/Aircrew	1
Total	514

The Queen's Colour is proudly paraded through the streets of Cheltenham for the last time. (*CFS Archive*)

Ceremonial Parade

On 3 April, personnel of Little Rissington held a Freedom of Cheltenham Parade, marching through the streets of the City with 'bayonets fixed, Colours flying and drums beating'. The Salute was taken by the Mayor as four Jet Provosts flew over the Saluting Base, and the March Past was followed by a motorcade. The Mayor had given a lunch for senior staff of CFS before the parade, during which he exchanged gifts with Air Cdre Sutton.

Graduation Dinner

Coincident with the move from Little Rissington, the tradition of a Dining out night was changed to a Graduation Dinner using the same format as before. The Dinner for No. 276 Course was held on 7 April in the Officers' Mess when the Guest of Honour, MRAF Sir Thomas Pike, presented the usual array of trophies.

Farewell CFS

And so, on 12 April 1976, the remaining aircraft of the Central Flying School, responsible for training the RAF's flying instructors and for setting the high standards demanded by the Service since 1912, took off from Little Rissington for the last time. The previous year's defence cuts had predicted the move and reports that the USAF might have been interested in using it as an airfield were unfounded. Instead, it was decided that the Army would take over the Cotswold site in the following September.

The Squadrons disperse

On the morning of the twelfth, a final flypast was led by nine Bulldogs in arrow formation, followed by a formation of five Jet Provost T.3s flanked on either side by a box formation of four Jet Provost T.5s. Bringing up the rear was a six-ship formation led by the Vintage Pair flanked by a pair of Gnats from the Kemble CFS detachment on either side. The complete formation could be held for a few seconds only because of the relative speeds; the Bulldogs cruised at 100kt very close to the stalling speed of the jets which cruised at about 240kt. The latter flew higher than Bulldogs so that they could overtake in clear air. After passing over the airfield the formations broke up and headed off for their respective destination airfields.

April 6th and practice for the final flypast, with nine Bulldogs leading five Jet Provost T.5s, followed by the Vintage Pair and four Gnats, with eight Jet Provost T.3s in two box formations on the flanks. (*CFS Archive*)

The Headquarters Central Flying School, Examining Wing, Jet Provost Squadron and the Vintage Pair moved from Little Rissington to RAF Cranwell, while the Bulldog Squadron headed for RAF Leeming. The CFS Gnats of 4 Squadron at Kemble transferred to No. 4 FTS at RAF Valley, Anglesey, to await the arrival of the first Hawker Siddeley Hawk advanced trainer later in the year.

Wg Cdr Cas Maynard (*right*) bids farewell to Wg Cdr Maurice Felton before climbing into a nearby Jet Provost T.3 XM419/60 and leading the final flypast. (*CFS Archive*)

Naturally, this separation of the various CFS flying units was unpopular with RAF personnel at Little Rissington as one school of thought suggested that the nearby RAF airfield at Fairford would have made an ideal alternative airfield from which to operate, particularly as the Concorde test programme had been forced to relinquish its facility there. But sadly it wasn't to be!

That was not quite the end of RAF flying on the airfield however, as recorded in the log book of former "Red Arrows" pilot Flt Lt Nigel Champness. *"We flew twice more at Little Rissington, once for a function on 2 July 1976 and finally, a pre-season practice display on 6 April 1977."*

To Brize Norton

With the closure of Little Rissington recalls Sgt Brian Goodfellow, *"responsibility for accommodation and administration for all 'Red Arrows' personnel on detachment at Kemble was transferred to RAF Brize Norton. Single individuals were billeted at Brize and bussed over each day while those in Quarters and Hirings remained where they were – the management of their residences having been passed on to Brize."*

Care and Maintenance

Throughout May the Station continued administrative close down procedures. By the end of the month most of the subsidiary activity clubs had closed and the tempo of normal station life slowed down considerably. Work continued closing down inventories, clearing buildings and preparing for the handover to the Army on 1 September. By 1 July, the 1st Battalion The Royal Irish Rangers had begun the occupation of married quarters as they prepared for the arrival of the advance party on 9 August.

Key to the Cotswolds

At 10:30 on 1 September, a Board of Officers assembled for the transfer of the lands, buildings, facilities and services. At 12:00 a simple handover parade took place when, symbolically, the Station was handed over to the Royal Irish Rangers. The parade consisted of 20 Airmen and NCOs and an Equal number of Rangers drawn up in front of the Station Flag Staff. The RAF Ensign was hauled down to the 'Last Post', played by buglers of the Royal Irish Rangers, and a formation of three CFS Jet Provost T.5s from RAF Cranwell flew over in formation. Wg Cdr Felton presented the "Key to the Cotswolds" to Lt Col Hiles commanding the 1st Battalion and received in exchange, the badge of the Royal Irish Rangers. The RAF contingent then marched out of the Main Gate as a solitary Gnat of "The Red Arrows", trailing smoke, flew over in salute.

Present at the parade was WO J. Baker MBE, who as a Corporal policeman was the first NCO to raise the Ensign at Little Rissington in 1937.

Its days as a flying station over, SWO Gill Davies continued to run a skeleton staff which he says *"was retained to maintain the base in working order and organise the removal of essential equipment to maintenance units and units at other airfields. After the Royal Irish Rangers took over in September and renamed Little Rissington 'Imjin Barracks', I retired to Little Rissington village where I still live."*

Civilian staff look on as Wg Cdr Felton hands over the 'Key to the Cotswolds' to Lt Col Hiles outside Station HQ, bringing to a close the tenure by the RAF of Little Rissington. (*CFS Archive*)

'Beating the Retreat'

In 1976, Gp Capt R D Bates, an earlier student on No. 196 course, was by then OC RAF Brize Norton, parenting Little Rissington in the final days of RAF activity. *"Mike Williams was the last Group Captain station commander of the active base. On 29 October 1976, my diary records the 'Beating the Retreat' ceremony at RAF Little Rissington. A little later, I recall receiving a plaintive phone call from the Flt Lt commanding the Rear Party, who had spent weeks saying farewell to his slowly diminishing team. Could he come and take his leave of me. 'Sic transit gloria mundi!'*

Regal maternal concerns for "The Reds"

Both before and after this major CFS move, 'The Red Arrows' changed bases more than once, prompting the apocryphal story of HM The Queen Mother, Commandant-in-Chief CFS, enquiring of the Commandant – 'The next time you move my 'Red Arrows', do you think someone would kindly let me know?' He is probably still trying to work out a reply."

A lifelong servant

As most of the stories in this account about life at post-war Little Rissington are from former air force personnel, we thought it would be a fitting tribute for the penultimate recollection to come from a gentleman who served as a civilian on the station throughout the CFS years. His name is John Stevens and he is probably remembered by everyone who lived or worked in the Officers' Mess.

"Known as Jack to all who knew me, I joined No. 8 Maintenance Unit at Little Rissington in 1946 after wartime service in the Army. Seven years later in 1953, I was appointed as the Officers' Mess Manager, a capacity in which I worked until the airfield closed as an Air Force base in 1976. For my services as Mess Manager, I was awarded the MBE on 1 June 1972, receiving the award from Queen Elizabeth II at Buckingham Palace on 5 December. In addition to my work at Rissington, I enjoyed my sport and was a leading member of both Bourton Vale Cricket Club and Bourton Ladies Hockey Club.

On 23 July 1976, my wife and I were the guests of Station Commander, Wg Cdr M.C.D. Felton along with 80 officers, honorary members and their ladies for dinner. This was the final social occasion to be held by RAF personnel in the Officers' Mess at Little Rissington before it was handed over to the 1st Battalion of the Royal Irish Rangers."

AM Sir John Sutton KCB

"In early 1976 I had taken over CFS from John Severne on 12th February and I see from my logbook that the formal fly in to Cranwell with 21 Jet Provosts beyond our final 28 aircraft flypast over Little Rissington was made on 12th April. I see that I personally flew more than 20 hours in March but there was some reduction in activity with

packing up and preparations for the move and the fact that we had a Royal Visit by HM the Queen Mother on 31st March.

Having been at Cranwell for a few months it became clear to me (not ever having been to CFS before so it was an objective view) that splitting up CFS was a mistake. Part of the strength of CFS had been undermined some years before when CFS itself, its agents apart and perhaps inevitably, ceased to fly operational aircraft. What was left was valuable provided Examining Wing and the CFS squadrons were kept together so that flying training techniques could be jointly developed and refined, standards set and maintained. Once CFS was split up much of that was lost and the value of having CFS at all could be questioned.

I wrote all this in a paper and sent it to Command Headquarters. Nothing at all happened. Then after about 6 months HQ asked for another copy of my paper as they had apparently lost the original. Following this, there was a rush to 'put CFS back together again' and rectify those shortcomings I had outlined. I was only at Cranwell for 15 months, being promoted and sent as ACAS (Pol) but before I left arrangements were made to reunify CFS. Shortly after I left, this was done first at Leeming and later still at Scampton. Since Command HQ had taken no interest whatsoever initially, all this sudden interest in putting the Central Flying School back together again seemed very odd. What occurred to me and might well have happened was that HM The Queen Mother was well informed and had asked some penetrating questions during her last visit to Little Rissington, to which there were no sensible answers. So on my ppc visit to Clarence House I said I was delighted at the HQ decision to put 'Her Flying School' back together again and asked if she had fixed it. 'Well,' she said, 'I did have a word with a few people'. And, of course, that was all it took. At the end of her life she must have been upset to see that the wheel had again turned full circle with CFS HQ again at Cranwell and the various bits split up around the country."

The CFS post-Little Rissington

The end of the Central Flying School's tenure at Little Rissington saw the dispersal of its individual units to stations across the UK. The Headquarters Central Flying School, Examining Wing and Jet Provost Squadron moved from Little Rissington to RAF Cranwell on 12 April 1976, while on the same date the Gnat Squadron moved from RAF Kemble to RAF Valley, where it was replaced by the Hawk Squadron the following November.

The Headquarters Central Flying School, which had effectively become a lodger unit, moved from RAF Cranwell to RAF Leeming on 5 September 1977 and from there to RAF Scampton on 1 September 1984. Five years later, on 1 February 1989, the Bulldog Squadron transferred from RAF Scampton to operate within No. 3 Flying Training School at RAF Cranwell, vacating facilities which were occupied by the newly formed Tucano Squadron on 1 September that year. The Refresher Flying Flight was incorporated into CFS for a short period from late 1991 until the demise of the Jet Provost in June 1992. Meanwhile the Hawk Squadron had become 19 (Reserve) Squadron at RAF Valley, remaining within No. 4 Flying Training School. Finally, the Headquarters Central Flying School left RAF Scampton and moved back to its former home at RAF Cranwell on 31 May 1995, where it currently resides.

A solitary Gnat of 'The Red Arrows' flies low over the station as the last contingent of RAF personnel perform the marching out ceremony through the main gate, 1 September, 1976. (*CFS Archive*)

CHAPTER 7

CFS Aerobatic Teams

No account of Little Rissington would be complete without covering the various CFS aerobatic teams. From the earliest days, the CFS realised that one of the ways in which pilots could develop their ability was through formation flying. When the Hendon Air Displays began in the 1920s, they became the medium for displaying the skills of RAF pilots. The first CFS aerobatic formation appeared at the 1921 Hendon show flying Sopwith Snipes and these were succeeded in 1927 by five De Havilland Genet Moths. These were replaced in 1931 by Gipsy Moths. This team of five included a flypast in vic formation with the leader inverted. Thus began a tradition of inverted flying that was continued by the 1933 team of Avro Tutors. Many famous personalities took part at various times. Young officers like A. Coningham, J.N. Boothman, G.H. Stainforth, R.L.R. Atcherley, D.A. Boyle, B.E. Embry and H.A. Constantine, to name but a few, added glory to the name of CFS and rightly won their place in aviation's hall of fame.

Post World War II, reference is made to a CFS five-ship Tiger Moth aerobatic team in 1947, although no record could be found as to whether it was an official RAF team. A three-ship Prentice display team existed for a while circa 1951, and subsequent CFS teams have performed in Meteors, Piston Provosts, Vampires, Jet Provosts, Chipmunks and the Gnat.

"The Meteorites"

Flt Lt Caryl Gordon, an instructor with the Central Flying School, led four Meteor T.7 aircraft in the first official post-war CFS display team for the 1952 season. Known as "The Meteorites" they are believed to be the first RAF aerobatic team to be given a name; until then individual teams were identified by their squadron numbers.

The team's aircraft retained their standard bare metal (silver) colours, although towards the end of the season they gained high visibility yellow anti-collision training bands round the fuselage and wings.

AV-M Sir John Severne has vivid memories of his tour as a Flight Lieutenant instructor on the Meteor Flight in the early fifties. At the same time he was also PA to the Commandant, Air Cdre 'Mark' Selway.

"One day I found in my In tray that famous photograph of the CFS Display Team of 1933 of the Tutors with the leader inverted. The Commandant had been a member of the team and he had simply written on the photo: "Re-do Meteors". And we did! Sqn Ldr George Brabyn, our New Zealand squadron commander, was the inverted leader and I flew the photographic aircraft. The tricky bit was that the Meteor was only cleared to fly upside down for 15 seconds. During that time the leader had to roll upside down, the other two members and I had to get into formation, take the photograph and then open out sufficiently for George Brabyn to be able to turn the right way up again. We found that if the leader's engines were not at full power, we could stay upside down for much longer than 15 seconds, although I was told subsequently that it did not do the oil pressure much good! Anyhow, we never had a flame-out. The Air Ministry photographer, Mike Chase, who flew in the back seat of my aircraft, took the picture which hit the world's press, including

A box-four Meteor T.7 formation of the appropriately named Meteorite team, pull up in this view, taken in 1953 by Russell Adams from a Meteor flown by Flt Lt Severne. (*John Severne*)

the New York Times. I believe it was published by about 160 newspapers. Flt Lt Jimmy James flew as No. 2 on the right and his passenger was Mr Coles from the Air Ministry. Flt Lt Johnny Price flew as No. 3 with Mr Young (also from the Air Ministry) who subsequently wrote an amusing article about the sortie in 'Punch' (see 'High level conversions' in Chapter 2).

The next logical stage was to attempt the first half of a loop with four aircraft and an inverted leader. This was achieved by our flight commander, Caryl Gordon, with me again flying the photographic aircraft. I believe this was the first time this had been done. I always felt that air-to-air photographs should be taken from ahead of the subject rather than from behind. This involved formating on the team during the loop by looking backwards! It is not as difficult as it sounds; try riding a bicycle by looking at another cyclist alongside but a little behind! Caryl Gordon subsequently taught the Duke of Edinburgh to fly."

More Meteor teams

Although "The Meteorites" disbanded at the end of the 1953 season, they were succeeded by other Meteor teams in successive years. The final Meteor T.7 team was a four-ship formation called "The Pelicans" and included a Fg Off Patrick Hine who recollects:

"The team started its work-up in February and progressively developed a more ambitious sequence of formation change manoeuvres during loops, rolls and steep wingovers. The most difficult one - certainly from my perspective as No.2 - was a change from echelon starboard (the unusual order then being 1, 3, 4 and 2 after my easing out as 3 and 4 slotted in) back to the basic box during a roll to port. It was a change that for me required stop-to-stop throttle movements and very rapid closure on the leader during the first part of the roll whilst keeping a wary eye on my colleagues, particularly No.4 as he moved back into line astern of the leader. We eventually hacked it but with inconsistent success, and so after much discussion in the bar decided to replace it with a line astern to box change during the roll (in order 1, 2, 3 and 4) which proved to be much easier.

While there were some 'hairy' moments during the season, we managed to avoid any collisions or mishaps and to give around a dozen well-received shows at major air displays up and down the country, including 3 on the Battle of Britain At Home Day. The team was disbanded, following a final photographic session with Russell Adams, in October 1956 when the leader, 'Frank' Franklin, was promoted and posted to the Handling Squadron at Boscombe Down. Matt Kemp and I later joined 'Treble One' Squadron's Black Arrows team on Hunters, whilst 'Mac' McArthur stayed at CFS until being selected as one of the first batch of RAF pilots to fly the U-2".

"The Sparrows"

Formed at South Cerney in the spring of 1957 the onus fell on Basic Squadron to provide a new display team for the coming season using the Piston Provost. As Flt Lts Charlie Kingsbury, Les Howes and Bert Lane had been 'playing' at formation aeros for some time, they were assigned to the team where they were joined by Flt Lt Mike Bradley, a recent arrival from 208 Squadron in the Middle East, and Flt Lt Black who was assigned as reserve.

Five aircraft with up-rated Leonides were prepared for their use and it was soon found that rapid opening of the throttle quickly moved the aircraft forward some five feet and ten feet to the right, so the highest level of concentration was called for from the pilots. As reported in the CFS Magazine for October, *"when viewed from the ground it is decidedly diverting, when viewed from the cockpit devastatingly disconcerting."*

Having transferred to Little Rissington in May, "The Sparrows" as the team became known, took part in displays at Squire's Gate, Woodvale, Baginton, Little Rissington (for the visit of HRH Princess Margaret), the SBAC show at Farnborough and Battle of Britain displays at Little Rissington and Colerne. Support was provided throughout by a dedicated team of eleven groundcrew under the charge of Sgt Gisbourne.

The team's Provosts were painted in the standard RAF training colours of the period, silver with yellow training bands.

The Sparrows flying their uprated Piston Provost T.1s in echelon port. *(CFS Archive)*

"The Helicans"

Undoubtedly the least known and shortest-lived of CFS teams, "The Helicans" was a three-ship formation comprising a single Hunter F.4 from the CFS Type Flight at Kemble leading two Rissington-based Meteor T.7s. Apart from appearing in the Little Rissington At Home day in July 1957, no record of their participation at other venues has come to light

"The CFS Jet Aerobatic Team"

In the spring of 1958, a new aerobatic team formed under the leadership of Flt Lt Norman Giffin. Flying four Jet Provost T.Mk.1s, five of the team's pool of seven aircraft, XD675-680, 693 were painted in a special scheme of white upper surfaces and red undersides. Looking back, Norman recalls,

"The team wanted to use the name 'The Pelicans' previously used by the Meteor team, but the Meteor Squadron opposed this as it had intentions of reviving a 'Meatbox' team. Although this never materialised, the JP team retained the official title 'The CFS Jet

Aerobatic Team'. Of the remaining pilots, Flt Lts Don McClen flew at No. 2, Freddie Packer at No. 3 and Pete Millington brought up the rear. Flt Lt Mike Edwards was the spare pilot.

When asked if we could paint the aircraft in a special colour scheme, AM Atcherley told us to paint them whatever colour we liked so I prepared a quick sketch on a small piece of card as guidance for the chaps at the St Athan MU. As a consequence, they mimicked my drawing exactly, including the miniscule roundel on the fuselage which became a topical subject of much comment. 'Be careful not to fly through a rain storm', was the advice from the NCO in charge, as they had applied a single coat only and would probably wash off. The split red and white colour scheme was designed to make it easier for spectators to identify which aircraft were being flown inverted during the display. Technical modifications were also incorporated to enable the aircraft to fly inverted for up to three minutes. Later in the season, a pair of smoke generators was fitted under the wings.

A dedicated groundcrew team was assembled and members took it in turns to fly in the spare seats on displays away from base. An engineer from Hunting Percival and another called Wilkinson from Armstrong Whitworth were on hand to solve any serious problems. The latter often flew as passenger to displays, but the Hunting's chap was afraid to fly and preferred to take the train or drive to the various venues.

Our first practice as a four-ship took place on 3 March 1958. In one memorable incident, we landed in formation at Rissy after a display for a visiting Thai Air Force delegation, but unknown to me, Pete Millington's wheels had not come down and, as he was concentrating on keeping formation, he forgot to check for three greens. He did a wheels-up behind us and it wasn't until I turned off the runway that I saw his aircraft, XD679, skidding across the grass. As we taxied in, the runway controller commented that he thought that as we were always doing different things it was part of the display.

On another occasion, 21 July, we had finished our display at RNAS Culdrose and, without filing a flight plan, took off in the direction of RAF Chivenor. The weather was poor and on arrival overhead I called the tower and got no response. To our surprise the airfield was closed for the weekend. Fortunately, the GCA controller lived nearby and on hearing us flying round dashed to the airfield, opened-up GCA and guided us in. As soon as we landed I was marched in front of the Wing Commander Flying and informed that Chivenor had been closed all day and what the hell were we doing there.

Participation at the SBAC Farnborough show was the undoubted highlight of the team's season, but it could have ended in tragedy. During one display we executed a barrel role and I must have been going too fast as Don McClen was thrown out of formation and as he closed in on the downward leg, our wingtips touched. Close inspection afterwards revealed nothing more than scratch marks on the two wingtips but, if the impact had been much heavier, the ailerons could have jammed."

View from No. 2

Flying at No. 2, gave Don McClen a different perspective.

"We worked up to display standard over a period of ten weeks, in over 40 sorties, practising between half an hour and an hour's duration. The main problem was that the JP1 had insufficient power for the leader to maintain height during a ten minute display, so he had to coax as much as he could from every manoeuvre, while still leaving us enough spare power to hold close formation. The result, especially in turbulent conditions, meant that we were often flying to the limit, while still losing height. The display season took us around the country and also to Jersey (where Norman met his future wife), later culminating in the SBAC show at Farnborough – a total of 20 displays in all.

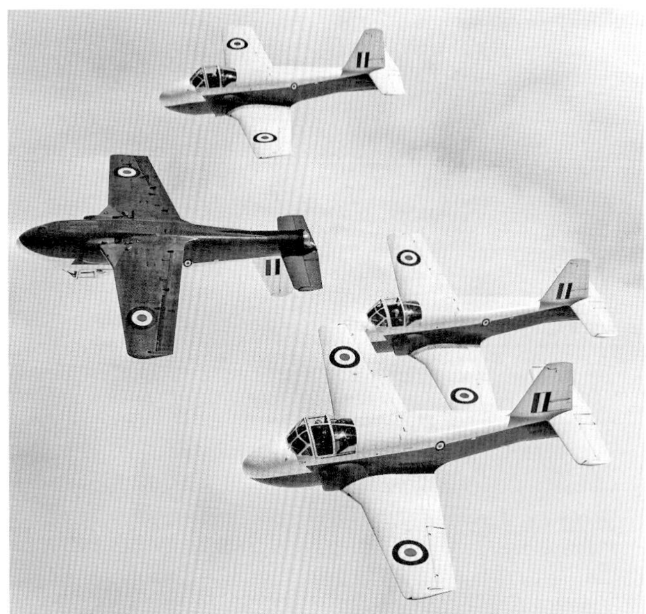

While Flt Lt Norman Giffin holds his Jet Provost T.1 inverted, the remaining three aircraft in the CFS Jet Aerobatic Team close in formation. (*Norman Giffin*)

Although we consoled ourselves that the cognoscenti appreciated our skills, our role was to entertain the public and we knew how much better we would be with an uprated engine. At Farnborough that year we were 'competing' with 'The Black Arrows', which specialised in performing a loop with 22 Hunters. Endeavouring to cheer us up, 'Batchy' Atcherley, our staunchest supporter, snorted 'Any self-respecting pilot can do a formation loop in a Hunter, but you chaps are up against the stops for your entire display!' Our spirits were also buoyed by a congratulatory letter from Air Cdre Sir Frank Whittle

We particularly enjoyed performing over water where there was usually less turbulence and where, therefore, we could conserve our height and fly more smoothly. So the displays over the Tall Ships outside Portsmouth Harbour, and in the harbour entrance to St Helier, Jersey, were undoubtedly the best. The worst was at the Farnborough Air Show one day when we had very severe turbulence and squally showers to contend with. Norman Giffin tried to judge the display so that we would finish at, or just above, our minimum permitted height, aiming to complete this particular display with a barrel roll continuing into a steep turn for a formation landing. Realising, when inverted, that he was lower than desirable, he tightened the roll to conserve height. I was initially thrown out of position and then found myself battling to regain close formation with my aircraft sliding towards the leading aircraft. It was an affair of seconds, but my violent control movements resulted in my left wing tip touching the leader's right wing tip. We didn't know this had happened until we landed, but both wing tips had to be replaced. It had been a close shave.

The only other incident was during a display at Little Rissington for a visiting Thai Air Force delegation. In concentrating on his formation during landing in the rear slot, Peter Millington forgot to lower his undercarriage. As he sank lower and lower he realised, too late, what had happened and suffered the indignity of finding his aircraft sliding along on its belly. Without waiting to transmit his intentions he vacated the aircraft as soon as it had stopped, in case it caught fire, while the rest of us taxied blithely to the dispersal wondering where the hell he was! We were not told what the Thai delegation made of this departure from the advised programme."

The team's performances were well received throughout the summer, although somewhat overshadowed by the incredible 22-aircraft loop performed by the Hunters of 111 Squadron's "Black Arrows" at the Farnborough Air Show.

"The Redskins"

When the "CFS Jet Aerobatic Team" disbanded at the close of the 1958 season three of its Jet Provost T.1s, were re-allocated for use by a new team for 1959. Called "The Redskins" and flown by Flt Lts P.J. 'Curly' Hirst and J.R. Rhind, they performed as a synchronised pair throughout the summer. 'Curly' Hirst:

"The Redskins team was an idea jointly formulated between Jim Rhind and myself. The title was a natural choice of name, chosen by Jim, because of the complete red colour scheme for each aircraft.

Jim Rhind and myself had considerable autonomy in the displays with regard to the content and arrangements and we devised a synchronised aerobatic sequence which looked quite spectacular from the ground. In particular, we included an item where we looped from opposite directions, and when alongside one another, facing opposite directions, executed a flick roll before completing the loop. I doubt whether anyone would be authorised for such a manoeuvre if one were to ask permission. The CFS engineers were very good and devised a white smoke system for the aircraft which involved fixing a large smoke cartridge under each wing which was ignited from a switch inside the cockpit. The smoke was very effective and lasted for between three and four minutes. I tried the system inadvertently (and the Fire Service!) just before a scheduled SBAC performance at Farnborough when the switch operated at start up – I had not switched it 'OFF' after the previous display.

For the flying displays, because of the relatively poor power/weight ratio we operated with minimum amounts of fuel and about 600lb. total was normally sufficient for a complete show where transit time was not required. But as mentioned earlier, aircraft control was excellent, particularly with the well balanced ailerons.

The first demo was at Hucknall on 18 May and the last one was at Shawbury on 22 October for the Duchess of Gloucester. A total of 34 displays were flown during the year."

"The Pelicans"

As the bird forms the crest of the Central Flying School coat of arms, the association with the Pelican came to symbolise many of the unit's aerobatic teams over the years. A Meteor T.7 team was the first to adopt it in 1956, but, curiously, two teams were flown using the 'Pelican' name in 1960.

First up was a Jet Provost T.3 four-ship formation which worked up on brand new aircraft as the season progressed. Flt Lt R. Langstaff was appointed team leader and the Nos. 2 to 4 positions were filled by Flt Lts F.R. Brambley and J.G. Nicklin, and Plt Off B.A. McDonald. They flew four silver and day-glo painted JPs equipped with the Viper 102 engine and fitted with underwing smoke generators. The team was not confined to displays in the UK; a trip to the French National Air Rally at L'Orient in August was one of the more notable overseas events. In September the Pelicans performed at the SBAC Farnborough Air Show.

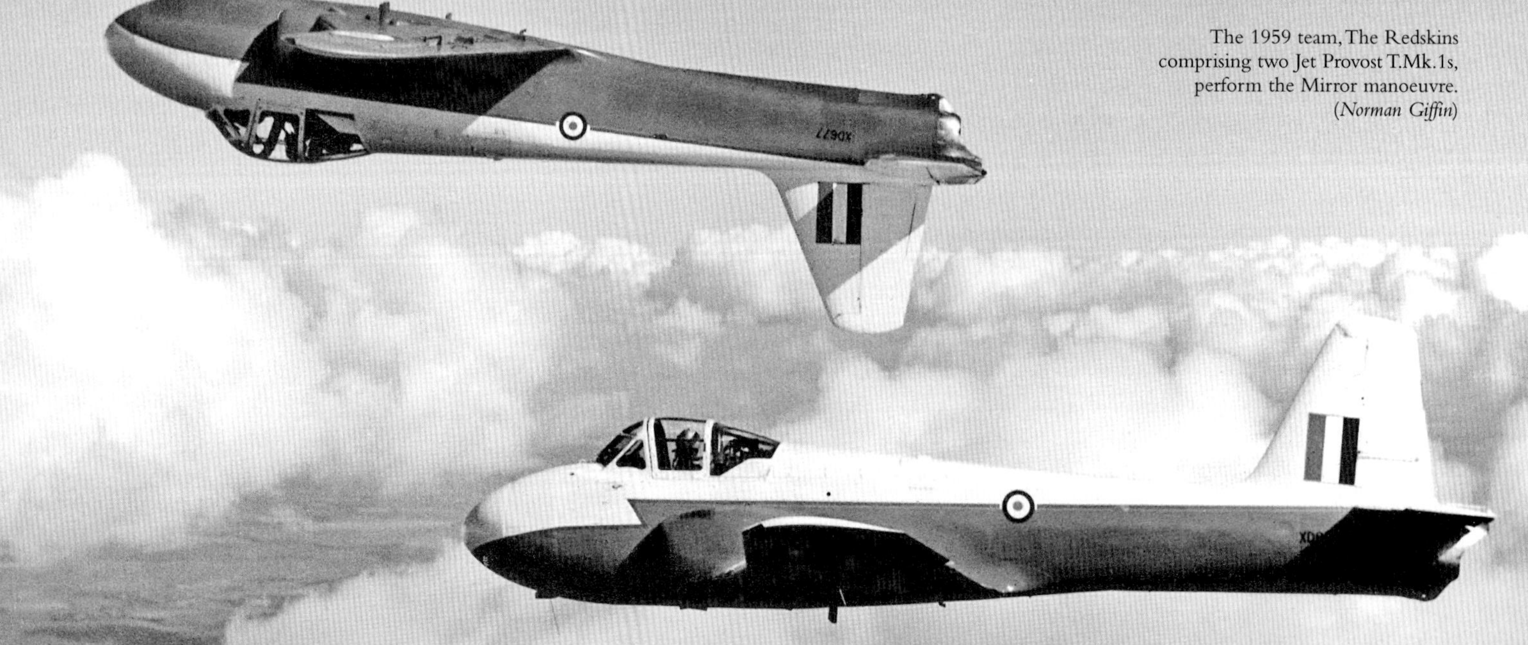

The 1959 team, The Redskins comprising two Jet Provost T.Mk.1s, perform the Mirror manoeuvre. (*Norman Giffin*)

Mission to Africa

After a short tour to Nigeria and Ghana in 1960, Air Clues wrote the following account of the flight home: "With October's display before the President of Ghana, Dr. Kwame Nkrumah, The CFS Pelican aerobatic team of four Jet Provost T.Mk.3 trainers (plus another in reserve) completed their mission in West Africa and a few days later began their flight back to Britain. Their uncomfortable homeward route across the French Sahara was similar to the route flown on the outward journey, except for an additional refuelling stop, which removed some of the hazards experienced on the way out. The party of some 29 officers and airmen, led by CFI Wg Cdr Kenneth Tapper, expected difficulties from the limited endurance of the Jet Provost, navigation over featureless country with limited aids, and the intense heat of the desert.

Any potential forced landing for the eight in five Jet Provosts (three carried spare pilots) had some cover from shuttles and leap-frogging stages planned by the two transport crews, with limited equipment and knowledge of the desert. Sqn Ldr John F.D. ('Tim') Elkington flew the Varsity and Fg Off Jack Goodwin, a former Ferry Wing pilot, captained the Valetta. One difficult stage was the 415 miles between Niamey and Tessalit, where the French Air Force, with their desert-flying experience, set up a rescue organisation especially for the RAF. For any flight over French-administered territory their Search and Rescue organisation is informed of the flight plan and an aircraft is positioned at the most suitable airfield for the area to be covered. A Dassault Flamant was positioned at Tessalit, with a C-47 earmarked for the next part of the route and a Constellation positioned in Algeria. In fact the Flamant was called away for an urgent casevac task but another was flown 600 nautical miles from Bamako to Niamey to provide rescue cover.

The route home was through Tamale, 300 miles north of Accra, to Niamey on the Niger, where they spent their first night. On 13 October three JPs went to Tessalit in the French Sudan, thence on to El Golea in Algeria to night stop. The two other trainers left Niamey on 15 October and stayed in Tessalit, before joining up with the others at El Golea. By the 17th all five aircraft reached Maison Blanche (Algiers Airport) where they split again, two leaving on the 17th and three the next day for Palma in the Balearic Islands. All five JPs left Palma on the 19th to fly via Orange and Dijon, crossing the Hampshire coast to land at Thorney Island for Customs, before flying their short final leg to Little Rissington.

Three of the Jet Provosts were specially fitted with Marconi sub-miniature radio compasses, which proved a boon to the pilots. The team found some voice bearings could be anything up to 50° out, whereas on several occasions the little radio compass locked on during the climb at the start of a 350 mile leg. VDF homers at Tessalit and elsewhere proved extremely accurate within normal operating range. An unforecast sandstorm blacking out an airfield was the team's chief concern, with a minimum holding off time on the approach when already with low fuel states. Even on take-off almost anything could happen on these desert strips. At Tessalit, for example, on the outward journey, the jet trainers were forced to take off with an 8-

No sooner had the Mark 3 Jet Provost entered service at CFS than No. 1 Squadron pilots used it to form The Pelicans aerobatic team. Smoke was provided by underwing generators. (*Ray Deacon*)

knot downwind in a sun temperature of 160° - taxiing down the runway for an upwind take-off would have consumed an extra 200 lbs. of precious fuel. On top of that, two donkeys appeared half-way along either side of the runway."

On their return to the UK, the underwing smoke generators were removed and a full smoke generation system using diesel fuel injected directly into the jet stream was installed ready for 1961, when Flt Lt F.R. Brambley took over as leader. In the following year, "The Pelicans" converted on to the Viper 202-powered Jet Provost Mark 4, with 50% extra thrust. The addition of a fifth aircraft increased the range and speed of formation changes in their displays. Flt Lt I.K. McKee was nominated leader for the 1962 season.

"Pelican Red"

Activities on the second aerobatic team for the 1960 season are recalled by Flt Lt Peter Frame.

"The team was led by Lt Dickie Wren RN with Flt Lt Pete Broughton as No. 2, me as No. 3 and Flt Lt John Mayes in the box. Unusually I flew the aircraft solo from the right hand seat, which caused some funny remarks from the groundcrew, especially when operating away from Rissington. Being built like a gorilla enabled me to reach the HP cock and pressurisation wheel from the right hand seat, though I had to turn on the pressurisation before getting airborne which was the incorrect method.

The second display team for the 1960 season, the Vampire T.11s of Pelican Red, take off for their slot in the 1960 ROC Day programme. (*Ray Deacon*)

The introduction of the 200-series Viper-powered Jet Provost T.4, enabled the 1961 Red Pelicans (*above*) to extend their repertoire (*Dave Watkins*), and the 1962 team (*below*) to be increased to a five-ship formation. (*Simon Watson*)

The team was formed just after I arrived in April 1960 and the first session took place on 4 May. There was a JP team and I think that they were called 'The Pelicans' so we had to call ourselves 'Pelican Red'. Our team was a bit unofficial in that it didn't have any back-up and we didn't carry out a lot of displays. Perhaps the two biggest displays we took part in were for the Queen Mother's visit on 16 November and a very large display at RNAS Culdrose on 15 July. There were quite a few displays at CFS for various visitors but I think that we only lasted the one season with the Queen Mother's show being our finale".

"The Red Pelicans"

The colour scheme on the Jet Provosts dramatically changed in 1963 to an all-over day-glo red scheme, and the team name revised to "The Red Pelicans". Nine production Jet Provost T.Mk.4s, XP549-554 and XP571-573, were assigned to the team, sufficient to operate a six-ship formation. During the season the team appeared at many air displays across the UK and Europe.

Having flown as No. 2 in the 1962 team, Flt Lt Ian Bashall took over as team leader for the 1963 season, and recalls one particular incident:

"Due to the amount of aircraft flying around Rissy, we used to go to Pershore for our practice sessions, or down to Kemble. One Friday afternoon when practising the mirror formation at Pershore, the two aircraft got a bit too close and the tops of their fins and rudders made contact. There was something of a muffled conversation over the R/T and I realised that all was not as it should be. So I led the team back to Rissy, and put the two offending aircraft out at Nos. 5 and 6. This was so as to make sure that they landed last and would be parked as far from the hangar as possible, hopefully to avoid anyone else seeing the damage.

When we went in to sign the F700s, I took the Chiefy aside and asked him to have a look at the two aircraft at the far end, as I think they may have had a bit of a bird strike. He came back a little while later, and with a wry smile said, 'The only bird strike they have had is with another Pelican'.

To my eternal gratitude, the two aircraft were secreted into the hangar

The pinnacle for the Jet Provost as a formation display aircraft came in 1963 with the Red Pelican team, led by Flt Lt Ian Bashall, seen here flying their six bright red Mark 4s. For the following season, the team had the honour to perform as the official aerobatic team of the RAF. (*Ian Bashall*)

and repaired over the weekend, without knowledge of the incident going any further. So I thought!!

At the end of the season in September, the whole team was invited to a reception by the Commandant, Air Cdre Bird-Wilson. To my amazement, he turned to me and said, 'How fortunate we are to have such excellent groundcrew who are able to repair two Pelicans' broken tail feathers so quickly and quietly.' Clearly, he had known about it all summer but was good enough not to take it any further."

FTC provides official RAF Aerobatic Teams

Until the early sixties the RAF's premier aerobatic teams were chosen from front line squadrons, but the exorbitant costs of operating fighter-based teams caused a major shift in Government policy in 1963; henceforth the official RAF aerobatic team would be formed of training aircraft operating from units within Flying Training Command. The consequence of this was that the 1964 "Red Pelicans" were appointed as the official aerobatic team of the RAF. Led by Flt Lt T.E.L. Lloyd, Flt Lts B.A. Nice, W.A. Langworthy, D.F. Southern, H.R. Lane and E.C.F. Tilsley flew in the Nos. 2 to 6 slots respectively.

The following extract is taken from the 1964 "Red Pelicans" official programme:

The 'hatching' process

"The 1964 'Red Pelicans Fledglings' foregathered early in February, when six pilots and ten ground personnel were selected from volunteers at the Central Flying School.

Formation practice commenced with three aircraft and the pilots practising basic manoeuvres in Echelon, Line-Abreast and Line-Astern positions. As experience was gained, the number of aircraft was increased until finally, after much hard work, the complete formation of six aircraft was flown for the first time late in March. Practice continued with six aircraft at 5,000 ft until a sequence of manoeuvres was finalised for presentation and clearance to fly down to 500 ft.

When watching a formation 'sequence' one little realises the amount of trial and error required to obtain a smooth-flowing display; changes of formation must follow in the correct order so that the most suitable formation patterns are used for the more difficult manoeuvres. This part of an aerobatic team's work is probably the most interesting – although sometimes frustrating! Once the sequence is finalised the aim is then PERFECTION.

During this time the groundcrew have been busy servicing the team aircraft and preparing the considerable technical backing for the display season. Additionally the task of respraying the red aircraft, proving of the smoke systems and other major servicing programmes have been carried out by the station's Technical Wing.

The display that you see today is the culmination of many weeks' practice, preparation and, above all, TEAMWORK."

The CFS Mascot

A Pelican was incorporated as part of the Armorial Bearings of the Central Flying School because of its heraldic representation as the mythical bird of learning. Thus when Patrick was presented to the School early in 1962, he naturally assumed the role of the CFS mascot.

'Performance' figures for this bird are still on the SECRET list, but it is known that he is strictly a subsonic aviator. He is highly respected by members of the staff, who consider that some of his less endearing traits make him a potentially devastating addition to the country's low-level 'strike' force.

Regrettably, his social habits leave much to be desired – in his own interests it was decided that he should be detached locally and he is now based in a well-known Cotswold aviary at Bourton-on-the-Water.

The 1964 "Red Pelican" Team's first performance took place at Little Rissington during the Wright Jubilee Trophy event on 28 April. It was a fitting prelude to subsequent appearances at 25 venues, including several on mainland Europe. The undoubted highlight of the season was a co-ordinated display of formation aerobatics with the Gnat-mounted "Yellowjacks" team of No. 4 FTS Valley at the SBAC Farnborough Airshow. "The Red Pelicans" disbanded at the end of September 1964.

"The CFS Jet Provost Team"

When not being used for display purposes, "The Red Pelicans" JPs were dispersed to various flights around CFS for student training, but this did not prevent a group of enthusiastic instructors deciding that they should form a new team. Flt Lt Derek Bell reminisces: *"After several years of establishing myself as an aerobatic pilot, I felt luck had dealt me a good hand when I was posted to CFS at Little Rissington. At the end of the 1964 season 'The Red Pelicans' were succeeded by 'The Red Arrows'. The red-painted JP4s were still at Rissington and Bill Langworthy, who had been on the Pelicans, convinced the powers that be that he should use four of these ex-Pelly birds to form a new CFS team. Now I was in a strong position, Bill and I were on the same Flight, I had done a number of displays in the JP, and I don't think very many others were that keen on coming to work early, flying an extra sortie each day and not getting too many Saturdays off during*

With the demise of the Red Pelicans, four instructors decided to form The CFS JP Team for 1965, using the previous team's aircraft. Here, the early morning sun reflects on the aircraft as they practise their routine over a quiet Rissy airfield below. (*Michael Rigby via Derek Bell*)

the summer. We were called 'The CFS Jet Provost Team' and we had a ball; thanks to Bill's efforts we did a lot of displays during 1965."

With Flt Lt Bill Langworthy leading the team and Flt Lt Derek Bell as his No. 2, the remaining positions were filled by Flt Lts Roy Booth and Cas Maynard. When Roy was on leave, Flt Lt M. Baston RAAF flew in his position for a couple of shows, and Sqn Ldr Don McClen took over from Derek Bell when he moved over to "The Red Arrows". The team's sixteenth and final display was given on 10 October at the RAF Chivenor ROC Day.

Grass strips and a 'burn up' on the Isle of Wight

Led by Wg Cdr Eddie Edmonds, the 1966 four-ship team comprised Sqn Ldr Don McClen at No. 2 with Flt Lts Chas Sturt, Colin Thomas, and Cas Maynard sharing the other two places during the season. The aircraft originally assigned to the team in 1962 were replaced by fully refurbished Mark 4s painted in a new deep red livery.

"One of our displays was at an air show at Bembridge, in the Isle of Wight," recalls Don McClen, *"where the organisers were keen that we should stay the night; I therefore agreed to see whether it was safe to land and take off from the airfield's grass strip of 933 yards. There was a longer grass strip at Sandown, on the south eastern side of the Isle of Wight, which it seemed sensible to try out before committing ourselves to Bembridge. With a trusting Colin Thomas as 2nd pilot, I flew to Sandown on 1 July, and thus became the first pilot to land a jet aircraft on the Isle of Wight. Five days later we flew to Bembridge and, after a couple of low-level flypasts to assess the approach and condition of the surface of the strip, I landed there without any difficulty as well.*

Being uncertain of how much the grass surface would retard acceleration for take off, I arranged for the ground crew to push the Jet Provost back so that it was only some ten yards from the boundary hedge. I then ran the engine up to full power before releasing the brakes. The aircraft bounded along the strip and got airborne with plenty of room to spare, so I radioed Bembridge's air traffic control to confirm my satisfaction with their airfield. They replied by advising me that my jet engine had set fire to the hedge and they had despatched a fire engine and crew to close the road behind the hedge before putting the fire out. In spite of this vandalism we would still be warmly welcomed back for the weekend.

A second 'Tay Bridge disaster'

Unknown to us at the time, a much more embarrassing fiasco was lying in store. The Queen Mother had been invited to open the new Tay Bridge on 18 August. As Commandant-in-Chief of the Central Flying School she had asked that the Red Pelicans should fly past over the bridge to coincide with her declaring it open. That was fine by us; we regarded it as a great honour. All we needed was the timing of events leading up to the speech and the length of time for her to deliver it. Our contact in Clarence House was evasive. She was sorry, but she could not guarantee that the programme times for the ceremony would be met exactly, though she was fairly confident about how long the Queen Mother would take to deliver her speech. Ever flexible, we arranged for a radio to be situated near the podium and for someone to give us a running commentary on the Queen Mother's movements leading up to when she began her speech. Meanwhile, we would orbit out of sight at a predetermined point up river and be prepared to vary the pattern of our turns so that we could set course when she started to speak, having timed our run to the bridge to equate precisely with the length of her speech.

We knew it might require what Eddie Edmonds referred to as 'a dirty dart' from wherever we were in our orbit to set course for the bridge. We were used to flinging our aircraft around to stick close to him, so we weren't too perturbed. These plans seemed to work perfectly on the day as we were able to set course in good order in response to a radio confirmation that HM The Queen Mother was starting her speech. We flew over the bridge at 200 ft, on time to the second, and waited for a word of congratulations from our ground controller. 'She hasn't finished speaking!' he squawked, and we returned to RAF Leuchars, where we were based for the occasion, with our proverbial four tails between our dozen undercarriage legs. It transpired that she had observed a respectful but spontaneous silence after referring to several accidental deaths during the construction of the bridge. We had not been advised of any pauses and had interrupted her uncompleted speech as we roared obliviously overhead. The station's switchboard was jammed by journalists demanding a reason for such discourtesy and incompetence. We could hardly blame the Queen Mother, though we silently cursed Clarence House, and took the insults and one sneering accusation on the chin."

As the display pilots were also fully employed in the instructional role, both practice and display flying took place outside normal working hours. The groundcrew team was initially provided by volunteer airmen such as SAC Peter Marshall, *"When the team went away for display a number of volunteer groundcrew went in support, occupying the spare seats in the JPs. On one occasion I flew with the team to Bembridge airfield on the Isle of Wight. Being a grass strip it was the first occasion a jet team had landed there and a very bumpy arrival it proved to be. Whether that was the cause for one of the aircraft developing a fuel leak or not, we had not taken an engine mechanic with us and had great difficulty fixing it. As a result, a dedicated groundcrew squad was formed under the leadership of Flt Sgt F.J. Coxon."*

The team gave 25 displays throughout the summer and early autumn, including two in Germany.

More Red Pelicans

The tradition of operating a second CFS aerobatic team continued with "The Red Pelicans" flying four-ship formations using Jet Provost T.4s from 1967 to 1969. Sqn Ldr P.J. 'Curly' Hirst, who flew in the "The Redskins" two-ship team in 1959, took over the reins in 1967 and he was succeeded in 1968 by Flt Lt D. Smith, and in 1969 by Flt Lt John Robinson. A spare aircraft was flown to overseas venues by Flt Lt John Davy who also provided the commentary for spectators during the final year of the T.Mk.4.

Pelicans change up a gear

For the 1970 season, the team exchanged its T.Mk.4s for more modern Jet Provost Mark 5s. Membership of the team was progressively changed during the preceding years, but for this season its constitution was entirely new. Sqn Ldr Eric Evers was appointed leader, with Flt Lts Terry Francis at No. 2, John Davy at No. 3 and Ken Tait in the box position filling the remaining slots. Flt Lt Rod Brown was detailed to fly the spare aircraft to overseas shows and he also commentated during the team's displays. The brand new T.Mk.5s carried standard RAF red and white training markings with "The Red Pelicans" title emblazoned on the rear fuselage and unit badge on top of the tail fin. Led by Ch Tech Dennis Holmes, a dedicated team of seven groundcrew was formed from airmen of No. 1 Handling Party. These keen volunteers were rewarded for their hard work by flying with the team on long distance trips and on overseas visits.

The long association of the Red Pelicans with the Jet Provost finally came to end in 1973. In this scene, the 1970 team, comprising new Mark 5 JPs and led by Sqn Ldr Eric Evers, climbs through the vertical over familiar territory. (*John Davy*)

Near miss!

Flt Lt John Davy passed through CFS as a student on the Jet Provost in 1966-67 and returned to take up a position as instructor on 1 Squadron in March 1969.

"For the 1969 season, I flew the spare Pelican aircraft to the various display venues and commentated while the team performed. In 1970 I took over the No. 3 position and during the pre-season work up we were flying over Moreton-in-Marsh when we spotted a Chipmunk, which had every right to be in the vicinity, heading straight towards us. Sqn Ldr Eric Evers, our team leader, took avoiding action as indeed did I, but in their efforts to avoid the Chippie, a wing of the No. 4 aircraft struck the tail of No. 2, causing its ailerons to lock in the level position. Fortunately, Ken Tait was able to fly his damaged JP back to Ris using small movements of rudder to adjust his heading. All aircraft landed safely with no injury to aircrew, but the incident prompted the issue of an instruction to all RAF aerobatic teams, to the effect that practice formations were to be carried out over active airfields only! This meant getting up extra early in the morning to practise in the still air over Little Rissington and before flying proper began. The disadvantage of this of course was that when the time came to perform on a Saturday afternoon somewhere, the air was on the bumpy side."

Low on fuel and another close shave

Eric Evers led the team on all 23 displays that year and one in particular stands out in his memory, not for the display itself but for a few hairy moments when returning from a display at Regensburg, Bavaria, about 20 nautical miles from the Czech border.

"The journey out from Rissy was uneventful and we staged through RAF Wildenrath for a refuelling stop. The display in front of a large crowd was well received helped, I suspect, by the fact that we were the only display team in the whole show. Later that evening we were guests of honour at a very enjoyable party laid on for us by the organisers of the show with lots of Bavarian beer and 'oompah oompah' music.

The next day we started on the return journey, aiming to stage through RAF Wildenrath again, then on to RAF Manston for HM Customs check and finally to Rissy. Ken Tait, whose team job was flight planning, told me that the first leg to Wildenrath, against the prevailing westerly wind, was going to be tight on fuel. On the forecast winds we had a little bit to spare but it needed a careful watch during the transit. Based on this information we flew as a loose five formation at 25,000 ft in the clear above thick cloud and with frequent fuel checks. These showed that we were all about the same on fuel state but that the actual headwinds were stronger than forecast. Furthermore, on contacting Wildenrath we were told that the cloud base was about 1,000 ft and visibility about one mile so a radar approach was mandatory. So my plan with our tight fuel state, for a gentle throttled back straight descent towards Wildenrath until below cloud then a run in and break, was quickly discarded. I decided that fuel was so low that we all had to descend as a single unit rather than split the formation and delay further the second pair of aircraft.

Now, in our early morning work-up practices at Rissy in preparation for the display season I had worked at and polished many aspects of our display but I had never considered the need to practise or even think about landing as a five aircraft formation from a radar approach! However, needs must and I had the utmost faith that my team would follow the instructions they were about to get. 'The Red Pelican' team would descend in close formation as a Box Four with Ken Tait in the box as normal. Rod Brown to fly as loose line astern as possible on Ken, commensurate with retaining good visual contact in cloud. On landing I would aim to land one third of the way up the runway on the centreline with Terry and John either side of me. Rod would land first however, as close as possible to the threshold of the runway and he was to call 'Down and Braking' to allow Ken to land ahead of him and then make the same call to allow me to land.

The descent, in cloud all the way, went as planned and we levelled at 1,500 ft asl. Take-off flap was lowered followed by undercarriage and approaching the glidepath still in cloud I was beginning to relax. Everything was nicely under control, fuel state low but not critical and in another few hundred feet we should see the ground and hopefully the runway lights. Now it's at this point that any experienced aviator will tell you that 'Sod's Law' usually takes over and destroys your complacency in a flash. Sure enough it did!

'Red Leader Radar, unidentified aircraft ahead crossing you left to right same height turn right immediately.' The economy with words and the urgency in his voice spoke volumes and stopped dead any idea I might have had of having a discussion about it. 'Pelicans turning right, turning right Go' was my immediate response. I suddenly felt as vulnerable as the lead duck in a flock just about to fly over the guns of the local annual duck shoot as this unguided missile of an aircraft headed towards us in cloud and we low and slow five aircraft in close formation, belly up towards him giving him a target the size of a football pitch to aim at! The next few seconds seemed like an eternity but thankfully the danger passed without incident and my next concern was our fuel state on having to go round again .... quick decision .... raise the undercarriages to reduce the drag and save fuel but leave the take-off flap down to give more control at the slow speed. Slowly we came round to line-up with the runway once again lowered the undercarriages and landed exactly as planned with very little fuel left in the tanks. The rest of the journey home was uneventful thank goodness but that approach and landing at Wildenrath thirty three years on remains as clear in my memory as if it were yesterday!"

Flt Lt Terry Francis took over the lead role in 1971, but due to Government cutbacks, the final CFS Jet Provost team was disbanded at the close of the 1973 season.

"The Skylarks"

Tentatively formed as "The Pink Penguins" in 1966, "The Skylarks" was one of the lesser-known CFS aerobatic teams. Flying at No.2 in the formation was Flt Lt John Merry who explains the name change. *"When we got four Chipmunks together we put our tongues in our cheeks and called the formation "The Pink Penguins". But that wouldn't do for public consumption – too much of an in joke. When we went properly public in 1967 it was suggested that we should be called "The Sparrows". 'Good name' we all thought, but then it was vetoed as being too close to the Arrows. Casting about for something of the flavour of our type of display someone thought of the local river and suggested that we should be known as "The Windrushers". We didn't like it very much, and fortunately it too was vetoed – on the grounds that someone might mishear us on the R/T and think we were the Wing-brushers. I think it was the then Station Commander who came up with the name "Skylarks", and as what we did was larking about in the sky it would be difficult to improve on the name."* The full team comprised Flt Lts Robert 'Chips' Wood, John F. Merry, Anthony C. Langmead and Peter Dummer and performed at a few minor displays in their first year, most notably at Shawbury and Tern Hill in the June.

Flying four de Havilland Canada Chipmunk T.10 trainers, it reformed in 1967 when the team was led by Flt Lt John Merry ably supported by Flt Lts Anthony Langmead, Brian Owen and Peter Dummer at Nos. 2, 3, 4 positions respectively. Flt Lt Jack Hindle was assigned as reserve pilot. The 'Chippies' were marked in standard flying training colours with a 'Skylark' badge on the tail fin and a green 'lightning flash' along the fuselage sides.

Sgt R.J.A Kinsey was assigned to "The Skylarks" for the 1967-69 seasons and flew in the back seat of one of the Chipmunks when the team displayed away from Little Rissington.

"The team leader when I was involved was Sqn Ldr Steve Holding. At Old Warden Aerodrome sometime in 1969, our four-ship formation arrived overhead of the airfield but were unable to make radio contact. After circling for a while and still unable to establish contact, the leader decided we would have to land anyway because of the wind strength and direction. The resulting landing must have been downwind because of the rate at which the boundary hedge approached, very nearly running into it! On further investigation into the cause of the communication

One of the Skylarks Chipmunk T.10s, WP844/04, displays the slightly modified livery applied to the team's aircraft - a lightning flash and Skylark badge on the fin. (*Rod Brown*)

'malfunction', it transpired that the radio bods back at Rissy had been given the wrong frequency for Old Warden and had installed the wrong crystals.

On another occasion we were scheduled to stage through RAF Manston and our arrival gave cause to be remembered. After being given landing clearance 'The Skylarks' leader asked if it was OK to land on the grass. ATC gave clearance but omitted to mention that the grass was over two feet high! The resulting landings were quite heavy and minor damage was caused to the aircraft undersides particularly the undercarriages. Looking back, we were lucky that none of the Chippies tipped onto their noses. However, we were able to continue to Germany for a display at RAF Brüggen, but had to divert to RAF Wildenrath because of accommodation shortages at Brüggen. Once again we had the wrong radio crystals fitted and couldn't raise Wildenrath. Luckily our repeated calls were picked up by a British Airways 'Speedbird' flight passing overhead and the crew relayed our message to Wildenrath. We were eventually contacted by Brüggen so we decided to land there.

A qualified Navigator had to be carried on that trip as the Chipmunk didn't have much in the way of navigation aids. He flew with Sqn Ldr Holding and I flew with Flt Lt John Snell. A rescue helicopter was placed on standby at Manston when we crossed the Channel as the top brass were nervous about flying Chipmunks over the sea for any distance.

On the way home, we landed at a Belgian airfield called Brugge to refuel prior to crossing the Channel for Manston. As (bad) luck would have it, the pre-arranged Avgas Bowser failed to turn up and we ended up spending the night there in the clothes we stood up in as all our luggage was in the accompanying Varsity which had continued on."

By 1970, Flt Lt Bill Hobson had taken over leadership of the team with the other pilots drawn from Flt Lts Michael McKinley, Michael Telford, Thomas Anderson and George Cullen.

Whilst lacking some of the noise and panache of the jet teams, "The Skylarks" flew their low-powered yet highly manoeuvrable aircraft, in a 10-minute repertoire that began with a four-ship loop and continued with a display of low-speed co-ordinated aerobatics in pairs. The team disbanded at the end of the 1970 season.

"The Red Arrows"

Teams from the RAF have performed formation aerobatics for over 80 years, but "The Red Arrows" are unique in that the team's sole function is display flying and that it has flown as the premier aerobatic display team for half that period, a truly remarkable record. Its roots go back to 1964, when a 36-year-old instructor and ex-fighter pilot, Flt Lt Lee Jones, led a formation of five all-yellow Folland Gnat trainers at the 4 FTS base at RAF Valley, Anglesey. Flt Lt Henry Prince was a member of that team and remembers that, *"For practice flying over Valley and to avoid confusion with the daily student formations who used various colour callsigns for identification, the suffix 'Jack' was used by the team. The idea was Lee Jones's who flew with "The Black Arrows" which used the callsign 'Blackjack'. A local reporter was in the Valley control tower to watch a practice display, heard the callsign 'Yellowjack' and the name appeared in the press. The highlight of the team's solitary season was a synchronised display with the CFS 'Red Pelicans' Jet Provosts at the 1964 Farnborough Air Show."*

Section of film taken by SAC Bill Hickman, depicts a low flypast of a Red Arrows Gnat T.1 flown by Flt Lt Henry Prince.

At the end of the '64 season, the 'Yellowjack' Gnats were flown to 5 MU at Kemble for repainting in a new all-over red scheme and re-issued to the Central Flying School at Little Rissington early in the following year. The Gnat's sleek appearance awakened memories the public had grown accustomed to in the formation displays of earlier years, so it was perhaps an obvious choice for this diminutive aircraft to replace 'The Red Pelicans' Jet Provosts in the cherished role as the RAF's premier aerobatic team. Lee Jones was appointed team leader and continuity was maintained by the inclusion of other former 'Yellowjack' pilots, Flt Lts Henry Prince, Gerry Ranscombe and Fg Off Peter Hay. For the 1965 season the display was increased to a seven-ship formation and new pilots were posted in to increase the complement. Among these were Flt Lts Ray Hanna and Bill Loverseed who had flown Meteors with the College of Air Warfare display team, "The Macaws", from RAF Manby, and both of whom were destined to become "Red Arrows" leaders.

"The Red Arrows" came directly under the jurisdiction of CFS and Sqn Ldr Dick Storer, who was appointed Team Manager, took over responsibilities for doing commentaries at air shows and managing the team's administration. Also responsible for flying the spare Gnat to display venues, Dick was perhaps the most overworked member of the team. To relieve some of his workload, two Engineering Officers, Fg Offs Cliff Harrow and Denis Whitby, were appointed to assume responsibility for "The Red Arrows" engineering and maintenance facilities. A 27-man team of airmen under Flt Sgt 'Jock' Hutson was selected to perform first line servicing at Fairford and on trips to other locations, while the CFS Gnat base engineering team rectified faults on the team's return. Flt Lt Ron Dench was appointed Team Adjutant in 1967, a post he was to occupy for the next three years.

Naming the team

As Ray Hanna explains in his excellent book on the "Red Arrows" (1974), *"The name itself was officially chosen, unlike the titles of some earlier teams which began as purely unofficial nicknames in press reports and elsewhere. The title of the team from which the Gnats took over – 'The Red Pelicans' – had entirely logical origins: the aircraft had a red paint-scheme and a Pelican is depicted in the official crest of the CFS. When the new CFS team*

Air and ground crews on the first Red Arrows team line up in front of their Gnats; *(standing, l to r)* Sqn Ldr Richard Storer, Flt Sgt Gordon Hutson, SAC H. Green, A.N. Other, Cpl Kellaher, J/T Ron Hargreaves, SAC 'Taff' Gardner, J/T Jimmy Mearns, Sgt Howard Smallman, SAC Tony Gannon, Cpl R. Mayes, A.N. Other, SAC C. Thomas, Cpls Wood, Casey, SAC Woodhead, Fg Off Cliff Harrow, SAC Bill Hickman. *(kneeling, l to r)* Flt Lts E. Tilsley, Henry Prince, Fg Off Peter Hay, Flt Lts Bryan Nice, Lee Jones, Ray Hanna, Gerry Ranscombe, Bill Loverseed. (*Tony Gannon*)

was formed, the red finish was retained for the aircraft to emphasise the continuity of CFS aerobatic teams, and it was logical to make 'red' part of the title. 'Arrows' not only suited the plan-form of the Gnat but also gave a link with the most famous of recent RAF aerobatic teams, 'The Black Arrows'."

Perfecting the formation

During the early months of 1965, the team flew practice sortie after practice sortie as it strived to attain the standards expected of the RAF's official aerobatic team. Debriefing by the Team manager and comments from those on the ground were taken on board but Lee wanted something more visual by which to make a judgement of progress. Experiments with a type G45 or G90 ciné-gun camera adapted for handheld purposes had proved to be only partially successful, and the time taken for the processed result to return to the team for assessment was often too long to be of immediate practical value.

The CFS, however, in the normal course of its operations, had no requirement for ciné assessment training as such, added to which the photographic section at Little Rissington had neither the space nor the facilities to undertake such a task. A volunteer was called for at RAF Honington, and a Senior Aircraftsman, Bill Hickman jumped at the chance. "The Red Arrows" got their temporary photographer and contrary to expectations, one who came with some three to four years first line experience in Fighter Command.

Bill takes up the story.

"When I arrived at Rissy, I reported to the Photo section to be told I was needed over at Fairford, where they were setting up a new aerobatic team. I duly reported to the Team Manager who in turn introduced me to Fg Off Pete Hay who had been designated Team Photo Officer. Pete handed me an unmodified G90 16mm ciné gun camera, straight from the nose of a Hunter and asked if I could do anything with it. We were joined a few moments later by Lee Jones who greeted me warmly and explained briefly what he required of me. The first task was to modify the camera.

My other task was to convert two rooms set aside for a darkroom and projection room respectively. With the camera ready for use I managed to obtain two 50 ft lengths of Kodak colour film from the photo section at Rissy, which were surplus to requirement. I loaded them into the G90 magazines and secretly filmed the team, under the pretext of it being a 'dry run'. I then sent them off to Kodak for processing and a few days later, I was able to give the team their first ever sight of themselves doing a full practice display – IN COLOUR. They were most impressed! The Wing Co Flying was immediately informed, as was the Commandant, Air Cdre Bird-Wilson, and both came down next day to see the film. In the meantime, 'Jock' Hutson and his lads on the line received a special showing later that afternoon.

Filming the practice sorties began in earnest and following each sortie I was able to get the processing and splicing time down to an average of 30 minutes before it was ready on the projector. This was another big plus factor which, according to Lee, had not been achieved at North Weald. The camera was so easy to use that others occasionally took turns, leaving me free to load further magazines for the day's use. From being an occasional 'added extra' tried out first on the Black Arrows, ciné assessment became an integral part of the Red Arrows training set up, and I am informed by Brian Goodfellow that the camera lasted without

Three images depicting minor changes to the Red Arrows livery in the early years; 1965 (*top*) XR996, parked outside 5 Hangar, carries the first scheme; in the 1966 (*centre*) view XS111, en-route to Ilfracombe on the slipper tank fuel flow test flight, an enlarged CFS crest adorns the forward fuselage and the Union Jack the top of the fin; starting up at Kemble, XR986 (*bottom*), displays the tricolour scheme applied to the fin for the 1967 season. It was another year before Sqn Ldr Ray Hanna achieved his desire for a lightning flash along the forward fuselage. (*Ray Deacon*)

further modification, until the introduction of video filming, some years later.

During my year on the team, I got to fly in the Gnat on two occasions, the first being with Pete Hay in XR996 to Bristol Siddeley Engines at Filton to discuss my contribution to the team programme they had undertaken to provide; the second occasion was later in the season in XS111 with Ben Lewis to Rimini for a display at Ravenna. For me, flying over the Alps at 48,000 ft as the sun was going down, more than made up for the excruciating pain in the sinuses occasioned by a rapid descent earlier into Chateauroux. Needless to say, I was not permitted to fly in the Gnat again."

On with the show!

"The Red Arrows" first public display was given at Clermont-Ferrand on 9 May 1965, and by the autumn the team had flown 60 shows and visited France and Belgium. The following year when newly promoted Sqn Ldr Ray Hanna took over as leader, the tally reached the high 80s and only the cancellation of two displays abroad prevented the team passing the 100 mark in 1968, the RAF's 50th anniversary year.

In 1966 the display formation was increased to nine Gnats drawn from a total allocation of just ten aircraft, reflecting the high serviceability levels of the aircraft and maintenance skills of the groundcrew. Having settled nicely into the modern facilities, the decision was taken to temporarily house the new VC10 and Belfast squadrons at Fairford while reconstruction work progressed at RAF Brize Norton, and to base the Concorde trials aircraft in the hangar occupied by the CFS Gnats. A pair of adjoining hangars was prepared at RAF Kemble for use by CFS and the detachment moved ten miles west to its new home on 26 September 1966.

During the first four years the team operated on a year-to-year basis as part of CFS, but in 1969 "The Red Arrows" gained status equivalent to that of a standard squadron, although its personnel continued to be based with CFS at Little Rissington. In 1970, Sqn Ldr Dennis Hazell took over from Ray Hanna and he was succeeded a year later by Sqn Ldr Bill Loverseed. In the following year, Sqn Ldr Ian Dick was appointed leader and he remained in charge for three seasons, although the team was briefly under the leadership of Sqn Ldr Peter Squire at the beginning of 1974. Due to the energy crisis in 1974, the display season was curtailed, the team's first public appearance not occurring until July. Sqn Ldr Dickie Duckett had the distinction of leading the team for the final year of CFS tenure at Little Rissington and he was still in charge when the unit departed in April 1976.

On the original 1965 all-red livery, the CFS badge was mounted above a sloping fin flash, the only deviation from standard markings allowed at the time, and the pilot's name and that of the airman regularly occupying the rear seat, were painted in white just below the canopy on the starboard side. Pressure from Ray Hanna to 'jazz' the aircraft up reaped a small concession in 1966, with the addition of the full CFS crest on the nose and union flag on the fin. One year later a further relaxation allowed the fins to be painted red, white and blue, and, in 1968, Ray finally got his wish for the addition of a white lightning cheat line along the fuselage sides forward of the engine air-intakes. This was modified to a straight white line with the words 'ROYAL AIR FORCE' emblazoned over it in the mid-seventies.

In the ten years that the "The Red Arrows" were associated with Little Rissington the team gave over 850 displays and were admired by millions of people at home and overseas. It continued to operate out of Kemble until it closed in 1983, when it moved north to RAF Cranwell. Forty years after its first public display, the team is still the RAF's premier aerobatic team, a fitting tribute to those involved at the beginning.

Joining the team

In those formative years, no pilot was accepted for membership of the team with less than 1,000 hours' first-pilot experience. Each year, three pilots were posted from the team to other jobs in the RAF, so

Good team spirit exudes from this view of the Red Arrows groundcrew taken at Farnborough in 1966. In relaxed mood are *(back row, l to r)*, SAC K. Boucher, Cpl Pete Chadburn, J/Ts G. Hurren, Eric Fennel, A.N. Other, SAC Tony Gannon. *(front row, l to r)*, J/T. Rick Howse, A.N. Other, A.N. Other, SAC R. Carroll, J/T Jimmy Mearns, Cpl R. Mayes, A.N. Other, J/T Bunny Austin, A.N. Other, J/T N. Scurr, Flt Sgt Gordon Hutson. *(Tony Gannon)*

that a typical tour of duty with the "Arrows" was about three years. At the end of 1965 there were a number of vacant slots on the team and Derek Bell was given the choice of either a tour with the 'Trappers' at CFS or of being put forward as a candidate for the team.

"No contest!!" says Derek. *"First came the conversion to the Gnat. I had been flying the JP for 5 years and jumping into the Gnat was a bit of cultural shock. I spent the first few hours trying to catch up with this little tiger and most of the time all I could do was to hang onto its tail. But with a lot of help from 'C' Flight we were eventually let loose on our own. The Gnat was a delightful aircraft to operate, it was highly manoeuvrable, had very precise sensitive controls, a very good power to weight ratio, the cockpit was ergonomically sound and the pilot was so close to the ground that low flying was a joy. What a great shame that we never had it as a fighter!*

Soon we were working up for the 1966 season. This was different – no more quick debriefs from mates on the ground who may have watched the practice – every sortie was filmed and debriefed by our eagle-eyed manager and groundcrew. Nothing was missed, every move was analysed, every mistake noted. The following couple of months were a hard grind for me. I found that getting to grips with the problem of constantly being in exactly the correct position and smoothly maintaining that position so that the guys flying outside and behind me could do their even harder job was extremely taxing. There were many days when I doubted that I would ever hack it and I don't think I would have done if it had not been for the support and encouragement I received from others. I have to mention in particular 'Big' Frank Hoare who spent many hours in the back of my aircraft. I can still hear his gentle Welsh brogue encouraging me to 'Keep at it Boyo, the left-hand side is struggling too and when you get a minute, pass the gravy!' This in the middle of a five abreast roll! Eventually it came good, how good you would need to ask others!

I was honoured to stay with the 'Red Arrows' for three full seasons. These were the finest days of my flying career and at the end of Farnborough week in 1968 I knew that life in the Royal Air Force could never get better. I started looking at new horizons in Civil Aviation."

Bird strikes – the ever present danger

Another member of the 1965 Jet Provost team to transfer to "The Red Arrows" was Flt Lt Roy Booth who recalls a few incidents that gave him cause for concern.

"Like all low level squadrons the team had its share of bird strikes. We were lucky in that the Gnat and Orpheus engine proved to be a robust combination. A typical incident occurred in August 1968 when my aircraft hit a large gull as we flew down the Bristol Channel en-route to Chivenor. A visual inspection confirmed damage to the left intake. Handling was normal and we landed at Chivenor without further incident. Post flight inspection showed the engine to be clear. However the damage to the intake was serious enough to ground the aircraft. I flew the spare for the rest of the day's programme, displays at Chivenor and Teeside, plus two transit flights. The groundcrew were brilliant in this kind of situation. By early evening they had effected a temporary repair and I ferried it back to Kemble.

My worst moment was a multiple strike at RNAS Culdrose in July 1966. As No. 5, I was close to the left hand edge of the runway during take-off. Seconds after lift-off I flew into a dense flock of birds which had broken cover out of the grass on my side. One moment it was raining birds then I was through. However I was slowly losing ground even with the throttle hard against the stop. A glance inside showed the engine rpm slowly winding down through 95%. For an awful moment it seemed I might have to eject in front of the crowd and with the back four close behind me. Suddenly there was a muffled bang from the back end, full power was restored and the cockpit filled with the acrid smell of burned feathers.

We turned left behind the crowd towards our holding point, a disused airfield nearby. I pulled clear of the formation and gingerly exercised the throttle back and forth. All seemed well except for a slight flat spot during acceleration. We were debating whether I should continue when the engine gave a couple of 'coughs' and handling became perfectly normal. I rejoined as Ray started the run in for what turned out to be an uneventful display.

The engine had ingested three birds cleanly, one down the right intake and two down the left. An exhaustive examination revealed no sign of damage whatever, rather surprising in the circumstances. Later that afternoon we took off for a high level transit to the USAF base at Chateauroux in France. That engine completed the season without further incident although the burned feathers smell lingered on for weeks."

Engine Fitter has time of his life

Although he spent some of his time rectifying problems on the Course Gnats, most of Cpl Peter Chadburn's working day was employed on the Aerobatic Team aircraft. On occasions when aircraft were left behind because of engine defects, he would be one of a team despatched to carry out repairs.

"There were two engine change detachments in 1965, one at Chateauroux in France and the other at RNAS Culdrose. On completion of the Culdrose task, the engine team made its way by road to St Mawgan to be picked up by the CFS Varsity – en-route we called into a Post Office somewhere in Cornwall to collect our pay, we didn't even have to salute the Postmistress. I think it was about this time that bank accounts started to come onto the scene.

To keep fit I drove a Ford Anglia (the one with the sloping back window) which kept running out of petrol, usually within walking distance of the main gate. The lack of money was always a factor. My main drinking hole was the New Inn at Nether Westcote run by Don and Audrey. The beers on Tuesdays were always bought by my pal Tony 'Geordie' Hurren. Sylvia, his wife who was still in Newcastle at the time, would send a few pounds to arrive on the day. One Tuesday the letter didn't arrive – disaster – I remember putting 800 Embassy cigarette coupons behind the bar at the New Inn (Audrey paid 10/- for 500). Thanks to Audrey we managed more than a few pints of Morrells at 1/11d per pint.

My last Red Arrows trip of 1965 confirmed my joining the 'Jet Set' when, on Battle of Britain day, we had breakfast in Jersey, lunch at Shawbury and an evening meal at Biggin Hill.

Winter servicing

The first Gnat Winter Servicing Team (GWS), which was formed at Little Rissington in October 1965, was comprised of airmen from the various servicing flights plus most of the 'Arrows' servicing team. We shared No. 5 Hangar with the Painters and Dopers. This was the first real sign that I was part of Little Rissington, although I had lived in Baldwin Block (the block across the road and nearest MQs) for about six months. The 'Red Arrow' Gnats were ferried from Fairford to the GWS for mods. and other servicing updates, and to prepare them for the 1966 season. It was during this first winter that the aircraft were modified for red and blue smoke. I remember Wg Cdr Thirwell and Ch Techs Ben Godfrey, Len Cherry and Willie Watson being in charge the GWS.

The Gnats were gradually returned to service in the early part of 1966 and the ground crew were soon back on the daily trip to Fairford. 'The Red Arrows' carthorse for 1966 was the Armstrong Whitworth Argosy, nicknamed the 'Flying Wheelbarrow'. 'The Red Arrows' ground crew became adept at unloading a fully laden Argosy in twenty minutes. With most displays at weekends, the team returned to Fairford on a Sunday or Monday. Tuesdays became the day of unpacking, washing and ironing ready for the next weekend. Thursdays and Fridays of most weeks were spent packing and preparing for the next trip. When not on a trip, I spent many a pleasant evening in The George at Kempsford playing darts or shove ha'penny. Not many pubs can boast a shove ha'penny board – I wonder if the board is still there. We invited the French Aero Team, 'La Patrouille de France', to a games night at The George. What the result was I don't recall but the local ladies enjoyed their company. I do, however, remember that they supped a lot of whisky.

With the arrival of Concorde at Fairford in 1966 the team moved to Kemble. As with the previous year, the winter servicing team was reformed back at Ris in November 1966, occupying the same hangar. By February 1967, the last of the Gnats was flown back to Kemble. After the GWS closed down, I rejoined the team and stayed with it until June 1967. My final trip with the team was the Paris Air Show when sadly a Fouga Magister of the French aerobatic team hit the ground killing the pilot. I was married on 7 June 1967 and departed RAF Little Rissington on a 13 month unaccompanied tour to Bahrain five days later.

I returned for a nostalgic look round in 1999 but I couldn't find the camp. Looking back I have some fantastic memories of Little Rissington and the Cotswolds but most of all I realise how lucky and privileged I was to be a member of the Royal Air Force and to be based at Little Rissington during that period of my life."

Post-winter servicing air tests

As the aircraft completed their winter service, the pressure was on to return them to Kemble for the new team pilots to practise for the new season. The final check was a full air test. One such test that sticks in Ch Tech Malcolm Thomas's mind was carried out on Sunday 13 December 1970 by Flt Lt Dougie Marr with Malcolm occupying the rear seat.

"The climb appeared normal and we arrived at 40,000 ft in the usual seven minutes. A Pressure Ratio Limiter (PRL) check was carried out and appeared OK. Next a check for surge-free engine response – one very nasty surge, so back down for some ground runs and Air Fuel Ratio Control Unit (AFRCU) checks and adjustment. Slam checks on the ground appeared normal. A further air test was carried out on Monday. The result at altitude was the same, or worse! Back on the ground the engine was replaced and everything 'worked as advertised'. When the old engine was stripped down we realised it could have all ended in disaster, but then number thirteen has always been lucky for me.

After another air test post winter servicing, when returning to Little Rissington the approach was normal but the aircraft stopped very quickly after touchdown, in fact it stopped on the runway intersection with both main wheel tyres burst and the wheel hubs and brake units quite badly damaged. The brake units and wheels were replaced and the system checked over. No fault could be found so a second air test was carried out some days later. The landing burst both tyres and some damage occurred to the wheels but not as drastic as on the first occasion. Lots of head scratching and a discussion with OC Engineering Wing, then to our amazement an air test on another aircraft ended in a 'brakes-on' landing.

This was cause for some serious thinking and testing. Flt Lt Dougie Marr decided to try some fast taxi runs down the runway using the brakes quite hard, while the team EO and I chased the aircraft in a Land Rover. The brakes became white hot but still worked perfectly, refusing to lock on. Next we pondered the modification programme and examined the differences between taxiing and flying. Jet aircraft are pressurised once airborne and the pressure differential increases with altitude. The higher you fly the colder it gets and temperatures of -50C or more are the norm. Hot air is blown into the cockpit to warm the crew. We decided to try and simulate the fault, first by raising the aircraft onto jacks so the wheels could be spun, then using a hot air blower to blow hot air into the cockpit. Within a few minutes the brakes came on! By carefully slackening the bleed screws on the brake valves one at a time we found that the rear seat bleed screws let the brakes off.

The fault was caused by over-long bolts, which had been supplied with the modification kits for the back seat rudder pedals. They caused the foot motors on the rear cockpit brakes to close. The hot air had increased the volume of brake fluid trapped in the lines and generated sufficient pressure over the 1½ hour flight to cause the brakes to jam on. Luckily, similar pressure was exerted to both brakes; imagine landing with one brake on and one off – ground looping at 150mph does not bear thinking about!"

Aerobatics in the blood

Flt Lt Ernie Jones joined No. 231 Course at Little Rissington early in November 1965 and had his first 'famil' flight on the 16th in a JP3 'clockwork mouse'. In January 1966 he was delighted to change to the Gnat about which he says *"I found it a wonderfully impressive and responsive aircraft to fly."*

Previous experience flying with "The Firebirds" Lightning display team and as the Fighter Command Hunter and Lightning solo display pilot, had earned Ernie respect as one of the top aerobatic pilots, and in early January 1967 he received a phone call from Ray Hanna.

"He asked me if I would like to pop down to Kemble to discuss the possibility of me joining his team. I felt very privileged to be asked and quickly got the necessary authority to leave Valley. It is interesting to compare the way 'Red Arrows' team selection was made in those early days with the fairly comprehensive method officially adopted later. I assumed at the time that Ray had made his call to me as a result of the number of times we had met when my Lightning solo displays coincided with the 'Arrows' displays, both in the UK and on the Continent. Better the devil you know, etc., etc.

I first flew with the team on 8 February 1967 with 'that very nice man' Henry Prince observing from the back seat. After another couple of sorties I was given a permanent slot as Red 7 and joined Henry as his 'synchro' partner, a position I particularly enjoyed flying as he was a professional down to his bootlaces. Henry has a reputation as a thoroughly nice guy whose jokes and witty anecdotes became legend in the RAF. My maxim was to always try to 'get one in first' otherwise, if I couldn't duck fast enough, I would undoubtedly find myself at the receiving end of his banter.

At the end of the season, I asked Ray if I could return to instructing at Valley and was duly released from the team. Looking back now I think I must have been mad! However, having been involved in display flying on and off for the previous five years, I really did want to try my hand at instructing on the Gnat at Valley. Later, between 1972-75 I was lucky enough to join the Battle of Britain Memorial Flight, before returning to Little Rissington as OC the CFS Gnat Detachment at Kemble in April 1976."

'The Flying Circus'

Sqn Ldr Ray Hanna once said that *"although trust and confidence were vital in the air, it was easier to maintain teamwork and discipline while flying than on the ground."* But teamwork on the ground was and still is, an integral part of the overall "Red Arrows" performance. And discipline even in the air may not be substantially greater than that demonstrated by the team's engineering ground staff.

When the groundcrew started flying in the Gnats it was very soon apparent that having engineers instantly available away from base reduced turn-round times during transit flights, and allowed the number of shows per day to be increased. It was quite easy to get the required mix of the correct aircraft tradesmen as nearly all of them were keen to fly. As all the team pilots were QFIs, it was quite natural during transit flights for the groundcrew to be given the opportunity to fly the aircraft. The chatter in the crewroom during coffee breaks inevitably turned to flying, with explanations of manoeuvres entered into intentionally or accidentally being graphically illustrated by hand movements accompanied by suitable noises. One day during such a coffee break, Pete Chadburn suddenly jumped up and declared: - *"I'm fed up with all this, you flying circus boys really piss me off!"* The gathering dissolved into laughter and "The Flying Circus" was born. From then on all those who flew in the back seats were known as "The Flying Circus" (from 'Monty Python's Flying Circus', a popular TV show at the time).

Ch Tech 'Tom' Thomas recalls that;

There were nine seats available in the Gnats so we could accommodate nine engineers. This gave us the ability to turn-round the aircraft – carrying out refuelling, re-loxing (liquid oxygen) and replenishing the diesel tanks (for smoke generation) and carrying out checks and tests before the next flight. We had a simple proforma made up for each aircraft which was signed by each tradesman as the checks were completed then countersigned by the SNCO i/c the Flying Circus, ready for the pilots to sign accepting his aircraft as ready for flight. These documents formed an extension of the Form 700 aircraft log books and could not be carried in the aircraft to which they related. Each member of the Circus therefore carried another's documents just in case of a mishap.

Use of the Flying Circus enabled "The Red Arrows" to carry out up to 100 shows in a season, plus another 300 or so practice displays. They were fabulous days, we worked hard and played hard, it was a joy to be

Nine members of the Flying Circus for the 1968 season with, *(standing, l to r)*, J/Ts Bruce Hudson, 'Wally' Walters, Cpls Ian Bennett, Graham Thomas, Sgt Malcolm 'Tom' Thomas, J/T Mick Harris; *(kneeling)* Cpls Ray Thurstons, Ron Turrell, Jeff Fletcher. *(Malcolm Thomas)*

The Red Pelicans also flew with a Circus on trips away from Rissy and the seven airmen pictured accompanied the team on detachment to RAF Leuchars in 1966; (*l to r*) Derek Henderson, Taff Jenkins, Brian Kevell, John Doleman, Geordie Sheen, AN Other, Graham Parkin. (*David Watkins*)

part of it, to be involved in new ideas and new methods. Many of us remember it as our own air force – it was unique, it will never happen again. We stayed in all sorts of accommodation from really rough French Air Force conscript's barracks to smart hotels; we flew in our own aircraft and attended some of the receptions. There were huge audiences at the displays and we met some wonderful people. We travelled Europe and the world and were spoiled, although we were always conscious that it would have to end one day. The team was extremely close, we loved the work and were very professional in its execution and looked after each other. It was something very special and was the happiest time of my life."

Competition among technicians for membership of the team was second only to that that among pilots. "Red Arrows" groundcrews had considerably more opportunity to fly than most tradesmen. Almost half of them flew with the team when displaying away from their Kemble base.

Although the engineering staff was subject to tours of duty, a tradition of carefully planned maintenance and systematic servicing had to be established. This resulted in an impeccable record which approached 100 per cent. And this was not because "The Red Arrows" had a large pool of aircraft from which to draw. Even though the formation grew from seven to nine Gnats, its display aircraft were still drawn from the original allocation of ten aircraft. They continued to operate with only one reserve Gnat although later on two additional aircraft were acquired from Valley but were not modified for smoke generation.

The demands of more than a hundred displays in five months were met only by complete co-operation and teamwork. The groundcrew team was led by Flt Sgt 'Jock' Hutson and included 60 NCOs and airmen. Ray Hanna often said: *"It was to the engineering staff that the greatest credit belongs."*

In those early years, the engineering team comprised two sections: the base groundcrew, and the travelling groundcrew, all under the command of the Team Engineering Officer. He was responsible for ensuring complete maintenance and serviceability. The base groundcrew carried out most engineering work on both the CFS Gnats operated by 4 Squadron and "The Red Arrows". Faults that arose during displays were rectified on the team's return and the crew even managed to squeeze in scheduled servicing as required.

The travelling groundcrew consisted of 27 technicians and a Flight Sergeant. Some accompanied the team in the support Beverley, Argosy or Hercules transport aircraft whenever they were away from base, while a member of the 'Flying Circus' flew in the rear seat of each aircraft. The Engineering Officer flew with the Team Manager in the reserve aircraft. They took with them a basic range of spares: in effect a portable engineering base. Just as each pilot was allotted his own Gnat so was each mechanic, the airman's name being painted below that of the pilot on the nose of the aircraft.

The major servicing of "The Red Arrows" aircraft was undertaken during the winter months. If the previous summer's season revealed any weaknesses, suitable modifications were carried out. After most winter servicing each aircraft was repainted, the existing coat of paint having been removed down to bare metal. This work was usually carried out by the resident servicing teams in 5 Hangar at Little Rissington. The newly serviced aircraft returned to Kemble during late February/early March.

The support aircraft were drawn from one of the Lyneham-based squadrons and would usually fly into Kemble the afternoon before the team was due to depart for a display, allowing ample time for the loading of ground equipment and spares. Loading was refined to a fine art and could be achieved in a surprisingly short time. Much of the cargo space was occupied by the team's Mini pick-up and Land-Rover, plus the large tool cabinet and the trolley used for priming the Gnats' dye-tanks. Also loaded were two Palouste engine starters, and the spare wheels – seventeen main undercarriage and four nosewheels.

Often the display aircraft would arrive at an airfield hours before the support aircraft, allowing the 'Flying Circus' to prepare for the display or carry out basic maintenance, clearing any snags that occurred in transit. Normally an hour was needed on the ground between displays to refuel, replenish dye-tanks and attend to other minor details. An hour was ideal but the turnround could be completed more quickly on tight schedules when three or four displays were performed in a day.

The groundcrew could relax only when the pilots taxied out for the display. They belonged to a highly disciplined team; the work could be very demanding. But this was tempered by the rewards of being part of the Royal Air Force Aerobatic Team. As the competition for places among the engineering staff showed, a tour with "The Red Arrows" was regarded as an elite posting.

Invitations to official receptions were often received by the support team, especially at overseas displays. That the groundcrew were always assumed to have been included indicated the team management's appreciation of their vital contribution to the team.

Turin Air Show and disaster avoided

Having reported 'something amiss' with the ailerons on his aircraft, XR986, Team Leader Sqn Ldr Dennis Hazell suggested it was left to be checked over during an Arrows day off prior to a trip to Italy in August 1970. Checks completed, Flt Lt Bill Loverseed decided to give the aircraft an air test with Ch Tech Thomas in the back seat.

"I asked to go along for the ride as being a 'rigger' I was interested to see or feel any difference in the controls. We took off and played about over the airfield doing lots of horizontal figure of eights with 'Derry turns'.

All seemed OK so we left the circuit and followed the railway line from Kemble Station toward Swindon. Soon we saw a train approaching so turned and followed it back to Kemble gauging our speed to arrive at the station as the passengers were leaving the train. We made a low pass with smoke on then pulled up vertically, rolling continually on the climb. Bill was expecting a visitor and the manoeuvre was to let the person know that they were at Kemble! We landed and declared the aircraft serviceable.

The following day the team flew a high level transit through Nice to Turin. Sunday was the big International Show and the team put on an immaculate performance. Monday morning pre-flight inspections were carried out and with no problems found, the paperwork completed. The crews clambered aboard for the return trip. I was in Red 7. Start-up was normal and we waited for clearance to taxi. Suddenly the Boss told us all to shut down. His aircraft was unserviceable, his ailerons were not working – no lateral control from either cockpit!! How fortunate it happened on the ground, imagine if it had snapped during the show!

On inspection a cable was found to have snapped where it crossed a pair of elliptical pulleys. A signal was sent to Kemble while we commenced checks on the other aircraft, which entailed removing the canopy and rear ejection seat – times nine! The team then took off leaving the Manager, EO and myself together with six airmen. Sgt Reg Spedding flew out with the new pulley assembly which we fitted, tested and signed off as serviceable. The aircraft took off with the Manager and EO aboard, the air test being carried out on the way home."

Social interludes!

On trips abroad it was usual for the pilots to be invited to various receptions and they would do their utmost to ensure that the groundcrew received invitations too. *"On one trip to Germany,"* recalls 'Tom' Thomas, *"a reception was held for the team, but only sixteen tickets had been supplied for 23 groundcrew. Being a resourceful bunch, a quantity of matching blue card was acquired and using a similar style of writing, a set of forged tickets was produced for the remaining seven members. The forgeries were so good, it was impossible to tell the real from the fake."*

From the back seat

In the autumn of 1961, Cpl Malcolm Thomas, 'Tom' to his friends, became the first Airframe Fitter to be trained on the Folland Gnat. Much of his training was carried out at Dunsfold aerodrome so he was well prepared for the arrival of the first Gnat into RAF service in February of the following year.

"In 1966 I moved from Fairford Rectification Flight to 'The Red Arrows' and had the good fortune to fly with Flt Lt Henry Prince (Red Six) leader of the two solo aircraft. I was to be in charge of the 'backseaters', later to be known as the 'Flying Circus'. I thought it right to fly with the solos as it could be one of the harder seats to fill but also likely to be even more exciting.

Henry was the chap who introduced me to a whole new world. I had flown before and always enjoyed it. I had some gliding experience but this was something else! It took almost two seasons before I could understand the radio calls fully and to find which way was up when pulling 'g'. It was a brilliant way to travel. I flew with Henry in 1966 and 1967 and I think my first sonic dive was with him. The effect of the trim changes, something I had up until then only known in theory, was exciting to find and feel working. A real adrenalin rush."

Apart from a one year tour in Borneo after the Gnat Project Team had disbanded, Tom spent the years up until 1973 working on and flying with "The Red Arrows", latterly as a 'Chiefy'. In 1968 he flew with Flt Lt Terry Kingsley, first as Red Seven and then again in 1969 when he was Red Six. On one occasion he had the rare experience of flying in the front seat on a return trip to Kemble from Mildenhall.

"Terry asked me to fly a 'Barrel Roll' – Yes! I ended up vertically and scared myself no end. Luckily we were over 5,000 ft when we started the manoeuvre. The second attempt with some very welcome tuition was much better. It was a lesson I will not forget and what a wonderful experience! Such a super little aeroplane."

So what was it like to fly in the back seat? Sit back and relive Tom's compelling account of what it was like to be a backseat driver.

"Red check in!". I sat and listened as the replies came, quick and sharp "1 - 2 - 3 - 4 - 5 - 6 - 7 - Eight's not started yet Boss" the unmistakable voice of Aussie Sqn Ldr Phil Dunn (Red 9) filled the headphones "9 – 10". "Loud and clear" came the Boss's reply.

I sat and watched the other ground crew pull chocks and Palouste starters clear of us and away towards the Argosy freight aircraft, to be loaded. I thought of the trip which was just beginning and of my luck and good fortune which had brought me onto the 'Flying Circus' side of the Red Arrows ground crew. This was indeed a job in a million! - everything after this must surely seem very humdrum and routine. This was the most thrilling experience of my life, to fly with the greatest Aerobatic Team in the world, to have an inside view of how it's done. I was one of the fortunate nine 'back seat men'. We were each allotted an aircraft and flew in it with the same pilot throughout the season. We had the distinction of having our names painted on the side of the cockpit beneath that of the pilot. For this honour we suffered the doubtful pleasures of decompression checks, wet dinghy drill and aircraft escape procedure lectures, not that anyone really disliked them!

"Kemble - Red taxi?" Sqn Ldr Ray Hanna's voice cut into my drifting thoughts "Red taxi, runway zero nine, QFE one thousand and four, wind westerly five knots", Kemble Tower answered with routine precision. We taxied forward checked the brakes and swung onto the

Heading off on another practice sortie, Flt Lt Derek Bell maintains perfect formation behind Ray Hanna. (*Ray Deacon*)

perimeter track. Waves and gestures were exchanged with the Argosy side of the ground crew. "Your straps tight, all that gear OK Tom?" Flt Lt Terry Kingsley's voice came over the intercom just that bit clearer and louder than other r/t messages (as I was sharing his aeroplane). "All set" I assured him. "Red line up?" Sqn Ldr Hanna asked Kemble. "Red line up - take off when ready". The QFE, wind direction and runway in use were repeated by Kemble. We lined up on the runway. I was sitting in the back of Red Six with Flt Lt Terry Kingsley (leading the second section of four aircraft). Ahead I could see the front five aeroplanes in vee across the runway. The tenth aircraft flown by the Manager Flt Lt Pete Macintosh, with Engineering Officer Flt Lt George White in the back-seat, took off independently afterwards.

"Up to 90, lights on go!" Sqn Ldr Hanna's short sharp routine messages continued. I watched our engine rpm build up as Terry Kingsley opened the throttle to 90 percent, the needle of the jet pipe temperature gauge leapt up then settled gently back. Clouds of red and blue smoke came towards us from the front section as the dye left in the diffuser pipes was drawn out and vaporised in the jet stream of the engines. "Front five - brakes off go!" Ray Hanna commanded. The front section were rolling. Terry Kingsley counted slowly then pressed the transmit button "Gippo section, brakes off go!" We surged forward straight down the centre line. The aircraft on either side of us gently reared as the aircraft nosewheels lifted off the runway. On our right behind Flt Lt Jack Rust sat Cpl Colin Blight, on our left, Sqn Ldr Phil Dunn with Sgt John Stuart in the back, and outboard of them was Flt Lt Ian (Widgie) Dick with Cpl Mick Harris as his rear seat man. I exchanged a rude sign with John Stuart and thought I could detect a grin beneath his oxygen mask. "Front five gear up go, wingover port!" the leader called. Then it was Terry Kingsley again, "Six Rotating!" and the rear section of four pulled up into a steep climb. "Gear up go!" Terry called. I waited for the thump of the doors closing after the undercarriage had retracted then checked the indicator lights were out. We turned gently left and as we did so the front five in perfect vee formation came up from beneath us about a mile ahead, also turning left. The wingover continued to 3,000 ft. "Two ten", the leader's voice calling the main formation's speed - "One ninety - One eighty", we slipped quietly closer, "One seventy" as the main formation turned at the top of the wingover. "One sixty" we slid into formation making the 'Diamond' complete. "All aboard!" Sqn Ldr Phil Dunn told the Boss. "Very nice" came back the reply - "Smoke on go!" The formation came out of the wingover and flew back across the airfield, nine beautiful red aeroplanes in 'Diamond' formation smoke streaming leaving a twisting swirling white ribbon. "Smoke off go!" the leader called and in the same transmission spoke to Kemble tower, "Red clearing, thank you Kemble". "Goodbye Red Lead, have a good trip" was Kemble's short reply.

"Red open up and relax" the Boss cued the team to gently break formation. The outside men acknowledged first "Five out – Four out – Eight out" all in rapid succession. "Red stud nine go!", the leader ordered to change radio frequency. This particular one was the team's own air-to-air frequency. "Can you see ten?" Terry asked me, meaning had Red 10 joined our loose formation. "Yes, he's with us" I confirmed. "Red check in!" the leader ordered. "Two – Three – Four – Five – Six – Seven – Eight – Nine – Ten" the voices rapidly report, rising and falling slightly in tone. "Loud and clear" responded the Boss. We now flew in two loose 'Battle' formations of five aircraft. Staying quite low we headed for Royal Naval Air Station Yeovilton. Just a short trip this one, less than 90 miles, about 16 minutes for us!.

"You have it" Terry said, "keep the others in your 10 o'clock". He meant I had control of the aircraft and I was to keep the front section on our left, they were about two miles ahead. This was one of the moments the 'Circus' waits for, to have a go at the 'pole'! We skimmed some low fluffy clouds and banked gently around a larger mountain of 'cotton' then turned back again to maintain our correct position relative to the front section. "One at three o'clock, five miles" someone called. "Contact" was the leader's instant reply. I looked right and eventually saw it, a small light aeroplane heading toward us and then passing behind.

One of the rear section aircraft slid in close to us in tight formation. Terry put his hands on his head to indicate that he was not flying our aeroplane, the other aircraft peeled away rapidly to a safer vantage point.

"Anyone got a Tacan?" the leader enquired, to enable him to check his heading (he meant had anyone a Tacan lock onto Yeovilton). "Two-oh-five, twenty four" came a reply, giving the compass bearing and the range. "Red set up two-nine-four decimal five; two-nine-four-five." The team leader prepared the team to change radio frequency to that of Yeovilton Tower! "I have control" Terry called as he pumped the throttle forward. With a surge the aeroplane slid into our slot behind and below the leader. The rest of the team followed into loose Diamond Nine. Yet no word was spoken. The discipline and anticipation of these pilots is remarkable. "Keep it loose" the leader called. "Two-nine-four-five-go!" I saw Terry lean forward to change frequency.

A few seconds later the leader called "Red check in!" Again the replies were short and sharp, the voices rising and falling as if singing an octave of some music, "2-3-4-5-6-7-8-9-10". "Loud and clear!" the leader confirmed; then went on "Yeovilton -Yeovilton Red Arrow lead, do you

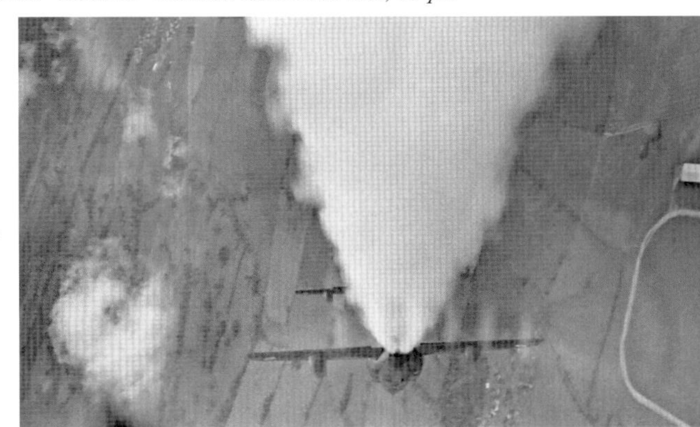

Rolling out over RAF Aston Down, one of a number of local airfields used by the Red Arrows to practise their display routines. (*Ray Deacon*)

read?". "Red lead – Yeovilton - I read you five by five-go ahead". A new voice in the head phones. "Yeovilton - Red Arrow lead, formation of ten aircraft at two thousand feet five miles northeast this time". The leader informed Yeovilton "Red leader I have you identified - QFE nine nine eight, runway two seven, left hand, circuit clear." The Yeovilton controller reported. "Red lead – thank you, may we use your circuit for fifteen minutes please?" the leader enquired. "Yeovilton - the circuit's all yours - no known traffic this time". The leader's transmit button just clicked as his acknowledgment of Yeovilton's message. "The VIP enclosure is on the north side of the runway intersection" the leader informed the two solo aircraft, ours (Six) and Flt Lt Ian Dick (Seven). "We'll use the runway intersection as datum" he continued. "The GCA van and the windsock" Terry called to Seven, meaning to use these points as markers for the solos' opposition manoeuvres!

"Big nine go!" the leader instructed. We (Red Six) slid to our right into the number four slot and Red seven had gone to the left into the number five slot, making up the Big nine formation. I looked left and watched the aeroplanes shining brightly and bobbing gently up and down against a blurred green background as we banked left toward Yeovilton airfield. The formation was now about 3 miles northeast of the airfield. The ground was getting closer now as the boss banked the formation and descended for the run in. "Thirty seconds" the leader told the team." No colour - all white". Sqn Ldr Hanna instructed his team not to use coloured smoke for this practice.

"Smoke on go!" The airfield and its buildings flashed by about 50 ft below. A brief glimpse of green turf and black tarmac runways, then "Pulling up - now!" The horizon slipped below the windscreen and down under the aircraft. The 'g' force came on forcing us down into our seats increasing our weight about four times so that I apparently weighed over 45 stone! I looked to my left the brilliant scarlet aeroplanes glinting in the sunshine, still rocking and bobbing gently. The formation pointed skyward trailing white smoke with an amazing background of green patchwork fields, brown stone walls, a small wood, a lake reflecting the yellow sunlight, and a beautiful blue sky with a few scattered woolly, cotton clouds. "Diamond nine go!" The calm quiet voice of the leader ordered. "Six" - "Seven"' came the crisp replies. The split second of the command, the answer hardly mouthed and we flashed down under the number two on our left, below the leader's tail and slid smoothly back into our slot. Other aircraft had also moved in that instant to form the "Diamond". We turned gently onto our backs, no 'g' force now, weightless for a few seconds; I noticed the undercarriage warning flag flicking in the airspeed indicator as our speed had dropped below that when the undercarriage should have been lowered in normal flight. The airfield, hangars, control tower, office buildings, parked aircraft and yellow-painted military vehicles all filled the canopy. Looking back over our heads I could see the smoke trail showing the path of our climb. Then we plunged downward, gathering speed, the 'g' force building as we descended, white vortices streaming from our wingtips and the altimeter unwinding madly from 4,800 ft to 100 ft. "Smoke off go, bending right." More instructions from the leader. We rolled into a wingover, I looked to my right, the ground seemed to be gently falling away as we climbed up into the turn. "Going down for a diamond roll" The leader called keeping the team informed of his intention, although each pilot knew the sequence inside out. We came out of the wingover descending from 3,000 ft gathering speed dropping to about 200 ft. "Smoke on go!" With the formation still banked the number four aircraft on the right wing seemed perilously close to the ground but Flt Lt Dickie Duckett's gaze never shifted from the number two aircraft. Each member of the team has implicit faith in the leader and in each other. "Pulling up - reversing" The boss's quiet voice commanding and confident, not a word wasted. The earth seemed to rock, drop and then climb up to fill the canopy then slide down as we completed the roll. "Smoke off go!" Bending left –"Arrow go!" More sharp cool orders. "Eight" – "Nine" snapped back the equally cool replies. A pause now as we turned through 90 degrees, roughly 200 ft above the airfield, holding a steady 3'g' turn. "Half swan go!" "Two" – "Three" clicked back the replies, sharp as any parade ground commands. "Smoke on go - playing it down" The leader told his team as he slipped off another 100 ft, for the fly-by past the VIP enclosure. I peered over the starboard cockpit coaming trying to see the VIP tent, but the angle of bank was too high. I looked left and down at the grass seemingly brushing number Five's wing tip, but both Flt Lt Euan Perreaux and his back seat man Cpl Mick Sivell were looking up at the formation and not at all perturbed. "Datum" the leader called as we flashed over the runway intersection. "Rolling out" the steady 3g of the turn slackened for an instant then as the leader called "Pulling up!" the force increased to 4g and the formation pulled up into a loop. "Arrow go!" from the boss, "Two" - "Three" came the replies. "More pull - more power" again the boss calling. Nearly 5,000 ft, on our backs, weightless again for a few moments. "Vixen go!" from the boss, then the answers - "Eight" – "Nine". Down from the loop, the speed building from 110 knots at the top of the loop to just over 300 at the bottom, the g force increasing with the speed to around 4g at the bottom. "Smoke off go!" from the leader as he pulls the formation up. "Wine glass go!" then continues into a barrel roll, at the bottom of the roll he calls "Concorde go!" the team sweep across the airfield in a low banked fly-by over the VIP enclosure. At the end of the fly-by the team change back into "Feathered arrow", as this is rather a mouthful to say as an order and with an oxygen mask clamped to one's chin as well, the call is made as "Fred go!". The leader turns the formation back toward the airfield holding it quite low and steering for the VIP enclosure, he calls "Smoke on go!" and pulls up into a loop. Only the two extreme wing men one each side of the formation and the two "stem" aircraft smoke. "Pulling up - split go!" The instant the command is made Terry's reply is made "Six clear!" as six and seven pull hard and climb vertically away from the formation. "Box go!" boss Hanna now ordering the main formation to change to box, the aircraft now climbing, belly toward the crowd snap crisply from vee to box in the blink of an eye. The skill and courage to carry out these manoeuvres require each pilot to have total faith in and 100 percent commitment to each other. The two aircraft from the "stem" meanwhile had also been busy, Six and Seven had split from the main formation and called "Clear" then as the boss had called "box" Terry called "Six split go!" Six and Seven still smoking, split from each other. From their vertical climb they pulled to the horizontal (inverted), so as the main formation changed from vee to box, I in Red six had an upside

down split second view of a very smart formation change, before we and Seven rolled the right way up and flew away from each other. The main formation now at 90 degrees to us continued their loop. Terry looking over his left shoulder watching for Red Seven turning, pulling 3 or 4g and diving gently from 3,000 ft to 50 ft at just under 300 knots.

This synchronisation of the two solo aircraft with each other and with the main formation is worked up over many, many practices but changes are made every time as the conditions for any two displays are never the same. The allowances for wind or cloud or airfield obstructions are continually changing. The ability to fly like this, to play it off the cuff, but to get it right every time is very special and very special to watch! To fly with these men, to share the thrill and spectacle of it all is incredible, a once in a lifetime chance, and a great honour. It takes a long time and many many 'back-seat rides' to remember the details and which manoeuvre follows which, but now after 3 years of solo rides I seem to be able to remember most of them.

The flying now is fast and furious, the g loads are never off and never constant – wonderful, I'm totally enthralled! The main formation now coming out of their loop, seven shining scarlet aeroplanes in perfect Vixen formation diving vertically down, "Smoke on go!" calls the leader. "Six turning" Terry calling to Ian (Widgie) Dick the other solo pilot "Seven", Ian using his callsign to acknowledge Terry's transmission. We are turning left toward the airfield, descending rapidly. Through the top of the canopy I can see the airfield, a whole expanse of green countryside, the hangars and buildings and the runway on which we are lining up. "Six smoke on go!" Terry orders the solos. Immediately a small stream of smoke appears about 4 miles away coming toward us in line with the runway and like us descending toward it. On our left the main formation has reached the bottom of their loop and fly across our path toward the VIP enclosure, Sqn Ldr Hanna calls "Red - break break go!" The formation fans out into the Vixen break. We flash down the runway at 30 ft beneath the main formation as they break. I look over Flt Lt Kingsley's shoulder and see Seven heading toward us at a closing speed of about 700 knots (750 mph) "Six pull - now!" as Terry calls he pulls sharply back, the aeroplane's nose lifts skywards and the g force again makes itself felt; as this happens Seven flashes past our left side seemingly at an angle of 45 degrees. We rocket up into a loop, a tighter loop than the normal formation one. The airfield and its buildings climb up into the canopy, we look over our heads craning our necks to see the white ribbon of smoke led by a scarlet arrow climbing toward us. Seven passes on our left slower now as we lay on our backs and slow to about 120 knots. "Holding" Terry calls and pushes the stick forward. The straps bite into my shoulders and my feet float up behind the instrument panel as negative g tries to propel me from my seat. Small particles of dust float up under my visor and around me. The two briefcases under my right arm are trying to join the dust up in the canopy. "Pull now" Terry calls, his voice steady and even. The negative g is released and I bump back onto my dinghy pack seat with a jar as the normal positive g increases. We hurtle earthwards once more. Looking over my head I briefly glimpse Seven, like us diving down streaming smoke. Our speed and g load increase and we pass again at about 100 ft above the ground continuing the now shallow dive down to 30 ft. "Smoke off go - clearing!" Terry calls. The ground streaks by our starboard wing tip as we bank into a tight turn. We roll out and head for a gap in some trees, then climb gently away about 45 degrees to the runway centre line and back up to 2,500 ft. Terry looks over his right shoulder and sees Seven making for the prearranged marker at the opposite end of the runway. "Exploded Arrow go!" Ray Hanna's voice fills the earphones. I look over my left shoulder, tilting my head up and back. The seven shining specks in arrow formation heading toward the runway down its extended centre line, "Smoke on go!" the leader calls the main formation, I can see the resulting white streams. Terry calls "Six turning!" the words hardly spoken as Ian Dick's reply is snapped back "Seven!" We turn left descending again. "Smoke off go - stabilise!". The boss brings the seven-ship section straight down the centre of the runway at 100 ft. Their speed is just over 400 knots as they hurtle toward us. "90" calls Terry to Seven. "Roll - roll - go!" Ray Hanna calls the main formation. The seven bright red sparkling aircraft each revolve around their longitudinal axes in the blink of an eye, the roll is completed in three quarters of a second - the name of the manoeuvre "Twinkle roll" describes it admirably. "Airbrakes go - bending right!" Hanna calls as they flash by us. We are down to 50 ft again. Terry calls "Roll" - a slight pause as we bank left, and then "Pull". The bank is reversed and we pull up into a tight barrel roll. Looking again over Terry's shoulder I can see Seven spiralling toward us, streaming smoke. We pass, both inverted at the apex of the roll, then down again very close to the ground. A flash of buildings, helicopters, parked vehicles, startled cattle looking skyward as we apparently brush their heads. Then we are climbing again, this time we stay about 500 ft. We keep turning until we are behind the crowd line, I look through the left side of the windscreen. "Contact!", Seven calling (he can see us). Both solo's are now heading toward each other. We bank hard right through about 150 degrees, I'm looking left for Seven, skidding in trying to get behind us. We reverse left, the g is constant and hard. I look at the fields and trees, looking for the shadow of our aircraft hurtling across the green turf and stone houses. Then I see a second shadow. Seven's with us I tell Terry. "Echelon port go!" we hear the boss again. "Smoke on go!". We complete about a 200 degree turn so we are now heading for the airfield from behind the crowd. "Pulling up!" calls the boss - pause, then "Rolling under - now!". The main formation is on our right, coming toward us in two sections, a four and a three in echelon port. The three are line astern of the four ship formation. They pull up into a climb and then peel under each other in succession, to carry out the "Twizzle". They flash past on our right. "Smoke off go!" The boss calls. We run in from behind the VIP enclosure at 50 ft, one or two startled white faces peering upward. We race on at 310 knots. "Datum" calls Terry as we cross the runway intersection two aircraft in tight line astern. He counts quietly to himself then calls "Six smoke on go!" The instant of the command we break hard right into an 80 degree bank, streaming smoke. Seven has gone left also trailing smoke. "290 holding this" Terry calls

'Break, break, go!' calls Sqn Ldr Ray Hanna and the nine aircraft disperse in all directions. *(Malcolm Thomas)*

indicating his speed to Red Seven. The turn is a constant 4g 270 degrees, so by maintaining 4g and 290 knots both aircraft should trace the same circle. Looking at the grass just below our right wing tip it seems to be getting a little foggy - I breeth deeply and tense the muscles in my chest, arms and legs. The fog clears as the blood is forced back to my brain. I look upward through the canopy and see a thin trail of white smoke describing an arc turning toward us, the distance is closing rapidly! At nearly 600 knots closing speed it should. Although we are on our side turning about 50 ft above the ground, because of the g forcing us into our seats, our brains think down is where our backsides are. I can see two white helmeted figures in the scarlet machine rushing toward us, then they are gone underneath our windscreen. There's a shock as we fly through their smoke trail, the bank and the g is suddenly released and the world suddenly turns the right way up. On the right the empty VIP tent flashes past, we hurtle down the runway at 350 knots seemingly skimming the tarmac. I feel a thrill as we bank left through some trees and climb gently to 2,500 ft and slow to 200 knots using the airbrakes. Terry looks left for Seven who is on a course like ours, but at the opposite end of the runway. I look right twisting around to look over my right shoulder my head tipped back, looking through the top of the canopy. I see the main formation climbing up into a loop in Leader's Benefit (that is line abreast with the leader's aircraft fifteen feet further forward than the other six). There are no guides to help to keep four feet between wing tips in this manoeuvre, just pure skill and judgement. I watch the formation with pride as they reach the top of the loop. The Boss calls "Arrow - go!" and the line abreast obediently swings back into arrow. "Smoke off go!" The formation tips graciously over the top of the loop and gather speed heading toward the crowd. "Smoke on go!" calls the Boss. "Break - break go!" commands the Boss. The seven brilliant shining aeroplanes drift gently apart, making (to my mind) the prettiest of all manoeuvres the 'Cascade'. We now have all nine aircraft behind the crowd heading away from the airfield. We see one aircraft smoking – that's the boss. Now all the aircraft have to turn back toward the airfield and keeping the Boss in sight, we all have to change sides of the scattered formation. How each one knows where the others are I will never know. We and Seven are turning and keeping very low. "Pulling up" calls Boss Hanna and the eight aircraft climb vertically after the leader and close on him. The altimeter winds around very quickly through 3,000 – 4,000-4,500 ft as we slide up line astern of the Boss with Seven close behind us. Other aircraft climbing, slide toward us from both sides, and as we reach 4,500 ft, Seven calls "All aboard." The formation is complete again in the basic 'Diamond' formation.

All nine aircraft seem to float momentarily, weightless, inverted, the panorama of the Somerset countryside, Mendip Hills, with the Bristol Channel ahead of us and the star cross of the airfield runways, hangars, parked aircraft and vehicles fills the canopy. The formation slowly completes the loop and increases speed, the 'Diamond' now pointing vertically toward the earth, "Break - Break - Go!" the Boss calls. "1 left - 2 left - 3 left – 4 left" the calls come back, the formation breaks into the 'Bomb-burst'. We turn slightly left of the Boss. All nine aircraft hurtling downward, the g force increases rapidly as we pull out of the dive. We pull the nose up gently and as we reach about 1,000 ft. "Smoke Off Go!" the last command of another practice. We turn left parallel to the runway just nineteen minutes from start to finish of the display.

It's been one terrific adventure, so much compressed into so short a time. The sights, the movements, changes, sounds, pressure on the body, movement of the aircraft, the adrenaline excitement, wonder, pride, so many feelings, so much life in such a short time. Life is amazing!

We continue our left turn using airbrakes to slow down. Ahead are three aircraft, I look left across the airfield, we are travelling downwind on the right of the active runway. Over to our left on the other side of the runway is another line of five aircraft. We land alternately from left and right. As each aircraft turns finals and calls "Three Greens", each in turn momentarily emits smoke to enable the aircraft next in line to identify the caller and turn into line behind him. We land and pull to the side of the runway and stop to wait for the Boss to land and taxi through. Then each aircraft in numerical order turns and taxi behind. Now the Circus's work begins – the preparation of ten beautifully polished aeroplanes for the highlight of the Yeovilton Show in three hours' time. It's a wonderful life!!"

Bad Weather Displays

One of the biggest fears any air show organiser has is that bad weather will prevent participants flying. While many displays were grounded, "The Red Arrows" would try to ensure that the public would at least see one performance. Roy Booth describes one such experience.

"The Gnat was the most delightful aircraft I ever flew. The controls were extraordinarily responsive, although that could be a mixed blessing in turbulence when the ride became very lively. It was all too easy to over control. Full display formation changes were made well away from the ground where the air was generally smoother. A low cloud base held us down in the worst of the turbulence. Even with smoke on, the Gnat could be hard to see against a grey sky, so we flew a tight pattern to keep us in sight of the crowd. Some flat displays were a real challenge, none more so than the 1967 Battle of Britain display at Biggin Hill.

The 16th of September was a gloomy day with low cloud covering the whole of southern England. Our first display, at Abingdon, went smoothly enough under a ceiling of around 900 ft. However the prospects for Biggin were poor, with reports of 600 ft and two miles visibility persisting throughout the afternoon. Much of their programme had been cancelled and they were desperate for us to make an appearance. A non-precision approach radar had been set up just for the show. It was decided that our safest bet was to fly an instrument transit and approach as a single formation which was most unusual.

After take-off from Abingdon we joined up and climbed into the overcast. Visibility inside the cloud was good enough for me, flying as 5 at outside left, to see Pete Evans (4) on the far side almost the whole time. Radar guided us to the east of Biggin before turning us in for the approach. The talkdown controller gave heading corrections, range and the height required for the glide-slope. This we flew at a higher than normal approach speed with speedbrake out. We emerged from cloud at 600 ft although it was so murky underneath that it took me a few moments to realise I could see the ground. Speedbrake in, power on, landing lights on and less than 30 seconds later we were smoking low along the crowd line.

Unfortunately we were flying the wrong way to go straight into the display. Once clear of the airfield we rolled into a steep right turn. Trees, cars and upturned faces whirled past seemingly just feet beyond Pete's wingtip. When the airfield reappeared we were slightly off line which led to an unexpectedly rapid reversal into the arrival manoeuvre. The display was low, tight and as difficult as it gets for the wingmen. It was also very rewarding. The spectators had expected little more than a flypast and landing, so they were thrilled when we reappeared and went into the full routine. Lew Willcox, team manager and a hard man to impress, was unusually fired up when he met us after shutdown. From the initial dramatic appearance of landing lights racing out of the gloom, to the final break, he reckoned it had been a spectacular show. We knew it must have been something special if even 'Big Louis' was excited!"

Well, blow me!!!

On returning directly to RAF Biggin Hill from a trip to Southern France in September 1969, the team announced its arrival at Biggin Hill with a formation fly-by and Diamond Nine loop, before finishing with a bomb-burst – nine aircraft scattered to the four corners of the airfield and beyond. Immediately after completing the manoeuvre, they began their downwind legs on both sides of the runway, some aircraft flying left hand circuits and some right hand circuits as usual. Having landed, they moved to the very edges of the runway, alternatively left and right, to leave the centre clear. This enabled each aircraft to resume its numerical sequence for the taxi back to the parking apron. On this occasion the team were fortunate in that the landing direction was away from the A233 main road and the steep drop into the tree covered valley beyond. Ch Tech Thomas was in Red Six:

"We were parked close to the left edge of the runway, listening to the R/T patter as the others were landing, when a quite casual Australian drawl announced 'Red Nine coming through' and a Gnat came steaming past us and off the end of the runway, disappearing in clouds of dust and straw, into a freshly harvested cornfield. As we taxied off to our parking spot we watched and waved as the occupants of the stranded aircraft clambered out.

Once the aircraft had been retrieved and placed in its normal slot in the parking area, we gathered around it, inspecting for damage; there was none – not a scratch, even the tyres were clean! The only problem, despite the engine having been stop-cocked long before the aircraft left the runway, that we could see was that the intakes were full of straw and possibly other debris. The intakes and jet trunks on the Gnat being long and too narrow for anyone to access left us with no option but to split the aircraft in two and take the engine out – an all night job. Or so we thought! As several of us were keen to get away that evening, I suggested that we try blowing the stuff out. So, with the help of Sgt John Stuart (the back seat man from the wayward aircraft) and Sgt Graham Thomas (the other engine technician) we moved a Palouste engine starter close by and while John removed one intake blank at a time and Graham bypassed the start switch to run the Palouste at full speed, I held the air nozzle as far down the aircraft's jet pipe as I could. Hey Presto, the straw and debris were blasted out! A thorough examination of the intake and engine revealed no damage and a ground run proved normal. The brake problem was traced to a faulty maxaret unit and once this was replaced, a taxi and air test was carried out. All was in order and the aircraft declared serviceable.

Some time later after we returned to Little Rissington, the OC Engineering Wing, Wg Cdr V.W. Holden, saw me and said sarcastically 'I've heard it all now – blowing an engine backwards!'"

Catching up

With the loss of Dennis Hazell as team leader, following his ejection from a Gnat in November 1970, Alan East was invited to join the team.

"The weather for the remainder of the year must have been reasonable because my log book shows some fairly intensive practice as I tried to catch up the other new pilots on the team. On occasions when the weather was poor over Kemble, we would fly to Manston and do a couple of practices there. Then as the weather approached Manston we would return to Kemble and take advantage of the improvement there. I do not remember why the long break, but I did not fly from mid-December until mid-January. Then disaster struck.

As more aircraft emerged from winter servicing, we would practise ever-larger segments of the formation. In between these sorties, Nos. 6 and 7, the synchro pair, would practise their manoeuvres separately. They were doing this on the morning of 20 January 1971, with Bill Loverseed observing from the control tower. I was alone in the crew room, which at Kemble was inside the hangar. Nevertheless, I was aware that I could no longer hear any aircraft flying, so I went out to see why they had landed early. Through the open hangar door I saw an unmistakable pall of smoke. I went outside, expecting to see the other aircraft positioning to land and saw another pall of smoke. Six and Seven had collided. Euan Perreaux and Johnnie Haddock had new pilots Colin Armstrong and John Lewis in their back seats. All four were killed and are buried side by side in Little Rissington churchyard. Three of them were married. The Friday before, Pete Mackintosh, team manager for the previous two years and now a full member, had lost his medical category. So there were four of us left: Bill Loverseed, Doug Marr, Chris Roberts and me.

An official statement was made in Parliament saying that the future of the team would depend upon the findings of the Board of Inquiry, but we had to assume that we had a future and planned accordingly.

It was not possible to take two replacement aircraft from Valley and modify them in time for the beginning of the season. But more importantly, a team of nine would now include seven new pilots, which was not thought to be a good idea. So we were joined by the late Bill Aspinall, Pete Day and Roy Somerville to create a team of seven, the number the team had started with in 1965. Also, the late Ken Tait joined us as Manager. There was no detachment to Cyprus in those days, so we practised as much as the UK weather allowed, often nipping over to RAF Manston in the morning until a weather front had cleared Kemble. Sometimes we would stay there overnight. On 20 April we had to leave two aircraft there after a 'coming-together'. Myself and Pete Day had to return to Rissy to explain to the Commandant what had happened. We also hoped that this incident would not adversely affect the eagerly awaited decision on the team's future. Meanwhile, the late George White and a small team of engineers stayed behind at Manston, working through the night to replace the pitot-head of my aircraft and an aileron and wing-tip of Pete's. In the true tradition of the team, both aircraft were serviceable by the next morning.

Eventually, a little later than usual, we received the C-in-C's approval on 13 May. Our first public display was at RAF Linton-on-Ouse the following day. From there we flew to RNAS Lossiemouth for a display over HMS Ark Royal. It was bigger then! This was interesting because for the comfort of crew seated on deck the ship was steaming gently with the wind so that there was no wind over the deck. So each time we returned for a manoeuvre the smoke of the previous one was still there. By the end of the display the spectators must have been wishing for a bit of deck wind! At another RN venue, Yeovilton, we met Lt Cdr Shepherd, who flew an impressive display in the Sea Vixen. He christened the team the Crimson Crabs and thereafter Bill used that as our callsign whenever calling navy controllers, but often they failed to respond.

For 1972, Ian Dick, a past team member, returned as leader, Ken Tait became a team pilot and was replaced as Manager by Bruce Donnelly. Dave Binnie and Ted Girdler made up the nine and Ian Brackenby replaced George White as Engineering Officer. We only had one in those days! And we bade farewell to Doug Marr. The practice period went well, again making much use of Manston and often using standard aircraft because that winter the team aircraft went to the factory at Bitteswell for major work. Ken Tait was an accomplished woodworker and had made some splendid pieces of furniture for his and Pam's home. On days when the weather prevented flying, he built a row of very attractive glass-fronted cabinets, mounted along the lengths of two walls of the crew room. In these we displayed the fine collection of mementos which had been presented to the team over the years. On 23 March the Senior Air Staff Officer, Flying Training Command, AV-M Freddie Sowrey, flew in my back seat on a full practice and gave us our clearance for the season. It is at that point that the pilots don their red flying suits again.

Our first public displays were at Kemble for the families and at Bitteswell for the civilian engineers who had worked so hard on the aircraft over the winter. But the highlight of the season for me was the visit to Canada and the US.

Early in the year the team had been invited to Transpo 72, a 10-day Transport Exposition at Dulles Airport, Washington DC. But how to get there? The maximum range of the Gnat in still air is 760 nautical miles. We suggested that Ark Royal owed us a favour; we could winch the Gnats aboard and sail across. In case she was not available, we calculated that five Gnats could be fitted into a C5 Galaxy, so we would need only two. But their Air-ships insisted that we fly there. Quite right, too! I was now Deputy Leader and also responsible for navigation and diplomatic clearances. In the spring a party comprising the Engineering Officer, Wing Commander Ops, a representative from FTC and myself, were flown in a Hercules to reconnoitre the route. We checked accommodation (which meant staying the night at each place), local engineering support (aircraft starters, compatibility of oxygen trolley connectors, etc.), navigation facilities (the Gnat had only TACAN and ILS) and not forgetting the suitability for our Hercules support aircraft.

Perfection! The Red Arrows, acknowledged as the best aerobatic team in the world climbing through clouds in Diamond Nine formation. (*Tony Gannon*)

From Stornoway we flew to the USN base at Keflavik; fine. Then to Narsarsuaq, from which the Gnats could have made Goose Bay in one hop. In earlier times, this had been a busy US base known as Bluie West 1; thousands of aircraft were ferried through there during and after WWII. Now it was very quiet with the one remaining hangar damaged by fire and the one remaining H-block serving as everything – offices, hotel, general store, the lot. There was a Danish helicopter and a DC-4 based there. We were also warned about the local Inuit girls; apparently they had either VD or TB, so the advice was: if tempted, pick one who coughs! The only Navigation Aids are two NDBs, one at the end of the fjord and the other on the airfield, which itself is at the base of a long steep glacier. Not having ADF, the Gnat could not carry out the cloud break procedure here if required. But, despite it being a clear day, we flew it in the Hercules out of interest. Having descended over the outer beacon, there was a choice of channels to follow by map reading. The ice was beginning to break up as we passed the still visible foundations of Leif Eriksson's settlement on one shore and a wrecked ship on another. Both were marked on the official Arrival chart. The sky was still clear the following morning, but a gale was blowing sheets of roof cladding across the ramp and alarmingly close to the Hercules. The resident Met. Officer apologised for not forecasting it, but explained that it was a katabatic wind. Rather more significant than the gentle breezes of the Cotswolds, but then it had flowed all the way down the Greenland ice cap. No way could we risk parking ten Gnats overnight there, so we flew up the coast to Sonderstromfjord, an operational USAF base. Here there was everything we needed, but from there we would have to route via Frobisher Bay on Baffin Island.

Another consideration was the possible incapacity of the leader for any reason while we were over there. After going all that way, could we really afford to have nothing to present? So, we flew several sorties with me leading, practising a 7-ship display similar to that of the previous season. Luckily, that was never needed. In 2003, I asked if the present team ever plan for such a contingency on their longer overseas tours and was told, 'If the leader cannot fly, nobody flies!'

We departed Stornoway on 16 May, the first RAF display team to visit North America since the Vampires of No. 54 Squadron in July, 1948. Normally on such transit flights we would have had our usual engineer in the back seat, but on these legs over cold sea or terrain we flew solo. Then, if the aircraft had to be abandoned for any reason, there would be only one person to rescue. Because we carried more spares, including a spare engine, on this important tour, there were two support Hercules; so there was plenty of room. We actually used that engine in Frobisher Bay. It was only a minor snag on the leader's aircraft, but, quite understandably, the engineers chose to do an engine change in a heated hangar rather than work on it outside in below zero temperatures.

On the long over-water legs we had a USAF 'Duckbut' Hercules beneath us watching us on his radar. In the event of an ejection, he claimed that he would reach us within 15 minutes; he would drop a larger dinghy and survival kit and orbit our position. Meanwhile, a Jolly Green Giant helicopter would have scrambled from whichever end of our route was nearer; they would home on to the Hercules, hoist us aboard, in-flight refuel from the Hercules and then fly us to somewhere warmer. The longest leg was 1 hr 45 mins. from Keflavik to Sonderstromfjord. It was very comforting to know that facility was available as we sat in our immersion suits, squeezed into the snug Gnat cockpit and looking down either at the beautiful patterns made by the breaking ice flowes as they drifted in the currents of the cold water below, or at the tracks where a ski-equipped C.130 had landed to service a remote TACAN beacon, a very small speck, but the only feature to be seen in the snow covered scene below..

Most of the time we were within range of a TACAN beacon, but not of a radio station. We had no long-range HF radio with which to obtain an up-to-date weather report from our destination as we reached the point of no return (PNR). So we had an escort to provide a radio link. I anticipated that this would be a Canberra but, surprisingly, the aircraft whose climb and cruise performance matched ours best was the Vulcan. In fact, we had two. One went ahead to be in the circuit of our destination as we approached PNR and he relayed his report of the weather to his buddy who was in loose formation with us. Another useful facility for us and a welcome 'jolly' for them. Their only embarrassment came at Goose Bay where, believing the local RAF personnel were familiar with the Vulcan, the crew chief left them to refuel it unsupervised. But they selected the wrong tanks first and tipped it on to its tail. It was very interesting watching the next bit as they assembled cranes and giant air bags in order to lower the nose gently without causing further damage. By now the ECM pod was at a very strange angle and the four jet pipes were decidedly oval.

We treated Goose Bay to a display before going on to Trenton, on the shore of Lake Ontario, where we stayed for four days. From here we flew a photographic sortie over Niagara Falls. If you have ever wondered why the smoke looks so thin in those photographs, it is because we had uplifted Canadian winter grade diesel fuel, which is very light. We also practised our American display. The displays of the American teams were very different to ours because FAA rules did not allow them to fly over the crowd, nor even towards the crowd. That meant that they could not even do a 360 degree turn in front of the crowd because at one stage they would obviously be flying towards it. To comply with all of that would have meant a complete redesign of the Red Arrows' display, so we had negotiated some concessions. But there were some significant adjustments which we had to practise.

At Dulles, we opened the flying display every afternoon. For the first five days it was closed by the USAF Thunderbirds, and for the second five by the USN Blue Angels. Both teams were using the Phantom at the time, which compared to the Gnat was very big and very noisy. When parked alongside them, a Gnat looked like a potential under-wing store waiting to be hoisted on to its pylon. They were fascinated by our tiny 24ft wing span toys. One found the VHF antenna under one wing and almost touching the ground. 'Look!' he said, 'Here's how these guys fly so low. Kerb feelers!' Hearing that we had no in-flight refuelling capability, another asked, 'How did you get these things over here?' I replied, 'Very carefully!' which became a useful answer to several other questions. The public had seen nothing like our display and it was very well received. After the tight overlapped position keeping of their national teams, to see us pull up in a wide gaggle and achieve the Diamond-9 by the time we were vertical, as part of the demonstration, they thought was rather audacious. At the time when Rolls-Royce had just gone bust and things were difficult in the UK, it was good to be over there showing off our British skills in British aircraft. From there we took part in the 3-day Reading Air Show in Pennsylvania and a smaller one at St Catharines, on the Canadian side of the Falls and whose date had been brought forward so we could be there. At Reading they locked on to the fact that I am originally from Reading, England. I was asked to convey a gift from their mayor to the mayor back home, which was a handy excuse to have to attend another reception when we got back. At the end of the year, I was awarded the AFC. Again, there was no citation, but I like to think that it was for what I did towards the success of this challenging Atlantic crossing for a most satisfying tour in North America.

My back seat man for both seasons was John Webb, whose name was painted under mine on the side of XR993. Indeed, my attitude was that it was his aircraft, which he allowed me to fly. After all, it was he who kept it clean! As with many of the other back-seaters, on transit flights, it was John who flew the aircraft for most of the flight. He became proficient at rejoining formation and maintaining station during selection of wheels and flaps. After I left he gained his PPL, going solo in less than five hours. Years later, he was to own a Bölkow 207 and earn his living servicing other people's light aircraft."

Aircraft Finishing Teams

Part of No. 5 MU's remit at Kemble was to repaint aircraft of all shapes and sizes. Gordon Chin joined 5 MU in 1973 and worked on the Aircraft Finishing Team responsible for returning "The Red Arrows" Gnats to pristine condition at the beginning of each new season. *"Each aircraft was stripped back to bare metal or rubbed right down before receiving primer and top coats. The job itself was quite involved and I found it very interesting and satisfying. We did everything including making the stencils. One thing that sticks in my mind was when I removed the stencil backing from 'The Red Arrows' badge on Flt Lt Barber's aircraft to expose the motto, 'Imprimis Praecepta' – 'Our teaching is everlasting'".*

Last of the Rissy "Arrows"

The final "Red Arrows" pilot selection for the 1976 team took place during the previous summer and in a break from tradition, new pilots did not have to be Qualified Flying Instructors in order to gain a place on the team. One of three newcomers, Flt Lt Nigel Champness was fresh from a tour on Harriers and was interviewed by a selection panel headed by team leader, Sqn Ldr 'Dickie' Duckett.

"On arrival at Little Rissington, Flt Lts Mike Phillips, Tim Curley and myself settled into our rooms in the Officers' Mess and, having completed our arrival procedures, made our way to Kemble to meet the then current team. By way of introduction to life on the "Arrows" and familiarisation with close formation flying, I converted onto the Gnat and was then flown in the back seat during both practice and live displays. I flew XS107 in the No. 9 position for my first year in 1976 and moved to No. 5 in the following year.

A close relationship that evolved during my time on the team was that with Dunlop Tyres, the tyre supplier for the Gnat. Someone on the team had noticed that the special tyres Dunlop produced for motor cycle racing had red arrows painted on them to indicate the direction of rotation for the mechanics. A goodwill visit to the factory outside Liverpool was arranged for the team and for it to display at the TT Races on the Isle of Man. In return, representatives from the company were invited to join us for a day at Kemble. Phil Read, who was a world class racer at the time and was sponsored by Dunlop, came down to Kemble with his racing machine. As the day progressed, the challenge was dropped for a race down the runway between Phil on his bike and Dickie Duckett in XS111, but I don't recall the outcome.

Motor bike racer Phil Read alongside Sqn Ldr Dickie Duckett in XS111 as they hurtle down the Kemble runway. (*inset*) Not all Red Arrows pilot training involves flying; in this nautical pose the 1976 team take a 'serious' approach to emergency ditching drill in Cirencester pool; (*l to r*), Flt Lts Nigel Champness, Tim Curley, Mel Cornwell, Sqn Ldr Brian Hoskins, Flt Lts Roy Barber, Dudley Carvell, Bob Eccles, Mike Phillips, Sqn Ldr Dickie Duckett. (*Nigel Champness*)

We had one aircraft, XR987, that used to 'flick' of its own accord. Following rigging checks Dudley Carvell took it up for a quick handling check while we were strapped in waiting for him to return before departing for a series of shows on the continent. Flying with him was Terry Whelan, a Sergeant Electrician and Dudley's regular back-seater. Shortly after take-off their intercom went dead but Dudley decided to continue with the test. As they went over the top of a loop the aircraft 'flicked' and Terry, thinking Dudley had lost control, panicked and ejected through the canopy. He landed safely but became the butt of jokes for the rest of his time on the team. Dudley meanwhile centralised the controls and landed safely back at Kemble. After further investigation, '987 had a wing change and this cured the problem.

One incident that sticks in my mind is the occasion when I landed my Gnat with the brakes full on at the end of a practice display. I didn't realise anything was wrong until suddenly the left main tyre burst, quickly followed by the right, and I was heading off the tarmac. Fortunately little damage was done, but the question arose as to whether I landed with my feet on the brakes or the main hydraulic valve feeding the brakes had jammed. Replacing it would have meant taking the aircraft apart and as I was prepared to put my hand up, the aircraft was signed-off as serviceable. I took a bit of stick when I got back to the Mess though."

Aircraft fatigue

By the time CFS departed Little Rissington, "The Red Arrows" had operated eleven full seasons from their Fairford and Kemble bases and accidents and fatigue had taken its toll on the team's aircraft. In 1970, XR992 and XR995 were replaced by XR545 and XS107, which were transferred from 4 FTS at Valley and brought up to display specifications, and the loss of two more aircraft in 1971 imposed a reduction in the size of the team to seven aircraft. Even so, following modification, XM708 and XS101 were transferred to the team from 4 Squadron CFS to make up the numbers. In the following year, a reduction in the established Gnat force at Valley enabled two additional aircraft, XR572 and XR981, to be transferred to the team. They were repainted in "Red Arrows" colours but were not fitted with the smoke generating system until some time later. By the time CFS departed Little Rissington, four of the original ten aircraft were still flying with the team: XR540, XR987, XR991 and XR993.

Display totals per season for "The Red Arrows"

After a steady first season on the display circuit, running-in as it were, the number of performances by "The Red Arrows" grew quite sharply over the ensuing years until the magic 100 was reached in 1973. A century would have been achieved as early as 1968 had it not been for two shows that were cancelled at the last minute due to bad weather.

The table below shows the number of public displays given by the team over the twelve years in which it was associated with CFS at Little Rissington:

Year	Annual Total	Cumulative Total
1965	41	41
1966	84	125
1967	77	202
1968	98	300
1969	87	387
1970	89	476
1971	74	550
1972	90	640
1973	103	743
1974	59	802
1975	56	858
1976	109	967

The average number of shows per annum = 80.6

The team continued to occupy the G-site hangar at Kemble until the airfield closed for RAF use in 1983, when it moved to Cranwell. Apart from a change of colour, the hangar is little changed today. It was used for parts storage by the USAF for a period, before being sold to its current occupier, Delta Jets. How apt then that the company now restores, maintains and operates a number of Hunters, Gnats and Jet Provosts, all former CFS types. One of its Hunters, T.Mk.7b, WV318, even operated with the CFS Type Flight at Kemble from 1960 to 1963.

"The Vintage Pair"

The final display team to be formed at RAF Little Rissington was the appropriately-named "Vintage Pair" in February 1972. Comprising a Meteor T.7 and Vampire T.11, the team performed as a duo at airshows throughout the country, both air and groundcrews being composed of volunteers.

The aircraft were flown by Sqn Ldrs Bruce McDonald and William Shrubsole in the Meteor and Flt Lts Peter Bouch and Alistair Holyoake in the Vampire, all instructors with Examining Wing. Wg Cdr Ian Brimson was the Team Manager and ground support was provided by a small team led by Sgt Stewart Morton. Peter Bouch takes up the story. *"We worked out a display routine and went and practised it over Chedworth before getting it approved by the Commandant, Air Cdre Roy Crompton. It came together very well but it was difficult to see each other in poor light (grey painted aircraft) in opposition manoeuvres. The Commandant suggested a trip with the 'Arrows' might help so I took him up on that and flew with the 'Synchro Pair', Dave Binnie and Roy Somerville. They were magic, but brightly coloured aircraft, bright lights and smoke did give them a small advantage. It didn't really help us but I was impressed with their skill and felt privileged to fly with them as no one but the Commandant and Red Leader could go with the pair on display."*

Over the years the team operated two Meteors and a single Vampire, each painted in a light, all-over grey finish with yellow training bands. The oldest was T.7, WA669, which first flew in March 1950 and was retired in October 1975, while sister-ship WF791 first took to the air in April 1951. This aircraft had a previous association with Little Rissington having served on the Meteor Type Flight (3 Squadron) from 1962 to 1965. It joined the team in March 1976. First flown in December 1955, the T.11, XH304, was already on the CFS inventory when the team formed and was the last airworthy Vampire to serve with the RAF.

By 1975 all the original crews had been posted out, their seats being filled by Sqn Ldr Tony Gregory and Flt Lt Ross Payne in the Vampire, and Wg Cdr 'Cas' Maynard and Flt Lt Derek Fitzsimmons in the Meteor. The same pair continued to fly the T.7 in 1976 while Flt Lts Dan Hicks and Rod Dowd took over in the T.11.

Wg Cdr 'Cas' Maynard recalls that;

"At the beginning of May, Flt Lt Dusty Rhodes of Examining Wing gave me a refresher course on the Meteor T.7, after which I started working up to fly as a member of the 'Vintage Pair'. Vintage was managed by Examining Wing and two pilots were assigned to each aircraft – I shared the Meteor with Derek Fitzsimmons and the T.11 was flown by Ross Payne and Tony Gregory. We all flew the same sequence and so were able to share the display workload. On landing-away displays our groundcrew would fly in the back seat. It is worth recording that without the engineering support the team could not have functioned. The aircraft were no longer in regular service, spares were scarce as indeed was manpower, so all the support had to be voluntary and in addition to normal duties. The smart appearance of the aircraft and their preparation did great credit to the groundcrew; LAC Colin Sexton flew with me throughout the 1975 season. All the team worked well together and I feel proud to have been part of it."

Although the aircraft were fully aerobatic, only basic manoeuvres were carried out during their 5-minute displays to ensure that their estimated fatigue lives could be extended for as long as possible. On 12 April 1976, the team moved with the Central Flying School to RAF Cranwell.

The Vintage Pair Vampire T.11, XH304, and Meteor T.7, WA669, perform a low flypast before separating for their solo displays. (*Tony Gregory*)

CHAPTER 8

View from the Ground

This chapter presents an intriguing insight into what life was like at Little Rissington from the perspective of some of the airmen and airwomen who were based there.

The considerable number and variety of aircraft flown by CFS required a force averaging 650 airmen, 70 airwomen and 300 civilians to keep them flying and other airfield facilities functioning. The mechanics and fitters working in the engine, radio, instrument, armament and electrical servicing bays, not to forget the MT drivers, parachute packers, administrators, clerks and cooks, all provided essential backup and support for the ground crews working on the flight lines.

Wartime posting to Ris

When AC2 Reg O'Neil joined the RAF in 1940 he had no idea what fate had in store for him. He had hoped to become a Wireless operator/Air gunner but was 'persuaded' on account of his background in Hotel and Restaurant Management to work in the Sergeants' Mess.

"My six weeks square bashing eventually came to an end, hopes that we might be given some leave to go and show off our uniforms to our folk at home were dashed when it was announced that we were to be posted directly to airfields around the country. We were to parade to be told of our postings and as each destination was called out there were hasty references made to pocket diaries to see if such a name was evident on the map section. 'Little Rissington'... 'Where is it?', we asked; couldn't see it on the map! But the following morning on receiving our travelling instructions we got some clue. We (six of us) were to travel to Worcester by train, there to change to a train going to Oxford but to alight at a place called Kingham! 'Where on earth is Kingham?' No one had ever heard of it, no town or city of that name was shown on any of our maps.

Kingham was but a few stops up the line and was the junction for the Cheltenham branch line. As we alighted from the train and dragged our kitbags onto the platform we asked a porter how we could get to Little Rissington. Being a very helpful person, he told us to leave our kit on the platform and cross over the bridge to a Salvation Army Canteen to take refreshment whilst he would contact the RAF Station to send transport for us. After some thirty minutes or so and several mugs of tea, a huge Crossley six-wheeled truck arrived into which we loaded our kit and ourselves and away we were transported through the Oxfordshire countryside and over the border into Gloucestershire where we found ourselves on what seemed to be, the top of the world! In fact we were on the top of the Cotswolds and from the airfield we could see for miles in all directions. On a summer's evening, to watch the sun setting in the west was a sight to behold. During the winter however, quite a considerable change to this scene was to unfold, a wilderness of ice and snow resembling the Polar Regions.

As it was late afternoon, we were hurried through the preliminaries of booking in and given instructions where to bed down for the night, etc. We found ourselves in a top room of a barrack block whose inmates soon put us in the picture of where to get food and other necessities and so eventually we turned in. Hardly had we dropped off to sleep when we were awakened by the sound of the air raid siren. Nobody seemed to take much notice and we were told, 'Not to worry, nothing ever happens here', so we returned to our beds and a few minutes later we heard the sound of an aircraft droning overhead followed by the whistle of a bomb falling, culminating in a shattering explosion. It turned out to be the first bomb to be heard at this station but fortunately it had fallen outside the camp in fields on the outskirts of a nearby village. Such was the welcome to what was to become my home for the next eighteen months.

Once a fortnight, on a Friday, we would attend Pay Parade. The whole camp would form up on the parade ground facing the NAAFI, in alphabetical order. Then to be marched into the establishment where a long table covered in blankets would confront us, behind which would be seated an Accounts Officer, Orderly Officer and various NCOs and accounts clerks. On the table would be the ledgers and little stacks of coins awaiting distribution. The Duty Officer would call out a man's surname, to which the man in question would acknowledge by springing to attention and shouting 'Sir,' and add his 'last three', the last three digits of his service number. He would then march to the table, come to the halt and salute. The Accounts Officer would then call out in a loud voice 'Fourteen Shillings' or whatever was due to the man. Sometimes a larger sum of 'One pound fifteen shillings' or some other large sum would be heard which would bring forth murmurs of 'Cor' or similar cry, to which the voice of the Orderly Officer would yell: 'Silence in the ranks'. After receiving his wages the airman would salute and smartly about turn and march off.

At this time, August 1940, an invasion was expected at any moment and in consequence plans had been drawn up for the defence of the station and airfield. The personnel were divided into two groups, one being confined to camp for one week on 'Anti-sabotage guard' whilst the other would have their freedom. This meant that the 'on duty' group had to draw rifles and bayonets from the armoury to be retained by each individual for 24 hours a day. Each morning from an hour before sunrise until an hour after, airmen had to position themselves 50 yards apart around the perimeter of the camp, watching out for enemy parachute troops descending to capture the establishment. There were one or two things amiss about this plan, one being that the number of rifles available were no more than 500, most of which were 'DP' (drill purposes) and had no firing pin! Also there was a complete shortage of ammunition. Five rounds for each serviceable rifle were all that could be spared. So the defence of this large RAF establishment at that time was 500 rifles and bayonets, a few rounds of .303 ammo. And 100 'Pikes'! And two Vickers machine guns mounted on the roof of one of the hangars. At first the whole thing was not taken too seriously and to while away these early morning hours, the 'sentries' would pass the time watching day break until one bright individual started up a chorus of 'Bless 'em all', which was quickly taken up by all. Later that morning, a message was relayed over the Tannoy system to the effect that 'Airmen on duty during night hours were to remain silent and not to disturb the rest of the camp, especially the Officers' Mess and Married Quarters.'

Turns were taken to perform the task of 'room orderly', the duties of which were to see that everything was shipshape in the billet prior to a visit from the orderly officer. At one time it was discovered that mice had found their way into the billet and a mousetrap was set. One morning the duty officer marched into the billet and saw the trap on the floor, to which he enquired of the room orderly 'What is that?', the orderly replied with a sheepish grin: 'A mousetrap, sir'. The officer then retorted that he could see that it was a mousetrap but what was it doing on the floor. The airman meekly replied that it was there to catch a mouse! There followed a discourse as to the legality of the situation, during which he was assured that this invasion had been reported and the trap had been allocated to deal with the situation. He accepted this statement but offered the advice that on the morrow, the trap must be out of sight. On the following morning the OO decided to check if the tops of the lockers had been dusted and ran his fingers along them until from the top of one came a resounding snap followed by a yell! The surprised officer calmed down a little and had to admit that he had given instructions that the offending article should be placed out of sight. It should be explained that the orderly officer happened to be none other than a very well known film star who had appeared in the film version of Shaw's 'Pygmalion' as the dustman father of Eliza Doolittle. He was suffering from a broken arm at the time and had been put on light duties and so was a semi permanent orderly officer. It just so happened that I was the 'room orderly' at the time of the first visit!"

Advance Party from Upavon

Sgt Joe Imber, an early Fitter IIE, remembers being in the first civilian contractor's lorry and Advance Party moving across from RAF Upavon to Little Rissington.

"RAF Upavon was the original CFS base in Wiltshire from 1912 to 1926 and from 1935 to the early years of WW2. Born in 1920 and brought-up in the village of Sherrington, 15 miles south-west Salisbury Plain from Upavon, I was always aware of CFS and its flying activities up until August 1937 when I joined the RAF as a Trenchard Brat with the 36th Entry at RAF Halton. To local people in earlier generations, RAF Upavon was referred to as 'Up-the-Flying-School'. After my WW2-accelerated Apprenticeship I passed out in December 1939 and was given a choice-of-posting, listing Upavon, Old Sarum or Boscombe Down so as to be near my home village. True to RAF procedure, I was posted to RAF Sealand up in Cheshire!

On returning from a posting as an instructor to the West African Air Corps in The Gambia in September 1945, once again I was given a 'choice-of-posting'. With my wife living at Shifnal near RAF Cosford, I had instructed there before my posting to Africa, and not wanting to return to Technical Training Command, I chose three aerodromes not too distant from Shifnal, namely Shawbury, Tern Hill and High Ercal. I was promptly posted to RAF Upavon, my original first choice in December 1939! During early WW2, RAF Upavon ceased to be called CFS and became No.7 FIS. During the April and May of 1946, the move from Upavon to Little Rissington took place and the original unit title of CFS was reinstated. A fleet of 3-ton lorries, hired from local civilian contractors, transported the bulk of Stores and Equipment with each truck carrying airmen escorts as the nucleus of the Advance Party. I was privileged to travel on the first lorry loaded with Stores, as Sergeant in charge of the Advance Party from the Repair & Inspection Section (R & I).

At that time, the camp was served by three local country bus firms, namely Pulham's, Scarrett's and Fluck's (Diana Dors maiden name!). Wives from the MQs had to travel weekly by bus down to Bourton-on-the-Water village Post Office to draw their Air Ministry marriage allowances.

My Rissy service lasted only until the end of 1946 and I was employed in the R & I Section, which was situated in the hangar behind the aerodrome Control Tower. R & I was commanded by an Admin. Flying Officer, who relied heavily on the Engineering Officer, WO Turnbull. During this time CFS experienced persistent defects with the Oxfords. Moisture from 'picketing-out' and landing on wet grass caused fungi growth in the tail unit near the tailwheel. A memorable experience I witnessed was a confrontation between Wg Cdr Jones, our CFI, and WO Turnbull. The former complained of how short he was of serviceable aircraft and he began to blame the R & I section for taking too much time over Major Inspections. WO Turnbull despatched him on his way with this memorable riposte: 'Sir, just remember – I am an aircraft engineer, not a bloody mushroom farmer!'

My next recall involved the Armament Officer and the Staff firework display for the MQ children to be held on the rugby field on 5 November. The children wanted a bonfire but were told 'No bonfire but good fireworks'. On the night, the armourers set-off a large number of Very Light cartridges and distress rockets, one of which set fire to a nearby cornrick on the arable land near the Officers' Mess. The Fire Section was called out but the small Karrier Bantam fire tender, with its tiny wheels, became bogged down trying to cross the arable field to reach the fire. The cornrick continued to burn merrily and was completely destroyed, much to the delight of the children, convinced the bonfire had been laid-on for

them after all.

As 1946 became 1947 I was posted to the Air Ministry Gas Factory at RAF Cardington to train with and become Crew Chief of an Oxygen Production Team for the Middle East. My wife remained at No. 26 MQ, thus enduring the great snowfall and freeze-up of 1947. Managing to travel back to our MQ on weekend pass, I had to walk cross-country from Kingham railway station, since all roads had completely disappeared under a deep blanket of snow. During my moonlight trek I even stumbled on and over the roof of a car, part hidden under the snow, as I crossed above what should have been the Burford to Stow-on-the-Wold road! The extreme temperatures froze the water supply to the Married Quarters for a full seven weeks and my wife, like others, had to melt snow to obtain her daily water needs. There were several imminent births in the MQs during this period and as the maternity hospital for Rissy was at Moreton-in-Marsh, an emergency transport convoy was assembled comprising a blower-type snowplough leading, followed by an ambulance ahead of a Coles mobile crane. The crane used its boom hoist as a winch for pulling out the snowplough or ambulance, both frequently stuck in deep snow.

After training at Cardington, both my team and I were drafted to SPDC Burtonwood in Cheshire to await our delayed embarkation by ship to the Middle East, arriving at the Oxygen Production Centre at 160 MU RAF Aqir, Palestine in July 1947."

Getting to grips with the first jets

Ted Sadler and Frank Stokes, both ex-47th Entry Halton fitters, were posted to CFS in the summer of 1947 following improvement (or was it improvisation?) at RAF St Athan.

"During our tour there the first Vampires arrived," says Frank, *"and since we both were the only jet-engine trained fitters on camp, we were assigned to the care of these two early Vampire single-seat aircraft.*

Our job included first-line servicing as well as 'chimney sweeping', so each morning would see one or both of us wheeling one or both of these machines out to the flight line. Normally both of us would be on duty and we would take turns with the pushing and the job of in-cockpit braking. The gradient, as others will recall, was slightly downhill from our hangar area to the flight line. Inevitably there were times when only one of us was on duty but these too were the times we enjoyed because, although we needed help to return the Vampires to the hangar after flying, one of us could manage by himself in the morning.

Firstly one would lean over the tailboom to lift the nose wheel and then pedal hard so as to swing the aircraft's nose around. By ourselves, after getting off the tail boom as we let the Vampire begin to trundle gently downhill, one had to run swiftly around the wingtip to overtake the aircraft then jump on to the side cockpit step. Up there we would have a hand on the brake lever and, when our final turning was necessary, abandon our braking. As the caption on our Winter 2004 Haltonian magazine says, 'You wouldn't get away with that today, Sir!', but great fun for a young teenager."

National Service

Les Lane was a fourth generation cabinet-maker who left technical college at the age of 18 and was called up to do National Service, which at that time was 18 months.

"I reported to RAF Padgate on 1 December 1948" recalls Les, *"and spent my first week or so 'kitting-out' along with several hundred other youths. I was then transferred to RAF West Kirby for 8 weeks 'square-bashing'. In early February 1949 I was posted to RAF Little Rissington. On a cold sunny day I and several other National Servicemen arrived at Kingham railway station where we were collected by lorry and taken to the airfield. On arrival we were allocated beds, I was lucky to be billeted in a new barrack block which had single rooms. I had my own door key – a great luxury in those days.*

Our first eight weeks were spent on practical and theoretical courses for our allocated trades, Airframe or Engine Assistants, designed especially for us.

To the best of my recollections, when I arrived at Rissy CFS had one Lancaster, one Spitfire, several Vampires, Tiger Moths, Mosquitos and several Harvards, plus a WWII German experimental rocket plane. Later other aircraft arrived, Chipmunks, Percival Prentices, two-seater Meteors and Balliol Trainers.

As a fully qualified Airframe Assistant, I was assigned to the Technical Wing to work in the Hydraulic Bay which was attached to the outside of the main servicing hangar, overlooking the airfield. It was a small workshop in which the main equipment was a large metal table with surrounding trough, with various connections for hydraulic pipes and hand operated pumps, in fact a Hydraulic Test Bench. I was introduced to Sgt Gore, an eccentric and slightly mad ex-Marine from Plymouth with 15 years' service behind him. He used hydraulic fluid as hair oil!

I was his entire staff and spent most of my working time servicing hydraulics on Harvards, Mosquitoes, Vampires and several other types. My main tasks were to service Harvard master brake-cylinders and Harvard oleo-legs which had developed oil leaks or been bent due to heavy landings. The bent legs often jammed and to release them I undid the top gland nut, connected the leg to the test bench and gradually increased the pressure to push out the bent section of leg. This had to be done with great care as it could be released with a mighty rush and not without some danger. I noticed that a window had been replaced; Sgt Gore told me his predecessor, a corporal, had jumped through the window when an oleo leg had suddenly become released. This made me very cautious indeed!

I guess Sgt Gore was in his late forties, but he had a young wife at home in Plymouth and she was expecting a baby. Learning that I was a skilled cabinet maker he persuaded me, against my better judgment, to construct a folding crib for the infant, during working hours, in the Bay. My doubts about his sanity were fed by the fact that he tried to convince me that he had invented a perpetual motion machine! He also brought the hydraulic-brake pipes from a friend's car into the Bay and attached them to the test-bench to look for leaks. When the pressure reached 2,000 lb. per sq. in. and the pipes began to straighten, I smartly left the Bay! Nevertheless he was very amiable and an easy task-master.

I remember the air displays very well, particularly the flying of a Lancaster across the airfield on one engine – albeit for a short distance as the aircraft was steadily losing height.

(*above*) Airmen from Technical Wing pose by a Harvard outside 1 Hangar in 1949. Among them are Jimmy Johnson, Les Lane and Phil Quantrill, 1st, 2nd and 3rd from the left in the back row; (*below*) Phil Quantril, Les Lane and fellow airman pause from their toil while working on a Harvard. (*Les Lane*)

The introduction of the Meteor to CFS got off to an ignominious start when the first aircraft, VW437, suffered a partial undercarriage collapse on landing. In another incident a Mosquito and Meteor collided and both aircraft landed safely, the Mosquito with several feet missing from one wing and a damaged propeller. The Meteor had a damaged wing tip and the top of its tailfin missing.

Rissy had its own farm, and sometimes you would see a pony and cart wandering around the camp, with an Airman at the reins and a small-bore shotgun by his side.

The camp Cinema was always popular and the local population was allowed in too. I particularly remember the high excitement when the Doris Day film 'It's Magic' was showing. There was a craze for launching paper aeroplanes whilst waiting for the films to begin and this developed into a competition to see who could fly the largest plane but when the planes reached poster size it all became very rowdy and the Station Police moved in to keep order.

I left Little Rissington at the end of May 1950 and was demobbed on the 1 June nearly two months before my 20th birthday. I always look back at my time at RAF Little Rissington with great nostalgia as it has had a great influence on my life. It was an experience I would not have missed. I enjoyed the frequent flying displays and the skill of the pilots. I still go and have a look at 'Rissy' when I am in that part of the country."

Six years in the Tower!

In June 1953, Ken Evans joined the RAF as a National Serviceman. Shortly after arriving at RAF Cardington, he turned down the chance to go aircrew, a five year commitment, and accepted the recruiter's advice that, if he signed on for three years, he could become an operations clerk – this he was assured, quite incorrectly, was the job seen in wartime newsreels, working underground pushing plaques about an ops table.

"After square bashing at West Kirby I arrived at Kingham station one evening and luckily found a driver, who had just dropped an officer off, to give me a lift to Little Rissington. After a night in transit accommodation I started the long 'arrival' process with a tedious tour round every section in correct order with the blue card for signature. The big surprise for me was to walk between the hangars and catch sight of the Control Tower for the first time, unaware that I would forever be grateful for that recruiter's duff information, as I would spend a happy life in the many Control Towers where I worked during my next 37 years. That first day I met the man of most influence in my future life, the SATCO, Sqn Ldr C. Holdway, well known throughout the RAF and on his last tour of duty at CFS. An imposing character, especially to this newly arrived AC2, for three years he encouraged me to take all exams and I was promoted to Corporal in 15 months. Next he persuaded me that my future lay with the RAF so away went thoughts of returning to Wales to become a solicitor. With his recommendation, I signed on to serve until my 55th birthday.

My first year I lived in the old huts, next to the Link Trainer and Officers' Mess, with a central stove fire, which, even if kept glowing red-hot, still failed to keep us warm during a Little Rissington winter. Later, moving into Trenchard Block next to the parade square, the central heating was great but the downside was that now we were always the block to be inspected by the many high-ranking visitors. At work there was plenty to learn, in the R/T cabin monitoring radio frequencies and giving pilots True Bearings on cross countries, operating the switchboard with its various landlines to contact other airfields in arranging flights, often for the Examining Wing to be dropped off by our Comm. Flight Ansons, flown by our two Flt Sgt Pilots, Hill and Hatton. Every time I could get off duty and there was a spare seat, I flew off with them. In the

Approach Room we kept the movements board up to date and had to operate the Jet Clock system – with the limited endurance of jets, it was vital to remind pilots formally after 45 minutes of flight and every 10 minutes thereafter until they were safely on recovery. In Flight Planning we had to keep the briefing boards and maps current with Danger Area details and all the various Notam warnings.

Great emphasis was always placed on Flight Safety so we had to be able to run down the stairs and cross the taxiway to start up the standby diesel if our ATC mains power failed. This entailed priming and swinging the starting handle, with its kick like a mule ensuring you soon learned to keep your thumb in the right place. In the event of a total communications failure we would fire a mortar, which went up to a thousand feet and had to be fired from a prone position, to avoid blowing one's head off. It was never used during my stay.

Before Night Flying we had to lay dozens of gooseneck paraffin flares and hundreds of glim lamps in case of electric failure, and check the Pundit was flashing 'LR' correctly. This meant we all had to know the Morse Code and be able to fire the Very pistol, which reminds me of an incident, serious but amusing once we found out no one was hurt. We frequently used Enstone as our relief landing ground and sent a Controller and Assistant there. Most airmen at this time were still National Servicemen, a few of whom had been to University before call up – unfortunately being clever did not always equate to common sense. The one at Enstone this particular day fired the Very pistol inside the Control Room and the round promptly bounced off roof, ceiling and windows before burning itself out at the Controller's feet. Once he had stopped shaking, he was on the phone asking me to send a relief down and to take our idiot graduate away.

Another incident recalled at Enstone, where firemen stopped the week to save driving their vehicles there and back every day, was when I was manning Rissy's switchboard. A call came from a fireman after the Controller had left for home. He told me an aircraft had just landed, not that unusual as light planes had landed by mistake there before. However he became excited and said this was really big. Once I asked him to describe it, I accused him of playing a joke on me. He repeated his story so I said I would get back to him. Ringing the USAF base at Upper Heyford, I asked if by any chance they had mislaid a B-36, Convair's famed 180 ton, 230 foot wingspan, intercontinental SAC bomber, with its 'six turning, four burning' combination of six Pratt & Whitney driven pusher props and four outboard J-47 jet engines. The reply came swiftly back – funny I should ask but one had just disappeared from their radar! Explaining one had landed safely at Enstone, I felt distinct relief at the far end tinged with concern since Enstone's runway was less than half their own runway length. With rockets fitted for more thrust, the B-36 later flew out OK but with a different pilot, as the one who landed there was sent back to USA.

Most memories are of people I met at CFS, some later gaining high rank. These included Flt Lt Severne, Flt Lt Hine, Flt Lt Tavanyar and Plt Off Rod Farley. Another was Jan (Johnnie) Masat, a Czech, who had made his way across Europe early in WW2 to join the RAF as a Sgt Pilot. Becoming the Link Trainer Instructor, he was a harsh disciplinarian. Once as Orderly Sergeant he was known to throw two or three rows out of the Astra Cinema when no one owned up to making certain noises when the National Anthem was being played. Anyone on 'Jankers' hoped he was not on duty because he would be worse than any Orderly Officer in awarding extra days. Suddenly informed one day that he only had acting rank and needed to remuster to a new trade or leave the service, he was heart broken and joined us in the tower, where I was given the job of training him. He was allowed to keep his rank and proved a good pupil, soon passing his exams and going off to the Air Traffic Control School at RAF Shawbury, ahead of me to qualify as a Runway Controller, which did not overly please me at the time.

Newly qualified, now I spent most time at the end of the active runway ensuring no pitot head covers had been left on, no ejection seat pins left in and that each aircraft looked safe to fly, without leaks and loose panels, before cleared for take off. Even more critical, all undercarriages had to be inspected as fully down before aircraft landed and care taken that nothing untoward was happening on the runway. A regular occurrence was stopping people returning from the pub just outside the airfield boundary and taking the short cut back to their quarters across the runways. We were fortunate during my period at CFS as there were no fatal accidents on the airfield. Quite a few 'near misses' occurred as air traffic circuit density meant our using two runways at the same time as well as the grass for take offs and landings. We were still finding pieces of metal from the Meteor, which crashed on the football pitch before I arrived. Also working in the Tower was a Corporal, severely injured when a Meteor smashed into the Caravan when practising asymmetric landings.

One night during night flying, a Derwent engine of a downwind Meteor in the circuit exploded but the pilot, Sqn Ldr Harkness, calmly landed despite a huge gaping hole where one of his two engines had been. If a Runway Controller saved someone landing with wheels up or taking off with a seat pin still in place, you would normally find a packet of cigarettes or a pint left behind the bar of The Old New Inn, the camp's favourite watering hole. Most entertainment in those days was on the station, as pay was so low that much off duty time was spent in the NAAFI, at the Astra Cinema or playing sport. Soccer played a big part in my life as I played for two teams and even had to run from one pitch to the other to pull on a different shirt most Wednesday sports afternoons. One night as we left the Cinema in a crowd, the Station rugby captain grabbed me to say 'You are 6ft 4in, could you play for the team?' I explained I was from Mid Wales and had never played but SAC Dave Cheshire with me said if they were short, he would help. He was only 5ft. 6ins. tall and the captain somewhat reluctantly said OK. We went to watch the match and Dave, who had been a regular in Aberavon's first team, had a great game and was kept in the team for the rest of his stay.

One evening, about to book out at the Guardroom to go for a drink down the village with my Fire Section friend, the Duty Policeman turned to two women waiting there and said: 'This is the chap who will know – Ken, when is this aeroplane landing back?' I explained that we had closed until Tuesday, as it was Bank Holiday. One woman, Flt Sgt Hatton's wife, was so sure her husband was returning, we turned around, went to the Fire Section, took out the Crash Land Rover and Tower keys to open up. When I spoke to Approach at RAF Waddington, they confirmed that an Anson was on its way to Rissy. We manned up another fire vehicle and sent him to find a Controller – I switched everything on including our runway lights, as it was getting dark. Flt Sgt Hatton called up on the R/T. I explained the position that we could not find a Controller but he was not worried in the least and landed safely. We also had called out the Duty Crew to open up the hangars to put the aircraft away. We closed everything down and continued on our evening out, with Flt Sgt Hatton later dropping in at the Old New Inn to buy us a pint. It proved a different matter on the Tuesday because the new SATCO gave me quite a telling off for not searching hard enough for a Controller!

By this time I had a single room in the block and was responsible for the twenty airmen living in the one main room. One Sunday a National Service airman, who worked in the Tower and had annoyed me by mouthing off or muttering under his breath, so much so that I had to find extra dirty jobs for him to do, knocked on my door. He said his dad and mum would like to see me. Going outside, I saw them both sitting in their Rolls-Royce. They said how pleased they were that I was able to discipline their son, as he never took any notice of them, and then took me out for Sunday Dinner! Around this time a new National Service airman named Martin (Bing) Crosby came to work in the Tower and, having worked down the mines, was older than others. When he found out how isolated we were, he was on the phone to his father asking him to buy him a car. He went home that weekend, returning on the Sunday night with a lovely car. From then on, Bing, I and our friend, Spud Murphy, could go wherever we wanted. We had a good system with our money, Bing paying for the beer on Thursday, Spud on Friday and I, best paid, covering Saturday and Sunday. On Monday Bing, having been on the phone to his Mum to plead poverty, received in the mail enough to last us until payday. In 1959, after nearly six years and now among the longest serving personnel at CFS, my posting came through and I was on my way to RAF Jever in Germany".

On secondment

As an Airframe Mechanic, SAC Tony Towers had been working on Vampires in 2nd Line Servicing with No. 7 FTS at RAF Swinderby when late in 1954 he was seconded to CFS to help start up a Vampire Flight.

"I think they wanted some in-depth experience!!! I was only there for about six months until they got organised and was then posted back to Swinderby. The Flight Commander at that time was a Major Emmons who was seconded from the USAF. As it was winter and Little Rissington being on top of a hill, we suffered from a lot of clamps(fog) and Major Emmons being American, used to organise volleyball competitions and awarded prizes for the best kept aircraft as each one had its own airframe and engine mechanic.

One of the Meteor Flights was situated in a tin hangar out in the airfield, and weather permitting, it used to be a race between a Vampire and a Meteor as to who could get in the air first in the early morning to do a weather check. The only personal incident I can remember is that one snowy day a few of us went to the Meteor Flight's hangar and blocked the coke fire chimney with snow before retreating to watch the exodus! They realised who it was and we were warned that they were retaliating by laying siege to our hangar with a snowplough and snowballs. As we had advance notice I suggested that we lay in a supply of snowballs just inside the hangar doors and at the appropriate time, load ourselves with them, open the door, and charge. At the appropriate time the doors were opened and I led the charge, however, as soon as I was outside, my mates closed the doors and I was left stranded to face the enemy alone!! At the time I was wearing a full denim overall and by the time they had finished with me I looked like a Michelin Man where they had stuffed my denims with snow and tied me to a tree. So much for my friends!! I also had my introduction to scrumpy in one of the locals and thought I was OK until I went outside and the fresh air hit me!!"

Variety, the spice of life

As a young lad from Dundee, Doug Sampson joined the RAF in 1953 and after all the usual training to Eng/Mech T, was posted to 23 Squadron at RAF Coltishall operating Venom 2 night fighters.

"A great outfit which was to shape my future approach to RAF life. After five years on Canberras with 102 Squadron, Swifts with 79 Squadron and Meteors, Javelins and Canberras with 228 OCU, I was demobbed at Leeming. My time in the RAF had been busy but enjoyable. Some of us adapt to the disciplined way of life, good or bad.

Once outside I was the one who couldn't adapt to civvy life although the job and money were good (after SAC wages it couldn't be anything else). The 8-5 and home to the family left me wanting the excitement, companionship and camaraderie of Service life. So it was back to Cardington and a blue/grey suit with shiny buttons.

Remember the old story about Prince Charles turning up at a remote spot in the Empire wearing a furry sort of bonnet? He was asked why he was wearing the odd headgear and replied that Her Majesty his mum had advised him to do so when he told her where he was going. 'Wearafoxhat' she told him and these were approximately the words I used when told I was posted to Little Rissington. The posting guys said it was in Gloucestershire and it was affectionately known as 'Little Riss' or 'Rissy'! And they thought it was a flying training school. Great, dirty hands from aircraft with props and piston engines spewing dirty black oil all over the place. Wonder who I'd upset at Innsworth to justify such a terrible future! But a few jars later things seemed much rosier after all it was just another posting, if only I had known how wrong I was. Not just another posting, it was RAF LITTLE RISSINGTON. A camp and local area with charm, friendliness and atmosphere, where IT all happened. The goings-on on camp and those wonderful little villages and country pubs dimmed the brightest city lights as I had pleasure in finding out.

I arrived at Kingham at about 14:00 (pub closing time in those days) phoned for transport – permission had to come from the Station Orderly Room. After a long discourse with a sergeant who I thought was a bit antisocial, it was decided I should catch the 16:30 bus. It was a double-decker and down those narrow Cotswold lanes it could be an interesting experience. However, I arrived at the guardroom booked in and proceeded to Transit, which was situated behind the guardroom and was definitely unsuitable for human habitation (airmen excepted!). It was an old type hut, asbestos panels, no door, broken windows, but a vast selection of furnishings (broken lockers and beds) and dodgy looking mattresses. However I did get bedding from the guardroom. After a visit to the

NAAFI and a broken night's sleep thanks to the noisy air conditioning, in the cold early dawn washed, shaved and dressed, I emerged ready to face whatever lay ahead of me (no memory of breakfast, so it must have been indifferent).

Over to the Station Orderly Room for my blue chit and another long chat with the 'attitude problem'. His parting words: 'you re-enlistments are all the same.' I wondered how many more handsome guys with my personality and charm he had met. Pitched up at Tech Wing HQ and found myself posted to Type Flight operating Canberras and Meteors (saved by the bell).

Type Flight (3 HP) run by Sergeant Barraclough (Barra) aided by some great characters, was a small but busy outfit and night flying was great (the Canberras went to Manby for a few nights) and ground crews stayed at home. Never play cards with Sergeant Barra unless you are his partner. We won a few whist evenings in the Families Club and 18 years later we met again in Saudi Arabia where we were bridge partners, but that's another story.

There were also plenty of opportunities to get some flying. I found out the unit test pilot, Flt Lt Alexander I think, was able to take an aircraft to Scotland at weekends. I was in like a shot not so much for a weekend at home, but for the flights. It was usually the station Anson but not always. One Saturday it was to be a Vampire (we worked Saturday mornings in those days), I had to be decompressed in the chamber that sat outside Sick Quarters, I passed OK except for toothache and had to get a tooth out. Our last trip in the Anson was just before Christmas 1958. On the way back we were to pick up a pilot from Manby but were lucky to get into Binbrook before 'Harry Clampers' shut everywhere down. A WRAF officer, Flt Lt Walker and another WRAF were also on board and we had to return to Rissy by train. Someone must have been a smooth talker as we were issued with duty travel warrants! The weather was so foggy the Anson didn't get back till New Year and someone missed his duty free run to Jersey – no more Scotland.

Type Flight like all sections had the occasional unfortunate incident such as a Canberra engine oil cap not properly secured. It would never have been noticed but the aircraft had a decompression at altitude making the aircrew descend rapidly causing the cap to burst open with resultant loss of oil pressure. The airman did his punishment and with the RAF-type sense of humour, was thereafter known as 'Caps'. The aircrew I believe received Commendations and much experience from an unfortunate incident.

To enable the Army Kinema Corps to make a safety film on actions after an A-Bomb explosion, a Hunter belonging to the Type Flight Detachment was flown in from Kemble. We simply had to tow the Hunter into the hangar and close the doors using 2 HP's end of 4 hangar. The tractor driver was Sid, I think, someone on brakes, and another someone and myself closing the doors dressed in cold wet gear. We were all in position raring to go when up came the guy with the black and white clapper board and called, 'Take One'. When we stop laughing it was 'Take 2', by take 20+something, even Josh the cleaner's Jack Russell had got into the picture. The director was having a fit, and the 2 HP guys were thoroughly enjoying themselves. How the Hunter wasn't written off by the hangar doors I'll never know. If you've been on the handles, you'll know what I mean. Once going they take some stopping. Anyone ever see the film? I never did, you'd think the stars would have been invited to the premiere.

Coming out of the Mousetrap pub one fine evening, I as usual Mr Nice Guy, and more sober than another member of our party, tried to assist him to the bus which we missed. He was 6ft tall and heavy, so I left him propped on a wall and tried for a taxi. When I returned I couldn't find him until an almighty commotion erupted from behind a house. How could he get stuck in a dustbin!! I couldn't move him and the householder must have dialled 999 because a young Constable appeared to arrest him, (he wasn't much cop) but with my help he managed to extract the inebriate and between us got him to the Bourton-on-the-Water police station with its lovely, highly polished brown lino floor (just like the RAF). The local Sergeant was called; his car duly screeched to a halt outside and he rushed in just in time to witness the heavy drinker having a heave all over his nice shiny floor. The Sergeant was not amused and called Rissy; the station ambulance duly arrived outside, using the Sergeant's car to assist in stopping. Well things got a bit heated then and we were returned to camp. The next day the SWO phoned and asked if I'd like to pay the Station Adj a visit (like yesterday) and not for morning coffee either. There I met the local bobby again – not a happy chappy. He charged the drunk and myself with being drunk and disorderly. Well, was I shocked, me having assisted the police in their constabulary duties to be done, etc. I'm glad to say the Gloucestershire Constabulary dropped the charges. After that when I went to Bourton-on-the-Water I always had a feeling of being watched."

Preparing the Canberras for an overseas visit

Engine Mechanic SAC Rod Brown was working in SSF in the spring of 1959 and was detailed to help prepare the three Canberras (one as reserve) for a trip to Southern Rhodesia by Examining Wing.

"It was soon realised that the fuel would have to be changed to the grade encountered overseas. On further investigation it was determined that this would reduce engine performance and that adjustments would have to be made with engines at full power to check the maximum r.p.m. Ch Tech Jim Stratton and I were detailed to carry out the checks and promptly started work on the first aircraft. The correct grade fuel was ordered from RAF Lyneham and it duly arrived in a huge bowser which contained enough for both the ground runs and first leg of the trip to Luqa.

The first two aircraft were refuelled and tested during normal working time, but the third aircraft decided to play up – the starboard engine refused to allow us to adjust it within specification. Time was short, so it was decided to work on the aircraft during an evening and into the night if necessary. Despite our best efforts and full power ground runs keeping the camp awake, the engine continued to play up so we packed up for the night to sleep on the problem. On the next day, with our stocks of Avtag running low, the aircraft was flown to Lyneham for topping up and on return to Rissy, the r.p.m. was found to be within limits, enabling the aircraft to depart on schedule.

It was around this time that the Wednesday afternoon sports period was abolished and a five-day working week established. Station parades were still held on occasions, usually Friday afternoons, which did away with the more usual Saturday affair. This was a great relief to us in SSF as we were working overtime until 21:00 two evenings per week and then losing that time on Saturday morning with parades.

Whilst with SSF, 'Pop', the NAAFI driver, had an unfortunate accident when starting the NAAFI wagon, a petrol-driven Ford Thames 3-tonner. His habit was to park the vehicle pointing in towards the building to protect it on three sides from the wind and weather. On one occasion he was hand swinging the engine between the front of the truck and the wall when the engine fired whilst in gear, pinning him to the wall."

(*above*) Having pushed 1 Squadron Piston Provost, XF895/PA, out of 2 Hangar, the groundcrew take a well earned rest; (*l to r*) J/T Phil Turner, SAC Sid xxxx, SAC Terry Chapman, AN Other, SAC Taff Evans. (*right*), Bob Kenna and colleague use subtle persuasion on an Anson's Cheetah engine, 1958. (*Rod Brown*)

You've been posted!

Very few airmen or airwomen, when informed that they had been posted to Little Rissington, had any idea where it was. SAC Roy Bagshaw spent the four years up until 1959 at RAF Manby in Lincolnshire and was busy at work when the Station WO called him in to tell him that he was being posted out. *"I asked him where I was going'* Roy recalls, *'China' he said. 'I'm going to China?, I responded inquisitively, to which he replied, 'Four seasons in a day. You're going to a place called Little Rissington and it's on a little hill.' He was of course referring to the weather in China where they experience all four seasons on the same day. I did not know then that Little Rissington had the same reputation. 'When you get to the top of the hill, you'll know you are there', he continued. I remember going from Kingham station and walking up the hill and could not believe that this was to be my new home. I was assigned to No. 2 Handling Party (HP) and little did I know how much I would become attached to the place."*

The Handling Parties

In the late fifties/early sixties, the flight line crews were known as Handling Parties (HP). Each HP had responsibility for 1st line servicing and support of a particular Squadron; 1 HP to 1 Squadron, 2 HP to 2 Squadron, 3 HP to 3 Squadron and 4 HP to the Handling Squadron. Manpower requirements for each were dependant on the type and number of aircraft allocated to each Squadron. No. 2 HP, for example, comprised twenty or so airmen under a Flight Sergeant, Sergeant and two Corporals, and was responsible for twenty Vampire T.11s, whereas 3 HP operated three Meteor T.7s and three Canberra T.4s only so fewer NCOs and other ranks were required.

From Brat to life on the line

Having passed-out from Boy Entrant Air Wireless Mechanic training at Cosford as an SAC, Ray Deacon arrived at Kingham Station during the late afternoon of 29 December 1959, en-route to Little Rissington.

"Transport up the hill was provided by a red City of Oxford double-deck bus operating on one of two daily services between Chipping Norton and the Airfield. As most people were still on Christmas leave the camp was deserted and had an icy cold feel about it.

Soon after completing my arrival procedure, I was assigned to the Scheduled Servicing Flight. Being an outdoor type I hated being shut up in a hangar and although most of the airmen working there were always up for a laugh, I worked for a dour Senior Technician (Air Radar) who was a real creep and not much liked by anyone. He saw me as someone to boss around but I was not going to stand any of that for long. About three months into my posting, I had just completed a Primary Inspection on the Examining Wing's Valetta, when he told me to rub down the aerials to the bare metal, clean them up and repaint them … again. As I knew I had done them as instructed per the manual, I refused and he stormed off in a huff muttering threatening words. A few minutes later I was summoned to explain myself to Sgt Pat Trumper in RSF who informed me in no uncertain terms that a Senior Tech had the same authority as a Sergeant. With the threat of a charge hanging over my head so early in my career, Pat let me off with a warning as to my future conduct and as punishment(!), transferred me to 2 HP. It was the best thing that could have happened to me and the next two years were some of the most entertaining of my life."

No. 2 Handling Party

To ensure that aircraft were available on time, the day began at 08:30 for Handling Party crews. After a hearty breakfast a ten-minute walk to their respective hangars, and a change into protective overalls, their

first task was to complete pre-flight checks on aircraft allocated for the first sorties of the day, a list having been produced by the line Chiefy. The Varsities were parked outside 1 Hangar overnight but on 2 HP, where three of the authors worked, and the three other HPs, it was all hands to the hangar doors. Each door was opened using a large winding handle and two men were usually needed to get these giant structures moving, with additional brawn supplied by half-a-dozen bodies propelling the trailing end. Each end of a hangar had six doors and when spirits were high, which was normally the case, the middle pair would be pushed as hard and fast as possible until they crashed at speed into the buffer stops, the objective being to see how far back along their tracks we could make them run. Each door weighed several tons and the consequences of one coming off the rails would have been catastrophic, but hey, life was fun on the line.

Some of the 2 HP groundcrew outside 4 Hangar in the autumn of 1960 with; (*l to r standing*), SAC Mick Bundy, Cpl Mick Brewer, LAC Bob 'Jock' Dargue, AN Other, SAC Bill Bailey, SAC 'Taff' Evans (his last day in the RAF), SAC Ray 'Ginge' Deacon, SAC Terry Bellis, SAC Mike Newman, SAC Mike 'Willy' Guilmant; (*kneeling*), SAC Dennis Horsfall, SAC John Hughes, SAC Mick Blundell, SAC David 'Dickie' Baston, SAC 'Flogger' Floyd. (*Ray Deacon*)

Jet experience!

Up until mid-1960, it had been rare for groundcrew to experience a trip in the Vampire's right hand seat, but this all changed when Sqn Ldr Peter Hicks took over as OC 2 Squadron.

"On one occasion", says Ray, *"when I was strapping him in for a solo flight, I enquired if it would be possible for some of the groundcrew to go up on sorties that would otherwise have empty seats. Within a few weeks, most of us would-be pilots had experienced their first jet-propelled flights and would enjoy several more over time.*

My first Vampire trip was on 9 September with Flt Lt Peter Broughton at the controls of XD383/VW. Having first taken us up to 40,000 ft Peter taught me how to perform loops and barrel rolls. Then, in appreciation for their hard work through the year, eight airmen were invited to fly in an eight-ship formation two days before Christmas 1960. I sat alongside Sqn Ldr Hicks in the lead aircraft, XK586/VO with the intention of taking photographs, but being at the front made it almost impossible to turn the camera far enough to the rear to get a decent shot.

We took off in two box-fours and headed towards the south west in a steady climb into clear air between cloud layers to reform into arrow formation. Sqn Ldr Hicks then led a series of practice manoeuvres before taking us down to 1,000 ft to overfly Kemble and Brize Norton. The aircraft then spilt into two groups of four and climbed back up into the murk for some close formation flying much of the time through dense clouds. All too soon it seemed, we were back at Little Rissington, breaking in sequence for a stream landing."

SACs Mickie Blundell and Dennis Horsfall were two other members of 2 HP who went on that trip. Dennis remembers;

"It was a dull, wet day and after going over a couple of things in the pre-flight briefing, my pilot said to me, 'If we have a problem and I say Eject, Eject, Go! and you say What, you will be talking to yourself.' That is something that will stay with me forever. During the trip, he had me changing the VHF radio to the required channel – to ensure that that was all I played with perhaps. On returning to the airfield we performed a formation break over the runway before making individual landings.

Rissy airfield was an excellent place to pick mushrooms. On many occasions over a weekend we would fill our baskets and take them to the Ground Radio station for a breakfast of eggs, sausages, bacon and mushrooms. Those guys had it made, night rations every night.

Roy Bagshaw was a fair footballer and played for one of the local teams. One thing that sticks in my mind about him was that he would wear a hair net to keep his hair in place and on cold days, a pair of nylons to keep his legs warm. His young lady if I recall lived in one of the last houses in the village before you left to go back up the hill to Rissy."

WZ416/VF was the third Vampire trainer off the production line back in 1953, and aircrew reported that it would flip onto its back during high speed stalls. The Station test pilot, Flt Lt Peter Marsh, was contacted and scheduled an air test on 30 October 1961. Ray badgered Flt Lt Marsh into taking him in the right hand seat.

"On what transpired to be my final flight in a jet, until a high speed thrash in a Hunter through the Radfan mountains in Aden two years later, I was about to experience the fright of my life. Peter had warned me that the test would be hairy but I was determined to give it a go. Following a standard take-off, Peter trimmed the aircraft for a steady

Flt Lt Peter Broughton flying T.11 XE994/VP, with 2 Squadron airman in the second seat, maintains close station with XK582/VO, flown by Sqn Ldr Peter Hicks, during the eight-ship Christmas formation, 23 December, 1960. (*Ray Deacon*)

climb with a high power setting on the throttle, and began writing notes on his knee pad. During the climb he explained the fundamentals of a high speed stall and how he proposed testing for the reported problem, quietly adding that if the aircraft misbehaved he would also need to check its behaviour in a spin. Only now did it dawn on me that I should have heeded his pre-flight warning and remained on the ground!

Some twenty minutes into the flight and with 40,000 ft indicating on the altimeter, we levelled out, accelerated to something approaching the Vampire's maximum speed, and began a slow bank to the right. With Peter pulling ever tighter on the stick the g-force increased and the plane began to shudder violently until suddenly, it flipped over to the left and onto its back, just as had been reported. Having regained control, Peter made a few notes and repeated the exercise with the same outcome. A few more notes and then two high speed stalls to the left. This time as the buffet came on the vibrations worsened as before but the aircraft remained under pilot control. More notes!

Now for the spins! Without knowing what to expect, we suddenly flipped over and headed downwards in a clockwise spiral at a disorientating and increasing rate of descent. When Peter applied what I now understand to be outspin aileron and opposite rudder to correct the spin, the combined effect of severe vibration and heavy stick forces prevented him from holding the column fully to the left with his right hand while extending the air brakes with his left. Having tried unsuccessfully a couple of times, he told me to help him hold the column over. I did as commanded without hesitation, but by now was 'passing bricks' and fearing those three dreaded words, 'Eject, Eject, Go', when the brakes extended and the Vampire slowly recovered in a controlled vertical dive. Yet more notes!

'Is that it, Sir?', I said in pleading voice. 'No Deacon it is not' came the sharp retort, 'Each test is performed twice'. So back up we climbed and we repeated a spin to the right with the same nerve-wracking effect. The final pair of tests comprised spinning to the left and as these were recovered without incident or passenger assist, we headed back to Rissy.

What a relief to feel my feet on terra firma. WZ416 was towed into a corner of the hangar to await rigging checks which were carried out by 'Tom' Thomas. Using a set of jigs he determined that one tailboom was higher than the other and that this was the probable cause of the high speed stall problem. A week or so later, Victor-Foxtrot was flown to St Athan, ostensibly for scrap, but records show that it was refurbished and re-issued to 1 FTS in 1963."

As time went by, competition for flights between the groundcrew intensified, and SAC Mickie Blundell is credited with using his initiative to best advantage. He recalls:

"When I arrived at the hangar each morning I would walk past the aircrew crew room and look at the flight board. If there was a slot with D.P. (dummy pilot) in it, I would go in, rub it out and insert my name. The aircrew got quite used to me and they even called me just before take-off time to give me a flying suit, electric hat and leg restrainers.

On one occasion, having been asked what I would like to do now that we are airborne, my reply was to fly as high as we can. So there we were at about 42,000 ft, ice on the instrument panel, when both the pilot and myself noticed the RPM gauge going in the wrong direction. The pilot's tone suddenly changed as he belted out the instruction, 'When I say prepare to eject, eject go, you had better be gone by the time the o is out of my mouth or you will be on your own'. It took two or three attempts to relight the Goblin and I remember thinking the ground looks a hell of a lot closer now than then it did a while ago.

I was also lucky enough to go up on a few air tests following minor inspections and the best bit to my mind was the loose article checks. This consisted of holding the stick and swirling it round as if stirring a cup of tea, then immediately inverting to pick bits of locking wire, etc., from the canopy. Fortunately there were never any tools!

I remember getting myself off the parade to welcome the return of the Commandant from an around-the-world trip. He was flying in a Canberra and had stopped at Lyneham for customs clearance. It was

(*above*) Civilian bowser drivers Vic Blunsdon, left, and Ted Connolly have unhooked the booms ready for SAC Dickie Baston (on the starboard wing) to refuel the T.11. (*below*) Ted 'supervises' Cpl Mick Brewer on the fuel hose while SAC 'Jock' Dargue aims his tank key at the camera and SAC Mick Blundell relaxes on the windscreen. (*Ray Deacon*)

The relaxed smile on SAC Ray Deacon's face before his 'terror' flight in Vampire T.11, WZ416, was notably absent on his return to the 2 Squadron apron, 30 October, 1961. (*Malcolm Thomas*)

decided that a Vampire and a JP should escort him back to Rissy and I managed to get myself in the Vamp. As the Canberra took off, we came in very low and slow to formate on him as he got airborne. As we climbed into thick cloud, lots of muttering was going on. On arrival back at Rissy, all three aircraft flew over the threshold in formation as if landing together and, as the Canberra touched down, the Vampire and JP went around again before landing."

Hangar allocations

Five main hangars were located on the north side of the airfield and these were numbered 1 to 4 from west to east, with number 5 almost hidden to the north of 3 Hangar. The Scheduled Servicing Flight (SSF) occupied 1 Hangar and was responsible for carrying out Minor and Major servicing on all aircraft plus the repair of any that sustained damage up to Cat. 3.

No. 1 Sqn and the Comms. Flight were assigned to 2 Hangar while Rectification Flight was located in 3 Hangar. Its responsibilities included the Primary servicing and repair of faults on aircraft that could not be undertaken quickly by the First Line teams on the flight lines. Nos. 2 and 3 Squadrons were located in the eastern and western halves respectively of 4 Hangar. No. 5 Hangar was equipped as a paint spray shop, its team of aircraft finishers being responsible for applying the CFS markings, and maintaining the fleet in a presentable condition.

As a flying training station, a five-day week Monday to Friday with normal working hours from 09:00 to 17:30 was in force, except on the rare occasions when night flying occurred or when the day was extended by an hour to make up for lost time during poor weather.

From Halton to Innsworth and where???

For an alternative insight into life as a tradesman we include this account from Engineering Officer, Sqn Ldr Michael Plimmer, who has clear memories of Little Rissington as an Instruments (General) Junior Technician.

"My first posting after completion of three years of apprentice training at RAF Halton was delayed by six months' hospitalisation at RAF Wroughton, courtesy of being sent, not volunteered, to the Aircrew Medical Centre at Hornchurch. My arrival and time at Rissy from January 1960, has stuck firmly in my memory. Discharged from hospital, I was held on the roll of that sinisterly named Personnel Disposal Unit at RAF Innsworth.

With no posting for me, I was sent on leave to await instructions. A fortnight later I rang Innsworth who, in an apparent fit of panic, quickly announced 'You're posted to Little Rissington'. 'Where's that?' I asked. 'Not sure', replies the national service clerk, 'but the nearest railway station is Kingham'. Armed with my railway warrant sent by post and some guidance from British Railways where Kingham might be, I thus arrived on its platform, situated roughly midway between Stow and Chipping Norton, one cold January Saturday morning. A porter tells me my best bet for Little Rissington is to take the local train to Bourton-on-the-Water, yet another unheard of place. At Bourton I find my way to the village high street to discover there is a bus to Little Rissington in an hour's time.

About ninety minutes later, one rather miffed J/T, laden with kit-bag and suitcase, is decanted at the guardroom. The civilian MoD police are singularly unimpressed with a Saturday midday arrival and I am put into transit and told to 'arrive properly' on Monday at SHQ. My first thoughts about Rissy were mainly 'Where in heaven's name am I?' – it seemed to be in the middle of nowhere but did have magnificent views. I spent the weekend cautiously exploring the camp and even found a welcoming booklet for new arrivals from which I learnt that I was in fact now at the home of the CFS. Monday was spent in the usual trawl around the station collecting signatures on my blue arrival card, but I did finally reach the office of my future boss Flt Lt De'ath, OC Electrical and Instrument Flight. The SNCO i/c the Instrument Bay, Flt Sgt Lockie, is called in and they decide that this new and inexperienced J/T instrument fitter will best be employed in the Scheduled Servicing Flight (SSF) under the charge of Cpl 'Jock' Ness. The SSF hangar, nearest to the main road, did only all the scheduled maintenance of the CFS fleet, which consisted mainly of Piston Provosts, Jet Provosts T.3s, Vampire T.11s, Canberra T.4s, and an assortment of Chipmunk, Anson, Valetta and Varsity trainers. The flow of work proved constant and heavy so our hangar was always full.

At that time we all were still issued with our individual tool kits and one vivid memory is the weekly tool check conducted by the Flt Sgt i/c SSF. On Friday afternoons we would sit on the hangar floor and, as our Flt Sgt called out any particular tool, we would all hold up that item from our tool kits.

The work itself was interesting for me because of the variety of aircraft coming into our hangar. Provosts had nice simple instrument panels, which hinged open for easy access and so could be quickly removed or re-fitted. Canberras had a hinged nose, which likewise made access easy for me, although other Canberra areas were more difficult to work in. The Vampire T.11 by contrast was a 'pig' to work on, with an instrument panel over 4 ft wide and which, when hinged down, fouled both control columns. Removing the panel required the hinge pins to be driven out while one took the weight of the entire assembly, always a sweaty struggle for removal or re-fitment.

Occasionally I would volunteer to help out during night flying down at the Vampire flight but dragging an oxygen trolley around between the aircraft and having to heave open the heavy Vampire cockpit canopies meant that you really did earn your night flying supper. Perhaps the worst job for an instrument 'basher' was adjusting the suction relief valve on the Piston Provost to provide the specified four inches of suction for the gyros. The valve is positioned on the engine firewall about 3 ft from the propeller and adjustments had to be done with the engine running. The slipstream and noise were bad enough on a good weather day but adjustments on a cold wet day were hellish. After five minutes you would be effectively frozen into a strange Nazi-like position with your one arm raised and body numbed. By comparison involvement in a compass swing was a doddle for us instrument men, as we sat in comfort in the cockpit while a gang of other trades pushed the aircraft around the compass base.

One day I got a pat on the back for discovering Avgas in the static drain traps of a Piston Provost. Initially the engine fitters did not believe me but, when I checked other aircraft and found the same problem, there was an almighty panic. A modification to introduce a source of static pressure to the Leonides engine was causing a syphoning effect from the fuel supply and allowing Avgas to enter the instrument pitot-static system. Other than that one eventful incident, I cannot claim to have distinguished myself – I was a small cog in a very large unit – from memory our CFS aircraft establishment was near enough seventy aircraft.

One disadvantage of working in SSF was that we rarely met any of the pilots, either staff or students. The only exception was when a post-major servicing air-test was required. The practice was for one of the tradesmen involved with the servicing to accompany the test pilot on the air-test. At Rissy still medically prohibited from flying in pressurized cabins, I was restricted to flying in Chipmunks or Provosts. Air-tests in a Provost certainly concentrated the mind wonderfully but were not recommended on a full stomach!

Social life at Ris for airmen (and the WRAF) was not too bad. Because our station was a long way from civilisation – the fleshpots of Cheltenham were twenty miles distant – we tended to inhabit the NAAFI. Being in rural Gloucestershire, we had scrumpy 'on tap' at ten old pence a pint or the smoother variety at one shilling and threepence (15 old pence equivalent later to just over 6p). Three pints of either version caused one to become tired and emotional, with a need for some 100% oxygen revival treatment the following morning. There was also a CFS flying club in being but to my everlasting regret I never took advantage of it. The corporal i/c my barrack room was a keen golfer and I would often caddy for him at the Burford course. There were always regular visits down to the pubs in Bourton and another pub often visited in the evenings was the Merrymouth located on the Burford road. This could be reached by walking across the airfield and various fields. I well recall that Station Routine Orders had a regular entry stating that airmen were not to walk across the runway when night flying was in progress but this did not deter many of us crossing our airfield.

After six months I had become accustomed to life at Little Ris and was happy to continue there but was called into the boss's office to be 'volunteered' for a transfer to the CFS Helicopter Squadron. This was located at RAF South Cerney about twenty miles away, where the corporal instrument fitter was off sick and there was no-one to over-sign the work of the other instrument tradesmen, all mechanics. So June 1960 saw me clearing from Rissy, putting my kit on the routine daily MT run to South Cerney and nursing my aged motorbike down the Fosse Way to Cirencester and then to Cerney. The CFS(H) squadron was in an odd situation as an autonomous squadron with its own CO, Sqn Ldr A.J. Clarke, and Engineering Officer, WO Tom Hayhow, but was a lodger unit on South Cerney, which provided all services except aircraft engineering support. Basically although the squadron could and did maintain its fleet of helicopters – mainly Sycamores and Whirlwinds plus two Dragonflies and a single Skeeter – all items removed from the 'choppers' had to be returned to Rissy for overhaul/rectification. To achieve this there was a daily MT run between the two stations to transport all such items back and forth. Unexpectedly urgent requirements were handled by a quick 'logistics' flight by helicopter and I had some most enjoyable flights in the Skeeter, clutching precious bits of helicopter on my lap. Skimming along at 50 ft and 80 knots over the Cotswold countryside was great fun, although cutting across to join the busy circuit at Little Rissington was very much a case of see and be seen. Soon I took a liking to helicopters and my boss at Ris decided that I was to stay at Cerney after promotion to Corporal Technician in July 1960. The squadron was reliant on Little Ris for our whole time at South Cerney but otherwise we were left to get on with our task.

Rumour had it that the expanding amount of chopper flying from Cerney was starting to infringe or affect Fairford's and other air traffic patterns. Ahead of our planned move in August 1961 and those relatively early days of helicopter development, it was virtually impossible to arrange for all our choppers to be serviceable on any given day. For our transfer to Tern Hill the Skeeter would go by road. Sixteen of us were selected to start up and then fly in our combined squadron formation up to Tern Hill – we had two Dragonflies at the front, followed by eight Sycamores and six Whirlwind Mk.2s and Mk.4s. In the third Sycamore, being flown by Flt Lt N.D. Fuller, I remember well my being simultaneously both shaken and stirred on this particular 90-minute flight. In our gaggle en route we had to be careful to stay out of each other's downwash and slipstream. En route we had two helicopters successively divert with problems, one early on back into Rissy and another much further north off into Shawbury.

Firstly our formation formally overflew Cirencester and then over Rissington. Cirencester was probably pleased to see the back of us – once I had had the dubious pleasure of being told to go into the town and report to the police station so as to collect a Whirlwind's front side vision panel. This, being slid back on its runners by the pilot, had kept going rearwards, on past the failing stoppers and fluttered down into the marketplace, fortunately without any damage or injury below!"

The last conscripts

Although conscription ended in 1960, four National Servicemen were still attached to 2 HP and none of them liked being in the RAF. SAC 'Taff' Evans was the more philosophical of the bunch and the first of the quartet to return to civvy street in the early autumn of that year. On his last day he was seen off with a huge party in the Old New Inn and being Welsh, led a repertoire of 'bawdy' songs that must have been audible along the high street at The Mousetrap. Another chap, Bob, came from Jersey and he also departed in October which left the Summers twins. Electricians by trade, one was very friendly and gregarious while the other was the complete opposite. Being identical, we had to take care when talking to one about the other just in case we offended the happy one, which we often did of course.

AOC-in-C's Parade

Once a year each Command took it in turn to hold the AOC-in-C's inspection and in 1960 it was the turn of Flying Training Command. In addition to the Station's Guard of Honour, a contingent of ninety other ranks was transported in RAF buses from Rissy to RAF

Oakington where the parade was being held. The first day was devoted to rehearsals and we were marched out to the huge ASP in two flights where we took up our positions at the extreme rear right corner. There must have been several thousand airmen on the pan by the time the parade had assembled.

Roy Bagshaw was in Little Rissington's Guard of Honour while Ray Deacon was in the supporting flight. Because of the vast size of the parade, instructions were given through a loudspeaker system. Roy continues the story; *"In preparation for the parade, a number of civilians had been employed to clean and paint the domed tops of the hangar roofs. Soon after we began marching, these guys sloped their brooms and started marching from one end to the other. With his back to the hangars, the Officer Commanding couldn't see them but everyone else could and an infectious wave of giggling quickly spread throughout the ranks, including some of the officers. This set the tone for the two days and helped make it more bearable. The parade was stood at ease while the Station Warrant Officer went over to call them down."*

Now this WO inadvertently took over as the centre of our amusement – Ray takes up the story. *"This poor chap had a bad nervous twitch and as he walked round the flights inspecting the men, his head would suddenly twitch to such an extent that you couldn't tell who he was addressing. After the debacle of the hangar roofs, that was all we needed, and as he passed through the flights in front of us, those in the Rissington ranks started sniggering, their shoulders rising and falling in an attempt to control any sudden exhalation. I've never seen so many airmen simultaneously place their right foot behind the left and reach for their hankies. Gradually the jollity spread to flights from other stations and it continued for much of the day. On the day of the parade, however, everyone behaved impeccably and everything went well. The Little Rissington contingent was even singled out for its splendid turn out and high standard of marching."*

(left) Civilian driver Sid Francis at the wheel of his trusty David Brown, waits to tow the 2 Squadron Vampires out of No.4 hangar, 1961. *(above)* What would we have done without them! Some of the civilian Refuelling Flight drivers outside their crewroom in 1961; *(l to r)* Frank Hunt, Charlie Smith, A.N. Other, Reg Avery, Sid Sandals, Alf Hartley, Sid Francis and John King. *(Ray Deacon)*

Let flying commence

Aircraft refuelling and tractor driving services were provided by civilian staff on the Refuelling Flight, a real bunch of characters from villages in the surrounding area with names such as Sid, Reg, Ted, Vic and Frank. The Flight was accommodated in a dedicated crewroom in 3 Hangar. A quick phone call to the Refuelling Flight by Chiefy would be responded to by one of the drivers, usually Sid or Reg, racing his David Brown tractor down the hardstanding, so keen were they to help 2 HP tow the first T.11s out to the flight pan. This was situated adjacent to the east end of 4 Hangar and could accommodate ten Vampires. A second driver would then appear with a line of recharged trolley-accs snaking out behind him which he deposited outside the crewroom. Once the aircraft were on the line, a message was passed through to the aircrew office to let them know flying could commence.

At the other end of the hangar, Flt Sgt 'Jock' Hutson would ensure his 3 HP team were busy preparing their Meteors and Canberras before towing them out to a hardstanding alongside 4 Hangar. The same ritual would be carried out by the crew at 1 HP, their Provosts, JPs and Chipmunks being aligned round the cramped confines of the hangar perimeter and the adjacent hardstanding. Completion of a new apron for the expanding JP fleet to the south of 2 Hangar late in 1961, made life a lot easier and safer for aircraft movements on this part of the airfield. The Varsities were operated from their overnight positions on the apron alongside 1 Hangar and the Ansons, when required, were parked in the space between 1 and 2 Hangars.

In 1960-62, the crew on 2 HP were a mix of 'old' lags, with active service on front line units, and keen young airmen on first postings. Apart from a couple of oddballs, it was a good mix and everyone got along fine. Except for the occasional incident necessitating his attention, 'Chiefy' Tucker kept himself to himself and Sgt Jack Castle kept out of the way, leaving the daily routine to Cpls 'Tom' Thomas and Des Mutton.

Cpl 'Tom' Thomas returned to the UK in the spring of 1960 after three years in the South Australian dry and dusty outback.

> *"The Gloucestershire countryside was a delight and Rissington held spectacular views across the lush green hills. My posting to No. 2 Handling Party was interesting to say the least. I and another corporal, Des Mutton, looked after a bunch of about twenty young airmen, a mixture of national service and regulars. It was a happy time and a lovely station to be on. I believe there were probably about 20 Vampires on the*

handling party although never more than 12 available at any one time as there were always some away on modification programmes or major servicing. We had some good times, morale was high and in the slack times, when the bad weather prevented flying, we played volley ball against the aircrew and got up to other mischief.

Generally Des and I stood back and 'encouraged' the lads to do the work, there were however occasions when I tried to show I could do their job just as well. One particular busy day one of the squadron Flight Commanders, Lt 'Dickie' Wren, a Navy pilot, was keen to get airborne to practise some solo aerobatics. Time was of the essence and most of our ground crew were busy so I endeavoured to strap him in, start him up and wave him off, after all I had seen our lads do it a thousand times. The most important job after strapping the crew in was to remove the safety pins from the ejection seats to make them live, one pin per seat. So I removed Dickie's pin, showed it to him in the prescribed manor and placed it in the stowage pocket in the side of the seat before closing the canopy. He started up and taxied out. Easy, I thought to myself. Then while watching one of the lads see off another aircraft as I walked back to the office, the thought struck me that I hadn't taken his pin out. As the doubts grew I ran into our office, phoned Air Traffic Control, gave the aircraft number and asked for it to be sent back for checking. By now the Vampire had begun its take-off run and it seemed an age before he throttled back. I met Lt Wren when he stopped and opened the canopy so that I could check his pin. I could see he was glaring at me as I mouthed 'OK' and gave the thumbs up. Slamming the canopy down he roared off. Yes, I had removed the pin but had probably upset him enough to prevent him enjoying his aerobatics. On his return he must have had words with Chiefy Tucker, who being a wise old bird said nothing to me about it. Next day, however, he gathered the ground crew around a T.11 in the hangar and told me to instruct them on the correct method of removal and stowage of ejection seat safety pins. A lesson I never forgot.

In the summer of 1961 I was sent to Folland's Apprentice Training School at Hamble for a three-week course on the new RAF trainer – the Folland Gnat. As part of the training I visited the flight test centre at Chilbolton airfield and the Gnat and Hunter production lines at Dunsfold. I returned to 2 HP after the course and stayed until February 1962 when the first Gnat arrived then I started work with the Gnat Project Team over at Kemble.

When the Gnat Project finished in July 1963 I moved on to the Gnat course line in brand new accommodation out on the airfield, adjacent to the new Air Traffic Control building. Gradually the Vampires departed as we re-equipped with the Gnat. I stayed with the Flight for another year during which time I had my first Gnat flight one lunch time with Aussie Sqn Ldr 'Benny' Raffin. We flew with another Gnat doing formation aerobatics and changing position from line astern to echelon port or starboard as the will took him. I enjoyed it to start with but became bored, very hot and then uncomfortable by the time our hour was up. I didn't feel hungry after we landed! A few days later while visiting Sqn Ldr Raffin at his house (my first wife was an Aussie and we used to baby sit for Benny and his wife), Benny said to me 'what did you think of the flight'. As I thought for a moment he said 'I'm sorry if I worried you'. 'No', I said, 'I quite enjoyed it.' 'Oh really', he said, followed by a pause, 'you do realise we very nearly crashed, I misjudged the line astern and almost collided with the other Gnat'.

In May 1964 I went to Borneo for a year and then on my return was posted back to Rissy where I joined "The Red Arrows" and stayed with them for the next seven years. Altogether I spent 11 years at Little Rissington, three of them living in the house situated just off the end of the main runway on the Barringtons road. They were 11 very good years."

As the first instructor/student pairs signed the F700s, Chiefy would slide back the wooden panel in the hatch linking his office with the Airmen's crewroom with a loud clonk, the signal to end our darts and card games and for starter crews to depart for the line. The starting procedure was straight forward, the instructor and pupil checking their T.11 externally for signs of damage, the flying control surfaces for full movement and that there was sufficient tread and air in the tyres, before removing the pitot head cover and climbing into the cockpit, having first verified that the safety pins were correctly inserted in the ejection seat guns. Meanwhile, the airman on starter duty had dragged a trolley-acc across the pan, plug it into the socket on the forward fuselage and check that the chain attached to the chock was not trapped under the nose wheel.

Having assisted the pilots to strap themselves in, handed them their helmets and plugged in their R/T leads, the ejector seat pins were removed, shown to the pilots and stowed in storage pockets on the side of the seats, the hood then closed and the steps moved away from the aircraft. With pre-flight cockpit checks completed, the twirl of a fore-finger from the captain (in the left seat) was reciprocated by the airman, giving the all-clear for the engine start button to be pressed. To the crackling of the igniters, the Goblin slowly wound up before igniting with a loud whoosh and sheet of flame from the short tailpipe; this made an illuminating sight at night. A final check of the instruments was followed by the chocks-away signal by the captain and the starter took up his position ready to marshal the aircraft safely away. Finally, the ground equipment on the empty pan was positioned ready to receive the aircraft on their return.

Time then to relax and return to the darts and cards and a mug of tea or coffee. On sunny days, high spirits could lead to all kinds of antics many of which would have got us into serious trouble had we been caught; scaling the unguarded ladder up the side of the hangar to hide on the roof to avoid Chiefy's hangar clean-ups, or racing the little flatbed trolleys across the pan and down through a natural water-splash by the rifle range, are antics that spring to mind. Another rather risky pastime involved chasing the civvy drivers on their tractors through the trees beside the hangar in a vain attempt to pull the engine cut-off as they tried to dodge us. It was a miracle no one got hurt.

Roy recollects one of the favourite epithets about Rissy: *"It could have four seasons in a day and one term in particular 'Harry Clampers' was used to describe foggy days. Days like this were worshipped by the groundcrew, as the Vampires could be moved to the sides of the hangar and the Officers challenged to a game of volleyball. The daily ritual of the mid-morning*

NAAFI van with its cups of chi (tea) and wads, was greeted by a shout of 'NAAFI-UP' which could be heard right across the hangar. One almost inedible delight, commonly known as the 'Sinker', consisted of a variety of crushed dried fruits lumped between two layers of granitised pastry. It could take an hour to eat and gained the name 'Sinker' on account of the effects on the stomach of eating two or more, something you only tried once."

All too soon the high-pitched whine of a Goblin engine could be heard approaching the threshold, the signal for us to present ourselves back on the line. Having marshalled the returning Vampires in and the cockpit access steps positioned alongside the fuselage, the ejection seat pins were inserted in the guns as the aircrew ran through their post flight checks. A pair of refuelling bowsers stationed at the edge of the pan, were moved to the front of the first two aircraft by Ted and Frank, and while some of the groundcrew got started on their turnround checks, those assigned to refuelling duties began the time consuming chore of filling the gravity-fed tanks. Air pockets would consistently build up and were removed by bouncing up and down on the wingtips, a bit like rocking one's car at the filling station until the bubbles stop. Twenty minutes or so later, the first two turnrounds were complete and the aircraft declared serviceable for their second sorties.

Similar procedures were followed on all Handling Parties throughout the day and were the staple diet for the first line servicing teams. When a problem arose it was the responsibility of the affiliated first line tradesman to verify the defect and to make repairs if possible. Certain problems, such as a wheel, radio and ejection seat changes, could be fixed on the line while aircraft with more complex defects were collected by Rectification Flight and towed up to 3 Hangar for attention.

As flying was continuous throughout the day, ground support was maintained over the lunch break by splitting the crews into shifts, the first departing for the Airmen's Mess at noon to return by 13:00, in time to enable the second shift to take an hour's break.

SAC Bob Dargue was an airframe mechanic on 2 HP in 1960-61 and he remembers the times we took the back road to the Mess for lunch. *"On occasions when we encountered a group of student pilots heading towards us we would spread ourselves out along the road so that they would have to give individual salutes as they passed each airman. Sometimes we reversed our tunics as the students approached and, although nothing was said, they would give us long peering glances when raising their hands to the salute. SAC Dickie Baston even had a kiddie's scooter which he rode to the Airmen's Mess without being challenged. It was this relaxed away-from-the-job discipline which contributed to the friendly atmosphere that existed at Little Rissington."*

Taking a break outside the 2 HP crewroom in the spring of 1961 are; (*l to r*) SACs Mike Newman, Mick Blundell, 'Jock' Dargue, Roy Bagshaw, J/T Johnny Johnson and civilian driver Sid Francis. (*Ray Deacon*)

The afternoon routine was similar to that of the morning, each aircraft flying a further two and occasionally three sorties. At the end of the day, as the aircraft were refuelled and the After Flight checks completed, the aircraft were towed back into their hangars and the hangar doors closed in double-quick time, for it was off to the Mess for a meal and an evening out in a pub somewhere. We often wondered how the Time and Motion boys commented on the leisurely pace with which aircraft appeared on the line in the mornings and the magical speed with which they disappeared into the hangars in the evenings!

Back to the subject of food, Roy describes the culinary delights for those on night flying duties. *"For a couple of evenings towards the end of each course, night flying was undertaken and the Airmen's Mess would deliver sandwiches in cardboard boxes to the HP crewrooms. Among the delicacies was a wonderful culinary delight called 'Prairie Chicken Sandwich', bread interlaced with synthetic cheese. At the end of the night flying session, which could be as late as 02:00 in the summer, it was off to the Mess for supper, a heaped plate of greasy chips, beans and rubberised eggs washed down with thick stewed tea. How did we manage to get to sleep after that!"*

Fortunately, accidents involving aircraft through negligence by airmen were rare, but a case that became the butt of jokes, could have had serious repercussions for the aircrew. It involved a radio mechanic who had been banned from working on aircraft on account of his absentmindedness. One lunch-time the VHF set in a Piston Provost went U/S and the NCO in charge at 1 HP called the Radio Bay to request a replacement set. As the mechanic in question was the only person in the bay at the time, he decided to carry a working set up to 2 Hangar and fit it himself. Having removed the duff set from its tray in the fuselage, fitted the new one and performed a ground test with the Control Tower, he signed the F700 and departed for his lunch. He had, however, forgotten to secure the wing nuts that locked the set in its mounting tray and it worked loose during a subsequent aerobatic sortie. On hearing a loud bang and feeling a thump behind him, the pilot returned to base under Mayday conditions, where the 30 lb metal box was found dangling on its cables through a hole it had punched through the fuselage side. A court martial sentenced the mechanic to a period at leisure in Her Majesty's Colchester Military Prison.

As the winter of 1960-61 progressed and several inches of ice-based snow lay over the airfield, impossible conditions for flying, 2 HP's groundcrew decided to build the biggest of snowmen out on the pan for all to see. Ray takes up the story,

> *"After an hour of hard toil the monster had grown so tall that we could not lift its head onto the shoulders, so the body was re-sculptured into a piece of 'modern' art. The light-hearted rivalry that existed between the*

(*above*) Having built a body so high it became impossible to lift the head on top of it, the 2 HP groundcrew, with SAC Dennis Horsfall prominent (*left*) on the shovel, resort to their more artistic talents. (*below*) 2 HP 'war council', Cpl 'Tom' Thomas and SAC Dennis Horsfall are prepared for the attack on 1 HP in 2 Hangar beyond. (*Ray Deacon*)

HPs was probably the reason for those from 1 HP pulverising our masterpiece while we were away at lunch. On our return we instinctively knew who was responsible for the destruction that had been wrought on our handiwork and attacked the 1 HP crewroom with a vengeance, a barrage of snowballs plastering the windows in seconds. Within minutes airmen from the other HPs had joined in what became a massive snowball fight that spread out on the airfield from 2 to 4 Hangars, much to the amusement of staff in the control tower. Words must have come down from on high as Chiefy Tucker told us he did not want to see a repeat performance.

On the following day, with frozen snow still covering the airfield, two Vampires were pushed outside the hangar and started up by a couple of instructors, the object of the exercise being to open up the Goblins to near full power and use them as simulated snow blowers. The loose snow blew away nicely but as the jets began to slide out of control on the compacted ice underneath, the groundcrew lined up along the wing leading edges and pushed against them as power came on to prevent them slipping forward. This did the trick and a few hours later much of the ice had been blasted away from the pan."

SAC Tony Algaze was a real character who hailed from Falmouth and on days when Rissy was clamped-in, he could talk continuously on any subject for hours in his strong, slightly stuttering Cornish accent. He would often burst into gobble-de-gook much to the delight of his captive audience who could hardly understand a word he was saying. As a variation to this, SAC Willy Guilmant came up with the idea of changing our names to read in reverse. *"We became so accustomed at calling each other Samoht, Wahsgab, Nocaed, etc., that Chiefy Tucker and the Officers had no idea what or who we were referring to. Visitors to the crewroom thought we were nuts"*, recalls Willy.

"The crewrooms were dingy and draughty and as the door on ours would not shut on its own, we attached a cord to the wall above it, routed it over the door and tied it to the duty roster board so that the weight of the heavy board would close the door. Every time the door opened the board went up and down which was fine until Chiefy came in to write on it just as someone opened the door to come in. He was not very pleased."

Trophy hunts!

"To brighten-up our crewroom", recalls Ray, *"the walls were adorned with beer mats and pinups and to improve the area outside, we collected 'trophies' on our evening trips to the local hotspots. A bus stop graced the corner of the hangar and a beautiful hanging basket hung above the doorway. This had been lifted from outside a pub called 'The Rampant Cat' which was located half way up Burford High Street. The pub is still there today but has a different name. After an evening's binge in the pub we carted it back to Tom Thomas's lovely old Austin Somerset but, as it was too large to fit inside with six inebriated airmen, we opened the boot lid, which was hinged at the bottom and perched it on top, crossing our fingers that it would still be there when we got back to camp. Tom kept a steady 35-40 mph pace all the way back through those narrow, winding lanes and try as he might to dislodge it, the basket was still there as we rode through the camp gates. Next item to arrive was a large folding ice cream sign, brought up on foot from a café in Bourton by two intrepid members of 2 HP and erected on the grass outside Chiefy's office. Both staff and students seemed to appreciate the unauthorised enhancements and would quietly smile as they walked past on their way to their aircraft, enquiring as to the flavours of our confectionery. Our new-found pleasure, however, was short-lived!"*

Ice cream sign – nothing to do with us, Corporal!

A few days later the ice cream sign was spotted by the Station's solitary RAF Policeman, Cpl Norman Ratcliffe, as he toured the camp on his bicycle. *"We had received a complaint from one of the café owners in Bourton that one of her signs had been stolen and the culprits had been identified as airmen from the camp. When I found it outside the 2 HP crew room I retrieved it with my Land Rover and took it back to the*

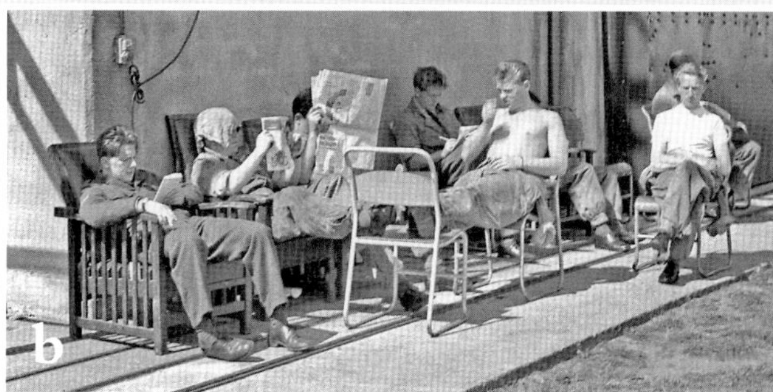

(a) Hunters from Kemble were regular visitors to 2 Sqn at Rissy. On this occasion, SAC Dave Lee leans out of the cockpit as a Summers twin, J/T Johnny Johnson and SAC 'Willy' Guilmant pose on the nose. (b) Break time! SAC Tony Algaze in white top, dozes beside SAC 'Jock' Dargue, as SAC John Hughes completes the crossword and SAC Bill Bailey hides under a makeshift 'hat'. (c) Up to their usual antics, Dickie Baston tops a pyramid supported by SACs John Hughes, Mick Blundell, 'Willy' Guilmant, AN Other, 'Jock' Dargue, J/T Johnny Johnson and SAC Dennis Horsfall. (d) Making life look grim while working on Jet Provost T.4, XP550, are SACs Dave Lee, in the cockpit, 'Taff' Langdon leaning on the fuselage and a colleague on the wing. (*below*) One way to clear compacted ice: light up a couple of Goblins and blast it away! Easier on the groundcrew despite their having to lean on the wings to prevent the aircraft sliding forwards. In this February 1961 view, the two Vampires being used are T.11s, XK627/VC-31 and XD376/VZ. (*all Ray Deacon*)

Guardroom where the duty officer told me to charge those responsible with theft. As soon as he left I contacted the Station Adjutant, Flt Lt Bunny Austin, and put it to him that it was unfair for airmen to be charged for bringing 'souvenirs' back from their nights out when the recent discovery of a number of tops from petrol pumps in the Officers' Mess was considered high spirits. I never heard anything more on the subject and, as I liked the sign so much, I set it up in the Guardroom."

When is a ban not a ban?

Roy Bagshaw remembers an episode involving SAC Les Carine, who had been posted to Rissy from overseas in the early sixties, when transportation was scarce and, like many other airmen on camp, he enjoyed a pint or four in the NAAFI.

> *"One drinking session took place on a Saturday afternoon and after several drinks to prepare his system for the evening session, it was off to the Airmen's Mess for an early tea. Little Rissington's mess had a reputation as one of the best in the RAF and it boasted a wonderful side table on which were laid a choice of salads. Having picked up a bowl of beetroot, Les stood at the end of an occupied dinner table and said, 'Right, who wants beetroot?' There was no response. So he then uttered the words, 'If I have beetroot you all have beetroot' and proceeded to empty the bowl's contents over the airmen.*
>
> *The following week Les was brought before his Flight Commander and asked to explain himself. 'Well sir' he began, 'It was like this. I was taking the beetroot to my colleagues and slipped on some chips that some fool had dropped on the floor. I lost control of the bowl and the beetroot went all over my colleagues'. Having not believed a word of Les's excuse, the officer turned to him and said, 'Carine, 5/- fine and banned from the NAAFI for two weeks'.*
>
> *About a week later, on a fine summer evening, as the Orderly Officer passed the NAAFI, who should he spot seated on the grass outside a window with a pint in his hand but Les. 'Carine, you are banned from the NAAFI, what are you doing here?' enquired the OO. 'Ah but I'm not in the NAAFI, Sir', replied Les. He was in fact obeying the banning*

order to the letter and receiving his cherished pints of beer from the airmen seated the other side of an open window. The OO turned and walked away and couldn't help smiling as he could obviously see the funny and ingenious ruse that all involved had devised to ensure Les did not go thirsty during his two-week ban."

Annual dance

The annual dance was held in a large upstairs function room attached to the NAAFI and attracted many young fillies brought in by bus from villages as far away as Broadway and Chipping Norton. These were invigorating occasions as they gave many airmen the chance to meet and sometimes marry local girls, not always to the liking of the

Favourite haunt for a night out was the Old New Inn in Bourton, where SAC Taff Evans (*second left*) is given a rousing demob party. Evident in this view are SACs Jock Dargue, Ginger Stevens and Sgt Pat Trumper. The painting depicting football in the river Windrush currently still adorns the wall of the lounge. (*Ray Deacon*)

local youth. Roy has every reason to remember his first encounter with a young lady at the dance:

"The band usually consisted of a pianist, drummer, bass and saxophonist, the latter occasionally being a vocalist. It was an occasion when most airmen attended dressed in a smart suit, tie and the traditional pocket-handkerchief. The dances were generally waltz, quickstep and the odd tango. During the interlude rock and roll records were played and it was great fun trying to spin your partner fast enough to lift the wide dresses and skirts they wore in those days.

On one occasion I spotted an elegantly dressed young lady and without hesitating I asked her, 'May I have the pleasure of the next dance' to which she agreed. We danced together for most of the evening and I jealously guarded her from other admiring airmen. After the dance we exchanged names and Hilary and I arranged to meet the next day on the village green in Bourton. At the designated time I arrived with no sign of Hilary. After hanging around for an hour, I picked up courage to knock on her front door and was greeted by her mother who quickly said 'When you know my daughter like I do you will understand that breaking dates is not unusual'. Not to be outdone I waited for her only to find out later she had been to a motor car hill climbing event at Prestcott with another airman. However, my perseverance was eventually rewarded and we were married in September 1961. In 1978 we finally came back to Bourton to live and have remained there to this day. Along the way we have been blessed with two children who in turn have returned the blessing with five grandchildren. Hilary and I are forever grateful for those far off days and the wonderful life we have enjoyed thanks to dear old Rissy. I often go past the old camp on my way to play golf and the wonderful memories of Rissy's days as an RAF base come flooding back."

Apart from stealing their young ladies, people in the local communities were very friendly and always made you feel welcome. Despite the daily aircraft noise and the pranks we pulled on them in the evenings, they generally enjoyed our company and could not resist the challenge of a game of darts or skittles with the military.

After hours

After an evening's drinking in the NAAFI the night was still young and a trip to the Windrush Transport café six miles away on the A40, was a popular destination for a fry-up. One night after a heavy session in the bar, Mickie Blundell and Willy Guilmant departed for the café on their Lambrettas with Dickie Baston and Ray Deacon on the rear seats. The lane from camp to the Barringtons was fairly straight but the final mile was narrow and twisty. Willy takes up the story: *"Getting there was no problem and we enjoyed a grease-laden meal before heading back. I was a bit slow starting my machine and as Mickie and Dickie shot off out of sight I tried to catch them up. The lane leading away from the A40 was narrow and steep with a sharp bend at the bottom and we approached it far too fast. Instinctively I lent the bike over but we slid sideways until the wheels hit the kerbing. The bike stopped dead and the force of the impact catapulted us over a low Cotswold stone wall into someone's front garden cabbage patch. On realising neither of us was hurt, we burst out laughing but when a light went on in the house, we quickly staggered back to the bike to assess the damage. The fairings were a little bent but it started OK so we departed the scene before anyone could identify us."*

On another night when the camp was shrouded in thick fog, SAC Dave Lee invited Mickie Blundell and Ray Deacon for a run to the A40 transport café in his brand new Ford Anglia; a present from his aunt, he said! Mickie takes up the story;

Every summer it was customary to hold a football match in the River Windrush in Bourton-on-the-Water. Among several CFS personnel to participate in this fun event was SAC Roy Bagshaw, seen standing third from right in this view of the victorious 1961 Bourton team. (*Roy Bagshaw*)

"We were well oiled after an evening in the NAAFI and although Dave managed to keep the verges on either side at a safe distance, he accelerated down the long straight towards Great Rissington, boasting how fast he could drive in dense fog. His tune quickly changed as we reached the junction for Great Rissington. Here the road to the Barringtons, the direction we should have taken, forked slightly to the left but Dave could not see a thing through the murk and his alcoholic haze, and we smashed into the bank and metal railings at the junction. With no seat belts in the car, we were tossed about and apart from a few dents and bruises, we escaped injury. With spirits dampened, we clambered out to find the front wheels pointing in opposite directions, leaving us no choice but to trudge back to camp leaving the vehicle protruding across the road in the hope that no one would run into it. The following morning, in front of his sniggering mates, a red-faced Dave had to explain to Chiefy why he needed a couple of hours off to retrieve his car."

Evenin' All!

An evening's entertainment in Bourton would often end with some prank or other and confrontation with the village bobby, a Sergeant Watts from bonnie Scotland. One evening, while walking back to catch the bus, Roy Bagshaw decided he would like to test his strength.

"On my way back from 'The Mousetrap' I walked past a pair of gateposts with concrete balls mounted on them. I managed to roll one of them off, lower it to the ground and proceed to roll it down the High Street when who should come along but Jock Watts. 'And what do we think we're doing with that, laddie? Take it back from where you found it'. So he made me roll it back to the gate and put it back on the post. Needless to say, I missed the bus and as I would have to walk back to camp, he let me off with a warning. The next time I went past the gateway I could not see how on earth I got the ball off let alone put it back.

A couple of weeks later, after an evening in 'The Old New Inn', and while waiting to catch the bus back, we lifted the big metal sign from outside the Witchcraft Centre carried it over to the river, climbed aboard and began paddling towards Birdland. As we approached one of the bridges who should be standing on it with his arms folded, but none other than Jock Watts. 'And wherrr do we think we'rrre goin with that, lads?' 'Back to camp, constable' came the resolute reply. 'Oh no yerr not, son, let's be having yerr'. And so once again we were forced to return our trophy from whence it came and trudge back up the hill."

The wonderful Tannoy system

Like most RAF stations, Little Rissington had a Tannoy system for broadcasting important information. More often than not, those at Rissy were read out by one of the elderly civilian policemen from the Main Guardroom. SAC Mick Bennett was an Instrument Mechanic assigned to the Instrument Bay. *"I always remember the announcements being made in a deep Gloucester accent. My favourite was when they announced a fire, it was always spoken very, very slowly and went something like; 'Foi – yer .....foi – yer .....foi – yer'; followed by an extra long pause, 'there is a foi - yer in the Airmen's Mess canteen' followed by another long pause, 'will all personnel manning foi - yer appliances and boooosster pomps please take up their positions immediately'. The delivery of this message took about two minutes by which time the place could have burned down."*

Five tours at Rissy!

The record for the highest number of tours undertaken by anyone at Little Rissington must surely belong to Flt Sgt 'Jock' Hutson, who was posted to the station no less than five times.

"In about September 1946, I was posted to Rissy for the first time but we lived in Married Quarters at South Cerney (which in those days was part of the Rissy set up). Travel from Cerney to Rissy was accomplished on occasions by borrowing a friend's motor cycle but with the chronic shortage of fuel, I mostly rode my pushbike which took me two hours each way. Boy was I fit!

A year later I was sent to RAF Locking for my Fitters I course, which covered all trades including Workshops and MT, but this had to be suspended after seven months to have an operation on my knees which had been postponed during the war. Following a full recovery I was posted back to Rissy and South Cerney. My first task was to replace a flap jack on a Lancaster but as there were none on camp, I had to scour round local airfields to try to find one. Fortunately brand new Lancasters were being cut up at RAF Aston Down so I went over and retrieved some jacks, fitted one to our Lanc and placed the rest in store.

During the summer of 1947 the CFS formed a five-ship Tiger Moth aerobatic team and being an NCO Airframe Fitter I was put in charge of the Airframe ground crew. During a practice session, one of the aircraft entered a spin from the top of a loop and crashed onto the airfield, killing the pilot.

In March 1948 I was posted to Khartoum for a two-year tour, at the conclusion of which I was posted back to Rissy, but had hardly unpacked my belongings when I was off to St Athan to complete my unfinished Fitters course. Then back to Rissy in 1951, this time to work on Harvards and Prentices at South Cerney. Soon my bags were being packed again this time for an Instructors Course followed by the A.I.D. Course. Flexibility was the name of the game, and shortly after my return I was put in charge of the MT section at Cerney despite my complaints. 'You are trained as a Fitter I and this includes MT' I was curtly informed. While I was there, the WO and a Flight Sergeant were caught running a fiddle and Court Martialled. After this I moved to the Workshops in charge of the Hydraulic, Pneumatic and Tyre bays. Bless my Fitter I Course!

In March 1953 I was posted out again, this time as NCO in charge of a jungle airstrip in Malaya during the Communist Terrorist war. November 1956 and, you've guessed it, I was posted back to Rissy, this time to work on the Vampire and Meteor Handling Parties and another set up for the first Jet Provosts when they arrived on the Station. I remember while doing an Independent Control Check on a Vampire I fell head first down the pit underneath the aircraft. It must have been a relief to those who came to help me that they couldn't understand a word I blasted forth, I created merry hell! In addition to my technical skills, the powers that be found out that in 1937 I had been trained in special

Command Drill for the RAF Guard of Honour and had participated in the Coronation Day parade, and completed a PT Drill Instructors Course in 1941. So, much against my will, they decided to place me in charge of the Guard of Honour, but that lasted for about four weeks only as the OC Engineering Wing got the Station RAF Regiment Sgt to replace me. What a carry on!

In 1959 I was selected to fly on a Military Mission to Spain and Portugal, all VIP stuff. We flew down in the Engineering Wing's Valetta and during the flight my task(s) were explained in more detail; Flight Engineer, Ground Engineer and Head VIP Escort. Kitted out in brand new overseas kit the trip lasted for two weeks and the 'Pig' did us proud. It wasn't all grind of course,

It was during this period that I began to enjoy playing sports and am proud to have played for the Station at Hockey, Tennis and Badminton and was a Station member of the Burford Golf Club. How on earth did I fit it all in I ask myself!

The University Air Squadron based at RAF Newton had been having serious technical problems for some time, so in October 1959, Air Cdre Whitworth called for me and told me I was being posted to Newton to sort the unit out. When I got there, the place was a shambles; no STIs, SIs or mods had been done on the Chipmunks for years. After what seemed an eternity at Newton ... yep ... back to Little Rissington this time as NCO i/c No. 3 HP. Three Meteor T.7s, three Canberra T.4s and a great bunch of lads, what else could one ask for.

Towards the end of 1961 I was sent over to RAF Gaydon to learn all about 'Drag-Off' equipment, a monstrous piece of iron and netting designed for the quick removal of an incapacitated aircraft from a runway. On completion of the course, we stripped it down and prepared it for shipping out to RAF Gan in the Maldive Islands. Back to Rissy, but for ten days only this time for I was posted to Gan as NCO in charge of the staging post. The 'Drag-Off' monster arrived soon afterwards and having assembled the beast, I instructed two teams how to use it. We got it down to such a fine art that had any aircraft pranged on our runway it would have been cleared in less than fifteen minutes. It had to, Gan was in the middle of the Indian Ocean and there were no diversion airfields.

November 1962 and as tour-ex approached I received my next posting. I suppose I half expected it, 'you're going to RAF Little Rissington' my CO kindly informed me. Just like coming home I thought. I arrived back just in time to take over the Gnat Project Team and a year later we formed the first Gnat Line Squadron operating from the new Visitors pan out on the airfield.

The mixed and crowded circuit at Rissy was, however, causing serious concerns about safety and the decision was taken to move the Gnat Squadron on permanent detachment to RAF Fairford, a former USAF base some twenty miles to the south. The transfer took place in October 1964 and a month later we were joined at Fairford by the pilots who were to form the first 'Red Arrows' aerobatic team. When our hangar was nominated as home for the Concorde, the Gnat detachment moved ten miles further west to the home of 5 MU at RAF Kemble.

Just over a year later, in November 1967, I departed Rissy for the last time on my way to RAF Laarbruch in Germany. During my various postings to Rissy we occupied two MQs at Cerney, three at Rissy, and lived in houses in Cheltenham, Whelford (Fairford) and Fosse Cross, and was awarded three commendations and a BEM. Looking back now I don't think I would have found the time to fit it all in had not been for the support of my wife and my most abiding memory is of all the friends we made, too numerous to mention."

The ground crews on 2 and 3 HPs got on well together and would help each other out when the need arose, in the hangar or at the bar. But this did not stop them playing practical jokes, such as the occasion when Bob Dargue hid Chiefy 'Jock' Hutson's bike by tying a rope to it and hauling it up a tree outside his office.

"Jock didn't spot it hanging there and I retrieved it a little while later while he was in the hangar looking for it. We didn't see his face but we heard the Gaelic verbals from our end of the hangar."

Memoirs of an 'Erk' at CFS

SAC Peter Marshall arrived at Little Rissington in January 1964 following a two year tour on Hunters with No. 8 Squadron at RAF Khormaksar.

"Coming from Aden, the five feet of snow and zero temperatures were a shock. I eventually regained some body heat by about June, by which time 'they' had moved me from Rectification Flight to 1 HP and the Jet Provosts of 1 Squadron. We would B/F (Before Flight) and tow out sometimes sixteen or so Jet Provosts and then wait for the first off. It was the custom, at this time, for the first aircraft airborne to beat up the line, and some of these 'wires', as they were known, were very low and fast for a JP. One naval instructor decided to do his beat up the other way round, very low and very slow. With full flap, he passed between the tower and a small brick store at about a knot and a half above the stall. I thought he was taxiing back in but then realised the undercarriage was up. Entertaining but I believe he was told 'don't do it again'.

In the Sixties and the Seventies there were two things an airman was keen to hear. 'Night flying for tonight is cancelled' and 'No, I am not pregnant'. I now refer to the former in that after night flying and the A/Fs (After Flights) were completed, it would be about four in the morning. The day crew would be depleted so, in order to speed up preparations for the following morning's flying, someone clever said 'Combine the A/Fs after night flying with the B/Fs, so all the day crew have to do is tow the aircraft out'. The night flying lot would turn up at four in the afternoon, and off we'd go again!

I strolled in one afternoon to be told one was in the 'poo', because an Instructor doing his walk round had found the engine panels on his aircraft were undone. I was charged with failing to ensure said panels were secure, etc., etc. These access panels were opened up to check hydraulics and engine oil. Ten minutes before my trial was due to start, the Flt Sgt running the line buttonholed me and said he could find no reference in the Servicing Schedule to closing these panels. I thought I hope he's right as shooting or 'jail' would seriously interfere with my nights in the Old New Inn in Bourton. We all stamped into the Engineering Officer's office and I trotted out my defence. Ten minutes

silence while his technicianship read the aforementioned servicing notes. Then – 'You are right' said he, and read them again. He was as astonished as I was. Case dismissed and the schedule amended. Flt Sgt Coxon – Thank you!

We were able to fly quite often and I spent many happy hours in one of the 'Red Pelicans'. This was after the 'Arrows' had taken over as the 'hot lot' in, I think, 1965. Reduced to four Jet Provosts and none of the smelly smoke, we (four ground crew) would don our red bone domes and step out to be flown around the UK with a free air show thrown in. Superb!

This went on for a while, until at Bembridge, Isle of Wight, the number four was seen to be trailing white vapour. On inspection after landing, there was much muttering and hopeful tapping of something clamped to the underside of the little Viper. As we had no engine man with us, I think the aircraft was left at Bembridge until an engine chappie was flown down to sort out the problem. This did not go down too well at Ris and the powers that were decreed that Pelican support be organised on something approaching a professional basis, with NCOs from each of the main trades, someone in the Office at weekends, etc.

Then 'they' said 'Go to Fairford!' Now the Gnat was something else. While the Jet Provost converted Avtur into noise, the Gnat got a move on and, with some of the early morning beat ups, it was a job to hear one approaching. The subsequent fright plus the Friday morning hangover – pay day being on a Thursday (brown envelopes) – led to vast quantities of black coffee and something that came in a miniature bottle sold by the pub which had inflicted the damage in the first place.

'They' moved the Gnats to Fairford because, I believe, the runway at Ris was a mite on the short side. I must point out that, when I talk about our Gnats, I mean 4 Squadron, CFS, not the Arrows. 4 Squadron ran the Course line with silver and dayglo Gnats.

One was able to travel to Fairford by standard NATO Bedford coach, driven by a doughty chap called Ted. On a good day he could get the thing wound up to about seventy and neatly cuff the odd pheasant which happened to be in the road. He did this one day and we grabbed the bird and hung it in a locker near the crew room, the idea being to cajole the cook into cooking it. He said pluck and gut first, then he would cook. After a few weeks, no joy, and with the locker jumping about the crew room, we threw the whole lot away.

And there was flying in the Gnats. There tended to be a gap in the courses and then we would fill our boots and take up the offers. I well remember a four ship trip where I was with the No. 4. We trotted into the briefing (professional stuff) and I think it was a formation practice around any airfield which would have us, plus a tail chase at the end. We flew a tour around central England and, as we approached each airfield, our leader requested a fly by, 4 Gnat formation. Some said 'yes'; others said 'push off!' – and the tail chase at the end tested my colon. A friend would tighten his face mask to an excruciating degree and this, coupled with the 'g' left deep crease marks on his cheeks. He thought they made him look rugged and might be handy as a weapon of seduction. We just ignored him – and I think the WRAFs did too!

Then 'they' said 'Go to Kemble; Concorde cometh!' I liked Kemble; away from the powers that were and a pub where we could hide the Bedford when the weather clamped. Poor old Ted; he had to make do with something fizzy while we threw it down us with gusto. We would arrive back at Ris in time for tea, stoned!

We had our own aerobatic 'ace' and, two or three times a week, he would nip off for a quick practice over the airfield. He was doing this one day and was pulling up for a loop. Halfway up he entered some cloud. The aircraft popped out of the cloud going one way and our man and his seat popped out going in the opposite direction. This was novel. Our man was alright and we learned later that the stick had 'gone all floppy' during the climb. A couple of months later he took another aircraft down to a big show at RAF Chivenor, but I think our little Gnat was rather lost among the afterburning Lightnings, F100s and French Navy Crusaders. We travelled by Varsity. I wonder if the Tucano chappies have as much fun."

A winter diversion

During the bad winter of 1962-63, when all aircraft at Rissy were grounded because of foul weather, seven groundcrew were crammed into a J2, each with sufficient overnight kit for two or three days, for a hazardous ride to Dunsfold. Cpl Tom Thomas was one of those lucky seven.

"Once there we were told our task was to load two production Gnats onto Queen Marys for transfer by road to Valley. The aircraft should have been flown to 4 FTS where they were desperately needed for the

No, not a Folland test flight, but the most convenient method of raising Gnat T.1, XP509, high enough for a Queen Mary transporter to slip underneath. A snowy Dunsfold on 7 February, 1963. (*Malcolm Thomas*)

Intensive Flying Trials, but it was impossible to clear the deep snow and as the forecast showed little sign of abating, the decision was taken to move them by road.

The J2 was driven by a young MT driver and we set off on extremely slippery roads. Not long after turning onto the Burford road, somewhere close to the Rissington runway approach lights, the driver cautiously braked as a convoy of HGVs approached from the opposite direction. Unfortunately due to the icy surface and inclined road, we slowly slid to a halt just short of the leading truck. Its driver was not very impressed and wound down his window to enquire 'why the bloody hell did you brake?' Further embarrassment ensued as the J2 refused to budge, so we all got out and eventually pushed the J2 onto the correct side of the road. No harm done except to the driver's pride. The journey continued in a deathly hush until we had regained confidence in our young chauffeur's driving ability.

After what seemed an eternity we arrived at Dunsfold and were greeted by W O Barber, who once worked as Engineering Coordinator at Little Rissington. He escorted us to a very nice canteen where we were served a first class meal by three very friendly young ladies, the elder one of the trio, who I assumed was the boss, was an Irish lass, but that is another story. Our accommodation for the next few nights was a nearby public house, not very smart but the ale was good and the landlord friendly. What more could a man ask for!

The next day after a hearty cooked breakfast, we returned to the airfield where two MT drivers and their co-drivers from No. 71 MU were waiting for us by two 60 ft long Queen Mary lorries. Before they could be loaded the aircraft had to be drained of fuel, the ejection seats disarmed and both wing tips removed to ensure these tiny aircraft were as safe, light and small as possible. As the draining and loading was completed on the first day, we thought we could hi-tail it for home, but no such luck. We had to hang around for the next four or five days as the roads were still too bad to attempt a drive through Welsh mountains. While awaiting further orders we occupied our time playing cards, investigating the hangars, looking round the Gnat, Hunter and Harrier production lines, chatting to employees and the canteen girls of course.

Day six dawned and we struggled down to the airfield, still cold and by now wet as the thaw gathered momentum. Mr Barber met us, 'good news', he said, 'you will love this – unload the Queen Marys, re-build the aircraft and fill them with fuel as the pilots are coming down to do the ground runs and fuel transfer checks. They will then wait for the weather to improve before flying them out. Valley is already open!'

Another couple of days passed and with no sign of the pilots we got into a routine of reading, sleeping and waiting. On about day nine we carried out the pre-flight checks and towed the aircraft out to the flight line – something we'd become very efficient at. As we scrambled back into the J2 to head for the canteen the aircrew turned up. 'We're off lads at long last!' Both aircraft were started up but XP507 experienced radio problems which required assistance from the production staff, and XP509 developed an oil leak in the brake system which was resolved by fitting a new brake unit. On the third start the pilot of XP509 reported hydraulic cycling was far too rapid. I checked the flexible hoses to the hydraulic gauges for leaks, a known defect on the early Gnats, and found one leaking. A new hose from the production line solved that and they were ready to go once more. I cannot recall the pilots' names but they thanked us for the hard work and complimented us on our quick diagnosis and sorting of the defects. 'Right' one said 'get the Palouste starters going while I sneak up from behind the bloody aeroplane, jump in and surprise it – this time we are going'. And they did. They were back at Valley before we had lunched and loaded our J2.

W O Barber invited me to ride back to Rissy in his car an offer I gladly accepted thinking how much warmer it would be! The journey back was much smoother and quicker. As we followed a market lorry across a roundabout, a sack of potatoes fell from the back. Without a word, Mr Barber stopped the car on the roundabout, opened the boot and we picked up the spuds, dumped them in the back and drove back to Rissy where the spoils were shared."

Scheduled Servicing Flight

Number 1 Hangar was divided up into bays each one responsible for carrying out 2nd line servicing of all the aircraft types operating from the base. To each bay was assigned a team of airmen made up of, two airframe and engine fitters known as Man 'A' and Man 'B', and an electrical, instrument, radio, radar and armament fitter. The teams worked to a schedule that contained the servicing plan for the particular type of aircraft being worked on and was calculated to entitle each tradesman access to certain areas of the aircraft to perform specific tasks over a specific time. Tasks that could not be completed within the allotted time were re-allocated to one of the spare slots in the schedule. The schedules were kept in small portakabins, one of which was assigned to each team and was used as an office by the Chief Technician in charge.

Each team had their own mobile general tool cabinet which could be secured from theft and were known as 'Shadow boards'. As a tool was removed a painted shadow of that tool on the board enabled any that went missing to be easily identified. Each set of tools was colour-coded to link them to a specific team and teams were not allowed to borrow tools from another team. To reduce the risk of losing tools, each one was signed out by the tradesman removing it and signed in at the completion of his task. At the end of each working period and before an aircraft was returned to the line, the tool cabinets were checked for a full complement and if any one tool was missing, everyone in the team remained until that item was found and the culprit was not a very popular person.

Fire drills were carried out regularly and when the alarm went everyone reported to an assembly point which was equipped with buckets of sand and water. A roll was called to account for everyone while they waited for the all-clear. On one particular day Roy recalls;

"A Piston Provost was in the corner of the hangar undergoing Primary Star servicing. The electrician who had been working on it had disconnected some wiring in order to inspect it and, as he did not have the required instruments with him, left the aircraft to get them. During his absence another airman plugged a trolley-acc into the Provost to carry some of checks of his own, when suddenly, a huge shower of sparks and

smoke appeared from the cockpit area. The Chiefy-in-charge, who happened to be in the cockpit, shouted 'Fire' and instead of rushing to his aid, the whole hangar emptied in seconds leaving him to his fate. Fortunately he was able to disconnect the trolley-acc and extinguished the fire. Needless to say, a succession of fire drills were carried out over the following weeks until they were coming out of our ears.

Playing cards during the lunch break was a great favourite with many of us, but one carefully selected one's partner. I used to partner an airframe fitter called Bill at Partner Whist and we developed a signalling system that worked as follows; hand on our forehead 'Hearts', on the chin 'spades', right ear 'Clubs' and left ear 'Diamonds'. More often than not we took the kitty which usually amounted to 2/6d, rich pickings in those days."

That feminine touch

In the early spring of 1964, SACW Cecilia Collier finished her trade training at Cosford and was given joining instructions for RAF Little Rissington.

"I had no idea where I had been posted," she says, *"and with only an hour to catch the train I had no time to find out. However, it was so exciting being on my way to my first real posting.*

So it was then, that I arrived at a dark railway station – to this day I don't know where it was! I found an airman with a clipboard and assumed I should go with him. As we meandered through country roads the headlights of the minibus picked out a sign to Stow-on-the-Wold.

'Ah the Wolds' I thought (none the wiser) 'Is that the Cotswolds?' I asked the driver. He grunted and muttered 'We're going to Little Rissington.'

Although very few airwomen were assigned to the squadron lines, they would turn up on rare weekend working at Ris, such as Battle of Britain days. Here, SACWs Eileen Scott, (*left*) and Carol have perched themselves on the wing of the 'spare' Vampire T.11 as the lads await the return of the display aircraft, September 1960. (*Ray Deacon*)

The WRAF block overlooked the parade ground – which had been turned into a car park for most of the time. The long barrack room had been divided into an office for the WRAF admin sergeant and two four-bedded rooms. It was at the time when some office workers in the City had come up with the idea of 'We're backing Britain' and stickers had appeared on the windows. I don't think anyone quite knew what to do about them – it was obviously not right to have stickers – but then, one couldn't NOT be patriotic – they eventually disappeared just before a pre-AOC's inspection!

As the first WRAF in Air Radar since the war, no-one quite knew what to do with me! I was placed on second line testing which was fine. There was another WRAF in the next hangar – her trade was Air Electronics and she was having the same problem. I longed to work on real aeroplanes, not just bits of them, after all, wasn't that why I had joined the RAF – Biggles was never stuck on second line servicing!

One day, just as the weather was turning cold, the station had a visit from the Queen Bee – the WRAF Big White Chief! Of course, as a girl working in the technical trades, I was called for an interview with her. I mentioned how I would love to work on first line. I thought nothing more about her visit until one day – winter was really biting with a vengeance by then – I was called into the section commander's office and he informed me that he had been told to put the two WRAFs on first line servicing – he was obviously not happy, I think it was more his sense of chivalry, I don't think he thought it a suitable place for two young women. He asked me how I felt about that; with hindsight, I believe that he wanted me to ask not to be put on first line – of course he didn't know my passion for aircraft and I jumped at the chance to be part of the real air force.

I admit it was very hard, manual work. It was exhausting having to lug the refuelling hose onto the wings of the Jet Provosts. Nevertheless, I loved it – this was what working in the air force was all about.

It was a particularly bad winter and we were buried in deep snow for days and days. As the spring came, so came the bright weather. The CFS courses changed and the instructors still had to keep flying. Often there was a spare seat and the Flight Sergeant was asked if they could take 'one of the birds up'. Of course, this 'bird' loved it!

Apart from flying in the JPs, there were Chipmunks and Varsities. All of which I made it a point to fly in. I went gliding at the gliding club and horse riding at the riding club. Football in the river at Bourton-on-the-Water – some sort of tradition according to a painting in the local pub. A great summer!

Night flying was always fun, especially on summer nights when it wasn't too cold. Everything then was a new adventure.

This was all long ago, the mid-sixties when mini-skirts were making a debut, the Beetles were singing about a Hard Day's Night and computers were the size of a large room.

Recently I was driving through the Cotswolds and I came across a sign for The Rissingtons. Of course I had to find Rissy. I walked past the hangars and saw huge trees where once had been bushes. I saw the remnants of roses that had once grown with pride outside the servicing bays. Rissy was empty and deserted. It was like walking on a film set – I almost expected to hear the aircraft and laughter. I remember Geordie (aren't the wags always called Geordie) humming 'Those Magnificent Men in their Flying Machines' as a new class walked out to the JPs. And the CO putting him i/c dead heading of roses for his cheek! I half expected to see tumbleweed rolling through the empty roads.

I did not spend long at Rissy – but they were good years – I grew up there."

Gnats detach to Fairford

As the number of Gnats using the busy Rissy circuit increased it soon became apparent that these fast jets were not compatible with the likes of Chipmunks and Provosts and that sooner or later an accident was bound to occur. The solution arrived at was the same as that taken for the Hunter Flight in the mid-fifties; the Gnats would have to be moved to another airfield on a permanent detachment basis. As the Americans had vacated the nearby base at RAF Fairford, the opportunity was taken to relocate C Flight to the former USAF airfield and the transfer took place in November 1964.

At Fairford, the Flight took up residence in a large modern hangar that had a domed roof and was almost hidden out of sight behind two 'tin' hangars. It was equipped with spacious office and groundcrew accommodation, superb servicing bays and a long gallery linking the first floor offices ran the length of one of the walls, giving a panoramic view of activities on the hangar floor. An extensive concrete apron between the CFS hangar and the tin hangars provided ample space from which to operate the Gnats. For the reason outlined above and with the additional requirement to be able to practise over the airfield up to four-times a day, "The Red Arrows" moved to Fairford soon after they were formed early in 1965, making use of the same hangar and operating facilities as C Flight.

From FEAF to Fairford

On completion of Cpl Peter Chadburn's tour with No. 20 Squadron in Singapore he departed the FEAF on 26 November 1964 and headed for RAF Syerston, near his home city of Nottingham. He had been there barely two months when a request for volunteers to join the RAF Aerobatic Team appeared in Engineering Wing orders.

"I didn't volunteer as having just returned to the UK from a 2½ year overseas tour I assumed I would be the last in a long queue. A few weeks later I was called into the Senior EO's office and 'invited' to apply for a position on the RAF Aero Team. Single-engine corporals, I learned later, were few and far between.

I arrived at Little Rissington on 1 March 1965. The message on the grapevine was that if the General Office didn't tell you to catch the 07:30 bus to Fairford then you had been misled – I did catch the bus to Fairford and found myself assigned to the Rectification Team looking after both the Aero Team Gnats and the silver and dayglo Gnats flown by the Course Line.

Any problems with the Bristol Siddeley Orpheus, like most jet engines, were solved by changing the engine. My first real encounter came at the end of June 1965 when a line Gnat had been snagged with a 'noisy' running engine. I did a ground test and checked that the prescribed run down time was within limits, and finding nothing wrong I cleared the F700. Later, that afternoon I was approached by a determined looking Flt Lt Alex Wickham who said "Come with me Corporal", and within the hour we were airborne over Fairford. 'Ready?', enquired the Flight Commander 'Yes' I replied. The nose dipped and I heard this horrible growl from the engine. 'OK, OK, OK', I said expecting that the more OKs I said the quicker we would level out. 'Again!' came the warning over the intercom and before I could utter the first of a long series of high pitched 'I've heard it, I've heard it', the nose dipped again. The second growl sounded more sickening than the first. To my relief, we landed twenty minutes later. Subsequent

Contemplation and relaxation at Fairford, 1965. (*Top*) Fg Off Bill Green, second left, in conversation with Ch Techs Jackson, 'Willie' Watson and SAC Tony Gannon, and (*right*), Sgt Pete Scott, left, enjoys a joke with three airmen. (*Alex Wickham*)

investigations revealed that the rear bearing had failed and the growl was caused by the turbine blades scraping the shroud. My only defence was that we can't simulate g-forces during engine ground runs."

Return to Ris

Following six months at Valley and another year on a Fitters Course at Cosford, Ray Deacon could not believe his luck – a posting back to Little Rissington.

"My second tour at Ris began in October 1965 with a stint on the 2 Squadron Varsities, but as I wanted to return to working on fast jets, my application to transfer to C Flight was granted in the spring of 1966. The move occurred directly on my return from honeymoon in May, my wife Rose and I having moved into a hiring near Northleach. My problem of getting the ten miles to Fairford was resolved when my friend Sgt Tom Thomas sold me his knackered old Lambretta scooter for £10. Within a week the exhaust fell off and as it didn't have enough power, Rose would have to get off every time we went up hill, but it didn't let me down – for a while anyway. As it had no value and as I was sure I wasn't going to run into anyone, I never did insure it!

I was assigned to the Rectification Team, working alongside Sgt Chris Armes and Cpl Ron Turrell. In addition to maintaining the Course Gnats we were responsible for rectifying defects on 'The Red Arrows' aircraft on their return from weekends away. Mondays were often hectic as the aircraft had to be available for practice flying on Tuesdays."

As the summer of 1966 progressed, and the refurbishment of RAF Brize Norton for Transport Command was ongoing, the decision was taken to temporarily house the new VC10 and Belfast fleets at Fairford. Consequently, No. 10 Squadron was assigned one of the tin hangars and 53 Squadron's Belfasts the other and with two new aircraft types on board, both squadrons began a period of training. As their numbers increased the circuit became more active and following the announcement that the Concorde Trials Unit would move to the 'Gnat' hangar, the CFS detachment prepared for another move – down the road to RAF Kemble.

No. 1 Handling Party

Shortly before leaving RAF St Athan as a newly qualified Airframe Mechanic in May 1966, SAC Dave Watkins was asked to short-list three postings of his preference.

"Spoilt for choice, I put down Singapore, Cyprus and Hong Kong, only to be informed that I was to be posted to RAF Little Rissington – a short distance from the small Gloucestershire mining town where I had been born and brought up!

Five of us arrived at Rissy from St Athan and, after a brief induction chat, one guy was told that he was being detached to RAF Fairford to work on the Folland Gnat, while the rest of us were sent to No. 1 Handling Party, which operated the Jet Provost T.3 and T.4. No. 1 HP's Line Chief was Flt Sgt Coxon, but he left after a short while and was replaced by Ch Tech Elmer George; I liked 'Chiefy' George because he would let me finish early on a Friday afternoon and go home for the weekend

We had about forty Jet Provosts on the line and the work was quite hard at times – especially in the winter. It was also extremely boring and gave us no chance to use our initiative or newly acquired skills. Despite being trained as an airframe mechanic, the CFS operated a 'composite trained' system on the JP line, which meant we had to carry out basic first-line servicing as airframe, engine, electrical and instrument tradesmen.

The Jet Provost was a basic aircraft and was easy to work on, having plenty of access panels; the engine had two large hinged panels on top of the fuselage, while the nose cone was also hinged to facilitate access to the radio equipment and to replenish the oxygen system. The engine would occasionally suffer a 'wet start', and this was remedied by lying on our backs and removing the two drain plugs on the underside of the fuselage to release the excess fuel – usually down our arms!

We came in early each morning and carried out two or three pre-flight inspections each to get the aircraft on the flight line before the first of the instructors and students came to collect them. After seeing the first wave off, we could relax for a while before they all came back and the aircraft had be 'turned-around', i.e., a quick inspection, refuelled, and the oxygen replenished, before the process would start all over again and continued until about 17:00 hours, when they were put away in the hangars. Towards the end of each course there was also a short period of night flying, usually two or three nights if the weather permitted. I quite liked night flying as the duty suppers showed a marked improvement over the normal quality of mess food – and the fact that we were stood down after the last night until the following Monday morning!

We also boasted our own Jet Provost aerobatic team – "The Red Pelicans". The team did not acquire the status of the "The Red Arrows", but it was very professional and comprised four aircraft, led by Sqn Ldr P.J. 'Curly' Hirst. The 'Pelicans' usually laid on about twenty displays throughout the year, and would occasionally venture as far a field as Istres in France and Koksijde in Belgium. The groundcrews were all volunteers, who were usually prepared to give up their weekends.

Situated on what must be the highest spot in the Cotswolds, the flying was subject to more than its fair share of 'Black Flag' days in the winter; fog, snow, and rain meant that the aircraft were grounded, and to enable the courses to catch up we were occasionally detached to such places as Pershore, near Malvern. In August 1966, the JPs were flown up to RAF Leuchars to provide a formation fly past when HM The Queen Mother officially opened a new bridge. I flew up to Leuchars in a Varsity with the guys' kit bags but was able to fly back in one of the Jet Provosts.

Rissy itself was quite a pleasant camp and, despite the weekly 'domestic evenings', the frequent, week-long fire picquet and occasional parades for visiting dignitaries, I made the most of being situated in what I considered to be the most beautiful part of the Cotswolds. I bought a car soon after arriving and, at every possible opportunity, would drive off with a new found friend or latest girlfriend to explore Oxford, Stratford-upon-Avon, Cirencester, etc. Occasionally, if my car was off the road for some reason, I would get a lift home on a Friday and catch the Pulhams coach back from Cheltenham on a Sunday night. It would leave the bus station at 21:00 hours and arrive at Bourton at 21:45 hrs, just in time to have a quick drink, before eventually dropping us off by the guardroom. The coach was always full and there was usually someone to chat to about the weekend.

Apart from the occasional end-of-course social evening in a local pub, we had very little to do with the instructors and students. In fact, some could be very disdainful towards us and it was quite unlike the attitude I was later to encounter once I was posted to an operational squadron.

My time at Little Rissington was one of mixed emotions, and eventually I managed to obtain an exchange posting because I was beginning to become concerned that my entire Service career was going to be spent on one camp. Looking back I suppose that I enjoyed my time at Rissy, and whenever I now have the opportunity to return and look over the small Cotswold stone wall that borders the western end of the airfield, I will admit to a tinge of sadness at what remains of the station since the RAF left in 1976."

The move to Kemble

For anyone with an interest in aircraft, Kemble was a fascinating airfield. Home to No. 5 MU since 1938, it was one of two Hunter maintenance and storage units (19 MU at St Athan being the other), and had facilities for the servicing, repainting and storage of all types of aircraft for the RAF, Royal Navy and foreign air forces. As no operational flying units were based there, it was an ideal base for the CFS Course and "Red Arrows" Gnats. Two 'tin' hangars on G-site were prepared for CFS occupation, newly constructed office and servicing facilities being provided inside each. C Flight was assigned to one hangar and the "Arrows" the other and the move was completed on 26 September 1966.

"It didn't take us long to settle into our new surroundings," says Ray Deacon, *"and once everything was unpacked and organised, we got down to the important task of marking out a volleyball court ready for the encroaching winter. As the new pan was still under construction, the Gnats operated from the end of the short runway for several months. When finished it had space for the ten Team Gnats only, so the short runway continued to be used as an apron.*

Watching the 'Flying Circus' taking off in the back seats of 'The Reds' gave me the urge to have a go and when in October 1966 Boscombe Down gave the all-clear for the Gnat to be flown in formation with slipper tanks fitted, and Sqn Ldr Ray Hanna decided to fly all ten aircraft on a fuel-flow test formation, I saw my chance. I asked Tom if he could arrange it and arrange it he did, as several others from the Recce Team were invited to partake in the trip. Flt Lt Bill Langworthy was my pilot and he flew XR993 at No.3. After a formation take-off, the team opened-up into loose formation and flew fast and low towards Ilfracombe, where we climbed to 10,000 ft for some formation loops and rolls. On arrival back at Kemble, the team formed line-astern for a tail chase over the airfield that seemed to go on and on. Exhilarating and terrific fun!

With comparatively few aircraft movements, the circuit at Kemble was usually quiet and tailor-made for the Gnats. Course aircraft could easily slot their circuits and bumps around the practice displays of the 'Arrows' and you could guarantee that at the end of a practice, at least one of the Gnats would sneak in dead-low and unseen across the line and cover everyone in an evil smelling cloud of diesel. Ray Hanna, Henry Prince and Terry Kingsley were masters at this.

In November 1966, Rose and I moved into a married quarter at Little Rissington, 16 Glebe Crescent I think it was, which meant getting up early to catch the RAF bus to Kemble. Ron and Ros Turrell lived round the corner in No. 14 and I would knock on their door on my way out to the pick-up point on the Great Rissington road. No sooner had we settled in than Rose got a job serving airmen and women in The Windrush Club. It didn't take her long to master the oblique banter unique to service life.

My second and last trip in a Gnat was on the day I left the RAF, 2 May 1967. Having suffered no ill effects from my first trip, I asked if I could go up on one of the team's practice sorties to take some photographs. 'Be kitted up and ready at 14:00', said Ray Hanna. What I didn't know was that this was to be no practice but a full display for an Officers' Passing Out parade at RAF South Cerney. It was the first full show I'd done and the effects of loop after loop and roll after roll, combined with continual changes from positive to negative g, I began to feel distinctly unwell and hardly able to lift my camera. I later found several shots of the inside of the cockpit! To my relief, the bomb-burst ending the show came and went and I asked my pilot, Flt Lt Frank Hoare, if he wouldn't mind darting back to Kemble as fast as he could. 'I thought you wanted to take some photographs, Deacon' he said. 'Yes I did but I think I've got all I wanted thank you, Sir', came my sheepish reply. I got out of the aircraft and sat on the grass by the pan for the hour or so it took to recover. What a great way to end a career!"

CHAPTER 9

Accommodation and Amenities

Accommodation

Approximately half of the airmen were single or unaccompanied and were billeted in one of two types of barrack block. Trenchard Block, a two-storey barrack located on the east side of the Square, dated from the late 1930s and comprised four barrack rooms with shared toilet and bathroom facilities. An adjacent block further to the east remained unoccupied for most of the year, being opened for use by air cadets on their summer camps. The thirty or so airmen quartered in each room were generally those that worked the standard 09:00-17:30 day in SSF, RF and the various equipment bays. Their quarters may not have been modernised since their construction but they did have the advantage of being closest to the camp facilities.

The remaining airmen were housed in two post-war blocks located outside the airfield perimeter on the west side of the Great Rissington road. These were two-storey constructions that comprised primarily single rooms and were assigned predominantly to the airmen who worked on the flight lines, as they were expected to work unsociable hours, night flying being a regular occurrence. With distant views across the hills, life in Baldwin and Burnett blocks was great in the summer but cold and exposed to the howling gales of winter. Access to the camp facilities and airfield was across the road and via a gap in the 3-foot high Cotswold stone wall and a footpath.

'Godfrey Paine' block was located on the west side of the Square and was occupied by the WRAF contingent.

The Square was probably the first feature that most people noticed on arrival at Rissy as half of it was cordoned-off to provide car parking space for airmen and airwomen. The other half was used only for the raising and lowering of the RAF Ensign at the beginning and end of each day. Official parades were rare events and were held on the aircraft pan by 1 Hangar.

The Airmen's married quarters were located on the north side of the camp and were constructed in three phases, the first, shortly before the war, were followed by more spacious designs in the fifties and sixties. A playing field separated these from the Officers' married quarters. As the number of quarters was insufficient for the camp's needs, many families lived in local houses hired out to the RAF.

One of two pre-fabricated airmen's barrack blocks built after the war, Burnett block, illustrated here, was located opposite the main gate. Single-room accommodation was provided for 84 airmen plus another 16 in four, four-man rooms. The latter were subsequently converted for use as reading and TV rooms. (*Les Lane*)

CFS Handbook

In 1968, the Station Commander, Gp Capt B. P. Mugford, wrote the following Foreword to the CFS Handbook which superseded the CFS magazine of earlier years: "I am pleased to welcome you to RAF Little Rissington the home of the fixed wing element of CFS, which is the oldest flying unit in the British Services. Our task here, to which every post on the station contributes, is to train qualified pilots from all three services and from abroad to be flying instructors. The level of skill which we manage to impart to these student flying instructors will be reflected very quickly in the future standard of flying of the Royal Air Force, and other Services, in terms of operational ability and flight safety. You will appreciate from this that our work at Little Rissington is vitally important, and only if we can do it to the best of our ability can we deserve the satisfaction of having such a worthwhile job.

The object of this booklet is to help you find your feet at Little Rissington, and amongst other things it will tell you about the many sporting and social activities which are available to you on the station.

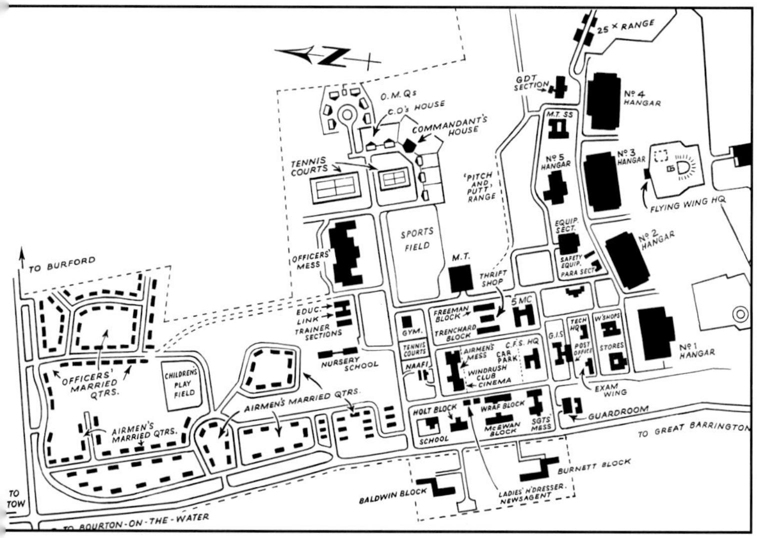

Map of the main site showing the officers' and airmen's married quarters, sports facilities, administration buildings, workshops and hangars. (*CFS Handbook*)

(*left*) A 1963 scene outside the Old New Inn in Bourton and (*below*), a recent photograph of The Fox Inn at Great Barrington. Both were popular haunts for Rissy personnel. (*Ray Deacon*)

Please take full advantage of these to make your off duty time more interesting and enjoyable. But remember that they represent a lot of hard effort freely given by men and women on the station at present; let their adage be yours for the future and do all you can to help others whilst you are stationed at Little Rissington.

I hope your tour here will be a happy one for you and your family."

Getting about

For many posted into Little Rissington, Kingham Station provided the first glimpse of the Cotswolds. On the main line between Paddington and Worcester, the station at one time provided an important junction for branch lines in the area. The line to Chipping Norton closed in the late fifties while that through Stow, Bourton and Andoversford to Cheltenham became a casualty of the Beeching closures in October 1963. The MT section ran a bus the six miles to Kingham Station on Friday evenings for those going home for the weekend and it returned at 23:00 on Sunday to pick them up. Weekends on camp were usually quiet affairs, a trip to Cheltenham via narrow winding country lanes on the top deck of Pulhams bright red ex-London Transport bus being perhaps the highlight.

At your leisure

After a hard day's work, it was time to relax! Little Rissington, like many RAF stations, was isolated from local amenities. Located on a ridge high above the Cotswold hills, winters could be severe with gales and blizzards accumulating several feet of snow, but in summer, it was an extremely pleasant place to live and work with distant views across beautiful countryside, leafy lanes and pleasant stone-clad Cotswold villages with wonderful names such as, Bourton-on-the-Water, Stow-on-the-Wold, Moreton-in-Marsh, Shipton-under-Wychwood, Upper and Lower Slaughter. The village of Little Rissington was nearest to the camp, but as it had no watering hole, The Lamb at Great Rissington, The Old New Inn and Mousetrap in Bourton were the most favoured haunts for airmen. Other popular venues included The Duke of Wellington and The Old Manse Hotel in Bourton, The Unicorn in Stow and Rampant Cat in Burford. For a more energetic evening's entertainment, the skittle alley in the Fox

The Landlord's Invitation.

Here's to Pands Penda's
Ocialh our in ha R M
Les Smir Tha ndfunle Tfr
iend ship Re ign Bejustan
Dkin Dan Devils Pe akof
n one.

Something to challenge your capabilities after a pint or four in the bar, this little teaser was mounted on a wall in the Old New Inn. (*Ray Deacon*)

Bourton-on-the-Water Railway Station on the last day of service. Closed by Dr Beeching, the line once provided a useful link between the village and Cheltenham to the west and the main line to Paddington at Kingham Junction to the east. (*Roy Bagshaw*)

Pulhams Coaches ex-London RTL-type bus passes Baldwin block en-route to Cheltenham on a Saturday afternoon. A couple of airmen have grabbed the front upper-deck seats to take in the magnificent views afforded of the Cotswold countryside. (*Ray Deacon*)

at Great Barrington was a popular attraction, an evening there invariably ending with a game of darts followed by a challenge for everyone to cross the narrow pipe that bridged the stream at the rear of the pub. After a pint or five of Donningtons finest ale, several would not make it across and end up with a soaking. A chap called 'Bo' Morris was the licensee at the Old New Inn, and this was a popular venue for de-mob and birthday parties.

In the early sixties, the few airmen who owned cars or scooters were high in the popularity stakes and in great demand especially at pub opening time. On weekdays Pulhams Coaches of Bourton ran buses from several localities in the mornings and evenings for civilians working on camp, and a late evening service would get you to the pubs in Bourton. Leave it too late at closing time and you had to make your own way back the 1½ miles up the steep hill. Civilian staff living on the bus route from Chipping Norton through Kingham to Little Rissington could use a twice-a-day double-deck service operated by The Oxford Bus Company to get to work.

Libraries

The following libraries were available to all station personnel; Reference and Textbook (4,000 volumes), Recreational (1,800 volumes), Children's (run by the Station Wives Club).

CFS Museum

A small museum, known as Airmanship Hall and depicting the history of CFS, contained a sectioned Derwent engine, a complete Vampire trainer and a broad selection of exhibits and artefacts. An excellent selection of 1/12th scale models, presented to CFS by Hawker Siddeley and De Havilland, hung from the roof of the Hall. The museum was located in an annexe of the Ground Instruction Squadron Building. It was open daily during working hours to everyone on the Station.

Hobbies and Pastimes

A wide range of hobbies and pastimes was provided over the years ranging from a Motor Cycle Club, Arts and Crafts Club, Scout Group, Dance Classes, Whist Drives, Chess Club, Bridge Club to a Photographic Club in the forties, but by the sixties and seventies the options had expanded considerably with greater emphasis being placed on activity and sporting pursuits. These included the following:

Amateur Radio Club

The Amateur Radio Club was situated behind the Officers' Mess and met on Monday evenings at 18:30. The Club had its own radio station with the call sign G3NG2 and communicated regularly with other RAF clubs at home and abroad and with civilian amateur radio clubs. Facilities were also available for training members in morse code and electronics theory up to the standard required for a GPO amateur licence.

Carpentry Club

The Carpentry Club was situated behind the Education Section and Club members were entitled to draw the keys any evening or weekend. The Club provided facilities for cabinet making, general woodwork and marquetry. Whenever possible, instruction was available to provide assistance to members. Plans and drawings which covered most of the 'do-it-yourself' enthusiasts' requirements were also available.

Photographic Society

There was a first rate Photographic Society on the station, situated in the Decontamination Centre next to the Primary School. The Society had a fully equipped studio and changing room, a dark room, chemical storage room, film drying facilities, enlargers and a coffee bar in the Society's own information and social room. Meetings were held weekly and frequent visits made to neighbouring civilian Photographic Clubs.

Rifle Club

The Rifle Club was located in the large wooden building behind the Guardroom. It had a well furnished clubroom, where meetings were held every Thursday evening throughout the year. There was a 25-yard range on the premises. Tuition was always available to beginners and advanced coaching to those who wished to improve their averages.

Games and Sports

RAF Little Rissington catered for a wide range of sporting interests and had ample facilities for personnel to take part in most sports. In addition to hockey, soccer, rugby and cricket pitches, and tennis and squash courts, a heated sports hangar was opened on the south side of the airfield previously occupied by Nos. 8 and 250 MUs. This had three tennis courts, three badminton courts, volleyball and basketball courts, a five-a-side football pitch, a mini-hockey pitch, boxing ring and archery range.

Archery

The Station had a limited amount of archery equipment which could be borrowed from the Sports Store.

Basketball

Any player, no matter how inexperienced was welcome provided that he brought with him the two vital qualities of enthusiasm and fitness. The team represented the Station in the usual RAF competitions and also in the local Cheltenham and District Basketball League. Most of the civilian fixtures were played in Cheltenham on Tuesday and Thursday evenings and they inevitably included an extremely enjoyable 'inquest' in the nearest local.

Little Rissington village football team, circa 1961, included several airmen. (*standing, l to r*), Tom Dalton, Eric Creed, Des Lewin, Derek Treaby, Norman Lane and Taff Edwards (RAF). (*kneeling, l to r*), Bob Dargue (RAF), Derek Hamilton, Scouse*, Jim Hughes, and Colin Sarahs (RAF). (*Robert Dargue*)

Badminton

The Badminton season extended from September to April but facilities were available all the year round. Station team practice and matches took place in the Sports Centre on Thursday evenings and an Inter Section league operated on Tuesday evenings. Ladies Badminton took place on Wednesday evenings after 'Keep Fit' classes either in the Gymnasium or the Sports Centre, depending on the numbers attending.

Expedition Training

Expeditions were organised throughout the year in Skiing, Canoeing, Mountain Walking and Camping. Some expeditions took the form of training for beginners and others provided a challenge to the more experienced. Training was given by qualified instructors.

Gliding

"The Windrushers", the CFS Gliding and Soaring Club, a branch of the RAFGSA, was formed on 1 April 1954. Its prime objective was to encourage non-flying personnel to sever their connection with the earth, temporarily that is, and experience the joys of controlled flight. Although theoretically differing from powered flight in that the old adage "all that goes up must come down," no longer applied, it was hoped that some of those who normally used an engine would also be undaunted by the thought of rising in ever decreasing circles. After all, rumour had it that many of them were switched off anyway.

In 1954, the C-in-C., Air Marshal L.F. Pendred CB MBE DFC was President of the club which also had the good fortune to have such splendid support from the Commandant, Air Cdre G.J.C. Paul DFC, who was an eminent gliding enthusiast. Ab initio instruction took

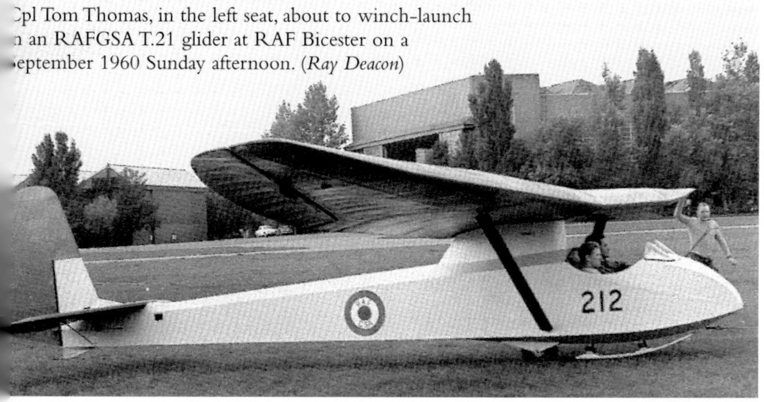

Cpl Tom Thomas, in the left seat, about to winch-launch in an RAFGSA T.21 glider at RAF Bicester on a September 1960 Sunday afternoon. (*Ray Deacon*)

place in the T.21 side-by-side dual trainer, after which pupils graduated to the Kirby Cadet and their first solo flight.

Gliding was then and probably still is, the cheapest form of flying. For an annual subscription of 10/-, and a monthly 5/-, it offered unparalleled value. Membership was open to anyone, whatever rank or sex.

Personnel serving at CFS were fortunate in being close to the RAFGS centre at RAF Bicester. Apart from normal week-end flying, ab initio courses were available in mid-week periods and soaring weeks for solo pilots. In 1967 it was possible to learn to fly up to solo standard for less than £5! The Centre had four dual aircraft and a full range of solo aircraft from early types up to the high performance competition aircraft.

Golf

All serving personnel and civilians working at Rissy were eligible to join the golf club at Burford, approximately 7 miles from the Station. The Station Golf team held many fixtures throughout the year and new golfers were encouraged to join.

Kart Club

The CFS Kart Club and track, which was situated on the old MU site on the south side of the airfield, was open to all CFS personnel and their families. The club possessed three Class I and two Class IV Karts at the end of the 1968 Season. The track was 1,200 yards long, included two good straights and a chicane, and became known nationally and was liked by many of the country's top drivers, including Bruno Ferrari and Chris Lambert. Racing took place every other Sunday during the Season – April to October – and on the alternate Sundays many of the existing members were at the club tuning up and testing the 'Karts'. Personnel were encouraged to bring their spouses for a trial ride. The subscription was £1 per annum, good value if you wanted to experience the fun and thrills of motor racing.

Rough Shooting

The Station had a small Rough Shooting Syndicate, which met once a month during the Rough Shooting Season. The Station Commander owned the shooting rights at Little Rissington. Members could also participate in Clay Pigeon Shooting once a fortnight from May to September, weather permitting. New members were welcomed but each shoot was usually limited to eight guns. Game licences were required in order to shoot on MoD property.

Sailing

Dinghy sailing facilities were available at the RAF Sailing Centre, Somerford Keynes, situated some three miles SW of Cirencester. Here suitably qualified helmsmen could use either of the Station's two Fireflies at any time for racing or just pottering about the 15-acre lake. A small charge was made for the use of the boats and the facilities at the centre. For those more interested in deep sea sailing there were often vacant berths on the RAF's 'Dambuster', 'Contrail', 'Jethou' or 'Watchful' yachts, cruising in the Solent, West Country waters or to France and the Channel Islands.

Tennis

The Station team ran practice nights on Mondays after working hours; anyone interested in playing tennis was welcome to attend. The Station, in addition to holding regular fixtures with neighbouring stations on Wednesdays, also played a number of evening matches with local civilian clubs. Tennis was played throughout the year being indoors during winter months.

WRAF Sports

Facilities were available for almost any sport in which airwomen were keen to participate and members of the WRAF were encouraged to join in sporting activities. Netball, Hockey, Tennis, Badminton, Athletics, Riding, Shooting, Squash and Table Tennis were all organised on the station. In addition, WRAF could also swim at Cheltenham, and join in the gliding at Bicester or sailing at South Cerney.

Entertainment

The severe weather that accompanied the winter months, encouraged many to make the most of the camp's limited entertainment facilities. These comprised a Cinema, NAAFI, a jazz club and a theatre group existed for a while, but its popularity tended to ebb and flow. As a consequence, the NAAFI was the hub of social life which enabled everyone to get acquainted.

The Windrush Club

In 1965, the NAAFI building was refurbished and re-opened as the social centre of the Station for airmen, airwomen and their families. Membership of the new 'Windrush Club' was open to airmen, airwomen, their spouses and members of other British Services and Allied Forces of equivalent rank who were posted or attached to Little Rissington. Members' children over the age of 18 were made honorary members and civilians could be made 'Friends of the Club' and attend functions for which a charge was made.

Located between the Station Cinema and the Airmen's Mess, the Windrush Club was in easy walking distance of both single and married quarters. The Club consisted of a Restaurant for light meals and refreshments and where dances were held on special occasions, a Cocktail Bar and lounge, opening off the Restaurant, the Tavern Bar and its Annexe, where social gatherings could be held and where the Windrush Wives Club held their functions. Upstairs there was a Snooker Room with three tables and a table tennis table, and a Games Room that saw regular use as a discotheque. A Services Shop was located in the Club foyer, stocked with gifts, chocolates, cigarettes and toilet requisites.

Pipes and Drums

Formed in 1958, the CFS Pipe Band was fortunate in being granted permission by Lord Lynch, King of Arms, to wear the Henderson Tartan. The pipes and drums performed at all the Station's ceremonial occasions and the band was in big demand by the organisers of fêtes and galas and similar functions in the local area in the summer months. One of the perks for the volunteer band members was that they were excused station duties, such as, Fire Picket and Guard of Honour.

The size of the band fluctuated as people were posted in and out. When Ray Deacon joined the drum section early in 1960 there were some eight or nine pipers and about half as many drummers. *"The lead drummer at that time was Sgt Pat Trumper a radio technician in RSF who, having found out that I had played trumpet and drums with the 'Brats' at Cosford, persuaded me to give it a go. I remember the Pipe Major as being dour Scottish Sergeant, quite short in stature, with cheeks that expanded like enormous red eggs when puffing into his 'doodle-sack'. He was an excellent piper but sometimes missed his note if he made too liberal a use of the hip flask he always carried with him, be it on station parade or civil function. The more he sipped, the more wrong notes crept into his playing and the more 'stick' we got from the lads afterwards. Still it was good fun."*

(*Left*) What was once the NAAFI restaurant and bar, the splendid Windrush Club Bar shortly after refurbishment in 1965, (*CFS Handbook, via Roy Bagshaw*) (*below*) Situated next door was the ever popular Astra Cinema, (*Graham Pitchfork collection*). Sadly both buildings were demolished circa 2000 to make way for new housing.

Domestic Supply Flight

The Station Clothing Store was open between 08:00 and 12:00 and from 13:00 to 15:30 hours daily. Clothing Parades for No. 1 Best Blue uniform were held at times notified in SROs, and were attended by the Clothing Contractor. The camp tailoress was in attendance from 10:00 to 15:30.

Individual laundry bundles were collected from barrack rooms on Thursdays between 08:00 and 09:30 when sheets and pillow cases could also be exchanged. Clean laundry was delivered back to barrack rooms on Wednesdays between 08:30 and 09:00 hours. Sheets and pillow cases could be exchanged at Airmen's married quarters on Wednesdays between 10:00 and 12:00 hours.

Friday mornings were allocated for the handing in of dry cleaning at the Barrack Stores and could be collected on the following Tuesday week.

NAAFI Grocery Shop

RAF Little Rissington was served by a NAAFI with a modern self-service shop, which, in effect was a miniature supermarket. It stocked everything needed for the normal requirements of families and personnel.

Local Traders

In addition to NAAFI, local traders visited the married quarters regularly, delivering vegetables, meat, milk, etc. A complete list was published in the Families Bulletin at regular intervals. Occupants of married quarters were advised that occasionally, high pressure salesmen visited the quarters with luxury items such as vacuum cleaners, washing machines, etc., and that any hire purchase agreement entered into with these salesmen should be fully read and the conditions of sale fully understood before any item was purchased.

Wives' Activities

There were a number of useful and interesting activities on the Station which were run and organised on a voluntary basis by the station wives. In consultation with the OC Administrative Wing and under the presidency of the Station Commander's wife, there were committees of wives to run the Nursery School, Welfare Clinic, Thrift Shop, NAAFI Customer Relations, Welcoming Committee, the Windrush Club Wives' Committee and the Officers' Wives Entertainment Committee. Details of the Station Wives' Activities were published in the Families Bulletin which was circulated to all married quarters. Copies were also available in the Messes, at the NAAFI and in the Windrush Club.

Scouts, Cubs and Brownies

The RAF Little Rissington Scout Troop and Cub and Brownie Packs met weekly in their hut near the Education Section.

CHAPTER 10

'We Shall Remember Them'

No historical account of RAF Little Rissington would be complete without reference to the twelfth century St. Peter's Church in the village of Little Rissington, as this is where airmen killed while serving on the station are buried. Reached via a path from the centre of the village, the church stands on a small promontory commanding beautiful views over the Windrush valley.

Both the church and its churchyard show the close connection between Little Rissington village and the RAF Station which was the home of No. 6 Service Flying Training School from 1938 and of the Central Flying School from 1946 until 1976. When the RAF left Little Rissington in 1976, the chapel altar cross and the churchwardens' staves were presented to the church. Made of plated steel, the cross was produced in the Station Workshops. Designed by J.A. Crombie, ARCA, and built by John Baker, the west window illustrates the badges of the Central Flying School, "The Red Arrows" and the RAF Association, with the crossed keys of St. Peter and the dove of peace above. It was dedicated by the then Bishop of Gloucester on Battle of Britain Sunday, 1983, as a memorial, to the men of the Royal Air Force and of the Commonwealth Air Forces who were stationed at RAF Little Rissington during the Second World War and especially those who lie buried in the churchyard.

Outside, on the east and highest side of the churchyard, there are seventy-six graves marked in moving simplicity by the customary stones, crosses and roses laid out by the Commonwealth War Graves Commission (CWGC) all over the world. Of the seventy-six men buried here, forty-five lost their lives in the Second World War, and that number includes four men from the Royal Australian Air Force and three from the Royal Canadian Air Force and five from the Royal New Zealand Air Force. A "Cross of Sacrifice" of white stone with a black sword affixed can be seen amongst the war graves.

To this day, on the Sunday before Battle of Britain Sunday, a service of thanksgiving is held in the church. The service is well supported by the village and some ex-CFS members travel long distances to attend. After the service, the village hosts an excellent tea in the village hall. On Sunday, 11 September 2003, AV-M Sir John Severne, on behalf of the then present CFS Commandant, Gp Capt Jon Fynes, presented a picture to the village representing 90 years of CFS. The montage included photographs of all 48 CFS Commandants.

The church is open to the public; entry is via a gate and door. Once inside, the stained-glass window to the left shows the badges of the Central Flying School, and a 'Gnat' in Red Arrows colours.

Further mementos, in the form of plaques mounted to certain pews and hassocks, record the affection of villagers and churchgoers for those who served at Rissy. Beneath the window there are three commemorative plaques.

The standard CWGC markers date from the late 1930s to the 1970s, reflecting RAF Little Rissington's long service history. Some of the graves from the 1960s and 1970s are those of Red Arrows pilots; whilst their aircraft were based at Kemble some 20 miles to the south, many of the 'Reds' made their home at Little Rissington, in the Central Flying School's officers' quarters.

Whilst all the graves appear similar at

(*below*) The tranquil setting of St Peter's Church on the fringe of Little Rissington village and (*right*), the ornate window in the west wing are a timely reminder of the close links that existed between the village and the RAF station. (*Ray Deacon*) first glance, the wartime graves are rounded at the top, whilst the post-war markers have a more pronounced curve at either side.

The grave of Flt Sgt Jack Hazeldene, commemorated on the plaque in "The Lamb", can be found mid-way along the wall of the churchyard in the war graves plot.

The full list of men buried in the churchyard follows at the end of this chapter.

A tragic night out

In Reg O'Neil's book, 'A lighter shade of Pale Blue', he tells the story of the bus trip to Cheltenham that was to end in disaster.

"There were times when things would go awfully wrong; being a school for flyers, accidents were bound to happen. Death always seemed to come in nines, as I was to experience later. Sometimes relatives would request that the victim be sent to their home town for interment but others would be buried in the churchyard of the local village church of St Peter's, Little Rissington. Victims would be given a full military funeral with the customary honours. A contingent of airmen would lead the cortege headed by the station band, and march down the hill to the village for the interment, at which an armed party would fire a salute. Following the ceremony the contingent would march back up the hill led by the Station Warrant Officer, who was an ex-guardsman, mature in years, but could leave the parade struggling behind as he strode out ahead!

On the night of 21 October 1941, 'Trafalgar Day' to be precise, a tragic accident was to happen which would affect most of the different sectors of the station in one way or another. An old commercial coach had been requisitioned for the MT section and had been camouflaged with green and black aircraft dope. This was used for transporting duty personnel between sites and it had been allowed to be used for recreational duties when free. Arrangements were made for it to convey bods into Cheltenham for an evening out once in a while and so it was on that fateful night. It had left Cheltenham at 23:00 as arranged for the return to camp. There were more passengers for the return trip than the outward run and in consequence it became overcrowded and many had to stand. The coach stopped on the outskirts of the town to pick up the camp photographer, close to his home. At 60, he must have been the oldest airman on the camp. He had served in the RFC in the First World War and had volunteered for this one. He was affectionately known as 'Pop' and was very popular with everyone. I happened to be sitting in the first seat by the door and so gave him my seat. A few minutes later as we were passing a reservoir on the outskirts of Andoversford, we ran into the back of a lorry laden with sheet steel that had broken down. The young driver of the bus (who had never driven a bus before) saw the lorry in the dim light of his headlamps and tried to take avoiding action. We were travelling at less than twenty miles per hour but unfortunately, he was too late and the nearside of the bus collided with the rear of the lorry. What happened after that I was not to know for a while until I came to, to find myself in a tunnel of flame. The whole coach was one huge ball of fire and somehow I was able to make my way through the tunnel and out over the engine. I was later informed that I was the last to escape from the inferno.

The military section of St Peter's cemetery, Little Rissington village, dominated by the Cross of Sacrifice, contains the graves of 76 airmen who died while serving at the RAF Station and several who died after it closed. (*Ray Deacon*)

As we were taken away in an ambulance, I held the hand of one young lad that I knew who was on a stretcher with a broken back. He mumbled a few words to me that I could not understand but after a little while the pressure of his hand in mine relaxed as it went limp. He was no longer in pain. We were taken to an ARP first aid centre where we were given mugs of Bovril and later transferred to the RAF Hospital at Innsworth Lane.

There were nine killed in that accident! The fateful 'nine'. Amazingly, considering the number of people on the bus, casualties were very light. Three of us sustained serious burns, one with a broken femur. There were several with light injuries and shock, I was not to really know the true facts for several days as the three of us were taken to the burns centre at RAF Cosford. I must admit that apart from an ache on the side of my face, which was thought to have been a broken jaw, I felt no pain from the burns, which proved to be severe, third degree.

Most of us were unable to return to camp that night and many sections had bods missing for work the next morning. Regretfully, the photographic section was to be one less as poor old 'Pop' did not survive. His gravestone is one of eight to be found in the Little Rissington churchyard. The other victim went 'home'.

After several months of treatment by Dr. McIndoe at RAF Cosford, I found myself back at Kingham awaiting transport to Little Rissington. I soon found my old bed-space which had been shifted into a hut, checked over my kit before making a visit to the NAAFI, where I was greeted by several pals. I reported next morning to the MO who sent me off on another twenty-one days sick leave. But not before I was to carry out a special task for him. It appeared that the young driver of the ill-fated coach had been charged with dangerous driving, exceeding the speed limit (20 mph) and driving under the influence of drink. (He had only taken a half pint of beer!). He was found guilty and awarded six months detention in the Glasshouse. This was reduced to six months confined to camp on compassionate grounds. When asked by the MO for my version of what had happened, he tended to agree with me that I considered the driver was not to blame. I had been questioned by the police after the accident, against the wishes of the medical people, who said that I was not in a fit state to be questioned at that moment in time. However, I felt that I could and told how I saw the rear of the lorry appear in the headlights of the coach and that I was able to quote the number plate, which was firmly imprinted in my memory. Hearing this, the police agreed that my memory was correct but there was some doubt as to whether the lorry was displaying rear lights. On hearing this question, my memory simply collapsed and I could not positively say yes or no. To this day I am convinced in my mind that there were no lights. The MO asked if I would go and have a chat with the young lad as he just wouldn't talk with anyone on the camp, but just kept himself to himself. I did this and tried to re-assure him that I was certain that he was not to blame. I hope that I was able to convince him as, on returning from my leave he had been posted to another Unit. I later learned that a question had been asked in the 'House of Commons' by an MP as to why an inexperienced 21 year-old had been detailed to drive that vehicle when there were seven ex-London bus drivers serving in the MT section. I was never to learn the outcome of the enquiry as I was posted shortly afterwards."

Name	Rank	Occupation	Service No.	Service	Date of Death	Age
R.G. James	Plt Off	Pilot	-	RAF	30/09/1938	18 yrs
J.G. Mason	Plt Off	Pilot	-	RAF	30/09/1938	24 yrs
J.E. Hull	Plt Off	Pilot	-	RNZAF	19/09/1939	24 yrs
D.K. Robertson	Plt Off	Pilot		RAF	07/11/1939	20 yrs
D. Duncan	Sgt	-	754488	RAF	17/08/1940	20 yrs
M.A.R. Sutherland	LAC	U/T Pilot	903457	RAF	20/09/1940	29 yrs
I.F. Davies	Fg Off	Pilot	-	RAF	23/10/1940	23 yrs
R.T. Shaw	Fg Off	Pilot	-	RAF	23/10/1940	Unknown
D.R. Tooth	LAC	U/T Pilot	905289	RAF	03/11/1940	28 yrs
F.S. Hucks	LAC	U/T Pilot	752146	RAF	14/04/1941	45 yrs
D.S. Temple	Cpl	U/T Pilot	967234	RAF	18/05/1941	18 yrs
G.J. Buckle	LAC	U/T Pilot	1263121	RAF	23/05/1941	Unknown
V.C.R.S. Newman	LAC	U/T Pilot	1290309	RAF	26/08/1941	Unknown
P. R. West	LAC	U/T Pilot	656077	RAF	18/09/1941	22 yrs
W.L. Falardeau	Sgt	Pilot	R80157	RCAF	14/10/1941	19 yrs
B.L. Hoese	Sgt	Pilot	R67911	RCAF	14/10/1941	26 yrs
K.J. Fuller	AC	Unknown	1317209	RAF	21/10/1941	20 yrs
J. Baseley	AC	Unknown	1084639	RAF	21/10/1941	Unknown
R.L. Coppin	AC	Unknown	1134494	RAF	21/10/1941	27 yrs
S.F. Andrews	Cpl	Unknown	1154921	RAF	21/10/1941	25 yrs
H.T. Stokes	LAC	Photographer	52152	RAF	21/10/1941	60 yrs
F. Poulter	AC	Unknown	1525727	RAF	21/10/1941	36 yrs
S.G.P. Medwin	LAC	Unknown	1315853	RAF	21/10/1941	19 yrs
M.B. De Maynard	LAC	Unknown	1331436	RAF	21/10/1941	Unknown
B.H. Sparrow	Unknown	Driver	1920470	Royal Engineers	08/02/1942	Unknown
A.W. Westgate	Sgt	Air Gunner	403630	RNZAF	25/03/1942	25 yrs
R.V. Daniels	Sgt	Unknown	404603	RAAF	25/03/1942	27 yrs
E.J. Biddulph	Sgt	Pilot	778574	RAF (South African)	25/03/1942	20 yrs
B. Noseworthy	Sgt	Unknown	798569	RAF (Newfoundland)	25/03/1942	20 yrs
J.R. Lee	Plt Off	Pilot	-	RAF	08/04/1942	21 yrs
W.F. Good	Sgt	Observer	1210053	RAF	08/04/1942	34 yrs
R.H. Imeson	Fg Off	Pilot Instructor	-	RAF	15/05/1942	21 yrs
D.G. Henderson	Sgt	Pilot	R93969	RCAF	24/07/1942	22 yrs
W.A.H. Millar	Plt Off	Pilot	-	RAF	17/08/1942	21 yrs
E.D. Francis	Sgt	Unknown	411137	RAAF	19/08/1942	24 yrs
J.D. Rankin	Sgt	Unknown	411829	RAAF	21/08/1942	25 yrs
M.S. Haynes	Sgt	Wireless Operator	1263649	RAF	21/08/1942	21 yrs
A.M. Henderson	Plt Off	Unknown	-	RAF	21/08/1942	30 yrs
R.G. McCarthy	Sgt	Pilot	415072	RNZAF	16/09/1942	27 yrs
W.J. Ferguson	Sgt	Observer	1387312	RNZAF	16/09/1942	23 yrs
H.W. Farquharson	Sgt	Pilot	416472	RNZAF	06/11/1942	20 yrs
G. Lardner	W O	-	351015	RAF	24/11/1942	Unknown

Name	Rank	Occupation	Service No.	Service	Date of Death	Age
P.F. Barker	Sgt	Pilot	1394394	RAF	12/06/1943	20 yrs
A.J. Greatbatch	Sgt	Pilot	1577478	RAF	14/06/1943	22 yrs
M. Gardener	Sgt	Air Bomber	1388174	RAF	17/06/1943	21 yrs
J.F. Page	Flt Lt	Instructor Navigator	-	RAF	22/07/1943	29 yrs
P. R. Hope	Sgt	Pilot	1338924	RAF	22/07/1943	19 yrs
G.E.K. Stone	Cadet 1st Class	Unknown		163 ATC	11/09/1943	16 yrs
J.A. Hazeldene	Flt Sgt	Unknown	19907	RAAF	07/10/1943	24 yrs
L.W.H. Craig	Fg Off	Pilot	-	RAF	22/11/1944	20 yrs
L. Gregory	Sqn Ldr	Unknown	-	RAF	25/07/1945	37 yrs
J.A. Shelley	Flt Lt	Pilot	-	RAF	04/02/1954	33 yrs
C.H. Lazenby	Flt Lt	Pilot Instructor	-	RAF	28/07/1954	32 yrs
R. Bennet	Flt Lt	Unknown	-	RAF	28/07/1954	30 yrs
B.G. Rendle	Flt Lt	Pilot	-	RAF	28/07/1954	25 yrs
A.R. Wardell	Fg Off	Pilot	-	RAF	09/03/1955	24 yrs
D.J. Cooper	Flt Sgt	Pilot	577409	RAF	09/03/1955	32 yrs
P. Millington	Flt Lt	Pilot	-	RAF	04/12/1958	28 yrs
J. Satchell	Sqn Ldr	Unknown	-	RAF	28/03/1959	41 yrs
J.H. Ardaker	Flt Lt	Unknown	-	RAF	26/08/1959	28 yrs
T.J. Doe	Flt Lt	Pilot	-	RAF	26/06/1962	38 yrs
H.W. Carter	Flt Lt	Pilot	-	RAF	26/06/1962	24 yrs
J. Donald	Sgt	Unknown	1920878	RAF	05/11/1962	30 yrs
E. Roberts	Flt Lt	Pilot	-	RAF	26/01/1965	40 yrs
K.T.A. O'Sullivan	Flt Lt	Pilot	-	RAF	21/02/1969	47 yrs
J.J. Bowler	Flt Lt	Pilot	-	RAF	26/03/1969	27 yrs
C. Armstrong	Flt Lt	Pilot	-	RAF	20/01/1971	26 yrs
J.S. Haddock	Flt Lt	Pilot	-	RAF	20/01/1971	27 yrs
J. Lewis	Flt Lt	Pilot	-	RAF	20/01/1971	27 yrs
E.R. Perreaux	Flt Lt	Pilot	-	RAF	20/01/1971	31 yrs
M.E. Dobson	Sgt	-	X4003831	RAF	27/03/1971	42 yrs
D.F. McIntosh	Flt Sgt	-	C1682080	RAF	27/03/1971	48 yrs
R.M. Storr	Flt Lt	Pilot	-	RAF	13/12/1971	26 yrs
D.C. Longden	Flt Lt	Pilot	-	RAF	13/12/1971	28 yrs
J.M. Collis	SAC	Unknown	B0595632	RAF	18/11/1974	23 yrs
A.J. Kershaw	Flt Sgt	Unknown	L4035565	RAF	05/10/1975	44 yrs
I.J. Douglas	Flt Lt		-	RAF	06/06/1976	50 yrs

The following personnel are buried in Little Rissington churchyard but died after the camp closed:

Name	Rank	Occupation	Service No.	Service	Date of Death	Age
B.E. Russel	Sqn Ldr	-	-	RAF	2001	-
K. McMaster Williamson	Flt Lt	-	-	RAF	-	-
K. Coombe	Sqn Ldr	-	-	RAF	1990	-
A.K. Harkness	Gp Capt	-	-	RAF	1986	-
Sir Ivor Broom	A M	-	-	RAF	22/01/2003	82 yrs

The following RAF Little Rissington personnel are buried in Great Rissington Churchyard:

Name	Rank	Occupation	Service No.	Service	Date of Death	Age
L.R. Bull	AC	Wireless Operator/Gunner	620416	RAF	09/12/1939	19 yrs
D.S. Dadson	Plt Off	Pilot	-	RAF	14/03/1940	25 yrs
F.E. Morris	Flt Lt	Pilot		RAF	30/10/1950	27 yrs

CHAPTER 11

Gate Guardians and Museum Aircraft

During the 1950s and 1960s several historic aircraft were retained at Little Rissington either for display by the main gate or as museum exhibits. A small museum known as Airmanship Hall, created in an annexe to the Ground School, contained artefacts depicting the history of CFS and Little Rissington. In this chapter we look at the part these aircraft played in the history of the airfield and to their ultimate fate.

Spitfire LF.Mk.XVIe, SL721

Before the Second World War, Air Chief Marshal Sir James Robb had a long association with CFS. He flew his first solo at the School and later completed his instructor's course there, before returning in 1927 for a three-year tour as a Staff instructor. He was a member of the 1928 display team at RAF Hendon and, following promotion to Group Captain, became CFS Commandant in 1936 contributing much to the rapid pre-war expansion of the RAF. He subsequently became C-in-C Fighter Command and retired as C-in-C Western Union Air Forces. On his last day in the Royal Air Force, 21 September 1951, he flew his personal Spitfire LF.Mk.XVIe, SL721, into Little Rissington and handed it to Air Cdre Selway as a gift to CFS. Painted all-over light blue and with his personal code 'JMR' behind the roundel, it had been specially prepared for Sir James and lightened by the removal of all armament, armour plate and a fuel tank, it boasted a remarkable turn of speed even for a Spitfire.

ACM Sir James Robb's personal transport, Spitfire LF.XVIe, SL721, was painted all-over blue and carried his pennant and initials along the fuselage sides. (*MAP*)

The aircraft remained airworthy at Little Rissington for displays and special events and was often flown by Flt Lt John Severne, a staff instructor and PA to the Commandant. However, in 1955 and despite vigorous objections from CFS Staff, the Air Ministry issued instructions for it to be flown to RAF Lyneham for scrapping. Fortunately it evaded the scrap man and was bought by a Sussex garage owner for £120 for display on his forecourt. Three years later, the aircraft was loaned to Lord Montagu for display outside his museum at Beaulieu.

In 1966 the Spitfire came on the market again and CFS staff officer Flt Lt Winterbourne made a valiant attempt to obtain the aircraft but the offer of Little Rissington's gate guardian, recently refurbished Spitfire, LA226, in exchange proved unsuccessful. Instead it was sold to an American who shipped it to the USA and restored it to airworthy condition. Seven years later it was purchased by Doug Arnold and brought back to the UK, but in 1975 it was offered for sale again. The then Commandant of CFS happened to be John Severne and he made a resolute attempt to buy the Spit from Doug Arnold on behalf of CFS but got no reply. SL721 was sold to an Arizona-based collector. In 2003 it was repainted in a wartime camouflage scheme by its current Ottawa-based owner and registered C-CVZB.

Vampire T.Mk.11, XD457

Although relatively young for a museum exhibit, XD457 was grounded after its wing attachment points were found to have oversized holes, a manufacturing defect that took three years to manifest itself. Instead of being sent for scrap it was moved into Airmanship Hall in April 1957 where it became a major exhibit.

Spitfire F.Mk.21, LA226

The association of the Spitfire with Little Rissington dates back to the Second World War when newly-built aircraft were prepared for service by 8 MU. Several were also used by CFS post-war so it was

(*above*) Spitfire F.21, LA226, after its starring role in the Battle of Britain film, was mounted on a pole outside Station HQ where it was photographed in 1965. Harvard T.2b, FS890, (*below*) pictured outside the GIS building where it stood for many years as Gate Guardian. Spitfire LA226 can be seen in the background, 1961. (*Ray Deacon*)

therefore fitting that a Spitfire should occupy an honoured and conspicuous position at the world's oldest air training establishment.

LA226 was first issued to No. 91 Squadron at RAF Manston during the war and its first operational sortie was an anti-submarine strike. After the war it passed from station to station from as far apart as Inverness to Exeter before being grounded in 1952. Two years later it was issued to an ATC Squadron at Albrighton, Salop, before being brought to Little Rissington on 9 February 1958. It stood on the grass outside Station HQ, opposite the Harvard, until 1964 when it was transported to 5 MU at Kemble for refurbishment. On its return in January 1965 it was mounted in flying attitude on a pole outside the HQ building, bearing the markings and codes of No. 91 Squadron, DL:E.

Like many other Spitfire guardians, LA226 was taken to RAF Henlow in 1967 and prepared for use as a static aircraft in the 1968 film 'Battle of Britain'. It never returned to Little Rissington but saw further gate guardian duties at the Vickers-Armstrongs works near Swindon and Biggin Hill and is currently in store as a reserve item with the RAF Museum at Cosford.

Harvard T.Mk.2b, FS890

Apart from the reported collision between FS890 and FT337 at Moreton-in-Marsh on June 26, 1952, nothing is known about this aircraft's operational background. Retired from service at Nottingham University Air Squadron on 25 October 1956, FS890 was despatched to 10 MU for storage. Two years later, it was selected to represent Little Rissington's long association with the type and was placed on the grass outside the Administration building on 10 January 1958. Here it remained for several years, but was subsequently moved into one of the hangars to prevent it deteriorating and was occasionally wheeled out as a static exhibit on special occasions. Although it was noted as still being on camp by aircraft spotters as late as 1971, no record of its removal from Little Rissington could be found.

Mosquito B(TT).Mk.35, TA639

One of the last Mosquitos in service with the RAF at No. 3 CAACU based at Exeter Airport, TA639 was withdrawn in October 1962. Along with several other former 3 CAACU Mossies it undertook a flying role in the film 633 Squadron before being allocated to the RAF Museum and flown to Little Rissington on 31 May 1963, for safe keeping with CFS. The Commandant, Air Cdre Bird-Wilson, was an accomplished Mosquito pilot and took great delight in displaying it at air shows during his tour at the School.

After Air Cdre Bird-Wilson departed in 1965, Flt Lt C. Kirkham took over as the Mosquito display pilot and, following his last display of the 1965 season, the ROC Day at RAF Stradishall on 3 October, the aircraft was placed aside in No. 4 Hangar for the winter.

Some years later, Flt Lt Mike Telford returned to Little Rissington on the staff, and retells a story passed on to him by Chipmunk staff member Sqn Ldr John Snell.

"John was trained during WWII and was an experienced, decorated test pilot, with probably a hundred or more types in his logbook. One day John was called to the office of the then Commandant of CFS, Air Cdre Frank Dodd. 'Doddy' said that though the Mossie was 'his', he had inadequate time and continuity to fly the machine, so would John like to take it on for the following year's display season. John was over the moon to accept such an offer. The following year John ran the engines up, pronouncing them both to be 'sweet as a nut' but sensed that old problem of 'something-feels-a-bit-loose-down-the-back-end'. He consulted a chum in the know about these things, whose rapid verdict was that this Mossie would never fly again, nor did it, I believe. John investigated matters further. Some Engineering Wing SNCOs, it appeared, had gone to OC Eng Wing, with frightening stories of the massive extra work the Mossie would involve for a technical staff already working to capacity. What could be done, then, asked OC Eng? Leave it to us, said our conspiratorial SNCOs as the Mosquito was put into Hangar 5. Alone among Rissy's hangars, this one had heating facilities: several hot air blowers were mounted on the hangar's roof girders, each with wide canvas

pipes reaching down to duct hot air to the working level, a few feet above the hangar floor. Our stage is now set for subsequent events.

The Mossie, nicknamed the 'Wooden Wonder' had glue joints used in a number of key areas of the aircraft's construction. Subjected to heat, these glues can eventually fail. Our clever plotters arranged for the Mossie to be 'stored' in the heated hangar for an entire winter, with its tail section strategically positioned under one of the canvas air ducts. Under constant strong heating, as found in some overseas WWII theatres, the glue failed with serious loss of structural integrity. The technical term, I believe, is crystallisation, when key joints were sprung, irreparably so."

Inspections early in 1967 revealed serious deterioration in the glue joints around the engine mountings, undercarriage and tail unit, and valiant attempts were made by Air Cdre Dodd to persuade the powers that be to get Maintenance Command at RAF Henlow to carry out repairs. Sadly his request was turned down and the aircraft was permanently grounded. The engines were occasionally ground run and it was included as a static exhibit on special occasions, but its days at Rissy were numbered and it departed for static display to the RAF Museum at Cosford on 5 July 1967.

Spitfire LF.Mk.XVIe, TE356

When its flying career with the RAF ended on 1 September 1952, TE356 was moved to RAF Bicester where it remained until 1967. After a period at RAF Henlow, when it was restored to taxiing condition for participation in the Battle of Britain film, the aircraft was transferred to 5 MU at RAF Kemble for refurbishment. It arrived at Little Rissington on 4 December 1970 and in March the following year it was mounted on a concrete plinth outside Station Headquarters. Three months later, a small ceremony was held at the site in which Mr W.W. Tait, who had generously donated the money for the plinth, unveiled a commemorative plaque.

The following tale was also imparted by Flt Lt Mike Telford.

"Illustrating partly understandable turf tensions, the station commander, Gp Capt Adams, and CFS Commandant, Air Cdre Hazlewood, fell out rather more spectacularly than usual. This resulted in the sensible arrangement of existing adjacent offices being changed, to be replaced by a newly built 'Air HQ' extension at the opposite end of the Station HQ building. Thus, looking at SHQ from the ground school block, the stationmaster's offices would be at the extreme right-hand end of the frontage of SHQ, while the Commandant's new Air HQ would be on the extreme left. There the story might well have ended had it not been for the Spitfire standing on a plinth in front of the left-hand side of SHQ. The stationmaster reportedly insisted that, since this was 'his' Spitfire, he wanted it in front of 'his' offices. Thus the aircraft had to be moved, so moved it was! The plinth was taken up and the resulting hole filled in, to be landscaped with a large flowerbed.

For several years the Spitfire had stood on its own plinth and wheels, assessed to be in potentially airworthy condition. The only problems concerned its Packard Merlin engine, where numerous complications over its engine re-certification boiled down to nobody wanting to 'sign it off' as fit for flight. Before these could be resolved, the Spitfire was put up on to its new, more dynamic, plinth in front of the station commander's (i.e. right hand) side of SHQ. This operation necessitated the embedding of a substantial steel pylon, after the digging of a very deep hole. On top of the pylon was a huge T-shaped bracket, with flanges, bolts and fastening points at each end, now actually located into the main wingspars. The Spitfire was displayed as though airborne, with wheels retracted, in a slightly nose-down, banked attitude. All this looked very pretty except, as hinted, those precious main spars had to be sawn through, thus rendering the aircraft effectively Cat 5.

The total cost of the operation hardly bears thinking about, while the loss of this rare airworthy and priceless historic airframe leaves one speechless. All this occurred at 'the home of the world's finest fliers', seemingly because two blokes just did not get on. Many years have passed since those events and some of the less flattering details may even be apocryphal. This tale IS correct to the best of my recollection – the building of the Air HQ extension is real enough, as was the moving of the Spitfire."

On 13 April 1976, TE356 was dismantled and transported by road as part of the move of CFS to RAF Cranwell. Sometime later it was sold to Doug Arnold who discovered that the aircraft could be returned to airworthy condition and soon set about the task of restoration. Subsequently sold to a new owner in the USA, the Spitfire is currently flying with the Evergreen Aviation Museum at McMinnville, Oregon, registered as N356TE.

Mosquito B.35, TA639, seen parked in 4 Hangar in late 1965, not long before the cracked glue joints were discovered. (*Ray Deacon*)

The second Spitfire to guard Rissy's gate was LF.XVIe, TE356. Subsequently sold on the civilian market, the aircraft was restored to airworthy condition in the USA. (*MAP*)

CHAPTER 12

Little Rissington Postscript

Royal Irish Rangers

Some time after Little Rissington was handed over to the Army, Sqn Ldr Dick Storer, one-time "Red Arrows" Team Manager, was working in his office at the MoD when a chap walked in who turned out to be the CO of the battalion then based at Rissy. *"I said to him, 'You lucky people, the RAF wept when we left there. It is such a wonderful place to be stationed'. He looked at me with an unsmiling face and said, 'You obviously don't understand soldiers. All they want on a night out is to get drunk, have a fight and find a woman. You can't do that in Bourton-on-the-Water.'"*

The Royal Irish Rangers tenancy at Little Rissington lasted a mere four years before they moved on to their next posting.

USAF Contingency Hospital for Europe

Eric Johnson was assigned to Little Rissington Airfield from 1981 to 1984 as part of a team that planned and created the USAF Contingency Hospital. During this period, Eric lived at 8 Smith-Barry Circus, close to the Officers' Mess and he kindly allowed us to use extracts from his webpage on the Little Rissington website.

For much of the 1980s the married quarters at Little Rissington were occupied by officers and men of the 20th Tactical Fighter Wing (20th TFW) from RAF Upper Heyford and the 'Listening Post' at RAF Croughton. During this period the USAF used many of the wartime technical buildings; the wartime main store was converted into a small medical centre and the armoury was again secured and used for the storage of medical drugs.

However, the main occupant during this period was the United States Air Force Contingency Hospital, an emergency facility available in the event of a major conflict. The duties of the hospital (one of three in the UK – the others being at RAF Bicester, Oxfordshire and RAF Nocton Hall, Lincolnshire) were the procurement and provision of medical equipment to front-line units, and to provide hospital facilities on a large scale, for casualties injured in conflict.

From the outset the Contingency Hospital was established as a detachment of the hospital at RAF Upper Heyford and was renamed several times before settling on the 870th USAF Contingency Hospital. The entire technical site was commandeered to support the prime and ancillary requirements of a military hospital: the hangars as emergency hospital wards and the Officers' Mess as a ward for 'walking wounded'.

One 'D'-type hangar on the main site was completely refurbished at great expense as a hospital unit and equipped with clean air units and ward facilities for up to 1,500 patients. Casualties from any conflict world wide would have been flown first to a casualty clearing centre at Zweibrücken in Germany and onward to one of the three Contingency Hospitals. Little Rissington was provisionally cleared for the operation of C-130 Hercules and C-5A Galaxy aircraft; the aircraft that would have flown them in.

One of the 'C'-type hangars on the MU site, believed to be the second hangar in from the Great Rissington road, had a very sophisticated high-density warehouse system installed and the annexe, on the airfield side, was equipped with an advanced materials management system.

Many other buildings were adapted for the storage of medical equipment, beds, 'emergency personal medical packs' and other essential items such as ambulances.

Once preparations were finished and the Hospital declared operational, it was placed on stand-by as the largest USAF medical facility outside of mainland USA. Medical staff were not assigned to the base at this time, but would have been flown in should an emergency have arisen. To keep everyone on their toes, exercises were regularly held when 'casualties' were brought in from a fictional war-zone. The exercises also helped prove the viability of the emergency hospitals and for adjustments to be made to their contingency plans. Due to their high cost, however, at no time was the facility ever tested to its full potential of up to 2,550 patients.

Desert Storm

Following the invasion of Kuwait by allied forces in the late summer of 1990, the decision was taken to activate all four USAF Europe Contingency Hospitals, Little Rissington, Bicester, Nocton Hall and Zweibrücken, as it was anticipated that a ground war with large numbers of casualties would be inevitable. On 30 October, USAF teams began assessments of each of the hospitals, to ensure they were ready should the need arise and Little Rissington and Bicester were declared operational on 14 November 1990.

Numbers 73 and 74 Sopwith Road, formerly semi-detached Airmen's married quarters, were converted to this attractive village store soon after the site was sold. (*Ray Deacon*)

Externally, the change of use was hard to detect. Anyone passing by on the Great Rissington road would have had no idea that the old RAF base had been converted to a huge hospital, ready to handle several hundred casualties a week. Thankfully there were far fewer casualties than had been forecast and none of them were treated at Little Rissington; the facilities in Saudi Arabia and Germany having been able to handle the low number.

The Contingency Hospital at Little Rissington was quietly stood-down late in 1991 and the emergency facility permanently closed during 1992.

From Little Rissington to Upper Rissington

After the Americans departed in 1994, the MoD decided to sell the whole of the north side of Little Rissington, excluding the runways and aircraft aprons, to Country & Metropolitan Homes for redevelopment and this occurred in 1996. The married quarters were sold on to a housing association and, following limited modernisation, most had been snapped up by eager buyers by the turn of the millennium. Two former quarters, Nos. 73 and 74 Sopwith Road, were rebuilt and knocked into one to provide a local village-style shop and this is currently run by a national supermarket chain. Well before the MoD sell-off, both Baldwin and Burnett Blocks had been demolished and the land disposed of for the construction of two exclusive housing complexes.

More recently, all buildings and facilities on a swathe of land south of the former married quarters and north of a line running behind the former Sergeants' Mess and Station HQ, including the barrack blocks, Windrush Club (NAAFI), Cinema, shop, gymnasium and Airmen's tennis courts, were demolished and the land cleared for an up-market housing development. Further housing development has also taken place in the area bounded by the old officers' married quarters.

In 2000, the revitalised 'village' gained a new identity being officially redesignated Upper Rissington.

The airfield site

All three wartime runways remain in situ, as do the miles of perimeter track. Apart from a few hangars that were demolished on the south side of the airfield, all the remaining hangars are still standing and several on the north side are in commercial use. The 'C' type hangar converted for use as a hospital by USAF is currently surrounded by barbed wire, leading to speculation that it could be re-activated in any future conflict.

Looking through the main gate with the Upper Rissington Business Park sign in 2003. The management company has taken great pride in restoring the site to a high standard which no doubt is why much of it is in use by commercial enterprise.
(*inset*) The Officers' and Airmen's married quarters are now privately owned, several having been modernised and extended as depicted in this recent view of Glebe Close. J/T Ray Deacon once lived in the extended corner quarter. (*Ray Deacon*)

Nos. 4 and 3 Hangars, and the old control tower as they are today. An Italian company uses 4 Hangar as its UK base for the importation, packaging and shipment of nuts and dried fruits from its home country to supermarkets around the U.K. (*Ray Deacon*)

The original control tower, which was converted for use as an Operations Block when the new tower was opened in 1962, can still be seen although, like much of the surviving infrastructure, it is in a dilapidated state. The area encompassing the aircraft aprons retains the wire security fencing erected by the Americans.

637 Volunteer Gliding School

The only aircraft flying from Little Rissington now are the Vigilant T.1 motor gliders of No. 637 Volunteer Gliding School. These aircraft are busy most weekends, weather permitting. Flt Lt Matt Lane, whose everyday job is Engineering Officer at RAF Cranwell and is also an instructor on the glider school, wrote the following summary:

"As part of the Air Cadet Organisation's Flying Branch, 637 VGS currently operates 3 Grob 109B motorgliders, Vigilant T.1 in RAF designation, from Little Rissington. The Vigilant is a tailwheel, side-by-side two seater 90hp motorglider which is an excellent introduction to light aircraft flying skills for hundreds of youngsters every year. Although the engine can be shut down in flight to experience true gliding, the Vigilant is effectively operated as a powered aircraft and the aircraft can be seen doing 'circuits and bumps' most weekends as the instructors try in vain to get their charges off solo!

Every year, scores of cadets get their first experience of light aviation by undertaking a Gliding Induction Course. This is a series of 3 short flights, during which cadets progressively learn about the primary flying controls and aircraft handling. Having achieved the age of 16, many cadets return for a Gliding Scholarship. They then attend for flying every weekend with the aim of getting the prized 'silver wings' following a solo circuit. The instructors are all volunteers, with some holding RAFVR commissions and executive appointments. Normal occupations range from policeman to advertising executive, and there are regular RAF volunteers from all ranks and branches.

The VGS operates from the former US Fire Station, located next to the now demolished control tower. A large 'Rubb' semi-permanent hangar is located on the old ASP nearby to house the aircraft. Interestingly, the width of the doors on this are less than the copious wingspan of the Vigilant and an intricate 'wiggle' is necessary to get the aircraft in and out!

A miniature castle, currently located outside the old Station HQ, is believed to have been built by German PoWs in May 1945 outside 5 Hangar. Although in a dilapidated state, the current site owner intends to have it fully restored in the near future. (*Ray Deacon*)

Little Rissington is a challenging airfield for the air cadets to learn at. The turbulence and winds created by the surrounding ridges and terrain make accurate flying crucial, and low-level orographic cloud can sweep in and catch out even the most experienced instructor. In addition, the sloping runways make a good 'three-pointer' a definite challenge! It is perhaps fitting that even in retirement, the airfield is still home to RAF flying training, and that many present and future pilots still have their first taste of aviation at Little Rissington."

Upper Rissington Business Park

Much of the Main Site is now incorporated in the Upper Rissington Business Park – an industrial and commercial enterprise owned by Country & Metropolitan Homes which leases many of the former offices, workshops and hangars to private companies.

The old Guardroom has been converted for use by C&M as its main office and a large sign giving the locations of the various companies stands on the opposite side of the road. Interestingly, the buildings retain the site numbers allocated to them back in 1938. Visitors are allowed onto the Park but access beyond the security fence to the airfield is prohibited. Having fallen into a state of disrepair, it is noticeable that the buildings and grounds are being returned to a standard reminiscent of RAF days; all that is missing are the Spitfire and Harvard. Street names remain as they were in RAF days but the actual signs were replaced by the brown style favoured by the Americans.

The Officers' Mess

This once elegant building has at various times been proposed for conversion to a hotel, conference centre, leisure and office complex, but no firm decision has been taken, as of yet, on its future. Until then it will be allowed to continue to deteriorate and is now in such a dilapidated condition that it would cost a small fortune to renovate.

Speculation on the airfield's future

During the early summer of 2004, a number of RAF Lyneham-based Hercules aircraft landed at Little Rissington during an exercise, enforcing local rumours that when Lyneham closes Little Rissington will be reactivated as a relief landing ground and for training purposes by the Hercules squadrons.

The once impressive Officers' Mess may be boarded up and in a shabby state after a decade of disuse, but the possibility of it being converted into an office complex, conference centre or hotel may hopefully come to fruition in the near future. (*Ray Deacon*)

APPENDIX 1

Course Dates and Trophy Winners

CFS Flying Instructors Courses at RAF Little Rissington

Course Numbers and Months of Completion

Year	Jan	Feb	Mar	Apr	May	Jun	Jul	Aug	Sep	Oct	Nov	Dec	Total
1946						91		92	93		94		4
1947	95+96				97	98	99	100		101			7
1948	102			103			104			105			4
1949	106		107		108	109		110			111		6
1950	112		113		114		115	116		117	118		7
1951	119	120	121	122	123	124	125	126+127	128	129+130	131	132+133	15
1952	134	135+136	137	138	139	140	141	142	143	144+145		146	13
1953	147	148	149	150+151		152	153	154	155	156		157	11
1954		158	159		160		161	162			163	164	7
1955		165	166	167		168	169	170		171	172		8
1956	173	174		175	176	177		178	179	180		181	9
1957	182		183	184		185	186		187+188			189	8
1958		190		191		192			193		194		5
1959				195	196	197			198			199	5
1960			200	201			202		203		204		5
1961		205		206		207			208		209		5
1962		210		211		212		213			214		5
1963		215			216	217			218		219		5
1964	220			221		222		223		224			5
1965	225			226		227		228		229			5
1966	230		231			232		233		234			5
1967	235		236		237		238			239		240	6
1968			241		242		243		244			245	5
1969			246		247			248		249			4
1970	250		251				252			253			4
1971	254			255			256			257		258	5
1972				259			260			261			3
1973	262			263			264		265				4
1974	266			267			268			269			4
1975	270		271			272		273			274		5
1976		275		276									2

Trophies competed for at CFS

The Brabyn Trophy

Brabyn trophy First awarded in 1953, the Brabyn Trophy was initially presented for the best individual aerobatic display by a student on the advanced part of the course. In 1962, before Course No. 213, the competition was re-categorised as an annual aerobatic competition for CFS staff instructors

The CFS Trophy

CFS trophy The CFS Trophy was presented to the Central Flying School by No. 101 Course when graduating in October 1947. It is awarded to the best all round student throughout the Course, on the recommendation of the Commandant. This award is not automatic and is only made when the Commandant is satisfied that a sufficiently high standard has been achieved

Clarkson trophy The Clarkson is the oldest CFS Trophy and incorporates an Avro 504K biplane, made of silver. It was presented to the Central Flying School in 1929 by Flying Officer C. Clarkson who served as an instructor on the unit and subsequently became the founding CFS Association Secretary. Initially it was a trophy for inter-flight aerobatics but after 1935 was awarded to the best all-round pilot on the course. Since the second world war the Clarkson has been awarded to the best individual aerobatic display by a student on the Applied Basic part of the course

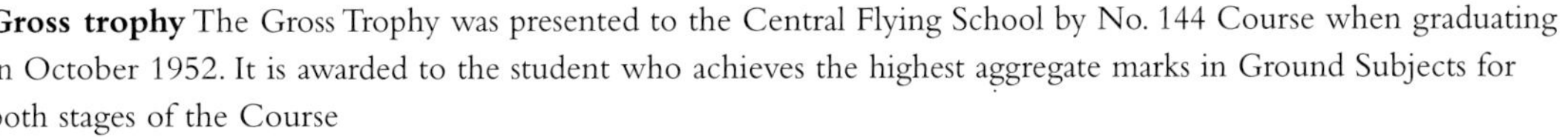

Gross trophy The Gross Trophy was presented to the Central Flying School by No. 144 Course when graduating in October 1952. It is awarded to the student who achieves the highest aggregate marks in Ground Subjects for both stages of the Course

The Gross Trophy

Hopewell trophy The Hopewell Trophy is presented to a student instructor for the best overall instructional ability

No.250 trophy As the name implies, No. 250 Trophy was first competed for by No. 250 course and is awarded to the student instructor with the highest marks for navigation

Wright Jubilee trophy Presented in 1953 by the Royal Air Forces Association to commemorate the 50th anniversary of powered flight, the Wright Jubilee trophy, first awarded in 1954, was competed for annually by a selected flying instructor from each of the jet flying training schools and RAF College, Cranwell, with the School of Refresher Flying at Manby included until its function was subsumed within CFS. The competition, which took the form of compulsory aerobatics, interspersed by voluntary manoeuvres in a continuous sequence, was held at Little Rissington each summer

The Clarkson Trophy

Central Flying School Trophy Winners

Brabyn Trophy for students – pre Course No. 213

Course	Winner	Course	Winner	Course	Winner	Course	Winner
138	Sgt Warden	157	Not awarded	176	Fg Off R.E. Holloway	195	Not awarded
139	Fg Off G.G. Farley	158	Plt Off K.S. O'Brien	177	Not awarded	196	Not awarded
140	Plt Off Bienick	159	Plt Off A.H.C. Back	178	Not Awarded	197	Not awarded
141	Plt Off D.E. Kinsey	160	Flt Lt R.R. Watson	179	Flt Lt D.P. English	198	Fg Off A.J.R. Doyle
142	Plt Off Bones	161	Sqn Ldr G.W.W. Waddington	180	Fg Off W.C. Mackison	199	Lt B.J. Bullivant RN
143	Flt Lt T.J. Doe	162	Fg Off A.R. Wardell	181	Fg Off P.G.C. Edwards	200	Not awarded
144	Flt Lt J.F. Walker	163	Flt Lt E.F. Hemming	182	Flt Lt B.W. Weskett	201	Fg Off D.E.A. Rees
145	Plt Off R.P. Woodward	164	Fg Off G.J. Bennett	183	Flt Lt B.B. Sharman	202	Fg Off D.E. Betts
146	Not Awarded	165	Fg Off B. Clayton	184	Flt Lt D.F. Moffat	203	Lt A.R.D. Copeland RN
147	Fg Off D.B. Craig	166	Fg Off N.R.C. Price	185	Fg Off J.A.D. Bradshaw	204	Not Awarded
148	Plt Off H.M. Archer	167	Fg Off J.M.D. Cowell	186	Fg Off D.J. Fewell	205	Not Awarded
149	Plt Off A. Bannerman	168	Flt Lt A.D.R. Dawes	187	Fg Off A.E. Pearce	206	Plt Off B.K. Walton
150	Plt Off G.J.A. Kerr	169	Fg Off M. Kemp	188	Fg Off V.W. Small	207	Flt Lt D.G. Hazell
151	Flt Lt Hughes	170	Fg Off C.B. Lewis	189	Flt Lt J.H. Gardner	208	Flt Lt J.G. McCluney
152	Flt Lt Saunders	171	Fg Off L.H. Harrison	190	Flt Lt D.H. Mills	209	Not Awarded
153	Fg Off Hall	172	Fg Off A.D. Saddington	191	Lt J.F.H.C. deWinton RN	210	Not Awarded
154	Plt Off Webster	173	Fg Off R.E. Chitty	192	Flt Lt D.A. Proctor	211	Not Awarded
155	Plt Off J.A. Wellerd	174	Flt Lt G.F.G. Dakyns	193	Fg Off E.W. Hopkins	212	Not Awarded
156	Lt Howard RN	175	Fg Off R.N. Rumbelow	194	Flt Lt J.R. Ayres		

Brabyn Trophy for instructors – annually from August 1962

Year	Winner	Year	Winner	Year	Winner	Year	Winner
1962	Flt Lt B.H. Dale	1966	Flt Lt R. Cope-Lewis	1970	Maj L.A. Hopgood USAF	1974	Not Awarded
1963	Not Awarded	1967	Flt Lt J. Merry	1971	Flt Lt R. Howell	1975	Flt Lt J.B. Swinhoe
1964	Not Awarded	1968	Maj J.K. Snow USAF	1972	Flt Lt M.A. Telford	1976	Flt Lt I. Hill
1965	Flt Lt R.K.J. Hadlow	1969	Flt Lt W.A.M. Tait	1973	Flt Lt I. Reilly		

CFS Trophy

Course	Winner	Course	Winner	Course	Winner	Course	Winner
101	Sqn Ldr L.J. Bunce	144	Flt Lt D.O. Luke	189	Flt Lt W.E. Waite	234	Flt Lt N.R.W. Whitling
102	Fg Off B.K. Chambra	145	Flt Lt D.C. Smith	190	Fg Off D.G. Murchie	235	Flt Lt J.E. Brown
103	Sqn Ldr S. Grant	146	Lt D.L. Crofts RN	191	Flt Lt R. Langstaff	236	Flt Lt B. Potter
104	Flt Lt L.L. Harland	147	Fg Off R.J. Bannard	192	Fg Off B.C. Farrer	237	Flt Lt P.P. Gilroy
105	Lt S.J.A. Richardson RN	148	Fg Off A. Turner	193	Fg Off A. Fraser	238	Flt Lt P.J. Wilkinson
106	Flt Lt F. Symmons	149	Flt Lt A.G. Whitbread	194	Fg Off B.J. Jones	239	Flt Lt R.K. Piggott
107	Lt M.A. Tibby RN	150	Plt Off R.J. Stroatfield	195	Fg Off J.F.C. Mayes	240	Flt Lt M.J. Phillips
108	Flt Lt F.J. Vickers	151	Flt Lt A. Tavanyar	196	Flt Lt P.D.G. Terry	241	Flt Lt R.B. Duckett
109	Sqn Ldr A.J. Hill	152	Sqn Ldr F.R. Foster	197	Fg Off K.F. Beck	242	Flt Lt R.J. Howard
110	Flt Lt Allen	153	Sqn Ldr E.A. Fairhurst	198	Fg Off B.W. Saunders	243	Flt Lt D.C. Coldicutt
111	Fg Off Ross	154	Fg Off A.K.E. Ibett	199	Plt Off R.J. Kemble	244	Capt A.A. Hussein RJAF
112	Sqn Ldr Pye	155	Sqn Ldr R.G. Knott	200	Flt Lt M.K. Adams	245	Fg Off H.V. Lether
113	Lt G.B. Newby RN	156	Flt Lt R. Dicker	201	Fg Off G.A. Smart	246	Plt Off D.R. Carvell
114	Fl Lt P.G. Honeyman	157	Flt Lt R.G. Ridley	202	Fg Off K.A. Ball	247	Flt Lt J. Staniforth
115	Flt Lt H.O. Forth	158	Flt Lt R.D. Doe	203	Flt Lt A. Tyldesley	248	Flt Lt A.M. Lovett
116	Sqn Ldr J.B.A. Fleming	159	Fg Off S. Pomfret	204	Flt Lt R.W. Glover	249	Flt Lt D.J. Hamilton-Rump
	Flt Lt N.R. Moss	160	Plt Off J.M. Henderson	205	Flt Lt R.B. Gubbins	250	Capt J.J. Wright Aust AVN
117	Flt Lt P.D.C. Street	161	Sqn Ldr G.W.W. Waddington	206	Lt D.M.L. McWilliam RN	251	Flt Lt A.H. Blake
118	Flt Lt R.J. Hough	162	Fg Off D.R.J. Hall	207	Flt Lt D.A.V. Johnson	252	Flt Lt W. Purchase
119	Flt Lt J.L. Bayley	163	Flt Lt A.H. Turner	208	Flt Lt B.A. Stead	253	Flt Lt P.T. Squire
120	Flt Lt A.D. Dick	164	Flt Lt W.E. Kelly	209	Flt Lt W.J.A. Innes	254	Flt Lt M.R. Hall
121	Flt Lt A.J. Steele	165	Fg Off P.B. Hine	210	Plt Off N.R. Hayward	255	Flt Lt K.R. Jackson
122	Sqn Ldr A. Mc Steedman	166	Fg Off L.J. Roberts	211	Flt Lt J.T.S. Lewis	256	Sqn Ldr D.I. Oakden
123	Flt Lt J. Towler	167	Flt Lt C.P. Francis	212	Flt Lt F.A. Mallet	257	Flt Lt M.N. Sawyer
124	Lt R.C. Stock RN	168	Flt Lt R.S. Eyre	213	Flt Lt J.B. Parkinson	258	Flt Lt W.L. Green
125	Flt Lt D.S. Bell	169	Fg Off D.T. Stephenson	214	Flt Lt B.A. Mitchell	259	Flt Lt G.L.S. Dyer
126	Flt Lt D.M. Scrimgeour	170	Flt Lt L.A. Stapleton	215	Flt Lt J.H. Harris	260	Flt Lt K.W. Jarvis
127	Flt Lt J. Corbishley	171	Fg Off P. Blake	216	Flt Lt J. Gibbon	261	Flt Lt J.D. Aldington
128	Flt Lt A.D. Lockyer	172	Fg Off D.J.R. Beard	217	Flt Lt P.J. Maitland	262	Fg Off F.L. Hart
129	Flt Lt K. Green	173	Fg Off R.A.E. Dunn	218	Lt J. Manley RN	263	Flt Lt C.P. Lumb
130	Flt Lt M.A. McNeile	174	Fg Off P.D. Austin	219	Plt Off W.I. Parker	264	Flt Lt S.J. Gowling
	Flt Lt J.F.W. Pembridge	175	Fg Off D. McClen	220	Flt Lt G.B. Browne	265	Flt Lt P.N.O. Plunkett
131	Flt Lt J. Cartwright	176	Lt C.S. Casperd RN	221	Flt Lt R.M. Turner	266	Flt Lt M.R. Cornwell
132	Fg Off R.D. Hillary	177	Fg Off W.J. Packer	222	Flt Lt J.N. Puckering	267	Flt Lt J.D. Kennedy
133	Flt Lt W. Park	178	Flt Lt R. Garland	223	Flt Lt B. Wooler	268	Flt Lt M.B. Stoner
134	Flt Lt D.H. Bennett	179	Lt A.H. Milnes RN	224	Flt Lt R. Cloke	269	Flt Lt R. McKendrick
135	Flt Lt J.R. Ritchie	180	Fg Off R.B.R. Dillon	225	Sqn Ldr R.J. Coleman	270	Flt Lt I.C. Lawrence
136	Wg Cdr D. Peveler	181	Plt Off D. Wells	226	Flt Lt G.W. Rushforth	271	Flt Lt P.G. Barton
137	Flt Lt I.K. Salter	182	Fg Off P.J. Hirst	227	Flt Lt R. Kidney	272	Flt Lt R. Handfield
138	Sqn Ldr A.W. Horne	183	Fg Off R. Wells	228	Flt Lt J. Nesbitt	273	Flt Lt J.N.L. Grisdale
139	Fg Off J. Primrose	184		229	Flt Lt B.E.C. Forse	274	Flt Lt G.B. Gray
140	Flt Lt M.F. Aldersmith	185	Fg Off D.R. Carr	230	Flt Lt F.K. Lundy	275	Flt Lt A.M. Keane
141	Lt V.A. Winterbotham RN	186	Fg Off D.J. Fewell	231	Flt Lt J. Delafield	276	Flt Lt P.R. Webb
142	Flt Lt J. Morgan	187	Flt Lt T. Parsons	232	Flt Lt A.J. Fairweather		
143	Flt Lt J.F. Manning	188	Flt Lt D. Mullarkey	233	Flt Lt W.P. Jago		

Clarkson Trophy

Course	Winner	Course	Winner	Course	Winner	Course	Winner
100	Flt Lt J.R. Gibbons	145	Plt Off M.A. Rasheed	190	Flt Lt D.A. Briggs	235	Lt C.J. Blower RN
101	Fg Off D.B. Piggott RIAF	146	Flt Lt B.T.S. Jones	191	Fg Off I.K. McKee	236	Flt Lt I.C.H. Dick
102	Lt J.O. Rowbottom RN	147	Lt A. Haidar Syrian AF	192	Flt Lt R. Humphreyson	237	Flt Lt M.N. Evans
103	Fg Off W.D. McNeil RIAF	148	Com Plt D.I. Collingwood	193	Flt Lt A.C. Ramsay	238	Fg Off J.J. Pook
104	Fg Off J. de M. Severne	149	Lt P.E. Bailey RN	194	Flt Lt R.T. Stock	239	Fg Off R.N. Kennedy
105	Flt Lt G.A. McDonald RCAF	150	Sgt C.J.B. Murdock	195	Not awarded	240	Lt T.J.H. Kedge RN
106	Fg Off N.W. KhanRPAF	151	Plt Off R. Bagshaw	196	Flt Lt G.S. Cameron	241	Fg Off J.L. Bishop
107	Fg Off F.M. Hosain	152	Sgt A.M. Webster	197	Fg Off J.A. Carter	242	Fg Off S. Robinson
108	Lt C.J. Lavender RN	153	Flt Lt A.E. Richmond	198	Flt Lt M.E. Kerr	243	Flt Lt H.H. Moses
109	Plt J. Plasil Czech	154	Flt Lt F.L. Latham	199	Plt Off R.J. Kemball	244	Fg Off R.A. Sargeant
110	Fg Off G.H. Farley	155	Sqn Ldr R.D. Gallanders	200	Not awarded	245	Fg Off H.V. Lether
111	Fg Off V.P. Hegde RIAF	156	Lt J.M. Barbour RN	201	Fg Off R.T. Foster	246	Plt Off D.R. Carvell
112	Fg Off H.C. Sahgal	157	Flt Lt P.A. Gifkins	202	Flt Lt H.W.J. Rigg	247	Lt G.A. Richardson RN

Course	Winner
113	Flt Lt B.N. Byrne
114	Fg Off T.W.F. De Sallis
115	Lt A.H. Smith RN
116	Flt Lt L.C. Glover
117	Flt Lt P.D.G. Street
118	Fg Off Abbasi RPAF
119	Flt Sgt F. Tomczak
120	Flt Lt A.D. Dick
121	Sgt P. Clark
122	Sqn Ldr A.M. Steedman
123	Capt Stern Israeli AF
124	Sgt G. deLouze
125	Plt Off F.G.H. Smith
126	Flt Lt D.M. Scrimgeour
127	Plt Off C. Bart
128	Flt Lt G.G. Smith
129	Flt Lt J.E. Bellingham
130	Sgt W.H. Black
131	Not awarded
132	Capt I. Yavneh IAF
133	Flt Lt R.H. Bennett
134	Com Plt P. Harvey RN
135	Flt Lt J.R. Ritchie
136	Fg Off K.P. Kelleher
137	Flt Lt B.S.E. Beattie
138	Fg Off G.C. Morton
139	Flt Lt K.I. Dolicher
140	Plt Off B.W. Woodfield
141	Lt J.A. Winterbotham RN
142	Com Plt R.A. Lister RN
143	Sqn Ldr C.H. Dyson
144	Plt Off J.S. Bates
158	Plt Off K.S. O'Brien
159	Fg Off P.H. Crawshaw
160	Flt Lt J.H.W. Grobler
161	Fg Off J.K. Jones
162	Fg Off A.E. Sadler
163	Flt Lt R. Hollingworth
164	Fg Off G.J. Bennett
165	Fg Off P.B. Hine
166	Fg Off N.R.C. Price
167	Fg Off C.T. Lake
168	Fg Off R. Dick
169	Fg Off D.L. Davies
170	Fg Off C.P. Lewis
171	Flt Lt J.M. McMinn
172	Fg Off J.L. Martin
173	Lt A.C.R. Fane RN
174	Fg Off J.D. Penrose
175	Fg Off R.N. Rumbelow
176	Fg Off F.W.H. Seaton
177	Flt Lt D.M.A. Samuels
178	Not Awarded
179	Fg Off K. Levitt
180	Fg Off W.C. Mackison
181	Flt Lt J.R. Rhind
182	Fg Off C.M. Christie
183	Flt Lt M.S. Langley
184	Not awarded
185	Flt Lt W.A. Gallienne
186	Fg Off D.F. Huggett
187	Fg Off C.E.W. Osborne
188	Fg Off S.G. Corps
189	Flt Lt N. Clayton
203	Flt Lt I.C.R. McIntosh
204	Flt Lt A.G. Newing
205	Not awarded
206	Flt Lt H.J.D. Prince
207	Flt Lt J.E.F. Hardcastle
208	Flt Lt P.D. Jennings
209	Flt Lt R.T.A. Innes
210	Flt Lt J.H. Newell
211	Not awarded
212	Flt Lt M.J.T. Heath
213	Lt A.T. Pinney RN
214	Not awarded
215	Not awarded
216	Flt Lt L. Jones
217	Flt Lt E.J. Nance
218	Fg Off A.G. Cleaver
219	Not awarded
220	Not awarded
221	Not awarded
222	Not awarded
223	Fg Off W.D. MacGillivray
224	Flt Lt A.I. Hickling
225	Flt Lt T.F.H Mermagen
226	Fg Off B.A.C. Chapple
227	Flt Lt A.A. MacKay
228	Flt Lt R.G. Macintosh
229	Flt Lt P.J. Blewitt
230	Flt Lt R.J. Manning
231	Flt Lt E.E. Jones
232	Flt Lt T.J. Burns
233	Flt Lt R.E. Pyrah
234	Flt Lt N.R.W. Whitling
248	Fg Off P.S. Owen
249	Fg Off W.A. Curtis
250	Flt Lt T.F.K. Miller
251	Fg Off M. Bowman
252	Flt Lt J.D. Clark
253	Flt Lt P.T. Squire
254	Not Flown
255	Not Flown
256	Sqd Ldr D.I. Oakden
257	Fg Off P.C. Hood
258	Not awarded
259	Flt Lt E.T.M. Danks
260	Flt Lt M. Underdown
261	Fg Off P.S. West
262	Flt Lt H.G. MacKay
263	Flt Lt D.L. Webley
264	Flt Lt R.H. Buncher
265	Flt Lt A. Moffat RN
266	Not awarded
267	Not awarded
268	Not awarded
269	Flt Lt P.J. Wood
270	Flt Lt R.A. Cole
271	Flt Lt A.K. Bryan
272	Flt Lt M.C. Hulyer
273	Flt Lt C. Hulyer
274	Flt Lt J.M. Leigh
275	Flt Lt R.M. Thomas
276	Flt Lt R. Lapraik

De Havilland Trophy (Chipmunk)

Course	Winner
225	Flt Lt P.L. Miller
226	Flt Lt D. Ward
227	Flt Lt G.S.R. Webb
228	Flt Lt C.H. Hilditch
229	Flt Lt R.B. Nelson
230	
231	Flt Lt P. Jones
232	Flt Lt T.L. Anderson
233	Fg Off R.S. Burrows
234	Capt A.S. Calder RE
235	Flt Lt A.C. Dix
236	Flt Lt J.C. Murray
237	Flt Lt P.J. Wilkinson
238	Flt Lt M.S.J. McKinley
239	Flt Lt C.R. Adams
240	
241	Flt Lt A.F.C. Hunter
242	Flt Lt D.M. Jones
243	Flt Lt A.C.C. Mason
244	Flt Lt C.J. Booth
245	Flt Lt J.H.M. Adam
246	Flt Lt R.T. Howell
247	Flt Lt A.T.H. Taylor
248	Flt Lt G.W. Morriss
249	Flt Lt V.C. Robertson
250	Flt Lt R.G. Davis
251	Flt. LT G. S. Foster
252	Fg Off F. Tiernan
253	Lt J.W. Bond RN
254	Lt E.D. Driver RAA
255	Flt Lt G. Dunn
256	Flt Lt G.B.N. McMurray
257	Lt N.W. Thomas RN
258	Flt Lt S.T. Logan
259	Flt Lt G.N. Dryland
260	Lt T. Bennett RN
261	Maj C.T. Barnett
262	Flt Lt C.P. Lumb
263	Flt Lt A.M. Tomalin
264	Flt Lt R.J.H. Fallis

Gross Trophy

Course	Winner
145	Fg Off R.J.P. Miers
146	Lt D.L. Crofts RN
147	Flt Lt J.F.M. Widmer
148	Flt Lt R.H.D. Dulieu
149	Flt Lt A.G. Whitbread
150	Flt Lt B. Day
151	Plt Off D.G. Slade
152	Fg Off J.D. Burgess
153	Fg Off P.O.R. Major
154	Fg Off A.K.E. Ibett
155	Sqn Ldr R.G. Knott
156	Flt Lt E.N. Barrington-Reinganum
157	Flt Lt G.R. Baxter
158	Plt Off R.J. Johnson
159	Fg Off R.H. Banff
160	Fg Off P. McDarmour
161	Lt G.A. Rowan-Thompson RN
162	Fg Off A.R. Wardell
163	Fg Off E.D. Mee
164	Flt Lt W.E. Kelly
165	Fg Off C.W. Curtis
166	Fg Off L.J. Roberts
178	Flt Lt R. Garland
179	Flt Lt S.E. King
180	Flt Lt B. Huxley
181	Flt Lt J.R. Rhind
182	Lt M.H. Coles RN
183	Fg Off R. Wells
184	Fg Off C.P. Sanderson
185	Fg Off D.R. Carr
186	Flt Lt G.C. Hutchinson
187	Fg Off A.B. Musgrave
188	Fg Off D.B. Hopkins
189	Flt Lt L.J. Otley
190	Flt Lt D.H. Mills
191	Flt Lt M.F. Goodwin
192	Fg Off R.D. Williamson
193	Fg Off R.E. Garwood
194	Flt Lt J.L. Spatcher
195	Fg Off T.H. Whittingham
196	Flt Lt P.D.G. Terry
197	Flt Lt I.D. Brimson
198	Flt Lt G. Roberts
199	Flt Lt R.E.W. Loverseed
200	Flt Lt M.K. Adams
212	Flt Lt D.V. Duval
213	Flt Lt M.N. Bond
214	Fg Off J.D. Blake
215	Sqn Ldr H.D. Iles
216	Flt Lt K.L. Hart
217	Flt Lt P.J. Maitland
218	Lt J. Manley RN
219	Plt Off W.I. Parker
220	Flt Lt D.J. Loveridge
221	Flt Lt D.J. Phillips
222	Flt Lt J.N. Puckering
223	Flt Lt B. Wooler
224	Flt Lt R. Jones
225	Sqn Ldr R.J. Coleman
226	Fg Off B.A. Salter
227	Flt Lt R. Kidney
228	Flt Lt D.M. Holliday
229	Flt Lt P.G. Pinney
230	Flt Lt M.J. Gibson
231	Lt C.A. Wheal RN
232	Fg Off J. Rudkins
233	Flt Lt A.A. Clark
234	Flt Lt D. Brooks
245	Flt Lt P.C. Norris
246	Plt Off D.R. Carvell
247	Flt Lt J.E. Jeffrey
248	Flt Lt K.G. Pollard
249	Fg Off W.A. Wainwright
250	Flt Lt T.F.K. Miller
251	Flt Lt A.H. Blake
252	Fg Off C.R. Ailkins
253	Flt Lt N. Crow
254	Flt Lt M.R. Hall
255	Flt Lt J.A. Foster
256	Sqn Ldr D.I. Oakden
257	Flt Lt J.E. Budd
258	Flt Lt W.L. Green
259	Flt Lt G.L.S. Dyer
260	Flt Lt T.P. Newman
261	Flt Lt J.H. Nutkins
262	Fg Off F.L. Hart
263	Flt Lt C.P. Lumb
264	Flt Lt R.A. Weetman
265	Lt C.K. Lee RSAF
266	Flt Lt P.C. Lee-Preston
267	Flt Lt D.G. Hawkins

167	Flt Lt T.A. Bennett
168	Flt Lt R.S. Eyre
169	Fg Off D.T. Stephenson
170	Flt Lt T. Davies
171	Fg Off P. Blake
172	Fg Off V.J. Nickson
173	Fg Off R.A.E. Dunn
174	Flt Lt M. Edwards
175	Flt Lt J.R. Aitken
176	Flt Lt A.P. Trowbridge
177	Fg Off F.W.J. Packer
201	Fg Off M.T. Chapman
202	Fg Off K.A. Ball
203	Flt Lt A. Tyldesley
204	Flt Lt R.W. Glover
205	Flt Lt R.B.Gubbins
206	Lt DM.L. McWilliam RN
207	Flt Lt D.A.V. Johnson
208	Flt Lt T.E. Gill
209	Flt Lt W.J. Innes
210	Fg Off A.P.W. Weiss
211	Flt Lt J.T.S. Lewis
235	Flt Lt F.G. Marshall
236	Flt Lt B. Potter
	Flt Lt A.C. Dix
237	Flt Lt P. Millar
238	Flt Lt R.K. Piggott
239	Flt Lt R.L. Joyce
240	Flt Lt M.J. Phillips
241	Flt Lt R.B. Duckett
242	Flt Lt I.E.D. Montgomerie
243	Fg Off T.V. Rogers
244	Flt Lt W.N. Blair-Hickman
268	Flt Lt P.R. Morley
269	Flt Lt R. McKendrick
270	Flt Lt R. Rackham
271	Flt Lt C.J. Taylor
272	Flt Lt D. Long
273	Flt Lt K.A. Jones
274	Flt Lt C.B. Gray
275	Flt Lt N.C.L. Hudson
276	Flt Lt Stacey

Hopewell Trophy

Course	Winner
225	Sqn Ldr R.J. Coleman
226	Plt Off B.A.C. Chapple
227	Fg Off L.J.E. Pinches
	Fg Off I.R. Spring
228	Fg Off P.G. Macintosh
229	Flt Lt B.E.C. Forse
230	Flt Lt F.K. Lundy
231	Flt Lt J. Delafield
232	Lt D.J. Starling RN
233	Flt Lt W.P. Jago
234	Flt Lt K. Winstanley
235	Flt Lt J.E. Brown
236	Flt Lt B. Potter
237	Lt D.R.G. Brittain
238	Flt Lt P.J. Wilkinson
239	Flt Lt D.R.G. Brittain
240	Fg Off K.J. Tait
241	Flt Lt R.B. Duckett
242	Flt Lt R.J. Howard
243	Flt Lt D.C. Coldicutt
244	Capt A.A. Hussein RJAF
245	Fg Off H.V. Lether
246	Flt Lt J.J. Blower
247	Flt Lt R.J. Dix
248	Flt Lt A.M. Lovett
249	Flt Lt D.J. Hamilton-Rump
250	Flt Lt I.D. MacFadyen
251	Flt Lt J.D. Kendrick
252	Flt Lt W. Purchase
253	Flt Lt P.T. Squire
254	Lt A.J. Crabb RN
255	Flt Lt R.K. Jackson
256	Sqn Ldr D.I. Oakden
257	Flt Lt M.N. Sawyer
258	Flt Lt W.L. Green
259	Flt Lt G.L.S. Dyer
260	W O I.L. Cornall
261	Flt Lt J.D. Aldington
262	Lt P. Chaplin RN
263	Flt Lt R.L. Dilworth
264	Flt Lt R.S. Munyard
265	Flt Lt V.A. Burt
266	Flt Lt M.R. Cornwell
267	Flt Lt J.D. Kennedy
268	Flt Lt M.B. Stoner
269	Flt Lt I.J. Sanford
270	Flt Lt I.C. Lawrence
271	Flt Lt C.W.D. Watson
272	Flt Lt R. Handfield
273	Flt Lt J.N.J. Grisdale
274	Flt Lt G.B. Gray
275	Flt Lt A.M. Keane
276	Flt Lt P.R. Webb

No. 250 Trophy

Course	Winner
250	Not awarded
251	Not awarded
252	Flt Lt W. Purchase
253	Fg Off J.A. Duckworth
254	Not awarded
255	Flt Lt G.L. Reynolds
256	Sqn Ldr D.I. Oakden
257	Flt Lt E.G.C. Rouse
258	Not awarded
259	Flt Lt D.G. Cadwallader
260	Flt Lt I.F. Clark
261	Lt M.C. Hagen RN
262	Flt Lt A.B. Fuller
263	Flt Lt R.L. Dilworth
264	Flt Lt I.S. Corbitt
265	Fg Off G.I. Hannam
266	Not awarded
267	Not flown
268	Flt Lt M.B. Stoner
269	Flt Lt I.J. Sanford
270	Flt Lt R.A. Cole
271	Flt Lt C.W.D. Watson
272	FLt Lt R.A. Mott
273	Flt Lt J.N.J. Grisdale
274	Flt Lt F.W. Foster
275	Flt Lt R.M. Thomas
276	Flt Lt P.R. Webb

Wright Jubilee Trophy

Year	Winner
1954	Fg Off R.P.V. Woodward
1955	Plt Off D.J. Lowery
	Flt Lt R. Dick
1956	Fg Off R.N. Rumblelow
1957	Fg Off G. Rorison
1958	Flt Lt R.E. Holloway
1959	Flt Lt D.P. Moffat
1960	Fg Off G. Rorison
1961	Flt Lt D.A. Proctor
1962	Flt Lt D.A. Proctor
1963	Fg Off T.J. Nash
1964	Flt Lt P.D. Jarvis
1965	Flt Lt P.D. Jarvis
1966	Flt Lt R. Turner
1967	Flt Lt R.E. Pyrah
1968	Flt Lt Bell
1969	
1970	Fg Off P. Dandeker
1971	Flt Lt P.C. Norris
1972	Flt Lt P.T. Squire
1973	Flt Lt W.F.C. Tyndall
1974	Flt Lt Ryott
1975	Flt Lt K. Marshall

APPENDIX 2

Facts and Figures

Monthly average Flying, Flights, Landings & Movements

Sampled months in calculated averages	(12) 1956	(41) 1957-60	(11) 1961	(12) 1964	(24) 1966-67	(12) 1971	(12) 1974	March 1976
Hours flown	999	1284	1665	1664	1643	1579	1193	1384
includes Night %	5.3%	4.4%	4.1%	4.5%	n.k.	n.k.	n.k.	n.k.
Flights	1228	1402	1708	1532	1666			
Av. Sortie (mins)	49	55	59	65	59			
Landings	3143	3446	3987	4407	3949	3959	3144	3472
Av. Landings per hr	3.1	2.7	2.4	2.7	2.4	2.5	2.6	2.5
Landings per sortie	2.6	2.5	2.3	2.9	2.4	n.k.	n.k.	n.k.
Movements	4450+	4380+	5044	5807	6676	6737		
includes Night %	n.k.	10%	14%	9%	10%	10%		
Jet % movements	89.5%	51.6%	71.9%	72.3%	76.5%	60.6%		
Piston % movements	10.5%	48.4%	28.1%	27.7%	23.5%	39.4%		
Night% jet movements	n.k.	10%	15%	7%	8%	9%		
Night% piston movements		9%	12%	13%	!2%	11%		

Footnotes: In 1948-49 and 1950-51 monthly flying hours (including night percentage) averaged 1775 (9.6%) and 3,140 (5.3%) respectively. In 1961 a monthly average total of 12 Flying Training Command, 13 CFS staff and 8 student instructors received Hunter F Mk4 check outs, several being already Hunter qualified.
In later years flight sorties were no longer recorded in Little Rissington Form 540s.

Monthly aircraft Utilisation hours & Serviceability percentage rates by type 1956-1976

Years sampled 1956-1976	Aircraft Type & Mark	Utilisation hours per a/c & av. month	Relevant years in sample	Average Percentage Serviceability Rate (years are from limited comparable records)			
				1956-58	1959-61	1964	1973-74
				%	%	%	%
1957-1964	Provost T.1	32.6	9	65.3	71.7	82	
1960-1976(Mar)	Chipmunk T.10	30.8	16+		67.3	76	64.4
1952-1971	Jet Provost T.4	30.6	10			both	
1960-1976(Mar)	Jet Provost T.3/3A*	29.8	16		52.3	64	57.2/63.4*
1970-1976(Mar)	Jet Provost T.5/5A*	29.5	6+				57.9/66.4*
1956-1960	Meteor T.7	27.1	5	61.0	50.5	68	65.4
1973-1976(Mar)	Bulldog T.1	25.6	3+				51.1
1959-1973	Varsity T.1	24.9	15		46.5	53	45.8
1956-1960	Vampire T.11	22.6	5	55.3	53.7	76	57.8
1962-1976(Mar)	Gnat Course	21.8	14+			38	43.0
1956-1960	Valetta C.1	20.3	5	47.3	41.5:59/60		
1956/7-1962	Hunter F.4	19.4	7	58.0	50.7		
1956-1965	Vampire T.11	18.6	10	55.3	53,7	76	57.8
1956-1970	Meteor T.7	18.5	15	61.0	50.5	68	65.4
1957-1961	Canberra T.4	17.6	5	41:57/58			
1956-1964	Anson C.19	15.6	9	57.3	53.3	(73)	
1965-1976(Mar)	Gnat Red Arrows	15.3	11+ :short years				65.6
1961-1962	Hunter T.7	14.7	2		38:1959		
1959-1960	Jet Provost T.1	7.7	2	51in1958	59:59/60		
1973-1975	Jetstream T.1	(very low)	(inadequate)				32in74

Footnotes: Figures are calculated by dividing the sum of raw annual monthly averages per type per year, although the Serviceability table has values for the shorter periods listed. The Red Arrows were role specific, with their Gnat utilisation hours reduced by an intensive shorter working year and demands for display availability. The validity of utilisation comparisons increases when recorded over long periods on types, both in quantity and beyond introductory problems. The Harvard serviceability rate was 70.5% and South Cerney's Prentice rate was 71.5% in 1952. The recorded Anson (73%) in 1964 was only for two months. The JP3A* 63.4% was the average serviceability over the last 7months of 1974. The JP5A* 66.4% average serviceability was over the last 5 months of 1974.

Monthly Average Aircraft on Inventory for the Period 1956-76

Years averaged	1956	1957	1958	1960	1961	1962	1963	1964	1965	1966	1968	1969	1971	1972	1973	1974	Mar 1976
Jet trainers																	
Canberra T.4		0.8	**2.9**	2.4	2.4	2.0											
Jetstream T.1															0.5	3.4#	
Vampire T.11	**20.5**	20.0	15.4	19.0	11.5	7.0	2.5	1.0	1.0	1.0	1.0	1.0	1.0	1.0	1.0	0.7	1.0
Meteor T.7	**4.9**	2.5	2.1	2.6	3.0	3.5	2.0	1.0	1.0	1.0	1.0	1.6	1.0	1.0	1.0	1.0	1.0
Hunter F.4	2.0	3.0	**5.0**	**5.0**	3.4	2.5	0.4										
Hunter T.7					1.6	**2.0**	0.2										
Gnat Course						2.5	5.0	10.9	**11.2**	11.0	8.8	8.5	6.0	5.8	7.3	5.5	5.0
Gnat Red Arrows									7.8	10.0	10.0	10.0	9.5	9.5	9.5	9.3	**12.0**
Jet Provost T5/5A												3.0	9.1	**11.0**	**11.0**	10.2	8.0
Jet Provost T4					0.6	11.0	13.1	**17.0**	12.3	12.4	11.2	10.5	1.0				
Jet Provost T3/3A				10.3	26.5	16.5	18.2	17.8	17.8	17.3	14.0	15.5	10.6	10.9	10.8	11.8	7.0
Jet Provost T.1		0.8	5.7														
Jet total	**27.4**	**27.1**	**31.1**	**39.3**	**49.0**	**47.0**	**41.4**	**47.7**	**51.1**	**52.7**	**46.0**	**50.1**	**38.2**	**39.2**	**41.1**	**41.9**	**34.0**
Piston trainers																	
Anson C.19	**2.7**	2.7	2.4	2.0	1.9	2.0	1.4	0.3									
Valetta C1	0.9	0.6	**1.1**	0.3													
Varsity T.1				2.9	2.9	4.5	4.0	4.4	5.8	6.0	5.0	5.7	6.4	5.4	5.0	3.9	
Chipmunk T10				2.5	3.5	4.0	4.3	4.6	6.3	8.6	10.2	12.7	7.4	7.0	7.3	1.1	1.0
Provost T.1	2.0*	15.7	**20.8**	19.4	7.5	5.5	4.9	2.9									
Bulldog T1															6.3	9.9	**11.0**
Piston total	**5.6***	**19.0**	**24.3**	**27.1**	**15.8**	**16.0**	**14.6**	**12.2**	**12.1**	**14.6**	**15.2**	**18.4**	**13.8**	**12.4**	**18.6**	**14.9**	**12.0**
Trainers total	**33***	**46.1**	**55.4**	**66.4**	**64.8**	**63.0**	**56.0**	**59.9**	**63.2**	**67.3**	**61.2**	**68.5**	**52.0**	**51.6**	**59.7**	**56.8**	**46.0**

Monthly Average Flying Hours for the Period 1956-76

Years averaged	1956	1957	1958	1960	1961	1962	1963	1964	1965	1966	1968	1969	1971	1972	1973	1974	Mar 1976
Jet Trainers																	
Canberra T.4		24	**58**	24	29	8											
Jetstream T.1															7	**58**	
Vampire T.11	**630**	520	366	292	203	104	32	13	6	8	10	7	6	3	3	4	6
Meteor T.7	**183**	76	59	45	57	58	18	8	17	13	11	11	6	3	4	5	6
Hunter F.4	51	58	76	76	**80**	51	2										
Hunter T.7					22	**31**											
Gnat Course						35	119	162	180	188	164	174	141	167	128	108	**207**
Gnat Red Arrows									102	146	189	172	145	174	173	160	**228**
Jet Provost T5/5A												9	304	289	257	191	**384**
Jet Provost T42					2	279	363	**497**	375	361	358	346	36				
Jet Provost T3/3A				167	848	448	478	578	**579**	531	549	524	413	372	270	262	141
Jet Provost T.1		6	**61**														
Jet total flying	**864**	**684**	**620**	**604**	**1241**	**1014**	**1012**	**1258**	**1259**	**1247**	**1281**	**1243**	**1051**	**1008**	**842**	**788**	**972**
Piston Trainers																	
Anson C.19	**59**	55	49	12	28	16	20	7									
Valetta C1	16	**20**	17	8													
Varsity T.1				51	56	103	108	130	115	138	**182**	139	145	151	130	71	
Chipmunk T10				43	78	101	121	163	201	239	360	303	**383**	352	221	15	29
Provost T.1	60*	476	**651**	643	265	180	156	106									
Bulldog T1															134	319	383
Piston total flying	**135***	**551**	**717**	**757**	**427**	**400**	**405**	**406**	**316**	**377**	**542**	**442**	**528**	**503**	**485**	**405**	**412**
Av. month flying	**999***	**1235**	**1337**	**1361**	**1668**	**1414**	**1417**	**1664**	**1575**	**1624**	**1823**	**1685**	**1579**	**1511**	**1327**	**1193**	**1384**
Av. Utilisation	30.3	26.8	24.1	20.5	25.7	22.4	25.3	27.8	24.9	24.1	29.8	24.6	30.4	29.3	22.2	21.0	30.1

Footnotes: Before 1956 most records were on a course basis and incomplete to calculate station totals. For brevity, the less accurate 1959, 1967, 1970 and 1975 records are omitted. Totals include only RAF Little Rissington fixed wing plus Kemble and Fairford Gnat flying. Year figures when monthly averages are highest are highlighted for easier comparative analysis. *NB These 1956 Little Rissington Form 540 records exclude the CFS (Basic) flying contribution at South Cerney with their monthly average of 27 Provost T.1s. Piston trainers produced an average extra 4.4% flying above their percentage proportion of the fleet inventory.

Little Rissington: Airfield Operational Details at closure in April 1976

This extract is from the 154 page RAF En-Route Supplement covering the British Isles and Atlantic. Designed for handy insertion in flying suit map pockets and updated every four weeks, this airfield directory listed all aerodromes, navigational aids and ground and in-flight facilities. An invaluable aircrew tool 'as a reference for the planning and safe conduct of air operations', this red En-Route Supplement was familiar to all aircrew (in particular for use before flying back to CFS or any other airfield and maybe covered during re-categorisation) and demonstrates the superior aids and facilities at the closure of CFS flying at Little Rissington, not there for earlier generations of QFI staff and students. This final Little Rissington Airfield information entry, beginning with 'EGVL', its International Civil Aviation Organisation's Location Indicator, covers its GMT airfield normal operating times and announces the airfield's historic closure wef 17:00 hrs on St George's Day, 23 April, 1976.

Little Rissington	**England**	**EGVL**
Tel. Bourton-on-the-Water 20606 Portland A S Rgn	RAF 51°52'N 01°42'W Elevation 730 ft	London FIR TAP 412S 415L 425L

TIME 07:00-16:00 Mon-Fri. PPR. CLOSED WEF 17:00 hrs 23 Apr 76

RWY **05/23** 4902 ft/1,494m, Asphalt, LCG V
05 (038·12°T) TORA/ASDA/LDA 4902 ft/1,494m, TODA 5000 ft/1,524m; T1, 4, 9
23 (218·12°T) TORA/ASDA/LDA 4902 ft/1,494m, TODA 5246 ft/l,599m; L1,4, 5, 6, 7, 9

STOP Rwy05 RAF Mk5 (50ft Ovrn) ———— RAF Mk5 Rwy23 (50ft Ovrn)

COM(E) **CAC** *Cotswold Radar* 269·4 (ICF), 134·3 (ICF), 247·3x (CAC). QFE
APP *ff Rissington App* 370·5 P, 362·3 Sx, 122·1¢, 142·29¢ , 126·5 M
SRE *ff Cotswold Radar* 247·3 PS, 358·2 SSD, 123·3 ¢
PAR(a) *ff Talkdown* 381·9 PF, 123·3 PF, 385·4 SF
TWR *ff Rissington Twr* 252·6 P, 257·8 Sx, 122·1 ¢, 142·29 ¢, 126·5 M

NAV **I Bn** *LR* Red UDF *ff*(U) (c) *Rissington App* 370·5P, 362·3Sx, 247·3x, 252·6x, 325·2x, 344·0x, 358·2x, 381·9x, 388·4x
ILS(d) *LR* 108·6/329·9 OM 222/4·7 MM222/0·6 GP3°

IAM **SRE** OCL O5/440, 23/440 DOA (A/D) 05/140, 23/140
PAR OCL 05/170 No GP 270, 23/170, No GP 270 DOA 05/70, No GP 70, 23/70, No GP 70
ILS OCL 23/170, No GP 270 D0A 23/70, No GP 70

SERV F18, 34. 0-117, 123, 128, 134, 136, 147, 149. S-745. H-515. E1, 3, 4, 11. A1. C1. LHOX, OXRB, (LOX (e))

RMKS 1. It is mandatory to obtain an overhead time and flight level before departure and to call App when 15 nm inbound

ANN (a) MP wkly 06:30-09:00 Mon & mthly 06:30-10:30 1st Mon
(b) MP 07:00-08:00 Tue
(c) MP 12:30-14:30 Thu
(d) Lczr offset 2·66° to right of rwy centreline. MP 07:00-12:00 2nd & 4th Wed
(e) Aval ¢ 24 hrs

Annotations, Abbreviations and Codes

Ff	Facility as aerodrome times *X On request can be provided in minutes from a request made in the air ¢* Can be made available by prior arrangement before flight
ANN	Annotations covering additional matters as maintenance periods and operating hours
APP	Approach
ASDA	Accelerate Stop Distance Available
ASR	Altimeter Setting Region
ATCC	Air Traffic Control Centre
Aval	Available
CAC	Centralised Approach Control
DOA	Dominant Obstacle Allowance (E) 243.0 and 121.5 emergency frequencies may only be monitored by ATCC
FIR	Flight Information Region
GP	Glidepath
IAM	Instrument Approach Minima
IBn	Identification Beacon (flashing light transmitting two letters in morse code)
ICF	Initial Contact Frequency
ILS	Instrument Landing System
Lczr	Localizer
LDA	Landing Distance Available
LCG	Load Classification Group indicates Runway strength: V here = Aircraft Load Classification Number 16-30 (16 000 to 30 000lb AUW) range
MM	Middle Marker
MP	Maintenance Period
NAV	Navigation
OCL	Obstacle Clearance Limit
OM	Outer Marker
P	Primary
PAR	Precision Approach Radar
PF	Primary/Final Talkdown
PPR	Prior Permission Required
PS	Primary/Search Director
QFE	Atmpospheric pressure at aerodrome elevation (or at runway threshold)
RWY	Runway
S	Secondary
SERV	Aircraft Servicing Facilities: Fuel: F18 = AVGAS F34 AVTUR O = various Oils S = De-Icing Fluids H = Hydraulic Fluids E = Electrical Servicing & Starting Trolleys A = Air Starting Trolleys C = Starter Cartridge LHOX Low & High Pressure Oxygen OXRB = Oxygen Replacement Bottles LOX = Liquid Oxygen Bottles
SF	Secondary/Final Talkdown
SRE	Secondary Radar Element
STOP	Arrester Barrier – here the RAF Mk.5 Barrier Arresting System – can be raised to prevent aircraft over-running the end of runway in emergency
TAP	Terminal Approach Procedures L Low Altitude Chart (after identification)
TODA	Take-off Distance Available
TORA	Take-off Run Available
TWR	Tower
UDF	Ultra High Frequency Direction Finder
WEF	with effect from

APPENDIX 3

CFS Aerobatic Team Personnel

Year	Team name	Aircraft Type & No.	Pilots	Support Teams/Flying Circus	
1949		3 x Meteor T.7	Flt Lt A.G. Brown Flt Lt G. Hulse Lt A.R. Rawbone RN		
1951		3 x Prentice T.1	Flt Lt Urwin Flt Lt Wood Flt Lt Sweetman		
1952	The Meteorites	4 x Meteor T.7	Flt Lt C.R. Gordon Flt Lt L.A. Titmus Flt Lt D.D. James M/Plt D. Fisher		
1953	The Meteorites	5 x Meteor T.7	Sqn Ldr Harkness Flt Lt A. Titmus Flt Lt D.D. James Fg Off Evans M/Plt D. Fisher		
1954		4 x Meteor T.7	Flt Lt R.G. Price Flt Lt J.R. Douche Flt Lt C.H. Lazenby Fg Off C. Bart		
1955		5 x Meteor T.7	Flt Lt H. Harrison Flt Lt D.G.T. Franklin Flt Lt T. Doe Flt Lt D. Hall Flt Lt M. Kemp		
1956	The Pelicans	4 x Meteor T.7	Flt Lt D.G.T. Franklin Fg Off P.B. Hine Flt Lt M.B. Kemp Flt Lt J.A. McArthur		
1957	The Sparrows	4 x Piston Provost T.1	Flt Lt J.H. Kingsbury Flt Lt H.L. Howes Flt Lt H.R. Lane Flt Lt M.G. Bradley Flt Lt W.A. Black (Res)		
1958	The CFS Jet Aerobatic Team	4 x Jet Provost T.1	Flt Lt N.H. Giffin Flt Lt D. McClen Flt Lt F.W.J. Packer Flt Lt D. Millington Flt Lt M. Edwards (Res)		
1959	The Redskins	2 x Jet Provost T.1	Flt Lt J.R. Rhind Flt Lt P.J. Hirst		
1960	Pelican Red	4 x Vampire T.11	Lt R. Wren RN Flt Lt P. Broughton Flt Lt P. Frame Flt Lt J. Mayes		
	The Pelicans	4 x Jet Provost T.3	Flt Lt R. Langstaff Flt Lt F.R. Brambley Plt Off B.A. McDonald Flt Lt J.G. Nicklin	Sgt O.M. Rose Cpl Mullins SAC Austin SAC Archer	SAC Burke SAC P.W. Lie SAC D.E. Webb LAC C. Hammonds
1961	The Pelicans	4 x Jet Provost T.3	Flt Lt F.R. Brambley Flt Lt D.T. McCann Plt Off B.A. McDonald Flt Lt T.H. Whittingham Flt Lt I.K. McKee Res) Flt Lt W.W. Elsegood (Res)		
1962	The Red Pelicans	5 x Jet Provost T.4	Flt Lt I.K. McKee Flt Lt K.F. Beck Flt Lt I. Bashall Flt Lt J.E.S. Rolfe Flt Lt R.G. Fox Flt Lt A.J.R. Doyle (Res)		

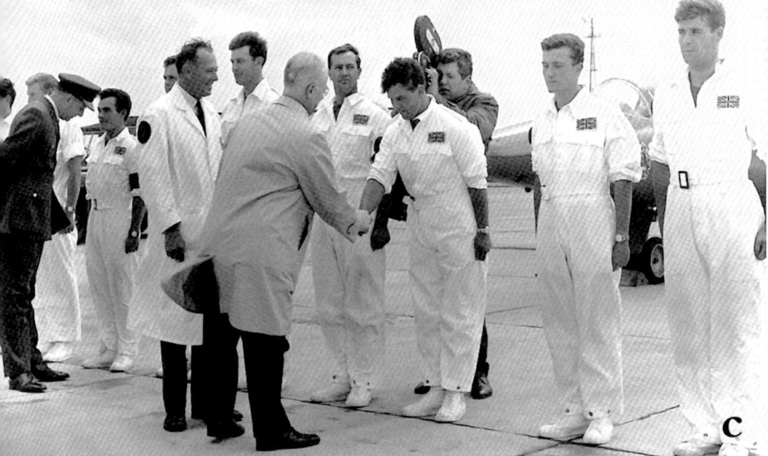

(a) The "Meteorites" team at the 1953 Jersey Air Show (*CFS Archive*).

(b) Seen at South Cerney before their transfer to Little Rissington in 1957, "The Sparrows" with, (*l to r*), Flt Lt 'Les' Howes, Flt Lt 'Charley' Kingsbury - leader, Flt Lt Mike Bradley, Flt Lt 'Bert' Lane (*Mike Bradley*).

(c) The 1965 Red Arrows support team are presented to the Chairman of a popular bicycle manufacturer, accompanied by Air Cdre Dodd and Flt Sgt 'Jock' Hutson, are (*l to r*) SAC Ivan Green, Cpls Fearnside, Jimmy Mearns, J/T Ricky Howse, Cpls Brian Wood, Ray Mayes, SAC Tony Gannon, J/T Jones and Cpl Pete Chadburn (*Tony Gannon*).

(d) With their brightly decorated helmets, the 1963 "Red Pelican" team of Flt Lts Ian Bashall - leader (*left*), Keith Beck, Tony Hawkes, Benny Raffin, Bryan Nice and Terry Lloyd (*Ian Bashall*).

(e) Having changed their name from "Pink Penguins" to "Skylarks", the 1967 team of Flt Lts Jack Hindle - reserve, John Merry - leader, Tony Langmead, Brian Owen and Peter Dummer pose by one of their mounts (*John Merry*).

(f) Dwarfed by the long-legged JP1, Flt Lts Don McClen, Norman Giffin - leader, Fred Packer and Pete Millington of the 1958 "CFS Jet Provost Aerobatic Team" (*Norman Giffin*).

Year	Team name	Aircraft Type & No.	Pilots	Support Teams/Flying Circus	
1963	The Red Pelicans	6 x Jet Provost T.4	Flt Lt I. Bashall	Snr Tech Smith	J/T Luff
			Flt Lt K.F. Beck	Cpl Bean	J/T Norton
			Flt Lt A.J. Hawkes	J/T Ashley	J/T Prior
			Flt Lt N.R. Raffin RAAF	J/T Baker	SAC Martin
			Flt Lt B.A. Nice	J/T Bulled	SAC Prosser
			Flt Lt T.E. Lloyd		
1964	The Red Pelicans	6 x Jet Provost T.4	Flt Lt T.E. Lloyd		
			Flt Lt B.A. Nice		
			Flt Lt M.R. Lane		
			Flt Lt W.A. Langworthy		
			Flt Lt D.F. Southern		
			Flt Lt E.C.F. Tilsley		
1965	The Red Arrows	7 x Gnat T.1	Flt Lt L. Jones	Flt Sgt G.F.J Hutson	J/T R. Howse
			Flt Lt B.A. Nice	Sgt Scott	J/T G. Hurren
			Flt Lt R.G. Hanna	Sgt Smallman	J/T J. Mearns
			Flt Lt G.L. Ranscombe	Cpl Casey	SAC Arliss
			Flt Lt R.E.W. Loverseed	Cpl P. Chadburn	SAC Boucher
			Flt Lt H.J.D. Prince	Cpl Fernside	SAC Dawson
			Fg Off P.G. Hay	Cpl Kellaher	SAC A. Gannon
			Flt Lt E.C.F. Tilsley (Res)	Cpl R. Mayes	SAC Green
			Fg Off C. Harrow (EO)	J/T Austin	SAC C. Thomas
			Fg Off D. Whitby (EO)	J/T R. Hargreaves	SAC W. Hickman
			Sqn Ldr. R. Storer (Man)		
			Flt Lt R. Dench(Adj)		
	CFS JP Aerobatic team	4 x Jet Provost T.4	Flt Lt W.A. Langworthy	Flt Sgt F.J. Coxon	SAC V. Gannon
			Flt Lt D.A. Bell	Ch Tech R.E. Goodfield	SAC T. Goodwillie
			Sqn Ldr D. McClen	Sgt A.L. Noble	SAC P.W. Hatch
			Flt Lt R. Booth	Cpl D. Parkinson	SAC D.C. Leach
			Flt Lt M. Baston RAAF (Res)	J/T A.G. Constable	SAC P.J. Blei
			Flt Lt J.J. Maynard (Res)	J/T A.R. Watson	
1966	The Red Arrows	7/9 x Gnat T.1	Sqn Ldr R.G. Hanna	Flt Sgt G.F.J Hutson	J/T G. Hurren
			Flt Lt D.R.H. McGregor	Sgt M. Thomas	J/T Jones
			Flt Lt H.J.D. Prince	Cpl P. Chadburn	J/T Scurr
			Sqn Ldr T.J.G. Nelson	Cpl Fernside	J/T Steer
			Flt Lt F.J. Hoare	Cpl R. Mayes	SAC Boucher
			Flt Lt P.R. Evans	Cpl J. Mearns	SAC R. Carroll
			Flt Lt D.A. Bell	Cpl Wood	SAC Dawson
			Flt Lt W.A. Langworthy	J/T Austin	SAC A. Gannon
			Flt Lt R. Booth	J/T E. Fennell	SAC Green
			Fg Off C. Harrow (EO)	J/T R. Hargreaves	SAC C. Thomas
			Fg Off D. Whitby (EO)	J/T R. Howse	SAC W. Hickman
			Sqn Ldr. R. Storer (Man)		
			Flt Lt R. Dench(Adj)		
	The Red Pelicans	4 x Jet Provost T.4	Wg Cdr D.L. Edmonds		
			Sqn Ldr D. McClen		
			Flt Lt C. Thomas		
			Flt Lt J.J. Maynard		
			Flt Lt C.J. Sturt		
	The Skylarks	4 x Chipmunk T.10	Flt Lt R. Wood		
			Flt Lt J.F. Merry		
			Flt Lt P.J. Dummer		
			Flt Lt A.C. Langmead		
1967	The Red Arrows	7 x Gnat T.1	Sqn Ldr R.G. Hanna	Flt Sgt G.F.J Hutson	J/T I. Dalgleish
			Flt Lt H.J.D. Prince	Ch Tech W. Watson	J/T E. Fennell
			Flt Lt F.J. Hoare	Sgt M. Thomas	J/T M. Harris
			Flt Lt D.A. Bell	Cpl I. Bennett	J/T R. Howse
			Flt Lt R. Booth	Cpl P. Chadburn	J/T McKnight
			Flt Lt P.R. Evans	Cpl J. Fletcher	SAC R. Carroll
			Flt Lt E.E. Jones	Cpl D. Nevard	SAC Dunn
			Fg Off D. Whitby (EO)	Cpl Smith	SAC Dawson
			Flt Lt L.G. Willcox(Man)	Cpl G. Thomas	SAC A. Gannon
			Flt Lt R. Dench(Adj)	Cpl R. Thurstans	SAC Smith
				Cpl R. Turrell	SAC D. Stidwell
				J/T Austin	
	The Red Pelicans	4 x Jet Provost T. 4	Sqn Ldr P.J. Hirst	Ch Tech E.P. George	SAC J. Trickey
			Capt J.K. Snow, USAF	Cpl G.D. Noyce	LAC A.R. Morgan
			Flt Lt D.J. Smith	Cpl P. Trunchion	LAC J.B. Pritchard
			Flt Lt M.S. Lovett	SAC A.E. Brewster	LAC L. Sheen
			Flt Lt J.K.A. Clark (Res)	SAC J. Dolman	
	The Skylarks	4 x Chipmunk T.10	Flt Lt J.F. Merry		
			Flt Lt B.A. Owen		
			Flt Lt P.J. Dummer		
			Flt Lt A.C. Langmead		
			Flt Lt J.S. Hindle (Res)		

Year	Team name	Aircraft Type & No.	Pilots	Support Teams/Flying Circus	
1968	The Red Arrows	9 x Gnat T.1	Sqn Ldr R.G. Hanna Flt Lt P.R. Evans Flt Lt D.A. Bell Flt Lt F.J. Hoare Flt Lt I.C. Dick Flt Lt R.B. Duckett Flt Lt J.T. Kingsley Flt Lt R. Booth Flt Lt D.A. Smith Fg Off D. Whitby (EO) Flt Lt L.G. Willcox(Man) Flt Lt R. Dench(Adj)	Ch Tech W. Watson Sgt M. Souter Sgt M. Thomas Cpl I. Bennett Cpl J. Fletcher Cpl D. Nevard Cpl Smith Cpl G. Thomas Cpl R. Thurstans Cpl R. Turrell J/T Austin J/T I. Dalgleish	J/T E. Fennell J/T B. Goodfellow J/T Harding J/T Harrington J/T M. Harris J/T B. Hudson J/T Walters SAC A. Bell SAC R. Carroll SAC B. Jones SAC Pinkerton SAC D. Stidwell
	The Red Pelicans	4 x Jet Provost T.4	Flt Lt D.J. Smith Flt Lt J.B. Robinson Flt Lt M.S. Lovett Flt Lt J.D. Blake		
	The Skylarks	4 x Chipmunk T.10	Sqn Ldr B.A. Owens Sqn Ldr R.B. Nelson Flt Lt P. Dummer Flt Lt G.S. Webb Flt Lt J.S. Hindle		
1969	The Red Arrows	9 x Gnat T.1	Sqn Ldr R.G. Hanna Sqn Ldr J.G. Nelson Flt Lt J. Rust Flt Lt J.T. Kingsley Flt Lt R.B. Duckett Flt Lt P.R. Evans Flt Lt D.A. Smith Flt Lt E. Perreaux Flt Lt I.C.H. Dick Sqn Ldr P. Dunn RAAF Fg Off G.E. White (EO) Flt Lt P. Mackintosh (Man) Flt Lt R. Dench (Adj)	Flt Sgt R. Young Ch Tech Loader Ch Tech M. Souter Ch Tech M. Thomas Sgt Dicker Sgt D. Fowler Sgt J. Stuart Sgt G. Thomas Cpl C. Blight Cpl M. Harris Cpl B. Hudson Cpl D. Jones Cpl Perrett Cpl M. Sivell	Cpl R. Turrell J/T Fothergill J/T B. Goodfellow J/T Keyworth J/T O. Scammell SAC A. Bell SAC Cresswell SAC Farra SAC A. Gannon SAC D. Hyland SAC B. Jones SAC Pinkerton SAC R. Williams
	The Red Pelicans	4 x Jet Provost T.4	Flt Lt J.B. Robinson Flt Lt A.J. Davies Flt Lt R.B. Mackenzie-Crooks Flt Lt R.M. Clayton Flt Lt J. Davy (Res)	Flt Sgt E. George Cpl A. Lines Cpl V. Prier SAC E. Irving	SAC L. Sheen SAC D. Thomas LAC K. Griffiths
	The Skylarks	4 x Chipmunk T.10	Sqn Ldr S.W.T. Holding Flt Lt R.W.K. Snell Flt Lt R.S. Burrows Flt Lt R.J. Snell Flt Lt W.R.T. Hobson (Res)	Sgt R.J. Kinsey SAC Newbury SAC Dawson SAC O'Brian SAC Postlethwait	
1970	The Red Arrows	9 x Gnat T.1	Sqn Ldr D.G. Hazell Flt Lt E.R. Perreaux Flt Lt D.A. Smith Flt Lt J.D. Rust Flt Lt J. Haddock Flt Lt I.C.H. Dick Flt Lt R.B. Duckett Flt Lt D.S.B. Marr Flt Lt R.E.W. Loverseed Flt Lt G.E. White (EO) Flt Lt P. Mackintosh (Man) W O L. Ludow (Adj)	Flt Sgt S. Arthur Ch Tech Dicker Ch Tech Fowler Ch Tech Francis Ch Tech M. Souter Ch Tech M. Thomas Sgt C. Blight Sgt J. Stuart Sgt R. Turrell Cpl B. Goodfellow Cpl D. Jones	Cpl O. Scammell Cpl M. Sivell J/T Heeley J/T Lagor SAC A. Bell SAC Cresswell SAC Crewe SAC Farra SAC Frampton SAC A. Gannon SAC O'Brian
	The Red Pelicans	4 x Jet Provost T.5	Sqn Ldr E.D. Evers Flt Lt T.R. Francis Flt Lt J. Davy Flt Lt K.J. Tait Flt Lt R.D. Brown (Res)	Ch Tech D. Holmes Cpl G. Parkin Cpl V. Prier Cpl G. White	SAC J. Dolman SAC M. Lever SAC D. Thomas
	The Skylarks	4 x Chipmunk T.10	Flt Lt W.R.T. Hobson Flt Lt M.S.J. McKinley Flt Lt M.A. Telford Flt Lt T. Anderson Flt Lt G. Cullen		
1971	The Red Arrows	7 x Gnat T.1	Sqn Ldr R.E.W. Loverseed Sqn Ldr D.S.B. Marr Flt Lt A.C. East Flt Lt W.B. Aspinall Flt Lt P.J.J. Day Flt Lt C.F. Roberts Flt Lt R.E. Somerville	Flt Sgt D. Fisk Ch Tech R. Dicker Ch Tech D. Fowler Ch Tech M. Souter Ch Tech M. Thomas Sgt Baker Sgt J. Stuart	Cpl O. Scammell Cpl J. Webb J/T M. Heeley J/T K. Lagor J/T G. Ruffle SAC A. Bell SAC Frampton

Year	Team name	Aircraft Type & No.	Pilots	Support Teams/Flying Circus	
			Flt Lt G.E. White (EO) Flt Lt K.J. Tait (Man) W O L. Ludow (Adj)	Cpl B. Armstrong Cpl R. Audley Cpl B. Hudson Cpl Jones Cpl D. Lawrence Cpl J. Perrett	SAC A. Gannon SAC J. Goddard SAC Howard SAC Marsh SAC Shorter SAC Thompson
	The Red Pelicans	4 x Jet Provost T.5	Flt Lt T. Francis Flt Lt B. Donnelly Flt Lt M. Langham Flt Lt R.Lewis		
1972	The Red Arrows	9 x Gnat T.1	Sqn Ldr I.C.H. Dick Flt Lt W.B. Aspinall Flt Lt A.C. East Flt Lt R.E. Somerville Flt Lt K.J. Tait Flt Lt P.J.J. Day Flt Lt D. Binnie Flt Lt E.E.G. Girdler Flt Lt C.F. Roberts Flt Lt I. Brackenbury (EO) Flt Lt B. Donnelly (Man) W O S. Wild (Adj)	Flt Sgt D. Fisk Ch Tech R. Dicker Ch Tech D. Fowler Ch Tech Martin Ch Tech Shea Sgt K. Ransome Sgt D. Sampson Cpl B. Armstrong Cpl B. Hudson Cpl D. Lawrence Cpl Parker-Ball Cpl Potter Cpl O. Scammell	Cpl R. Walton Cpl J. Webb J/T Blandford J/T G. Ruffle SAC A. Bell SAC V. Cresswell SAC A. Gannon SAC J. Goddard SAC Marsh SAC Radge SAC Shorter SAC Tarte SAC W. Worthington
	The Red Pelicans	4 x Jet Provost T.5	Flt Lt C. Mitchell Flt Lt R. Lewis Capt R.F. Lord USAF Flt Lt P. Tait		
	The Vintage Pair	1 x Meteor T.7 1 x Vampire T.11	Sqn Ldr B.A. McDonald Sqn Ldr R. Johnson Flt Lt G. Lee Flt Lt A. Holyoake Flt Lt P.A. Bouch		
1973	The Red Arrows	9 x Gnat T.1	Sqn Ldr I.C.H. Dick Flt Lt W.B. Aspinall Flt Lt B. Donnelly Flt Lt E.E.G. Girdler Flt Lt K.J. Tait Flt Lt D. Binnie Flt Lt R.E. Somerville Flt Lt D.J. Sheen Flt Lt P.J.J. Day Flt Lt I. Brackenbury (EO) Flt Lt R.M. Joy (Man) W O H.E.D. Rundstrom (Adj)	Flt Sgt D. Fisk Ch Tech Hosking Ch Tech Martin Ch Tech Shea Sgt I. Dalgleish Sgt K. Ransome Sgt D. Sampson Cpl B. Armstrong Cpl B. Hudson Cpl Marson Cpl Parker-Ball Cpl Potter Cpl O. Scammell Cpl R. Walton	Cpl J. Webb J/T Blandford J/T Lee J/T G. Ruffle SAC A. Bell SAC Chandler SAC Clay SAC V. Cresswell SAC G. Dallison SAC J. Radge SAC Shorter SAC D. Vale SAC W. Worthington
	The Red Pelicans	4 x Jet Provost T.5	Sqn Ldr I. Gibbs Lt M. Edwards RN Capt. R.F. Lord USAF Flt Lt B. Byron RAAF		
	The Vintage Pair	1 x Meteor T.7 1 x Vampire T.11	Sqn Ldr B.A. McDonald Sqn Ldr W.R. Shrubsole Flt Lt P.A. Bouch Flt Lt A.A. Holyoake Wg Cdr I.D. Brimson (Man)	Sgt S. Morton Cpl T. Owens J/T S. Coles	SAC B. Beach SACW M. Hart LAC P. Holcroft
1974	The Red Arrows	9 x Gnat T.1	Sqn Ldr I.C.H. Dick Flt Lt K.J. Tait Flt Lt B. Donnelly Flt Lt E.E.G. Girdler Flt Lt C.M. Phillips Flt Lt D. Binnie Flt Lt R.E. Somerville Flt Lt D.J. Sheen Flt Lt R. Eccles Flt Lt I. Brackenbury (EO) Flt Lt R.M. Joy (Man) W O H.E.D. Rundstrom (Adj)	Flt Sgt G. Bennett Ch Tech Hoskins Ch Tech Martin Ch Tech Hambrook Sgt I. Dalgleish Sgt K. Ransome Sgt D. Sampson Sgt T. Whelan Sgt Dave Rees Cpl R. Utting Cpl Lee Cpl Potter	Cpl Mackinder Cpl Marsden J/T Lee J/T Blandford SAC A. Bell SAC Chandler SAC Coates SAC G. Dallison SAC C. Ellis SAC Hoddy SAC R. Worthington SAC D. Vale
	The Vintage Pair	1 x Meteor T.7 1 x Vampire T.11	Sqn Ldr W.R. Shrubsole Flt Lt A.A. Holyoake Sqn Ldr A. Gregory Flt Lt P.A. Bouch	Cpl P. Thomas SAC B. Beach SAC F. Howard	

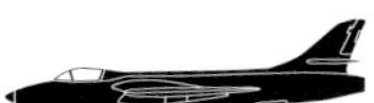

Year	Team name	Aircraft Type & No.	Pilots	Support Teams/Flying Circus	
1975	The Red Arrows	9 x Gnat T.1	Sqn Ldr R.B. Duckett Flt Lt C.M. Phillips Flt Lt B. Donnelly Flt Lt R. Eccles Flt Lt J. Blackwell Flt Lt D.J. Sheen Sqn Ldr B.R. Hoskins Flt Lt M.R. Cornwell Flt Lt R.S. Barber Flt Lt A. Hunt (EO) Sqn Ldr A.L. Wall (Man) W O H.E.D. Rundstrom (Adj)	Flt Sgt D. Rockett Ch Tech J. Rapley Ch Tech K. Ransom Ch Tech Hambrook Sgt I. Dalgleish Sgt M. Brewer Sgt T. Whelan Sgt D. Rees Cpl C. Cameron Cpl K. Homewood Cpl B. Kilgariffe Cpl Mackinder Cpl C. Greenhalgh	Cpl R. Marsden J/T T. Trim SAC Branson SAC Cross SAC Coates SAC G. Dallison SAC C. Ellis SAC Hoddy SAC Noble SAC D. Powell SAC W. Worthington SAC Slater SAC Edlin
	The Vintage Pair	1 x Meteor T.7 1 x Vampire T.11	Wg Cdr J.J. Maynard Flt Lt D. Fitzsimmons Sqn Ldr A. Gregory Flt Lt R. Payne	Sgt H. Chapel Cpl R. Vosper J/T L. Hearfield	J/T R. Jones LAC C. Sexton
1976	The Red Arrows	9 x Gnat T.1	Sqn Ldr R.B. Duckett Flt Lt C.M. Phillips Flt Lt R. Eccles Flt Lt D.R. Carvell Flt Lt R.S. Barber Sqn Ldr B.R. Hoskins Flt Lt M.R. Cornwell Flt Lt M.T. Curley Flt Lt N.S. Champness Flt Lt A. Hunt (EO) Sqn Ldr A.L. Wall (Man) W O H.G. Thorne (Adj)	Flt Sgt D. Rockett Ch Tech J. Rapley Ch Tech Hambrook Sgt M. Brewer Sgt B. Goodfellow Sgt Ryan Sgt B. Kilgariffe Sgt C. Greenhalgh Sgt T. Whelan Sgt D. Rees Cpl C. Cameron Cpl K. Homewood Cpl A. Pugh Cpl Mackinder	Cpl R. Marsden J/T T. Trim SAC Branson SAC Cross SAC Coates SAC G. Dallison SAC C. Ellis SAC Hoddy SAC Noble SAC D. Powell SAC W. Worthington SAC Slater SAC Edlin
	The Vintage Pair	1 x Meteor T.7 1 x Vampire T.11	Wg Cdr J.J. Maynard Flt Lt D. Fitzsimmons Flt Lt D. Hicks Flt Lt R. Payne		

(a) Wg Cdr D.L. Edmonds - leader, Sqn Ldr D. McClen, Flt Lt C. Thomas and Flt Lt J.J. 'Cas' Maynard flew four JP T.4s in the 1966 "Red Pelican" team. (*Cas Maynard*)

(b) Lined up behind Flt Lts Ken Tait, Terry Francis, Sqn Ldr Eric Evers - leader and Flt Lt John Davy, are Ch Tech Dennis Holmes and his crew comprising; Cpls Gordon Parkin, Victor Prier, George White, SACs John Dolman, Michael Lever and David Thomas, members of the 1970 "Red Pelican" team. (*Eric Evers*)

(c) The last team to form under CFS at Little Rissington was the "Vintage Pair" depicted here with the 1975 crews. (*l to r*) Sgt Harry Chappel, LAC Colin Sexton, J/T Lindsey Hearfield, Flt Lt Derek Fitzsimmons, Wg Cdr Cas Maynard, Flt Lt Ross Payne, Sqn Ldr Tony Gregory, Cpl Roy Vosper and J/T Raymond Jones. (*CFS Archive*)

APPENDIX 4

CFS Aircraft Inventory

Training aircraft in use at RAF Little Rissington, 1946-1976

Year	Type	Mark	Year	Type	Mark	Year	Type	Mark
1946-47	Oxford	C.1	1948-52	Prentice	T.1	1953-64	Piston Provost	T.1
1946-54	Harvard	T.2	1949-50	Balliol	T.2	1953-76	Vampire	T.11
1946-48	Anson	C.1	1949-50	Athena	T.2	1955-55	Pembroke	C.1
1946-50	Tiger Moth	T.2	1949-76	Meteor	T. 7	1955-63	Hunter	F.4
1947-51	Tiger Moth	T.1	1950	Meteor	F.3 & F.4	1957-59	Jet Provost	T.1
1946-64	Anson	C.19	1950-51	Dakota	C.4	1957-62	Canberra	T.4
1946	Magister	T.1	1950-51	Chipmunk	T.10	1958-76	Chipmunk	T.10
1946-49	Lancaster	B.7	1950-51	Balliol	T.1	1959-76	Jet Provost	T.3
1947-48	Mosquito	FB.6	1951-51	Buckmaster	T.1	1960-74	Varsity	T.1
1947-51	Mosquito	T.3	1951-51	Brigand	B.1	1960-63	Hunter	T.7
1947-48	Buckmaster	T.1	1951-55	Auster	T. 7	1961-70	Jet Provost	T.4
1947-48	Auster	AOP.6	1952-55	Vampire	F.5	1962-76	Gnat	T.1
1948-51	Auster	AOP.5	1952-60	Valetta	C.1	1969-76	Jet Provost	T.5
1947-55	Spitfire	F.9 & LFe.16	1952-55	Anson	C.12	1973-76	Bulldog	T.1
1947-48	Vampire	F.1	1952-54	Sea Fury	T.20	1973-75	Jetstream	T.1
1948-49	Vampire	F.3	1953-54	Venom	FB.1			

As not all F540 Aircraft Record cards are in the safe keeping of the RAF Museum Archive, the following tables do not give full details of every aircraft issued to CFS over the period 1946 to 1976. They should be viewed in the context of a guide rather than a definitive list. The arrival and departure dates for each aircraft are included where known and indicated as nn-nn-nn where unknown. Also included are the details of aircraft that were not issued to CFS but loaned from other units or establishments for short durations. Until 1951 aircraft codes were carried on the fuselage sides and comprised four alpha characters beginning with the letters 'FD'. By the mid-fifties the coding system had changed and consisted of two alpha characters until superseded by a two-digit numerical coding system, commencing at '01', in 1961. "The Red Arrows" Gnats remained uncoded until the early seventies when they received single-digit alpha codes commencing at 'A'.

Type	Mark	Serial No./Code	Issued to CFS	Mark	Serial No./Code	Issued to CFS
Tiger Moth	T.2	N5471 FDL F	07-05-46 – 22-07-47	T.2	T7094 FDL K	15-08-47 – 01-10-48
	T.2	N6647	09-10-47 – 01-10-48	T.2	T7121 FDL P	07-05-46 – 25-09-47
	T.2	N6725 FDL E	07-05-46 – 14-08-48	T.2	T7750	03-09-47 – 09-12-47
	T.2	N6776 FDL S	07-05-46 – 30-10-47	T.2	T7870	04-02-48 – 22-09-48
	T.2	N6792	11-03-48 – 29-12-48	T.2	DE136	03-09-47 – 08-12-47
	T.2	N9368	09-10-47 – 08-01-51	T.2	DE253	11-03-48 – 22-12-48
	T.2	N9369	04-02-48 – 05-10-48	T.2	DE255 FDL X	09-10-47 – 06-01-49
	T.2	N9461 FDL V	09-10-47 – 17-09-48	T.2	DE459 FDL J	13-07-49 – 28-12-50
	T.2	R4924 FDL A	09-05-46 – 01-10-47	T.2	DE523	07-05-46 – 21-05-46
	T.2	R5136	15-08-47 – 14-12-48	T.2	DE718 FDL R	07-05-46 – 30-10-47
	T.2	R5140 FDL H	07-05-46 – 22-07-47	T.2	DE854	20-10-47 – 28-09-48
	T.2	T5371 FDL C	07-05-46 – 22-07-47	T.2	DE856 FDL J	07-05-46 – 07-10-47
	T.2	T5716 G-AODX	nn-nn-57 – nn-nn-60 FC	T.2	DE904 FDL O	07-05-46 – 25-09-47
	T.2	T6109 FDL F	15-08-47 – 14-10-48	T.2	DE941	09-10-47 – 10-02-49
	T.2	T6170 FDL K	07-05-46 – 22-07-47	T.2	DE957	09-10-47 – 14-10-48
	T.2	T6256 FDL H	15-08-47 – 28-12-50	T.2	DF138	11-03-48 – 22-12-48
	T.2	T6274 FDL M	13-07-49 – 29-09-49	T.2	NL776 FDL D	07-05-46 – 07-10-47
	T.2	T6555 FDL G	07-05-46 – 01-10-48	T.2	NL782 FDL A	07-05-46 – 14-08-47
	T.2	T6708	29-08-47 – 17-01-49	T.2	NL784 FDL M	07-05-46 – 01-07-47
	T.2	T6777 FDL N	09-05-46 – 05-09-47	T.1	NL980 FDL W	09-10-47 – 08-01-51
	T.2	T7017	04-02-48 – 05-02-49			
Harvard	T.2b	FS742 FDN J	17-01-47 – 26-01-50	T.2b	FX369 FDM Z	nn-05-46 – nn-05-47
	T.2b	FS744 FDO U: O	16-05-50 – 31-12-53	T.2b	FX382	nn-05-46 – nn-05-47
	T.2b	FS753 FDN A	nn-03-48 – nn-12-49	T.2b	FX389	nn-05-46 – nn-05-47
	T.2b	FS813	nn-02-47 – nn-12-47	T.2b	FX391 FDO P	nn-05-46 – nn-08-54
	T.2b	FS819 FDN K	nn-05-46 – nn-12-49	T.2b	FX403 FDN Y	nn-05-46 – nn-10-53
	T.2b	FS822 FDO V	16-05-50 – 28-07-52	T.2b	FX434 FDO L	nn-10-51 – 22-06-53
	T.2b	FS837 FDO W	16-03-50 – 27-11-53	T.2b	FX438	nn-06-47 – 26-04-51
	T.2b	FS841 FDN J	nn-02-47 – nn-12-49	T.2b	FX470 FDM W: N I	nn-02-48 – nn-07-54
	T.2b	FS849 FDO Y	nn-07-49 – nn-07-54	T.2b	KF127 FDM A	nn-07-51 – nn-11-53
	T.2b	FS883 FDO Z	04-10-48 – 09-01-51	T.2b	KF142 FDM B	08-12-49 – 04-02-54
	T.2b	FS884 FDN O	04-10-48 – 20-06-51	T.2b	KF150 FDN T	nn-07-51 – nn-11-53

2 Squadron Vampire T.11, XD376-VZ. (*Ray Deacon*)

Prentice T.1, VS369-FDIL, in standard training livery during a visit to RAF Wyton in 1951. (*Ray Sturtivant*)

Hunter T.7, WV318, at Kemble in 1962. (*Ray Deacon*)

3 Squadron Meteor T.7, WF826. (*Ray Deacon*)

The Commandant's Anson C.19, VP517, complete with pennant, CFS crest and red and silver-striped colour scheme outside 2 Hangar in 1961. (*Ray Deacon*)

Hunter F.4, XF944-A visiting Little Rissington in 1961. (*Ray Deacon*)

Two 1 Squadron Piston Provosts shown here, XF680-PT (*left*) and XF900-03 (*above left*), illustrate the changes in colour scheme for the type in the early sixties. (*Ray Deacon*)

Aircraft	Mark	Serial/Codes	Dates	Mark	Serial/Codes	Dates
	T.2b	FS890	10-01-58 – nn-nn-7n GG	T.2b	KF156 FDM B	nn-07-49 – nn-05-50
	T.2b	FS899 FDO M	nn-nn-nn – nn-nn-nn	T.2b	KF169 FDO A	nn-nn-nn – nn-nn-nn
	T.2b	FT158 FDM C	nn-05-46 – nn-12-49	T.2b	KF182 FDM H	nn-02-48 – nn-01-50
	T.2b	FT165 FDN H	nn-12-49 – 11-10-51	T.2b	KF206 FDM F	nn-05-46 – nn-06-47
	T.2b	FT213 FDN L	27-02-47 – 20-07-54	T.2b	KF211 FDN Q	22-10-51 – 04-02-53
	T.2b	FT245 FDN A	14-12-49 – 28-09-54	T.2b	KF241 FDO E	nn-nn-nn – nn-02-54
	T.2b	FT246 FDM X	12-11-46 – 20-07-54	T.2b	KF244 FDM S: N E	02-03-48 – 03-02-53
	T.2b	FT270	12-11-46 – 19-12-46	T.2b	KF268	nn-nn-nn – 01-12-49
	T.2b	FT279	25-03-47 – 25-06-47	T.2b	KF276 FDM X	nn-02-48 – nn-04-51
	T.2b	FT313 FDM O	nn-02-47 – nn-01-53	T.2b	KF289 FDO B: D	06-12-50 – 04-10-54
	T.2b	FT321 FDM D	nn-05-46 – nn-05-52	T.2b	KF307	nn-03-47 – nn-10-53
	T.2b	FT331 FDM K	09-07-46 – 06-12-49	T.2b	KF315 FDO C: D	nn-nn-nn – nn-nn-nn
	T.2b	FT332 FDM K	26-02-47 – 26-06-47	T.2b	KF320 FDM V	22-09-51 – 16-04-54
	T.2b	FT346 FDM W: N G	01-01-51 – 01-10-54	T.2b	KF321 FDM U	nn-nn-nn – 20-05-52
	T.2b	FT348 FDN C	nn-12-49 – nn-08-54	T.2b	KF338 FDM T	nn-nn-nn – 21-07-52
	T.2b	FT354 FDO K	nn-07-49 – nn-07-54	T.2b	KF339	nn-05-46 – 16-09-47
	T.2b	FT361 FDN X: O O	26-09-51 – 20-07-54	T.2b	KF352 FDM A	08-12-49 – 28-07-54
	T.2b	FT364 FDM D: R	01-12-49 – 20-07-54	T.2b	KF464	nn-nn-nn – nn-nn-nn
	T.2b	FT397 FDO J	nn-07-49 – nn-08-54	T.2b	KF468 FDO Q	nn-07-49 – nn-08-54
	T.2b	FT424 FDM F	nn-nn-nn – 28-09-54	T.2b	KF473 FDO H: N H	16-03-50 – 18-10-54
	T.2b	FT450 FDO N	16-03-50 – 25-08-52	T.2b	KF541	nn-02-47 – nn-06-47
	T.2b	FT496	nn-nn-nn – 26-02-51	T.2b	KF563 FDN C	nn-05-46 – nn-12-49
	T.2b	FX199 FDM P	nn-05-46 – nn-07-52	T.2b	KF564 FDN D	nn-05-46 – nn-02-50
	T.2b	FX221	12-08-48 – nn-07-52	T.2b	KF572 FDN O	11-10-51 – nn-10-54
	T.2b	FX227 FDN B	26-12-49 – 20-07-54	T.2b	KF584	30-07-52 – 11-12-53
	T.2b	FX234 FDM K: N D	nn-05-46 – nn-04-52	T.2b	KF588 FDN E	26-02-53 – 14-12-54
	T.2b	FX240 FDM S	nn-05-46 – nn-07-50	T.2b	KF695 FDN H	nn-nn-nn – nn-07-54
	T.2b	FX254 FDN T	04-10-46 – 07-07-54	T.2b	KF698	25-07-52 – nn-07-54
	T.2b	FX291 FDN F: O F	02-02-51 – 18-10-54	T.2b	KF702 FDM Q	16-03-50 – 09-12-54
	T.2b	FX301 FDM V: Q: N	02-02-48 – 26-04-51	T.2b	KF755 FDO T	02-09-52 – 04-10-54
	T.2b	FX307 FDO I	12-11-46 – 24-01-51	T.2b	KF937 FDN M	nn-12-49 – 15-09-51
	T.2b	FX350 FDM A: N Z	20-03-51 – 07-07-54	T.2b	KF948	08-01-52 – 28-07-52
	T.2b	FX362 FDN U	nn-nn-nn – nn-nn-nn	T.2b	KF959	nn-02-47 – nn-06-47
Anson	C.1	MG446	09-08-46 – 25-02-48	C.19	TX225 M K: 10	21-06-60 – 22-04-64
	C.12	PH538	nn-nn-nn – nn-nn-nn	C.19	TX232 M C	15-08-55 – 16-07-58
	C.12	PH810 M A	23-06-52 – 30-08-55	C.19	VM315	16-06-59 – 12-08-60
	C.19	PH843 FCV J	17-06-46 – 06-07-49	C.19	VP517 M J: 11	11-07-55 – 10-06-63
		FCV S	03-05-50 – 09-01-51	C.19	VP521 M A	03-10-55 – 20-07-59
	C.19	PH844	17-06-46 – 13-08-49	T.20	VS507	21-08-51 – 01-04-52
			10-03-50 – 07-03-51	C.21	VS575	13-11-50 – 02-04-51
	C.19	TX191 G I	01-08-51 – 15-07-52	T.21	VV981	04-07-52 – 28-08-52
			13-08-52 – 24-11-52	T.21	WB454	03-10-57 – 04-02-60
	C.19	TX192	28-05-50 – 02-11-51	T.21	WB463	04-07-52 – 28-08-52
	C.19	TX209	20-11-53 – 24-04-54			
Oxford	C.1	V3880 FDL C	nn-nn-nn – nn-nn-nn	C.1	NM521	12-11-46 – 19-12-46
	C.1	X6872 FDJ G	08-06-47 – 27-10-47	C.1	NM548	12-11-46 – 01-05-47
	C.1	BG244	nn-nn-nn – nn-nn-nn	C.1	NM710	13-12-46 – 01-05-47
	C.1	EB863	nn-nn-nn – nn-nn-nn	C.1	NM808	12-11-46 – 31-12-46
	C.1	HM696 FDL F	nn-05-46 – nn-nn-nn	C.1	PH186	nn-05-46 – 30-07-46
	C.1	HN667 FDL Z	nn-nn-nn – nn-nn-nn	C.1	PH372	12-11-46 – 19-12-46
	C.1	NJ399	12-11-46 – 25-04-47	C.1	PH462	12-11-46 – 08-05-47
Magister	T.1	L8262 FDL H	14-11-46 – 19-12-46	T.1	N3978 FDJ G	nn-nn-nn – nn-nn-nn
Lancaster	B.7	NX629	21-05-48 – 27-04-50	B.7	NX737 FDI B	04-04-49 – 05-04-50
	B.7	NX696 FDI C	11-09-47 – 08-11-49	B.7	NX754	19-08-48 – 20-04-50
	B.7	NX735	25-07-47 – 28-07-49	B.7	RT681	20-12-48 – 13-04-50
Mosquito	FB.6	RS551 FDO T	16-04-47 – 17-02-48	T.3	TW116	11-04-47 – 04-08-48
	FB.6	RS698	17-03-47 – 16-02-48	T.3	VA886	12-11-48 – 13-05-49
	T.3	HJ885 FDO U	08-12-48 – 15-08-49	T.3	VA889	06-03-50 – 12-04-50
	T.3	HJ978	15-08-47 – 27-08-47	T.3	VA891	27-10-47 – 08-02-49
	T.3	HJ991	24-04-47 – 06-05-48	T.3	VA892	14-01-48 – 10-08-50
	T.3	LR520	02-01-50 – 11-08-50	T.3	VT581	08-12-48 – 08-04-49
	T.3	LR539	27-10-49 – 24-03-50	T.3	VT586	08-12-48 – 01-09-49
	T.3	LR556	15-08-47 – 04-07-49	T.3	VT588 FDO D	24-05-49 – 13-12-50
	T.3	RR290	10-06-49 – 16-10-50	T.3	VT590	27-01-48 – 26-10-48
	T.3	RR298	20-08-47 – 07-06-48	T.3	VT591 FDO Y	13-10-47 – 01-12-49
	T.3	RR303	14-01-48 – 07-06-48	T.3	VT594	30-01-48 – 12-02-48
	T.3	RR308	26-08-48 – 04-11-48	T.3	VT604 FDO N	14-01-48 – 12-05-49

	T.3	RR317	22-09-47 – 07-06-48	T.3	VT605	21-08-48 – 26-10-48
	TT.35	TA639	31-05-63 – 05-07-67 M	T.3	VT608	09-02-48 – 20-01-49
	T.3	TV967	21-04-47 – 22-10-48	T.3	VT613	10-11-49 – 17-07-50
	T.3	TV983	14-03-50 – 12-02-51			
Buckmaster	T.1	RP173	22-04-47 – 25-02-48	T.1	RP230	10-04-47 – 25-02-48
	T.1	RP182 FDO E	27-03-47 – 25-02-48	T.1	VA360	19-07-51 – 06-09-51
	T.1	RP212	03-03-47 – 25-02-48	T.1	VA365	02-04-47 – 09-03-48
Vampire	F.1	TG295	28-08-47 – 27-05-48	T.11	XD454	27-04-54 – 15-03-56
	F.1	TG444	19-02-48 – 01-06-48	T.11	XD455 V G	10-12-60 – 29-05-61
	F.1	VF270	18-07-47 – 15-04-48	T.11	XD456 V E	02-04-58 – 03-03-61
	F.1	VF274	28-08-47 – 15-04-48	T.11	XD457 I W	29-08-56 – 12-04-57 M
	F.3	VF332	02-05-49 – 01-12-49	T.11	XD512 V T	09-07-59 – 21-12-59
	F.3	VF342	26-10-48 – 15-09-49	T.11	XD523 N D	17-06-54 – 10-10-56
	F.3	VT798	05-11-48 – 16-03-49	T.11	XD526 I P	03-12-54 – 16-03-56
	F.3	VT854	09-03-48 – 29-07-48	T.11	XD527 I Q	03-12-54 – 13-12-56
	F.3	VT856 FDJ L	23-02-48 – 04-10-49	T.11	XD531 N A	06-10-54 – 10-10-56
	F.3	VT860	09-03-48 – 07-09-49	T.11	XD532 N E	06-10-54 – 10-10-56
	FB.5	VV455 I P	05-02-52 – 29-05-54	T.11	XD534	03-12-54 – 16-03-56
	FB.5	VV559 I N	29-01-52 – 29-06-54	T.11	XD538 N M	17-12-54 – 13-09-56
	FB.5	VV600 I O	29-01-52 – 10-04-53	T.11	XD541 IT: N C	06-10-54 – 18-09-56
	FB.5	VZ868 I Q	12-02-52 – 08-02-54	T.11	XD543	03-12-54 – 03-03-55
	FB.5	VZ876 I R	03-03-52 – 29-08-54	T.11	XD550 V L: 32	01-07-59 – 16-01-67
	FB.5	WA215 I U	02-07-52 – 12-03-54	T.11	XD553 N F	07-10-54 – 08-11-56
	FB.5	WA216 I S	17-04-52 – 31-10-52	T.11	XD590 I V	13-10-54 – 13-12-56
	FB.5	WA250	16-12-54 – 19-09-55	T.11	XD593 V X: 36	04-10-60 – 19-12-62
	FB.5	WA359 I V	03-07-52 – 09-06-54	T.11	XD600 I C	01-02-55 – 21-12-56
	FB.5	WA381	20-08-52 – 19-08-54	T.11	XD603 N K	09-12-54 – 22-11-56
	FB.5	WA424 I T	25-04-52 – 20-06-53	T.11	XD605 I U	28-06-54 – 12-09-56
	FB.5	WE830 I H	30-04-52 – 21-05-52	T.11	XD612 I Z	23-08-55 – 12-09-56
	T.11	WZ416 V F	27-05-59 – 31-12-61	T.11	XD614	12-01-62 – 07-08-63
	T.11	WZ417	24-02-53 – 16-02-54	T.11	XD617 N O	26-09-55 – 24-10-56
	T.11	WZ466	13-10-55 – 16-11-55	T.11	XD621 I O	06-10-55 – 18-09-56
	T.11	WZ505	17-12-54 – 10-02-55	T.11	XD626	20-04-54 – 22-07-55
	T.11	WZ510 N L:V L	01-12-54 – 21-12-59	T.11	XE831 N H:V H	14-10-54 – 11-07-61
	T.11	WZ516	07-11-56 – 23-06-58	T.11	XE859	03-07-59 – 27-05-60
	T.11	WZ547	28-09-53 – 08-12-53	T.11	XE864 I R	10-12-54 – 11-05-56
	T.11	WZ550 N F	29-09-55 – 01-10-57	T.11	XE872 I P	18-04-55 – 22-10-57
	T.11	WZ551 N J:V J	03-12-54 – 27-04-61	T.11	XE876 V T	01-07-59 – 28-07-61
	T.11	WZ571	13-07-59 – 01-01-60	T.11	XE891 N O	11-03-55 – 24-08-55
	T.11	WZ574	07-11-56 – 26-07-57	T.11	XE893 I S:V S: 34	03-09-56 – 17-07-62
	T.11	WZ576 I Y	03-12-54 – 10-02-55	T.11	XE921 I R:V R: 33	03-09-56 – 27-06-63
	T.11	WZ585 I X:V X	22-08-56 – 29-08-60	T.11	XE994 I P:V P	05-09-56 – 24-05-61
	T.11	WZ617	26-11-53 – 31-03-55	T.11	XH304 71	09-12-71 – 12-04-76
	T.11	XD376 I Z:V Z: 37	03-10-56 – 27-09-62	T.11	XH322 V K	10-10-58 – 27-03-61
	T.11	XD379 I V	29-10-56 – 04-11-57	T.11	XK582 N B:V B	30-05-56 – 28-07-61
	T.11	XD381 I Y: N G	31-12-53 – 25-10-56	T.11	XK586 V O	04-02-57 – 30-05-61
	T.11	XD383 V W: 35	10-07-59 – 06-06-63	T.11	XK624 32	16-01-67 – 14-12-71
	T.11	XD389 I X	05-12-53 – 04-12-56	T.11	XK627 V C: 31	21-09-56 – 03-08-62
	T.11	XD393 I C: I S	06-10-54 – 23-06-56	T.11	XK628 I T:V T	12-09-56 – 24-07-59
	T.11	XD405 N B	06-10-54 – 22-06-56	T.11	XK629 V N	14-09-56 – 05-12-57
	T.11	XD436 I B	01-02-55 – 18-09-56	T.11	XK630 N E:V E	26-09-56 – 04-09-58
	T.11	XD443	12-01-62 – 06-04-62	T.11	XK631 N D:V F	04-10-56 – 07-04-59
	T.11	XD446 V G	30-04-59 – 31-12-60	T.11	XK632 N G:V G	12-10-56 – 02-12-58
	T.11	XD448 I A	01-02-55 – 13-11-56	T.11	XK633 N A:V A: 30	30-10-56 – 27-06-63
Spitfire	F.9	BS348 FCW C	nn-nn-nn – nn-nn-nn	LF.16e	TD284	03-07-47 – 20-01-48
	F.21	LA226 QL E	09-02-58 – nn-nn-67 GG	LF.16e	TD376 FDJ O	13-05-48 – 27-10-49
	F.9	MJ216 FCW F	nn-nn-nn – nn-nn-nn	LF.16e	TE193	20-04-49 – 01-07-49
	LF.16e	SL721 JMR	21-09-51 – nn-nn-55	LF.16e	TE200	21-08-47 – 27-09-49
	LF.16e	SL731	04-08-51 – 30-11-53	LF.16e	TE356	04-12-70 – 13-04-76 GG
	LF.16e	SM330	02-02-48 – 26-05-49	LF.16e	TE460	11-04-47 – 21-04-48
	LF.16e	SM340	14-04-47 – 29-04-48			
Auster	AOP.5	TW440 FDM Z	11-03-48 – 05-06-51	T.7	WE569	01-09-51 – 26-01-55
	AOP.6	VF611	12-12-47 – 27-02-48	T.7	WE570	01-09-51 – 12-01-55
	AOP.6	VF639	12-12-47 – 27-02-48	T.7	WE571	04-10-54 – 05-11-54
	T.7	WE568	04-09-53 – 04-02-54			
Prentice	T.1	VN687 FDI M	20-01-48 – 08-07-48	T.1	VS275 FDI O	16-08-48 – 03-01-49
	T.1	VN702 FDI O	20-01-48 – 08-07-48	T.1	VS276	11-09-51 – 14-04-51

	Mark	Serial / Code	Dates
	T.1	VR190	01-09-51 – 30-09-51
	T.1	VR192	01-09-51 – 14-11-51
	T.1	VR196 N J:T: L T	01-09-51 – 11-01-54
	T.1	VR200	01-09-51 – 09-07-52
	T.1	VR205 L E	01-09-51 – 19-01-54
	T.1	VR206 L M	01-09-51 – 22-06-53
	T.1	VR207	01-09-51 – 22-09-53
	T.1	VR208 L P	01-09-51 – 22-09-53
	T.1	VR209	01-09-51 – 23-02-54
	T.1	VR221	01-09-51 – 06-11-51
	T.1	VR237	01-09-51 – 13-11-51
	T.1	VR240 FDI L	01-09-51 – 10-07-53
	T.1	VR241 FDI K	30-07-48 – 04-06-51
	T.1	VR246 FDI N	16-08-48 – 27-01-49
	T.1	VR247 FDI O	16-08-48 – 11-11-48
	T.1	VR251 FDI P	23-08-48 – 03-09-48
	T.1	VR252	23-08-48 – 22-04-49
	T.1	VR263	01-09-51 – 12-01-54
	T.1	VR267 FDI O: N C	04-09-50 – 04-06-51
	T.1	VR270	01-09-51 – 07-09-54
	T.1	VR275 FDI U	01-09-51 – 13-12-53
	T.1	VR276	04-09-52 – 22-06-53
	T.1	VR287	01-09-51 – 15-11-51
	T.1	VR293 J Q	01-09-51 – 02-02-54
	T.1	VR307	01-09-51 – 28-11-51
	T.1	VR316 L L	01-09-51 – 29-01-54
	T.1	VS241 FDI K	01-09-51 – 14-11-51
	T.1	VS244	01-09-51 – 14-11-51
	T.1	VS251	04-09-50 – 04-06-51
	T.1	VS268	16-08-48 – 17-01-49
	T.1	VS272 FDI T	16-08-48 – 14-12-48
	T.1	VS273 FDI U	16-08-48 – 11-07-51
	T.1	VS274	16-08-48 – 29-01-49
	T.1	VS278	16-08-48 – 17-02-49
	T.1	VS279 FDI Y	16-08-48 – 04-06-51
	T.1	VS319 N I	01-05-51 – 18-01-54
	T.1	VS320 N X	01-09-51 – 29-01-54
	T.1	VS332	01-09-51 – 11-01-54
	T.1	VS356	01-09-51 – 18-01-54
	T.1	VS369 FDI L	11-07-49 – 05-06-51
	T.1	VS373	01-09-51 – 31-10-51
	T.1	VS385	03-12-50 – 26-07-51
	T.1	VS388	01-09-51 – 04-01-54
	T.1	VS389 FDI M	18-07-49 – 11-07-51
	T.1	VS394	01-09-51 – 26-08-52
	T.1	VS395 N R	01-09-51 – 04-01-54
	T.1	VS396 FDI L: MV	01-09-51 – 19-01-54
	T.1	VS410	01-09-51 – 06-11-51
	T.1	VS619 N A	01-09-51 – 18-06-53
	T.1	VS620	01-09-51 – 14-11-51
	T.1	VS621	01-09-51 – 19-01-54
	T.1	VS623	01-09-51 – 19-01-54
	T.1	VS624 L J: N J	01-09-51 – 22-06-53
	T.1	VS625 FDI F	01-09-51 – 14-01-54
	T.1	VS626	01-09-51 – 06-11-51
	T.1	VS627	01-09-51 – 18-06-53
	T.1	VS628 N J	01-09-51 – 19-01-54
	T.1	VS630	01-09-51 – 04-01-54
	T.1	VS644	01-09-51 – 31-12-53
	T.1	VS724	01-09-51 – 12-08-53
	T.1	VS727 N B	01-09-51 – 31-10-51
	T.1	VS731 N K	01-09-51 – 22-06-53
	T.1	VS732	01-09-51 – 19-01-54
	T.1	VS733 L B: N B	01-09-51 – 14-01-54
	T.1	VS744	01-09-51 – 29-01-54
	T.1	VS745 FDI N	05-06-50 – 11-07-51
Meteor	F.3	EE282	07-11-50 – 29-12-50
	F.3	EE287	07-11-50 – 29-12-50
	F.3	EE426 FDU 6	07-11-50 – 29-12-50
	F.4	EE474	27-11-50 – 29-12-50
	T.7	VW419	21-02-52 – 10-03-52
	T.7	VW421	16-04-57 – 30-04-57
	T.7	VW433	28-06-49 – 12-07-49
	T.7	VW434	nn-nn-49 – nn-nn-nn
	T.7	VW435	28-06-49 – 14-04-57
	T.7	VW437	30-04-49 – 12-01-51
	T.7	VW438 FDJ P	12-05-49 – 11-04-51
	T.7	VW450 FDJ R	18-05-49 – 11-01-51
	T.7	VW455	20-02-52 – 20-04-52
	T.7	VW472	20-02-52 – 20-12-54
	T.7	VW475 FDJ A	22-10-50 – 15-11-51
	T.7	VW478 25	15-03-61 – 18-04-63
	T.7	VW481 FDJ U: O A	05-07-49 – 15-02-55
	T.7	VW485 26	12-04-61 – 28-08-63
	T.7	VZ635	15-10-52 – 18-12-52
	T.7	VZ642	08-08-49 – 05-11-51
	T.7	WA597	05-02-51 – 28-02-51
	T.7	WA615	12-06-53 – 14-04-54
	T.7	WA660 O D	31-12-53 – 08-07-55
	T.7	WA663 O Q	20-11-53 – 05-03-54
			06-02-56 – 11-05-56
	T.7	WA664	18-01-54 – 02-02-55
	T.7	WA666	23-06-52 – 11-10-52
	T.7	WA668	14-03-50 – 29-06-50
	T.7	WA669 27	24-04-69 – 27-10-75
	T.7	WA673	01-05-50 – 30-10-50
	T.7	WA678	01-05-50 – 20-02-51
	T.7	WA679	01-05-50 – 20-02-51
	T.7	WA682	08-05-52 – 25-02-53
	T.7	WA686	28-06-54 – 09-11-54
	T.7	WA688 FDJ Q: O Q	05-07-50 – 27-07-55
	T.7	WA691 FDJ Y: O Y	22-06-50 – 20-08-52
	T.7	WA698 O Z	30-08-50 – 04-03-54
	T.7	WF840 O G	26-11-53 – 19-07-55
	T.7	WF844	10-03-52 – 29-04-52
	T.7	WF851 O P	03-01-56 – 18-04-56
	T.7	WF852 O C	15-06-51 – 31-12-52
	T.7	WG962 O P: 27	24-11-52 – 23-12-55
			20-11-60 – 26-06-62
	T.7	WG964	21-07-54 – 15-10-54
	T.7	WG969	29-03-57 – 01-08-57
	T.7	WG979	21-07-54 – 14-10-54
	T.7	WG980	09-08-54 – 31-12-54
	T.7	WG981 O T	19-01-56 – 18-02-57
	T.7	WG987 O B	21-02-52 – 21-04-53
	T.7	WG993	27-07-53 – 12-11-54
	T.7	WH118	05-02-52 – 27-05-52
	T.7	WH131	04-03-52 – 10-11-53
	T.7	WH132	30-06-60 – 15-03-61
	T.7	WH166 27	26-01-65 – 12-09-69
	T.7	WH172 O K	07-02-56 – 17-10-56
	T.7	WH177 O H	05-08-52 – 12-07-54
	T.7	WH178 O N	05-03-56 – 24-07-57
	T.7	WH182	29-06-59 – 22-12-60
	T.7	WH183 O K	06-05-57 – 08-03-58
	T.7	WH184	14-09-54 – 15-10-54
	T.7	WH187 O X	16-03-56 – 23-05-57
	T.7	WH192 O U	17-09-54 – 16-08-57
	T.7	WH200	25-06-54 – 09-03-55
	T.7	WH217 O S	24-04-52 – 09-10-52
	T.7	WH218	22-06-52 – 20-01-55
	T.7	WH219	26-03-56 – 17-10-56
	T.7	WH225	11-06-52 – 19-09-52
	T.7	WH241 O N	05-03-52 – 07-12-53
	T.7	WH245 O M	05-03-52 – 04-12-53
	T.7	WH246	27-03-52 – 23-07-52
	T.7	WH247	12-03-52 – 27-10-54
	T.7	WH248	10-03-52 – 28-05-52
	T.7	WL359 O T	23-04-52 – 31-01-56
	T.7	WL364	07-09-54 – 21-04-55

	T.7	WA707	01-12-53 – 05-03-54	T.7	WL367 O F	15-12-53 – 16-08-55
	T.7	WA708	01-09-50 – 22-02-51			20-06-62 – 05-09-63
	T.7	WA714	17-06-52 – 03-11-53	T.7	WL369	10-06-51 – 16-06-52
	T.7	WA727	09-09-54 – 23-10-54	T.7	WL370 O K	15-07-52 – 15-02-56
	T.7	WA737	15-03-51 – 21-08-51	T.7	WL371 O E	21-05-54 – 12-01-55
	T.7	WA741 FDJ D: O D	01-02-51 – 01-10-52	T.7	WL373 O N	07-05-54 – 27-03-56
	T.7	WF766	31-01-51 – 20-04-51	T.7	WL374 O V	10-06-52 – 28-07-54
	T.7	WF769 FDJ E: O E	01-02-51 – 17-12-54	T.7	WL381 O I	12-06-52 – 25-02-53
	T.7	WF772	04-04-51 – 31-08-53	T.7	WL403 O K	24-04-58 – 08-09-60
	T.7	WF776	01-07-54 – 12-01-55	T.7	WL457	21-12-53 – 28-07-54
	T.7	WF791 27	14-07-62 – 26-01-65	T.7	WL458	03-11-53 – 09-11-53
			19-03-76 – 12-04-76	T.7	WL460	03-05-57 – 08-12-59
	T.7	WF826	15-09-60 – 24-04-61	T.7	WL481 O A	30-10-52 – 17-03-55
	T.7	WF829	20-11-53 – 29-12-53			
Balliol	T.1	VL892	nn-10-50 – 09-01-51	T.2	VR594	21-10-49 – 27-07-50
	T.2	VR593 FDO O	21-10-49 – 27-07-50			
Athena	T.2	VR566	31-10-49 – 02-02-50	T.2	VR567	31-10-49 – 29-06-50
Chipmunk	T.10	WB550 08	02-11-65 – 16-04-69	T.10	WG479 11	nn-nn-69 – nn-06-73
	T.10	WB551 FDL X	07-02-50 – 15-01-51	T.10	WG480 13	nn-nn-nn – nn-nn-nn
	T.10	WB562 10	02-11-65 – 26-09-69	T.10	WG483	21-07-54 – 12-08-54
	T.10	WB586 03	13-01-65 – 19-06-69	T.10	WK521 12	09-09-66 – 24-10-73
	T.10	WB613	20-05-50 – 18-07-50	T.10	WK573 M A: 12	30-11-60 – 12-09-66
	T.10	WB648	13-06-50 – 27-07-50	T.10	WK590 M B	nn-nn-nn – nn-nn-nn
	T.10	WB649	13-06-50 – 22-02-51	T.10	WK591 15	23-06-61 – 29-09-66
	T.10	WB650 09	14-01-66 – 24-10-73	T.10	WK628 13	09-09-66 – 22-09-69
	T.10	WB654	07-04-64 – 30-09-64	T.10	WK633	30-04-64 – 07-07-64
	T.10	WB684 08	30-10-69 – 24-10-73	T.10	WK634	05-08-55 – 29-09-55
	T.10	WB697	11-07-61 – 31-07-61	T.10	WK643	nn-nn-nn – nn-nn-nn
	T.10	WB738 06: 10: 15	31-01-66 – 09-02-67	T.10	WP797	16-06-75 – 20-08-75
			05-07-68 – 18-05-71	T.10	WP807 15	24-02-70 – 15-05-74
	T.10	WB760	16-08-68 – 13-09-68	T.10	WP844 02	30-07-57 – 05-02-60
	T.10	WB765	nn-nn-nn – nn-nn-nn			26-09-69 – 06-04-73
	T.10	WD299 06: 15	11-03-57 – 21-05-57	T.10	WP848 06	06-04-67 – 04-08-67
			01-09-67 – 22.10.73	T.10	WP850	21-03-68 – 30-04-68
	T.10	WD347	26-09-69 – 22-10-73	T.10	WP868	30-07-57 – 07-10-58
	T.10	WD361	29-03-57 – 03-05-57	T.10	WP897	21-07-54 – 25-08-54
	T.10	WG290	nn-nn-nn – nn-nn-nn	T.10	WP905	27-02-57 – 27-04-57
	T.10	WG299 M C: 14	28-04-59 – 22-06-66	T.10	WP912	04-02-65 – 02-04-65
	T.10	WG305	07-02-57 – 20-05-57	T.10	WP924 02: 07	30-12-65 – 22-09-69
	T.10	WG307	18-09-68 – 27-09-68	T.10	WP984	27-02-67 – 10-03-67
	T.10	WG317 02	25-06-69 – 17-08-69			30-09-67 – 07-12-67
	T.10	WG348 11	17-11-64 – 22-09-69	T.10	WZ847 01	nn-09-69 – nn-nn-73
	T.10	WG364 07	15-09-69 – 24-10-73	T.10	WZ855	23-03-56 – 06-04-56
	T.10	WG403 04	28-08-63 – 26-09-63	T.10	WZ873 15	31-01-66 – 09-02-67
			25-03-68 – 02-08-75	T.10	WZ874 15	16-02-68 – 02-05-68
	T.10	WG407 13	nn-11-69 – nn-06-73	T.10	WZ875 10	02-11-65 – nn-09-66
	T.10	WG422	04-02-70 – 06-04-70	T.10	WZ877 05	16-05-58 – 28-05-58
	T.10	WG430 14	nn-01-67 – nn-04-69			18-12-63 – 24-09-73
	T.10	WG431	29-03-57 – 13-05-57	T.10	WZ879 14	04-04-74 – 08-04-76
	T.10	WG469	nn-nn-nn – nn-nn-nn			
Dakota	C.4	KN506	06-10-50 – 07-01-51			
Brigand	B.1	RH759	09-10-51 – 12-10-51			
Valetta	C.1	VW195	16-12-55 – 31-12-55	C.1	WD163	16-04-52 – 18-08-52
	C.1	VW843 M F	24-11-52 – 04-11-58	C.1	WJ496 496: M F	25-09-58 – 24-05-60
	C.1	VX483	22-09-52 – 06-01-53			
Piston Provost	T.1	WV422	08-10-53 – 10-09-54	T.1	WV638 O W	23-06-54 – 10-05-56
	T.1	WV423	26-06-53 – 28-03-56	T.1	WV639 O Z	01-07-54 – 07-06-57
	T.1	WV424 X A	20-06-53 – 04-02-56	T.1	WV640	01-07-54 – 21-10-55
	T.1	WV427	22-06-53 – 23-07-53	T.1	WV641 X C	05-07-54 – 02-05-56
	T.1	WV429 O N	22-06-53 – 23-07-53	T.1	WV642 X D	05-07-54 – 14-07-57
			09-07-54 – 11-05-57	T.1	WV670 N C	23-08-54 – 24-01-56
	T.1	WV430 O A	09-11-53 – 06-12-53	T.1	WV678 N Q	03-09-54 – 16-01-56
			29-11-55 – 14-08-56	T.1	WV681 O B: P F	03-09-56 – 19-12-60
	T.1	WV431 X F	25-06-53 – 25-07-57	T.1	WV682 OF	03-09-54 – 16-08-57
	T.1	WV432 O J	28-05-53 – 31-03-57	T.1	WW386 P G	15-06-59 – 19-12-60
	T.1	WV433	08-06-53 – 14-03-56	T.1	WW392 P J: 05	11-05-57 – 01-08-62

Type	Mark	Serial	Dates	Mark	Serial	Dates
	T.1	WV434	15-06-53 – 22-07-53	T.1	WW397	07-10-68 – 28-10-68
	T.1	WV435	15-06-53 – 22-07-53	T.1	WW426	04-10-60 – 21-12-60
	T.1	WV436 O S	23-06-53 – 19-12-57	T.1	WW439 M G: P R	22-12-59 – 31-08-60
	T.1	WV438 O Q: X B	15-07-53 – 23-04-57	T.1	XE506	28-09-53 – 31-12-53
	T.1	WV439	07-06-57 – 10-09-57	T.1	XF542 M E	22-12-54 – 04-12-58
	T.1	WV440 N H	29-04-55 – 23-06-56	T.1	XF544 N K	10-01-55 – 23-02-55
	T.1	WV471 01	14-03-63 – 27-07-64	T.1	XF558	20-08-57 – 22-11-57
	T.1	WV472	28-09-53 – 02-08-57	T.1	XF560	10-01-55 – 23-02-55
	T.1	WV475 X B	28-06-54 – 22-04-57	T.1	XF563 X H	12-04-55 – 22-04-57
	T.1	WV476 X H	14-09-53 – 06-10-54	T.1	XF565 P L	13-04-55 – 20-12-60
	T.1	WV477 N J: X L	28-09-53 – 25-04-57	T.1	XF600 O V	05-04-55 – 22-04-57
	T.1	WV478 X J	28-09-53 – 10-07-57	T.1	XF604 O D: P H	18-03-55 – 31-10-60
	T.1	WV479	08-10-53 – 01-12-54	T.1	XF605 O M	18-03-55 – 16-01-59
	T.1	WV480 X N	02-10-53 – 15-09-57	T.1	XF606 P K: 04	13-05-57 – 26-11-62
	T.1	WV481 X D	02-10-53 – 11-07-57	T.1	XF607 X G: P E	05-04-55 – 01-12-59
	T.1	WV494 04	16-11-62 – 27-07-64	T.1	XF609 X K: P D	05-04-55 – 22-11-60
	T.1	WV505	25-08-54 – 04-02-55	T.1	XF614 P Z	09-08-57 – 22-08-60
	T.1	WV506 X E	07-06-54 – 16-07-57	T.1	XF678 X R: P N	14-10-55 – 19-12-60
	T.1	WV508	12-07-54 – 05-08-57	T.1	XF679 02	10-09-63 – 27-07-64
	T.1	WV509	29-09-54 – 23-02-55	T.1	XF680 P P: P T: 06	26-09-57 – 26-11-62
	T.1	WV510	07-09-54 – 16-01-56	T.1	XF681 P Q	09-08-57 – 19-12-60
	T.1	WV512	07-06-57 – 14-06-57	T.1	XF689 P P	30-04-59 – 01-06-60
	T.1	WV532	29-09-54 – 13-01-56	T.1	XF837 P C	30-05-57 – 18-07-61
	T.1	WV533	28-09-54 – 16-01-56	T.1	XF841 03	11-12-63 – 18-09-64
	T.1	WV536 O B	31-08-54 – 26-10-55	T.1	XF891 P W	01-08-57 – 01-01-60
	T.1	WV537	05-04-55 – 23-02-56	T.1	XF892 P B	30-05-57 – 29-01-62
	T.1	WV570	07-08-54 – 22-04-55	T.1	XF895 P A: 01	30-05-57 – 21-02-63
	T.1	WV575	31-08-54 – 18-01-56	T.1	XF896 05	26-10-62 – 18-09-64
	T.1	WV576 P M	31-08-54 – 21-12-60	T.1	XF897	01-08-57 – 22-04-59
	T.1	WV579 N G: N J	31-08-54 – 18-01-56	T.1	XF898 P Z: 02	14-10-60 – 12-09-63
	T.1	WV604 N G	07-08-54 – 24-01-56	T.1	XF900 P P: 03	18-03-60 – 22-11-63
	T.1	WV608	07-06-57 – 14-06-57	T.1	XF909	01-08-57 – 22-11-57
	T.1	WV611	31-08-54 – 22-12-54	T.1	XF911 P S	22-07-57 – 19-12-60
	T.1	WV618	07-06-57 – 14-06-57	T.1	XF913 P X	01-08-57 – 20-12-60
	T.1	WV620	07-09-54 – 18-01-56	T.1	XF914 P V	09-08-57 – 17-08-59
	T.1	WV637 X R	23-06-54 – 30-09-55			
Venom	FB.1	WE263	16-09-53 – 15-01-54	FB.1	WE264	02-02-54 – 03-05-54
Sea Fury	T.20	WE821	nn-nn-nn – 04-02-54			
Pembroke	C.1	WV738	14-02-55 – 01-03-55			
Hunter	T.7	WV318	23-11-60 – 11-03-63	F.4	XF934 C	13-02-59 – 15-06-61
	F.4	WV319	07-11-55 – 13-01-56	F.4	XF935 D	28-11-58 – 15-03-61
	F.4	WV325 C	09-11-55 – 10-03-59	F.4	XF943 B	30-10-58 – 27-06-62
	F.4	WV331 B	07-11-55 – 11-12-58	F.4	XF944 A	28-10-58 – 11-03-63
	F.4	WT806 A	01-03-57 – 04-11-57	F.4	XF973 E W	27-08-57 – 11-03-63
	F.4	XE704 A	11-11-57 – 14-11-58	F.4	XF980	25-07-56 – 24-08-56
	F.4	XF313 D	04-05-57 – 04-02-59	F.4	XF999	07-09-56 – 24-10-56
	F.4	XF933	31-08-60 – 06-09-61	T.7	XL611	18-05-61 – 11-03-63
Canberra	T.4	WD944 C A: 20	20-06-57 – 03-10-62	T.4	WJ991 C B: 21	12-08-57 – 13-01-59
	B.2	WH712	03-10-57 – 28-11-57			26-02-60 – 13-11-62
	B.2	WH878	03-10-57 – 28-11-57	T.4	WT480 C C: 22	nn-nn-57 – nn-nn-62
Jet Provost	T.1	XD675	19-11-57 – 10-11-59	T.3	XN584 78	28-11-75 – 12-04-76
	T.1	XD676	19-11-57 – 12-11-59	T.3	XN586 73	03-10-69 – 12-02-70
	T.1	XD677	19-11-57 – 10-11-59	T.3	XN591 S K: 69	28-06-61 – 10-03-65
	T.1	XD678	19-11-57 – 10-11-59	T.3	XN595 69	17-07-69 – 26-06-75
	T.1	XD679	19-11-57 – 10-11-59	T.3	XN640 74	01-09-64 – 05-08-75
	T.1	XD680	19-11-57 – 10-11-59	T.3	XN643	18-03-63 – 30-07-63
	T.1	XD693	19-11-57 – 16-11-59	T.4	XP549 40	23-11-61 – 18-05-66
	T.2	XD694	nn-nn-57 – nn-nn-57	T.4	XP550 41	23-11-61 – 20-05-66
	T.3	XM346 R R	31-08-60 – 31-07-61	T.4	XP551 42	07-12-61 – 18-05-66
	T.3	XM349 68	30-09-69 – 12-04-76	T.4	XP552 43	07-12-61 – 16-05-66
	T.3	XM355 R A: 74	31-07-59 – 22-03-62	T.4	XP553 44	11-12-61 – 22-03-67
	T.3	XM356 R B: 70	31-07-59 – 22-03-62	T.4	XP554 45	07-12-61 – 12-04-67
	T.3	XM357 R C	31-07-59 – 23-02-62	T.4	XP570 46	13-03-62 – 30-04-66
	T.3	XM358 70	30-06-66 – 12-04-76	T.4	XP571 47	02-03-62 – 21-05-66
	T.3	XM359 R D: 76	31-07-59 – 22-03-62	T.4	XP572 48	13-03-62 – 24-02-67
	T.3	XM360 R E: 71	31-07-59 – 24-01-69	T.4	XP573 49	13-03-62 – 16-05-66
	T.3	XM361 R F: 82	31-07-59 – 22-03-62	T.4	XP575 50	13-03-62 – 12-03-65

	T.3	XM364 68	18-03-62 – 26-08-69	T.4	XP588 51	27-04-62 – 02-05-63
	T.3	XM366 61	14-07-69 – 29-12-75	T.4	XP632 52	27-06-62 – 12-03-65
	T.3	XM371 66	24-09-75 – 12-04-76	T.4	XP639 53	20-07-62 – 12-03-64
	T.3	XM374 71	21-07-69 – 03-02-70	T.4	XP640 51	10-04-64 – 26-02-65
	T.3	XM375 S J	19-06-61 – 05-10-61	T.4	XP641	20-07-62 – 21-12-62
	T.3	XM378 60	09-05-69 – 30-10-75	T.4	XP642	20-07-62 – 21-12-62
	T.3	XM386 69	10-09-65 – 17-07-68	T.4	XP675 48	24-02-67 – 26-02-68
	T.3	XM401	18-03-63 – 10-09-63	T.4	XP679 45	12-04-67 – 26-01-68
	T.3	XM411 R G: 73	22-03-60 – 26-08-69	T.4	XR670 51	05-06-63 – 12-03-64
	T.3	XM413 R H: 68	22-03-60 – 22-03-62	T.4	XR671 48: 54	05-06-63 – 31-05-66
	T.3	XM418 S B	01-03-61 – 14-12-61			18-02-69 – 14-10-69
	T.3	XM419 60	14-10-75 – 12-04-76	T.4	XR678 55	03-07-63 – 20-02-69
	T.3	XM421 S C: 80	01-03-61 – 08-08-62	T.4	XR680 45	08-03-68 – 17-03-70
	T.3	XM422 S D	31-03-61 – 14-12-61	T.4	XR704 56	16-01-64 – 26-02-65
	T.3	XM423 R J	17-05-60 – 30-08-61	T.4	XR705 57	16-01-64 – 26-02-65
	T.3	XM424 R K: 72	17-05-60 – 20-08-70	T.4	XR706 48	08-10-69 – 22-01-70
	T.3	XM425 R L: 75	24-05-60 – 03-06-75	T.4	XS175 44	23-03-67 – 06-11-69
	T.3	XM426 R N	10-06-60 – 11-01-62	T.4	XS178 53	20-11-63 – 11-03-65
	T.3	XM428 R M	30-08-60 – 13-10-61	T.4	XS182 58	02-02-64 – 19-03-65
	T.3	XM460 70	01-09-64 – 14-12-64	T.4	XS212 40	06-05-66 – 18-02-70
	T.3	XM461	19-02-74 – 31-07-74	T.4	XS213 46	20-05-66 – 18-02-69
	T.3	XM466	21-07-75 – 01-09-75	T.4	XS217 50	24-04-66 – 09-02-73
	T.3	XM470 63	09-05-69 – 01-07-75			07-03-74 – 16-07-74
	T.3	XM471 R O	01-09-60 – 11-01-62	T.4	XS222 43	22-04-66 – 15-12-69
	T.3	XM472 R P: 81	01-09-60 – 05-06-62	T.4	XS225 47	06-05-66 – 17-03-70
	T.3	XM473 61	27-08-64 – 06-02-68	T.4	XS226 42	17-04-66 – 08-12-69
	T.3	XM474 R Q	31-08-60 – 14-12-61	T.4	XS229 49	22-04-66 – 26-02-68
	T.3	XN137 R S: 77	28-09-60 – 10-09-63	T.5	XW287 80	04-09-69 – 15-08-74
	T.3	XN462 62	31-01-69 – 27-10-75	T.5	XW288 81	25-09-69 – 28-01-76
	T.3	XN464 R T	01-11-60 – 04-12-61	T.5	XW289 82	06-10-69 – 15-10-75
	T.3	XN465 R U	01-11-60 – 09-11-61	T.5	XW290 83	08-10-69 – 08-12-75
	T.4	XN467 49	17-07-69 – 15-06-70	T.5	XW291 84	23-10-69 – 03-10-74
	T.4	XN468 41	22-05-66 – 23-10-69	T.5	XW292 85	14-11-69 – 18-11-75
	T.3	XN472 R V: 78	23-11-60 – 06-08-71	T.5	XW293 86	13-11-69 – 18-04-75
	T.3	XN502 66	18-07-69 – 01-10-75	T.5	XW294 87	26-11-69 – 09-05-75
	T.3	XN506 74	12-11-75 – 12-04-76	T.5	XW295 88	09-12-69 – 30-01-75
	T.3	XN511 R W: 64	27-02-61 – 13-10-69	T.5	XW297 90	15-12-69 – 20-01-70
	T.3	XN512 R X: 65	27-02-61 – 14-10-69	T.5	XW315 83	27-11-75 – 12-04-76
	T.3	XN548 R Z: 67	27-02-61 – 22-01-76	T.5	XW316 82	27-11-75 – 12-04-76
	T.3	XN549 R Y: 66	27-02-61 – 26-01-68	T.5	XW414 89	16-11-71 – 12-04-76
	T.3	XN550 S A: 63	07-03-61 – 30-05-69	T.5	XW421 90	06-12-71 – 12-04-76
	T.3	XN554 S E: 60	27-03-61 – 30-05-69	T.5	XW425 84	06-06-74 – 12-04-76
	T.3	XN557 S F	14-04-61 – 27-07-62	T.5	XW434 92	07-08-73 – 12-04-76
	T.3	XN573 S G: 62	27-04-61 – 03-04-68	T.5	XW435 93	26-03-74 – 12-04-76
	T.3	XN576 S H: 79	27-04-61 – 29-09-69	T.5	XW437 91	30-07-73 – 12-04-76
	T.3	XN581 77	19-01-72 – 12-04-76			
Varsity	T.1	WF325 18	18-03-63 – 22-06-66	T.1	WJ920 M D	29-02-60 – 31-03-61
	T.1	WF377	07-07-72 – 23-09-74	T.1	WJ942	12-11-69 – 04-02-70
	T.1	WF389	15-10-69 – 15-11-69	T.1	WJ945 21	27-02-67 – 26-10-74
	T.1	WF409 20	08-05-63 – 06-12-63	T.1	WJ948	19-09-60 – 10-01-62
	T.1	WF410	05-08-65 – 10-03-66	T.1	WJ949 19	05-04-62 – 01-05-67
			31-01-69 – 13-08-69			03-04-68 – 01-10-74
	T.1	WF411 18	16-12-66 – 27-11-73	T.1	WL623	13-02-68 – 24-04-68
	T.1	WF412 M G: 17	28-07-60 – 23-05-67	T.1	WL628	29-06-72 – 06-07-72
	T.1	WF418	18-03-70 – 02-10-70	T.1	WL666 18	03-11-61 – 24-08-62
	T.1	WF424 17	17-01-68 – 07-10-74	T.1	WL670	15-07-70 – 18-05-71
	T.1	WJ886 23	13-04-62 – 21-04-72	T.1	WL671 20	28-10-64 – 14-08-72
	T.1	WJ889	03-01-69 – 18-07-69	T.1	WL680	18-03-60 – 09-06-60
	T.1	WJ908 M E: 29	27-04-60 – 01-03-63	T.1	WL689 M H	27-06-61 – 29-09-61
	T.1	WJ919	19-02-60 – 26-05-60	T.1	XD366 M F: 16	06-05-60 – 06-01-69
Gnat	T.1	XM704 90: 95	13-12-63 – 28-09-66	T.1	XR544 B	18-01-72 – 12-04-76
	T.1	XM705 91: 98: B	07-12-62 – 08-02-71	T.1	XR545	03-04-70 – 20-01-71
			08-02-72 – 11-05-72	T.1	XR567 B	14-07-71 – 13-12-71
	T.1	XM706 92: 94: D	11-05-62 – 15-05-72	T.1	XR569 105: 90	05-11-63 – 31-01-67
	T.1	XM707 93: 91	16-07-63 – 30-06-67			06-01-69 – 28-04-69
	T.1	XM708 94: 99	10-05-62 – 09-02-72	T.1	XR572 R	31-10-72 – 12-04-76
	T.1	XM709 95: 92: C	02-02-62 – 14-04-71	T.1	XR573 97	22-08-68 – 26-03-69
	T.1	XP501 96	05-11-62 – 13-06-69	T.1	XR574	23-03-72 – 03-05-72
	T.1	XP504 95: K	30-12-67 – 23-09-70			01-08-74 – 28-02-75

	T.1	XP505	28-02-66 – 01-04-66
	T.1	XP511	23-03-72 – 02-08-72
	T.1	XP514	29-04-71 – 02-07-71
	T.1	XP515 98: 102: A	02-04-63 – 27-07-65
			02-01-69 – 21-01-70
			02-01-73 – 08-10-74
	T.1	XP516	23-03-72 – 13-04-72
			05-01-76 – 12-04-76
	T.1	XP530 97	24-03-63 – 03-01-66
	T.1	XP531 99	07-05-63 – 15-11-65
			23-03-72 – 16-02-76
	T.1	XP532	25-10-72 – 30-05-73
	T.1	XP534 101: E	23-05-63 – 23-04-65
			23-03-72 – 18-04-72
			30-05-73 – 04-09-73
	T.1	XP535 102	29-05-63 – 13-04-65
	T.1	XP536 103: 106	30-05-63 – 26-04-65
			03-01-69 – 08-05-69
	T.1	XP537 100	17-05-63 – 31-05-65
			23-03-72 – 13-04-72
			28-02-75 – 03-09-75
	T.1	XP538 K	28-06-71 – 25-07-72
			23-09-75 – 05-12-75
	T.1	XP539 L	04-04-73 – 12-04-76
	T.1	XP541	23-09-72 – 23-05-72
			23-09-75 – 05-12-75
	T.1	XP542	07-11-72 – 16-07-74
	T.1	XR534 104: 93: L	05-07-63 – 03-06-70
			23-09-75 – 03-12-75
	T.1	XR537	23-03-72 – 18-04-72
	T.1	XR540	27-01-65 – 12-04-76
	T.1	XR541 98: C	20-06-68 – 12-05-69
			25-10-72 – 12-04-76
			23-09-75 – 05-12-75
	T.1	XR951	08-02-72 – 14-04-72
			23-09-74 – 12-04-76
	T.1	XR954	23-09-75 – 03-12-75
	T.1	XR955	28-04-72 – 12-04-76
	T.1	XR977	22-03-76 – 12-04-76
	T.1	XR980 H	23-02-71 – 13-08-73
			23-09-75 – 12-04-76
	T.1	XR981 100: J: H	07-10-68 – 12-04-76
	T.1	XR983	23-11-71 – 19-06-72
	T.1	XR986	04-02-65 – 20-01-71
	T.1	XR987	03-02-65 – 12-04-76
	T.1	XR991	10-02-65 – 12-04-76
	T.1	XR992	12-02-65 – 16-12-69
	T.1	XR993	18-02-65 – 12-04-76
	T.1	XR994	17-02-65 – 13-11-70
	T.1	XR995	22-02-65 – 16-12-69
	T.1	XR996	25-03-65 – 08-06-73
	T.1	XR998	27-03-72 – 12-04-72
	T.1	XS101 101: H	07-10-64 – 12-04-76
	T.1	XS103 D	31-10-72 – 03-09-75
	T.1	XS104	14-07-75 – 12-04-76
	T.1	XS105 C	30-09-71 – 13-08-73
			23-09-75 – 28-11-75
	T.1	XS106	08-09-72 – 13-08-73
	T.1	XS107	25-03-70 – 12-04-76
	T.1	XS109 A	15-03-71 – 08-03-73
			23-09-75 – 05-12-75
	T.1	XS110 103	02-01-69 – 24-05-72
			07-11-72 – 08-03-73
			23-09-75 – 04-12-75
	T.1	XS111	14-05-65 – 12-04-76
Bulldog	T.1	XX514 44	02-05-73 – 12-04-76
	T.1	XX515 40	23-03-73 – 12-04-76
	T.1	XX516 41	26-03-73 – 12-04-76
	T.1	XX517 42	06-04-73 – 12-04-76
	T.1	XX518 43	09-04-73 – 12-04-76
	T.1	XX519	18-04-73 – 25-05-73
	T.1	XX520	08-05-73 – 31-05-73
	T.1	XX521	08-05-73 – 08-06-73
	T.1	XX522	08-05-73 – 18-06-73
	T.1	XX523	31-05-73 – 26-06-73
	T.1	XX526	31-05-73 – 04-07-73
	T.1	XX527	07-06-73 – 13-07-73
	T.1	XX528	31-05-73 – 09-07-73
	T.1	XX529	07-06-73 – 13-07-73
	T.1	XX538 45	26-07-73 – 12-04-76
	T.1	XX539 46	26-07-73 – 12-04-76
	T.1	XX540 47	22-08-73 – 12-04-76
	T.1	XX541 48	22-08-73 – 12-04-76
	T.1	XX542 49	29-08-73 – 04-03-76
	T.1	XX553 07	01-01-74 – 12-04-76
	T.1	XX554 09	01-01-74 – 12-04-76
Jetstream	T.1	XX476	16-10-73 – 13-11-75
	T.1	XX477	30-09-73 – 01-11-74
	T.1	XX478	19-12-73 – 24-11-75
	T.1	XX479	31-12-74 – 24-11-75
	T.1	XX480	20-03-74 – 17-12-75
	T.1	XX482	16-05-74 – 16-07-74
	T.1	XX483	30-12-74 – 27-10-75
	T.1	XX484	30-12-74 – 04-11-75
	T.1	XX485	18-12-74 – 26-09-75
	T.1	XX486	30-12-74 – 27-10-75

Suffixes: GG = Gate Guardian; M = Museum; FC = CFS Flying Club.

Pre-production Gnat T.1, XM704-95, Fairford, 1966

Chipmunk T.10, WK591-15

Jet Provost Mk4 XS217-50, Fairford, August 1966

Canberra T.4, WT480-CC

The last production Varsity T.1, XD366-MF

Jetstream T.1, XX475 *(Dennis Barber)*

Jet Provost T.3, XM355-RA

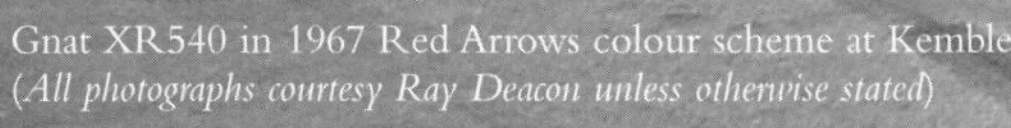

Gnat XR540 in 1967 Red Arrows colour scheme at Kemble.
(All photographs courtesy Ray Deacon unless otherwise stated)

APPENDIX 5

Accidents Involving CFS Aircraft

Date **Serial** **Aircraft** **Place** **Casualties**

21-05-46 **DE523** **Tiger Moth T.2** **Poulton, Gloucestershire** **2**
The aircraft stalled and crashed whilst the crew were carrying out aerobatics at a dangerously low height.
WO William Gallagher Gordon
Flt Lt Desmond Fred Ruchwaldy, 25, DFC

30-07-46 **PH186** **Oxford T.1** **Akeman Street** **0**
The aircraft took off with a crosswind of 25 to 30 knots at 25 degrees to the runway. As soon as the tail came off the ground, a swing developed and the pilot over corrected this before deciding to abandon the take-off. He closed the throttle and applied the brakes but, the aircraft's tail was still off the ground the aircraft pitched onto its nose.

16-03-47 **NC481** **Wellington T.10** **RAF Little Rissington** **0**
There were major gales in the local area and 74 Wellingtons and 4 Tiger Moths were damaged at RAF Little Rissington. Of the Wellingtons, this aircraft was pulled from its pickets and damaged beyond repair.

01-07-47 **NL784** **Tiger Moth T.2** **RAF Little Rissington** **1**
The pilot was carrying out rehearsals of low level aerobatics for the Blackpool Air Pageant. At the top of a loop at 1,000 ft, the pilot spun the aircraft but failed to initiate recovery action quickly enough and, although the spin had stopped, the aircraft struck the ground before pulling out of the dive. The pilot had not taken recovery action until the aircraft reached 250 ft, despite a height limit of 500 ft for the display.
Flt Lt Terence Martin Helmore

27-08-47 **HJ978** **Mosquito T.3** **RAF Little Rissington** **0**
The pilot was practising asymmetric approaches but allowed the speed to fall off. He realised that the aircraft would undershoot the runway and judged that it might strike an aircraft at the marshalling point. Consequently, he decided to crash land the aircraft in a field adjacent to the airfield and this he did. Aircraft SOC on 28-08-47.

16-09-47 **KF339** **Harvard T.2B** **RAF Little Rissington** **0**
Following a night take-off and at a height of 250 ft, the aircraft's engine failed. The pilot turned the aircraft to avoid trees and crash landed the aircraft. The cause of the engine failure was not recorded.

20-01-48 **TD284** **Spitfire LF.XVI** **RAF Little Rissington** **0**
The pilot did not complete his vital actions prior to take-off and left the throttle friction nut untightened. During take-off, the propeller pitch lever vibrated from the 'fully fine' position and the throttle also slipped back causing a loss of engine power. The pilot realised that the engine was not delivering full power and attempted to abandon the take-off. The aircraft ran off the end of the runway and was damaged when it passed through a wire fence.

12-02-48 **VT594** **Mosquito T.3** **RAF Moreton-in-Marsh** **0**
The aircraft was overshooting from an asymmetric approach but the student pilot allowed the speed to fall below the single-engined safety speed and height could not be maintained. The instructor force landed the aircraft in a field whilst he could still retain control.

06-05-48 **HJ991** **Mosquito T.3** **near RAF Morton-in-Marsh** **0**
The crew, who were student instructors, were engaged on a mutual asymmetric training sortie, taking turns to play the parts of student and instructor. The aircraft was overshooting from a single-engined approach but the pilot could not maintain height because he had commenced the overshoot at too low an airspeed. Some height was then lost as the pilot attempted to gain airspeed but the flaps were left down and the pilot then became disconcerted because the undercarriage lights were showing red despite the undercarriage having been raised. The aircraft did not recover and crashed about 2 miles north of the airfield, struck some trees and burst into flames.

29-07-48 **VT854** **Vampire F.3** **RAF Little Rissington** **0**
Overshot the runway and was badly damaged. Aircraft returned to De Havilland.

04-08-48 **TW116** **Mosquito T.3** **RAF Moreton-in-Marsh** **0**
The aircraft landed and an initial swing was corrected before a juddering was felt and the port undercarriage collapsed, followed by the starboard. The aircraft slid along the ground and caught fire. The initial collapse was caused by a structural failure within the undercarriage mechanism.

12-08-48 **FX221** **Harvard T.2B** **RAF Moreton-in-Marsh** **0**
The pilot did not handle the fuel controls properly and did not switch tanks until the one in use ran dry and the engine stopped. He then failed to pump fuel for long enough to ensure it was feeding and the engine would not, therefore, restart. The aircraft undershot the forced landing at base and ploughed through two hedges, fracturing the undercarriage. The aircraft was sent for repair at Halliwells but scrapped eleven months later.

03-09-48 **XXXXX** **Prentice T.1** **xxxxxx** **n**
The aircraft was put into an intentional spin to the right and the pilot tried both normal and emergency methods of recovery but without effect. The two crew, Flt Lt K.L. Hughes and Plt Off I.I.J. Bush, were able to abandon the aircraft and parachuted safely to the ground.

20-01-49 **VT608** **Mosquito T.3** **RAF Moreton-in-Marsh** **0**
The pilot attempted to initiate an overshoot from a normal approach but left the flaps down fully. The aircraft would not accelerate in this condition and the pilot closed the throttles and made a wheels up landing.

16-03-49 **VT798** **Vampire F.3** **near Stow-on-the-Wold** **1**
The aircraft was seen to spin into the ground in a flat attitude but the reason for the accident was not discovered.
Plt Off Thomas Millward Jacks 27

Date	Serial	Aircraft	Place	Casualties

08-04-49 **VT581** **Mosquito T.3** **RAF Moreton-in-Marsh** **0**
The student pilot failed to correct a swing to port quickly enough and the instructor pilot took control but overcorrected and induced a sharp swing to starboard before the undercarriage collapsed.

12-05-49 **VT604** **Mosquito T.3** **RAF Little Rissington** **0**
The pilot was making a practice single-engined approach but failed to begin his overshoot from 800 ft and the speed decayed, the aircraft touched down but overshot the landing into a field. Aircraft SOC 21-06-49.

13-05-49 **VA886** **Mosquito T.3** **near RAF Little Rissington** **0**
The crew was simulating an engine failure on take-off and feathered the port engine. Immediately, the starboard engine failed and caught fire because of a fracture of the connecting rods to both right and left No. 4 cylinders, puncturing of the crankcase and extensive damage to the sump. The crew; Flt Lt J.G. Crosshow and Lt. M.W. Rudolph RN, landed the aircraft straight ahead but it struck a wall and killed several cattle. The station commander commented that the crew had done extremely well but might have used more flap for the landing — a somewhat unkind observation given the circumstances and speed of the events.

01-07-49 **TE193** **Spitfire LF.XVI** **RAF South Cerney** **0**
The engine failed at 8,000 ft and the pilot attempted an emergency landing on the base airfield. However, in setting up his final approach, the pilot lowered the undercarriage too soon and the aircraft undershot the runway

04-07-49 **LR556** **Mosquito T.3** **near Moreton-in-Marsh** **0**
The pilot intended to overshoot an asymmetric approach and make a further circuit but did not realise that he still had full flap selected and hence the aircraft would not maintain height nor would it accelerate. A forced landing was made.

28-07-49 **NX735** **Lancaster B.7** **RAF Little Rissington** **0**
The aircraft was being used for circuit training but the pilot touched down short of the runway on a surface of loose stones and rubble. The stones were thrown up by the force of the landing and caused serious damage to the skin of the tailplane.

15-08-49 **HJ885** **Mosquito T.3** **RAF Little Rissington** **0**
The pilot had intended to make a single-engined overshoot from a height of 800 ft. However, he selected full flap instead of take-off flap and was unable to maintain speed or full control in this configuration. When the aircraft had descended to 200 ft he closed the throttle to the live engine and the aircraft touched down over 1,000 yds inside the airfield boundary and the pilot retracted the undercarriage to stop.

01-12-49 **VT591** **Mosquito T.3** **RAF Little Rissington** **0**
On take-off the aircraft swung to port and the pilot corrected but a swing to starboard developed. The instructor took control but the aircraft skidded on wet grass and the undercarriage collapsed.

06-12-49 **FT331** **Harvard T.2** **South of RAF Little Rissington** **1**
The pilot decided to abandon the sortie because of poor weather but failed to set the regional pressure setting on his altimeter, even though he knew he was flying into an area of lower pressure. Whilst climbing in cloud, the aircraft struck the top of a hill at a height of 930 ft. Although the student; Captain Mahmood of the Royal Iraqi Air Force was hurt, the pilot received fatal injuries.
Flt Lt William Patrick O'Kane, 29, DFM

05-04-50 **VW481** **Meteor T.7** **RAF Little Rissington** **0**
On the final leg of a single-engined approach, the nose of the aircraft rose and it turned through 90 degrees before crashing from about 500 ft and 1,100 yards short of the runway. Sqn Ldr C.T. Stimpson seriously injured.

12-04-50 **VA889** **Mosquito T.3** **RAF Little Rissington** **0**
The aircraft swung during the take-off and was damaged when the undercarriage collapsed as it ran into soft ground at the side of the runway.

29-06-50 **WA668** **Meteor T.7** **near RAF Little Rissington** **0**
The aircraft ran in for a high speed run at about 50 ft and then pulled up, when it suffered a structural failure and began to break up. The pilot, Flt Lt G. Hulse, baled out successfully.

30-10-50 **WA673** **Meteor T.7** **Salperton, Gloucestershire** **2**
The aircraft broke up in the air, possibly because the undercarriage dropped under high speed and 'g' loadings.
Flt Lt Francis Edward Morris, 27
Flt Lt Brian Ray Marks, 27, DFC, AFC

09-01-51 **FS883** **Harvard T.2B** **RAF Moreton-in-Marsh** **0**
Whilst taking off at night, the engine failed at about 150 to 200 ft and the aircraft then struck a building, believed to have been the WRAF block. The crew, Flt Lt G.L. Pendred and Siamese pilot, Fg Off Santai Siang Suke, escaped, although Flt Lt Pendred lost an eye.

24-01-51 **FX307** **Harvard T.2B** **Near Pebworth, Warwickshire** **2**
The aircraft dived into the ground at high speed and under power after emerging from low cloud.
Flt Lt Richard Brian Jackson, DFC
Flt Lt Leonard Arthur Green, DFC

26-02-51 **FT496** **Harvard T.2B** **Moreton-in-Marsh** **0**
During the landing, the aircraft nosed over and subsequently caught fire.

26-04-51 **FX301** **Harvard T.2B** **Moreton-in-Marsh** **0**
This aircraft and FX438, below, collided whilst they were making their approaches to land.

26-04-51 **FX438** **Harvard T.2B** **Moreton-in-Marsh** **1**
This aircraft and FX301, collided during their approaches to land. Although one of the crew of this aircraft, Flt Lt D.F. Orchard, was injured, he survived but the other crewman died of his injuries.
Flt Lt Douglas Charles Wilson Fortier, DFC

Date	Serial	Aircraft	Place	Casualties

20-06-51 **FS884** **Harvard T.2B** **Moreton-in-Marsh** **0**

The starboard fuel tank had been drained prior to removal and the fuel gauge disconnected but there was a residue of petrol fumes in the cockpit. An airman was cleaning out the cockpit and altered the position of his lamp to improve visibility. However, an electrical lead was exposed and this led to a short circuit and a spark when the bare wire touched metal in the cockpit. The fuel tank exploded and an airman working under the wing, J/T D.M. Short, was injured.

15-09-51 **KF937** **Harvard T.2B** **RAF St Athan** **1**

The pilot was operating from RAF Little Rissington at the RAF St Athan Battle of Britain Display. The aircraft began a spin at 2,500 ft and stopped at about 800 ft, when it went into a steep dive to 300 ft where recovery action was started. However, insufficient height remained to effect a successful recovery and the aircraft mushed into the ground.
Flt Lt John Martin Maynard, 27

11-10-51 **FT165** **Harvard T.2B** **Icomb, Gloucestershire** **2**

The aircraft was seen to be spinning at high altitude but the spin continued until very close to the ground, when the aircraft twisted over and crashed.
Plt Off Leonard Arthur Coxill, 28, DFC
Fg Off Leslie Arthur Trodd

05-11-51 **VZ642** **Meteor T.7** **RAF Little Rissington** **0**

The aircraft was landing in poor weather and restricted visibility. It struck overhead cables and then trees and was extensively damaged. The aircraft should have diverted to RAF Blakehill Farm, where the conditions were much better.

10-12-51 **RH759** **Brigand B.1** **RAF Little Rissington** **0**

The aircraft swung on take-off and crashed into trucks parked nearby.

21-01-52 **LA331** **Spitfire F.21** **RAF Llandow** **0**

On landing the undercarriage collapsed and the aircraft was damaged beyond repair. The CFS student pilot, Plt Off B.E. Than, was unhurt.

22-01-52 **FT424** **Harvard T.2B** **Stow-on-the-Wold** **0**

The aircraft flew into trees during a low flying sortie and crashed.

21-05-52 **WE830** **Vampire FB.5** **RAF Little Rissington** **0**

The aircraft crash-landed after it stalled in the latter stages of its approach.

16-06-52 **WL369** **Meteor T.7** **RAF Little Rissington** **0**

The aircraft was at the final stages of an asymmetric approach when it began to undershoot and the pilot applied power to the starboard engine and to control the yaw with rudder. The aircraft struck the undershoot heavily on its port wheel and headed for the runway caravan. The pilot tried to correct the swing but the port wing struck the caravan and injured the occupants, Cpl K. McAlister and AC1 M.C. Harvey. The two pilots, Fg Off D.J. Mountford and Plt Off W.B.C. Morgan, were uninjured.

21-07-52 **KF338** **Harvard T.2B** **RAF Little Rissington** **0**

The aircraft was making 'touch and go' landings but stalled and crashed, bursting into flames.

28-07-52 **FS822** **Harvard T.2B** **Near Calmsden, Gloucestershire** **2**

This aircraft and KF948, below, were involved in a mid air collision.
Flt Lt Alan Leonard Jose May
Flt Sgt Walter Stokes

28-07-52 **KF948** **Harvard T.2B** **Near Calmsden** **2**

Mid-air collision with FS822 during an instrument flying training sortie.
Flt Lt Timothy Allman Bridge, DFC
Flt Sgt Douglas Gordon Hughes

20-08-52 **WA691** **Meteor T.7** **South of RAF Little Rissington** **0**

The aircraft was returning to base with the starboard engine shut down to conserve fuel. On the final stages of the asymmetric approach, the port engine failed and a wheels down landing was made in a field short of the runway. The undercarriage legs were ripped off when the aircraft went through a stone wall. The cause of the accident was the pilot's failure to maintain a safe margin of fuel to complete a circuit.

26-08-52 **VS394** **Prentice T.1** **RAF Fairford** **0**

This aircraft and VS293 were involved in a mid-air collision. Although the other aircraft landed safely, the pilot of this aircraft baled out when control could not be maintained.

09-10-52 **WH217** **Meteor T.7** **Enstone, Oxfordshire** **0**

The aircraft was on its third landing when it stalled from a height of about 10 ft and struck the ground. When the port undercarriage leg collapsed, it slewed off the runway and struck a building before coming to a stop.

31-10-52 **WA216** **Vampire FB.5** **RAF Little Rissington** **0**

The brakes had failed on landing, the aircraft overran the runway and the undercarriage was raised to stop.

04-12-52 **LA253** **Spitfire F.21** **Llandow** **0**

The pilot, Plt Off Au Min, raised the tail too early on the take-off run and the propeller struck the runway. In the subsequent crash the aircraft overturned and was damaged extensively.

31-12-52 **WF852** **Meteor T.7** **RAF Little Rissington** **1**

The aircraft was on an aerobatic sortie, the pilot practising for the Brabyn Trophy. The aircraft crossed the airfield in a shallow high speed dive and then pulled up into cloud at an angle of about 45 degrees. It emerged briefly from cloud and then re entered cloud before being seen spinning out of the cloud. Although the spin was corrected, the aircraft immediately started to spin to the left and struck the ground, injuring Miss Pratt and Miss Mustow, LAC Hooper and ACs Allport, Cooksey and Kempton.
Plt Off Jack William Ward, 22

03-02-53 **KF244** **Harvard T.2B** **Near Moreton-in-Marsh** **0**

The aircraft belly-landed in a field 5 miles from Moreton-in-Marsh

Date	Serial	Aircraft	Place	Casualties
04-02-53	**KF211**	**Harvard T.2B**	**Near Naunton, Gloucestershire**	**2**

The aircraft climbed to a height of 4 to 5,000 ft and was seen to enter a spin. It was then seen at 1,500 ft spinning rapidly to the right and to crash into the ground.
Mtr Plt Francis Hubert Bloomer, 33
Sgt Barry Peter Morgan

25-02-53	**WL381**	**Meteor T7**	**About 3 miles west of Swindon**	**2**

The aircraft was carrying out a slow roll at about 3,000 ft when a puff of smoke was seen to come from the aircraft. It then appeared to stall and spin to the right before striking the ground.
Fg Off Ronald Taylor
Flt Lt Fred Stanley Woods

20-06-53	**WA424**	**Vampire FB.5**	**RAF Little Rissington**	**0**

Stalled over the runway and resulting heavy landing caused the undercarriage to collapse.

22-06-53	**FX434**	**Harvard T.2B**	**RAF South Cerney**	**0**

The engine failed on take-off and the aircraft was damaged in the subsequent forced landing.

09-11-53	**WL458**	**Meteor T.7**	**Kingham, Oxfordshire**	**2**

Whilst carrying out an asymmetric sortie, the aircraft became inverted and struck trees.
Flt Lt Richard Anthony Fox-Linton, 32, MRCS, LRCP
Flt Lt Raymond Geoffrey Mead

10-11-53	**WH131**	**Meteor T.7**	**near Stow-on-the-Wold**	**0**

During the execution of a loop, the aircraft flicked into a spin to the left. Recovery action was taken and the spin stopped and immediately, the aircraft went into an inverted spin to the right. Neither pilot, Plt Offs J. Armstrong, 21 nor S.R. Jones, 28, could effect recovery and so they baled out safely.

11-12-53	**KF584**	**Harvard T.2B**	**3 miles north-north-west of Winchcombe**	**0**

The aircraft took off for a sortie of aerobatics and controlled let downs. After completing the aerobatics and at a height of 4,200 ft and a speed of 150 knots, the engine failed and the oil pressure dropped. The aircraft glided down and a forced landing site selected and the approach begun. However, the crew, Plt Off G.C. Taylor and Fg Off P.J.B. Tucker, were forced to change direction when overhead power lines were seen and touchdown was made in a small field, having passed beneath some cables. The aircraft ran across the field, struck a cow, went through a hedge and came to rest in another field. The engine failure was caused by the oil pump seizing.

04-02-54	**WE821**	**Sea Fury FB.11**	**Stow-on-the-Wold**	**1**

The aircraft became uncontrollable in a spin and was abandoned. Although Flt Lt J.H. Verrall, 32, escaped, his colleague did not.
Flt Lt Jack Alan Shelley, 32

28-07-54	**WL374**	**Meteor T.7**	**2 miles south of RAF Upper Heyford**	**2**

Two Meteors were flying in close formation at about 1,000 ft when they collided during a formation change. Neither crew were able to escape in the height and time available.
Flt Lt Charles Harris Lazenby, 32, Pilot Instructor
Flt Lt Ronald Bennett, 30, Pilot

28-07-54	**WL457**	**Meteor T.7**	**2 miles south of RAF Upper Heyford**	**2**

Collided in the circumstances described above.
Flt Lt John Rowland Douche,28, DFC, Pilot Instructor
Flt Lt Brian Geoffrey Rendle, 26, Pilot

01-12-54	**WV479**	**Provost T.1**	**About ¾ mile east of South Cerney**	**0**

Whilst carrying out practice forced landings, the aircraft struck a wall and was damaged beyond repair.

14-12-54	**KF588**	**Harvard T.2B**	**South east of Thame, Buckinghamshire**	**0**

Belly landed in a field after communications difficulties.

09-03-55	**WH200**	**Meteor T.7**	**Broadwell Airfield**	**2**

The aircraft went into a spin during an instructional sortie of asymmetric flying after the air brakes were left out.
Fg Off Anthony Robert Wardell, 24
Flt Sgt David John Cooper, 32

21-04-55	**WL364**	**Meteor T.7**	**RAF Little Rissington**	**0**

The undercarriage collapsed after the aircraft touched down in the undershoot.

22-04-55	**WV570**	**Provost T.1**	**near RAF Kemble**	**1**

During an aerobatic sortie the student pulled out of a dive very harshly and the instructor, Flt Lt J.W. Thompson, blacked out. On recovering, the aircraft was diving steeply and the student said he could get no response from the controls. The instructor ordered the aircraft to be abandoned, at which point the starboard wing failed and the aircraft began to spin rapidly. The instructor abandoned the aircraft with some difficulty but despite releasing his harness and deploying his parachute the student remained in the aircraft.
Fg Off Peter Robert Moulden, 22

30-09-55	**WV637**	**Provost T.1**	**near RAF South Cerney**	**0**

Following an engine failure, the aircraft was force landed but the undercarriage collapsed and the aircraft was badly damaged. The two crew; Flt Lt J.M. Williams and Plt Off P.J. Izzard survived.

28-03-56	**WV423**	**Provost T.1**	**Hillcott End, near RAF South Cerney**	**1**

The instructor opened the throttle to demonstrate the maximum climb rate but there was a thud and the engine failed. Although initially intending to land at Fairford, smoke then appeared in the cockpit and so the canopy was jettisoned and a decision taken to abandon the aircraft. Although the student, Flt Lt C.A. Coatesworth parachuted to safety, the instructor did not leave the aircraft until a late stage and his parachute did not deploy fully.
Flt Lt Kenneth John Evans, 35

Date	Serial	Aircraft	Place	Casualties

24-08-56 **XF980** **Hunter F.4** **Wotton-under-Edge, Gloucestershire** **0**
This aircraft was climbing at full throttle when, at a height of 10,000 ft it was involved in a mid-air collision with a Javelin (XA644) making a rapid descent. The fin ripped through the Javelin and the fuselage buckled. The pilot, Flt Lt P.K.V. Hicks ejected through the canopy and was injured.

24-10-56 **XF999** **Hunter F.4** **3 miles east of RAF Kemble** **1**
On joining the circuit, the pilot reported hydraulic failure and was not able to lower the undercarriage properly. The aircraft began a turn to port, probably in manual control, when the aircraft rolled to port and the nose dropped. With the aircraft nearly inverted, the pilot ejected through the canopy but the ejection sequence did not complete. The accident was caused by hydraulics failure leading to control difficulties and out of balance forces in turbulent conditions.
Flt Lt Charles Martin Harcourt, 27

26-07-57 **WZ574** **Vampire T.11** **2 miles from Farringdon, Oxon** **0**
The aircraft was put into a spin by the student pilot and then recovery action was initiated. When this proved ineffective, the instructor took control but was also unable to control the aircraft and the crew, Flt Lt R.M. Agate, 35 (RCAF - an 'Al' category instructor) and Lt C.W. Barras, 26 RN, ejected with some difficulty. It seems likely that the crew did not recognise an inverted spin because they were disorientated and this particular aircraft had a history of unusual spinning characteristics.

08-03-58 **WH183** **Meteor T.7** **RAF Little Rissington** **0**
Badly damaged in a landing accident after striking a fence in the undershoot. The pilot, Wg Cdr R.C. Knott, 40, escaped uninjured.

28-08-58 **XD679** **Jet Provost T.1** **RAF Little Rissington** **0**
Having completed a practice display session, "The CFS Jet Provost Aerobatic Team" approached the runway for a formation landing. The pilot of the box aircraft, Flt Lt Peter Millington, was so busy keeping formation that he forgot to check for three greens and he made a wheels-up landing on the runway before skidding to a halt on the grass. The aircraft was repaired and returned to the team.

07-10-58 **WP868** **Chipmunk T.10** **Near Bibury, Gloucestershire** **2**
The aircraft had been airborne for about 7 minutes on a sortie to include practice circuits, landings, turns, stalls, spins and aerobatics. It was seen to drop its starboard wing and spiral into the ground from a height of about 600 ft. The reason for the accident could not be determined, although it is possible that one of the crew undid his harness straps to reach forward to an inaccessible switch and in doing so pushed the control column forward.
Sqn Ldr William Edward Caldecott, 40
Sqn Ldr John Stewart Lamplough

04-12-58 **XF542** **Provost T.1** **1½ miles from Kingham, Oxfordshire** **2**
This aircraft was leader of a pair in a tailchase and made three steep turns to port at low altitude. It then made a steep dive to port, pulled up sharply to about 500 ft and then, in a semi-stalled condition, the port wing dropped and the aircraft struck a tree and dived into the ground.
Flt Lt Peter Millington, 28, Instructor
Fg Off David Graham Hough, 22, Student

07-04-59 **XK631** **Vampire T.11** **near Bromyard, Hereford** **0**
Capt John Smitherman USAF and Flt Lt Dennis Allison were carrying out a low level mission when the fire warning light came on and the engine failed. Both crew safely abandoned the aircraft.

15-08-60 **XF614** **Provost T.1** **RAF Little Rissington** **0**
Overshot on landing and nosed over.

30-08-61 **XM423** **Jet Provost T.3** **3m south-east of Kidderminster** **0**
Abandoned after engine failed during night navigation exercise by Flt Lt I.K. McKee and Plt Off J. Armstrong.

28-02-62 **XM709** **Gnat T.1** **RAF Kemble** **0**
Sank back onto the runway after take-off with undercarriage partially retracted. Damage to starboard undercarriage leg enforced a two-wheel landing. Both crew safely abandoned the aircraft.

26-06-62 **WG962** **Meteor T.7** **RAF Little Rissington** **2**
Rolled into the ground after engine failure on take off and failure to correct quickly the asymmetric condition. The Meteor was notorious for problems in asymmetric flight if the speed and lateral control were not monitored very carefully and if the correct use of flaps and undercarriage were not followed.
Flt Lt Trevor James Doe, 38, Pilot Instructor
Flt Lt Henry William Carter, 24, Student Instructor

27-06-62 **XF943** **Hunter F.4** **RAF Kemble** **0**
Crashed into a wall having overshot the runway after an hydraulics failure.

21-02-63 **XF895** **Provost T.1** **RAF Little Rissington** **0**
Hit a snow bank while landing at night; starboard undercarriage collapsed.

02-05-63 **XP588** **Jet Provost T.4** **Near Chedworth Airfield** **0**
While practising for the Clarkson Trophy low over the disused Chedworth airfield, Flt Lt Charles Sturt abandoned the aircraft after the fire warning came on.

16-05-63 **XM705** **Gnat T.1** **RAF Little Rissington** **0**
Flt Lt Bill Loverseed was flying an instructional sortie with a student when the undercarriage failed to lock down. The aircraft made a wheels-up landing at Rissington. Returned to HAS at Dunsfold for Cat.4 repairs.

14-12-64 **XM460** **Jet Provost T.3** **RAF Little Rissington** **1**
Crashed after overshooting and hitting power lines. The Flight Line Controller and Deputy Unit Test Pilot was severely injured and died in January 1965 as a result of his burns.
Flt Lt Edward Berts, DFC

28-09-66 **XM704** **Gnat T.1** **RAF Kemble** **0**
Having made a heavy touchdown and suspecting that the undercarriage was damaged, the pilot was able to get airborne again and received confirmation from the tower that the port leg was not fully extended. A textbook two-wheeled landing was subsequently made and the aircraft returned to the hangar for inspection, which revealed a cracked main undercarriage casting, Cat 5.

Date	Serial	Aircraft	Place	Casualties
07-04-67	**XM705**	**Gnat T.1**	**RAF Kemble**	**0**

The aircraft lost power during take-off and, although the pilot managed to land back on the runway, the aircraft ran off the end and through the landing light poles into a field. Sustained Cat.4 damage, repaired and returned to CFS on 07-10-68.

30-06-67 | XM707 | Gnat T.1 | 2½ m west-north-west of RAF Kemble | 0

Abandoned after loss of tailplane control – Hobson unit seal blew and tail plane jammed full nose down. Aircraft completed outside loop. Pilot was Flt Lt R. Cope-Lewis who rolled the aircraft through 90 degrees and continued with the aircraft flying in circles still with negative g. He abandoned the aircraft which continued flying inverted but levelled off once the pilot ejection seat and canopy had left. The aircraft crashed close to the airfield.

26-02-68 | XP675 | Jet Provost T.4 | Hanling, Gloucestershire | 0

Mid-air collision with XS229.

26-02-68 | XS229 | Jet Provost T.4 | Hanling, Gloucestershire | 0

Mid-air collision with XP675. The two pilots Flt Lt D.J. Smith and Fg Off J. Tye escaped without serious injury.

02-05-68 | WZ874 | Chipmunk T.10 | Moreton-in-Marsh | 1

While performing low-level aerobatics over Moreton-in-Marsh airfield the engine cut at the top of a loop and the aircraft crashed heavily onto the runway. Student pilot Flt Lt Robin K.C. Melville escaped with moderate injuries.

Sqn Ldr Brian. A. Owens

24-01-69 | XM360 | Jet Provost T.3 | Brown Clee Hill, Abdon, Shropshire | 2

Flew into ground in low cloud.

Flt Lt John Sims Watson, 31, Instructor
Plt Off Ian Scott Primrose, 21

26-03-69 | XR573 | Gnat T.1 | RAF Kemble | 1

During an 'Arrows' formation practice over Kemble, the aeroplane flew into trees whilst positioning for join-up loop. The pilot Flt Lt Jerry Bowler was killed and the aircraft crashed against the car park fencing at the rear of the G-site hangar.

Flt Lt Jeremy John Bowler, 27

13-06-69 | XP501 | Gnat T.1 | RAF Fairford | 0

This was the eleventh aircraft accompanying Red Arrows en-route to the continent. The Commandant was flying the aircraft with an SAC in the back seat. An hydraulic failure was experienced and an attempt was made to return to Fairford. The aircraft undershot the airfield and hit a pile of manure before bouncing over a road and perimeter fence and stopping in the undershoot. Air Cdre Broom suffered two broken feet. The aircraft caught fire and the airman assisted him from the aeroplane.

29-09-69 | XN576 | Jet Provost T.3 | Northleach, Gloucester | 0

Abandoned after engine failure.

16-12-69 | XR992 | Gnat T.1 | Latton, near Cirencester, Gloucestershire | 0

Abandoned following report of engine fire during "Red Arrows" practice sortie.

16-12-69 | XR995 | Gnat T.1 | Latton, near Cirencester, Gloucestershire | 0

Abandoned after erroneous call that engine was on fire during "Red Arrows" practice sortie.

13-11-70 | XR994 | Gnat T.1 | RAF Kemble | 0

Aircraft suffered an engine failure during aerobatics practice with "Red Arrows" over Kemble airfield and was abandoned. Sqn Ldr Dennis Hazell ejected and suffered a broken thigh in the process.

20-01-71 | XR545 | Gnat T.1 | RAF Kemble | 2

Mid-air collision between "Red Arrows" synchro-pair. Collided with XR986 over the airfield while practising the Roulette manoeuvre and crashed within the boundary.

Flt Lt John Stuart Haddock
Flt Lt Colin Armstrong

20-01-71 | XR986 | Gnat T.1 | RAF Kemble | 2

Mid-air collision between "Red Arrows" synchro pair, as for XR545 above.

Flt Lt Euan Robert Perreaux
Flt Lt John Lewis

13-12-71 | XR567 | Gnat T.1 | RAF Upper Heyford | 2

Crashed while rolling at low level. The tail fin broke off, causing a grounding order to be issued against all Gnat aircraft while investigations ensued.

Flt Lt D.C. Longden
Flt Lt R.M. Storr

27-11-73 | WF411 | Varsity T.1 | RAF Little Rissington | 0

Damaged beyond repair when control lost after engine failed during a roller landing. Pilots were Flt Lts Roger Goff and Mike Preston.

01-11-74 | XX477 | Jetstream T.1 | RAF Little Rissington | 0

Double engine failure after a roller landing caused the aircraft to overshoot the runway and to be damaged beyond repair.

03-09-75 | XS103 | Gnat T.1 | Leck, Germany | 0

Mid-air collision with Italian Air Force F-104S.

24-06-76 | XS111 | Gnat T.1 | RAF Kemble | 0

Damaged beyond repair after undercarriage raised to stop aircraft after brakes failed on landing.

Reference Sources and Further Reading

Books

C.F.S. Birthplace of Air Power
John W. R. Taylor
ISBN 0 7106 0486 6
Published 1987 by Jane's Publishing Co Ltd
238 City Road, London. EC1V 2PU

Red Arrows
Ray Hanna
ISBN 0 85944 014 1
Published 1973 by Photo Precision Ltd
St Ives. Huntingdon

Folland Gnat: Sabre slayer and Red Arrow
Victor F. Bingham
ISBN 1 900511 78 9
Published 2000 by J&KH Publishing
PO Box 13, Hailsham. East Sussex. BN27 3XQ

De Havilland Vampire: The Complete History
David Watkins
ISBN 07509 1250 2
Published 1996 by Sutton Publishing Ltd
Pheonix Mill, Thrupp, Stroud. Gloucestershire. GL5 2BU

Autobiographical

My Story
Air Cdre Christopher Paul
Unpublished

In The Red
Terry Kingsley
ISBN 1 85821 754 7
Published 2000 by The Pentland Press Ltd
Bishop Auckland. Durham

Phantom Leader
Cdr Michael Doust
ISBN 0 946958 42 4
Published by Roger Chesneau/Ad Hoc Publications

A lighter shade of Pale Blue
Reg O'Neil
ISBN 1-873203-45-4
Published by Woodfield Publications
Bognor Regis, West Sussex

Periodicals and magazines

RAF Flying Review, Air Clues, Flight International, Aviation News

Websites

Central Flying School Association
http://www.centralflyingschool.org.uk/
Webmaster –

RAF Little Rissington
http://members.aol.com/airfields2000/glos.htm
Webmaster – Ashley Bailey

Service Pals
http://www.servicepals.com/
Webmaster – Ross Williams

Archives

Central Flying School Archive
RAF Cranwell, Lincs.

Royal Air Force Museum
Hendon, Middlesex

National Archives (Public Record Office)
Kew, Surrey.

List of documents accessed:
AIR 2/17127, 17876, 17879, 17933
AIR 20/7753, 7845, 9718, 10250-51, 10670, 10672-77, 10892, 11110
AIR 28/2049-59
AIR 29/1787-88, 2298, 2310-13, 2589, 2636, 2702, 2763, 2846, 3111, 3159, 3492, 548, 3591, 3628-33, 3725-27, 3765-3779 4183-4191

Index